Authors

Edward B. Burger, Ph.D., is the Francis Christopher Oakley Third Century Professor of Mathematics at Williams College, an educational and business consultant, and a former vice provost at Baylor University. He has authored or coauthored more than sixty-five articles, books, and video series; delivered over five hundred addresses and workshops throughout the world; and made more than fifty radio and television appearances. He is a Fellow of the American Mathematical Society as well as having earned many national honors, including the Robert Foster Cherry Award for Great Teaching in 2010. In 2012, Microsoft Education named him a "Global Hero in Education."

Juli K. Dixon, Ph.D., is a Professor of Mathematics Education at the University of Central Florida. She has taught mathematics in urban schools at the elementary, middle, secondary, and post-secondary levels. She is an active researcher and speaker with numerous publications and conference presentations. Key areas of focus are deepening teachers' content knowledge and communicating and justifying mathematical ideas. She is a past chair of the NCTM Student Explorations in Mathematics Editorial Panel and member of the Board of Directors for the Association of Mathematics Teacher Educators.

Timothy D. Kanold, Ph.D., is an award-winning international educator, author, and consultant. He is a former superintendent and director of mathematics and science at Adlai E. Stevenson High School District 125 in Lincolnshire, Illinois. He is a past president of the National Council of Supervisors of Mathematics (NCSM) and the Council for the Presidential Awardees of Mathematics (CPAM). He has served on several writing and leadership commissions for NCTM during the past decade. He presents motivational professional development seminars with a focus on developing professional learning communities (PLC's) to improve the teaching, assessing, and learning of students. He has recently authored nationally recognized articles, books, and textbooks for mathematics education and school leadership, including *What Every Principal Needs to Know about the Teaching and Learning of Mathematics.*

Matthew R. Larson, Ph.D., is the K-12 mathematics curriculum specialist for the Lincoln Public Schools and served on the Board of Directors for the National Council of Teachers of Mathematics from 2010-2013. He is a past chair of NCTM's Research Committee and was a member of NCTM's Task Force on Linking Research and Practice. He is the author of several books on implementing the Common Core Standards for Mathematics. He has taught mathematics at the secondary and college levels and held an appointment as an honorary visiting associate professor at Teachers College, Columbia University.

Steven J. Leinwand is a Principal Research Analyst at the American Institutes for Research (AIR) in Washington, D.C., and has over 30 years in leadership positions in mathematics education. He is past president of the National Council of Supervisors of Mathematics and served on the NCTM Board of Directors. He is the author of numerous articles, books, and textbooks and has made countless presentations with topics including student achievement, reasoning, effective assessment, and successful implementation of standards.

Martha E. Sandoval-Martinez is a mathematics instructor at El Camino College in Torrance, California. She was previously a Math Specialist at the University of California at Davis and former instructor at Santa Ana College, Marymount College, and California State University, Long Beach. In her current and former positions, she has worked extensively to improve fundamental pre-algebra and algebra skills in students who have historically struggled with mathematics.

Consulting Reviewers

Anne Papakonstantinou, Ed.D.
Director - Rice University School
Mathematics Project
Rice University
Houston, Texas

Richard Parr
Executive Director - Rice University
School
Mathematics Project
Rice University
Houston, Texas

Susan Troutman
Associate Director for Secondary
Programs - Rice University School
Mathematics Project
Rice University
Houston, Texas

Carolyn White
Associate Director for Elementary
and Intermediate Programs - Rice
University School Mathematics
Project
Rice University
Houston, Texas

Valerie Johse
Texas Council for Economics
Education (TCEE) consultant
Houston, Texas

Texas Reviewers

Margaret R. Barron
Mathematics Specialist
Brownsville Independent School
District
Brownsville, Texas

Susan Jones
Lake Travis Middle School
Austin, Texas

Lauren Lindley
Middle School Math Specialist
Aldine ISD
Aldine, Texas

Lance Mangham
Carroll ISD
Carroll, Texas

Mary Elizabeth Rigsby
Hamilton Middle School
Houston ISD
Houston, Texas

David Surdovel
21st Century Academic Coordinator
of Mathematics
Manor ISD
Manor, Texas

Andrew D. Werner
Science Facilitator
Socorro ISD
El Paso, Texas

© Houghton Mifflin Harcourt Publishing Company

UNIT 1 Number and Operations

MODULE 1 Rational Numbers

UNIT 2 — Ratios and Proportional Relationships

MODULE 2 — Rates and Proportionality

MODULE 3 — Proportions and Percent

 **Proportionality in Geometry**

 **Probability**

 MODULE 5 **Experimental Probability**

 **TEKS**

MODULE 6 **Theoretical Probability and Simulations**

TEKS

UNIT 4 Multiple Representations of Linear Relationships

MODULE 7 Linear Relationships

MODULE 8 Equations and Inequalities

UNIT 5 Geometric Relationships

MODULE 9 Applications of Geometry Concepts

MODULE 10 Volume and Surface Area

UNIT 6 Measurement and Data

MODULE 11 Analyzing and Comparing Data

TEKS

MODULE 12 Random Samples and Populations

TEKS

MODULE 13 Taxes, Interest, and Incentives

TEKS

MODULE 14 Planning Your Future

TEKS

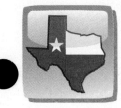

Texas Essential Knowledge and Skills for Mathematics

Correlation for HMH Texas Go Math Grade 7

Standard	Descriptor	Citations
7.1	**Mathematical process standards. The student uses mathematical processes to acquire and demonstrate mathematical understanding. The student is expected to:**	*The process standards are integrated throughout the book. See, for example, the citations below.*
7.1.A	apply mathematics to problems arising in everyday life, society, and the workplace;	SE: 19, 23, 30, 63, 91
7.1.B	use a problem-solving model that incorporates analyzing given information, formulating a plan or strategy, determining a solution, justifying the solution, and evaluating the problem-solving process and the reasonableness of the solution;	SE: 105, 177, 407
7.1.C	select tools, including real objects, manipulatives, paper and pencil, and technology as appropriate, and techniques, including mental math, estimation, and number sense as appropriate, to solve problems;	SE: 61, 85, 103, 115, 172
7.1.D	communicate mathematical ideas, reasoning, and their implications using multiple representations, including symbols, diagrams, graphs, and language as appropriate;	SE: 13, 17, 19, 67, 194
7.1.E	create and use representations to organize, record, and communicate mathematical ideas;	SE: 40, 74, 97, 187, 193
7.1.F	analyze mathematical relationships to connect and communicate mathematical ideas; and	SE: 37, 69, 75, 108, 189
7.1.G	display, explain, and justify mathematical ideas and arguments using precise mathematical language in written or oral communication.	SE: 66, 78, 120, 122, 162

Standard	Descriptor	Taught	Reinforced
7.2 Number and operations. The student applies mathematical process standards to represent and use rational numbers in a variety of forms. The student is expected to:			
7.2	extend previous knowledge of sets and subsets using a visual representation to describe relationships between sets of rational numbers.	SE: 7–10, 13–16	SE: 11–12, 17–18, 47–48
7.3 Number and operations. The student applies mathematical process standards to add, subtract, multiply, and divide while solving problems and justifying solutions. The student is expected to:			
7.3.A	add, subtract, multiply, and divide rational numbers fluently; and	SE: 19–21, 23–24, 27–29, 31, 35–36, 38, 41–44	SE: 25–26, 32–34, 39–40, 45–48, 49–50, 51–52, 53–54
7.3.B	apply and extend previous understandings of operations to solve problems using addition, subtraction, multiplication, and division of rational numbers.	SE: 22, 24, 30, 31, 37–38	SE: 25–26, 32–34, 39–40, 47–48, 49–50, 51–52, 53–54

Standard	Descriptor	Taught	Reinforced
7.4	**Proportionality. The student applies mathematical process standards to represent and solve problems involving proportional relationships. The student is expected to:**		
7.4.A	represent constant rates of change in mathematical and real-world problems given pictorial, tabular, verbal, numeric, graphical, and algebraic representations, including $d = rt$;	SE: 61–64, 67–70, 73–76	SE: 65–66, 71–72, 77–79, 141, 146
7.4.B	calculate unit rates from rates in mathematical and real-world problems;	SE: 61–62, 64	SE: 65–66, 141, 146, 148
7.4.C	determine the constant of proportionality ($k = \frac{y}{x}$) within mathematical and real-world problems;	SE: 69–70	SE: 71–72, 141
7.4.D	solve problems involving ratios, rates, and percents, including multi-step problems involving percent increase and percent decrease, and financial literacy problems; and	SE: 63–64, 67–70, 73–76, 86–88, 91–94, 97–100, 103–106	SE: 65–66, 71–72, 77–78, 89–90, 95–96, 101–102, 107–110, 141–143, 147–148
7.4.E	convert between measurement systems, including the use of proportions and the use of unit rates.	SE: 85–88	SE: 89–90, 109–110, 142–143
7.5	**Proportionality. The student applies mathematical process standards to use geometry to describe or solve problems involving proportional relationships. The student is expected to:**		
7.5.A	generalize the critical attributes of similarity, including ratios within and between similar shapes;	SE: 115–118, 121–124	SE: 119–120, 125–126, 139–140
7.5.B	describe π as the ratio of the circumference of a circle to its diameter; and	SE: 133–136	SE: 137–138, 145, 148
7.5.C	solve mathematical and real-world problems involving similar shape and scale drawings.	SE: 127–130	SE: 131–131, 139–140, 143–145, 148

Standard	Descriptor	Taught	Reinforced
7.6 Proportionality. The student applies mathematical process standards to use probability and statistics to describe or solve problems involving proportional relationships. The student is expected to:			
7.6.A	represent sample spaces for simple and compound events using lists and tree diagrams;	SE: 157, 160, 165, 170, 194–195	SE: 161–162, 173–174, 181, 197–198
7.6.B	select and use different simulations to represent simple and compound events with and without technology;	SE: 165–166, 171–172, 205–206	SE: 167–168, 173–174, 209–210, 211
7.6.C	make predictions and determine solutions using experimental data for simple and compound events;	SE: 165–166, 175, 178	SE: 167–168, 179–181, 213–215
7.6.D	make predictions and determine solutions using theoretical probability for simple and compound events;	SE: 189–190, 195–196, 199–202	SE: 191–192, 197–198, 203–204, 211, 217
7.6.E	find the probabilities of a simple event and its complement and describe the relationship between the two;	SE: 158–160	SE: 161–162
7.6.F	use data from a random sample to make inferences about a population;	SE: 373–376, 381–382	SE: 377–378, 383–384, 395–396
7.6.G	solve problems using data represented in bar graphs, dot plots, and circle graphs, including part-to-whole and part-to-part comparisons and equivalents;	SE: 349–352	SE: 353–354, 367–368
7.6.H	solve problems using qualitative and quantitative predictions and comparisons from simple experiments; and	SE: 176–178, 199–202	SE: 179–180, 203–204, 214–216, 218
7.6.I	determine experimental and theoretical probabilities related to simple and compound events using data and sample spaces.	SE: 155–156, 160, 163–164, 166, 169–170, 175–178, 187–188, 193–194, 199–202	SE: 161–162, 167–168, 172–174, 179–180, 181, 203–204, 211, 213–216, 217–218

© Houghton Mifflin Harcourt Publishing Company

Standard	Descriptor	Taught	Reinforced
7.7 Expressions, equations, and relationships. The student applies mathematical process standards to represent linear relationships using multiple representations. The student is expected to:			
7.7	represent linear relationships using verbal descriptions, tables, graphs, and equations that simplify to the form $y = mx + b$.	SE: 225–229, 233–236	SE: 230–232, 237–238, 239–240, 271–272, 274, 275–276
7.8 Expressions, equations, and relationships. The student applies mathematical process standards to develop geometric relationships with volume. The student is expected to:			
7.8.A	model the relationship between the volume of a rectangular prism and a rectangular pyramid having both congruent bases and heights and connect that relationship to the formulas;	SE: 317–318	319–320
7.8.B	explain verbally and symbolically the relationship between the volume of a triangular prism and a triangular pyramid having both congruent bases and heights and connect that relationship to the formulas; and	SE: 324, 325	326
7.8.C	use models to determine the approximate formulas for the circumference and area of a circle and connect the models to the actual formulas.	SE: 297–298	299–300
7.9 Expressions, equations, and relationships. The student applies mathematical process standards to solve geometric problems. The student is expected to:			
7.9.A	solve problems involving the volume of rectangular prisms, triangular prisms, rectangular pyramids, and triangular pyramids;	SE: 315–317, 319–320, 323, 325–326	SE: 321–322, 327–328, 335–336, 338, 341
7.9.B	determine the circumference and area of circles;	SE: 291–294, 298–300	SE: 295–296, 301–302, 309–310, 338, 342
7.9.C	determine the area of composite figures containing combinations of rectangles, squares, parallelograms, trapezoids, triangles, semicircles, and quarter circles; and	SE: 303–306	SE: 307–308, 309–310, 337–338
7.9.D	solve problems involving the lateral and total surface area of a rectangular prism, rectangular pyramid, triangular prism, and triangular pyramid by determining the area of the shape's net.	SE: 329–332	SE: 333–334, 335–336, 339–340, 341

	7.10 Expressions, equations, and relationships. The student applies mathematical process standards to use one-variable equations and inequalities to represent situations. The student is expected to:		
7.10.A	write one-variable, two-step equations and inequalities to represent constraints or conditions within problems;	SE: 246, 248, 257–258	SE: 249–250, 261–262, 269, 272, 275
7.10.B	represent solutions for one-variable, two-step equations and inequalities on number lines; and	SE: 252, 254, 264, 266	SE: 255–256, 267–268, 272–273, 276
7.10.C	write a corresponding real-world problem given a one-variable, two-step equation or inequality.	SE: 247–248, 259–260	SE: 249–250, 261–262
	7.11 Expressions, equations, and relationships. The student applies mathematical process standards to solve one-variable equations and inequalities. The student is expected to:		
7.11.A	model and solve one-variable, two-step equations and inequalities;	SE: 245, 248, 251, 254, 263–264	SE: 249–250, 255–256, 267–268, 269–270, 273
7.11.B	determine if the given value(s) make(s) one-variable, two-step equations and inequalities true; and	SE: 253–254, 265–266	SE: 255–256, 267–268, 270, 272–273
7.11.C	write and solve equations using geometry concepts, including the sum of the angles in a triangle, and angle relationships.	SE: 283–288	SE: 289–290, 237
	7.12 Measurement and data. The student applies mathematical process standards to use statistical representations to analyze data. The student is expected to:		
7.12.A	compare two groups of numeric data using comparative dot plots or box plots by comparing their shapes, centers, and spreads;	SE: 355–358, 361–364	SE: 359–360, 365–366, 367–368, 393–394, 397–398
7.12.B	use data from a random sample to make inferences about a population; and	SE: 379–380, 382, 386–387	SE: 383–384, 389–390, 391, 395–396, 397–398
7.12.C	compare two populations based on data in random samples from these populations, including informal comparative inferences about differences between the two populations.	SE: 385–388	SE: 389–390, 391, 395–396, 397–398

Standard	Descriptor	Taught	Reinforced
7.13	**Personal financial literacy. The student applies mathematical process standards to develop an economic way of thinking and problem solving useful in one's life as a knowledgeable consumer and investor. The student is expected to:**		
7.13.A	calculate the sales tax for a given purchase and calculate income tax for earned wages;	SE: 103, 106, 405–408	SE: 107–108, 409–410, 423–424, 451, 455
7.13.B	identify the components of a personal budget, including income; planned savings for college, retirement, and emergencies; taxes; and fixed and variable expenses, and calculate what percentage each category comprises of the total budget;	SE: 429–434	SE: 435–436, 449–450, 453
7.13.C	create and organize a financial assets and liabilities record and construct a net worth statement;	SE: 443–446	SE: 447–448, 449–450, 453, 456
7.13.D	use a family budget estimator to determine the minimum household budget and average hourly wage needed for a family to meet its basic needs in the student's city or another large city nearby;	SE: 437–440	SE: 441–442, 453
7.13.E	calculate and compare simple interest and compound interest earnings; and	SE: 104, 106, 411–414	SE: 415–416, 452
7.13.F	analyze and compare monetary incentives, including sales, rebates, and coupons.	SE: 417–420	SE: 421–422, 423–424, 454–455

Texas English Language Proficiency Standards (ELPS)

HMH Texas Go Math supports English language learners at all proficiency levels. The HMH Texas Go Math Student Edition provides integrated resources to assist all levels of learners, as shown in the correlation tables provided below.

In addition, students at various levels may benefit from additional program support:

Beginning - Students at a Beginning level are supported by *Spanish Student Edition, Spanish Assessment Resources*, Success for Every Learner and Leveled Practice A worksheets in *Differentiated Instruction, Math On the Spot* videos with Spanish closed captioning, and the *Multilingual Glossary.*

Intermediate - Students at the Intermediate level may use any of the resources above, and may also use Reading Strategies in *Differentiated Instruction.*

Advanced and Advanced High - Students at these levels will be successful as the *Student Edition* promotes vocabulary development through visual and context clues. The Multilingual Glossary may also be helpful.

ELPS	Student Edition Citations
c.1.A use prior knowledge and experiences to understand meanings in English	This standard is met in: Reading Startup in each module—Examples: 5, 59, 83, 113 Unpacking the TEKS in each module—Examples: 6, 84, 154, 186
c.1.D speak using learning strategies such as requesting assistance, employing non-verbal cues, and using synonyms and circumlocution (conveying ideas by defining or describing when exact English words are not known)	This standard is met in Math Talk in most lessons—Examples: 116, 128, 156, 165
c.2.C learn new language structures, expressions, **and basic and academic vocabulary heard during classroom instruction and interactions**	This standard is met in: Math Talk in most lessons—Examples: 128, 156, 165, 170 Reflect questions in most lessons—Examples: 86, 93, 97, 127
c.2.D monitor understanding of spoken language during classroom instruction and interactions and **seek clarification [of spoken language] as needed**	This standard is met in: Math Talk in most lessons—Examples: 22, 128, 223, 156 Reflect questions in most lessons—Examples: 20, 86, 93, 97
c.2.E use visual, contextual, and **linguistic support to enhance and confirm understanding of increasingly complex and elaborated spoken language**	This standard is met in Visualize Vocabulary in each module—Examples: 5, 59, 83, 113
c.2.I demonstrate listening comprehension of increasingly complex spoken English by following directions, retelling or summarizing spoken messages, **responding to questions and requests,** collaborating with peers, **and taking notes commensurate with content and grade-level needs**	This standard is met in: Math Talk in most lessons—Examples: 22, 116, 128, 156 My Notes in many lessons— Examples: 14, 87, 128, 165
c.3.B expand and internalize initial English vocabulary by learning and using high-frequency English words necessary for identifying and describing people, places, and objects, by retelling simple stories and basic information represented or supported by pictures, and by learning and using **routine language needed for classroom communication**	This standard is met in: Vocabulary Puzzle in each unit—Examples: 2, 56, 150, 220 Active Reading in each module—Examples: 59, 83, 113, 223 Unpacking the TEKS in each module—Examples: 6, 60, 84, 154 Reflect questions in most lessons—Examples: 75, 86, 97, 99 Math Talk in most lessons—Examples: 99, 116, 128, 156 Explore Activities in many lessons—Examples: 67, 73, 85, 115

ELPS	Student Edition Citations
c.3.C speak using a variety of grammatical structures, sentence lengths, sentence types, and **connecting words with increasing accuracy and ease as more English is acquired**	This standard is met in Math Talk in most lessons—Examples: 116, 128, 156, 165
c.3.D speak using grade-level content area vocabulary in context to internalize new English words and build academic language proficiency	This standard is met in: Vocabulary Puzzle in each unit—Examples: 2, 56, 150, 220 Active Reading in each module—Examples: 59, 113, 153, 185 Math Talk in most lessons—Examples: 75, 116, 128, 156
c.3.E share information in cooperative learning interactions	This standard is met in: Math Talk in most lessons—Examples: 116, 128, 156, 165 Explore Activities in many lessons—Examples: 67, 73, 85, 115
c.3.F ask [for] and give information ranging from using a very limited bank of high-frequency, high-need, concrete vocabulary, including key words and expressions needed for basic communication in academic and social contexts, to using abstract and content-based vocabulary during extended speaking assignments	This standard is met in: Math Talk in most lessons—Examples: 75, 116, 156, 165 Explore Activities in many lessons—Examples: 67, 85, 115, 127
c.3.H narrate, describe, and **explain with increasing specificity and detail as more English is acquired**	This standard is met in: Reflect questions in most lessons—Examples: 115, 127, 134, 156 Math Talk in most lessons—Examples: 75, 116, 128, 156 Independent Practice exercises in each lesson—Examples: 77, 119, 131, 161
C.4.C develop basic sight vocabulary, derive meaning of environmental print, and comprehend English vocabulary and language structures used routinely in written classroom materials	This standard is met in: Vocabulary Puzzle in each unit—Examples: 2, 56, 150, 220 Active Reading in each module—Examples: 59, 113, 153, 185 Unpacking the TEKS in each module—Examples: 6, 114, 154, 186 Highlighted vocabulary at point of use in instruction—Examples: 7, 8, 13, 128
c.4.D use prereading supports such as graphic organizers, illustrations, and pretaught topic-related vocabulary and other prereading activities to enhance comprehension of written text	This standard is met in Active Reading in each module—Examples: 59, 113, 153, 185
c.4.F use visual and contextual support and support from peers and teachers to read grade-appropriate content area text, enhance and confirm understanding, and develop vocabulary, grasp of language structures, and background knowledge needed to comprehend increasingly challenging language	This standard is met through photographs, illustrations, and diagrams throughout instruction—Examples: 13, 36, 87, 133
c.4.G demonstrate comprehension of increasingly complex English by participating in shared reading, **retelling or summarizing material, responding to questions, and taking notes commensurate with content area and grade level needs**	This standard is met in: Math Talk in most lessons—Examples: 75, 116, 128, 156 Reflect questions in most lessons—Examples: 127, 128, 133, 156 Essential Question Check In exercises in each lesson—Examples: 124, 130, 160, 166 H.O.T.S. exercises in each lesson—Examples: 90, 120, 126, 162

Succeeding with HMH Texas Go Math

Actively participate in your learning with your write-in Student Edition. Explore concepts, take notes, answer questions, and complete your homework right in your textbook!

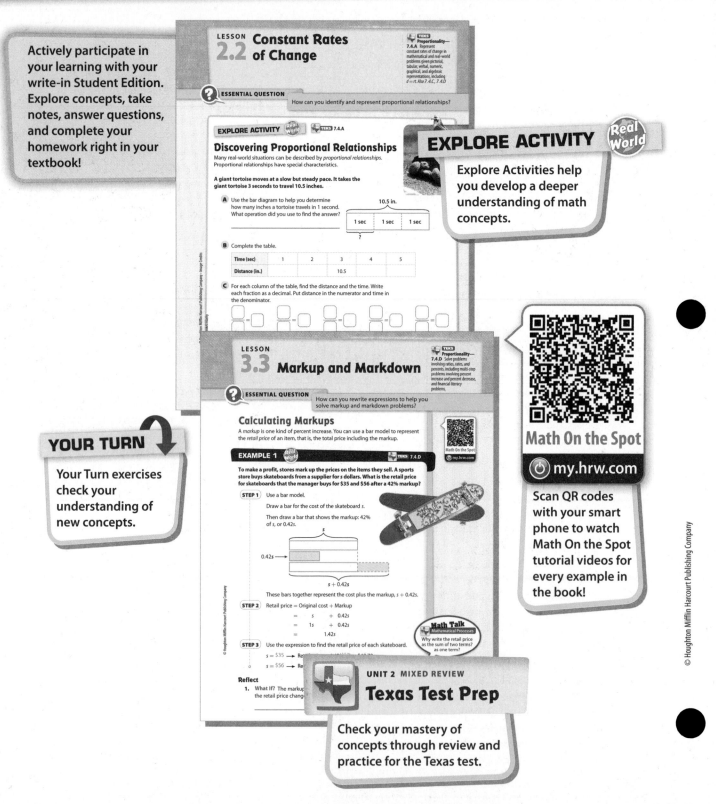

EXPLORE ACTIVITY *Real World*

Explore Activities help you develop a deeper understanding of math concepts.

YOUR TURN

Your Turn exercises check your understanding of new concepts.

Math On the Spot
⏻ my.hrw.com

Scan QR codes with your smart phone to watch Math On the Spot tutorial videos for every example in the book!

UNIT 2 MIXED REVIEW
Texas Test Prep

Check your mastery of concepts through review and practice for the Texas test.

© Houghton Mifflin Harcourt Publishing Company

GO DIGITAL

my.hrw.com

Enhance Your Learning!

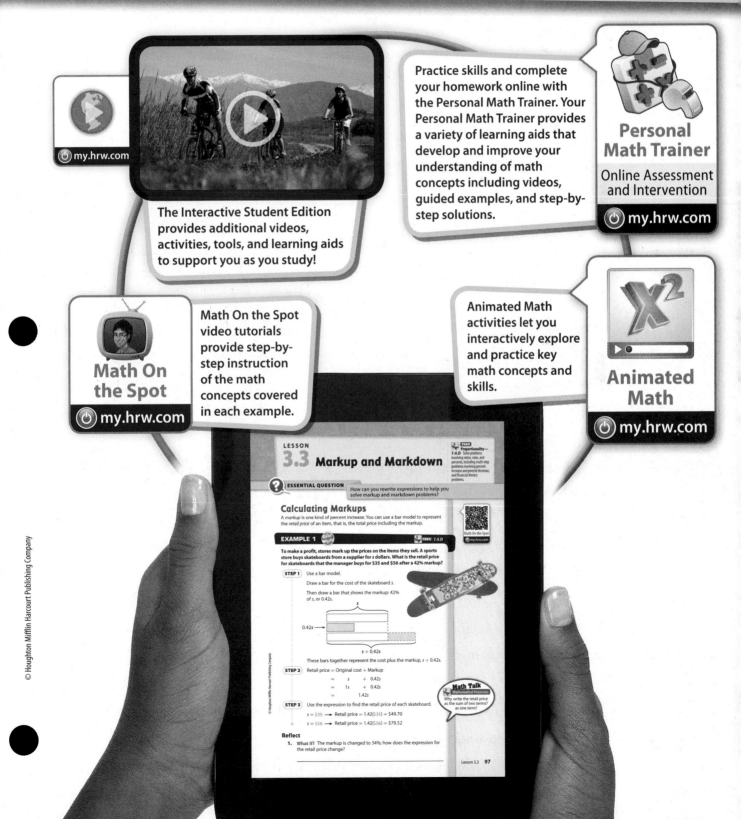

my.hrw.com

The Interactive Student Edition provides additional videos, activities, tools, and learning aids to support you as you study!

Practice skills and complete your homework online with the Personal Math Trainer. Your Personal Math Trainer provides a variety of learning aids that develop and improve your understanding of math concepts including videos, guided examples, and step-by-step solutions.

Personal Math Trainer

Online Assessment and Intervention

my.hrw.com

Math On the Spot

my.hrw.com

Math On the Spot video tutorials provide step-by-step instruction of the math concepts covered in each example.

Animated Math activities let you interactively explore and practice key math concepts and skills.

Animated Math

my.hrw.com

© Houghton Mifflin Harcourt Publishing Company

Mathematical Process Standards

7.1 **Mathematical process standards.** The student uses mathematical processes to acquire and demonstrate mathematical understanding.

7.1.A Everyday Life

The student is expected to apply mathematics to problems arising in everyday life, society, and the workplace.

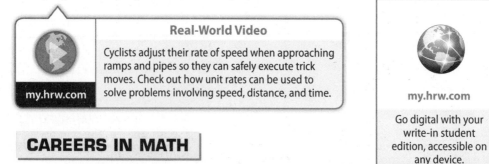

Real-World Video

Cyclists adjust their rate of speed when approaching ramps and pipes so they can safely execute trick moves. Check out how unit rates can be used to solve problems involving speed, distance, and time.

my.hrw.com

CAREERS IN MATH

my.hrw.com

Go digital with your write-in student edition, accessible on any device.

7.1.B Use a Problem-Solving Model

The student is expected to use a problem-solving model that incorporates analyzing given information, formulating a plan or strategy, determining a solution, justifying the solution, and evaluating the problem-solving process and the reasonableness of the solution.

Analyze Information

What are you asked to find?

What are the facts?

Is there any information given that you will not use?

Formulate a Plan

What strategy or strategies can you use?

Have you solved any similar problems before?

Solve

Follow your plan.

Show the steps in your solution.

Justify and Evaluate

Did you answer the question?

Is your answer reasonable?

Are there other strategies that you could use?

7.1.C Select Tools

The student is expected to select tools, including real objects, manipulatives, paper and pencil, and technology as appropriate, and techniques, including mental math, estimation, and number sense as appropriate, to solve problems.

EXPLORE ACTIVITY Real World

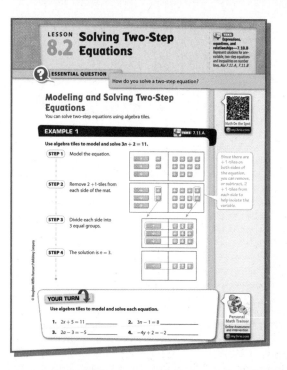

7.1.D Multiple Representations

The student is expected to communicate mathematical ideas, reasoning, and their implications, using multiple representations, including symbols, diagrams, graphs, and language as appropriate.

7.1.E Use Representations

The student is expected to create and use representations to organize, record, and communicate mathematical ideas.

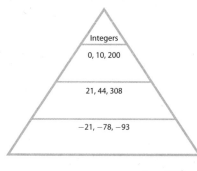

Integers

0, 10, 200

21, 44, 308

−21, −78, −93

7.1.F Analyze Relationships

The student is expected to analyze mathematical relationships to connect and communicate mathematical ideas.

H.O.T. FOCUS ON HIGHER ORDER THINKING

Reflect

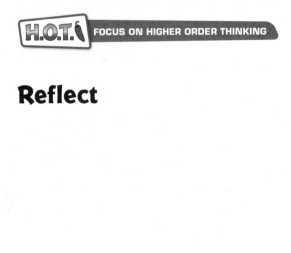

LESSON 7.1 Linear Relationships in the Form $y = mx + b$

Expressions, equations, and relationships—7.7 The student applies mathematical process standards to represent linear relationships using multiple representations...

ESSENTIAL QUESTION How do you use tables and verbal descriptions to describe a linear relationship?

EXPLORE ACTIVITY TEKS 7.7

Discovering Linear Relationships

Many real-world situations can be described by linear relationships.

Jodie pays $5 per ticket for a play and a one-time $2 convenience fee. The table shows the total cost for different numbers of tickets.

Number of tickets	1	2	3	4	5
Total cost ($)	7	12	17	22	27

A Describe a pattern for the row showing the number of tickets bought.

B Describe the pattern for the row showing total cost.

C Out of the total cost paid, how much does the actual ticket account for?

Reflect

1. How much more than $5 does Jodie pay for one ticket? What if she buys 5 tickets? Explain.

2. **Analyze Relationships** Describe the total amount paid in dollars based on the number of tickets.

Lesson 7.1 **225**

7.1.G Justify Arguments

The student is expected to display, explain, and justify mathematical ideas and arguments using precise mathematical language in written or oral communication.

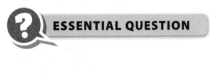

? **ESSENTIAL QUESTION**

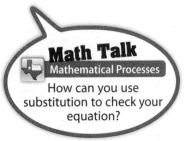

Math Talk
Mathematical Processes

How can you use substitution to check your equation?

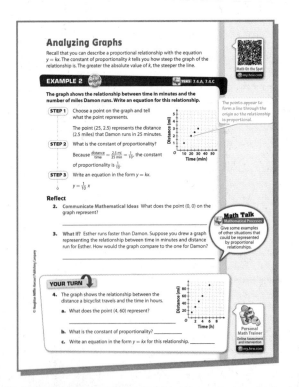

Analyzing Graphs

Recall that you can describe a proportional relationship with the equation $y = kx$. The constant of proportionality k tells you how steep the graph of the relationship is. The greater the absolute value of k, the steeper the line.

EXAMPLE 2 TEKS 7.4.A, 7.4.C

The graph shows the relationship between time in minutes and the number of miles Damon runs. Write an equation for this relationship.

STEP 1 Choose a point on the graph and tell what the point represents.

The point (25, 2.5) represents the distance (2.5 miles) that Damon runs in 25 minutes.

STEP 2 What is the constant of proportionality?

Because $\frac{distance}{time} = \frac{2.5 \text{ mi}}{25 \text{ min}} = \frac{1}{10}$, the constant of proportionality is $\frac{1}{10}$.

STEP 3 Write an equation in the form $y = kx$.

$y = \frac{1}{10} x$

The points appear to form a line through the origin so the relationship is proportional.

Reflect

2. **Communicate Mathematical Ideas** What does the point (0, 0) on the graph represent?

3. **What If?** Esther runs faster than Damon. Suppose you drew a graph representing the relationship between time in minutes and distance run for Esther. How would the graph compare to the one for Damon?

Math Talk
Mathematical Processes

Give some examples of other situations that could be represented by proportional relationships.

YOUR TURN

4. The graph shows the relationship between the distance a bicyclist travels and the time in hours.

a. What does the point (4, 60) represent?

b. What is the constant of proportionality? _____

c. Write an equation in the form $y = kx$ for this relationship. _____

Personal Math Trainer
Online Assessment and Intervention
my.hrw.com

GRADE 6 PART 1

Review Test

Personal
Math Trainer
Online
Assessment and
Intervention

my.hrw.com

Selected Response

1. Which temperature is warmest?

Ⓐ 16 °F   Ⓒ −21 °F

Ⓑ −16 °F   Ⓓ 21 °F

2. Which group of numbers is in order from least to greatest?

Ⓐ $-2.3, -\frac{2}{3}, 0.23, \frac{2}{3}$

Ⓑ $-\frac{2}{3}, -2.3, 0.23, \frac{2}{3}$

Ⓒ $0.23, -\frac{2}{3}, \frac{2}{3}, -2.3$

Ⓓ $-2.3, -\frac{2}{3}, \frac{2}{3}, 0.23$

3. Grant and Pedro are comparing the result of their stocks at the end of the week. Grant's result was a loss of $4. Pedro's result was the opposite of Grant's. How would you graph the results on a number line?

Ⓐ Grant's point is 4 units to the right of 0 on a number line, and Pedro's point is 4 units to the left of 0.

Ⓑ Grant's point is 4 units to the right of 0 on a number line, and Pedro's point is the same point.

Ⓒ Grant's loss is a point 4 units to the left of 0 on a number line, and Pedro's point is 4 units to the right of 0.

Ⓓ Grant's loss is a point 4 units to the left of 0 on a number line, and Pedro's point is the same point because it's already negative.

4. Evaluate $a + b$ for $a = 34$ and $b = -6$.

Ⓐ 40   Ⓒ −28

Ⓑ 28   Ⓓ −40

5. One winter day, the temperature ranged from a high of 20 °F to a low of −25 °F. By how many degrees did the temperature change?

Ⓐ −5 °F   Ⓒ −15 °F

Ⓑ 55 °F   Ⓓ 45 °F

6. Find the quotient.
$7\frac{1}{6} \div \frac{5}{9}$

Ⓐ $1\frac{13}{30}$ Ⓒ $12\frac{9}{10}$

Ⓑ 12   Ⓓ $13\frac{1}{2}$

7. Stephen purchased 4.7 pounds of coffee at a cost of $4.75 per pound. What was the cost of the coffee?

Ⓐ $223.25   Ⓒ $22.33

Ⓑ $9.45   Ⓓ $2.23

8. Carla is building a table out of boards that are 4.25 inches wide. She wants the table to be at least 36 inches wide. How many boards does she need?

Ⓐ 8   Ⓒ 9.5

Ⓑ 9   Ⓓ 153

9. You are working as an assistant to a chef. The chef has 8 cups of berries and will use $\frac{2}{3}$ cup of berries for each dessert he makes. How many desserts can he make?

Ⓐ 4 desserts   Ⓒ 12 desserts

Ⓑ $5\frac{1}{3}$ desserts   Ⓓ 16 desserts

10. Valerie sold 6 tickets to the school play and Mark sold 16 tickets. What is the ratio of the number of tickets Valerie sold to the number of tickets Mark sold?

Ⓐ 16 to 6 Ⓒ 2 to 8

Ⓑ 2 to 3 Ⓓ 3 to 8

11. Patricia paid $584 for 8 nights at a hotel. Find the unit rate.

Ⓐ $\frac{\$37}{1 \text{ night}}$ Ⓒ $\frac{\$146}{1 \text{ night}}$

Ⓑ $\frac{\$73}{1 \text{ night}}$ Ⓓ $\frac{\$584}{1 \text{ night}}$

12. A grocery store sells the brands of yogurt shown in the table.

Brand	Size (ounces)	Price ($)
Sunny	12	2.16
Fruity	14	2.34
Smooth	18	2.40
Yummy	16	2.24

For which brand of yogurt is the unit price cheapest?

Ⓐ Sunny Ⓒ Smooth

Ⓑ Fruity Ⓓ Yummy

13. The fuel for a chainsaw is a mix of oil and gasoline. The label says to mix 5 ounces of oil with 15 gallons of gasoline. How much oil would you use if you had 45 gallons of gasoline?

Ⓐ 1.67 ounces Ⓒ 21 ounces

Ⓑ 15 ounces Ⓓ 135 ounces

14. School A has 216 students and 12 classrooms. School B has 432 students. How many classrooms would School B need for the ratios of students to classrooms at both schools to be the same?

Ⓐ 16 Ⓒ 24

Ⓑ 20 Ⓓ 28

15. Terry drove 300 miles in 5 hours at a constant speed. How long would it take him to drive 420 miles at the same speed?

Ⓐ 5.6 hours Ⓒ 7 hours

Ⓑ 6.5 hours Ⓓ 62 hours

16. Lamar paid $93 for a bicycle that was on sale for 60% of its original price. What was the original price of the bicycle?

Ⓐ $33.00 Ⓒ $153

Ⓑ $55.80 Ⓓ $232.50

17. Selma rented a car for $29 per day plus a one-time charge of $14 for insurance. If d represents the number of days for which the car is rented, which equation represents the total cost c of the rental?

Ⓐ $c = 29d + 14$ Ⓒ $c = (29 + 14)d$

Ⓑ $c = 14d + 29$ Ⓓ $c = 29d - 14$

Gridded Response

18. To find the mileage, or how many miles a car can travel per gallon of gasoline, you can use the expression $\frac{m}{g}$, where m is the distance in miles and g is the number of gallons of gas used. Find the mileage in miles per gallon for a car that travels 585 miles on 18 gallons of gas.

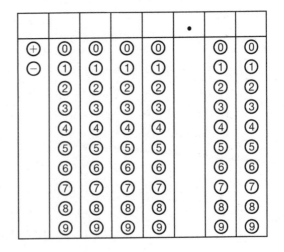

Selected Response

1. Suppose you have developed a scale that indicates the brightness of sunlight. Each category in the table is 5 times brighter than the next category. For example, a day that is dazzling is 5 times brighter than a day that is radiant. How many times brighter is a dazzling day than a dim day?

Sunlight Intensity	
Category	**Brightness**
Dim	2
Illuminated	3
Radiant	4
Dazzling	5

(A) 625 times brighter

(B) 125 times brighter

(C) 25 times brighter

(D) 3 times brighter

2. Which are possible side lengths of a triangle?

(A) 15, 9, 3   (C) 11, 6, 3

(B) 6, 12, 19   (D) 4, 8, 10

3. A triangle has sides with lengths of $5x - 7$, $3x - 4$, and $2x - 6$. What is the perimeter of the triangle?

(A) $10x - 17$ (C) $4x - 9$

(B) $6x - 17$ (D) $-7x$

4. A driveway is 162 feet long, 6 feet wide, and 4 inches deep. How many cubic feet of concrete will be required for the driveway?

(A) 254 ft³   (C) 355 ft³

(B) 324 ft³   (D) 3888 ft³

5. Wilson bought gift cards for some lawyers and their assistants. Each lawyer got a gift card worth $\$\ell$. Each assistant got a gift card worth $\$a$. There are 14 lawyers. Each lawyer has three assistants. The expression for total cost of the gift cards is $14\ell + 42a$. Write an expression that is equivalent to the given expression.

(A) $14(\ell + 2a)$ (C) $14(\ell + 42a)$

(B) $14(\ell + 3a)$ (D) $42(\ell + 3a)$

6. Find the volume of the rectangular prism.

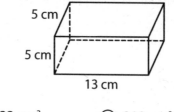

5 cm

5 cm

13 cm

(A) 23 cm³   (C) 310 cm³

(B) 184 cm³   (D) 325 cm³

7. Write an equation for the function. Tell what each variable you use represents. A plant's height is 1.6 times its age in months.

(A) x = plant's height; y = plant's age; $1.6 = xy$

(B) x = plant's height; y = plant's age; $y = 1.6x$

(C) x = plant's age; y = plant's height; $x = 1.6y$

(D) x = plant's height; y = plant's age; $x = 1.6y$

8. Justin is redoing his bathroom floor with tiles measuring 6 in. by 13 in. The floor has an area of 8,500 in². What is the least number of tiles he will need?

(A) 448 tiles   (C) 108.97 tiles

(B) 109 tiles   (D) 108 tiles

9. What value of s makes the equation true?
$s + 2.8 = 6.59$

Ⓐ $s = 3$ Ⓒ $s = 4.13$

Ⓑ $s = 3.79$ Ⓓ $s = 9.39$

10. Write an equation that models the situation and find its solution.
It will be Lindsay's birthday soon, and her friends Mary, Mikhail, Anne, Kim, Makoto, and Isabel have contributed equal amounts of money to buy her a present. They have a total of $36.00 to spend. Determine how much each friend contributed.

Ⓐ $6x = \$36.00; x = \$108.00$

Ⓑ $7x = \$36.00; x = \$5.14$

Ⓒ $6x = \$36.00; x = \$216.00$

Ⓓ $6x = \$36.00; x = \$6.00$

11. The table shows the results of a survey in which 200 people were asked about their favorite food. What percent of people surveyed said macaroni and cheese is their favorite food?

Food	Frequency
Hamburger	98
Macaroni and cheese	?
Spaghetti	44
Taco	28

Ⓐ 15% Ⓒ 49%

Ⓑ 30% Ⓓ 170%

12. In a box-and-whisker plot, the interquartile range is a measure of the spread of the middle half of the data. Find the interquartile range for the data set 10, 3, 7, 6, 9, 12, 13.

Ⓐ 12 Ⓒ 7

Ⓑ 8 Ⓓ 6

13. What is the interquartile range of the data represented by the box-and-whisker plot?

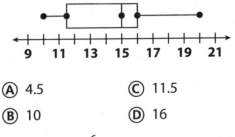

Ⓐ 4.5 Ⓒ 11.5

Ⓑ 10 Ⓓ 16

14. In a fish tank, $\frac{6}{7}$ of the fish have a red stripe on them. If 18 of the fish have red stripes, how many total fish are in the tank?

Ⓐ 26 fish Ⓒ 23 fish

Ⓑ 25 fish Ⓓ 21 fish

Gridded Response

15. What is the area of the polygon in square centimeters?

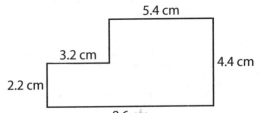

Selected Response

1. A store decreases the price of an item from $120 to $96. What is the percent decrease?

Ⓐ 20%

Ⓑ 24%

Ⓒ 25%

Ⓓ 80%

2. Juan plays on the school baseball team. In the last 9 games, Juan was at bat 28 times and got 6 hits. What is the experimental probability that Juan will get a hit during his next time at bat? Express your answer as a fraction in simplest form.

Ⓐ $\frac{14}{3}$

Ⓒ $\frac{3}{11}$

Ⓑ $\frac{3}{14}$

Ⓓ $\frac{11}{14}$

3. It took Jayla 40 seconds to rip half a DVD. What is Jayla's "ripping rate" in DVDs per minute?

Ⓐ $\frac{3}{4}$ DVD per minute

Ⓑ $\frac{7}{10}$ DVD per minute

Ⓒ $1\frac{2}{5}$ DVDs per minute

Ⓓ $1\frac{3}{7}$ DVDs per minute

4. A deli offers a lunch special that comes with soup, a sandwich, and a dessert. The soup choices are tomato or onion; the sandwich choices are ham, chicken, tuna, or pastrami; and the dessert choices are cake or pie. How many different lunch specials are in the sample space?

Ⓐ 8

Ⓒ 16

Ⓑ 12

Ⓓ 32

5. A coin-operated machine sells plastic rings. It contains 6 yellow rings, 11 blue rings, 15 green rings, and 3 black rings. Sarah puts a coin into the machine. Find the theoretical probability that Sarah gets a black ring, rounded to the nearest thousandth.

Ⓐ 0.914

Ⓒ 0.094

Ⓑ 0.171

Ⓓ 0.086

6. What are the actual dimensions of the Books section?

Floor Plan of Library

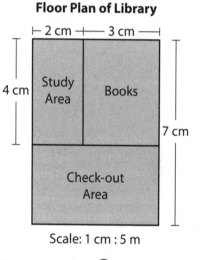

Scale: 1 cm : 5 m

Ⓐ 25 m × 35 m

Ⓒ 15 m × 35 m

Ⓑ 15 m × 20 m

Ⓓ 2 m × 4 m

7. In the gift shop of the History of Flight museum, Elisa bought a kit to make a model of a jet airplane. The actual plane is 21 feet long with a wingspan of 17.5 feet. If the finished model will be 10.5 inches long, what will the wingspan be?

Ⓐ 30.6 inches

Ⓒ 8.75 inches

Ⓑ 14.4 inches

Ⓓ 5 inches

8. An experiment consists of rolling two fair number cubes. What is the probability that the sum of the two numbers will be 4?

Ⓐ $\frac{1}{18}$ Ⓒ $\frac{1}{11}$

Ⓑ $\frac{1}{12}$ Ⓓ $\frac{1}{6}$

9. Iris wants to buy two necklaces, one for her sister and one for herself. The necklace for her sister costs $42.00, and the necklace for herself costs $28.00. The sales tax on the purchases is 8%. Find the total cost of Iris's purchases, including sales tax.

Ⓐ $5.60   Ⓒ $70.00

Ⓑ $64.40   Ⓓ $75.60

10. Tell whether the data show a proportional relationship. If so, identify the constant of proportionality.

Number of Baskets	Cost
3	$12
5	$20
6	$24
8	$32
15	$60

Ⓐ not proportional

Ⓑ proportional; $k = 9$

Ⓒ proportional; $k = \frac{1}{4}$

Ⓓ proportional; $k = 4$

11. Four sisters bought a present for their mother. They received a 10% discount on the original price of the gift. After the discount was taken, each sister paid $9.00. What was the original price of the gift?

Ⓐ $40.00   Ⓒ $36.00

Ⓑ $39.60   Ⓓ $32.73

12. Terry drove 366 miles in 6 hours at a constant speed. How long would it take him to drive 427 miles at the same speed?

Ⓐ 5.14 hours   Ⓒ 6.5 hours

Ⓑ 6.1 hours   Ⓓ 7 hours

13. Which set of numbers is *not* a subset of the rational numbers?

Ⓐ negative integers

Ⓑ negative repeating decimals

Ⓒ square roots of whole numbers

Ⓓ terminating decimals

14. The ratio of adults to children attending a new exhibit one day at the museum was found to be 7:3. Based on this ratio, if 370 people attended that day, how many were children?

Ⓐ 101   Ⓒ 159

Ⓑ 111   Ⓓ 259

Gridded Response

15. The graph shows the proportional relationship between the total cost and the number of pounds of cashews purchased. What would the total price in dollars be for 11.5 pounds of cashews?

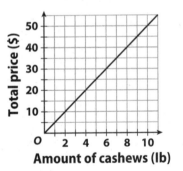

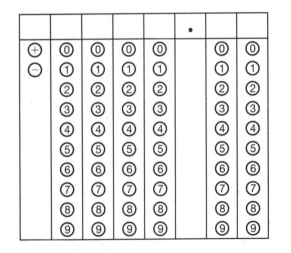

GRADE 7 PART 2

Benchmark Test

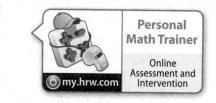

Personal
Math Trainer

Online
Assessment and
Intervention

my.hrw.com

Selected Response

1. Gina made 13 of 20 free throws in basketball practice. Predict the number of free throws she would make if she attempted 100 free throws.

   (A) 40   (C) 65

   (B) 50   (D) 73

2. A manufacturer inspects 500 personal video players and finds that 496 of them have no defects. The manufacturer sent a shipment of 2,000 video players to a distributor. Predict the number of players in the shipment that are likely to have no defects.

   (A) 16   (C) 1,840

   (B) 496   (D) 1,984

3. It costs $9 to go to Pete's Pottery Place to paint custom bowls at a cost of $3 per bowl. Natalie plans to paint bowls 5 days this month and to paint b bowls on each day so she can sell them at a craft fair. Which equation represents Natalie's total cost c for the month?

   (A) $c = 5(3b + 9)$ (C) $c = 5(9b + 3)$

   (B) $c = 3(5b + 9)$ (D) $c = 3(9b + 5)$

4. Find the area of the circle to the nearest tenth. Use 3.14 for π.

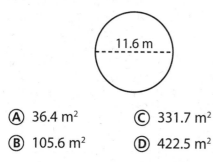

11.6 m

   (A) 36.4 m²   (C) 331.7 m²

   (B) 105.6 m²   (D) 422.5 m²

5. At the beginning of the year, Jason had $80 in his savings account. Each month, he added $15 to his account. Write an equation for the amount of money A in Jason's savings account each month. Then use the equation to find the amount of money in his account at the end of the year.

Month	1	2	3	m
Amount	$95	$110	$125	$?

   (A) $A = 95 + 15m$; $275

   (B) $A = 95 + m$; $107

   (C) $A = 80 + 12m$; $224

   (D) $A = 15m + 80$; $260

6. Which equation is represented by the graph?

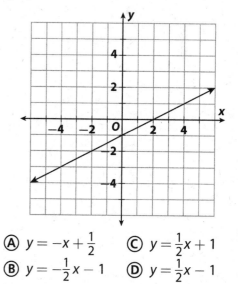

   (A) $y = -x + \frac{1}{2}$ (C) $y = \frac{1}{2}x + 1$

   (B) $y = -\frac{1}{2}x - 1$ (D) $y = \frac{1}{2}x - 1$

7. Write an equation to represent the linear relationship.

   The temperature of a pot of water is 72 °F. The temperature increases by 25 °F per minute when being heated.

   (A) $y = 72x + 25$ (C) $y = 72 + 25$

   (B) $y = 25x + 72$ (D) $y = (72 + 25)x$

8. For a history fair, a school is building a circular wooden stage that will stand 2 feet off the ground. Find the area of the stage if the radius of the stage is 4 meters. Use 3.14 for π.

Ⓐ 12.56 m²   Ⓒ 50.24 m²

Ⓑ 25.12 m²   Ⓓ 100.48 m²

9. Roselia built a cabinet in the shape of a rectangular prism. The cabinet was 30 inches wide, 4 feet tall, and 18 inches deep. What is the volume of the cabinet in cubic feet?

Ⓐ 12 ft³   Ⓒ 18 ft³

Ⓑ 15 ft³   Ⓓ 2,160 ft³

10. Find the surface area of the triangular prism.

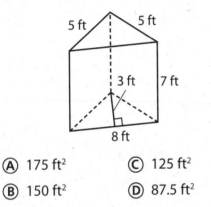

Ⓐ 175 ft²   Ⓒ 125 ft²

Ⓑ 150 ft²   Ⓓ 87.5 ft²

11. Ben and his friends are making a video to post online. The three friends all made video segments of the same length. Ben's video segment is at least 4 minutes long. Let s represent the length of each of the friend's segments. Write an inequality to represent the length ℓ of the combined video.

Ⓐ $\ell \geq 3s + 4$ Ⓒ $\ell \leq 3s + 4$

Ⓑ $\ell > 3s + 4$ Ⓓ $\ell \geq 4s + 3$

12. The number line shows the solutions to an inequality. Which inequality does not match the graph?

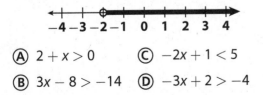

Ⓐ $2 + x > 0$ Ⓒ $-2x + 1 < 5$

Ⓑ $3x - 8 > -14$ Ⓓ $-3x + 2 > -4$

13. Ralph is an electrician. He charges an initial fee of $24, plus $33 per hour. If Ralph earned $189 on a job, how long did the job take?

Ⓐ 4 hours   Ⓒ 6.5 hours

Ⓑ 5 hours   Ⓓ 132 hours

14. Write and solve an equation to find the measure of the missing angle in the triangle.

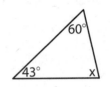

Ⓐ $60 - x > 43; x = 17°$

Ⓑ $60 + 43 + x = 180; x = 77°$

Ⓒ $x + 90 = 43 + 60; x = 13°$

Ⓓ $x = 60 + 43; x = 103°$

Gridded Response

15. Sara purchased a skirt for $15.99 and two shirts for $12.50 each. The sales tax in her town in 7.5%. What was the total cost of Sara's purchase in dollars including sales tax? Round to the nearest penny.

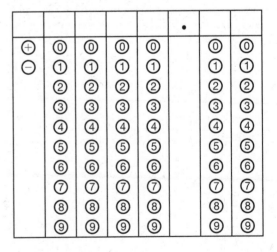

UNIT 1

Number and Operations

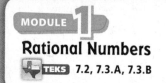

MODULE 1
Rational Numbers
TEKS 7.2, 7.3.A, 7.3.B

CAREERS IN MATH

Urban Planner An urban planner creates plans for urban, suburban, and rural communities and makes recommendations about locations for infrastructure, such as buildings, roads, and sewer and water pipes. Urban planners perform cost-benefit analysis of projects, use measurement and geometry when they design the layout of infrastructure, and use statistics and mathematical models to predict the growth and future needs of a population.

If you are interested in a career as an urban planner, you should study these mathematical subjects:
- Algebra
- Geometry
- Trigonometry
- Statistics

Research other careers that require using measurement, geometry, and mathematical modeling.

Unit 1 Performance Task

At the end of the unit, check out how **urban planners** use math.

© Houghton Mifflin Harcourt Publishing Company

Unit 1   **1**

Vocabulary Preview

Use the puzzle to preview key vocabulary from this unit. Unscramble the circled letters within found words to answer the riddle at the bottom of the page.

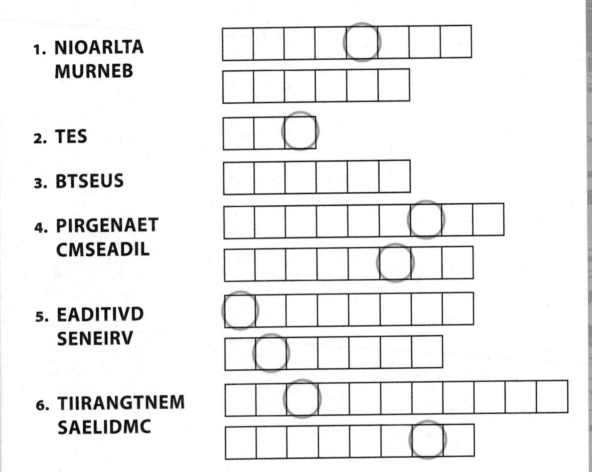

1. **NIOARLTA MURNEB**

2. **TES**

3. **BTSEUS**

4. **PIRGENAET CMSEADIL**

5. **EADITIVD SENEIRV**

6. **TIIRANGTNEM SAELIDMC**

1. Any number that can be written as a ratio of two integers. (Lesson 1-1)
2. A group of items. (Lesson 1-2)
3. A set that is contained within another set. (Lesson 1-2)
4. Decimals in which one or more digits repeat infinitely. (Lesson 1-1)
5. The opposite of any number. (Lesson 1-3)
6. Decimals that have a finite number of digits. (Lesson 1-1)

Q: Why were the two fractions able to settle their differences peacefully?

A: They were both __ __ __ __ __ __ __ __ __!

Rational Numbers

? ESSENTIAL QUESTION

How can you use rational numbers to solve real-world problems?

Real-World Video

In many competitive sports, scores are given as decimals. For some events, the judges' scores are averaged to give the athlete's final score.

my.hrw.com

GO DIGITAL
my.hrw.com

my.hrw.com

Go digital with your write-in student edition, accessible on any device.

Math On the Spot

Scan with your smart phone to jump directly to the online edition, video tutor, and more.

Animated Math

Interactively explore key concepts to see how math works.

Personal Math Trainer

Get immediate feedback and help as you work through practice sets.

Are YOU Ready?

Complete these exercises to review skills you will need for this chapter.

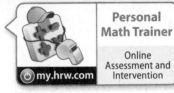

Personal Math Trainer
Online Assessment and Intervention
my.hrw.com

Multiply Fractions

EXAMPLE $\frac{3}{8} \times \frac{4}{9}$

$$\frac{3}{8} \times \frac{4}{9} = \frac{\overset{1}{\cancel{3}}}{\underset{2}{\cancel{8}}} \times \frac{\overset{1}{\cancel{4}}}{\underset{3}{\cancel{9}}}$$ Divide by the common factors.

$$= \frac{1}{6}$$ Simplify.

Multiply. Write the product in simplest form.

1. $\frac{9}{14} \times \frac{7}{6}$ _____
2. $\frac{3}{5} \times \frac{4}{7}$ _____
3. $\frac{11}{8} \times \frac{10}{33}$ _____
4. $\frac{4}{9} \times 3$ _____

Operations with Fractions

EXAMPLE $\frac{2}{5} \div \frac{7}{10} = \frac{2}{5} \times \frac{10}{7}$ Multiply by the reciprocal of the divisor.

$$= \frac{2}{\underset{1}{\cancel{5}}} \times \frac{\overset{2}{\cancel{10}}}{7}$$ Divide by the common factors.

$$= \frac{4}{7}$$ Simplify.

Divide.

5. $\frac{1}{2} \div \frac{1}{4}$ _____
6. $\frac{3}{8} \div \frac{13}{16}$ _____
7. $\frac{2}{5} \div \frac{14}{15}$ _____
8. $\frac{4}{9} \div \frac{16}{27}$ _____

9. $\frac{3}{5} \div \frac{5}{6}$ _____
10. $\frac{1}{4} \div \frac{23}{24}$ _____
11. $6 \div \frac{3}{5}$ _____
12. $\frac{4}{5} \div 10$ _____

Order of Operations

EXAMPLE $50 - 3(3 + 1)^2$ To evaluate, first operate within parentheses.

$50 - 3(4)^2$ Next simplify exponents.

$50 - 3(16)$ Then multiply and divide from left to right.

$50 - 48$ Finally add and subtract from left to right.

2

Evaluate each expression.

13. $21 - 6 \div 3$ ____
14. $18 + (7 - 4) \times 3$ ____
15. $5 + (8 - 3)^2$ ____

16. $9 + 18 \div 3 + 10$ ____
17. $60 - (3 - 1)^4 \times 3$ ____
18. $10 - 16 \div 4 \times 2 + 6$ ____

Reading Start-Up

Visualize Vocabulary

Use the ✔ words to complete the graphic. You can put more than one word in each section of the triangle.

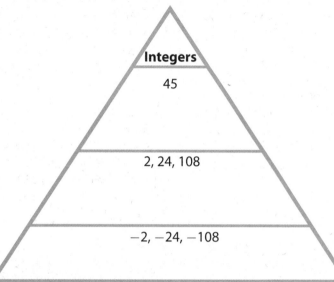

Integers

45

2, 24, 108

−2, −24, −108

Vocabulary

Review Words

   integers *(enteros)*

✔ negative numbers *(números negativos)*

   pattern *(patrón)*

✔ positive numbers

✔ whole numbers *(números enteros)*

Preview Words

   additive inverse *(inverso aditivo)*

   opposite *(opuesto)*

   rational number *(número racional)*

   repeating decimal *(decimal periódico)*

   set *(conjunto)*

   subset *(subconjunto)*

   terminating decimal *(decimal finitos)*

Understand Vocabulary

Complete the sentences using the preview words.

1. A group of items is a _____. A set contained within

   another set is a _____.

2. The _____ of a number is the same distance from 0 on a number line as the original number, but on the other side of 0.

3. A _____ can be expressed as a ratio of two integers.

Active Reading

Layered Book Before beginning the module, create a layered book to help you learn the concepts in this module. At the top of the first flap, write the title of the module, "Rational Numbers." Label the other flaps "Adding," "Subtracting," "Multiplying," and "Dividing." As you study each lesson, write important ideas, such as vocabulary and formulas, on the appropriate flap.

MODULE 1

Unpacking the TEKS

Understanding the TEKS and the vocabulary terms in the TEKS will help you know exactly what you are expected to learn in this module.

TEKS 7.3.A

Add, subtract, multiply, and divide rational numbers fluently.

Key Vocabulary

rational number (*número racional*)
Any number that can be expressed as a ratio of two integers.

What It Means to You

You will add, subtract, multiply, and divide rational numbers.

UNPACKING EXAMPLE 7.3.A

$$15 \cdot \frac{2}{3} - 12 \div 1\frac{1}{3}$$

$$\frac{15}{1} \cdot \frac{2}{3} - \frac{12}{1} \div \frac{4}{3} \qquad$$ Write the whole numbers and mixed number as fractions. Convert division to multiplication by the reciprocal.

$$\frac{15}{1} \cdot \frac{2}{3} - \frac{12}{1} \cdot \frac{3}{4}$$

$$\frac{\overset{5}{\cancel{15}} \cdot 2}{1 \cdot \underset{1}{\cancel{3}}} - \frac{\overset{3}{\cancel{12}} \cdot 3}{1 \cdot \underset{1}{\cancel{4}}} \qquad$$ Simplify.

$$\frac{10}{1} - \frac{9}{1} = 10 - 9 = 1 \qquad$$ Multiply numerators. Multiply denominators.

TEKS 7.3.B

Apply and extend previous understandings of operations to solve problems using addition, subtraction, multiplication, and division of rational numbers.

What It Means to You

You will solve real-world and mathematical problems involving the four operations with rational numbers.

UNPACKING EXAMPLE 7.3.B

In 1954, the Sunshine Skyway Bridge toll for a car was $1.75. In 2012, the toll was $\frac{5}{7}$ of the toll in 1954. What was the toll in 2012?

$$1.75 \cdot \frac{5}{7} = 1\frac{3}{4} \cdot \frac{5}{7} \qquad$$ Write the decimal as a fraction.

$$= \frac{7}{4} \cdot \frac{5}{7} \qquad$$ Write the mixed number as an improper fraction.

$$= \frac{\overset{1}{\cancel{7}} \cdot 5}{4 \cdot \underset{1}{\cancel{7}}} \qquad$$ Simplify.

$$= \frac{5}{4} = 1.25 \qquad$$ Convert the improper fraction to a decimal.

The Sunshine Skyway Bridge toll for a car was $1.25 in 2012.

Visit **my.hrw.com** to see all the **TEKS** unpacked.

my.hrw.com

© Houghton Mifflin Harcourt Publishing Company • Image Credits: ©Ilene MacDonald/Alamy

LESSON
1.1 Rational Numbers and Decimals

TEKS
Number and operations—7.2 The student applies mathematical process standards to represent and use rational numbers in a variety of forms. . . .

ESSENTIAL QUESTION

How can you convert a rational number to a decimal?

EXPLORE ACTIVITY TEKS 7.2

Describing Decimal Forms of Rational Numbers

A **rational number** is a number that can be written as a ratio of two integers a and b, where b is not zero. For example, $\frac{4}{7}$ is a rational number, as is 0.37 because it can be written as the fraction $\frac{37}{100}$.

A Use a calculator to find the equivalent decimal form of each fraction. Remember that numbers that repeat can be written as 0.333... or $0.\overline{3}$.

Fraction	$\frac{1}{4}$	$\frac{5}{8}$	$\frac{2}{3}$	$\frac{2}{9}$	$\frac{12}{5}$		
Decimal Equivalent						0.2	0.875

B Now find the corresponding fraction of the decimal equivalents given in the last two columns in the table. Write the fractions in simplest form.

C **Conjecture** What do you notice about the digits after the decimal point in the decimal forms of the fractions? Compare notes with your neighbor and refine your conjecture if necessary.

_____

Reflect

1. Consider the decimal 0.101001000100001000001.... Do you think this decimal represents a rational number? Why or why not?

_____

_____

2. Do you think a negative sign affects whether or not a number is a rational number? Use $-\frac{8}{5}$ as an example.

_____

_____

3. Do you think a mixed number is a rational number? Explain.

_____

_____

_____

Math On the Spot

my.hrw.com

Writing Rational Numbers as Decimals

You can convert a rational number to a decimal using long division. Some decimals are **terminating decimals** because the decimals come to an end. Other decimals are **repeating decimals** because one or more digits repeat infinitely.

EXAMPLE 1

TEKS 7.2

Write each rational number as a decimal.

A $\frac{5}{16}$

Divide 5 by 16.
Add a zero after the decimal point.
Subtract 48 from 50.
Use the grid to help you complete the long division.

Add zeros in the dividend and continue dividing until the remainder is 0.

The decimal equivalent of $\frac{5}{16}$ is 0.3125.

			0.	3	1	2	5
1	6	)5.	0	0	0	0	
		−4	8				
			2	0			
			−1	6			
				4	0		
				−3	2		
					8	0	
					−8	0	
						0	

B $\frac{13}{33}$

Divide 13 by 33.
Add a zero after the decimal point.
Subtract 99 from 130.
Use the grid to help you complete the long division.

You can stop dividing once you discover a repeating pattern in the quotient.

Write the quotient with its repeating pattern and indicate that the repeating numbers continue.

The decimal equivalent of $\frac{13}{33}$ is 0.3939…, or $0.\overline{39}$.

			0.	3	9	3	9
3	3	)1	3.	0	0	0	0
		−9	9				
		3	1	0			
		−2	9	7			
			1	3	0		
			−9	9			
			3	1	0		
			−2	9	7		
				1	3		

Math Talk

Mathematical Processes

Do you think that decimals that have repeating patterns always have the same number of digits in their pattern? Explain.

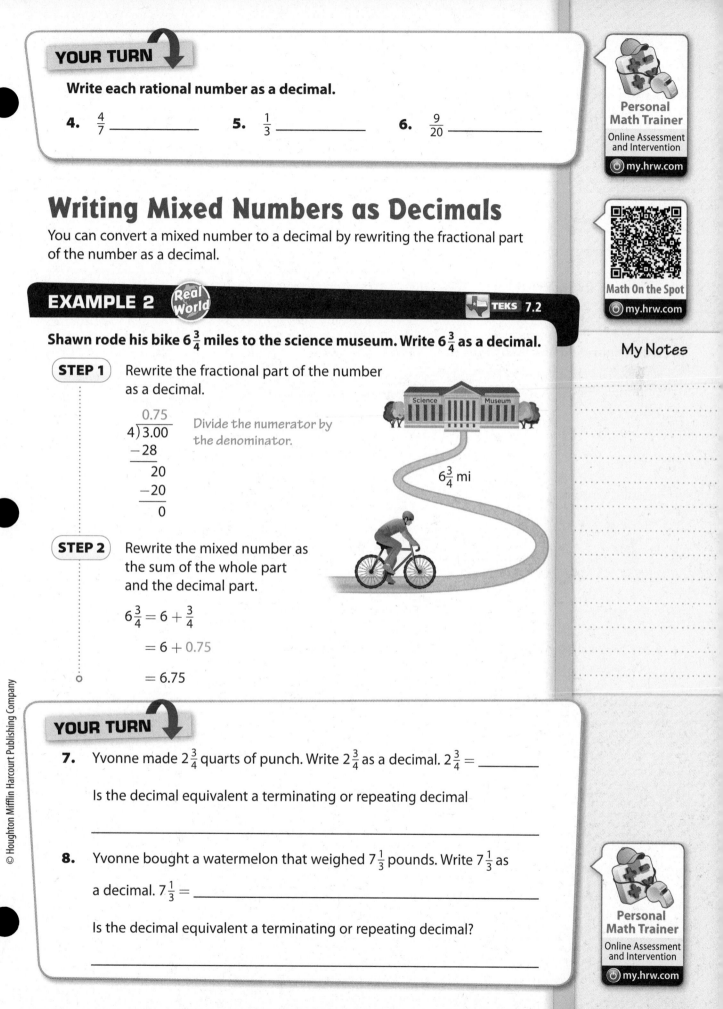

YOUR TURN

Write each rational number as a decimal.

4. $\frac{4}{7}$ _____ **5.** $\frac{1}{3}$ _____ **6.** $\frac{9}{20}$ _____

Writing Mixed Numbers as Decimals

You can convert a mixed number to a decimal by rewriting the fractional part of the number as a decimal.

EXAMPLE 2   Real World   TEKS 7.2

Shawn rode his bike $6\frac{3}{4}$ miles to the science museum. Write $6\frac{3}{4}$ as a decimal.

My Notes

STEP 1   Rewrite the fractional part of the number as a decimal.

$$
\begin{array}{r}
0.75 \\
4\overline{)3.00} \\
-28 \\
\hline
20 \\
-20 \\
\hline
0
\end{array}
$$

Divide the numerator by the denominator.

$6\frac{3}{4}$ mi

STEP 2   Rewrite the mixed number as the sum of the whole part and the decimal part.

$$6\frac{3}{4} = 6 + \frac{3}{4}$$

$$= 6 + 0.75$$

$$= 6.75$$

YOUR TURN

7. Yvonne made $2\frac{3}{4}$ quarts of punch. Write $2\frac{3}{4}$ as a decimal. $2\frac{3}{4} =$ _____

Is the decimal equivalent a terminating or repeating decimal

_____

8. Yvonne bought a watermelon that weighed $7\frac{1}{3}$ pounds. Write $7\frac{1}{3}$ as

a decimal. $7\frac{1}{3} =$ _____

Is the decimal equivalent a terminating or repeating decimal?

_____

Write each rational number as a decimal. Then tell whether each decimal is a terminating or a repeating decimal. (Explore Activity and Example 1)

1. $\frac{3}{5} = $ _____

_____

2. $\frac{89}{100} = $ _____

_____

3. $\frac{4}{12} = $ _____

_____

4. $\frac{25}{99} = $ _____

_____

5. $\frac{7}{9} = $ _____

_____

6. $\frac{9}{25} = $ _____

_____

7. $\frac{1}{25} = $ _____

_____

8. $\frac{25}{176} = $ _____

_____

9. $\frac{12}{1,000} = $ _____

_____

Write each mixed number as a decimal. (Example 2)

10. $11\frac{1}{6} = $ _____

11. $2\frac{9}{10} = $ _____

12. $8\frac{23}{100} = $ _____

13. $7\frac{3}{15} = $ _____

14. $54\frac{3}{11} = $ _____

15. $3\frac{1}{18} = $ _____

16. Maggie bought $3\frac{2}{3}$ lb of apples to make some apple pies. What is the weight of the apples written as a decimal? (Example 2)

$3\frac{2}{3} = $ _____

17. Harry's dog weighs $12\frac{7}{8}$ pounds. What is the weight of Harry's dog written as a decimal? (Example 2)

$12\frac{7}{8} = $ _____

? ESSENTIAL QUESTION CHECK-IN

18. Tom is trying to write $\frac{3}{47}$ as a decimal. He used long division and divided until he got the quotient 0.0638297872, at which point he stopped. Since the decimal doesn't seem to terminate or repeat, he concluded that $\frac{3}{47}$ is not rational. Do you agree or disagree? Why?

_____

_____

_____

_____

_____

1.1 Independent Practice

TEKS 7.2

Use the table for 19–23. Write each ratio in the form $\frac{a}{b}$ and then as a decimal. Tell whether each decimal is a terminating or a repeating decimal.

Team Sports	
Sport	**Number of Players**
Baseball	9
Basketball	5
Football	11
Hockey	6
Lacrosse	10
Polo	4
Rugby	15
Soccer	11

19. basketball players to football players

_____

20. hockey players to lacrosse players

_____

21. polo players to football players

_____

22. lacrosse players to rugby players

_____

23. football players to soccer players

_____

24. **Look for a Pattern** Beth said that the ratio of the number of players in any sport to the number of players on a lacrosse team must always be a terminating decimal. Do you agree or disagree? Why?

_____

_____

_____

_____

25. Yvonne bought $4\frac{7}{8}$ yards of material to make a dress.

a. What is $4\frac{7}{8}$ written as an improper fraction? _____

b. What is $4\frac{7}{8}$ written as a decimal? _____

c. **Communicate Mathematical Ideas** If Yvonne wanted to make 3 dresses that use $4\frac{7}{8}$ yd of fabric each, explain how she could use estimation to make sure she has enough fabric for all of them.

_____

_____

_____

26. Vocabulary A rational number can be written as the ratio of one

_____ to another and can be represented by a repeating

or _____ decimal.

27. Problem Solving Marcus is $5\frac{7}{24}$ feet tall. Ben is $5\frac{5}{16}$ feet tall. Which of the two boys is taller? Justify your answer.

_____

28. Represent Real-World Problems If one store is selling $\frac{3}{4}$ of a bushel of apples for $9, and another store is selling $\frac{2}{3}$ of a bushel of apples for $9, which store has the better deal? Explain your answer.

_____

_____

_____

_____

H.O.T. FOCUS ON HIGHER ORDER THINKING

29. Analyze Relationships You are given a fraction in simplest form. The numerator is not zero. When you write the fraction as a decimal, it is a repeating decimal. Which numbers from 1 to 10 could be the denominator?

_____

_____

30. Communicate Mathematical Ideas Julie got 21 of the 23 questions on her math test correct. She got 29 of the 32 questions on her science test correct. On which test did she get a higher score? Can you compare the fractions $\frac{21}{23}$ and $\frac{29}{32}$ by comparing 29 and 21? Explain. How can Julie compare her scores?

_____

_____

_____

_____

31. Look for a Pattern Look at the decimal 0.121122111222.... If the pattern continues, is this a repeating decimal? Explain.

_____

_____

_____

Work Area

© Houghton Mifflin Harcourt Publishing Company

LESSON
1.2 Relationships Between Sets of Rational Numbers

TEKS
Number and operations—7.2 The student is expected to extend previous knowledge of sets and subsets using a visual representation to describe relationships between sets of rational numbers.

? ESSENTIAL QUESTION

How can you describe relationships between sets of rational numbers?

Classifying Rational Numbers

A group of items is called a **set.** A Venn diagram uses intersecting circles to show relationships among sets of numbers or things. The Venn diagram below shows how the sets of whole numbers, integers, and rational numbers are related to each other.

Math On the Spot
⏻ my.hrw.com

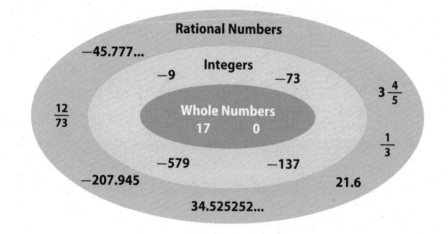

When a set is contained within a larger set in a Venn diagram, the numbers in the smaller set are also members of the larger set.

EXAMPLE 1   TEKS 7.2

Classify each number by naming the set or sets to which it belongs.

A 37
whole, integer, rational

37 is a whole number. All whole numbers are integers. All integers are rational numbers.

> When you classify a number, you can use the Venn diagram to help figure out which other sets, if any, it belongs to.

B −56.12
rational

−56.12 is rational number. It is not a whole number because it is negative. It is not an integer because there are non-zero digits after the decimal point.

C −98
integer, rational

−98 is an integer. All integers are rational numbers.

D $\frac{7}{8}$
rational

$\frac{7}{8}$ is a rational number. It is not a whole number because it is a fraction of a whole number. It is not an integer because it is not a whole number or the opposite of a whole number.

YOUR TURN

Classify each number by naming the set or sets to which it belongs.

1. −8

_____

_____

2. −102.55…

_____

_____

3. $\frac{9}{2}$

_____

_____

4. 3

_____

_____

Understanding Sets and Subsets of Rational Numbers

When one set is entirely contained in another set, we say the first set is a **subset** of the second set. You can use the Venn diagram to decide whether or not a given set of numbers is a subset of another set.

EXAMPLE 2   TEKS 7.2

Tell whether the given statement is true or false. Explain your choice.

A All integers are rational numbers.

True. Every integer is included in the set of rational numbers.

Integers are a subset of the set of rational numbers.

B All integers are whole numbers.

False. Every whole number is an integer, but it is not true that every integer is a whole number.

Integers such as −1 and −6 are not whole numbers.

Reflect

5. **Make a Conjecture** Jared said that every prime number is an integer. Do you agree or disagree? Explain.

_____

_____

_____

_____

My Notes

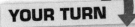

6. Tell whether the statement "Some rational numbers are integers" is true or false. Explain your choice.

   _____

   _____

7. Describe a real-world situation that is best described by the set of rational numbers.

   _____

   _____

Personal Math Trainer

Online Assessment and Intervention

⏻ my.hrw.com

Math Talk
Mathematical Processes

Are there any integers that are not rational numbers? Explain.

Identifying Sets for Real-World Situations

Numbers in real-world situations can be whole numbers, integers, rational numbers, or some combination of the three sets. When you have a choice of sets to describe a number in a real-world situation, you may be able to choose one that gives a more precise description than the others.

Math On the Spot

⏻ my.hrw.com

EXAMPLE 3 Real World   TEKS 7.2

Identify the set of numbers that best describes each situation. Explain your choice.

A the number of bills in a person's wallet

The set of whole numbers best describes the situation.
The wallet may contain no bills or any counting number of bills.
The possible numbers of bills 0, 1, 2, 3,… are whole numbers.

Whole numbers are also integers and rational numbers.
But since there cannot be a negative or a fractional number of bills,
the set of whole numbers is the most precise description.

B golf scores shown on a golf leaderboard

The set of integers best describes the situation. The
scores are also rational numbers. But since there
cannot be fractional scores, the set of integers is the
more precise description.

Leaderboard			
Position	Player	Score	Hole
1	Chin	−5	16
2	Smith	−2	14
3	Mehta	−1	12
4	Adams	0	15
5	Ramirez	+1	13

Classify each number by naming the set or sets to which it belongs. (Example 1)

1. 5

whole number, _____

_____

2. $-\frac{3}{14}$

_____

_____

3. −23

integer, _____

_____

4. 4.5

_____

_____

Tell whether the given statement is true or false. Explain your choice.
(Example 2)

5. All rational numbers are integers.   **True / False**

_____

_____

6. Some integers are whole numbers.   **True / False**

_____

_____

Identify the set of numbers that best describes each situation. Explain your choice. (Example 3)

7. the number of students in a school

The set of _____ best describes the situation because

_____

8. possible points in a certain board game (...−3, −2, −1, 0, 1, 2, 3,...)

The set of _____ best describes the situation because

_____

? ESSENTIAL QUESTION CHECK-IN

9. How can you represent how the sets of whole numbers, integers, and rational numbers are related to each other?

_____

_____

_____

1.2 Independent Practice

TEKS 7.2

Classify each number by naming the set or sets to which it belongs.

10. −9

_____

11. 7.5

_____

12. 789

_____

_____

13. $5\frac{3}{4}$

_____

_____

Fill in each Venn diagram with the whole numbers from 1 to 15. Remember that a composite number is a whole number greater than 1 that is not a prime number.

14.

Whole Numbers from 1 to 15

Divisible by 3

Divisible by 4

15.

Whole Numbers from 1 to 15

Composite Numbers

Odd Numbers

Tell whether the given statement is true or false. Explain your choice.

16. All rational numbers are whole numbers.

_____

_____

_____

_____

17. All whole numbers are integers.

_____

_____

_____

_____

18. Some whole numbers are negative.

_____

_____

19. No positive numbers are integers.

_____

_____

Identify the set of numbers that best describes each situation. Explain your choice.

20. possible number of miles you can walk in 1 hour

_____

_____

_____

21. possible number of marbles in a jar

_____

_____

22. **Represent Real-World Problems** Using what you know of rational numbers, describe a real-world situation where a doctor might use the set of rational numbers on a daily basis.

_____

_____

H.O.T. FOCUS ON HIGHER ORDER THINKING

23. **Communicate Mathematical Ideas** The letters in the Venn diagram represent whole numbers. Describe the numbers you would find in Section *c*, Section *d*, and Section *e*.

_____

_____

_____

_____

Divisible by 2   **Divisible by 3**

a   *b*   *c*

e

d   *f*

g

Divisible by 5

24. **Analyze Relationships** Explain how the set of integers differs from the set of whole numbers.

_____

_____

25. **Justify Reasoning** Explain why a mixed number is not in the set of integers or whole numbers.

_____

_____

_____

Adding Rational Numbers

TEKS
Number and operations—7.3.A Add, subtract, multiply, and divide rational numbers fluently.
Also 7.3.B

? ESSENTIAL QUESTION

How can you add rational numbers?

Adding Rational Numbers with the Same Sign

To add rational numbers with the same sign, apply the rules for adding integers. The sum has the same sign as the sign of the rational numbers.

Math On the Spot
⊙ my.hrw.com

EXAMPLE 1 Real World
TEKS 7.3.A

A Malachi hikes for 2.5 miles and stops for lunch. Then he hikes for 1.5 more miles. How many miles did he hike altogether?

STEP 1 Use positive numbers to represent the distance Malachi hiked.

STEP 2 Find $2.5 + 1.5$.

STEP 3 Start at 2.5.

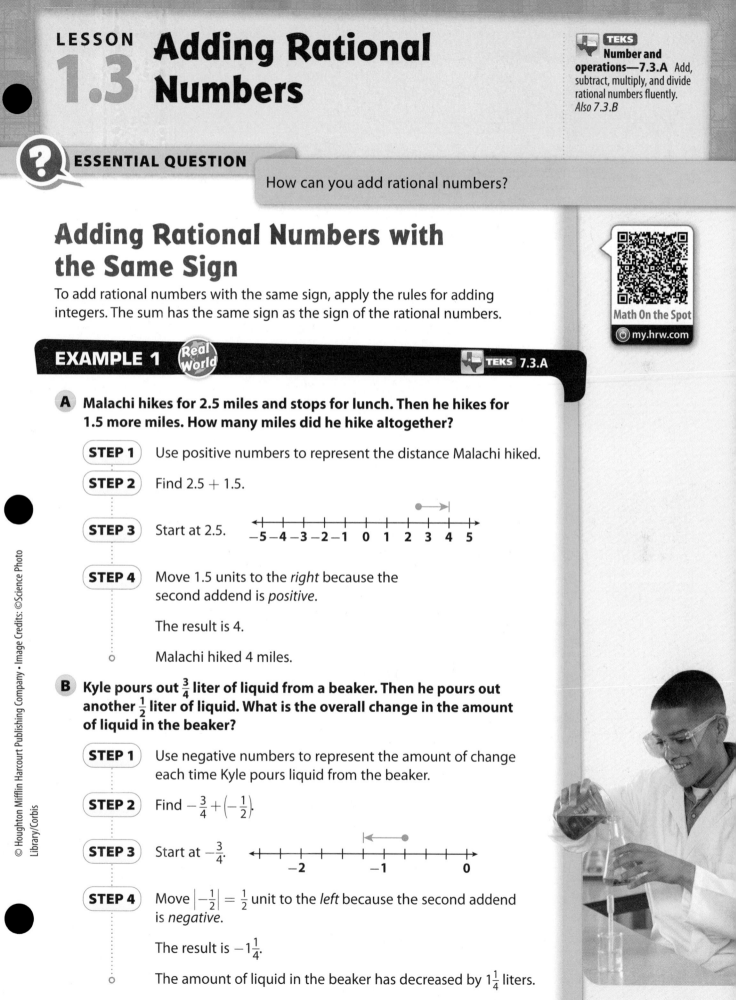

STEP 4 Move 1.5 units to the *right* because the second addend is *positive*.

The result is 4.

Malachi hiked 4 miles.

B Kyle pours out $\frac{3}{4}$ liter of liquid from a beaker. Then he pours out another $\frac{1}{2}$ liter of liquid. What is the overall change in the amount of liquid in the beaker?

STEP 1 Use negative numbers to represent the amount of change each time Kyle pours liquid from the beaker.

STEP 2 Find $-\frac{3}{4} + \left(-\frac{1}{2}\right)$.

STEP 3 Start at $-\frac{3}{4}$.

STEP 4 Move $\left|-\frac{1}{2}\right| = \frac{1}{2}$ unit to the *left* because the second addend is *negative*.

The result is $-1\frac{1}{4}$.

The amount of liquid in the beaker has decreased by $1\frac{1}{4}$ liters.

Reflect

1. Explain how to determine whether to move right or left on the number line when adding rational numbers.

_____

_____

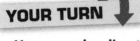

Use a number line to find each sum.

2. $3 + 1\frac{1}{2} =$ _____

3. $-2.5 + (-4.5) =$ _____

Adding Rational Numbers with Different Signs

To add rational numbers with different signs, find the difference of their absolute values. Then use the sign of the rational number with the greater absolute value.

EXAMPLE 2 Real World   ⬛ TEKS 7.3.A

A **During the day, the temperature increases by 4.5 degrees. At night, the temperature decreases by 7.5 degrees. What is the overall change in temperature?**

STEP 1 Use a positive number to represent the increase in temperature and a negative number to represent a decrease in temperature.

STEP 2 Find $4.5 + (-7.5)$.

STEP 3 Start at 4.5.

STEP 4 Move $|-7.5| = 7.5$ units to the *left* because the second addend is *negative*.

The result is -3.

The temperature decreased by 3 degrees overall.

B Ernesto writes a check for $2.50. Then he deposits $6 in his checking account. What is the overall increase or decrease in the account balance?

STEP 1 Use a positive number to represent a deposit and a negative number to represent a withdrawal or a check.

STEP 2 Find $-2.5 + 6$.

STEP 3 Start at -2.5.

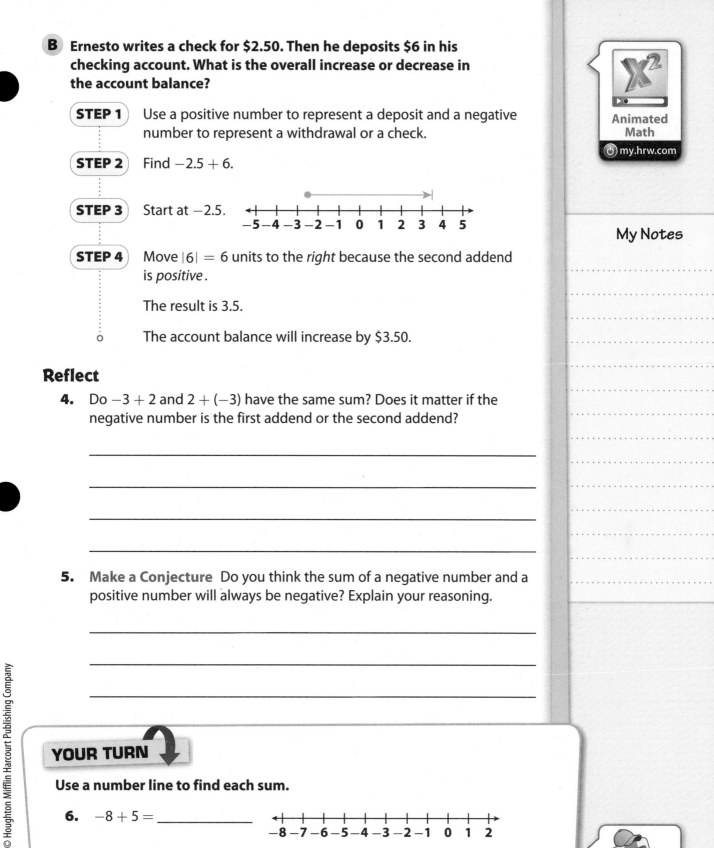

STEP 4 Move $|6| = 6$ units to the *right* because the second addend is *positive*.

The result is 3.5.

The account balance will increase by $3.50.

Reflect

4. Do $-3 + 2$ and $2 + (-3)$ have the same sum? Does it matter if the negative number is the first addend or the second addend?

_____

_____

_____

_____

5. **Make a Conjecture** Do you think the sum of a negative number and a positive number will always be negative? Explain your reasoning.

_____

_____

_____

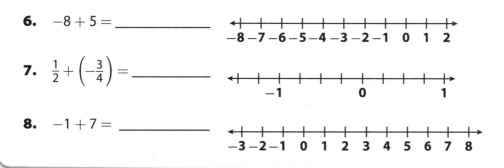

YOUR TURN

Use a number line to find each sum.

6. $-8 + 5 =$ _____

7. $\frac{1}{2} + \left(-\frac{3}{4}\right) =$ _____

8. $-1 + 7 =$ _____

© Houghton Mifflin Harcourt Publishing Company

Personal Math Trainer

Online Assessment and Intervention

⏻ my.hrw.com

Animated Math

⏻ my.hrw.com

My Notes

Finding the Additive Inverse

The **opposite**, or **additive inverse**, of a number is the same distance from 0 on a number line as the original number, but on the other side of 0. The sum of a number and its additive inverse is 0. Zero is its own additive inverse.

EXAMPLE 3 *Real World*   TEKS 7.3.B

Math Talk
Mathematical Processes

Explain how to use a number line to find the additive inverse, or opposite, of −3.5.

A A football team loses 3.5 yards on their first play. On the next play, they gain 3.5 yards. What is the overall increase or decrease in yards?

STEP 1 Use a positive number to represent the gain in yards and a negative number to represent the loss in yards.

STEP 2 Find $-3.5 + 3.5$.

STEP 3 Start at -3.5.

STEP 4 Move $|3.5| = 3.5$ units to the *right*, because the second addend is *positive*.

The result is 0. This means the overall change is 0 yards.

B Kendrick adds $\frac{3}{4}$ cup of chicken stock to a pot. Then he takes $\frac{3}{4}$ cup of stock out of the pot. What is the overall increase or decrease in the amount of chicken stock in the pot?

STEP 1 Use a positive number to represent chicken stock added to the pot and a negative number to represent chicken stock taken out of the pot.

STEP 2 Find $\frac{3}{4} + \left(-\frac{3}{4}\right)$.

STEP 3 Start at $\frac{3}{4}$.

STEP 4 Move $\left|-\frac{3}{4}\right| = \frac{3}{4}$ units to the *left* because the second addend is *negative*.

The result is 0. This means the overall change is 0 cups.

My Notes

YOUR TURN

Use a number line to find each sum.

9. $2\frac{1}{2} + \left(-2\frac{1}{2}\right) = $ _____

10. $-4.5 + 4.5 = $ _____

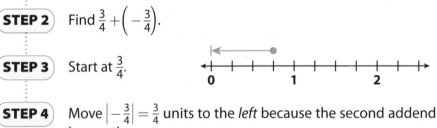

© Houghton Mifflin Harcourt Publishing Company

Adding Three or More Rational Numbers

Recall that the Associative Property of Addition states that when you are adding more than two numbers, you can group any of the numbers together. This property can help you add numbers with different signs.

Math On the Spot
⏱ my.hrw.com

EXAMPLE 4 *Real World*
★ **TEKS** 7.3.A

Tina spent $5.25 on craft supplies to make friendship bracelets. She made $3.75 on Monday. On Tuesday, she sold an additional $4.50 worth of bracelets. What was Tina's overall profit or loss?

STEP 1 Use *negative* numbers to represent the amount Tina *spent* and *positive* numbers to represent the money Tina *earned*.

> Profit means the difference between income and costs is positive.

STEP 2 Find $-5.25 + 3.75 + 4.50$.

STEP 3 Group numbers with the same sign.

$-5.25 + (3.75 + 4.50)$ Associative Property

STEP 4 $-5.25 + 8.25$ Add the numbers inside the parentheses.

Find the difference of the absolute values: $8.25 - 5.25$.

3 Use the sign of the number with the greater absolute value. The sum is positive.

Tina earned a profit of $3.00.

YOUR TURN

Find each sum.

11. $-1.5 + 3.5 + 2 =$ _____

12. $3\frac{1}{4} + (-2) + \left(-2\frac{1}{4}\right) =$ _____

13. $-2.75 + (-3.25) + 5 =$ _____

14. $15 + 8 + (-3) =$ _____

Personal Math Trainer
Online Assessment and Intervention
⏱ my.hrw.com

© Houghton Mifflin Harcourt Publishing Company

Use a number line to find each sum. (Example 1 and Example 2)

1. $-3 + (-1.5) =$ _____

$$-5 \ -4 \ -3 \ -2 \ -1 \ \ 0 \ \ 1 \ \ 2 \ \ 3 \ \ 4 \ \ 5$$

2. $1.5 + 3.5 =$ _____

$$-5 \ -4 \ -3 \ -2 \ -1 \ \ 0 \ \ 1 \ \ 2 \ \ 3 \ \ 4 \ \ 5$$

3. $\frac{1}{4} + \frac{1}{2} =$ _____

$$-1 \ \ -0.5 \ \ \ 0 \ \ \ 0.5 \ \ \ 1$$

4. $-1\frac{1}{2} + \left(-1\frac{1}{2}\right) =$ _____

$$-5 \ -4 \ -3 \ -2 \ -1 \ \ 0 \ \ 1 \ \ 2 \ \ 3 \ \ 4 \ \ 5$$

5. $3 + (-5) =$ _____

$$-5 \ -4 \ -3 \ -2 \ -1 \ \ 0 \ \ 1 \ \ 2 \ \ 3 \ \ 4 \ \ 5$$

6. $-1.5 + 4 =$ _____

$$-5 \ -4 \ -3 \ -2 \ -1 \ \ 0 \ \ 1 \ \ 2 \ \ 3 \ \ 4 \ \ 5$$

7. Victor borrowed $21.50 from his mother to go to the theater. A week later, he paid her $21.50 back. How much does he still owe her? (Example 3)

_____

8. Sandra used her debit card to buy lunch for $8.74 on Monday. On Tuesday, she deposited $8.74 back into her account. What is the overall increase or decrease in her bank account? (Example 3)

_____

Find each sum without using a number line. (Example 4)

9. $2.75 + (-2) + (-5.25) =$ _____

10. $-3 + \left(1\frac{1}{2}\right) + \left(2\frac{1}{2}\right) =$ _____

11. $-12.4 + 9.2 + 1 =$ _____

12. $-12 + 8 + 13 =$ _____

13. $4.5 + (-12) + (-4.5) =$ _____

14. $\frac{1}{4} + \left(-\frac{3}{4}\right) =$ _____

15. $-4\frac{1}{2} + 2 =$ _____

16. $-8 + \left(-1\frac{1}{8}\right) =$ _____

? ESSENTIAL QUESTION CHECK-IN

17. How can you use a number line to find the sum of -4 and 6?

_____

_____

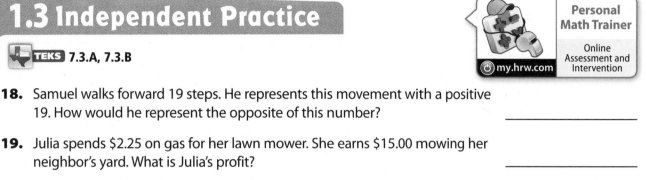

1.3 Independent Practice

TEKS 7.3.A, 7.3.B

18. Samuel walks forward 19 steps. He represents this movement with a positive 19. How would he represent the opposite of this number? _____

19. Julia spends $2.25 on gas for her lawn mower. She earns $15.00 mowing her neighbor's yard. What is Julia's profit? _____

20. A submarine submerged at a depth of -35.25 meters dives an additional 8.5 meters. What is the new depth of the submarine? _____

21. Renee hiked for $4\frac{3}{4}$ miles. After resting, Renee hiked back along the same route for $3\frac{1}{4}$ miles. How many more miles does Renee need to hike to return to the place where she started? _____

22. **Geography** The average elevation of the city of New Orleans, Louisiana, is 0.5 m below sea level. The highest point in Louisiana is Driskill Mountain at about 163.5 m higher than New Orleans. How high is Driskill Mountain? _____

23. **Problem Solving** A contestant on a game show has 30 points. She answers a question correctly to win 15 points. Then she answers a question incorrectly and loses 25 points. What is the contestant's final score?

_____

Financial Literacy Use the table for 24–26. Kameh owns a bakery. He recorded the bakery income and expenses in a table.

24. In which months were the expenses greater than the income? Name the month and find how much money

was lost. _____

25. In which months was the income greater than the expenses? Name the months and find how much money was gained each of those months.

Month	Income ($)	Expenses ($)
January	1,205	1,290.60
February	1,183	1,345.44
March	1,664	1,664.00
June	2,413	2,106.23
July	2,260	1,958.50
August	2,183	1,845.12

_____

26. **Communicate Mathematical Ideas** If the bakery started with an extra $250 from the profits in December, describe how to use the information in the table to figure out the profit or loss of money at the bakery by the end of August. Then calculate the profit or loss.

_____

_____

_____

_____

27. Vocabulary −2 is the _____ of 2.

28. The basketball coach made up a game to play where each player takes 10 shots at the basket. For every basket made, the player gains 10 points. For every basket missed, the player loses 15 points.

   a. The player with the highest score sank 7 baskets and missed 3. What was the highest score?

   _____

   b. The player with the lowest score sank 2 baskets and missed 8. What was the lowest score?

   _____

   c. Write an expression using addition to find out what the score would be if a player sank 5 baskets and missed 5 baskets.

   _____

   _____

H.O.T.   **FOCUS ON HIGHER ORDER THINKING**

29. Communicate Mathematical Ideas Explain the different ways it is possible to add two rational numbers and get a negative number.

_____

_____

_____

_____

30. Explain the Error A student evaluated $-4 + x$ for $x = -9\frac{1}{2}$ and got the answer of $5\frac{1}{2}$. What might the student have done wrong?

_____

_____

31. Draw Conclusions Can you find the sum $[5.5 + (-2.3)] + (-5.5 + 2.3)$ without performing any additions?

_____

_____

_____

Work Area

Subtracting Rational Numbers

TEKS
Number and operations—7.3.A Add, subtract, multiply, and divide rational numbers fluently. *Also 7.3.B*

? ESSENTIAL QUESTION

How do you subtract rational numbers?

Math On the Spot
my.hrw.com

Subtracting Positive Rational Numbers

To subtract rational numbers, you can apply the same rules you use to subtract integers.

EXAMPLE 1 Real World TEKS 7.3.A

The temperature on an outdoor thermometer on Monday was 5.5 °C. The temperature on Thursday was 7.25 degrees less than the temperature on Monday. What was the temperature on Thursday?

Subtract to find the temperature on Thursday.

STEP 1 Find 5.5 − 7.25.

STEP 2 Start at 5.5.

STEP 3 Move |7.25| = 7.25 units to the *left* because you are subtracting a *positive number*.

The result is −1.75.

The temperature on Thursday was −1.75 °C.

YOUR TURN

Use a number line to find each difference.

1. −6.5 − 2 = _____

2. $1\frac{1}{2} - 2 =$ _____

3. −2.25 − 5.5 = _____

Personal Math Trainer

Online Assessment and Intervention

my.hrw.com

© Houghton Mifflin Harcourt Publishing Company

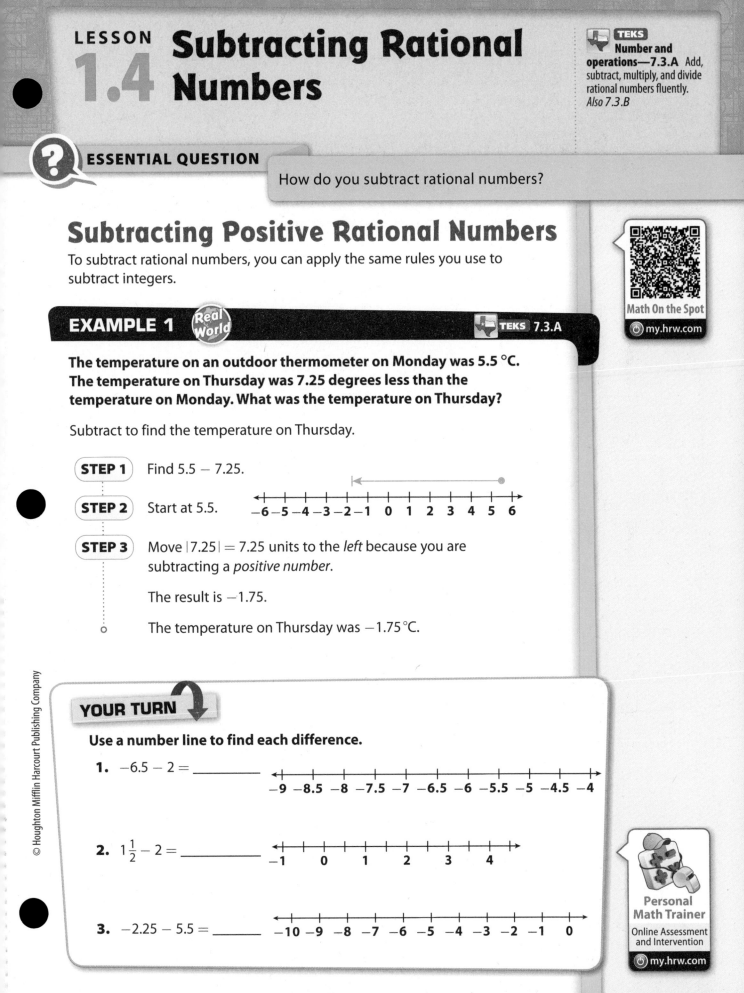

Subtracting Negative Rational Numbers

To subtract negative rational numbers, move in the opposite direction on the number line.

EXAMPLE 2 *(Real World)*   🗺 **TEKS** 7.3.A

During the hottest week of the summer, the water level of the Muskrat River was $\frac{5}{6}$ foot below normal. The following week, the level was $\frac{1}{3}$ foot below normal. What is the overall change in the water level?

Subtract to find the difference in water levels.

STEP 1   Find $-\frac{1}{3} - \left(-\frac{5}{6}\right)$.

STEP 2   Start at $-\frac{1}{3}$.

STEP 3   Move $\left|-\frac{5}{6}\right| = \frac{5}{6}$ to the *right* because you are subtracting a *negative* number.

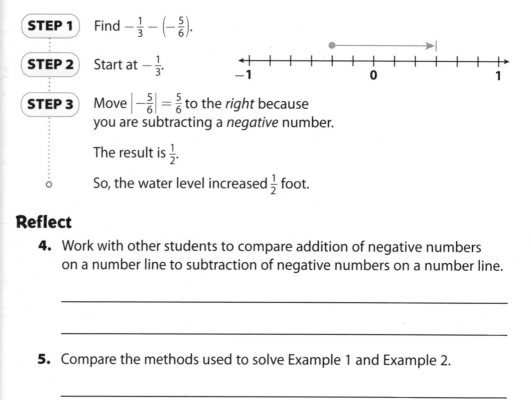

The result is $\frac{1}{2}$.

So, the water level increased $\frac{1}{2}$ foot.

Reflect

4. Work with other students to compare addition of negative numbers on a number line to subtraction of negative numbers on a number line.

_____

_____

5. Compare the methods used to solve Example 1 and Example 2.

_____

_____

_____

_____

Personal Math Trainer

Online Assessment and Intervention

⏱ my.hrw.com

YOUR TURN

Use a number line to find each difference.

6. $0.25 - (-1.50) =$ _____

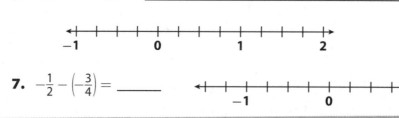

7. $-\frac{1}{2} - \left(-\frac{3}{4}\right) =$ _____

Adding the Opposite

Joe is diving $2\frac{1}{2}$ feet below sea level. He decides to descend $7\frac{1}{2}$ more feet. How many feet below sea level is he?

STEP 1 Use negative numbers to represent the number of feet below sea level.

STEP 2 Find $-2\frac{1}{2} - 7\frac{1}{2}$.

STEP 3 Start at $-2\frac{1}{2}$.

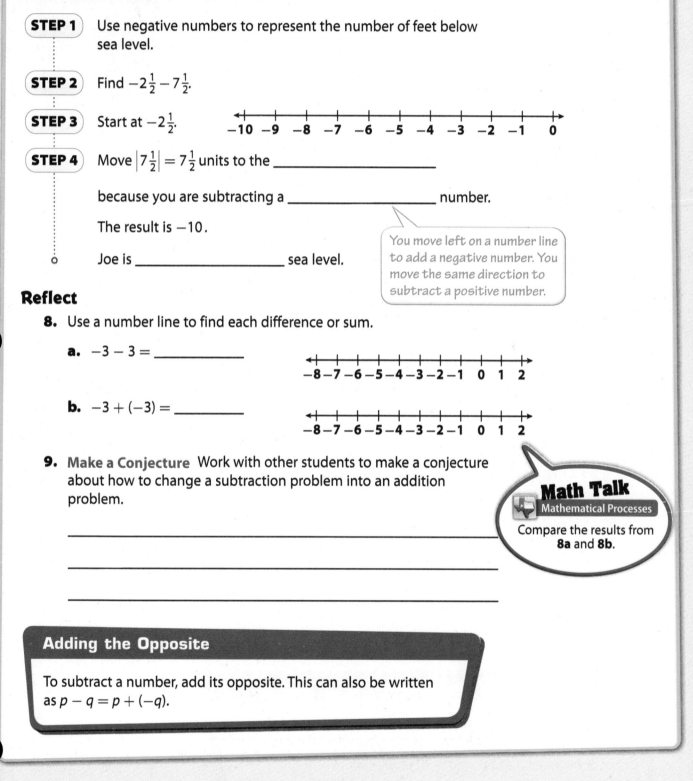

STEP 4 Move $\left|7\frac{1}{2}\right| = 7\frac{1}{2}$ units to the _____

because you are subtracting a _____ number.

The result is -10.

Joe is _____ sea level.

> You move left on a number line to add a negative number. You move the same direction to subtract a positive number.

Reflect

8. Use a number line to find each difference or sum.

   a. $-3 - 3 =$ _____

   b. $-3 + (-3) =$ _____

9. Make a Conjecture Work with other students to make a conjecture about how to change a subtraction problem into an addition problem.

_____

_____

_____

> **Math Talk**
> Mathematical Processes
> Compare the results from **8a** and **8b**.

Adding the Opposite

To subtract a number, add its opposite. This can also be written as $p - q = p + (-q)$.

Finding the Distance between Two Numbers

A cave explorer climbed from an elevation of −11 meters to an elevation of −5 meters. What vertical distance did the explorer climb?

There are two ways to find the vertical distance.

A Start at _____.

Count the number of units on the vertical number line up to −5.

The explorer climbed _____ meters.

This means that the vertical distance between

−11 meters and −5 meters is _____ meters.

B Find the difference between the two elevations and use absolute value to find the distance.

$-11 - (-5) =$ _____

Take the absolute value of the difference because distance traveled is always a nonnegative number.

$|-11 - (-5)| =$ _____

The vertical distance is _____ meters.

Vertical number line:
```
  0
 −1
 −2
 −3
 −4
 −5
 −6
 −7
 −8
 −9
−10
−11
```

Reflect

10. Does it matter which way you subtract the values when finding distance? Explain.

_____

_____

11. Would the same methods work if both the numbers were positive? What if one of the numbers were positive and the other negative?

_____

Distance Between Two Numbers

The distance between two values a and b on a number line is represented by the absolute value of the difference of a and b.

Distance between a and $b = |a - b|$ or $|b - a|$.

Guided Practice

Use a number line to find each difference. (Example 1, Example 2 and Explore Activity 1)

1. $5 - (-8) =$ _____

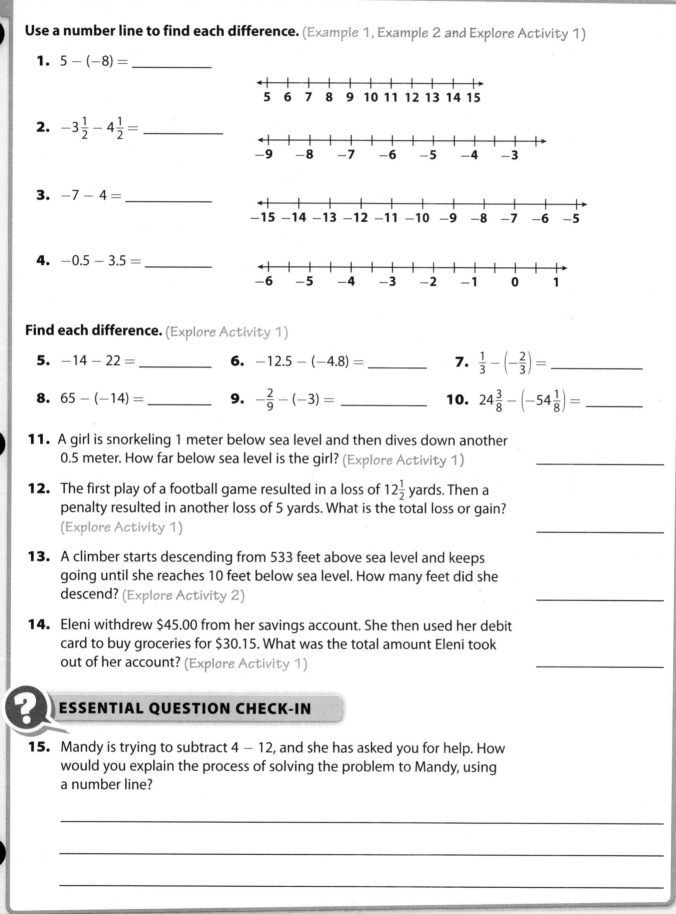

2. $-3\frac{1}{2} - 4\frac{1}{2} =$ _____

3. $-7 - 4 =$ _____

4. $-0.5 - 3.5 =$ _____

Find each difference. (Explore Activity 1)

5. $-14 - 22 =$ _____

6. $-12.5 - (-4.8) =$ _____

7. $\frac{1}{3} - \left(-\frac{2}{3}\right) =$ _____

8. $65 - (-14) =$ _____

9. $-\frac{2}{9} - (-3) =$ _____

10. $24\frac{3}{8} - \left(-54\frac{1}{8}\right) =$ _____

11. A girl is snorkeling 1 meter below sea level and then dives down another 0.5 meter. How far below sea level is the girl? (Explore Activity 1) _____

12. The first play of a football game resulted in a loss of $12\frac{1}{2}$ yards. Then a penalty resulted in another loss of 5 yards. What is the total loss or gain? (Explore Activity 1) _____

13. A climber starts descending from 533 feet above sea level and keeps going until she reaches 10 feet below sea level. How many feet did she descend? (Explore Activity 2) _____

14. Eleni withdrew $45.00 from her savings account. She then used her debit card to buy groceries for $30.15. What was the total amount Eleni took out of her account? (Explore Activity 1) _____

? ESSENTIAL QUESTION CHECK-IN

15. Mandy is trying to subtract $4 - 12$, and she has asked you for help. How would you explain the process of solving the problem to Mandy, using a number line?

_____

_____

_____

1.4 Independent Practice

TEKS 7.3.A, 7.3.B

Personal Math Trainer

Online Assessment and Intervention

my.hrw.com

16. Science At the beginning of a laboratory experiment, the temperature of a substance is $-12.6\,°C$. During the experiment, the temperature of the substance decreases $7.5\,°C$. What is the final temperature of the substance?

_____

17. A diver went 25.65 feet below the surface of the ocean, and then 16.5 feet further down, he then rose 12.45 feet. Write and solve an expression to find the diver's new depth.

_____

_____

18. A city known for its temperature extremes started the day at -5 degrees Fahrenheit. The temperature increased by 78 degrees Fahrenheit by midday, and then dropped 32 degrees by nightfall.

   a. What expression can you write to find the temperature at nightfall? _____

   b. What expression can you write to describe the overall change in temperature? *Hint*: Do not include the temperature at the beginning of the day since you only want to know about how much the temperature changed. _____

   c. What is the final temperature at nightfall? What is the overall change in temperature? _____

19. Financial Literacy On Monday, your bank account balance was $-\$12.58$. Because you didn't realize this, you wrote a check for $30.72 for groceries.

   a. What is the new balance in your checking account? _____

   b. The bank charges a $25 fee for paying a check on a negative balance. What is the balance in your checking account after this fee? _____

   c. How much money do you need to deposit to bring your account balance back up to $0 after the fee? _____

Astronomy **Use the table for problems 20–21.**

20. How much deeper is the deepest canyon on Mars than the deepest canyon on Venus?

_____

Elevations on Planets		
	Lowest (ft)	**Highest (ft)**
Earth	−36,198	29,035
Mars	−26,000	70,000
Venus	−9,500	35,000

21. Persevere in Problem Solving What is the difference between Earth's highest mountain and its deepest ocean canyon? What is the difference between Mars' highest mountain and its deepest canyon? Which difference is greater? How much greater is it?

_____

_____

_____

22. Pamela wants to make some friendship bracelets for her friends. Each friendship bracelet needs 5.2 inches of string.

    a. If Pamela has 20 inches of string, does she have enough to make bracelets for 4 of her friends?

_____

_____

    b. If so, how much string would she have left over? If not, how much more string would she need?

_____

23. Jeremy is practicing some tricks on his skateboard. One trick takes him forward 5 feet, then he flips around and moves backwards 7.2 feet, then he moves forward again for 2.2 feet.

    a. What expression could be used to find how far Jeremy is from his starting position when he finishes the trick?

_____

    b. How far from his starting point is he when he finishes the trick? Explain

_____

_____

24. Esteban has $20 from his allowance. There is a comic book he wishes to buy that costs $4.25, a cereal bar that costs $0.89, and a small remote control car that costs $10.99.

    a. Does Esteban have enough to buy everything?

_____

    b. If so, how much will he have left over? If not, how much does he still need?

_____

_____

Work Area

25. Look for a Pattern Show how you could use the Commutative Property to simplify the evaluation of the expression $-\frac{7}{16} - \frac{1}{4} - \frac{5}{16}$.

_____

_____

_____

26. Problem Solving The temperatures for five days in Kaktovik, Alaska, are given below.

$-19.6\ °F,\ -22.5\ °F,\ -20.9\ °F,\ -19.5\ °F,\ -22.4\ °F$

Temperatures over the same 5-day period last year were 12 degrees lower. What were the highest and lowest temperatures over this period last year?

_____

_____

27. Make a Conjecture Must the difference between two rational numbers be a rational number? Explain.

_____

_____

_____

_____

_____

28. Look for a Pattern Evan said that the difference between two negative numbers must be negative. Was he right? Use examples to illustrate your answer.

_____

_____

_____

_____

Multiplying Rational Numbers

TEKS
Number and operations—7.3.A Add, subtract, multiply, and divide rational numbers fluently.
Also 7.3.B

? ESSENTIAL QUESTION

How do you multiply rational numbers?

Multiplying Rational Numbers with Different Signs

The rules for the signs of products of rational numbers with different signs are summarized below. Let p and q be rational numbers.

Products of Rational Numbers

Sign of Factor p	Sign of Factor q	Sign of Product pq
+	−	−
−	+	−

Math On the Spot
my.hrw.com

You can also use the fact that multiplication is repeated addition.

EXAMPLE 1 (Real World)

TEKS 7.3.A

Gina hiked down a canyon and stopped each time she descended $\frac{1}{2}$ mile to rest. She hiked a total of 4 sections. What is her overall change in elevation?

STEP 1 Use a negative number to represent the change in elevation.

STEP 2 Find $4\left(-\frac{1}{2}\right)$.

STEP 3 Start at 0. Move $\frac{1}{2}$ unit to the left 4 times.

The result is −2.

The overall change is −2 miles. $-3 \quad -2 \quad -1 \quad 0$

Check: Use the rules for multiplying rational numbers.

$$4\left(-\frac{1}{2}\right) = \left(-\frac{4}{2}\right)$$ A negative times a positive equals a negative.

$$= -2 \checkmark$$ Simplify.

Personal Math Trainer

Online Assessment and Intervention

my.hrw.com

YOUR TURN

1. Use a number line to find 2(−3.5). _____

$-8 \quad -7 \quad -6 \quad -5 \quad -4 \quad -3 \quad -2 \quad -1 \quad 0$

Multiplying Rational Numbers with the Same Sign

The rules for the signs of products with the same signs are summarized below.

Products of Rational Numbers

Sign of Factor p	Sign of Factor q	Sign of Product pq
+	+	+
−	−	+

You can also use a number line to find the product of rational numbers with the same signs.

My Notes

EXAMPLE 2

TEKS 7.3.A

Multiply $-2(-3.5)$.

STEP 1 First, find the product $2(-3.5)$.

$$+(-3.5) \qquad +(-3.5)$$

-8 -7 -6 -5 -4 -3 -2 -1 0

STEP 2 Start at 0. Move 3.5 units to the left two times.

STEP 3 The result is -7.

STEP 4 This shows that 2 groups of -3.5 equals -7.

So, -2 groups of -3.5 must equal the *opposite* of -7.

-8 -7 -6 -5 -4 -3 -2 -1 0 1 2 3 4 5 6 7 8

STEP 5 $-2(-3.5) = 7$

Check: Use the rules for multiplying rational numbers.

$-2(-3.5) = 7$ *A negative times a negative equals a positive.*

YOUR TURN

2. Find $-3(-1.25)$. _____

-4 -3 -2 -1 0 1 2 3 4

Multiplying More Than Two Rational Numbers

If you multiply three or more rational numbers, you can use a pattern to find the sign of the product.

EXAMPLE 3

TEKS 7.3.B

Multiply $\left(-\frac{2}{3}\right)\left(-\frac{1}{2}\right)\left(-\frac{3}{5}\right)$.

STEP 1 First, find the product of the first two factors. Both factors are negative, so their product will be positive.

STEP 2 $\left(-\frac{2}{3}\right)\left(-\frac{1}{2}\right) = +\left(\frac{\cancel{2}}{3} \cdot \frac{1}{\cancel{2}}\right)$

$= \frac{1}{3}$

STEP 3 Now, multiply the result, which is positive, by the third factor, which is negative. The product will be negative.

STEP 4 $\frac{1}{3}\left(-\frac{3}{5}\right) = \frac{1}{\cancel{3}}\left(-\frac{\cancel{3}}{5}\right)$

STEP 5 $\left(-\frac{2}{3}\right)\left(-\frac{1}{2}\right)\left(-\frac{3}{5}\right) = -\frac{1}{5}$

Reflect

3. **Look for a Pattern** You know that the product of two negative numbers is positive, and the product of three negative numbers is negative. Write a rule for finding the sign of the product of n negative numbers.

_____

_____

_____

Math Talk
Mathematical Processes

Suppose you find the product of several rational numbers, one of which is zero. What can you say about the product?

YOUR TURN

Find each product.

4. $\left(-\frac{3}{4}\right)\left(-\frac{4}{7}\right)\left(-\frac{2}{3}\right)$ _____

5. $\left(-\frac{2}{3}\right)\left(-\frac{3}{4}\right)\left(\frac{4}{5}\right)$ _____

6. $\left(\frac{2}{3}\right)\left(-\frac{9}{10}\right)\left(\frac{5}{6}\right)$ _____

Use a number line to find each product. (Example 1 and Example 2)

1. $5\left(-\frac{2}{3}\right) =$ _____

2. $3\left(-\frac{1}{4}\right) =$ _____

3. $-3\left(-\frac{4}{7}\right) =$ _____

4. $-\frac{3}{4}(-4) =$ _____

5. $4(-3) =$ _____

6. $-1.8(5) =$ _____

7. $-2(-3.4) =$ _____

8. $0.54(8) =$ _____

9. $-5(-1.2) =$ _____

10. $-2.4(3) =$ _____

Multiply. (Example 3)

11. $\frac{1}{2} \times \frac{2}{3} \times \frac{3}{4} = \boxed{} \times \frac{3}{4} =$ _____

12. $-\frac{4}{7}\left(-\frac{3}{5}\right)\left(-\frac{7}{3}\right) = \boxed{} \times \left(-\frac{7}{3}\right) =$ _____

13. $-\frac{1}{8} \times 5 \times \frac{2}{3} =$ _____

14. $-\frac{2}{3}\left(\frac{1}{2}\right)\left(-\frac{6}{7}\right) =$ _____

15. The price of one share of Acme Company declined $3.50 per day for 4 days in a row. What is the overall change in price of one share? (Example 1)

_____

16. In one day, 18 people each withdrew $100 from an ATM machine. What is the overall change in the amount of money in the ATM machine? (Example 1)

_____

? ESSENTIAL QUESTION CHECK-IN

17. Explain how you can find the sign of the product of two or more rational numbers.

_____

_____

_____

1.5 Independent Practice

TEKS 7.3.A, 7.3.B

Personal Math Trainer

Online Assessment and Intervention

my.hrw.com

18. Financial Literacy Sandy has $200 in her bank account.

a. If she writes 6 checks for exactly $19.98, what expression describes the change in her bank account?

_____

b. What is her account balance after the checks are cashed?

_____

19. Communicating Mathematical Ideas Explain, in words, how to find the product of $-4(-1.5)$ using a number line. Where do you end up?

_____

_____

_____

_____

_____

20. Greg sets his watch for the correct time on Wednesday. Exactly one week later, he finds that his watch has lost $3\frac{1}{4}$ minutes. What is the overall change in time after 8 weeks?

_____

21. A submarine dives below the surface, heading downward in three moves. If each move downward was 325 feet, where is the submarine after it is finished diving?

_____

_____

22. Multistep For Home Economics class, Sandra has 5 cups of flour. She made 3 batches of cookies that each used 1.5 cups of flour. Write and solve an expression to find the amount of flour Sandra has left after making the 3 batches of cookies.

_____

_____

23. Critique Reasoning In class, Matthew stated, "I think that a negative is like an opposite. That is why multiplying a negative times a negative equals a positive. The opposite of negative is positive, so it is just like multiplying the opposite of a negative twice, which is two positives." Do you agree or disagree with this statement? What would you say in response to him?

_____

_____

_____

_____

_____

_____

_____

_____

24. Kaitlin is on a long car trip. Every time she stops to buy gas, she loses 15 minutes of travel time. If she has to stop 5 times, how late will she be getting to her destination?

_____

_____

© Houghton Mifflin Harcourt Publishing Company

25. The table shows the scoring system for quarterbacks in Jeremy's fantasy football league. In one game, Jeremy's quarterback had 2 touchdown passes, 16 complete passes, 7 incomplete passes, and 2 interceptions. How many total points did Jeremy's quarterback score?

Quarterback Scoring	
Action	**Points**
Touchdown pass	6
Complete pass	0.5
Incomplete pass	−0.5
Interception	−1.5

_____

 FOCUS ON HIGHER ORDER THINKING

Work Area

26. Represent Real-World Problems The ground temperature at Brigham Airport is 12 °C. The temperature decreases by 6.8 °C for every increase of 1 kilometer above the ground. What is the temperature outside a plane flying at an altitude of 5 kilometers?

_____

27. Identify Patterns The product of four numbers, *a*, *b*, *c*, and *d*, is a negative number. The table shows one combination of positive and negative signs of the four numbers that could produce a negative product. Complete the table to show the seven other possible combinations.

a	*b*	*c*	*d*
+	+	+	−

28. Reason Abstractly Find two integers whose sum is −7 and whose product is 12. Explain how you found the numbers.

_____

_____

_____

_____

LESSON
1.6 Dividing Rational Numbers

TEKS
Number and operations—7.3.A Add, subtract, multiply, and divide rational numbers fluently.
Also 7.3.B

? ESSENTIAL QUESTION

How do you divide rational numbers?

EXPLORE ACTIVITY 1 *Real World* **TEKS 7.3.A**

Dividing Rational Numbers

A diver needs to descend to a depth of 100 feet below sea level. She wants to do it in 5 equal descents. How far should she travel in each descent?

A To solve this problem, you can set up a division problem: $\dfrac{-100}{\boxed{}} = ?$

B Rewrite the division problem as a multiplication problem. Think: Some number multiplied by 5 equals −100.

_____ × ? = −100

C Remember the rules for integer multiplication. If the product is negative, one of the factors must be negative. Since _____ is positive, the unknown factor must be **positive / negative.**

D You know that 5 × _____ = 100. So, using the rules for integer multiplication you can say that 5 × _____ = −100.

The diver should descend _____ feet in each descent.

Reflect

1. What do you notice about the quotient of two rational numbers with different signs?

_____

_____

2. What do you notice about the quotient of two rational numbers with the same sign? Does it matter if both signs are positive or both are negative?

_____

_____

Let p and q be rational numbers.

Quotients of Rational Numbers

Sign of Dividend p	Sign of Divisor q	Sign of Quotient $\frac{p}{q}$
+	−	−
−	+	−
+	+	+
−	−	+

Also, $-\left(\dfrac{p}{q}\right) = \dfrac{-p}{q} = \dfrac{p}{-q}$, for q not zero.

EXPLORE ACTIVITY 2   TEKS 7.3.A

Placement of Negative Signs in Quotients

Quotients can have negative signs in different places.

Are the rational numbers $\dfrac{12}{-4}$, $\dfrac{-12}{4}$, and $-\left(\dfrac{12}{4}\right)$ equivalent?

A Find each quotient. Then use the rules you found in Explore Activity 1 to make sure the sign of the quotient is correct.

$\dfrac{12}{-4} =$ _____ $\dfrac{-12}{4} =$ _____ $-\left(\dfrac{12}{4}\right) =$ _____

B What do you notice about each quotient?

_____

C The rational numbers ⟨ **are / are not** ⟩ equivalent.

D **Conjecture** Explain how the placement of the negative sign in the rational number affects the sign of the quotients.

_____

_____

Reflect

Write two equivalent expressions for each quotient.

3. $\dfrac{14}{-7}$ _____ , _____   **4.** $\dfrac{-32}{-8}$ _____ , _____

Quotients of Rational Numbers

The rules for dividing rational numbers are the same as dividing integers.

EXAMPLE 1 | Real World | TEKS 7.3.A

A Over 5 months, Carlos wrote 5 checks for a total of $323.75 to pay for his cable TV service. His cable bill is the same amount each month. What was the change in Carlos' bank account each month to pay for cable?

Find the quotient: $\frac{-323.75}{5}$

STEP 1 Use a negative number to represent the withdrawal from his account each month.

STEP 2 Find $\frac{-323.75}{5}$.

STEP 3 Determine the sign of the quotient.

The quotient will be negative because the signs are different.

STEP 2 Divide.

$$\frac{-323.75}{5} = -64.75$$

Carlos withdrew $64.75 each month to pay for cable TV.

B Find $\frac{\frac{7}{10}}{\frac{-1}{5}}$.

STEP 1 Determine the sign of the quotient.
The quotient will be negative because the signs are different.

STEP 2 Write the complex fraction as division: $\frac{\frac{7}{10}}{\frac{-1}{5}} = \frac{7}{10} \div \frac{-1}{5}$

STEP 3 Rewrite using multiplication: $\frac{7}{10} \times \left(-\frac{5}{1}\right)$ *Multiply by the reciprocal.*

STEP 3 $\frac{7}{10} \times \left(-\frac{5}{1}\right) = -\frac{35}{10}$ *Multiply.*

$= -\frac{7}{2}$ *Simplify.*

$$\frac{\frac{7}{10}}{\frac{-1}{5}} = -\frac{7}{2}$$

YOUR TURN

Find each quotient.

5. $\frac{2.8}{-4}$ = _____

6. $\frac{-\frac{5}{8}}{-\frac{6}{7}}$ = _____

7. $-\frac{5.5}{0.5}$ = _____

Math On the Spot
my.hrw.com

Personal Math Trainer
Online Assessment and Intervention
my.hrw.com

Find each quotient. (Explore Activity 1 and 2, Example 1)

1. $\dfrac{0.72}{-0.9} =$ _____

2. $\left(\dfrac{-\frac{1}{5}}{\frac{7}{5}}\right) =$ _____

3. $\dfrac{56}{-7} =$ _____

4. $\dfrac{251}{4} \div \left(-\dfrac{3}{8}\right) =$ _____

5. $\dfrac{75}{-\frac{1}{5}} =$ _____

6. $\dfrac{-91}{-13} =$ _____

7. $\dfrac{-\frac{3}{7}}{\frac{9}{4}} =$ _____

8. $-\dfrac{12}{0.03} =$ _____

9. A water pail in your backyard has a small hole in it. You notice that it has drained a total of 3.5 liters in 4 days. What is the average change in water volume each day? (Example 1)

_____

10. The price of one share of ABC Company declined a total of $45.75 in 5 days. What was the average change of the price of one share per day? (Example 1)

_____

11. To avoid a storm, a passenger-jet pilot descended 0.44 mile in 0.8 minute. What was the plane's average change of altitude per minute? (Example 1)

_____

? ESSENTIAL QUESTION CHECK-IN

12. Explain how you would find the sign of the quotient $\dfrac{32 \div (-2)}{-16 \div 4}$.

_____

_____

_____

_____

_____

_____

1.6 Independent Practice

TEKS 7.3.A, 7.3.B

Personal
Math Trainer

my.hrw.com Online
Assessment and
Intervention

13. $\dfrac{\frac{5}{2}}{\frac{-2}{8}} =$ _____

14. $5\frac{1}{3} \div \left(-1\frac{1}{2}\right) =$ _____

15. $\dfrac{-120}{-6} =$ _____

16. $\dfrac{-\frac{4}{5}}{-\frac{2}{3}} =$ _____

17. $1.03 \div (-10.3) =$ _____

18. $\dfrac{-0.4}{80} =$ _____

19. $1 \div \frac{9}{5} =$ _____

20. $\dfrac{\frac{-1}{4}}{\frac{23}{24}} =$ _____

21. $\dfrac{-10.35}{-2.3} =$ _____

22. Alex usually runs for 21 hours a week, training for a marathon. If he is unable to run for 3 days, describe how to find out how many hours of training time he loses, and write the appropriate integer to describe how it affects his time.

_____

_____

_____

_____

_____

_____

_____

23. The running back for the Bulldogs football team carried the ball 9 times for a total loss of $15\frac{3}{4}$ yards. Find the average change in field position on each run.

_____

24. The 6:00 a.m. temperatures for four consecutive days in the town of Lincoln were $-12.1\,°C$, $-7.8\,°C$, $-14.3\,°C$, and $-7.2\,°C$. What was the average 6:00 a.m. temperature for the four days?

_____

25. Multistep A seafood restaurant claims an increase of $1,750.00 over its average profit during a week where it introduced a special of baked clams.

a. If this is true, how much extra profit did it receive per day?

_____

b. If it had, instead, lost $150 per day, how much money would it have lost for the week?

_____

c. If its total loss was $490 for the week, what was its average daily change?

_____

26. A hot air balloon descended 99.6 meters in 12 seconds. What was the balloon's average rate of descent in meters per second?

_____

_____

27. Sanderson is having trouble with his assignment. His work is as follows:

$$\frac{-\frac{3}{4}}{\frac{4}{3}} = -\frac{3}{4} \times \frac{4}{3} = -\frac{12}{12} = -1$$

However, his answer does not match the answer that his teacher gives him. What is Sanderson's mistake? Find the correct answer.

_____

_____

_____

_____

28. Science Beginning in 1996, a glacier lost an average of 3.7 meters of thickness each year. Find the total change in its thickness by the end of 2012.

_____

 **FOCUS ON HIGHER ORDER THINKING**

29. Represent Real-World Problems Describe a real-world situation that can be represented by the quotient $-85 \div 15$. Then find the quotient and explain what the quotient means in terms of the real-world situation.

_____

_____

_____

_____

30. Construct an Argument Divide 5 by 4. Is your answer a rational number? Explain.

_____

_____

_____

31. Critical Thinking Is the quotient of an integer divided by a nonzero integer always a rational number? Explain.

_____

_____

_____

Ready to Go On?

1.1 Rational Numbers and Decimals

Write each mixed number as a decimal.

1. $4\frac{1}{5}$ _____

2. $12\frac{14}{15}$ _____

3. $5\frac{5}{32}$ _____

1.2 Relationships Between Sets of Numbers

4. Are all whole numbers rational numbers? Explain.

_____

_____

1.3 Adding Rational Numbers

Find each sum.

5. $4.5 + 7.1 =$ _____

6. $5\frac{1}{6} + \left(-3\frac{5}{6}\right) =$ _____

1.4 Subtracting Rational Numbers

Find each difference.

7. $-\frac{1}{8} - \left(6\frac{7}{8}\right) =$ _____

8. $14.2 - (-4.9) =$ _____

1.5 Multiplying Rational Numbers

Multiply.

9. $-4\left(\frac{7}{10}\right) =$ _____

10. $-3.2(-5.6)(4) =$ _____

1.6 Dividing Rational Numbers

Find each quotient.

11. $-\frac{19}{2} \div \frac{38}{7} =$ _____

12. $\frac{-32.01}{-3.3} =$ _____

? ESSENTIAL QUESTION

13. How can you use rational numbers to represent real-world problems?

_____

_____

_____

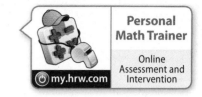
Selected Response

1. What is $-7\frac{5}{12}$ written as a decimal?

- (A) -7.25
- (B) $-7.333\ldots$
- (C) $-7.41666\ldots$
- (D) -7.512

2. Which set or sets does the number $-9\frac{1}{2}$ belong to?

- (A) Integers only
- (B) Rational numbers only
- (C) Integers and rational numbers only
- (D) Whole numbers, integers, and rational numbers

3. Renee ate $\frac{1}{4}$ of a pizza, and Sumi ate $\frac{1}{3}$ of the same pizza. How much of the pizza did they eat in all?

- (A) $\frac{1}{7}$ of the pizza
- (B) $\frac{2}{7}$ of the pizza
- (C) $\frac{5}{12}$ of the pizza
- (D) $\frac{7}{12}$ of the pizza

4. Kareem had $25 in his bank account on Monday. The table shows his account activity for the next four days. What was the balance in Kareem's account on Friday?

Day	Deposit	Withdrawal
Monday	none	$13.50
Tuesday	$85.10	none
Wednesday	none	$55.32
Thursday	$17.95	none

- (A) $59.23
- (C) $-$9.23
- (B) $9.23
- (D) $-$59.23

5. A used boat is on sale for $2,400. Austin makes an offer equal to $\frac{2}{3}$ of this price. How much does Austin offer for the boat?

- (A) $3,600
- (C) $1,600
- (B) $1,800
- (D) $800

6. Working together, 9 friends pick $23\frac{2}{5}$ bags of apples at an orchard. They divide the bags of apples equally between them. How many bags does each friend get?

- (A) $32\frac{2}{5}$ bags
- (C) $2\frac{3}{5}$ bags
- (B) $14\frac{2}{5}$ bags
- (D) $2\frac{5}{9}$ bags

7. The Flathead Rail Tunnel in Montana is about $7\frac{3}{4}$ miles long. A train travels at a speed of $\frac{3}{4}$ mile per minute. How long will it take the train to go through the tunnel?

- (A) $\frac{7}{16}$ minute
- (B) $5\frac{3}{16}$ minutes
- (C) $8\frac{1}{3}$ minutes
- (D) $10\frac{1}{3}$ minutes

Gridded Response

8. What is the value of $(-2.75)(-1.16)$?

⊕	⓪	⓪	⓪	⓪	•	⓪	⓪
⊖	①	①	①	①		①	①
	②	②	②	②		②	②
	③	③	③	③		③	③
	④	④	④	④		④	④
	⑤	⑤	⑤	⑤		⑤	⑤
	⑥	⑥	⑥	⑥		⑥	⑥
	⑦	⑦	⑦	⑦		⑦	⑦
	⑧	⑧	⑧	⑧		⑧	⑧
	⑨	⑨	⑨	⑨		⑨	⑨

© Houghton Mifflin Harcourt Publishing Company

Study Guide Review

MODULE 1 Rational Numbers

Key Vocabulary

rational number *(número racional)*

repeating decimal *(decimal periódico)*

set *(conjunto)*

subset *(subconjunto)*

terminating decimal *(decimal cerrado)*

? ESSENTIAL QUESTION

How can you use rational numbers to solve real-world problems?

EXAMPLE 1

Eddie walked $1\frac{2}{3}$ miles on a hiking trail. Write $1\frac{2}{3}$ as a decimal. Use the decimal to classify $1\frac{2}{3}$ by naming the set or sets to which it belongs.

$$1\frac{2}{3} = \frac{5}{3}$$ *Write $1\frac{2}{3}$ as an improper fraction.*

$$\begin{array}{r} 1.66 \\ 3\overline{)5.00} \\ -3 \\ \hline 2\,0 \\ -1\,8 \\ \hline 20 \\ -18 \\ \hline 2 \end{array}$$ *Divide the numerator by the denominator.*

The decimal equivalent of $1\frac{2}{3}$ is 1.66…, or $1.\overline{6}$. It is a repeating decimal, and therefore can be classified as a rational number.

EXAMPLE 2

Find each sum or difference.

A. $-2 + 4.5$

Start at -2 and move 4.5 units to the right. $-2 + 4.5 = 2.5$

B. $-\frac{2}{5} - \left(-\frac{4}{5}\right)$

Start at $-\frac{2}{5}$. Move $\left|-\frac{4}{5}\right| = \frac{4}{5}$ unit to the right because you are subtracting a negative number. $-\frac{2}{5} - \left(-\frac{4}{5}\right) = \frac{2}{5}$

EXAMPLE 3

Find the product: $3\left(-\frac{1}{6}\right)\left(-\frac{2}{5}\right)$.

$3\left(-\frac{1}{6}\right) = -\frac{1}{2}$

Find the product of the first two factors. One is positive and one is negative, so the product is negative.

$-\frac{1}{2}\left(-\frac{2}{5}\right) = \frac{1}{5}$

Multiply the result by the third factor. Both are negative, so the product is positive.

$3\left(-\frac{1}{6}\right)\left(-\frac{2}{5}\right) = \frac{1}{5}$

EXAMPLE 4

Find the quotient: $\frac{15.2}{-2}$.

$\frac{15.2}{-2} = -7.6$

The quotient is negative because the signs are different.

EXERCISES

Write each mixed number as a whole number or decimal. Classify each number by naming the set or sets to which it belongs: rational numbers, integers, or whole numbers. (Lessons 1.1, 1.2)

1. $\frac{3}{4}$ _____

2. $\frac{8}{2}$ _____

3. $\frac{11}{3}$ _____

4. $\frac{5}{2}$ _____

Find each sum or difference. (Lessons 1.3, 1.4)

5. $-5 + 9.5$ _____

6. $\frac{1}{6} + \left(-\frac{5}{6}\right)$ _____

7. $-0.5 + (-8.5)$ _____

8. $-3 - (-8)$ _____

9. $5.6 - (-3.1)$ _____

10. $3\frac{1}{2} - 2\frac{1}{4}$ _____

Find each product or quotient. (Lessons 1.5, 1.6)

11. $-9 \times (-5)$ _____

12. $0 \times (-7)$ _____

13. -8×8 _____

14. $\frac{-56}{8}$ _____

15. $\frac{-130}{-5}$ _____

16. $\frac{34.5}{1.5}$ _____

17. $-\frac{2}{5}\left(-\frac{1}{2}\right)\left(-\frac{5}{6}\right)$ _____

18. $\left(\frac{1}{5}\right)\left(-\frac{5}{7}\right)\left(\frac{3}{4}\right)$ _____

19. Lei withdrew $50 from her bank account every day for a week. What was the change in her account in that week?

_____

20. In 5 minutes, a seal descended 24 feet. What was the average rate of change in the seal's elevation per minute?

_____

1. **CAREERS IN MATH** | Urban Planner Armand is an urban planner, and he has proposed a site for a new town library. The site is between City Hall and the post office on Main Street.

City Hall   Library site   Post Office

The distance between City Hall and the post office is $6\frac{1}{2}$ miles. The library site is $1\frac{1}{4}$ miles closer to City Hall than it is to the post office.

a. Write $6\frac{1}{2}$ miles and $1\frac{1}{4}$ miles as decimals.

_____

b. Let *d* represent the distance from City Hall to the library site. Write an expression for the distance from the library site to the post office.

_____

c. Write an equation that represents the following statement: The distance from City Hall to the library site plus the distance from the library site to the post office is equal to the distance from City Hall to the post office.

_____

d. Solve your equation from part **c** to determine the distance from City Hall to the library site, and the distance from the post office to the library site.

_____

_____

2. Sumaya is reading a book with 240 pages. She has already read 90 pages. She plans to read 20 more pages each day until she finishes the book.

a. Sumaya writes the equation $330 = -20d$ to find the number of days she will need to finish the book. Identify the errors that Sumaya made.

_____

_____

b. Write and solve an equation to determine how many days Sumaya will need to finish the book. In your answer, count part of a day as a full day.

_____

_____

c. Estimate how many days you would need to read a book about the same length as Sumaya's book. What information did you use to find the estimate?

_____

_____

_____

3. Jackson works as a veterinary technician and earns $12.20 per hour.

a. Jackson normally works 40 hours a week. In a normal week, what is his total pay before taxes and other deductions?

_____

b. Last week, Jackson was ill and missed some work. His total pay before deductions was $372.10. Write and solve an equation to find the number of hours Jackson worked.

_____

c. Jackson records his hours each day on a time sheet. Last week when he was ill, his time sheet was incomplete. How many hours are missing? Show your work.

Mon	Tues	Wed	Thurs	Fri
8	$7\frac{1}{4}$	$8\frac{1}{2}$		

_____

_____

d. When Jackson works more than 40 hours in a week, he earns 1.5 times his normal hourly rate for each of the extra hours. Jackson worked 43 hours one week. What was his total pay before deductions? Justify your answer.

_____

_____

e. What is a reasonable range for Jackson's expected yearly pay before deductions? Describe any assumptions you made in finding your answer.

_____

_____

_____

UNIT 1 MIXED REVIEW

Texas Test Prep

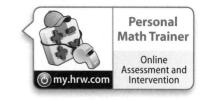

Personal
Math Trainer

Online
Assessment and
Intervention

my.hrw.com

Selected Response

1. What is $-6\frac{9}{16}$ written as a decimal?

(A) -6.625

(B) -6.5625

(C) -6.4375

(D) -6.125

2. Working together, 6 friends pick $14\frac{2}{5}$ pounds of pecans at a pecan farm. They divide the pecans equally among themselves. How many pounds does each friend get?

(A) $20\frac{2}{5}$ pounds

(B) $8\frac{2}{5}$ pounds

(C) $2\frac{3}{5}$ pounds

(D) $2\frac{2}{5}$ pounds

3. What is the value of $(-3.25)(-1.56)$?

(A) -5.85

(B) -5.07

(C) 5.07

(D) 5.85

4. Ruby ate $\frac{1}{3}$ of a pizza, and Angie ate $\frac{1}{5}$ of the pizza. How much of the pizza did they eat in all?

(A) $\frac{1}{15}$ of the pizza

(B) $\frac{1}{8}$ of the pizza

(C) $\frac{3}{8}$ of the pizza

(D) $\frac{8}{15}$ of the pizza

5. Jaime had $37 in his bank account on Sunday. The table shows his account activity for the next four days. What was the balance in Jaime's account after his deposit on Thursday?

Jamie's Bank Account		
Day	**Deposit**	**Withdrawal**
Monday	$17.42	none
Tuesday	none	$-$12.60
Wednesday	none	$-$9.62
Thursday	$62.29	none

(A) $57.49

(B) $59.65

(C) $94.49

(D) $138.93

6. A used motorcycle is on sale for $3,600. Erik makes an offer equal to $\frac{3}{4}$ of this price. How much does Erik offer for the motorcycle?

(A) $4,800

(B) $2,700

(C) $2,400

(D) $900

7. To which set or sets does the number -18 belong?

(A) integers only

(B) rational numbers only

(C) integers and rational numbers only

(D) whole numbers, integers, and rational numbers

8. Mrs. Rodriguez is going to use $6\frac{1}{3}$ yards of material to make two dresses. The larger dress requires $3\frac{2}{3}$ yards of material. How much material will Mrs. Rodriguez have left to use on the smaller dress?

Ⓐ $1\frac{2}{3}$ yards

Ⓑ $2\frac{1}{3}$ yards

Ⓒ $2\frac{2}{3}$ yards

Ⓓ $3\frac{1}{3}$ yards

9. Winslow buys 1.2 pounds of bananas. The bananas cost $1.29 per pound. To the nearest cent, how much does Winslow pay for the bananas?

Ⓐ $1.08

Ⓑ $1.20

Ⓒ $1.55

Ⓓ $2.49

Gridded Response

10. Roberta earns $7.65 per hour. How many hours does Roberta need to work to earn $24.48?

11. What is the product of the following expression?

$$(-2.2)(1.5)(-4.2)$$

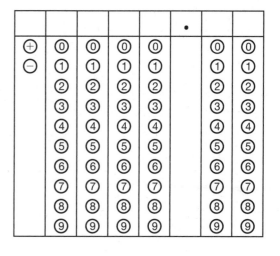

> **Hot Tip!** Correct answers in gridded problems can be positive or negative. Enter the negative sign in the first column when it is appropriate. Check your work!

12. Victor is ordering pizzas for a party. He would like to have $\frac{1}{4}$ of a pizza for each guest. He can only order whole pizzas, not part of a pizza. If he expects 27 guests, how many pizzas should he order?

Ratios and Proportional Relationships

CAREERS IN MATH

Landscape Architect Landscape architects design and create beautiful and functional outdoor spaces, such as city parks, college campuses, and arboretums. They use financial math when estimating and calculating costs of labor and supplies, and scaling and geometry when creating models and implementing their designs. If you are interested in a career as a landscape architect, you should study these mathematical subjects:

- Algebra
- Geometry
- Trigonometry

Research other careers that require geometry and scaling.

Unit 2 Performance Task

At the end of the unit, check out how **landscape architects** use math.

Vocabulary Preview

Use the puzzle to preview key vocabulary from this unit. Unscramble the circled letters within found words to answer the riddle at the bottom of the page.

1. A relationship between two quantities in which the rate of change or the ratio of one quantity to the other is constant. (Lesson 2-2)

   ◯ __ ◯ __ __ __ __ __ __ __
   ◯ __ __ ◯ __ __ __ __

2. Describes how much a quantity decreases in comparison to the original

   amount. (Lesson 3-2) __ __ ◯ __ __ __ __

   __ __ __ __ __ __ __

3. A fixed percent of the principal. (Lesson 3-4)

   __ __ __ __ __ ◯ __ __ __ __ ◯

4. Angles of two or more similar shapes that are in the same relative position. (Lesson 4-1)

   __ ◯ __ __ __ ◯ __ __ __ __ __
   __ __ __ __ __

5. A proportional two-dimensional drawing of an object. (Lesson 4-3)

   __ __ __ __ ◯ __ ◯ __

Q: What did the athlete order when he needed a huge helping of mashed potatoes?

A: __ __ __ __ – __ __ __ __ __ __ __ __ __!

Rates and Proportionality

? ESSENTIAL QUESTION

How can you use rates and proportionality to solve real-world problems?

Real-World Video

You can use rates to describe lots of real-world situations. A cyclist can compute rates such as miles per hour or rotations per minute.

my.hrw.com

GO DIGITAL
my.hrw.com

my.hrw.com
Go digital with your write-in student edition, accessible on any device.

Math On the Spot
Scan with your smart phone to jump directly to the online edition, video tutor, and more.

Animated Math
Interactively explore key concepts to see how math works.

Personal Math Trainer
Get immediate feedback and help as you work through practice sets.

Are YOU Ready?

Complete these exercises to review skills you will need for this chapter.

Operations with Fractions

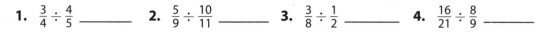

EXAMPLE $\frac{3}{10} \div \frac{5}{8} = \frac{3}{10} \times \frac{8}{5}$ Multiply by the reciprocal of the divisor.

$= \frac{3}{10_5} \times \frac{8^4}{5}$ Divide by the common factors.

$= \frac{12}{25}$ Simplify.

Divide.

1. $\frac{3}{4} \div \frac{4}{5}$ _____

2. $\frac{5}{9} \div \frac{10}{11}$ _____

3. $\frac{3}{8} \div \frac{1}{2}$ _____

4. $\frac{16}{21} \div \frac{8}{9}$ _____

Ordered Pairs

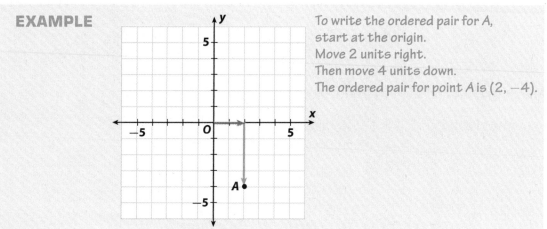

EXAMPLE

To write the ordered pair for A, start at the origin.
Move 2 units right.
Then move 4 units down.
The ordered pair for point A is $(2, -4)$.

Write the ordered pair for each point.

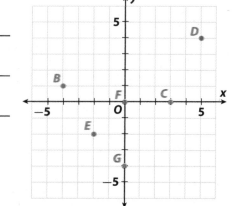

5. B _____

6. C _____

7. D _____

8. E _____

9. F _____

10. G _____

Reading Start-Up

Visualize Vocabulary

Use the ✔ words to complete the graphic. You can put more than one word in each bubble.

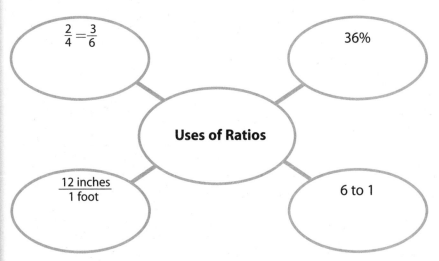

$\frac{2}{4} = \frac{3}{6}$

36%

Uses of Ratios

$\frac{12 \text{ inches}}{1 \text{ foot}}$

6 to 1

Vocabulary

Review Words

  constant *(constante)*

✔ conversion factor *(factor de conversión)*

✔ equivalent ratios *(razones equivalentes)*

✔ percent *(porcentaje)*

  rate *(tasa)*

✔ ratio *(razón)*

Preview Words

  complex fraction *(fracción compleja)*

  constant of proportionality *(constante de proporcionalidad)*

  proportion *(proporción)*

  proportional relationship *(relación proporcional)*

  rate of change *(tasa de cambio)*

  unit rates *(tasas unitarias)*

Understand Vocabulary

Match the term on the left to the definition on the right.

1. rate of change   **A.** Statement that two rates or ratios are equivalent.

2. proportion   **B.** A rate that describes how one quantity changes in relation to another quantity.

3. unit rate   **C.** Rate in which the second quantity is one unit.

Active Reading

Three-Panel Flip Chart Before beginning the module, create a three-panel flip chart to help you organize what you learn. Label each flap with one of the lesson titles from this module. As you study each lesson, write important ideas like vocabulary, properties, and formulas under the appropriate flap.

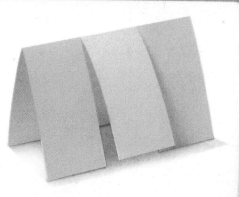

Unpacking the TEKS

Understanding the TEKS and the vocabulary terms in the TEKS will help you know exactly what you are expected to learn in this module.

TEKS 7.4.B

Calculate unit rates from rates in mathematical and real-world problems.

Key Vocabulary

rate *(tasa)*
A ratio that compares two quantities measured in different units.

unit rate *(tasa unitaria)*
A rate in which the second quantity in the comparison is one unit.

What It Means to You

Given a rate, you can find the equivalent unit rate by dividing the numerator by the denominator.

UNPACKING EXAMPLE 7.4.B

Lisa hikes $\frac{1}{3}$ mile every $\frac{1}{6}$ hour. How far does she hike in 1 hour?

$$\frac{\frac{1}{3}}{\frac{1}{6}} = \frac{1}{3} \div \frac{1}{6}$$

$$= \frac{1}{\cancel{3}_1} \cdot \frac{\cancel{6}^2}{1}$$

$$= 2 \text{ miles}$$

TEKS 7.4.C

Determine the constant of proportionality $(k = \frac{y}{x})$ within mathematical and real-world problems.

Key Vocabulary

constant *(constante)*
A value that does not change.

constant of proportionality *(constante de proporcionalidad)*
A constant ratio of two variables related proportionally.

What It Means to You

You will determine the constant of proportionality for proportional relationships.

UNPACKING EXAMPLE 7.4.C

The graph shows the distance a bicyclist travels over time. How fast does the bicyclist travel?

$$\text{slope (speed)} = \frac{\text{rise (distance)}}{\text{run (time)}}$$

$$= \frac{15}{1}$$

The bicyclist travels at 15 miles per hour.

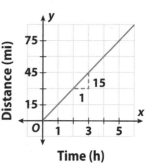

Visit **my.hrw.com** to see all the **TEKS** unpacked.

my.hrw.com

LESSON
2.1 Unit Rates

TEKS
Proportionality—
7.4.B Calculate unit rates from rates in mathematical and real-world problems.
Also 7.4.A, 7.4.D

? ESSENTIAL QUESTION

How do you find and use unit rates?

EXPLORE ACTIVITY **TEKS** 7.4.B

Exploring Rates

Commonly used rates like miles per hour make it easy to understand and compare rates.

Jeff hikes $\frac{1}{2}$ mile every 15 minutes, or $\frac{1}{4}$ hour. Lisa hikes $\frac{1}{3}$ mile every 10 minutes, or $\frac{1}{6}$ hour. How far do they each hike in 1 hour? 2 hours?

A Use the bar diagram to help you determine how many miles Jeff hikes. How many $\frac{1}{4}$-hours are in 1 hour? How far does Jeff hike in 1 hour?

? miles

| $\frac{1}{4}$ hour | $\frac{1}{4}$ hour | $\frac{1}{4}$ hour | $\frac{1}{4}$ hour |

$\frac{1}{2}$ mile

_____

B Complete the table for Jeff's hike.

Distance (mi)	$\frac{1}{2}$				
Time (h)	$\frac{1}{4}$	$\frac{1}{2}$	$\frac{3}{4}$	1	2

C Complete the bar diagram to help you determine how far Lisa hikes. How many miles does she hike in 1 hour?

| $\frac{1}{6}$ hour | $\frac{1}{6}$ hour | $\frac{1}{6}$ hour | $\frac{1}{6}$ hour | $\frac{1}{6}$ hour | $\frac{1}{6}$ hour |

_____

D Complete the table for Lisa's hike.

Distance (mi)	$\frac{1}{3}$				
Time (h)	$\frac{1}{6}$	$\frac{1}{3}$	$\frac{1}{2}$	1	2

Reflect

1. How did you find Jeff's distance for $\frac{3}{4}$ hour?

_____

2. Which hiker walks farther in one hour? Which is faster?

_____

Finding Unit Rates

A rate is a comparison of two quantities that have different units, such as miles and hours. Rates are often expressed as **unit rates**, that is, with a denominator of 1 unit.

$$\frac{60 \text{ miles} \div 2}{2 \text{ hours} \div 2} = \frac{30 \text{ miles}}{1 \text{ hour}}$$ This means 30 miles per hour.

When the two quantities being compared in the rate are both fractions, the rate is expressed as a *complex fraction*. A **complex fraction** is a fraction that has a fraction in its numerator, denominator, or both.

$$\frac{\frac{a}{b}}{\frac{c}{d}} = \frac{a}{b} \div \frac{c}{d}$$

EXAMPLE 1   Real World   TEKS 7.4.B

While remodeling her kitchen, Angela is repainting. She estimates that she paints 55 square feet every half-hour. How many square feet does Angela paint per hour?

STEP 1   Determine the units of the rate.

The rate is **area in square feet** per **time in hours**.

STEP 2   Find Angela's rate of painting in area painted per time.

area painted: 55 sq ft   **time:** $\frac{1}{2}$ hour

$$\frac{\text{area painted}}{\text{time}} = \frac{55 \text{ square feet}}{\frac{1}{2} \text{ hour}}$$

> The fraction represents area in square feet per time in hours.

STEP 3   Find Angela's unit rate of painting in square feet per hour.

$$\frac{55}{\frac{1}{2}} = 55 \div \frac{1}{2}$$ Rewrite the fraction as division.

$$= \frac{55}{1} \times \frac{2}{1}$$ Multiply by the reciprocal.

$$= \frac{110 \text{ square feet}}{1 \text{ hour}}$$

> The unit rate has a denominator of 1.

Angela paints 110 square feet per hour.

3. Paige mows $\frac{1}{6}$ acre in $\frac{1}{4}$ hour. How many acres does Paige mow per hour?

_____

4. Greta uses 3 ounces of pasta to make $\frac{3}{4}$ of a serving of pasta. How many ounces of pasta are there per serving?_____

Using Unit Rates

You can use unit rates to simplify rates that appear complicated, such as those containing fractions in both the numerator and denominator.

EXAMPLE 2 🌐 Real World   TEKS 7.4.D

Two pools are leaking. After 15 minutes, pool A has leaked $\frac{2}{3}$ gallon. After 20 minutes, pool B has leaked $\frac{3}{4}$ gallon. Which pool is leaking faster?

My Notes

STEP 1 Find the rate in volume (gallons) per time (hours) at which each pool is leaking. First convert minutes to hours.

Pool A

$$\frac{\frac{2}{3}\text{ gal}}{15\text{ min}} = \frac{\frac{2}{3}\text{ gal}}{\frac{1}{4}\text{ h}}$$

$15\text{ min} = \frac{1}{4}\text{ h}$

Pool B

$$\frac{\frac{3}{4}\text{ gal}}{20\text{ min}} = \frac{\frac{3}{4}\text{ gal}}{\frac{1}{3}\text{ h}}$$

$20\text{ min} = \frac{1}{3}\text{ h}$

STEP 2 To find the unit rates, first rewrite the fractions.

Pool A

$$\frac{\frac{2}{3}\text{ gal}}{\frac{1}{4}\text{ h}} = \frac{2}{3} \div \frac{1}{4}$$

Pool B

$$\frac{\frac{3}{4}\text{ gal}}{\frac{1}{3}\text{ h}} = \frac{3}{4} \div \frac{1}{3}$$

STEP 3 To divide, multiply by the reciprocal.

Pool A

$$\frac{2}{3} \div \frac{1}{4} = \frac{2}{3} \times \frac{4}{1}$$
$$= \frac{8}{3}, \text{ or } 2\frac{2}{3}\text{ gal per h}$$

Pool B

$$\frac{3}{4} \div \frac{1}{3} = \frac{3}{4} \times \frac{3}{1}$$
$$= \frac{9}{4}, \text{ or } 2\frac{1}{4}\text{ gal per h}$$

STEP 4 Compare the unit rates.

Pool A   Pool B

$$2\frac{2}{3} > 2\frac{1}{4}$$

So, Pool A is leaking faster.

Math Talk
Mathematical Processes

How do you compare mixed numbers?

Personal
Math Trainer

Online Assessment
and Intervention

my.hrw.com

5. One tank is filling at a rate of $\frac{3}{4}$ gallon per $\frac{2}{3}$ minute. A second tank is filling at a rate of $\frac{5}{8}$ gallon per $\frac{1}{2}$ minute. Which tank is filling faster?

_____

Guided Practice

1. Brandon enters bike races. He bikes $8\frac{1}{2}$ miles every $\frac{1}{2}$ hour. Complete the table to find how far Brandon bikes for each time interval. (Explore Activity)

Distance (mi)	$8\frac{1}{2}$				
Time (h)	$\frac{1}{2}$	1	$1\frac{1}{2}$	2	$2\frac{1}{2}$

Find each unit rate. (Example 1)

2. Julio walks $3\frac{1}{2}$ miles in $1\frac{1}{4}$ hours.

_____

3. Kenny reads $\frac{5}{8}$ page in $\frac{2}{3}$ minute.

_____

4. A garden snail moves $\frac{1}{6}$ foot in $\frac{1}{3}$ hour.

_____

5. A fertilizer covers $\frac{5}{8}$ square foot in $\frac{1}{4}$ hour.

_____

Find each unit rate. Determine which is lower. (Example 2)

6. Brand A: 240 mg sodium for $\frac{1}{3}$ pickle or Brand B: 325 mg sodium for $\frac{1}{2}$ pickle

_____

_____

_____

7. Ingredient C: $\frac{1}{4}$ cup for $\frac{2}{3}$ serving or Ingredient D: $\frac{1}{3}$ cup for $\frac{3}{4}$ serving

_____

_____

_____

? **ESSENTIAL QUESTION CHECK-IN**

8. How can you find a unit rate when given a rate?

_____

_____

_____

_____

2.1 Independent Practice

TEKS 7.4.A, 7.4.B, 7.4.D

Personal Math Trainer

Online Assessment and Intervention

my.hrw.com

9. The information for two pay-as-you-go cell phone companies is given.

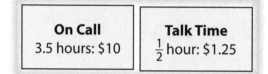

On Call	Talk Time
3.5 hours: $10	$\frac{1}{2}$ hour: $1.25

a. What is the unit rate in dollars per hour for each company?

_____

_____

b. **Analyze Relationships** Which company offers the best deal? Explain your answer.

_____

_____

c. **What If?** Another company offers a rate of $0.05 per minute. How would you find the unit rate per hour?

_____

_____

d. **Draw Conclusions** Is the rate in part **c** a better deal than On Call or Talk Time? Explain.

_____

_____

10. **Represent Real-World Problems** Your teacher asks you to find a recipe that includes two ingredients with a rate of $\frac{2 \text{ units}}{3 \text{ units}}$.

a. Give an example of two ingredients in a recipe that would meet this requirement.

_____

_____

b. If you needed to triple the recipe, would the rate change? Explain.

_____

_____

_____

_____

11. A radio station requires DJs to play 2 commercials for every 10 songs they play. What is the unit rate of songs to commercials?

_____

12. **Multistep** Terrance and Jesse are training for a long-distance race. Terrance trains at a rate of 6 miles every half hour, and Jesse trains at a rate of 2 miles every 15 minutes.

a. What is the unit rate in miles per hour for each runner?

_____

_____

b. How long will each person take to run a total of 50 miles at the given rates?

_____

_____

c. Sandra runs at a rate of 8 miles in 45 minutes. How does her unit rate compare to Terrance's and to Jesse's?

_____

_____

_____

13. **Analyze Relationships** Eli takes a typing test and types all 300 words in $\frac{1}{10}$ hour. He takes the test a second time and types the words in $\frac{1}{12}$ hour. Was he faster or slower on the second attempt? Explain.

____

____

Work Area

H.O.T. FOCUS ON HIGHER ORDER THINKING

14. **Justify Reasoning** An online retailer sells two packages of protein bars.

Package	10-pack of 2.1 ounce bars	12-pack of 1.4 ounce bars
Cost ($)	15.37	15.35

a. Which package has the better price per bar?

____

____

____

b. Which package has the better price per ounce?

____

____

____

c. Which package do you think is a better buy? Justify your reasoning.

____

____

15. **Check for Reasonableness** A painter painted about half a room in half a day. Coley estimated the painter would paint 7 rooms in 7 days. Is Coley's estimate reasonable? Explain.

____

____

16. **Communicate Mathematical Ideas** If you know the rate of a water leak in gallons per hour, how can you find the number of hours it takes for 1 gallon to leak out? Justify your answer.

____

____

____

Constant Rates of Change

TEKS
Proportionality—
7.4.A Represent constant rates of change in mathematical and real-world problems given pictorial, tabular, verbal, numeric, graphical, and algebraic representations, including $d = rt$. Also 7.4.C, 7.4.D

? ESSENTIAL QUESTION

How can you identify and represent proportional relationships?

EXPLORE ACTIVITY Real World **TEKS** 7.4.A

Discovering Proportional Relationships

Many real-world situations can be described by *proportional relationships*. Proportional relationships have special characteristics.

A giant tortoise moves at a slow but steady pace. It takes the giant tortoise 3 seconds to travel 10.5 inches.

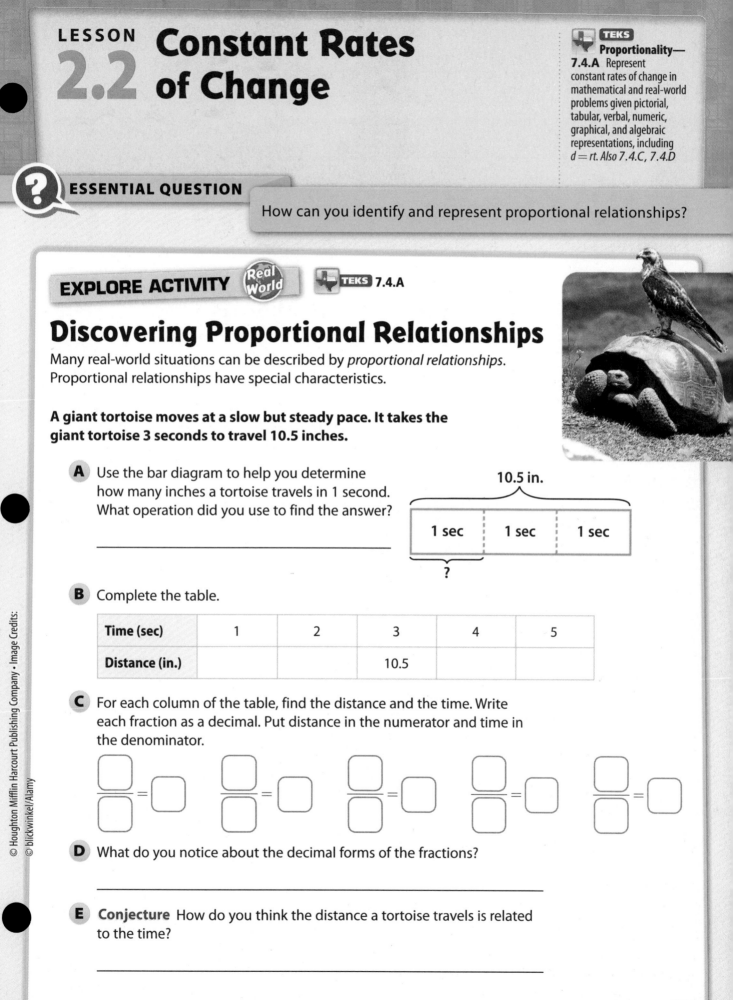

A Use the bar diagram to help you determine how many inches a tortoise travels in 1 second. What operation did you use to find the answer?

_____

10.5 in.

| 1 sec | 1 sec | 1 sec |

?

B Complete the table.

Time (sec)	1	2	3	4	5
Distance (in.)			10.5		

C For each column of the table, find the distance and the time. Write each fraction as a decimal. Put distance in the numerator and time in the denominator.

$$\frac{\square}{\square} = \square \qquad \frac{\square}{\square} = \square \qquad \frac{\square}{\square} = \square \qquad \frac{\square}{\square} = \square \qquad \frac{\square}{\square} = \square$$

D What do you notice about the decimal forms of the fractions?

_____

E **Conjecture** How do you think the distance a tortoise travels is related to the time?

_____

Reflect

1. Suppose the tortoise travels for 12 seconds. Explain how you could find the distance the tortoise travels.

   _____

2. How would you describe the rate of speed at which a tortoise travels?

   _____

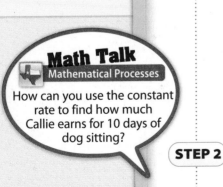

Proportional Relationships

A **rate of change** is a rate that describes how one quantity changes in relation to another quantity. A **proportional relationship** between two quantities is one in which the rate of change is constant, or one in which the ratio of one quantity to the other is constant.

Any two rates or ratios based on a given proportional relationship can be used to form a *proportion*. A **proportion** is a statement that two rates or ratios are equivalent, for example, $\frac{6 \text{ mi}}{2 \text{ h}} = \frac{3 \text{ mi}}{1 \text{ h}}$, or $\frac{2}{4} = \frac{1}{2}$.

EXAMPLE 1 Real World

TEKS 7.4.A

My Notes

Callie earns money by dog sitting. Based on the table, is the relationship between the amount Callie earns and the number of days a proportional relationship?

Number of Days	1	2	3	4	5
Amount Earned ($)	16	32	48	64	80

STEP 1 Write the rates.

$\dfrac{\text{Amount earned}}{\text{Number of days}} = \dfrac{\$16}{1 \text{ day}}$ Put the amount earned in the numerator and the number of days in the denominator.

$\dfrac{\$32}{2 \text{ days}} = \dfrac{\$16}{1 \text{ day}}$

$\dfrac{\$48}{3 \text{ days}} = \dfrac{\$16}{1 \text{ day}}$ Each rate is equal to $\dfrac{\$16}{1 \text{ day}}$, or $16 per day.

$\dfrac{\$64}{4 \text{ days}} = \dfrac{\$16}{1 \text{ day}}$

$\dfrac{\$80}{5 \text{ days}} = \dfrac{\$16}{1 \text{ day}}$

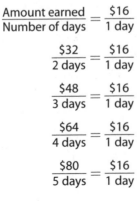

Math Talk
Mathematical Processes

How can you use the constant rate to find how much Callie earns for 10 days of dog sitting?

STEP 2 Compare the rates. The rates are all equal. This means the rate is constant, so the relationship is proportional.

The constant rate of change is $16 per day.

3. The table shows the distance Allison drove on one day of her vacation. Is the relationship between the distance and the time a proportional relationship? Did she drive at a constant speed? Explain.

Time (h)	1	2	3	4	5
Distance (mi)	65	120	195	220	300

Writing an Equation for a Proportional Relationship

If there is a proportional relationship between *x* and *y*, you can describe that relationship using the equation $y = kx$. The variable *k* is called the **constant of proportionality**, and it represents the constant rate of change or constant ratio between *x* and *y*. The value of *k* is represented by the equation $k = \frac{y}{x}$.

EXAMPLE 2 Real World   TEKS 7.4.A

Two pounds of cashews shown cost $19, and 8 pounds cost $76. Show that the relationship between the number of pounds of cashews and the cost is a proportional relationship. Then write an equation for the relationship.

STEP 1 Make a table relating cost in dollars to pounds.

Number of Pounds	2	3	8
Cost ($)	19	28.50	76

STEP 2 Write the rates. Put cost in the numerator and pounds in the denominator. Then simplify each rate.

$$\frac{\text{Cost}}{\text{Number of Pounds}} \longrightarrow \quad \frac{19}{2} = 9.50 \qquad \frac{28.50}{3} = 9.50 \qquad \frac{76}{8} = 9.50$$

The rates are all equal to $9.50 per pound. They are constant, so the relationship is proportional. The constant rate of change is $9.50 per pound.

STEP 3 To write an equation, first tell what the variables represent.

- Let *x* represent the number of pounds of cashews.
- Let *y* represent the cost in dollars.
- Use the numerical part of the constant rate of change as the constant of proportionality.

So, the equation for the relationship is $y = 9.5x$.

Math Talk
Mathematical Processes

How can you use your equation to find the cost of 6 pounds of cashews?

© Houghton Mifflin Harcourt Publishing Company

YOUR TURN

4. For a school field trip, there must be 1 adult to accompany 12 students, 3 adults to accompany 36 students, and 5 adults to accompany 60 students. Show that the relationship between the number of adults and the number of students is a proportional relationship. Then write an equation for the relationship.

Number of students	12	36	60
Number of adults	1	3	5

_____

_____

Guided Practice

1. Based on the information in the table, is the relationship between time and the number of words typed a proportional relationship?
   (Explore Activity and Example 1)

Time (min)	1	2	3	4
Number of words	45	90	135	180

$\dfrac{\text{Number of words}}{\text{Minutes}}$: $\dfrac{45}{1} = \boxed{}$ $\dfrac{\boxed{}}{\boxed{}} = \boxed{}$ $\dfrac{\boxed{}}{\boxed{}} = \boxed{}$ $\dfrac{\boxed{}}{\boxed{}} = \boxed{}$

The relationship ⟨ **is / is not** ⟩ proportional.

Find the constant of proportionality k. Then write an equation for the relationship between x and y. (Example 2)

2.

x	2	4	6	8
y	10	20	30	40

_____

3.

x	8	16	24	32
y	2	4	6	8

_____

? ESSENTIAL QUESTION CHECK-IN

4. How can you represent a proportional relationship using an equation?

_____

_____

2.2 Independent Practice

TEKS 7.4.A, 7.4.C, 7.4.D

Information on three car-rental companies is given.

5. Write an equation that gives the cost y of renting a car for x days from Rent-All. _____

6. What is the cost per day of renting a car from A-1? _____

7. **Analyze Relationships** Which company offers the best deal? Why?

_____

_____

Rent-All				
Days	3	4	5	6
Total Cost ($)	55.50	74.00	92.50	111.00

A-1 Rentals	**Car Town**
The cost y of renting a car for x days is $10.99 for each half day.	The cost of renting a car from us is just $19.25 per day!

8. **Critique Reasoning** A skydiver jumps out of an airplane. After 0.8 second, she has fallen 100 feet. After 3.1 seconds, she has fallen 500 feet. Emtiaz says that the skydiver should fall about 187.5 feet in 1.5 seconds. Is his answer reasonable? Explain.

_____

_____

_____

Steven earns extra money babysitting. He charges $31.25 for 5 hours and $50 for 8 hours.

9. Explain why the relationship between how much Steven charges and time is a proportional relationship.

_____

10. **Interpret the Answer** Explain what the constant rate of change means in the context.

_____

11. Write an equation to represent the relationship. Tell what the variables represent.

_____

_____

12. How much would Steven charge for 3 hours? _____

A submarine dives 300 feet every 2 minutes, and 6,750 feet every 45 minutes.

13. Find the constant rate at which the submarine dives. Give your answer in feet per minute and in feet per hour.

_____

14. Let x represent the time of the dive. Let y represent the depth of the submarine. Write an equation for the proportional relationship using the rate in feet per minute.

_____

15. Draw Conclusions If you wanted to find the depth of a submarine during a dive, would it be more reasonable to use an equation with the rate in feet per minute or feet per hour? Explain your reasoning.

_____

_____

H.O.T. ❱ **FOCUS ON HIGHER ORDER THINKING**

16. Make a Conjecture There is a proportional relationship between your distance from a thunderstorm and the time from when you see lightning to when you hear thunder. If there are 9 seconds between lightning and thunder, the storm is about 3 kilometers away. If you double the amount of time between lightning and thunder, do you think the distance in kilometers also doubles? Justify your reasoning.

_____

_____

_____

_____

17. Communicate Mathematical Ideas A store sells 3 ears of corn for $1. They round prices to the nearest cent as shown in the table. Tell whether you would describe the relationship between cost and number of ears of corn as a proportional relationship. Justify your answer.

Ears of corn	1	2	3	4
Amount charged ($)	0.33	0.67	1.00	1.34

_____

_____

_____

_____

LESSON
2.3

TEKS
Proportionality—

7.4.A Represent constant rates of change in mathematical and real-world problems given pictorial, tabular, verbal, numeric, graphical, and algebraic representations, including $d = rt$. Also 7.4.C, 7.4.D

Proportional Relationships and Graphs

? ESSENTIAL QUESTION

How can you use graphs to represent and analyze proportional relationships?

EXPLORE ACTIVITY  TEKS 7.4.A

Graphing Proportional Relationships

You can use a graph to explore proportional relationships.

Most showerheads that were manufactured before 1994 use 5 gallons of water per minute. Is the relationship between the number of gallons of water and the number of minutes a proportional relationship?

> Each minute, 5 gallons of water are used. So for 2 minutes, 2 · 5 gallons are used.

A Complete the table.

Time (min)	1	2	3		10
Water Used (gal)	5			35	

B Based on the table, is this a proportional relationship? Explain your answer.

_____

C Write the data in the table as ordered pairs (time, water used).

(1, 5), (2, ___), (3, ___), (___ , 35), (10, ___)

D Plot the ordered pairs.

E If the showerhead is used for 0 minutes, how many gallons of water will be used? What ordered pair represents this situation? What is this location called?

_____

F **Draw Conclusions** If you continued the table to include 23 minutes, would the point (23, 125) be on this graph? Why or why not?

_____

_____

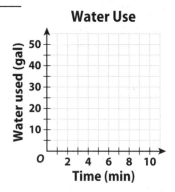

Water Use

Identifying Proportional Relationships

In addition to using a table to determine if a relationship is proportional, you also can use a graph. A relationship is a proportional relationship if its graph is a straight line through the origin.

EXAMPLE 1 Real World

TEKS 7.4.A

A house cleaning company charges $45 per hour. Is the relationship a proportional relationship? Explain.

> Each hour costs $45. So for 2 hours, the cost is 2 · $45 = $90.

STEP 1 Make a table.

Time (h)	1	2	3	5	8
Total cost ($)	45	90	135	225	360

STEP 2 Write the data in the table as ordered pairs (time, cost).

(1, 45), (2, 90), (3, 135), (5, 225), (8, 360)

STEP 3 Graph the ordered pairs.

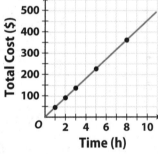

Place time on the x-axis and total cost on the y-axis.

Plot each point.

Connect the points with a line.

The graph is a line that goes through the origin.

So, the relationship is proportional.

YOUR TURN

1. Jared rents bowling shoes for $6 and pays $5 per bowling game. Graph the data. Is the relationship a proportional relationship? Explain.

Games	1	2	3	4
Total Cost ($)	11	16	21	26

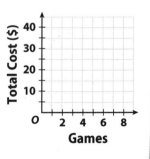

_____

_____

© Houghton Mifflin Harcourt Publishing Company

Analyzing Graphs

Recall that you can describe a proportional relationship with the equation $y = kx$. The constant of proportionality k tells you how steep the graph of the relationship is. The greater the absolute value of k, the steeper the line.

EXAMPLE 2 *Real World*　　　TEKS 7.4.A, 7.4.C

The graph shows the relationship between time in minutes and the number of miles Damon runs. Write an equation for this relationship.

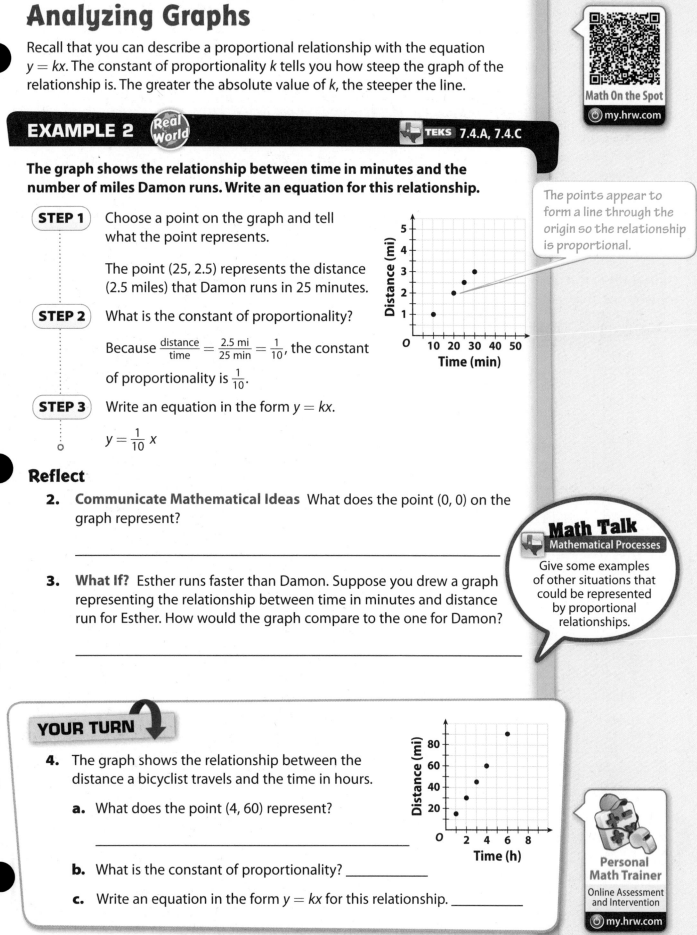

STEP 1 Choose a point on the graph and tell what the point represents.

The point (25, 2.5) represents the distance (2.5 miles) that Damon runs in 25 minutes.

> The points appear to form a line through the origin so the relationship is proportional.

STEP 2 What is the constant of proportionality?

Because $\frac{\text{distance}}{\text{time}} = \frac{2.5 \text{ mi}}{25 \text{ min}} = \frac{1}{10}$, the constant of proportionality is $\frac{1}{10}$.

STEP 3 Write an equation in the form $y = kx$.

$$y = \frac{1}{10} x$$

Reflect

2. **Communicate Mathematical Ideas** What does the point (0, 0) on the graph represent?

   _____

3. **What If?** Esther runs faster than Damon. Suppose you drew a graph representing the relationship between time in minutes and distance run for Esther. How would the graph compare to the one for Damon?

   _____

> **Math Talk**
> **Mathematical Processes**
> Give some examples of other situations that could be represented by proportional relationships.

YOUR TURN

4. The graph shows the relationship between the distance a bicyclist travels and the time in hours.

   a. What does the point (4, 60) represent?

   _____

   b. What is the constant of proportionality? _____

   c. Write an equation in the form $y = kx$ for this relationship. _____

Complete each table. Tell whether the relationship is a proportional relationship. Explain why or why not. (Explore Activity)

1. A student reads 65 pages per hour.

Time (h)	3	5		10
Pages			585	

_____

_____

2. A babysitter makes $7.50 per hour.

Time (h)	2		5	
Pages		22.50		60

_____

_____

Tell whether the relationship is a proportional relationship. Explain why or why not. (Explore Activity and Example 1)

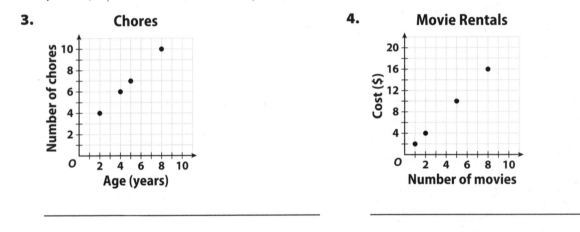

3. Chores

_____

_____

4. Movie Rentals

_____

_____

Write an equation of the form $y = kx$ for the relationship shown in each graph. (Example 2)

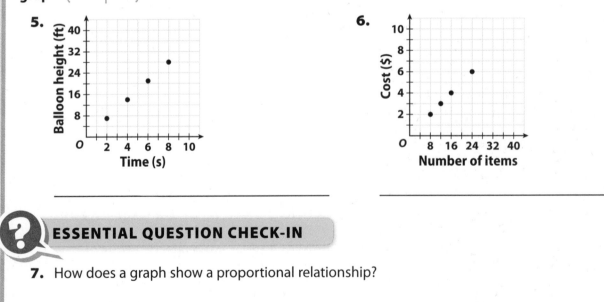

5.

_____

6.

_____

? ESSENTIAL QUESTION CHECK-IN

7. How does a graph show a proportional relationship?

_____

2.3 Independent Practice

TEKS 7.4.A, 7.4.C, 7.4.D

For Exercises 8–12, the graph shows the relationship between time and distance run by two horses.

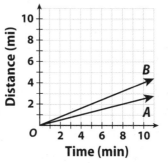

8. Explain the meaning of the point (0, 0).

_____

_____

9. How long does it take each horse to run a mile?

_____

_____

10. Multiple Representations Write an equation for the relationship between time and distance for each horse.

_____

11. Draw Conclusions At the given rates, how far would each horse run in 12 minutes?

_____

_____

12. Analyze Relationships Draw a line on the graph representing a horse than runs faster than horses A and B.

_____

_____

13. A bullet train can travel at 170 miles per hour. Will a graph representing distance in miles compared to time in hours show a proportional relationship? Explain.

_____

_____

_____

_____

14. Critical Thinking When would it be more useful to represent a proportional relationship with a graph rather than an equation?

_____

_____

_____

15. Multiple Representations Bargain DVDs cost $5 each at Mega Movie.

a. Graph the proportional relationship that gives the cost *y* in dollars of buying *x* bargain DVDs.

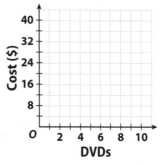

b. Give an ordered pair on the graph and explain its meaning in the real world context.

_____

_____

The graph shows the relationship between distance and time as Glenda swims.

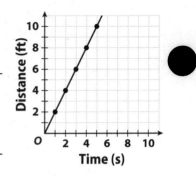

16. How far did Glenda swim in 4 seconds? _____

17. Communicate Mathematical Ideas Is this a proportional relationship? Explain your reasoning.

_____

18. Multiple Representations Write an equation that shows the relationship

between time and distance. _____

 **FOCUS ON HIGHER ORDER THINKING**

Work Area

19. Make a Conjecture If you know that a relationship is proportional and are given one ordered pair other than (0, 0), how can you find another pair?

_____

_____

_____

_____

The tables show the distance traveled by three cars.

Car 1	
Time (h)	Distance (mi)
0	0
2	120
3	180
5	300
6	360

Car 2	
Time (h)	Distance (mi)
0	0
5	200
10	400
15	600
20	800

Car 3	
Time (h)	Distance (mi)
0	0
1	65
2	85
3	105
4	125

20. Communicate Mathematical Ideas Which car is not traveling at a constant speed? Explain your reasoning.

_____

_____

21. Make a Conjecture Car 4 is traveling at twice the rate of speed of car 2. How will the table values for car 4 compare to the table values for car 2?

_____

_____

_____

© Houghton Mifflin Harcourt Publishing Company

Ready to Go On?

Personal Math Trainer

Online Assessment and Intervention

⊙ my.hrw.com

2.1 Unit Rates

Find each unit rate. Round to the nearest hundredth, if necessary.

1. $140 for 18 ft² _____

2. $2.99 for 14 lb _____

Circle the better deal in each pair. Then give the unit rate for the better deal.

3. $\dfrac{\$56}{25\,\text{gal}}$ or $\dfrac{\$32.05}{15\,\text{gal}}$ _____

4. $\dfrac{\$160}{5\,\text{g}}$ or $\dfrac{\$315}{9\,\text{g}}$ _____

2.2 Constant Rates of Change

5. The table shows the amount of money Tyler earns for mowing lawns. Is the relationship a proportional relationship? Why or why not?

Number of Lawns	1	2	3	4
Amount Earned ($)	15	30	48	64

_____

6. On a recent day, 8 euros were worth $9 and 24 euros were worth $27. Write an equation of the form $y = kx$ to show the relationship between the number of euros and the value in dollars.

_____ , where y is dollars and x is euros

2.3 Proportional Relationships and Graphs

7. The graph shows the number of servings in different amounts of frozen yogurt listed on a carton. Write an equation that gives the number of servings y in x pints.

_____

8. A refreshment stand makes 2 large servings of frozen yogurt from 3 pints. Add the line to the graph and write its equation.

_____

Frozen Yogurt

❓ ESSENTIAL QUESTION

9. How can you use rates to determine whether a situation is a proportional relationship?

_____

_____

MODULE 2 MIXED REVIEW

Texas Test Prep

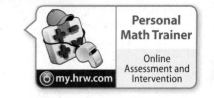

Personal
Math Trainer

Online
Assessment and
Intervention

my.hrw.com

Selected Response

1. Kori spent $46.20 on 12 gallons of gasoline. What was the price per gallon?

(A) $8.35

(C) $2.59

(B) $3.85

(D) $0.26

2. A rabbit can run 35 miles per hour. A fox can run 21 miles in half an hour. Which animal is faster, and by how much?

(A) The rabbit is faster by 7 miles per hour.

(B) The fox is faster by 7 miles per hour.

(C) The rabbit is faster by 14 miles per hour.

(D) The fox is faster by 14 miles per hour.

3. A pet survey found that the ratio of dogs to cats is $\frac{2}{5}$. Which proportion shows the number of dogs if the number of cats is 140?

(A) $\frac{2 \text{ dogs}}{5 \text{ cats}} = \frac{140 \text{ dogs}}{350 \text{ cats}}$

(B) $\frac{2 \text{ dogs}}{5 \text{ cats}} = \frac{140 \text{ cats}}{350 \text{ dogs}}$

(C) $\frac{2 \text{ dogs}}{5 \text{ cats}} = \frac{28 \text{ dogs}}{140 \text{ cats}}$

(D) $\frac{2 \text{ dogs}}{5 \text{ cats}} = \frac{56 \text{ dogs}}{140 \text{ cats}}$

4. What is the cost of 2 kilograms of flour, if 3 kilograms cost $4.86 and the unit price for each package of flour is the same?

(A) $0.81

(C) $3.24

(B) $2.86

(D) $9.72

5. One gallon of paint covers about 450 square feet. How many square feet will 1.5 gallons of paint cover?

(A) 300 ft²

(C) 675 ft²

(B) 451.5 ft²

(D) 900 ft²

6. The graph shows the relationship between the late fines the library charges and the number of days late.

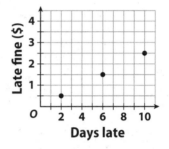

What is an equation for the relationship?

(A) $y = 0.25x$

(C) $y = 0.50x$

(B) $y = 0.40x$

(D) $y = 0.75x$

Gridded Response

7. School is 2 miles from home along a straight road. The table shows your distance from home as you walk home at a constant rate. Give the constant of proportionality as a decimal.

Time (min)	10	20	30
Distance from home (mi)	1.5	1	0.5

Proportions and Percent

ESSENTIAL QUESTION

How can you use proportions and percent to solve real-world problems?

40% OFF

Real-World Video

A store may have a sale with deep discounts on some items. They can still make a profit because they first markup the wholesale price by as much as 400%, then markdown the retail price.

my.hrw.com

GO DIGITAL

my.hrw.com

my.hrw.com

Go digital with your write-in student edition, accessible on any device.

Math On the Spot

Scan with your smart phone to jump directly to the online edition, video tutor, and more.

Animated Math

Interactively explore key concepts to see how math works.

Personal Math Trainer

Get immediate feedback and help as you work through practice sets.

Are YOU Ready?

Complete these exercises to review skills you will need for this chapter.

Percents and Decimals

EXAMPLE

$147\% = 100\% + 47\%$ Write the percent as the sum of 1 whole and a percent remainder.

$= \frac{100}{100} + \frac{47}{100}$ Write the percents as fractions.

$= 1 + 0.47$ Write the fractions as decimals.

$= 1.47$ Simplify.

Write each percent as a decimal.

1. 22% _____   **2.** 75% _____   **3.** 6% _____   **4.** 189% _____

Write each decimal as a percent.

5. 0.59 _____   **6.** 0.98 _____   **7.** 0.02 _____   **8.** 1.33 _____

Find the Percent of a Number

EXAMPLE

30% of 45 = ?

$30\% = 0.30$ Write the percent as a decimal.

$\begin{array}{r} 45 \\ \times 0.3 \\ \hline 13.5 \end{array}$ Multiply.

Find the percent of each number.

9. 50% of 64 _____   **10.** 7% of 30 _____   **11.** 15% of 160 _____

12. 32% of 62 _____   **13.** 120% of 4 _____   **14.** 6% of 1,000 _____

Reading Start-Up

Visualize Vocabulary

Use the ✔ words to complete the graphic. You can put more than one word in each bubble.

Measurement Systems

→ | feet, inches |

→ | grams, kilograms |

→ | ounce, pound |

→ | liter, milliliters |

Vocabulary

Review Words
- ✔ capacity (capacidad)
- ✔ customary system (sistema usual)
- ✔ length (longitud)
- ✔ mass (masa)
- ✔ metric system (sistema métrico)
-   proportion (proporción)
-   percent (porcentaje)
-   ratio (razón)
- ✔ weight (peso)

Preview Words
-   conversion factor (factor de conversión)
-   percent decrease (porcentaje de disminución)
-   percent increase (porcentaje de aumento)
-   principal (capital)
-   simple interest (interés simple)

Understand Vocabulary

Complete the sentences using the preview words.

1. A fixed percent of the principal is _____.

2. The original amount of money deposited or borrowed is the _____.

3. A _____ is a ratio of two equivalent measurements.

Active Reading

Tri-Fold Before beginning the module, create a tri-fold to help you learn the concepts and vocabulary in this module. Fold the paper into three sections. Label the columns "What I Know," "What I Need to Know," and "What I Learned." Complete the first two columns before you read. After studying the module, complete the third.

Unpacking the TEKS

Understanding the TEKS and the vocabulary terms in the TEKS will help you know exactly what you are expected to learn in this module.

TEKS 7.4.E

Convert between measurement systems, including the use of proportions and the use of unit rates.

Key Vocabulary

conversion factor *(factor de conversión)*
A fraction whose numerator and denominator represent the same quantity but use different units.

proportion *(proporción)*
An equation that states that two ratios are equivalent.

What It Means to You

You will convert between measurement systems by using a conversion factor.

UNPACKING EXAMPLE 7.4.E

A bookcase is 50 inches tall. Find the height of the bookcase in centimeters. The conversion factor is $\frac{2.54 \text{ cm}}{1 \text{ in.}}$.

$$50 \text{ in.} \cdot \frac{2.54 \text{ cm}}{1 \text{ in.}}$$

$$= \frac{50 \text{ in.}}{1} \cdot \frac{2.54 \text{ cm}}{1 \text{ in.}}$$

$$= 127 \text{ cm}$$

The bookcase is 127 cm tall.

TEKS 7.4.D

Solve problems involving ratios, rates, and percents, including multi-step problems involving percent increase and percent decrease, and financial literacy problems.

Key Vocabulary

percent increase *(porcentaje de aumento)*
A percent of change describing an increase in a quantity.

percent decrease *(porcentaje de disminución)*
A percent of change describing a decrease in a quantity.

What It Means to You

You will apply your understanding of proportional relationships to solve problems involving percents.

UNPACKING EXAMPLE 7.4.D

The original price of a bike helmet is $35. During a sale, the price is marked down by 20%. What is the discounted price of the helmet?

The percent decrease in the price is 20%, so the discounted price is 100% − 20% = 80% of the original price.

$$80\% \text{ of } \$35 = 0.80 \cdot 35$$
$$= 28$$

The discounted price of the helmet is $28.

Visit **my.hrw.com** to see all the **TEKS** unpacked.

my.hrw.com

LESSON 3.1 Converting Between Measurement Systems

TEKS
Proportionality—
7.4.E Convert between measurement systems, including the use of proportions and the use of unit rates. *Also 7.4.D*

? ESSENTIAL QUESTION

How can you use ratios and proportions to convert measurements?

EXPLORE ACTIVITY   TEKS 7.4.E

Converting Inches to Centimeters

Measurements are used when determining the length, weight, or capacity of an object. The two most common systems of measurement are the *customary system* and the *metric system*.

The table shows equivalencies between the customary and metric systems. You can use these equivalencies to convert a measurement in one system to a measurement in the other system.

Length	Weight/Mass	Capacity
1 inch = 2.54 centimeters	1 ounce ≈ 28.4 grams	1 fluid ounce ≈ 29.6 milliliters
1 foot ≈ 0.305 meter	1 pound ≈ 0.454 kilogram	1 quart ≈ 0.946 liter
1 yard ≈ 0.914 meter		1 gallon ≈ 3.79 liters
1 mile ≈ 1.61 kilometers		

Most conversions are approximate, as indicated by the symbol ≈.

The length of a sheet of paper is 11 inches. What is this length in centimeters?

A You can use a bar diagram to solve this problem. Each part represents 1 inch.

1 inch = _____ centimeter(s)

11 in.

1 in.										

☐ cm

B How does the diagram help you solve the problem?

_____

C 11 inches = _____ centimeters

Reflect

1. Communicate Mathematical Ideas Suppose you wanted to use a diagram to convert ounces to grams. Which unit would the parts in your diagram represent?

_____

_____

Math On the Spot

⏱ my.hrw.com

Using Conversion Factors

Another way to convert measurements is by using a ratio called a *conversion factor*. A **conversion factor** is a ratio of two equivalent measurements. Since the two measurements in a conversion factor are equivalent, a conversion factor is equal to 1.

EXAMPLE 1 🌎 Real World   🇺🇸 **TEKS** 7.4.E

While lifting weights, John adds 11.35 kilograms to his bar. About how many pounds does he add to his bar?

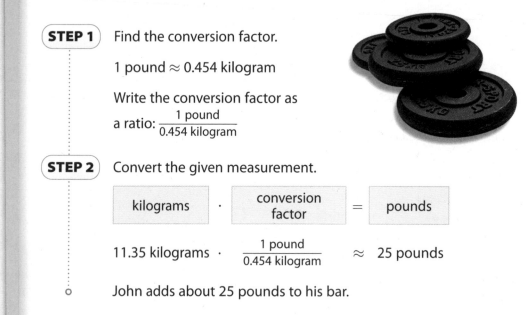

STEP 1 Find the conversion factor.

1 pound ≈ 0.454 kilogram

Write the conversion factor as a ratio: $\dfrac{1 \text{ pound}}{0.454 \text{ kilogram}}$

STEP 2 Convert the given measurement.

kilograms	·	conversion factor	=	pounds

11.35 kilograms · $\dfrac{1 \text{ pound}}{0.454 \text{ kilogram}}$ ≈   25 pounds

John adds about 25 pounds to his bar.

Personal Math Trainer

Online Assessment and Intervention

⏱ my.hrw.com

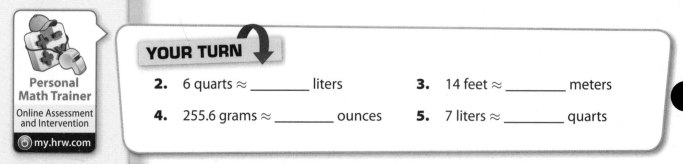

YOUR TURN

2. 6 quarts ≈ _____ liters

3. 14 feet ≈ _____ meters

4. 255.6 grams ≈ _____ ounces

5. 7 liters ≈ _____ quarts

Using Proportions to Convert Measurements

You can also convert a measurement from one unit to another by using a proportion. First write the conversion factor as a ratio, then multiply by a form of 1 to generate an equivalent ratio. Recall that two equal ratios form a proportion.

Proportions: $\dfrac{3 \text{ inches}}{2 \text{ feet}} = \dfrac{6 \text{ inches}}{4 \text{ feet}}$ $\qquad \dfrac{5}{10} = \dfrac{1}{2}$

EXAMPLE 2 Real World

TEKS 7.4.E

Bob's driveway is 45 feet long by 18 feet wide. He plans to pave the entire driveway. The asphalt paving costs $24 per square meter. What will be the total cost of the paving?

45 ft

18 ft

STEP 1 First find the area of the driveway in square meters.

Convert each measurement to meters.
Use 1 foot ≈ 0.305 meter.

$$\dfrac{1 \text{ foot}}{0.305 \text{ meter}} \overset{\times 45}{\underset{\times 45}{=}} \dfrac{45 \text{ feet}}{13.725 \text{ meters}}$$

Length ≈ 13.725 meters

$$\dfrac{1 \text{ foot}}{0.305 \text{ meter}} \overset{\times 18}{\underset{\times 18}{=}} \dfrac{18 \text{ feet}}{5.49 \text{ meters}}$$

Width ≈ 5.49 meters

The length and width are approximate because the conversion between feet and meters is approximate.

STEP 2 Find the area.

Area = length · width

= 13.725 · 5.49

= 75.35 square meters

STEP 3 Now find the total cost of the paving.

square meters · cost per square meter = total cost
75.35 · $24 = $1,808.40

Math Talk
Mathematical Processes

How much does the paving cost per square foot? Explain.

Reflect

6. **Error Analysis** Yolanda found the area of Bob's driveway in square meters as shown. Explain why Yolanda's answer is incorrect.

Area = 45 · 18 = 810 square feet

810 square feet · $\dfrac{0.305 \text{ meter}}{1 \text{ foot}}$ ≈ 247.1 square meters

_____

_____

YOUR TURN

7. A flower bed is 2 meters wide and 3 meters long. What is the area of the flower bed in square feet? Round intermediate steps and your answer to the nearest hundredth.

_____ square feet

Guided Practice

Complete each diagram to solve the problem. (Explore Activity)

1. Kate ran 5 miles. How far did she run in kilometers?

   5 miles = _____ kilometers

2. Alex filled a 5-gallon jug with water. How many liters of water are in the container?

   5 gallons ≈ _____ liters

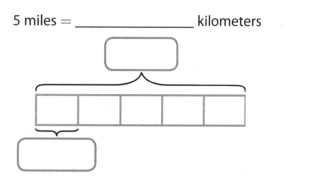

Use a conversion factor to convert each measurement. (Example 1 and 2)

3. A ruler is 12 inches long. What is the length of this ruler in centimeters?

   _____ centimeters

4. A kitten weighs 4 pounds. What is the approximate mass of the kitten?

   _____ kilograms

Use a proportion to convert each measurement. (Example 2)

5. 20 yards ≈ _____ meters

6. 12 ounces ≈ _____ grams

7. 5 quarts ≈ _____ liters

8. 400 meters ≈ _____ yards

9. 10 liters ≈ _____ gallons

10. 137.25 meters ≈ _____ feet

11. 165 centimeters ≈ _____ inches

12. 10,000 kilometers ≈ _____ miles

? ESSENTIAL QUESTION CHECK-IN

13. Write and solve a proportion that can be used to convert 60 inches to centimeters.

_____

3.1 Independent Practice

TEKS 7.4.E, 7.4.D

Tell which measure is greater.

14. Six feet or two meters _____

15. One inch or one centimeter _____

16. One yard or one meter _____

17. One mile or one kilometer _____

18. One ounce or one gram _____

19. One quart or one liter _____

20. 10 pounds or 10 kilograms _____

21. Four liters or one gallon _____

22. Two miles or three kilometers _____

23. What is the limit in kilograms?

weight limit for checked baggage: 50 pounds

_____

24. What is the limit in miles per hour?

BOGGY SWAMP CREEK

55 km/h

_____

25. Which container holds more, a half-gallon milk jug or a 2-liter juice bottle?

_____

26. The label on a can of lemonade gives the volume as 12 fl oz, or 355 mL. Verify that these two measurements are nearly equivalent.

_____

27. The mass of a textbook is about 1.25 kilograms. About how many pounds is this?

_____

28. Critique Reasoning Michael estimated his mass as 8 kilograms. Is his estimate reasonable? Justify your answer.

_____

29. Your mother bought a three-liter bottle of water. When she got home, she discovered a small leak in the bottom and asked you to find a container to transfer the water into. All you could find were two half-gallon jugs.

a. Will your containers hold all of the water?

_____

_____

b. What If? Suppose an entire liter of water leaked out in the car. In that case, would you be able to fit all of the remaining water into one of the half-gallon jugs? Explain.

_____

_____

_____

30. The track team ran a mile and a quarter during their practice.

How many kilometers did the team run? _____

31. A countertop is 16 feet long and 3 feet wide.

a. What is the area of the countertop in square meters? _____
square meters

b. Tile costs $28 per square meter. How much will it cost to cover the

countertop with new tile? $ _____

32. At a school picnic, your teacher asks you to mark a field every ten yards so students can play football. The teacher accidentally gave you a meter stick instead of a yard stick. How far apart in meters should you mark the lines if you still want them to be in the right places?

_____

33. You weigh a gallon of 2% milk in science class and learn that it is approximately 8.4 pounds. You pass the milk to the next group, and then realize that your teacher wanted an answer in kilograms, not pounds. Explain how you can adjust your answer without weighing the milk again. Then give the weight in kilograms.

_____

H.O.T. FOCUS ON HIGHER ORDER THINKING

34. Analyze Relationships Annalisa, Keiko, and Stefan want to compare their heights. Annalisa is 64 inches tall. Stefan tells her, "I'm about 7.5 centimeters taller than you." Keiko knows she is 1.5 inches shorter than Stefan. Give the heights of all three people in both inches and centimeters to the nearest half unit.

_____

_____

_____

_____

35. Communicate Mathematical Ideas Mikhael wanted to rewrite the conversion factor "1 yard ≈ 0.914 meter" to create a conversion factor to convert meters to yards. He wrote "1 meter ≈ _____. " Tell how Mikhael should finish his conversion, and explain how you know.

_____

_____

_____

Percent Increase and Decrease

TEKS
Proportionality—
7.4.D Solve problems involving ratios, rates, and percents, including multi-step problems involving percent increase and percent decrease, and financial literacy problems.

? ESSENTIAL QUESTION

How do you use percents to describe change?

Finding Percent Increase

Percents can be used to describe how an amount changes.

$$\text{Percent Change} = \frac{\text{Amount of Change}}{\text{Original Amount}}$$

The change may be an increase or a decrease. **Percent increase** describes how much a quantity increases in comparison to the original amount.

Math On the Spot
my.hrw.com

EXAMPLE 1 Real World   TEKS 7.4.D

Amber got a raise, and her hourly wage increased from $8 to $9.50. What is the percent increase?

STEP 1 Find the amount of change.

Amount of Change = Greater Value − Lesser Value

= 9.50 − 8.00   Substitute values.

= 1.50   Subtract.

STEP 2 Find the percent increase. Round to the nearest percent.

$$\text{Percent Change} = \frac{\text{Amount of Change}}{\text{Original Amount}}$$

$$= \frac{1.50}{8.00}$$ Substitute values.

$$= 0.1875$$ Divide.

$$\approx 19\%$$ Write as a percent and round.

Reflect

1. What does a 100% increase mean?

_____

_____

YOUR TURN

2. The price of a pair of shoes increases from $52 to $64. What is the

percent increase to the nearest percent? _____

Personal Math Trainer
Online Assessment and Intervention
my.hrw.com

Finding Percent Decrease

When the change in the amount decreases, you can use a similar approach to find percent decrease. **Percent decrease** describes how much a quantity decreases in comparison to the original amount.

My Notes

EXAMPLE 2 Real World

TEKS 7.4.D

David moved from a house that is 89 miles away from his workplace to a house that is 51 miles away from his workplace. What is the percent decrease in the distance from his home to his workplace?

STEP 1 Find the amount of change.

Amount of Change = Greater Value − Lesser Value

$= 89 - 51$ Substitute values.

$= 38$ Subtract.

STEP 2 Find the percent decrease. Round to the nearest percent.

Percent Change $= \dfrac{\text{Amount of Change}}{\text{Original Amount}}$

$= \dfrac{38}{89}$ Substitute values.

≈ 0.427 Divide.

$\approx 43\%$ Write as a percent and round.

Reflect

3. **Critique Reasoning** David considered moving even closer to his workplace. He claims that if he had done so, the percent of decrease would have been more than 100%. Is David correct? Explain your reasoning.

_____

_____

_____

YOUR TURN

4. The number of students in a chess club decreased from 18 to 12. What is the percent decrease? Round to the nearest percent. _____

5. Officer Brimberry wrote 16 tickets for traffic violations last week, but only 10 tickets this week. What is the percent decrease? _____

Using Percent of Change

Given an original amount and a percent increase or decrease, you can use the percent of change to find the new amount.

Math On the Spot
my.hrw.com

EXAMPLE 3 Real World

TEKS 7.4.D

The grizzly bear population in Yellowstone National Park in 1970 was about 270. Over the next 35 years, it increased by about 115%. What was the population in 2005?

STEP 1 Find the amount of change.

$1.15 \times 270 = 310.5$ Find 115% of 270. Write 115% as a decimal.

≈ 311 Round to the nearest whole number.

STEP 2 Find the new amount.

New Amount = Original Amount + Amount of Change

$= 270 + 311$ Substitute values.

$= 581$ Add.

> Add the amount of change because the population increased.

The population in 2005 was about 581 grizzly bears.

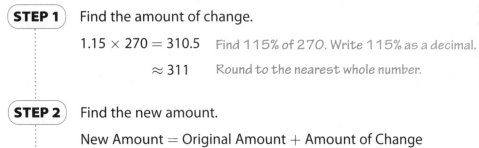

Reflect

6. Why will the percent of change always be represented by a positive number?

_____

_____

_____

7. **Draw Conclusions** If an amount of $100 in a savings account increases by 10%, then increases by 10% again, is that the same as increasing by 20%? Explain.

_____

_____

_____

YOUR TURN

A TV has an original price of $499. Find the new price after the given percent of change.

8. 10% increase _____

9. 30% decrease _____

Personal Math Trainer

Online Assessment and Intervention

my.hrw.com

Guided Practice

Find each percent increase. Round to the nearest percent. (Example 1)

1. From $5 to $8 _____

2. From 20 students to 30 students _____

3. From 86 books to 150 books _____

4. From $3.49 to $3.89 _____

5. From 13 friends to 14 friends _____

6. From 5 miles to 16 miles _____

7. Nathan usually drinks 36 ounces of water per day. He read that he should drink 64 ounces of water per day. If he starts drinking 64 ounces, what is the percent increase? Round to the nearest percent. (Example 1) _____

Find each percent decrease. Round to the nearest percent. (Example 2)

8. From $80 to $64 _____

9. From 95°F to 68°F _____

10. From 90 points to 45 points _____

11. From 145 pounds to 132 pounds _____

12. From 64 photos to 21 photos _____

13. From 16 bagels to 0 bagels _____

14. Over the summer, Jackie played video games 3 hours per day. When school began in the fall, she was only allowed to play video games for half an hour per day. What is the percent decrease? Round to the nearest percent. (Example 2) _____

Find the new amount given the original amount and the percent of change. (Example 3)

15. $9; 10% increase _____

16. 48 cookies; 25% decrease _____

17. 340 pages; 20% decrease _____

18. 28 members; 50% increase _____

19. $29,000; 4% decrease _____

20. 810 songs; 130% increase _____

21. Adam currently runs about 20 miles per week, and he wants to increase his weekly mileage by 30%. How many miles will Adam run per week? (Example 3) _____

? **ESSENTIAL QUESTION CHECK-IN**

22. What process do you use to find the percent change of a quantity?

_____

_____

3.2 Independent Practice

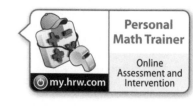

Personal Math Trainer

Online Assessment and Intervention

my.hrw.com

23. Complete the table.

Item	Original Price	New Price	Percent Change	Increase or Decrease
Bike	$110	$96		
Scooter	$45	$56		
Tennis Racket	$79		5%	Increase
Skis	$580		25%	Decrease

24. Multiple Representations The bar graph shows the number of hurricanes in the Atlantic Basin from 2006–2011.

a. Find the amount of change and the percent of decrease in the number of hurricanes from 2008 to 2009 and from 2010 to 2011. Compare the amounts of change and percents of decrease.

_____

_____

_____

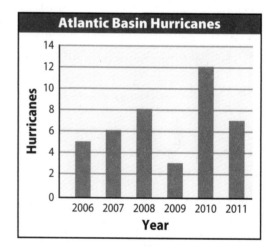

b. Between which two years was the percent of change the greatest? What was the percent of change during that period?

_____

25. Represent Real-World Problems Cheese sticks that were previously priced at "5 for $1" are now "4 for $1".

a. Find the percent decrease in the number of cheese sticks you can buy for $1.

_____

b. Find the percent increase in the price per cheese stick.

_____

_____

26. Percent error calculations are used to determine how close to the true values, or how accurate, experimental values really are. The formula is similar to finding percent of change.

$$\text{Percent Error} = \frac{|\text{Experimental Value} - \text{Actual Value}|}{\text{Actual Value}} \times 100\%$$

In chemistry class, Charlie records the volume of a liquid as 13.3 milliliters. The actual volume is 13.6 milliliters. What is his percent error? Round to

the nearest percent. _____

FOCUS ON HIGHER ORDER THINKING

27. Look for a Pattern Leroi and Sylvia both put $100 in a savings account. Leroi decides he will put in an additional $10 each week. Sylvia decides to put in an additional 10% of the amount in the account each week.

a. Who has more money after the first additional deposit? Explain.

_____

_____

b. Who has more money after the second additional deposit? Explain.

_____

_____

c. How do you think the amounts in the two accounts will compare after a month? A year?

_____

_____

_____

28. Critical Thinking Suppose an amount increases by 100%, then decreases by 100%. Find the final amount. Would the situation change if the original increase was 150%? Explain your reasoning.

_____

_____

29. Look for a Pattern Ariel deposited $100 into a bank account. Each Friday she will withdraw 10% of the money in the account to spend. Ariel thinks her account will be empty after 10 withdrawals. Do you agree? Explain.

_____

_____

_____

TEKS
Proportionality—
7.4.D Solve problems involving ratios, rates, and percents, including multi-step problems involving percent increase and percent decrease, and financial literacy problems.

? ESSENTIAL QUESTION

How can you rewrite expressions to help you solve markup and markdown problems?

Calculating Markups

A *markup* is one kind of percent increase. You can use a bar model to represent the *retail price* of an item, that is, the total price including the markup.

EXAMPLE 1 Real World   TEKS 7.4.D

Math On the Spot
my.hrw.com

To make a profit, stores mark up the prices on the items they sell. A sports store buys skateboards from a supplier for s dollars. What is the retail price for skateboards that the manager buys for $35 and $56 after a 42% markup?

STEP 1   Use a bar model.

Draw a bar for the cost of the skateboard s.

Then draw a bar that shows the markup: 42% of s, or $0.42s$.

$$s$$

$0.42s \longrightarrow$

$$s + 0.42s$$

These bars together represent the cost plus the markup, $s + 0.42s$.

STEP 2   Retail price = Original cost + Markup

$$= \quad s \quad + \quad 0.42s$$
$$= \quad 1s \quad + \quad 0.42s$$
$$= \quad 1.42s$$

STEP 3   Use the expression to find the retail price of each skateboard.

$s = \$35 \longrightarrow$ Retail price $= 1.42(\$35) = \$49.70$

$s = \$56 \longrightarrow$ Retail price $= 1.42(\$56) = \$79.52$

Math Talk
Mathematical Processes

Why write the retail price as the sum of two terms? as one term?

Reflect

1. **What If?** The markup is changed to 34%; how does the expression for the retail price change?

YOUR TURN

2. Rick buys remote control cars to resell. He applies a markup of 10%.

   a. Write two expressions that represent the retail price of the cars.

   _____

   b. If Rick buys a remote control car for $28.00, what is his selling price?

   _____

3. An exclusive clothing boutique triples the price of the items it purchases for resale.

   a. What is the boutique's markup percent? _____

   b. Write two expressions that represent the retail price of the clothes.

   _____

Calculating Markdowns

An example of a percent decrease is a *discount*, or *markdown*. A price after a markdown may be called a sale price. You can also use a bar model to represent the price of an item including the markdown.

EXAMPLE 2   Real World

 TEKS 7.4.D

A discount store marks down all of its holiday merchandise by 20% off the regular selling price. Find the discounted price of decorations that regularly sell for $16 and $23.

STEP 1   Use a bar model.

Draw a bar for the regular price p.

Then draw a bar that shows the discount: 20% of p, or $0.2p$.

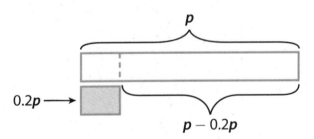

The difference between these two bars represents the price minus the discount, $p - 0.2p$.

STEP 2 Sale price = Original price − Markdown

$$= \quad p \quad - \quad 0.2p$$

$$= \quad 1p \quad - \quad 0.2p$$

$$= \quad 0.8p$$

STEP 3 Use the expression to find the sale price of each decoration.

$p = \$16$ ⟶ Retail price = 0.8($16) = $12.80

$p = \$23$ ⟶ Retail price = 0.8($23) = $18.40

Reflect

4. **Conjecture** Compare the single term expression for retail price after a markup from Example 1 and the single term expression for sale price after a markdown from Example 2. What do you notice about the coefficients in the two expressions?

_____

_____

Math Talk
Mathematical Processes

Is a 20% markup equal to a 20% markdown? Explain.

YOUR TURN

5. A bicycle shop marks down each bicycle's selling price *b* by 24% for a holiday sale.

   a. Draw a bar model to represent the problem.

   b. What is a single term expression for the sale price? _____

6. Jane sells pillows. For a sale, she marks them down 5%.

   a. Write two expressions that represent the sale price of the pillows.

   _____

   b. If the original price of a pillow is $15.00, what is the sale price?

   _____

Personal Math Trainer

Online Assessment and Intervention

my.hrw.com

© Houghton Mifflin Harcourt Publishing Company

1. Dana buys dress shirts from a clothing manufacturer for *s* dollars each, and then sells the dress shirts in her retail clothing store at a 35% markup. (Example 1)

   a. Write the markup as a decimal. _____

   b. Write an expression for the retail price of the dress shirt. _____

   c. What is the retail price of a dress shirt that Dana purchased for $32.00? _____

   d. How much was added to the original price of the dress shirt? _____

List the markup and retail price of each item. Round to two decimal places when necessary. (Example 1)

	Item	Price	Markup %	Markup	Retail Price
2.	Hat	$18	15%		
3.	Book	$22.50	42%		
4.	Shirt	$33.75	75%		
5.	Shoes	$74.99	33%		
6.	Clock	$48.60	100%		
7.	Painting	$185.00	125%		

Find the sale price of each item. Round to two decimal places when necessary. (Example 2)

8. Original price: $45.00; Markdown: 22%

   _____

9. Original price: $89.00; Markdown: 33%

   _____

10. Original price: $23.99; Markdown: 44%

    _____

11. Original price: $279.99, Markdown: 75%

    _____

? ESSENTIAL QUESTION CHECK-IN

12. How can you determine the sale price if you are given the regular price and the percent of markdown?

    _____

    _____

3.3 Independent Practice

TEKS 7.4.D

Personal Math Trainer

Online Assessment and Intervention

my.hrw.com

13. A bookstore manager marks down the price of older hardcover books, which originally sell for *b* dollars, by 46%.

   a. Write the markdown as a decimal. _____

   b. Write an expression for the sale price of the hardcover book.

   _____

   c. What is the sale price of a hardcover book for which the original retail

   price was $29.00? _____

   d. If you buy the book in part **c**, how much do you save by paying the

   sale price? _____

14. Raquela's coworker made price tags for several items that are to be marked down by 35%. Match each Regular Price to the correct Sale Price, if possible. Not all sales tags match an item.

| Regular Price $3.29 | Regular Price $4.19 | Regular Price $2.79 | Regular Price $3.09 | Regular Price $3.77 |

| Sale Price $2.01 | Sale Price $2.45 | Sale Price $1.15 | Sale Price $2.72 | Sale Price $2.24 |

15. **Communicate Mathematical Ideas** For each situation, give an example that includes the original price and final price after markup or markdown.

   a. A markdown that is greater than 99% but less than 100%

   _____

   b. A markdown that is less than 1%

   _____

   c. A markup that is more than 200%

   _____

16. Represent Real-World Problems Harold works at a men's clothing store, which marks up its retail clothing by 27%. The store purchases pants for $74.00, suit jackets for $325.00, and dress shirts for $48.00. How much will Harold charge a customer for two pairs of pants, three dress shirts, and a suit jacket?

_____

17. Analyze Relationships Your family needs a set of 4 tires. Which of the following deals would you prefer? Explain.

(I) Buy 3, get one free   **(II)** 20% off   **(III)** $\frac{1}{4}$ off

_____

_____

18. Critique Reasoning Margo purchases bulk teas from a warehouse and marks up those prices by 20% for retail sale. When teas go unsold for more than two months, Margo marks down the retail price by 20%. She says that she is _breaking even_, that is, she is getting the same price for the tea that she paid for it. Is she correct? Explain.

_____

_____

_____

19. Problem Solving Grady marks down some $2.49 pens to $1.99 for a week and then marks them back up to $2.49. Find the percent of increase and the percent of decrease to the nearest tenth. Are the percents of change the same for both price changes? If not, which is a greater change?

_____

_____

20. Persevere in Problem Solving At Danielle's clothing boutique, if an item does not sell for eight weeks, she marks it down by 15%. If it remains unsold after that, she marks it down an additional 5% each week until she can no longer make a profit. Then she donates it to charity.

Rafael wants to buy a coat originally priced $150, but he can't afford more than $110. If Danielle paid $100 for the coat, during which week(s) could Rafael buy the coat within his budget? Justify your answer.

_____

_____

_____

© Houghton Mifflin Harcourt Publishing Company

Work Area

Applications of Percent

TEKS
Proportionality—
7.4.D Solve problems involving ratios, rates, and percents, including multi-step problems involving percent increase and percent decrease, and financial literacy problems. *Also 7.13.E*

? ESSENTIAL QUESTION

How do you use percents to solve problems?

Finding Total Cost

Sales tax, which is the tax on the sale of an item or service, is a percent of the purchase price that is collected by the seller.

Math On the Spot
my.hrw.com

EXAMPLE 1 Real World

TEKS 7.4.D

Marcus buys a varsity jacket from a clothing store in Arlington. The price of the jacket is $80 and the sales tax is 8%. What is the total cost of the jacket?

STEP 1 Use a bar model to find the amount of the tax.

Draw a bar for the price of the jacket, $80. Divide it into 10 equal parts. Each part represents 10% of $80, or $8.

Then draw a bar that shows the sales tax: 8% of $80.

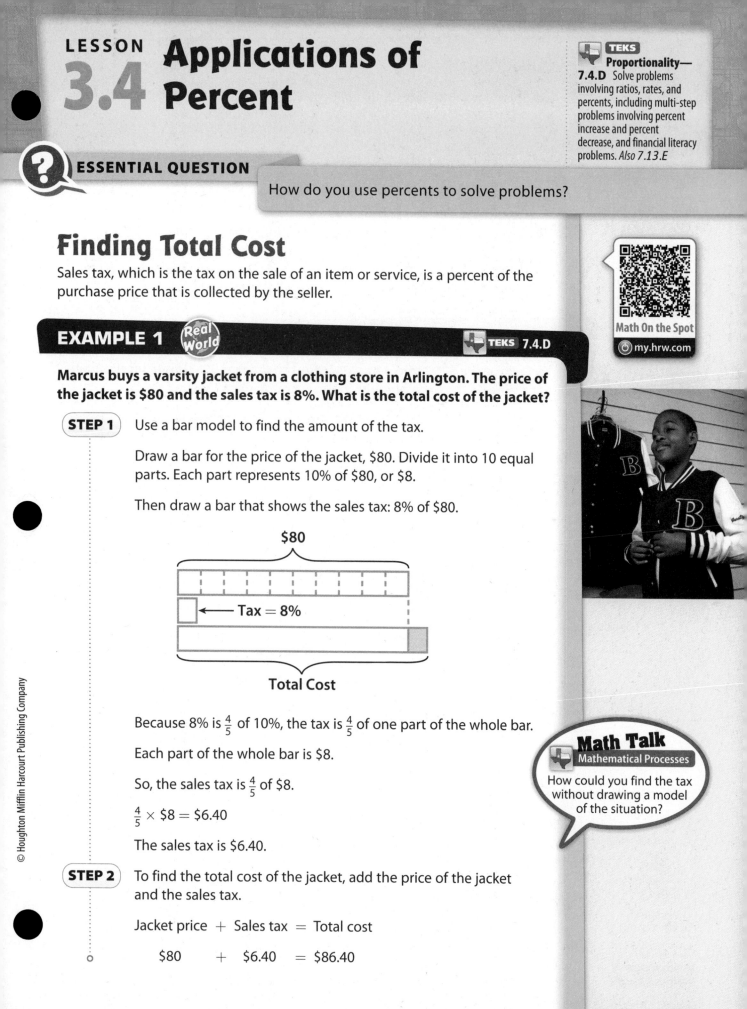

$80

Tax = 8%

Total Cost

Because 8% is $\frac{4}{5}$ of 10%, the tax is $\frac{4}{5}$ of one part of the whole bar.

Each part of the whole bar is $8.

So, the sales tax is $\frac{4}{5}$ of $8.

$\frac{4}{5} \times \$8 = \$6.40$

The sales tax is $6.40.

Math Talk
Mathematical Processes

How could you find the tax without drawing a model of the situation?

STEP 2 To find the total cost of the jacket, add the price of the jacket and the sales tax.

Jacket price + Sales tax = Total cost

$80 + $6.40 = $86.40

YOUR TURN

1. Sharon wants to buy a shirt that costs $20. The sales tax is 5%. How much is the sales tax? What is her total cost for the shirt? _____

Finding Simple Interest

When you deposit money in a savings account, your money usually earns interest. When you borrow money, you must pay back the original amount of the loan plus interest. **Simple interest** is a fixed percent of the *principal*. The **principal** is the original amount of money deposited or borrowed.

EXAMPLE 2 🌎 Real World   TEKS 7.4.D

Terry deposits $200 into a bank account that earns 3% simple interest per year. What is the total amount in the account after 2 years?

My Notes

STEP 1   Find the amount of interest earned in one year. Then calculate the amount of interest for 2 years.

Write 3% as a decimal: *0.03*

Interest Rate × Initial Deposit = Interest for 1 year

   0.03   × $200   = $6

Interest for 1 year × 2 years = Interest for 2 years

      $6   ×   2   = $12

STEP 2   Add the interest for 2 years to the initial deposit to find the total amount in his account after 2 years.

Initial deposit + Interest for 2 years = Total

   $200   + $12   = $212

The total amount in the account after 2 years is $212.

Reflect

2. Write an expression you can use to find the total amount in Terry's account.

_____

YOUR TURN

3. Ariane borrows $400 on a 4-year loan. She is charged 5% simple interest per year. How much interest is she charged for 4 years? What is the total amount she has to pay back? _____

© Houghton Mifflin Harcourt Publishing Company

Using Multiple Percents

Some situations require applying more than one percent to a problem. For example, when you dine at a restaurant, you might pay a tax on the meal, and pay a tip to the wait staff. The tip is usually paid on the amount before tax. When you pay tax on a sale item, you pay tax only on the discounted price.

EXAMPLE 3   Problem Solving   TEKS 7.4.D

The Maxwell family goes out for dinner, and the price of the meal is $60. The sales tax on the meal is 7%, and they also want to leave a 15% tip. What is the total cost of the meal?

Analyze Information

Identify the important information.
- The bill for the meal is $60.
- The sales tax is 7%, or 0.07.
- The tip rate is 15%, or 0.15.

The total cost will be the sum of the bill for the meal, the sales tax, and the tip.

Formulate a Plan

Calculate the sales tax separately, then calculate the tip, and then add the sales tax and the tip to the bill for the meal to find the total.

Solve

Sales tax: $0.07 \times \$60 = \$4.20$ Tip: $0.15 \times \$60 = \$9.00$

Meal + Sales tax + Tip = Total cost

$60 + $4.20 + $9 = $73.20

The total cost is $73.20.

Justify and Evaluate

Estimate the sales tax and tip. Sales tax is about 10% plus 15% for tip gives 25%. Find 25% of the bill: $0.25 \times \$60 = \$15$. Add this to the bill: $60 + $15 = $75. The total cost should be about $75.

YOUR TURN

4. Samuel orders four DVDs from an online music store. Each DVD costs $9.99. He has a 20% discount code, and sales tax is 6.75%. What is the total cost of his order?

_____

1. 5% of $30 = _____

2. 15% of $70 = _____

3. 0.4% of $100 = _____

4. 150% of $22 = _____

5. 1% of $80 = _____

6. 200% of $5 = _____

7. Brandon buys a radio for $43.99 in a state where the sales tax is 7%. (Example 1)

    a. How much does he pay in taxes? _____

    b. What is the total Brandon pays for the radio? _____

8. Luisa's restaurant bill comes to $75.50, and she leaves a 15% tip. What is Luisa's total restaurant bill? (Example 1)

_____

9. Joe borrowed $2,000 from the bank at a rate of 7% simple interest per year. How much interest did he pay in 5 years? (Example 2)

_____

10. You have $550 in a savings account that earns 3% simple interest each year. How much will be in your account in 10 years? (Example 2)

_____

11. Martin finds a shirt on sale for 10% off at a department store. The original price was $20. Martin must also pay 8.5% sales tax. (Example 3)

    a. How much is the shirt before taxes are applied? _____

    b. How much is the shirt after taxes are applied? _____

12. Teresa's restaurant bill comes to $29.99 before tax. If the sales tax is 6.25% and she tips the waiter 20%, what is the total cost of the meal? (Example 3)

_____

? ESSENTIAL QUESTION CHECK-IN

13. How can you determine the total cost of an item including tax if you know the price of the item and the tax rate?

_____

_____

3.4 Independent Practice

TEKS 7.4.D, 7.13.E

Personal Math Trainer

Online Assessment and Intervention

my.hrw.com

14. Emily's meal costs $32.75 and Darren's meal costs $39.88. Emily treats Darren by paying for both meals, and leaves a 14% tip. Find the total cost.

_____

15. The Jayden family eats at a restaurant that is having a 15% discount promotion. Their meal costs $78.65, and they leave a 20% tip. If the tip applies to the cost of the meal before the discount, what is the total cost of the meal?

_____

16. A jeweler buys a ring from a jewelry maker for $125. He marks up the price by 135% for sale in his store. What is the selling price of the ring with 7.5% sales tax?

_____

17. Luis wants to buy a skateboard that usually sells for $79.99. All merchandise is discounted by 12%. What is the total cost of the skateboard if Luis has to pay a state sales tax of 6.75%?

_____

18. Kedar earns a monthly salary of $2,200 plus a 3.75% *commission* on the amount of his sales at a men's clothing store. What would he earn this month if he sold $4,500 in clothing? Round to the nearest cent.

_____

19. Danielle earns a 7.25% commission on everything she sells at the electronics store where she works. She also earns a base salary of $750 per week. How much did she earn last week if she sold $4,500 in electronics merchandise? Round to the nearest cent.

_____

20. Francois earns a weekly salary of $475 plus a 5.5% commission on sales at a gift shop. How much would he earn in a week if he sold $700 in goods? Round to the nearest cent.

_____

21. Sandra is 4 feet tall. Pablo is 10% taller than Sandra, and Michaela is 8% taller than Pablo.

a. Explain how to find Michaela's height with the given information.

_____

_____

_____

_____

_____

_____

_____

b. What is Michaela's approximate height in feet and inches?

_____

22. Eugene wants to buy jeans at a store that is offering a $10 discount on every item. The tag on the jeans is marked 50% off. The original price is $49.98.

a. Find the final cost if the 50% discount is applied before the $10 discount.

_____

b. Find the final cost if the $10 discount is applied before the 50% discount.

_____

23. Multistep Eric downloads the coupon shown and goes shopping at Gadgets Galore, where he buys a digital camera for $95 and an extra battery for $15.99.

Gadgets Galore

It's Our Birthday **10%** Discount on any 1 item

a. What is the total cost if the coupon is applied to the digital camera?

_____

b. What is the total cost if the coupon is applied to the extra battery?

_____

c. To which item should Eric apply the discount? Explain.

_____

d. Eric has to pay 8% sales tax after the coupon is applied. How much is his total bill if he applies the coupon to the digital camera?

_____

24. Two stores are having sales on the same shirts. The sale at Store 1 is "2 shirts for $22" and the sale at Store 2 is "Each $12.99 shirt is 10% off".

a. Explain how much will you save by buying at Store 1.

_____

_____

b. If Store 3 has shirts originally priced at $20.98 on sale for 55% off, does it have a better deal than the other stores? Justify your answer.

_____

 FOCUS ON HIGHER ORDER THINKING

Work Area

25. Analyze Relationships Marcus can choose between a monthly salary of $1,500 plus 5.5% of sales or $2,400 plus 3% of sales. He expects sales between $5,000 and $10,000 a month. Which salary option should he choose? Explain.

_____

_____

_____

26. Multistep In chemistry class, Bob recorded the volume of a liquid as 13.2 mL. The actual volume was 13.7 mL. Use the formula to find percent error of Bob's measurement to the nearest tenth of a percent.

$$\text{Percent Error} = \frac{|\text{Experimental Value} - \text{Actual Value}|}{\text{Actual Value}} \times 100\%$$

_____

Ready to Go On?

Personal Math Trainer

Online Assessment and Intervention

⏱ my.hrw.com

3.1 Converting Between Measurement Systems

Convert each measurement.

1. 20 gallons ≈ _____ liters

2. 36 ounces ≈ _____ grams

3. 43 yards ≈ _____ meters

4. 5 miles ≈ _____ kilometers

3.2 Percent Increase and Decrease

Find the percent change from the first value to the second.

5. 36; 63 _____

6. 50; 35 _____

7. 40; 72 _____

8. 92; 69 _____

3.3 Markup and Markdown

Use the original price and the markdown or markup to find the retail price.

9. Original price: $60; Markup: 15%; Retail price: _____

10. Original price: $32; Markup: 12.5%; Retail price: _____

11. Original price: $50; Markdown: 22%; Retail price: _____

12. Original price: $125; Markdown: 30%; Retail price: _____

3.4 Applications of Percent

13. Mae Ling earns a weekly salary of $325 plus a 6.5% commission on sales at a gift shop. How much would she make in a work week if she sold $4,800 worth

of merchandise? _____

14. Ramon earns $1,735 each month and pays $53.10 on electricity. To the nearest tenth of a percent, what percent of Ramon's earnings are spent on electricity

each month? _____

? ESSENTIAL QUESTION

15. Give three examples of how percents are used in the real-world. Tell whether each situation represents a percent increase or a percent decrease.

_____

_____

Selected Response

1. Zalmon walks $\frac{3}{4}$ of a mile in $\frac{3}{10}$ of an hour. What is his speed in miles per hour?

Ⓐ 0.225 miles per hour

Ⓑ 2.3 miles per hour

Ⓒ 2.5 miles per hour

Ⓓ 2.6 miles per hour

2. Shaylyn measured her house as 5 meters tall. Which of these is an equivalent measurement?

Ⓐ 0.3 miles   Ⓒ 16.4 feet

Ⓑ 7.3 yards   Ⓓ 27.2 inches

3. Find the percent change from 70 to 56.

Ⓐ 20% decrease   Ⓒ 25% decrease

Ⓑ 20% increase   Ⓓ 25% increase

4. Delia uses 3.5 skeins of yarn to knit one scarf. How many scarves can she complete if she has 19 skeins of yarn?

Ⓐ 4 scarves   Ⓒ 6 scarves

Ⓑ 5 scarves   Ⓓ 7 scarves

5. The rainfall total two years ago was 10.2 inches. Last year's total was 20% greater. What was last year's rainfall total?

Ⓐ 8.16 inches   Ⓒ 12.24 inches

Ⓑ 11.22 inches   Ⓓ 20.4 inches

6. A pair of basketball shoes was originally priced at $80, but was marked up 37.5%. What was the retail price of the shoes?

Ⓐ $50   Ⓒ $110

Ⓑ $83   Ⓓ $130

7. The day after Halloween, candy was marked down 40%. Which expression represents the new retail price?

Ⓐ 0.4p   Ⓒ 1.4p

Ⓑ 0.6p   Ⓓ 1.6p

8. The sales tax rate in Jan's town is 7.5%. If she buys 3 lamps for $23.59 each and a sofa for $769.99, how much sales tax does she owe?

Ⓐ $58.85   Ⓒ $67.26

Ⓑ $63.06   Ⓓ $71.46

9. A bank offers an annual simple interest rate of 8% on home improvement loans. How much would Tobias owe if he borrowed $17,000 over a period of 2 years?

Ⓐ $1,360   Ⓒ $18,360

Ⓑ $2,720   Ⓓ $19,720

Gridded Response

10. The granola Summer buys used to cost $6.00 per pound, but it has been marked up 15%. How much in dollars and cents will Summer pay for 2.6 pounds of granola at the new price?

$\oplus$	⓪	⓪	⓪	⓪	•	⓪	⓪
$\ominus$	①	①	①	①		①	①
	②	②	②	②		②	②
	③	③	③	③		③	③
	④	④	④	④		④	④
	⑤	⑤	⑤	⑤		⑤	⑤
	⑥	⑥	⑥	⑥		⑥	⑥
	⑦	⑦	⑦	⑦		⑦	⑦
	⑧	⑧	⑧	⑧		⑧	⑧
	⑨	⑨	⑨	⑨		⑨	⑨

Proportionality in Geometry

ESSENTIAL QUESTION

How can you use proportions to solve real-world geometry problems?

Real-World Video

Architects make blueprints and models of their designs to show clients and contractors. These scale drawings and scale models have measurements in proportion to those of the project when built.

⊙ my.hrw.com

© Houghton Mifflin Harcourt Publishing Company • Image Credits: ©Photo Researchers/Getty Images

GO DIGITAL

my.hrw.com

my.hrw.com

Go digital with your write-in student edition, accessible on any device.

Math On the Spot

Scan with your smart phone to jump directly to the online edition, video tutor, and more.

Animated Math

Interactively explore key concepts to see how math works.

Personal Math Trainer

Get immediate feedback and help as you work through practice sets.

Are YOU Ready?

Complete these exercises to review skills you will need for this chapter.

Simplify Fractions

EXAMPLE   Simplify $\frac{18}{30}$.

18: 1, 2, 3, ⑥, 9, 18
30: 1, 2, 3, 5, ⑥, 10, 30

$\frac{18 \div 6}{30 \div 6} = \frac{3}{5}$

List all the factors of the numerator and denominator.
Circle the greatest common factor (GCF).
Divide the numerator and denominator by the GCF.

Write each fraction in simplest form.

1. $\frac{25}{30}$ _____

2. $\frac{27}{36}$ _____

3. $\frac{14}{16}$ _____

4. $\frac{15}{45}$ _____

Write Fractions as Decimals

EXAMPLE

$$\frac{7}{25} \rightarrow 25\overline{)7.00}$$

$$\begin{array}{r} 0.28 \\ 25\overline{)7.00} \\ -5\,0 \\ \hline 2\,00 \\ -2\,00 \\ \hline 0 \end{array}$$

$2 \times 25 = 50$
$8 \times 25 = 200$

Write the fraction as a division problem.
Write a decimal point and a zero in the dividend.
Place a decimal point in the quotient.
Write more zeros in the dividend if necessary.

Write each fraction as a decimal.

5. $\frac{4}{5}$ _____

6. $\frac{3}{8}$ _____

7. $\frac{15}{16}$ _____

8. $\frac{13}{20}$ _____

Area of Squares, Rectangles, and Triangles

EXAMPLE

5 cm

9 cm

$A = l \times w$ Formula for the area of a rectangle
$= 9 \times 5$ Substitute the length and width.
$= 45$ cm^2 Simplify.

Find the area of each rectangle.

9. $l = 10$ cm, $w = 4$ cm _____

10. $l = 14$ in., $w = 9.5$ in. _____

11. $l = 0.7$ cm, $w = 0.35$ cm _____

12. $l = \frac{2}{3}$ yd, $w = \frac{1}{2}$ yd _____

Reading Start-Up

Visualize Vocabulary

Use the ✔ words to complete the graphic. You may put more than one word on each line.

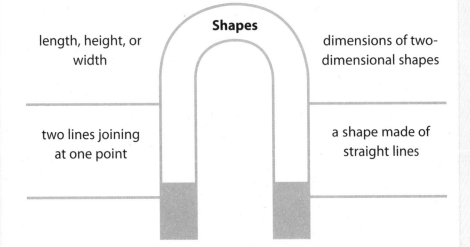

length, height, or width

Shapes

dimensions of two-dimensional shapes

two lines joining at one point

a shape made of straight lines

Understand Vocabulary

Complete the sentences using the preview words.

1. What is a proportional two-dimensional drawing of an object?

   _____

2. What is the distance around a circle? _____

3. What is a line segment that passes through the center of a circle and

   has both endpoints on the circle? _____

Active Reading

Key-Term Fold Before beginning the module, create a key-term fold to help you learn the vocabulary in this module. Write each highlighted vocabulary word on one side of a flap. Write the definition for each word on the other side of the flap. Use the key-term fold to quiz yourself on the definitions in this module.

Unpacking the TEKS

Understanding the TEKS and the vocabulary terms in the TEKS will help you know exactly what you are expected to learn in this module.

TEKS 7.5.A

Generalize the critical attributes of similarity, including ratios within and between similar shapes.

Key Vocabulary

similar shapes *(formas semejantes)* Figures with the same shape but not necessarily the same size are similar.

What It Means to You

You will use the properties of similar figures to solve mathematical and real-world problems.

UNPACKING EXAMPLE 7.5.A

A rectangle has a length of 14 inches and a width of 9 inches. A second rectangle has a length of 42 inches. The two rectangles are similar. What is the width of the second rectangle?

The two similar rectangles have the same shape, so the ratio of width (shorter side) to length (longer side) is the same for each rectangle.

$$\frac{9}{14} = \frac{w}{42}$$
$$\frac{9 \times 3}{14 \times 3} = \frac{w}{42}$$
$$9 \times 3 = w$$
$$27 = w$$

The width of the second rectangle is 27 inches.

TEKS 7.5.C

Solve mathematical and real-world problems involving similar shape and scale drawings.

Key Vocabulary

scale *(escala)*
The ratio between two sets of measurements.

What It Means to You

You will learn how to calculate actual measurements from a scale drawing.

UNPACKING EXAMPLE 7.5.C

A photograph of a painting has dimensions 5.4 cm and 4 cm. The scale factor is $\frac{1}{15}$. Find the length and width of the actual painting.

$$\frac{1}{15} = \frac{5.4}{l} \qquad\qquad \frac{1}{15} = \frac{4}{w}$$
$$\frac{1 \times 5.4}{15 \times 5.4} = \frac{5.4}{l} \qquad\qquad \frac{1 \times 4}{15 \times 4} = \frac{4}{w}$$
$$15 \times 5.4 = l \qquad\qquad 15 \times 4 = w$$
$$81 = l \qquad\qquad 60 = w$$

The painting is 81 cm long and 60 cm wide.

Visit **my.hrw.com** to see all the **TEKS** unpacked.

⏻ my.hrw.com

Similar Shapes and Proportions

TEKS
Proportionality—
7.5.A Generalize the critical attributes of similarity, including ratios within and between similar shapes.

? ESSENTIAL QUESTION

How can you use ratios to determine if two figures are similar?

EXPLORE ACTIVITY TEKS 7.5.A

Similar Shapes and Proportions

Similar shapes have the same shape but not necessarily the same size. You can use square tiles to model similar figures.

A rectangle made of square tiles measures 5 tiles long and 2 tiles wide. Find the length of a similar rectangle that measures 6 tiles wide.

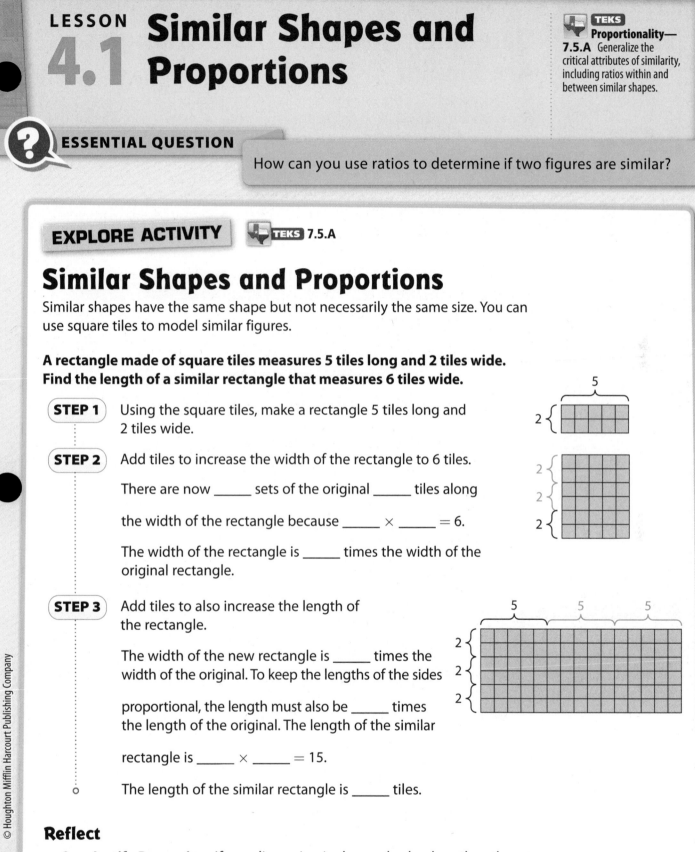

STEP 1 Using the square tiles, make a rectangle 5 tiles long and 2 tiles wide.

STEP 2 Add tiles to increase the width of the rectangle to 6 tiles.

There are now _____ sets of the original _____ tiles along

the width of the rectangle because _____ × _____ = 6.

The width of the rectangle is _____ times the width of the original rectangle.

STEP 3 Add tiles to also increase the length of the rectangle.

The width of the new rectangle is _____ times the width of the original. To keep the lengths of the sides

proportional, the length must also be _____ times the length of the original. The length of the similar

rectangle is _____ × _____ = 15.

The length of the similar rectangle is _____ tiles.

Reflect

1. **Justify Reasoning** If one dimension is changed, why does the other dimension have to change to create a similar figure?

_____

_____

my.hrw.com

Determining Whether Two Triangles Are Similar

Similar shapes have the same shape, but not necessarily the same size. **Corresponding angles** and **corresponding sides** of two or more similar shapes are in the same relative position.

The symbol ~ means "is similar to." In the figure shown, sides and angles that are the same color correspond to each other. $\triangle ABC \sim \triangle DEF$.

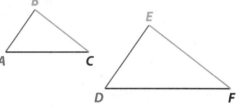

Similar Figures

In two similar figures:

- the measures of their corresponding angles are equal, and
- the lengths of their corresponding sides are proportional.

EXAMPLE 1

TEKS 7.5.A

Explain whether the triangles are similar.

STEP 1 Check that the corresponding angles of the triangles have equal measures.

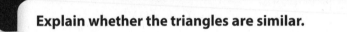

$m\angle E = m\angle R = 106°$ $\angle E$ corresponds to $\angle R$

$m\angle F = m\angle S = 34°$ $\angle F$ corresponds to $\angle S$

$m\angle D = m\angle Q = 40°$ $\angle D$ corresponds to $\angle Q$

Math Talk
Mathematical Processes

Are all equilateral triangles similar? Explain.

STEP 2 Check that the corresponding side lengths are proportional.

$\overline{DE}$ corresponds to $\overline{QR}$. $\overline{EF}$ corresponds to $\overline{RS}$.

$\overline{DF}$ corresponds to $\overline{QS}$.

> A side of a figure can be named by its endpoints with a bar above.

$\dfrac{DE}{QR} \overset{?}{=} \dfrac{EF}{RS} \overset{?}{=} \dfrac{DF}{QS}$ Write ratios using the lengths of corresponding sides.

$\dfrac{7}{21} \overset{?}{=} \dfrac{8}{24} \overset{?}{=} \dfrac{12}{36}$ Substitute the lengths of the sides.

$\dfrac{1}{3} \overset{?}{=} \dfrac{1}{3} \overset{?}{=} \dfrac{1}{3}$ ✓   Simplify.

Since the measures of the corresponding angles are equal and the corresponding sides are proportional, the triangles are similar.

Explain whether the triangles are similar.

2.

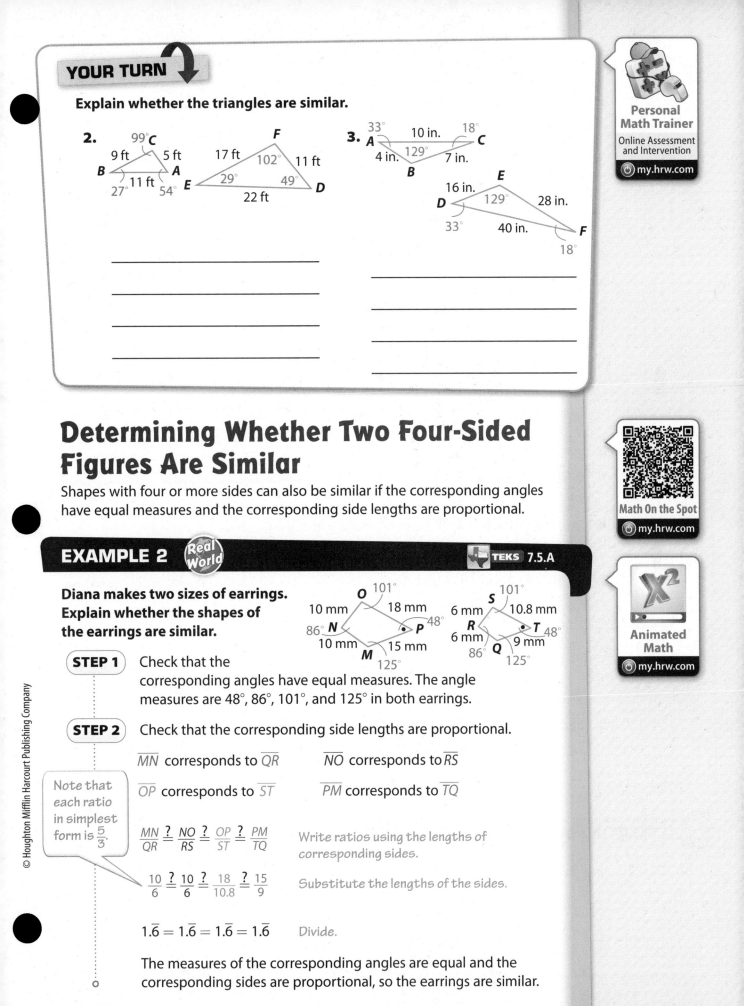

3.

_____

_____

_____

_____

_____

_____

_____

_____

Determining Whether Two Four-Sided Figures Are Similar

Shapes with four or more sides can also be similar if the corresponding angles have equal measures and the corresponding side lengths are proportional.

EXAMPLE 2 Real World   TEKS 7.5.A

Diana makes two sizes of earrings. Explain whether the shapes of the earrings are similar.

STEP 1 Check that the corresponding angles have equal measures. The angle measures are 48°, 86°, 101°, and 125° in both earrings.

STEP 2 Check that the corresponding side lengths are proportional.

$\overline{MN}$ corresponds to $\overline{QR}$ $\overline{NO}$ corresponds to $\overline{RS}$

$\overline{OP}$ corresponds to $\overline{ST}$ $\overline{PM}$ corresponds to $\overline{TQ}$

Note that each ratio in simplest form is $\frac{5}{3}$.

$\dfrac{MN}{QR} \overset{?}{=} \dfrac{NO}{RS} \overset{?}{=} \dfrac{OP}{ST} \overset{?}{=} \dfrac{PM}{TQ}$ Write ratios using the lengths of corresponding sides.

$\dfrac{10}{6} \overset{?}{=} \dfrac{10}{6} \overset{?}{=} \dfrac{18}{10.8} \overset{?}{=} \dfrac{15}{9}$ Substitute the lengths of the sides.

$1.\overline{6} = 1.\overline{6} = 1.\overline{6} = 1.\overline{6}$ Divide.

The measures of the corresponding angles are equal and the corresponding sides are proportional, so the earrings are similar.

YOUR TURN

Explain whether the shapes are similar.

4. rectangle *ABCD* with sides of 7 and 5 and rectangle *MNOP* with sides of 21 and 15

_____

_____

5.

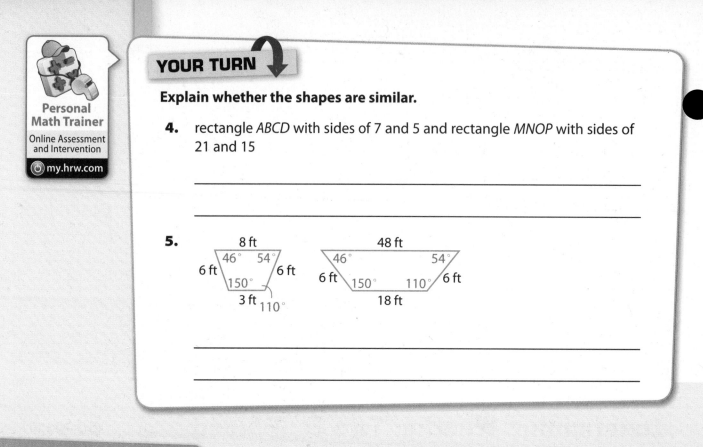

_____

_____

Guided Practice

1. A rectangle made of square tiles measures 7 tiles long and 3 tiles wide. What is the length of a similar rectangle whose width is 9 tiles?
(Explore Activity)

_____

Explain whether the shapes are similar. (Examples 1 and 2)

2.

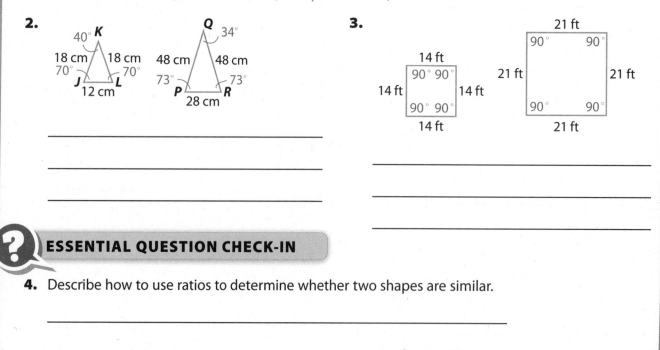

_____

_____

_____

3.

_____

_____

_____

? ESSENTIAL QUESTION CHECK-IN

4. Describe how to use ratios to determine whether two shapes are similar.

_____

_____

4.1 Independent Practice

TEKS 7.5.A

Personal
Math Trainer

Online
Assessment and
Intervention

my.hrw.com

Determine if each statement is true or false. Justify your answer.

5. All squares are similar. _____

6. All right triangles are similar. _____

_____

_____

_____

_____

_____

_____

_____

Art For 7–10, use the table. Assume all angle measures are equal to 90°.

7. Hugo has a small print of one of the paintings in the table. It is similar in size to the original. The print measures 11 in. × 10 in. Of which painting is this a print? Explain.

_____

_____

_____

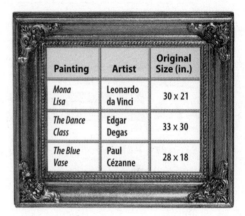

Painting	Artist	Original Size (in.)
Mona Lisa	Leonardo da Vinci	30 x 21
The Dance Class	Edgar Degas	33 x 30
The Blue Vase	Paul Cézanne	28 x 18

8. A local artist painted a copy of Cezanne's painting. It measures 88 in. × 74 in. Is the copy similar to the original? Explain.

_____

_____

9. A company made a poster of da Vinci's painting. The poster is 5 feet long and 3.5 feet wide. Is the poster similar to the original *Mona Lisa*? Explain.

_____

_____

_____

10. The same company made a poster of *The Blue Vase*. The poster is 36 inches long and 26 inches wide. Is the poster similar to the original *The Blue Vase*? Explain.

_____

_____

Problem Solving The figure shows a 12 ft by 15 ft garden divided into four rectangular parts, each planted with a different vegetable. Explain whether the rectangles in each pair are similar and why.

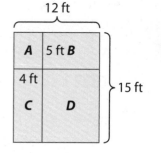

11. rectangle *A* and the original rectangle

_____

_____

12. the original rectangle and rectangle *D*

_____

_____

13. rectangle *C* and rectangle *B*

_____

_____

_____

![H.O.T.] **FOCUS ON HIGHER ORDER THINKING**

14. Analyze Relationships Which of these four-sided shapes are similar?

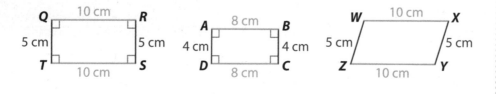

_____

15. Communicate Mathematical Ideas Describe the two tests two polygons must pass to be proven similar.

_____

_____

_____

16. Make a Conjecture Using what you know of similar figures, explain whether you believe all rectangles are similar. Give an example or a counterexample.

_____

_____

_____

_____

Work Area

© Houghton Mifflin Harcourt Publishing Company

TEKS
Proportionality—
7.5.A Generalize the critical attributes of similarity, including ratios within and between similar shapes.

? **ESSENTIAL QUESTION**

How can you use similar shapes to find unknown measures?

Finding Unknown Measures in Similar Triangles

When you measure the height of a door with a measuring tape, you are using direct measurement. The process of using similar shapes and proportions to find a measure is called **indirect measurement**. You can use indirect measurement to measure things that are difficult to measure directly, like the height of a tree.

Math On the Spot
⊙ my.hrw.com

EXAMPLE 1

TEKS 7.5.A

$\triangle ABC \sim \triangle JKL$. **Find the unknown measures.**

A Find the unknown side, x.

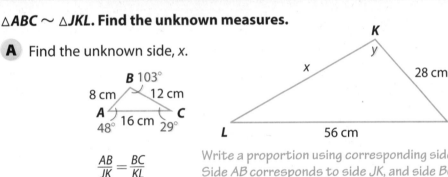

$$\frac{AB}{JK} = \frac{BC}{KL}$$

$$\frac{8}{28} = \frac{12}{x}$$

$$\frac{8 \div 4}{28 \div 4} = \frac{2}{7}$$

$$\frac{2}{7} = \frac{12}{x}$$
×6 ↗ ×6 ↘

$$x = 42 \text{ cm}$$

Write a proportion using corresponding sides. Side AB corresponds to side JK, and side BC corresponds to side KL.
Substitute the known lengths of the sides.

Simplify $\frac{8}{28}$ to help you find a factor of 12.
2 is a factor of 12.

Since 2 times 6 is 12, multiply 7 times 6 to find the value of x.

B Find y.

$\angle K$ corresponds to $\angle B$.

$y = 103°$

Corresponding angles of similar triangles have equal angle measures.

Reflect

1. **Analyze Relationships** What other proportion could be used to find the value of x in the example? Explain.

_____

_____

YOUR TURN

△ABC ~ △JGH. Find the unknown measures.

2.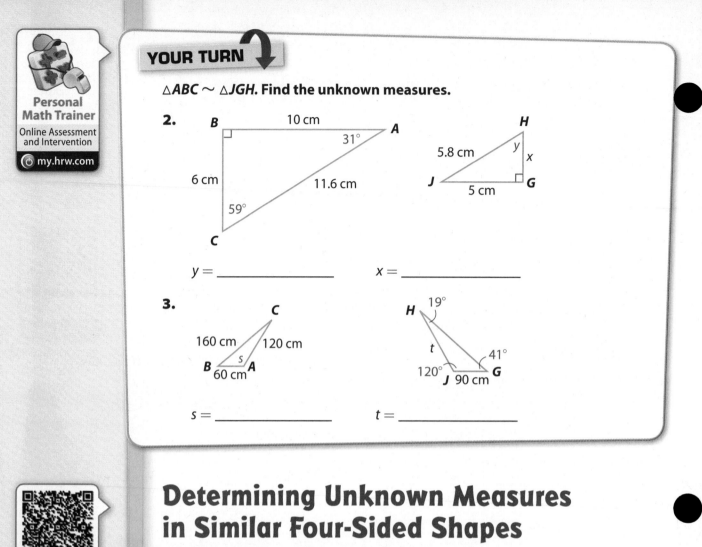

y = _____   x = _____

3.

s = _____   t = _____

Determining Unknown Measures in Similar Four-Sided Shapes

You can use similar shapes and proportions to find measures of sides in rectangles and other four-sided shapes.

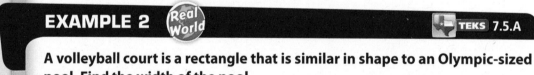

EXAMPLE 2   Real World   TEKS 7.5.A

A volleyball court is a rectangle that is similar in shape to an Olympic-sized pool. Find the width of the pool.

Math Talk
Mathematical Processes

With similar triangles, you need to find missing sides and angles. Why do you need to find only missing sides with rectangles?

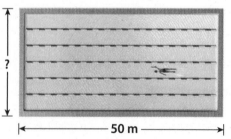

Let w = the width of the pool.

$$\frac{18}{50} = \frac{9}{w}$$ Write a proportion using corresponding sides.

 $\frac{18}{50} = \frac{9}{w}$ Since 18 divided by 2 is 9, divide 50 by 2 to find the value of w.

$$w = 25$$

The pool is 25 meters wide.

4. These rectangular gardens are similar in shape. Find the width of the smaller garden.

_____

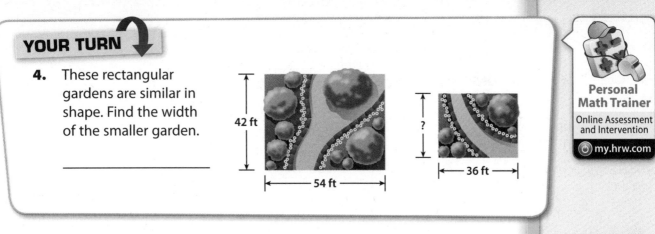

42 ft
54 ft
?
36 ft

Using Indirect Measurement

When you write a proportion to calculate a measurement, you can write ratios comparing measures of the same object. For example, use the ratio formed by the height of an object and the length of its shadow.

EXAMPLE 3 Real World

TEKS 7.5.A

Find the height of the totem pole.

$$\frac{\text{height of person}}{\text{shadow of person}} = \frac{\text{height of totem pole}}{\text{shadow of totem pole}}$$ Write a proportion.

$$\frac{5}{4} = \frac{h}{16}$$ Substitute known values.

$$\frac{5}{4} \overset{\times 4}{=} \frac{h}{16}$$ Since $4 \times 4 = 16$, multiply 5 by 4 to find the value of h.

$$h = 20$$

The totem pole is 20 feet tall.

h
16 ft
5 ft
4 ft

5. A student who is 4 feet tall stands beside a tree. The tree has a shadow that is 12 feet long at the same time that the shadow of the student is

   6 feet long. Find the height of the tree. _____

6. A photographer is taking a photo of a statue of Paul Bunyan, the legendary giant lumberjack. He measures the length of his shadow and the shadow cast by the statue. Find the height of the

   Paul Bunyan statue. _____

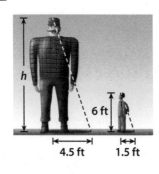

h
6 ft
4.5 ft
1.5 ft

△**ABC** ∼ △**XYZ** in each pair. Find the unknown measures (Example 1)

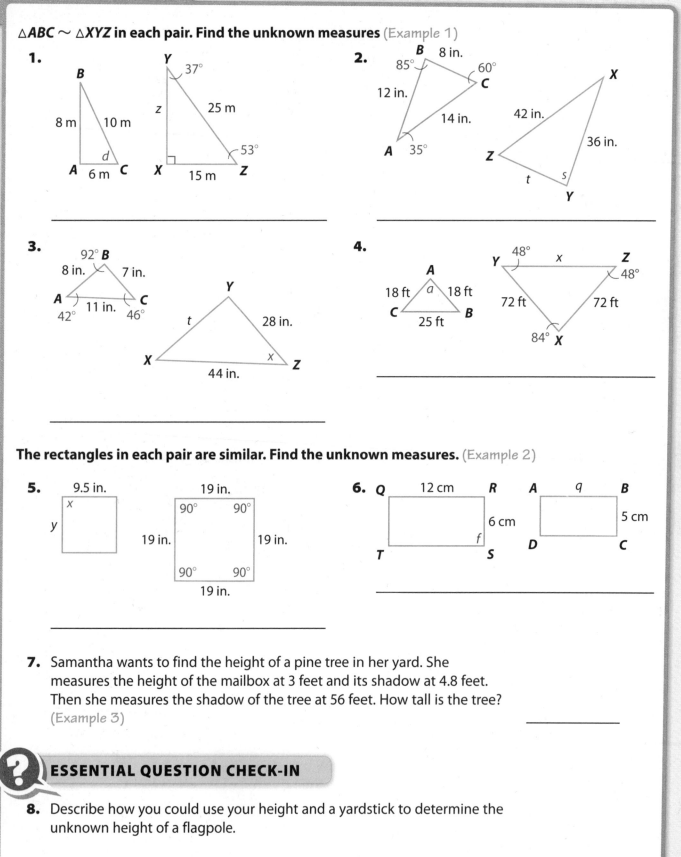

1.

2.

_____

_____

3.

4.

_____

_____

The rectangles in each pair are similar. Find the unknown measures. (Example 2)

5.

6.

_____

_____

7. Samantha wants to find the height of a pine tree in her yard. She
measures the height of the mailbox at 3 feet and its shadow at 4.8 feet.
Then she measures the shadow of the tree at 56 feet. How tall is the tree?
(Example 3)

_____

? ESSENTIAL QUESTION CHECK-IN

8. Describe how you could use your height and a yardstick to determine the
unknown height of a flagpole.

_____

_____

4.2 Independent Practice

Personal Math Trainer

Online Assessment and Intervention

my.hrw.com

TEKS 7.5.A

9. A cactus casts a shadow that is 15 ft long. A gate nearby casts a shadow that is 5 ft long. Find the height of the cactus.

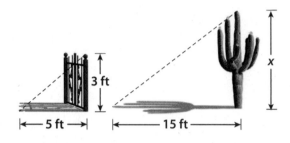

3 ft

x

|← 5 ft →| |← 15 ft →|

_____

10. Two ramps modeled with triangles are similar. Which side of triangle *KOA* corresponds to $\overline{JN}$? Explain.

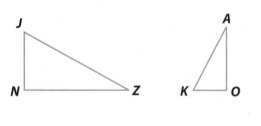

J

A

N   Z   K   O

_____
_____
_____

11. A building with a height of 14 m casts a shadow that is 16 m long while a taller building casts a 24 m long shadow. What is the height of the taller building?

_____

12. Katie uses a copy machine to enlarge her rectangular design that is 6 in. wide and 8 in. long. The new width is 10 in. What is the new length?

_____

13. **Art** An art exhibit at a local museum features several similarly shaped metal cubes welded together to make a sculpture. The smallest cube has a edge length of 6 inches.

a. What are the edge lengths of the other cubes if the ratios of similarity to the smallest cube are 1.25, $\frac{4}{3}$, 1.5, $\frac{7}{4}$, and 2 respectively?

_____
_____

b. If the artist wanted to add a smaller cube with an edge length with a ratio of $\frac{2}{3}$ to the sculpture, what size would the cube be?

_____

c. Why do you only have to find the length of one edge for each cube?

_____
_____

$\triangle XYZ \sim \triangle PQR$ in each pair. Find the unknown measures.

14.

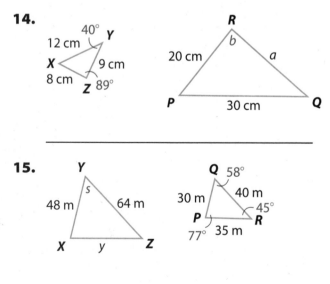

40° Y
12 cm

X
       9 cm
8 cm
      Z 89°

R
    b
20 cm   a

P   30 cm   Q

_____

15.

Y
     s
48 m   64 m

X   y   Z

Q 58°
30 m   40 m
            45°
P
77° 35 m   R

_____

16. Two common envelope sizes are $3\frac{1}{2}$ in. $\times$ $6\frac{1}{2}$ in. and 4 in. $\times$ $9\frac{1}{2}$ in. Are these envelopes similar? Explain.

_____

_____

17. A pair of rectangular baking pans come in a set together for $15. One pan is 13 inches by 9 inches and the other pan is 6 inches by 6 inches. Without doing any calculations, how can you tell that these pans are not similar?

_____

_____

_____

_____

 **FOCUS ON HIGHER ORDER THINKING**

Work Area

18. Draw Conclusions In the similar triangles used in indirect measurement with the shadows of a flagpole and a person, which sides of the triangles represent the rays of the sun?

_____

19. Make a Conjecture Do you think it is possible to use indirect measurement with shadows if the sun is directly overhead? Explain.

_____

_____

_____

20. Analyze Relationships Joseph's parents have planted two gardens. One is square and has an area of 25 ft². The other one has two sides equal to $\frac{2}{3}$ of one side of the square, and the other two sides equal to $\frac{5}{2}$ of one side of the square.

a. Find the dimensions of the other garden. Explain how you found your answer.

_____

_____

_____

_____

b. Find the area of the other garden.

_____

TEKS
Proportionality—
7.5.C Solve mathematical and real-world problems involving similar shape and scale drawings.

? ESSENTIAL QUESTION

How can you use scale drawings to solve problems?

EXPLORE ACTIVITY 1 *Real World* **TEKS** 7.5.C

Finding Dimensions

Scale drawings and scale models are used in mapmaking, construction, and other trades.

A blueprint is a technical drawing that usually displays architectural plans. Pete's blueprint shows a layout of a house. Every 4 inches in the blueprint represents 3 feet of the actual house. One of the walls in the blueprint is 24 inches long. What is the actual length of the wall?

16 in.

24 in.

A Complete the table to find the actual length of the wall.

Blueprint length (in.)	4	8	12	16	20	24
Actual length (ft)	3	6				

Reflect

1. In Pete's blueprint the length of a side wall is 16 inches. Find the actual length of the wall.

   _____

2. The back wall of the house is 33 feet long. What is the length of the back wall in the blueprint?

   _____

3. **Check for Reasonableness** How do you know your answer to **2** is reasonable?

   _____

   _____

   _____

   _____

Using a Scale Drawing to Find Area

A **scale drawing** is a proportional two-dimensional drawing of an object. Scale drawings can represent objects that are smaller or larger than the actual object.

A **scale** is a ratio between 2 sets of measurements. It shows how a dimension in a scale drawing is related to the actual object. Scales are usually shown as two numbers separated by a colon such as 1:20 or 1 cm:1 m. Scales can be shown in the same unit or in different units.

You can solve scale-drawing problems by using proportional reasoning.

My Notes

EXAMPLE 1 Real World   TEKS 7.5.C

The art class is planning to paint a mural on an outside wall. This figure is a scale drawing of the wall. What is the area of the actual wall?

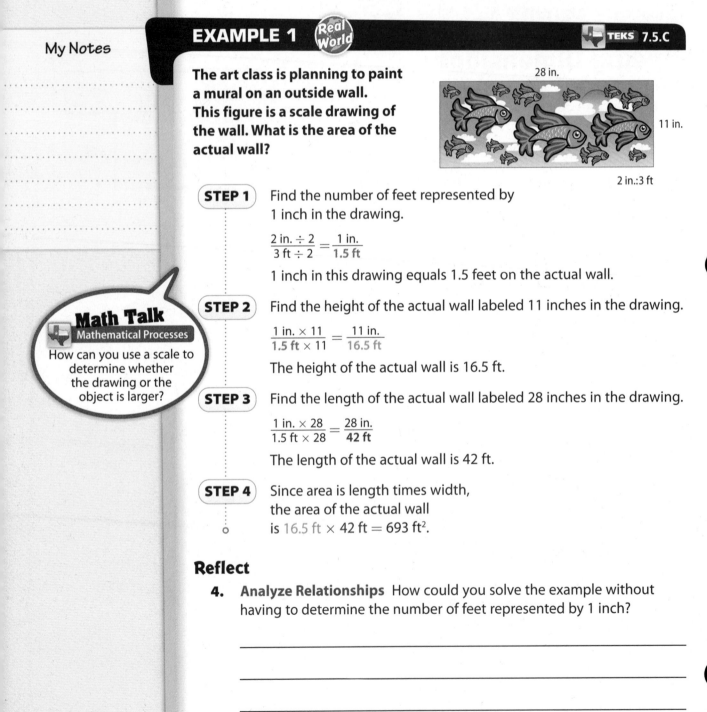

28 in.

11 in.

2 in.:3 ft

STEP 1 Find the number of feet represented by 1 inch in the drawing.

$$\frac{2 \text{ in.} \div 2}{3 \text{ ft} \div 2} = \frac{1 \text{ in.}}{1.5 \text{ ft}}$$

1 inch in this drawing equals 1.5 feet on the actual wall.

Math Talk
Mathematical Processes

How can you use a scale to determine whether the drawing or the object is larger?

STEP 2 Find the height of the actual wall labeled 11 inches in the drawing.

$$\frac{1 \text{ in.} \times 11}{1.5 \text{ ft} \times 11} = \frac{11 \text{ in.}}{16.5 \text{ ft}}$$

The height of the actual wall is 16.5 ft.

STEP 3 Find the length of the actual wall labeled 28 inches in the drawing.

$$\frac{1 \text{ in.} \times 28}{1.5 \text{ ft} \times 28} = \frac{28 \text{ in.}}{42 \text{ ft}}$$

The length of the actual wall is 42 ft.

STEP 4 Since area is length times width, the area of the actual wall is $16.5 \text{ ft} \times 42 \text{ ft} = 693 \text{ ft}^2$.

Reflect

4. **Analyze Relationships** How could you solve the example without having to determine the number of feet represented by 1 inch?

_____

_____

_____

_____

5. Find the length and width of the actual room, shown in the scale drawing. Then find the area of the actual room. Round your answer to the nearest tenth.

6.5 in.

5 in.

3 in.:8 ft

_____

_____

6. The drawing plan for an art studio shows a rectangle that is 13.2 inches by 6 inches. The scale in the plan is 3 in.:5 ft. Find the length and width of the actual studio. Then find the area of the actual studio.

_____

_____

EXPLORE ACTIVITY 2 *Real World*   **TEKS** 7.5.C

Drawing in Different Scales

A A scale drawing of a meeting hall is drawn on centimeter grid paper as shown. The scale is 1 cm:3 m.

Suppose you redraw the rectangle on centimeter grid paper using a scale of 1 cm:6 m. In the new scale, 1 cm

represents [**more than/less**] than 1 cm in the old scale.

The measurement of each side of the new drawing will

be [**twice/half**] as long as the measurement of the

original drawing.

B Draw the rectangle for the new scale 1 cm:6 m.

Reflect

7. Find the actual length of each side of the hall using the original drawing. Then find the actual length of each side of the hall using the your new drawing and the new scale. How do you know your answers are correct?

_____

_____

_____

_____

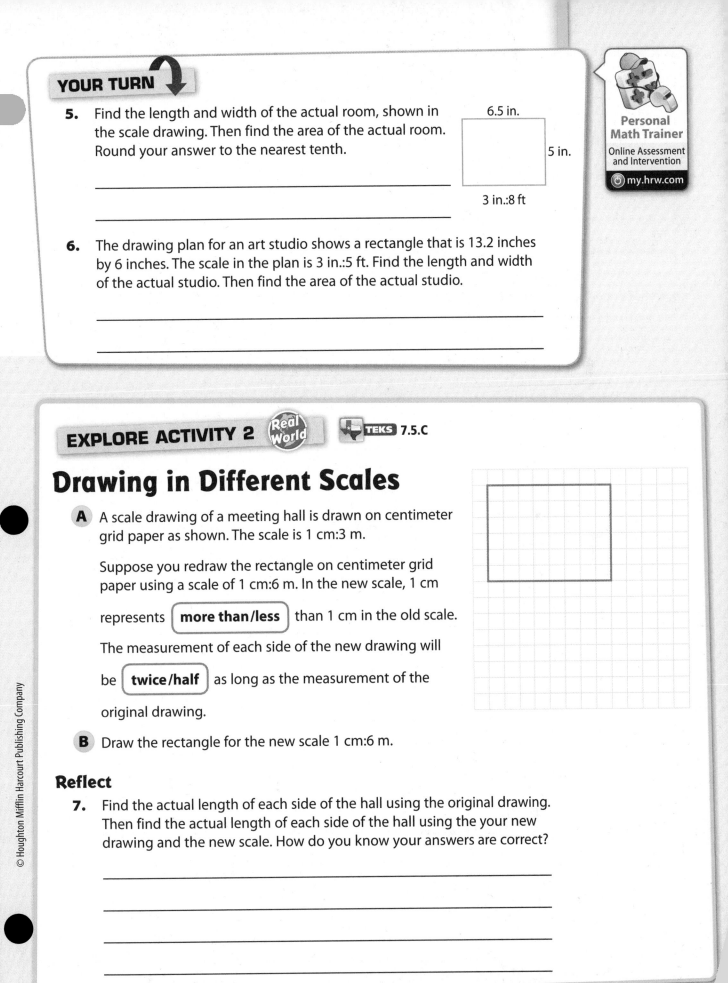

1. The scale of a room in a blueprint is 3 in : 5 ft. A wall in the same blueprint is 18 in. Complete the table. (Explore Activity 1)

Blueprint length (in.)	3	6	9	12	15	18
Actual length (ft)						

    a. How long is the actual wall? _____

    b. A window in the room has an actual width of 2.5 feet.
        Find the width of the window in the blueprint. _____

2. The scale in the drawing is 2 in. : 4 ft. What are the length and width of the actual room? Find the area of the actual room. (Example 1)

14 in.

7 in.

_____

_____

3. The scale in the drawing is 2 cm : 5 m. What are the length and width of the actual room? Find the area of the actual room. (Example 1)

10 cm

6 cm

_____

4. A scale drawing of a cafeteria is drawn on centimeter grid paper as shown. The scale is 1 cm : 4 m. (Explore Activity 2)

    a. Redraw the rectangle on centimeter grid paper using a scale of 1 cm:6 m.

    b. What is the actual length and width of the cafeteria using the original scale? What are the actual dimensions of the cafeteria using the new scale?

_____

? **ESSENTIAL QUESTION CHECK-IN**

5. If you have an accurate, complete scale drawing and the scale, which measurements of the object of the drawing can you find?

_____

_____

4.3 Independent Practice

Personal Math Trainer

Online Assessment and Intervention

my.hrw.com

TEKS 7.5.C

6. **Art** Marie has a small copy of Rene Magritte's famous painting, *The Schoolmaster*. Her copy has dimensions 2 inches by 1.5 inches. The scale of the copy is 1 in:40 cm.

   a. Find the dimensions of the original painting.

   _____

   b. Find the area of the original painting.

   _____

   c. Since 1 inch is 2.54 centimeters, find the dimensions of the original painting in inches.

   _____

   d. Find the area of the original painting in square inches.

   _____

7. A game room has a floor that is 120 feet by 75 feet. A scale drawing of the floor on grid paper uses a scale of 1 unit:5 feet. What are the dimensions of the scale drawing?

   _____

8. **Multiple Representations** The length of a table is 6 feet. On a scale drawing, the length is 2 inches. Write three possible scales for the drawing.

   _____

9. **Analyze Relationships** A scale for a scale drawing is 10 cm:1 mm. Which is larger, the actual object or the scale drawing? Explain.

   _____

   _____

10. **Architecture** The scale model of a building is 5.4 feet tall.

    a. If the original building is 810 meters tall, what was the scale used to make the model?

    _____

    b. If the model is made out of tiny bricks each measuring 0.4 inch in height, how many bricks tall is the model?

    _____

11. You have been asked to build a scale model of your school out of toothpicks. Imagine your school is 30 feet tall. Your scale is 1 ft:1.26 cm.

   a. If a toothpick is 6.3 cm tall, how many toothpicks tall will your model be?

   _____

   b. Your mother is out of toothpicks, and suggests you use cotton swabs instead. You measure them, and they are 7.6 cm tall. How many cotton swabs tall will your model be?

   _____

FOCUS ON HIGHER ORDER THINKING

Work Area

12. **Draw Conclusions** The area of a square floor on a scale drawing is 100 square centimeters, and the scale of the drawing is 1 centimeter:2 ft, What is the area of the actual floor? What is the ratio of the area in the drawing to the actual area?

_____

13. **Multiple Representations** Describe how to redraw a scale drawing with a new scale.

_____

_____

_____

_____

_____

_____

14. **Represent Real-World Problems** Describe how several jobs or professions might use scale drawings at work.

_____

_____

_____

_____

_____

_____

_____

TEKS
Proportionality—
7.5.B Describe π as the ratio of the circumference of a circle to its diameter.

? ESSENTIAL QUESTION

What is the relationship between the circumference of a circle and its diameter?

EXPLORE ACTIVITY 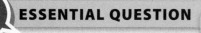 **TEKS** 7.5.B

Exploring Circumference

A circle is a set of points in a plane that are a fixed distance from the center.

A **radius** is a line segment with one endpoint at the center of the circle and the other endpoint on the circle. The length of a radius is called the radius of the circle.

A **diameter** of a circle is a line segment that passes through the center of the circle and whose endpoints lie on the circle. The length of the diameter is twice the length of the radius. The length of a diameter is called the diameter of the circle.

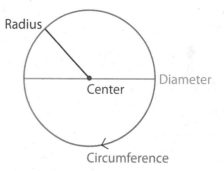

The **circumference** of a circle is the distance around the circle.

A Use a measuring tape to find the circumference of five circular objects. Then measure the distance across each item to find its diameter. Record the measurements of each object in the table below.

Object	Circumference C	Diameter d	$\frac{C}{d}$

B Divide the circumference of each object by its diameter. Round your answer to the nearest hundredth.

Reflect

1. **Make a Conjecture** Describe what you notice about the ratio $\frac{C}{d}$ in your table.

_____

Determining Proportionality in Circles

The ratio of the circumference to the diameter $\frac{C}{d}$ of any circle is the same for all circles. This ratio $\frac{C}{d}$ is represented by the Greek letter π, called **pi**. As you calculated in the Explore Activity, the value of π is close to 3. You can approximate π as 3.14 or $\frac{22}{7}$.

Later, you can use this ratio to find a formula for circumference. Circles do not have sides and angles, but every circle has a radius and diameter whose lengths you can measure and compare.

EXAMPLE 1

TEKS 7.5.B

Determine if the radius and diameter of the two circles are proportional.

STEP 1 Find the radius and diameter of each circle.

Larger circle		**Smaller circle**	
$r = 5$ in.	The radius is given.	$r = 3$ in.	
$d = 10$ in.	To find the diameter, multiply the radius by 2.	$d = 6$ in.	

> The diameter is 2 times the length of the radius.

STEP 2 Set up a proportion using the corresponding lengths of the radius and diameter.

$\frac{r}{r} = \frac{d}{d}$ Set up a proportion.

$\frac{5}{3} \overset{?}{=} \frac{10}{6}$ Substitute the values for r and d.

$\frac{5}{3} \overset{?}{=} \frac{10 \div 2}{6 \div 2}$ Simplify.

$\frac{5}{3} = \frac{5}{3}$ ✓   The two ratios are equal so the corresponding lengths are proportional.

The radius and diameter of the two circles are proportional.

$r = 5$ in.

$r = 3$ in.

Reflect

2. In every circle, what is the ratio of the radius to the diameter? What is the ratio of the circumference to the diameter?

_____

_____

3. **Draw Conclusions** Based on the ratios of the radius to diameter and circumference to diameter, are all circles proportional? Is the ratio of circumference to the diameter of any circle the same for all circles?

_____

_____

_____

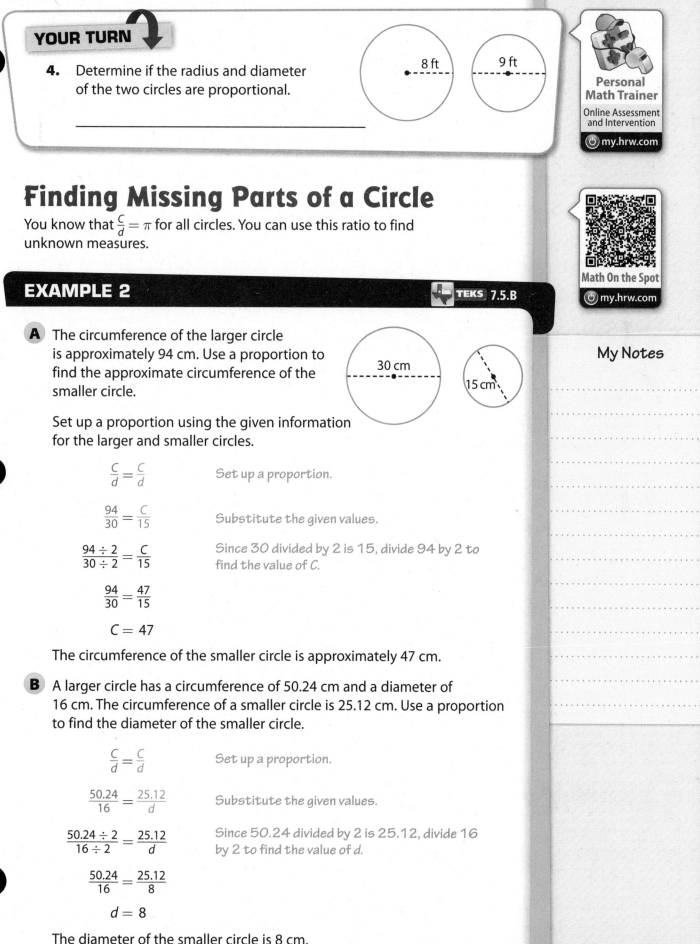

4. Determine if the radius and diameter of the two circles are proportional.

_____

8 ft   9 ft

Personal Math Trainer

Online Assessment and Intervention

my.hrw.com

Finding Missing Parts of a Circle

You know that $\frac{C}{d} = \pi$ for all circles. You can use this ratio to find unknown measures.

EXAMPLE 2

TEKS 7.5.B

Math On the Spot

my.hrw.com

A The circumference of the larger circle is approximately 94 cm. Use a proportion to find the approximate circumference of the smaller circle.

30 cm   15 cm

My Notes

Set up a proportion using the given information for the larger and smaller circles.

$$\frac{C}{d} = \frac{C}{d}$$ Set up a proportion.

$$\frac{94}{30} = \frac{C}{15}$$ Substitute the given values.

$$\frac{94 \div 2}{30 \div 2} = \frac{C}{15}$$ Since 30 divided by 2 is 15, divide 94 by 2 to find the value of C.

$$\frac{94}{30} = \frac{47}{15}$$

$$C = 47$$

The circumference of the smaller circle is approximately 47 cm.

B A larger circle has a circumference of 50.24 cm and a diameter of 16 cm. The circumference of a smaller circle is 25.12 cm. Use a proportion to find the diameter of the smaller circle.

$$\frac{C}{d} = \frac{C}{d}$$ Set up a proportion.

$$\frac{50.24}{16} = \frac{25.12}{d}$$ Substitute the given values.

$$\frac{50.24 \div 2}{16 \div 2} = \frac{25.12}{d}$$ Since 50.24 divided by 2 is 25.12, divide 16 by 2 to find the value of d.

$$\frac{50.24}{16} = \frac{25.12}{8}$$

$$d = 8$$

The diameter of the smaller circle is 8 cm.

YOUR TURN

5. The circumference of the larger circle is approximately 44 meters and the circumference of the smaller circle is approximately 11 meters. Use a proportion to find the approximate

diameter of the smaller circle. _____

d   14 m

Guided Practice

Fill in the blanks. (Explore Activity)

1. Vocabulary In any circle, the ratio of the _____ to the diameter is pi.

2. Vocabulary In any circle, the ratio of the _____ to the radius is 2.

3. You can use the decimal number _____ or the fraction _____ as an approximation for pi.

4. Determine if the radius and diameter of a circle with a diameter of 100 mm and a circle with a diameter of 10 mm are proportional. (Example 1)

_____ = _____

5. Is the circle represented by a penny similar to the one of a quarter? Explain. (Example 1)

_____

_____

6. The circumference of the larger circle is about 18.8 centimeters and the circumference of the smaller circle is about 6.3 centimeters. Find the approximate diameter of the smaller circle.

(Example 2) _____

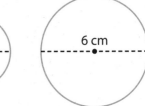

?   6 cm

❓ ESSENTIAL QUESTION CHECK-IN

7. What is the result of dividing the distance around a circle by the distance across the same circle? What number can you use as an approximate value for this ratio?

_____

4.4 Independent Practice

TEKS 7.5.B

Personal Math Trainer

Online Assessment and Intervention

my.hrw.com

8. Measurement Jillian measured the distance around a small fishpond as 27 yards. Which would be a good estimate for the distance across the pond, 14 yards, 9 yards, or 7 yards? Explain how you decided.

_____

_____

_____

_____

9. A rotating wind turbine has a diameter of about 185 feet and its circumference is about 580 feet. A smaller model of the turbine has a circumference of about 10 feet. What will the diameter of the model be?

_____

10. Multistep Andrew has a flying disc with a radius of 10 centimeters. What is the circumference of the disc? (Remember $\frac{C}{d} = 3.14$.)

_____

11. Mandie wants to put some lace trim around the outside of a round tablecloth she expanded. The original tablecloth had a radius of 2 feet and a circumference of 12.56 feet. If the tablecloth now has a radius of 3 feet, is 15 feet of lace enough? Explain.

_____

_____

_____

12. Marta is making two different charms for a necklace. One charm has a 1 centimeter diameter and a 3.14 centimeter circumference. A similar charm has a diameter of 4 centimeters. What is the circumference?

_____

13. Randy is putting bricks around the outside of his round flower bed to protect the plants.

a. If the diameter of his flower bed is 100 inches, what is the distance around the garden? (Remember $\frac{C}{d} = 3.14$.)

_____

b. If the curved bricks he wants to buy are each half a foot long, how many will he need to put around the outside of the garden? Explain.

_____

_____

_____

c. If each brick costs $0.68, and he can only buy whole bricks, how much will it cost him to get the material to put around the outside of his garden?

_____

d. If his mother decides he can only have half of that diameter for his flower bed, how will the cost of the bricks be affected? Explain?

_____

_____

_____

_____

14. Your grandmother is teaching you how to make a homemade pie. The pie pan has a diameter of 9 inches.

   a. If she asks you to cut a strip of pie crust long enough to go around the outside of the pan, how long does it need to be? (Remember $\frac{C}{d} = 3.14$.)

   _____

   b. If another pie pan is 8 inches across the diameter, how long does that piece of crust need to be?

   _____

FOCUS ON HIGHER ORDER THINKING

Work Area

15. Make a Conjecture You know that all squares are similar and all circles are similar. An equilateral triangle has 3 equal sides and 3 angles of 60 degrees each. Are all equilateral triangles similar?

_____

_____

16. Multiple Representations You know three different number representations for pi that you can use to approximate the answer to a problem. Describe a situation when you might choose to use $\frac{22}{7}$.

_____

_____

17. Represent Real-World Problems Describe an example in your daily life where you might be able to measure around something but could not measure across it.

_____

_____

18. Critical Thinking Every morning Jesse runs 3 laps on a circular track. One morning the track is closed, but the straight path from one side of the track to the other is open. How many times should Jesse run across the path if he wants to run his usual distance? Explain your answer.

_____

_____

_____

Ready to Go On?

4.1 Similar Shapes and Proportions

1. Explain whether the shapes are similar.

_____

_____

_____

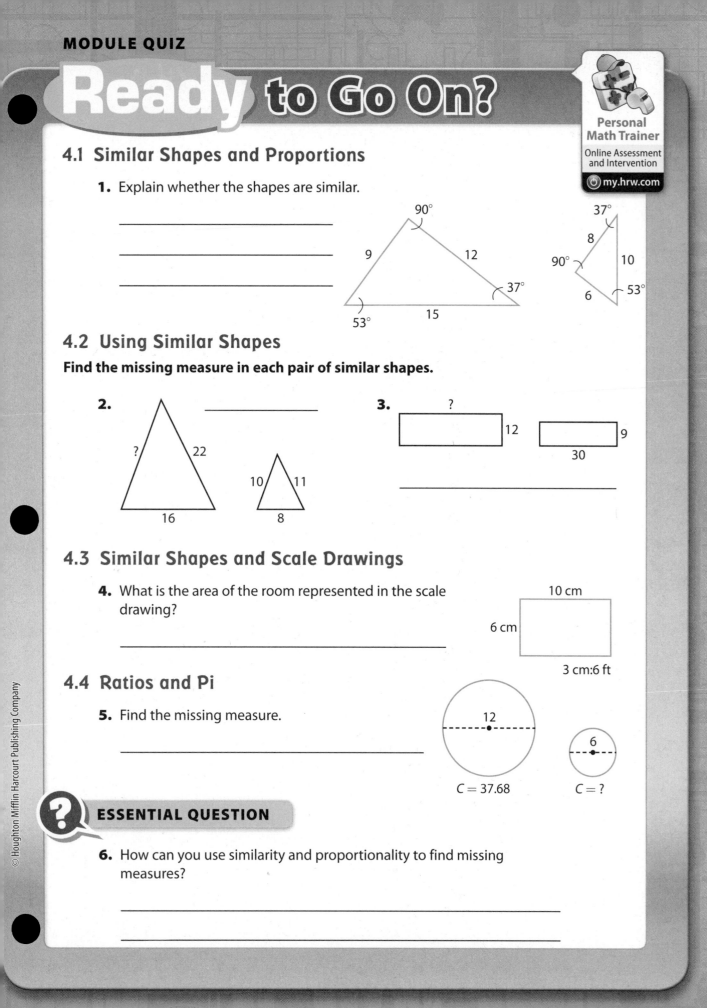

4.2 Using Similar Shapes

Find the missing measure in each pair of similar shapes.

2. _____

3. _____

4.3 Similar Shapes and Scale Drawings

4. What is the area of the room represented in the scale drawing?

_____

4.4 Ratios and Pi

5. Find the missing measure.

_____

? ESSENTIAL QUESTION

6. How can you use similarity and proportionality to find missing measures?

_____

_____

Selected Response

1. Which shows a pair of shapes that are **not** similar? All corresponding angles have equal measure.

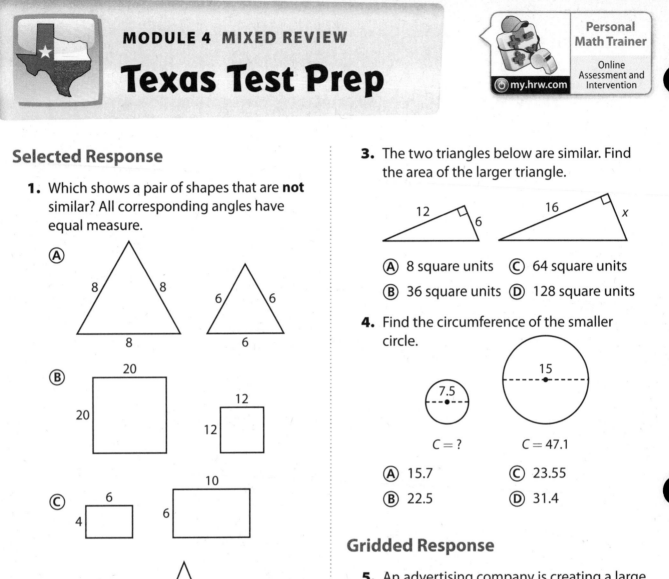

Ⓐ

8 8
8

6 6
6

Ⓑ

20
20

12
12

Ⓒ

6
4

10
6

Ⓓ

9 9
6

12 12
8

2. A scale drawing of a rectangular deck is shown below.

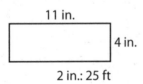

11 in.
4 in.

2 in.: 25 ft

What is the perimeter of the actual deck?

Ⓐ 187.5 ft   Ⓒ 550 ft

Ⓑ 375 ft   Ⓓ 750 ft

3. The two triangles below are similar. Find the area of the larger triangle.

12
6

16
x

Ⓐ 8 square units   Ⓒ 64 square units

Ⓑ 36 square units   Ⓓ 128 square units

4. Find the circumference of the smaller circle.

7.5
15

C = ?   C = 47.1

Ⓐ 15.7   Ⓒ 23.55

Ⓑ 22.5   Ⓓ 31.4

Gridded Response

5. An advertising company is creating a large wall banner and a smaller flyer that are similar figures. What percent of the area of the banner is the area of the flyer?

40 in.
15 in.

24 in.
x

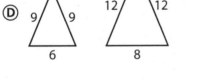

MODULE 2 # Rates and Proportionality

Key Vocabulary

complex fraction *(fracción compleja)*

constant of proportionality *(constante de proporcionalidad)*

proportion *(proporción)*

proportional relationship *(relación proporcional)*

rate of change *(tasa de cambio)*

unit rate *(tasa unitaria)*

? ESSENTIAL QUESTION

How can you use rates and proportionality to solve real-world problems?

EXAMPLE 1

A store sells onions by the pound. Is the relationship between the cost of an amount of onions and the number of pounds proportional? If so, write an equation for the relationship, and represent the relationship on a graph.

Number of pounds	2	5	6
Cost ($)	3.00	7.50	9.00

Write the rates.

$$\frac{\text{cost}}{\text{number of pounds}} : \frac{\$3.00}{2 \text{ pounds}} = \frac{\$1.50}{1 \text{ pound}}$$

$$\frac{\$7.50}{5 \text{ pounds}} = \frac{\$1.50}{1 \text{ pound}}$$

$$\frac{\$9.00}{6 \text{ pounds}} = \frac{\$1.50}{1 \text{ pound}}$$

The rates are constant, so the relationship is proportional.

The constant rate of change is $1.50 per pound, so the constant of proportionality is 1.5. Let x represent the number of pounds and y represent the cost.

The equation for the relationship is $y = 1.5x$.

Plot the ordered pairs (pounds, cost): (2, 3), (5, 7.5), and (6, 9).

Connect the points with a line.

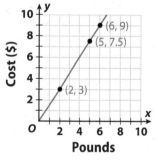

Cost of Onions

EXERCISES

1. Steve uses $\frac{8}{9}$ gallon of paint to paint 4 identical birdhouses. How many gallons of paint does he use for each birdhouse?

   (Lesson 2.1) _____

2. Ron walks 0.5 mile on the track in 10 minutes. Stevie walks 0.25 mile on the track in 6 minutes. Find the unit rate for each walker in miles per hour. Who is the faster walker?

   (Lesson 2.1) _____

   _____

3. (Lessons 2.2, 2.3) The table below shows the proportional relationship between Juan's pay and the hours he works. Complete the table. Plot the data and connect the points with a line. (Lessons 2.2, 2.3)

Juan's Pay

Hours worked	2		5	6
Pay ($)	40	80		

Key Vocabulary

conversion factor *(factor de conversión)*

percent decrease *(porcentaje de disminución)*

percent increase *(porcentaje de aumento)*

principal *(capital)*

simple interest *(interés simple)*

MODULE 3 Proportions and Percent

? ESSENTIAL QUESTION

How can you use proportions and percent to solve real-world problems?

EXAMPLE 1

June's garden is in the shape of a rectangle with a width of 20 yards and a length of 40 yards. She plans to fence it in, using fencing that costs $30 per meter. What will be the total cost of the fencing?

Convert each measurement to meters. Use 1 yard ≈ 0.914 meter.

Length: $\dfrac{1 \text{ yard}}{0.914 \text{ meter}} = \dfrac{40 \text{ yards}}{36.56 \text{ meters}}$ Width: $\dfrac{1 \text{ yard}}{0.914 \text{ meter}} = \dfrac{20 \text{ yards}}{18.28 \text{ meters}}$

Find the perimeter P: $P = 2\ell + 2w = 2(36.56) + 2(18.28) = 109.68$ meters

The total cost of the fencing is $30(109.68) = \$3,290.40$.

EXAMPLE 2

Donata had a 25-minute commute from home to work. Her company moved, and now her commute to work is 33 minutes long. Does this situation represent an increase or a decrease? Find the percent increase or decrease in her commute to work.

This situation represents an increase. Find the percent increase.

amount of change = greater value − lesser value

$33 - 25 = 8$

percent increase $= \dfrac{\text{amount of change}}{\text{original amount}}$

$\dfrac{8}{25} = 0.32 = 32\%$

Donata's commute increased by 32%.

© Houghton Mifflin Harcourt Publishing Company

142 Unit 2

EXERCISES

Convert each measurement. (Lesson 3.1)

1. 7 centimeters ≈ _____ inches

2. 10 pounds ≈ _____ kilograms

3. 24 kilometers ≈ _____ miles

4. 12 quarts ≈ _____ liters

5. Michelle purchased 25 audio files in January. In February she purchased 40 audio files. Find the percent increase.

(Lesson 3.2) _____

6. Sam's dog weighs 72 pounds. The vet suggests that for the dog's health, its weight should decrease by 12.5 percent. According to the vet, what is a healthy weight

for the dog? (Lesson 3.2) _____

7. The original price of a barbecue grill is $79.50. The grill is marked down 15%. What is the sale price of the grill?

(Lesson 3.3) _____

8. A sporting goods store marks up the cost *s* of soccer balls by 250%. Write an expression that represents the retail cost of the soccer balls. The store buys soccer balls for $5.00 each. What is the retail price of the soccer balls?

(Lesson 3.3) _____

MODULE **4** # Proportionality in Geometry

? ESSENTIAL QUESTION

How can you use proportionality in geometry to solve real-world problems?

Key Vocabulary

circumference
 (circunferencia)
corresponding angles
 (ángulos
 correspondientes)
corresponding sides (lados
 correspondientes)
diameter (diámetro)
indirect measurement
 (medición indirecta)
pi (pi)
radius (radio)
scale (escala)
scale drawing (dibujo a
 escala)
similar shapes (formas
 semejantes)

EXAMPLE 1

△*NOP* ~ △*QRS*. **Find the unknown measures.**

A. Find the unknown side *x*.

Write a proportion using corresponding sides *NO* and *QR*, *NP* and *QS*.

$\dfrac{NO}{QR} = \dfrac{NP}{QS}$ *Write a proportion using corresponding sides NO and QR, NP and QS.*

$\dfrac{4}{8} = \dfrac{x}{14}$ *Substitute the known lengths of the sides.*

$\dfrac{1}{2} = \dfrac{x}{14}$ *Simplify $\frac{4}{8}$ to find a factor of 14. 2 is a factor of 14.*

$\dfrac{1 \times 7}{2 \times 7} \dfrac{x}{14}$ *Since 2 × 7 = 14, multiply 1 by 7 to find the value of x.*

$x = 7$ cm

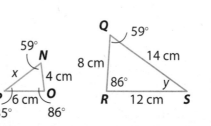

B. Find the unknown angle measure y.

$y = 35°$ ∠*S* and ∠*P* are corresponding angles.

EXAMPLE 2

Use the scale drawing to find the perimeter of Tim's yard.

$\dfrac{2 \text{ cm}}{14 \text{ ft}} = \dfrac{1 \text{ cm}}{7 \text{ ft}}$ 1 cm in the drawing equals 7 feet in the actual yard.

$\dfrac{1 \text{ cm} \times 15}{7 \text{ ft} \times 15} = \dfrac{15 \text{ cm}}{105 \text{ ft}}$ 15 cm in the drawing equals 105 feet in the actual yard. Tim's yard is 105 feet long.

$\dfrac{1 \text{ cm} \times 4}{7 \text{ ft} \times 4} = \dfrac{4 \text{ cm}}{28 \text{ ft}}$ 4 cm in the drawing equals 28 feet in the actual yard. Tim's yard is 28 feet wide.

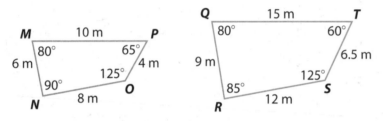

15 cm

4 cm

2 cm : 14 ft

Perimeter is twice the sum of the length and the width. So the perimeter of Tim's yard is 2(105 + 28) = 2(133), or 266 feet.

EXERCISES

1. Are the four-sided shapes similar? Explain. (Lesson 4.1)

_____

_____

_____

_____

_____

2. △*JNZ* ~ △*KOA*. Find the unknown measures. (Lesson 4.2)

$x =$ _____

$y =$ _____

$r =$ _____

$s =$ _____

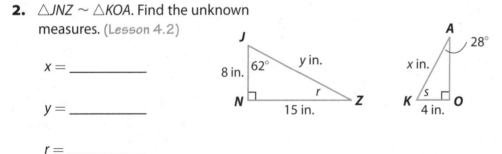

3. In the scale drawing of a park, the scale is 1 cm: 10 m. Find the area of the actual park.

(Lesson 4.3) _____

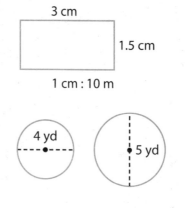

3 cm

1.5 cm

1 cm : 10 m

4. The circumference of the larger circle is 15.7 yards. Find the circumference of the smaller circle.

(Lesson 4.4) _____

4 yd

5 yd

Unit 2 Performance Tasks

1. **CAREERS IN MATH** Landscape Architect A landscape architect creates a scale drawing of her plans for a garden. She draws the plans on a sheet of paper that measures $8\frac{1}{2}$ inches by 11 inches. On the right-hand side of the paper, there is a column $2\frac{1}{2}$ inches wide that includes the company name and logo. The drawing itself is $5\frac{1}{2}$ inches by $7\frac{1}{2}$ inches. The scale of the drawing is 1 inch = 10 feet.

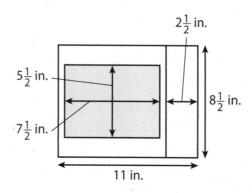

$2\frac{1}{2}$ in.

$5\frac{1}{2}$ in.

$7\frac{1}{2}$ in.

$8\frac{1}{2}$ in.

11 in.

a. The landscape architect wants to make a larger drawing on a sheet of paper that measures 11 inches by 17 inches. The larger drawing should include the same $2\frac{1}{2}$ inch column on the side. There should be at least $\frac{1}{2}$ inch of space on all sides of the drawing. What are the dimensions of the area she can use to make the new drawing?

_____

b. How large can she make the scale drawing without changing any of the proportions? Justify your reasoning.

_____

_____

_____

_____

_____

2. The table below shows how far several animals can travel at their maximum speeds in a given time.

Animal Distances		
Animal	**Distance traveled (ft)**	**Time (s)**
elk	33	$\frac{1}{2}$
giraffe	115	$2\frac{1}{2}$
zebra	117	2

a. Write each animal's speed as a unit rate in feet per second.

_____

_____

_____

b. Which animal has the fastest speed?

_____

c. How many miles could the fastest animal travel in 2 hours if it maintained the speed you calculated in part **a**? Use the formula $d = rt$ and round your answer to the nearest tenth of a mile. Show your work.

_____

_____

_____

d. The data in the table represents how fast each animal can travel at its maximum speed. Is it reasonable to expect the animal from part **b** to travel that distance in 2 hours? Explain why or why not.

_____

_____

_____

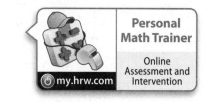
Selected Response

1. If the relationship between distance y in feet and time x in seconds is proportional, which rate is represented by $\frac{y}{x} = 0.6$?

ⓐ 3 feet in 5 s

ⓑ 3 feet in 9 s

ⓒ 10 feet in 6 s

ⓓ 18 feet in 3 s

2. The Baghrams make regular monthly deposits in a savings account. The graph shows the relationship between the number x of months and the amount y in dollars in the account.

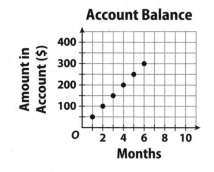

Account Balance

What is the equation for the deposit?

ⓐ $\frac{y}{x} = \$25/\text{month}$

ⓑ $\frac{y}{x} = \$40/\text{month}$

ⓒ $\frac{y}{x} = \$50/\text{month}$

ⓓ $\frac{y}{x} = \$75/\text{month}$

Hot Tip! Read graphs and diagrams carefully. Look at the labels for important information.

3. Rosa's room is 4 meters wide. Which of these is an equivalent measurement?

ⓐ 0.28 mile

ⓑ 4.38 yards

ⓒ 12.4 feet

ⓓ 136.2 inches

4. What is the decimal form of $-4\frac{7}{8}$?

ⓐ -4.9375

ⓑ -4.875

ⓒ -4.75

ⓓ -4.625

5. Find the percent change from 72 to 90.

ⓐ 20% decrease

ⓑ 20% increase

ⓒ 25% decrease

ⓓ 25% increase

6. A store had a sale on art supplies. The price p of each item was marked down 60%. Which expression represents the new price?

ⓐ $0.4p$ ⓒ $1.4p$

ⓑ $0.6p$ ⓓ $1.6p$

7. Clarke borrows $16,000 to buy a car. He pays simple interest at an annual rate of 6% over a period of 3.5 years. How much does he pay altogether?

ⓐ $18,800

ⓑ $19,360

ⓒ $19,920

ⓓ $20,480

8. To which set or sets does the number 37 belong?

(A) integers only

(B) rational numbers only

(C) integers and rational numbers only

(D) whole numbers, integers, and rational numbers

9. The two triangles below are similar. What is the missing length?

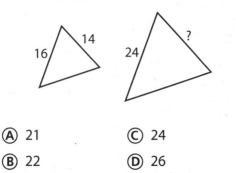

(A) 21

(C) 24

(B) 22

(D) 26

Gridded Response

10. The smaller circle has a diameter that is half the size of the larger circle. What is the missing circumference in centimeters?

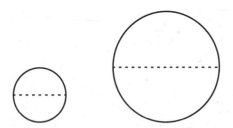

Circumference: ? Circumference: 53.38 cm

11. Jermaine paid $37.95 for 11 gallons of gasoline. What was the price in dollars per gallon?

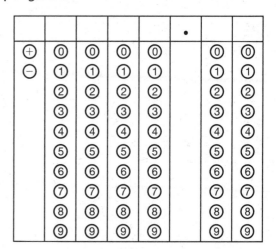

Pay attention to the units given in a test question, especially if there are mixed units, such as inches and feet.

12. Shown below is a scale drawing of a rectangular patio.

21 cm

12 cm

2 cm : 1 ft

What is the perimeter of the actual patio in feet?

Probability

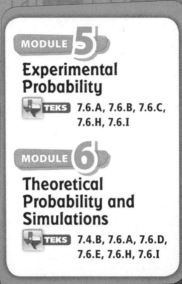

CAREERS IN MATH

Meteorologist Meteorologists use scientific principles to explain, understand, observe, and forecast atmospheric phenomena and how the atmosphere affects us. They use math in many ways, such as calculating wind velocities, computing the probabilities of weather conditions, and creating and using mathematical models to predict weather patterns. If you are interested in a career as a meteorologist, you should study these mathematical subjects:

- Algebra
- Geometry
- Trigonometry
- Calculus
- Probability and Statistics

Research other careers that require computing probabilities and using mathematical models.

Unit 3 Performance Task

At the end of the unit, check out how **meteorologists** use math.

© Houghton Mifflin Harcourt Publishing Company • Image Credits ©Imac/Alamy Images

Vocabulary Preview

Use the puzzle to preview key vocabulary from this unit. Unscramble the circled letters within found words to answer the riddle at the bottom of the page.

```
Y  R  F  S  P  D  A  U  L  B  S  T  Y  C  P
T  N  U  E  A  G  V  V  X  I  Y  R  C  A  R
N  N  B  A  H  M  C  P  M  F  U  I  Y  H  O
R  E  E  X  C  K  P  P  L  O  O  A  A  X  B
K  V  H  M  H  O  L  L  D  G  H  L  T  O  A
Q  L  R  B  I  E  W  V  E  Z  V  I  W  S  B
L  F  E  B  E  R  X  E  X  S  I  F  Y  I  I
Q  V  I  V  T  N  E  M  E  L  P  M  O  C  L
Q  O  E  S  H  J  R  P  S  R  K  A  L  E  I
A  N  H  C  J  D  D  O  X  H  P  F  C  X  T
T  P  Z  K  V  Z  V  F  N  E  P  F  U  E  Y
U  V  K  S  I  M  U  L  A  T  I  O  N  P  J
K  X  O  L  P  M  O  M  S  U  Z  J  W  A  P
R  O  C  P  T  U  N  D  N  V  E  R  T  U  A
U  W  O  G  L  B  U  H  K  E  S  F  A  P  B
```

- An activity based on chance in which results are observed. (Lesson 5-1)
- The set of all outcomes that are not included in the event. (Lesson 5-1)
- Each observation of an experiment. (Lesson 5-1)
- A model of an experiment that would be difficult or too time-consuming to perform. (Lesson 5-2)
- Measures the likelihood that the event will occur. (Lesson 5-1)
- An event with only one outcome (2 words). (Lesson 5-2)
- A set of all possible outcomes for an event (2 words). (Lesson 5-1)

Q: Why was there little chance of success for the clumsy thieves?

A: Because they had low ___ ___ ___ – ___ ___ ___ ___ ___ ___ ___!

Experimental Probability

? ESSENTIAL QUESTION

How can you use experimental probability to solve real-world problems?

Real-World Video

Meteorologists use sophisticated equipment to gather data about the weather. Then they use experimental probability to forecast, or predict, what the weather conditions will be.

my.hrw.com

GO DIGITAL
my.hrw.com

my.hrw.com

Go digital with your write-in student edition, accessible on any device.

Math On the Spot

Scan with your smart phone to jump directly to the online edition, video tutor, and more.

Animated Math

Interactively explore key concepts to see how math works.

Personal Math Trainer

Get immediate feedback and help as you work through practice sets.

Complete these exercises to review skills you will need for this chapter.

Personal Math Trainer

Online Assessment and Intervention

my.hrw.com

Simplify Fractions

EXAMPLE   Simplify $\frac{12}{21}$.

12: 1, 2, ③ 4, 6, 12   List all the factors of the numerator and denominator.
21: 1, ③ 7, 21   Circle the greatest common factor (GCF).

$\frac{12 \div 3}{21 \div 3} = \frac{4}{7}$ Divide the numerator and denominator by the GCF.

Write each fraction in simplest form.

1. $\frac{6}{10}$ _____

2. $\frac{9}{15}$ _____

3. $\frac{16}{24}$ _____

4. $\frac{9}{36}$ _____

5. $\frac{45}{54}$ _____

6. $\frac{30}{42}$ _____

7. $\frac{36}{60}$ _____

8. $\frac{14}{42}$ _____

Write Fractions as Decimals

EXAMPLE $\frac{13}{25} \rightarrow$

$$\begin{array}{r} 0.52 \\ 25\overline{)13.00} \\ -12.5 \\ \hline 50 \\ -50 \\ \hline 0 \end{array}$$

Write the fraction as a division problem.
Write a decimal point and a zero in the dividend.
Place a decimal point in the quotient.
Write more zeros in the dividend if necessary.

Write each fraction as a decimal.

9. $\frac{3}{4}$ _____

10. $\frac{7}{8}$ _____

11. $\frac{3}{20}$ _____

12. $\frac{19}{50}$ _____

Percents and Decimals

EXAMPLE $109\% = 100\% + 9\%$
$= \frac{100}{100} + \frac{9}{100}$
$= 1 + 0.09$
$= 1.09$

Write the percent as the sum of 1 whole and a percent remainder.
Write the percents as fractions.
Write the fractions as decimals.
Simplify.

Write each percent as a decimal.

13. 67% _____

14. 31% _____

15. 7% _____

16. 146% _____

Write each decimal as a percent.

17. 0.13 _____

18. 0.55 _____

19. 0.08 _____

20. 1.16 _____

Reading Start-Up

Visualize Vocabulary

Use the ✔ words to complete the graphic. You can put more than one word in each box.

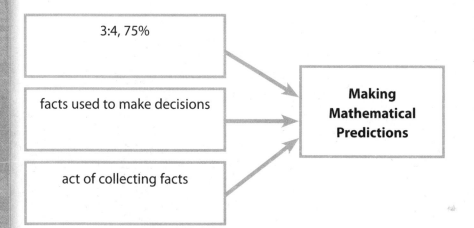

| 3:4, 75% |
| facts used to make decisions |
| act of collecting facts |

→ **Making Mathematical Predictions**

Understand Vocabulary

Match the term on the left to the definition on the right.

1. probability   **A.** Measures the likelihood that the event will occur.

2. trial   **B.** A set of one or more outcomes.

3. event   **C.** Each observation of an experiment.

© Houghton Mifflin Harcourt Publishing Company

Vocabulary

Review Words
✔ data (datos)
✔ observation (observación)
✔ percent (porcentaje)
✔ ratio (razón)

Preview Words
complement (complemento)
compound event (suceso compuesto)
event (suceso)
experiment (experimento)
experimental probability (probabilidad experimental)
outcome (resultado)
probability (probabilidad)
simple event (suceso simple)
simulation (simulación)
trial (prueba)

Active Reading

Pyramid Before beginning the module, create a rectangular pyramid to help you organize what you learn. Label each side with one of the lesson titles from this module. As you study each lesson, write important ideas, such as vocabulary, properties, and formulas, on the appropriate side.

MODULE 5

Unpacking the TEKS

Understanding the TEKS and the vocabulary terms in the TEKS will help you know exactly what you are expected to learn in this module.

TEKS 7.6.C

Make predictions and determine solutions using experimental data for simple and compound events.

Key Vocabulary

simple event *(suceso simple)*
An event consisting of only one outcome.

compound event *(suceso compuesto)*
An event made of two or more simple events.

experimental probability *(probabilidad experimental)*
The ratio of the number of times an event occurs to the total number of trials, or times that the activity is performed.

What It Means to You

You will use experimental probabilities to make predictions and solve problems.

UNPACKING EXAMPLE 7.6.C

Caitlyn finds that the experimental probability of her making a goal in hockey is 30%. Out of 500 attempts to make a goal, about how many could she predict she would make?

$$\frac{3}{10} \cdot 500 = x$$

$$150 = x$$

Caitlyn can predict that she will make about 150 of the 500 goals that she attempts.

TEKS 7.6.I

Determine experimental and theoretical probabilities related to simple and compound events using data and sample spaces.

Key Vocabulary

sample space *(espacio muestral)*
All possible outcomes of an experiment.

What It Means to You

You will use data to determine experimental probabilities.

UNPACKING EXAMPLE 7.6.I

Anders buys a novelty coin that is weighted more heavily on one side. He flips the coin 60 times and a head comes up 36 times. What is the experimental probability of flipping a head?

$$\text{experimental probability} = \frac{\text{number of times event occurs}}{\text{total number of trials}}$$

$$= \frac{36}{60} = \frac{3}{5}$$

The experimental probability of flipping a head is $\frac{3}{5}$.

Visit **my.hrw.com** to see all the **TEKS** unpacked.

⊕ my.hrw.com

© Houghton Mifflin Harcourt Publishing Company • Image Credits: ©Zuma Press, Inc/Alamy Images

5.1 Probability

TEKS
Proportionality—
7.6.E Find the probabilities of a simple event and its complement and describe the relationship between the two. *Also 7.6.A, 7.6.B, 7.6.I*

? **ESSENTIAL QUESTION**

How can you describe the likelihood of an event?

EXPLORE ACTIVITY **TEKS** 7.6.I

Finding the Likelihood of an Event

Each time you roll a number cube, a number from 1 to 6 lands face up. This is called an *event*.

Work with a partner to decide how many of the six possible results of rolling a number cube match the described event.

Then order the events from least likely (1) to most likely (9) by writing a number in each box to the right.

Rolling a number less than 7 _____ ⬜

Rolling an 8 _____ ⬜

Rolling a number greater than 4 _____ ⬜

Rolling a 5 _____ ⬜

Rolling a number other than 6 _____ ⬜

Rolling an even number _____ ⬜

Rolling a number less than 5 _____ ⬜

Rolling an odd number _____ ⬜

Rolling a number divisible by 3 _____ ⬜

Reflect

1. Are any of the events impossible? _____

_____

Describing Events

An **experiment** is an activity involving chance in which results are observed. Each observation of an experiment is a **trial**, and each result is an **outcome**. A set of one or more outcomes is an **event**.

The **probability** of an event, written *P*(event), measures the likelihood that the event will occur. Probability is a measure between 0 and 1 as shown on the number line, and can be written as a fraction, a decimal, or a percent.

If the event is not likely to occur, the probability of the event is close to 0. If an event is likely to occur, the event's probability is closer to 1.

Impossible	Unlikely	As likely as not	Likely	Certain

0		$\frac{1}{2}$		1
0		0.5		1.0
0%		50%		100%

EXAMPLE 1    🔲 **TEKS** 7.6.I

Tell whether each event is impossible, unlikely, as likely as not, likely, or certain. Then, tell whether the probability is 0, close to 0, $\frac{1}{2}$, close to 1, or 1.

A You roll a six-sided number cube and the number is 1 or greater.

> *Because you can roll the numbers 1, 2, 3, 4, 5, and 6 on a number cube, there are 6 possible outcomes.*

This event is certain to happen. Its probability is 1.

B You roll two number cubes and the sum of the numbers is 3.

This event is unlikely to happen. Its probability is close to 0.

C A bowl contains disks marked with the numbers 1 through 10. You close your eyes and select a disk at random. You pick an odd number.

This event is as likely as not. The probability is $\frac{1}{2}$.

D A spinner has 8 equal sections marked 0 through 7. You spin and land on a prime number.

This event is as likely as not. The probability is $\frac{1}{2}$.

> *Remember that a prime number is a whole number greater than 1 and has exactly 2 divisors, 1 and itself.*

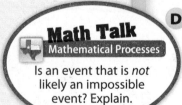

Math Talk
Mathematical Processes

Is an event that is *not* likely an impossible event? Explain.

Reflect

2. The probability of event *A* is $\frac{1}{3}$. The probability of event *B* is $\frac{1}{4}$. What can you conclude about the two events?

_____

_____

YOUR TURN

3. A hat contains pieces of paper marked with the numbers 1 through 16. Tell whether picking an even number is impossible, unlikely, as likely as not, likely, or certain. Tell whether the probability is 0, close to 0, $\frac{1}{2}$, close to 1, or 1.

_____

Finding Probability

The **sample space** is a set of all possible outcomes for an event. A sample space can be small, such as the 2 outcomes when a coin is flipped. Or a sample space can be large, such as the possible number of Texas Classic automobile license plates. Identifying the sample space can help you calculate the probability of an event.

Probability of An Event

$$P(\text{event}) = \frac{\text{number of times the event occurs}}{\text{total number of equally likely possible outcomes}}$$

EXAMPLE 2 *Real World*

TEKS 7.6.A

What is the probability of rolling an even number on a standard number cube?

STEP 1 Find the sample space for a standard number cube.

{1, 2, 3, 4, 5, 6}   *There are 6 possible outcomes.*

STEP 2 Find the number of ways to roll an even number.

2, 4, 6   *The event can occur 3 ways.*

STEP 3 Find the probability of rolling an even number.

$$P(\text{even}) = \frac{\text{number of ways to roll an even number}}{\text{number of faces on a number cube}}$$

$$= \frac{3}{6} = \frac{1}{2}$$ *Substitute values and Simplify.*

The probability of rolling an even number is $\frac{1}{2}$.

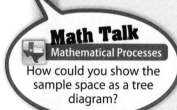

Math Talk

Mathematical Processes

How could you show the sample space as a tree diagram?

YOUR TURN

Find each probability. Write your answer in simplest form.

4. Picking a purple marble from a jar with 10 green and 10 purple marbles. _____

5. Rolling a number greater than 4 on a standard number cube.

_____

Using the Complement of an Event

The **complement** of an event is the set of all outcomes in the sample space that are *not* included in the event. For example, in the event of rolling a 3 on a number cube, the complement is rolling any number other than 3, which means the complement is rolling a 1, 2, 4, 5, or 6.

> **An Event and Its Complement**
>
> The sum of the probabilities of an event and its complement equals 1.
>
> $$P(\text{event}) + P(\text{complement}) = 1$$

You can apply probabilities to situations involving random selection, such as drawing a card out of a shuffled deck or pulling a marble out of a closed bag.

EXAMPLE 3 Real World   TEKS 7.6.E

There are 2 red jacks in a standard deck of 52 cards. What is the probability of not getting a red jack if you select one card at random?

$P(\text{event}) + P(\text{complement}) = 1$

$P(\text{red jack}) + P(\text{not a red jack}) = 1$ *The probability of getting a red jack is $\frac{2}{52}$.*

$\frac{2}{52} + P(\text{not a red jack}) = 1$ *Substitute $\frac{2}{52}$ for $P(\text{red jack})$.*

$\frac{2}{52} + P(\text{not a red jack}) = \frac{52}{52}$ *Write 1 as a fraction with denominator 52.*

$\underline{-\frac{2}{52}\qquad\qquad\qquad -\frac{2}{52}}$ *Subtract $\frac{2}{52}$ from both sides.*

$P(\text{not a red jack}) = \frac{50}{52}$ *Simplify.*

$P(\text{not a red jack}) = \frac{25}{26}$ *Simplify.*

The probability that you will not draw a red jack is $\frac{25}{26}$. It is likely that you will not select a red jack.

Reflect

6. Why do the probability of an event and the probability of its complement add up to 1?

_____

_____

_____

_____

_____

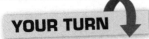 **YOUR TURN**

Personal Math Trainer

Online Assessment and Intervention

ⓞ my.hrw.com

7. A jar contains 8 marbles marked with the numbers 1 through 8. You pick a marble at random. What is the probability of not picking the marble marked with the number 5? _____

8. You roll a standard number cube. Use the probability of rolling an even number to find the probability of rolling an odd number. _____

Guided Practice

1. In a hat, you have index cards with the numbers 1 through 10 written on them. Order the events from least likely to happen (1) to most likely to happen (8) when you pick one card at random. In the boxes, write a number from 1 to 8 to order the eight different events. (Explore Activity)

You pick a number greater than 0. ▢

You pick an even number. ▢

You pick a number that is at least 2. ▢

You pick a number that is at most 0. ▢

You pick a number divisible by 3. ▢

You pick a number divisible by 5. ▢

You pick a prime number. ▢

You pick a number less than the greatest prime number. ▢

© Houghton Mifflin Harcourt Publishing Company

Determine whether each event is impossible, unlikely, as likely as not, likely, or certain. Then, tell whether the probability is 0, close to 0, $\frac{1}{2}$, close to 1, or 1. (Example 1)

2. randomly picking a green card from a standard deck of playing cards.

_____

3. randomly picking a red card from a standard deck of playing cards

_____

4. picking a number less than 15 from a jar with papers labeled from 1 to 12

_____

5. picking a number that is divisible by 5 from a jar with papers labeled from 1 to 12

_____

Find each probability. Write your answer in simplest form. (Example 2)

6. Spinning a spinner that has 5 equal sections marked 1 through 5 and landing on an even number. Use a tree diagram to find the sample space.

_____

7. Picking a diamond from a standard deck of playing cards which has 13 cards in each of four suits: spades, hearts, diamonds and clubs.

_____

Use the complement to find each probability. (Example 3)

8. What is the probability of not rolling a 5 on a standard number cube?

_____

9. A spinner has 3 equal sections that are red, white, and blue. What is the probability of not landing on blue?

_____

10. A spinner has 5 equal sections marked 1 through 5. What is the probability of not landing on 4?

_____

11. There are 4 queens in a standard deck of 52 cards. You pick one card at random. What is the probability of not picking a queen?

_____

? **ESSENTIAL QUESTION CHECK-IN**

12. Describe an event that has a probability of 0% and an event that has a probability of 100%.

_____

_____

_____

5.1 Independent Practice

TEKS 7.6.E, 7.6.A, 7.6.B, 7.6.I

Personal Math Trainer

Online Assessment and Intervention

my.hrw.com

13. There are 4 aces and 4 kings in a standard deck of 52 cards. You pick one card at random. What is the probability of selecting an ace or a king? Explain your reasoning.

_____

_____

14. There are 12 pieces of fruit in a bowl. Seven of the pieces are apples and two are peaches. What is the probability that a randomly selected piece of fruit will not be an apple or a peach? Justify your answer.

_____

_____

15. **Critique Reasoning** For breakfast, Clarissa can choose from oatmeal, cereal, French toast, or scrambled eggs. She thinks that if she selects a breakfast at random, it is likely that it will be oatmeal. Is she correct? Explain your reasoning. Use a tree diagram to determine your sample space.

_____

_____

_____

16. **Draw Conclusions** A researcher's garden contains 90 sweet pea plants, which have either white or purple flowers. About 70 of the plants have purple flowers, and about 20 have white flowers. Would you expect that one plant randomly selected from the garden will have purple or white flowers? Explain.

_____

_____

_____

17. The power goes out as Sandra is trying to get dressed. If she has 4 white T-shirts and 10 colored T-shirts in her drawer, is it likely that she will pick a colored T-shirt in the dark? What is the probability she will pick a colored T-shirt? Explain your answers.

_____

_____

18. James counts the hair colors of the 22 people in his class, including himself. He finds that there are 4 people with blonde hair, 8 people with brown hair, and 10 people with black hair. What is the probability that a randomly chosen student in the class does not have red hair? Explain.

_____

_____

19. Persevere in Problem Solving A bag contains 8 blue coins and 6 red coins. A coin is removed at random and replaced by three of the other color.

a. What is the probability that the removed coin is blue?

_____

b. If the coin removed is blue, what is the probability of drawing a red coin after three red coins are put in the bag to replace the blue one?

_____

c. If the coin removed is red, what is the probability of drawing a red coin after three blue coins are put in the bag to replace the red one?

_____

 **FOCUS ON HIGHER ORDER THINKING**

© Houghton Mifflin Harcourt Publishing Company

Work Area

20. Draw Conclusions Give an example of an event in which all of the outcomes are not equally likely. Explain.

_____

_____

_____

21. Critique Reasoning A box contains 150 black pens and 50 red pens. Jose said the sum of the probability that a randomly selected pen will not be black and the probability that the pen will not be red is 1. Explain whether you agree.

_____

_____

_____

22. Communicate Mathematical Ideas A spinner has 7 identical sections. Two sections are blue, 1 is red, and 4 of the sections are green. Suppose the probability of an event happening is $\frac{2}{7}$. What does each number in the ratio represent? What outcome matches this probability?

_____

_____

Experimental Probability of Simple Events

TEKS
Proportionality—
7.6.I Determine experimental and theoretical probabilities related to simple and compound events using data and sample spaces. *Also 7.6.A, 7.6.B, 7.6.C*

? ESSENTIAL QUESTION

How do you find the experimental probability of a simple event?

EXPLORE ACTIVITY **TEKS** 7.6.I

Finding Experimental Probability

You can toss a paper cup to demonstrate *experimental probability*.

A Consider tossing a paper cup. Fill in the Outcome column of the table with the three different ways the cup could land.

B Toss a paper cup twenty times. Record your observations in the table.

Outcome	Number of Times

Reflect

1. Which outcome do you think is most likely?

_____

2. Describe the three outcomes using the words *likely* and *unlikely*.

_____

_____

3. Use the number of times each event occurred to calculate the probability of each event.

4. What do you think would happen if you performed more trials?

_____

_____

_____

5. What is the sum of the three probabilities in the table?

_____

Outcome	Experimental Probability
Open-end up	$\dfrac{\text{open-end up}}{20} = \dfrac{\boxed{}}{20}$
Open-end down	$\dfrac{\text{open-end down}}{20} = \dfrac{\boxed{}}{20}$
On its side	$\dfrac{\text{on its side}}{20} = \dfrac{\boxed{}}{20}$

Calculating Experimental Probability

You can use *experimental probability* to estimate the probability of an event. The **experimental probability** of an event is found by comparing the number of times the event occurs to the total number of trials. When there is only one outcome for an event, it is called a **simple event**.

Experimental Probability

$$\text{experimental probability} = \frac{\text{number of times the event occurs}}{\text{total number of trials}}$$

EXAMPLE 1   Real World   TEKS 7.6.I

Martin has a bag of marbles. He removed one marble, recorded the color and then placed it back in the bag. He repeated this process several times and recorded his results in the table. Find the probability of drawing each color. Write your answers in simplest form.

Color	Frequency
Red	12
Blue	10
Green	15
Yellow	13

A   Number of trials = 50

B   Complete the table of experimental probabilities. Write each answer as a fraction in simplest form.

> Substitute the results recorded in the table.

Color	Experimental Probability
Red	$\dfrac{\text{frequency of the event}}{\text{total number of trials}} = \dfrac{12}{50} = \dfrac{6}{25}$
Blue	$\dfrac{\text{frequency of the event}}{\text{total number of trials}} = \dfrac{10}{50} = \dfrac{1}{5}$
Green	$\dfrac{\text{frequency of the event}}{\text{total number of trials}} = \dfrac{15}{50} = \dfrac{3}{10}$
Yellow	$\dfrac{\text{frequency of the event}}{\text{total number of trials}} = \dfrac{13}{50}$

Reflect

6. What are two different ways you could find the experimental probability of the event that you do not draw a red marble?

_____

_____

_____

_____

© Houghton Mifflin Harcourt Publishing Company

7. A spinner has three unequal sections: red, yellow, and blue. The table shows the results of Nolan's spins. Find the experimental probability of landing on each color. Write your answers in simplest form.

Color	Frequency
Red	10
Yellow	14
Blue	6

Math Talk
Mathematical Processes
Will everyone who does this experiment get the same results?

Making Predictions with Experimental Probability

A **simulation** is a model of an experiment that would be difficult or inconvenient to actually perform. You can use a simulation to find an experimental probability and make a prediction.

Math On the Spot
my.hrw.com

EXAMPLE 2   Real World

TEKS 7.6.B

My Notes

A baseball team has a batting average of 0.250 so far this season. This means that the team's players get hits in 25% of their chances at bat. Use a simulation to predict the number of hits the team's players will have in their next 34 chances at bat.

STEP 1 Choose a model.

Batting average $= 0.250 = \frac{250}{1,000} = \frac{1}{4}$

A standard deck of cards has four suits, hearts, diamonds, spades, and clubs. Since $\frac{1}{4}$ of the cards are hearts, you can let hearts represent a "hit." Diamonds, clubs, and spades then represent "no hit."

STEP 2 Perform the simulation.

Draw a card from the deck, record the result, and put the card back into the deck. Continue until you have drawn and replaced 34 cards in all.

Since the team has 34 chances at bat, you must draw a card 34 times.

(H = heart, D = diamond, C = club, S = spade)

H D D S H C H S D H C D C C D H H
S D D H C C H C H H D S S S C H D

STEP 3 Make a prediction.

Count the number of hearts in the simulation.

Since there are 11 hearts, you can predict that the team will have 11 hits in its next 34 chances at bat.

© Houghton Mifflin Harcourt Publishing Company

YOUR TURN

8. A toy machine has equal numbers of red, white, and blue rubber balls. Ross wonders which color ball will come out of the machine next. Describe how you can use a standard number cube to model this situation. Then use a simulation to predict the color of the next ball.

_____

_____

_____

Guided Practice

1. Toss a coin at least 20 times. (Explore Activity and Example 1)

   a. Record the results in the table.

   b. What do you think would happen if you performed more trials?

   _____

   _____

Outcome	Number of Times	Experimental Probability
Heads		
Tails		

2. Rachel's free-throw average for basketball is 60%. Describe how you can use 10 index cards to model this situation. Then use a simulation to predict how many times in the next 50 tries Rachel will make a free throw. (Example 2)

   _____

   _____

   _____

❓ ESSENTIAL QUESTION CHECK-IN

3. **Essential Question Follow Up** How do you find the experimental probability of a simple event?

   _____

   _____

   _____

5.2 Independent Practice

TEKS 7.6.I, 7.6.A, 7.6.B, 7.6.C

Personal Math Trainer

Online Assessment and Intervention

my.hrw.com

4. Dree rolls a strike in 6 out of the 10 frames of bowling. What is the experimental probability that Dree will roll a strike in the first frame of the next game? Explain why a number cube would not be a good way to simulate this situation.

_____

_____

5. To play a game, you spin a spinner like the one shown. You win if the arrow lands in one of the areas marked "WIN". Lee played this game many times and recorded her results. She won 8 times and lost 40 times. Use Lee's data to explain how to find the experimental probability of winning this game.

_____

_____

6. Critique Reasoning A meteorologist reports an 80% chance of precipitation. Is this an example of experimental probability, written as a percent? Explain your reasoning.

_____

7. The names of the students in Mr. Hayes' math class are written on the board. Mr. Hayes writes each name on an index card and shuffles the cards. Each day he randomly draws a card, and the chosen student explains a math problem at the board. What is the probability that Ryan is chosen today? What is the probability that Ryan is not chosen today?

Anna	Alisha	Kenna	Bridget
Meghan	Cody	Parker	Grace
Michael	Gabe	Taylor	Joel
Kate	Kaylee	Shaw	Tessa
Jon	Ryan	Morgan	Leo

_____

8. Mica and Joan are on the same softball team. Mica got 8 hits out of 48 times at bat, while Joan got 12 hits out of 40 times at bat. Who do you think is more likely to get a hit her next time at bat? Explain.

_____

_____

9. Make a Prediction In tennis, Gabby serves an ace, a ball that can't be returned, 4 out of the 10 times she serves. What is the experimental probability that Gabby will serve an ace on the first serve of the next game? Make a prediction about how many aces Gabby will make on her next 40 serves. Justify your reasoning.

_____

Work Area

10. Represent Real-World Problems Patricia finds that the experimental probability of her dog wanting to go outside between 4 p.m. and 5 p.m. is $\frac{7}{12}$. About what percent of the time does her dog not want to go out between 4 p.m. and 5 p.m.?

_____

_____

11. Critique Reasoning Talia tossed a penny many times; she got 40 heads and 60 tails. She said the experimental probability of getting heads was $\frac{40}{60}$. Explain the error and correct the experimental probability.

_____

_____

12. Communicate Mathematical Ideas A high school has 438 students, with about the same number of males as females. Describe a simulation to predict how many of the first 50 students who leave school at the end of the day are female.

_____

_____

_____

13. Critical Thinking For a scavenger hunt, Chessa put one coin in each of 10 small boxes. Four coins are quarters, 4 are dimes, and 2 are nickels. How could you simulate choosing one box at random? What problem would there be if you planned to put these coins in your pocket and pick one?

_____

_____

_____

_____

Experimental Probability of Compound Events

TEKS
Proportionality—
7.6.B Select and use different simulations to represent ... compound events without technology.
Also 7.6.A, 7.6.C, 7.6.I

? ESSENTIAL QUESTION

How do you find the experimental probability of a compound event?

EXPLORE ACTIVITY  **TEKS** 7.6.I

Exploring Compound Probability

A **compound event** is an event that includes two or more simple events, such as flipping a coin *and* rolling a number cube. A compound event can include events that depend on each other or are independent. Events are independent if the occurrence of one event does not affect the probability of the other event, such as flipping a coin and rolling a number cube.

A What are the possible outcomes of flipping a coin once? _____

B What are the possible outcomes of rolling a standard number cube once? _____

C Complete the list for all possible outcomes for flipping a coin *and* rolling a number cube.

H1, H2, _____, _____, _____, _____, T1, _____, _____, _____, _____, _____

There are _____ possible outcomes for this compound event.

D Flip a coin and roll a number cube 50 times. Use tally marks to record your results in the table.

> H1 would mean the coin landed on heads, and the number cube showed a 1.

	1	2	3	4	5	6
H						
T						

E Based on your data, which compound event had the greatest experimental probability and what was it? The least experimental

probability? _____

F **Draw Conclusions** Did you expect to have the same probability for each possible combination of flips and rolls? Why or why not?

_____

_____

Calculating Experimental Probability of Compound Events

The experimental probability of a compound event can be found using recorded data.

EXAMPLE 1 Real World

TEKS 7.6.A

A food trailer serves chicken and records the order size and sides on their orders, as shown in the table. What is the experimental probability that the next order is for 3 pieces with cole slaw?

	Green Salad	Macaroni & Cheese	French Fries	Cole Slaw
2 pieces	33	22	52	35
3 pieces	13	55	65	55

STEP 1 Find the total number of trials, or orders.

$$33 + 22 + 52 + 35 + 13 + 55 + 65 + 55 = 330$$

STEP 2 Find the number of orders that are for 3 pieces with cole slaw: 55.

STEP 3 Find the experimental probability.

$$P(3 \text{ piece} + \text{slaw}) = \frac{\text{number of 3 piece} + \text{slaw}}{\text{total number of orders}}$$

$$= \frac{55}{330} \quad \text{Substitute the values.}$$

$$= \frac{1}{6} \quad \text{Simplify.}$$

The experimental probability that the next order is for 3 pieces of chicken with cole slaw is $\frac{1}{6}$.

Math Talk
Mathematical Processes

Javier said the total number of orders is 8 and not 330. Is he correct? Explain.

YOUR TURN

Personal Math Trainer

Online Assessment and Intervention

my.hrw.com

1. Drink sales for an afternoon at the school carnival were recorded in the table. What is the experimental probability that the next drink is a small coffee?

	Soda	Water	Coffee
Small	77	98	60
Large	68	45	52

_____

Using a Simulation to Make a Prediction

You can use a simulation or model of an experiment to find the experimental probability of compound events.

EXAMPLE 2 Real World   TEKS 7.6.B

At a street intersection, a vehicle is classified either as a *car* or a *truck*, and it can turn *left*, *right*, or go *straight*. About an equal number of cars and trucks go through the intersection and turn in each direction. Use a simulation to find the experimental probability that the next vehicle will be a car that turns right.

My Notes

STEP 1 Choose a model.
Use a coin toss to model the two vehicle types.
Let Heads = **C**ar and Tails = **T**ruck

Use a spinner divided into 3 equal sectors to represent the *three* directions as shown.

(spinner shows: Left, Right, Straight)

STEP 2 Find the sample space for the compound event.

There are 6 possible outcomes: **C**L, **C**R, **C**S, **T**L, **T**R, **T**S

STEP 3 Perform the simulation.

A coin was tossed and a spinner spun 50 times. The results are shown in the table.

	Car	Truck
Left	8	9
Right	6	11
Straight	9	7

STEP 4 Find the experimental probability that a car turns right.

$$P(\text{Car turns right}) = \frac{\text{frequency of compound event}}{\text{total number of trials}}$$

$$= \frac{6}{50} \qquad \text{Substitute the values.}$$

$$= \frac{3}{25} \qquad \text{Simplify.}$$

Based on the simulation, the experimental probability is $\frac{3}{25}$ that the next vehicle will be a car that turns right.

Reflect

2. **Make a Prediction** Predict the number of cars that turn right out of 100 vehicles that enter the intersection. Explain your reasoning.

_____

_____

YOUR TURN

3. A jeweler sells necklaces made in three sizes and two different metals. Use the data from a simulation to find the experimental probability that the next necklace sold is a 20-inch gold necklace.

	Silver	Gold
12 in.	12	22
16 in.	16	8
20 in.	5	12

_____

Guided Practice

1. A dentist has 400 male and female patients that range in ages from 10 years old to 50 years old and up as shown in the table. What is the experimental probability that the next patient will be female and in the age range 22–39? (Explore Activity and Example 1)

	Range: 10–21	Range: 22–39	Range: 40–50	Range: 50+
Male	44	66	32	53
Female	36	50	45	74

_____

2. At a car wash, customers can choose the type of wash and whether to use the interior vacuum. Customers are equally likely to choose each type of wash and whether to use the vacuum. Use a simulation to find the experimental probability that the next customer purchases a deluxe wash and no interior vacuum. Describe your simulation. (Example 2)

_____

_____

_____

❓ ESSENTIAL QUESTION CHECK-IN

3. How do you find the experimental probability of a compound event?

_____

_____

5.3 Independent Practice

TEKS 7.6.B, 7.6.A, 7.6.C, 7.6.I

Personal Math Trainer

Online Assessment and Intervention

my.hrw.com

4. Represent Real-World Problems For the same food trailer mentioned in Example 1, explain how to find the experimental probability that the next order is two pieces of chicken with a green salad.

_____

_____

The school store sells spiral notebooks in four colors and three different sizes. The table shows the sales by size and color for 400 notebooks.

	Red	Green	Blue	Yellow
100 Pages	55	37	26	12
150 Pages	60	44	57	27
200 Pages	23	19	21	19

5. What is the experimental probability that the next customer buys a red notebook with 150 pages?

_____

6. What is the experimental probability that the next customer buys any red notebook?

_____

7. Analyze Relationships How many possible combined page count and color choices are possible? How does this number relate to the number of page size choices and to the number of color choices?

_____

_____

A middle school English teacher polled random students about how many pages of a book they read per week.

	6th	7th	8th
75 Pages	24	18	22
100 Pages	22	32	24
150 Pages	30	53	25

8. Critique Reasoning Jennie says the experimental probability that a 7th grade student reads at least 100 pages per week is $\frac{16}{125}$. What is her error and the correct experimental probability?

_____

9. Analyze Relationships Based on the data, which group(s) of students should be encouraged to read more? Explain your reasoning.

_____

_____

© Houghton Mifflin Harcourt Publishing Company

Work Area

10. Make a Conjecture Would you expect the probability for the simple event "rolling a 6" to be greater than or less than the probability of the compound event "rolling a 6 and getting heads on a coin"? Explain.

_____

_____

11. Critique Reasoning Donald says he uses a standard number cube for simulations that involve 2, 3, or 6 equal outcomes. Explain how Donald can do this.

_____

_____

_____

12. Draw Conclusions Data collected in a mall recorded the shoe styles worn by 150 male and 150 female customers. What is the probability that the next customer is male and has an open-toe shoe (such as a sandal)? What is the probability that the next male customer has an open-toe shoe? Are the two probabilities the same? Explain.

	Male	**Female**
Open toe	11	92
Closed toe	139	58

_____

_____

_____

13. What If? Suppose you wanted to perform a simulation to model the shoe style data shown in the table. Could you use two coins? Explain.

_____

_____

14. Represent Real-World Problems A middle school is made up of grades 6, 7, and 8, and has about the same number of male and female students in each grade. Explain how to use a simulation to find the experimental probability that the first 50 students who arrive at school are male and 7th graders.

_____

_____

_____

_____

Making Predictions with Experimental Probability

TEKS
Proportionality—
7.6.C Make predictions and determine solutions using experimental data for simple and compound events. *Also* 7.6.H, 7.6.I

? **ESSENTIAL QUESTION**

How do you make predictions using experimental probability?

Using Experimental Probability to Make a Prediction

Scientists study data to make predictions. You can use probabilities to make predictions in your daily life.

Math On the Spot
my.hrw.com

EXAMPLE 1 Real World   TEKS 7.6.C

Danae found that the experimental probability of her making a bull's-eye when throwing darts is $\frac{2}{10}$, or 20%. Out of 75 throws, about how many bull's-eyes could she predict she would make?

Method 1: Use a proportion.

$$\frac{2}{10} = \frac{x}{75}$$
Write a proportion. 2 out of 10 is how many out of 75?

$$\frac{2}{10} = \frac{x}{75}$$
$\times 7.5$

$$\frac{2}{10} = \frac{15}{75}$$
$\times 7.5$

Since 10 times 7.5 is 75, multiply 2 times 7.5 to find the value of x.

$$x = 15$$

Method 2: Use a percent equation.

$$0.20 \cdot 75 = x$$ Find 20% of 75.

$$15 = x$$

You can write probabilities as ratios, decimals, or percents.

Danae can predict that she will make about 15 bull's-eye throws out of 75.

YOUR TURN

1. A car rental company sells accident insurance to 24% of its customers. Out of 550 customers, about how many customers are predicted to

purchase insurance? _____

Personal Math Trainer

Online Assessment and Intervention
my.hrw.com

Using Experimental Probability to Make a Qualitative Prediction

A prediction is something you reasonably expect to happen in the future. A qualitative prediction helps you decide which situation is more likely in general.

EXAMPLE 2 🌐 Real World   ▣ TEKS 7.6.H

A doctor's office records data and concludes that, on average, 11% of patients call to reschedule their appointments per week. The office manager predicts that 23 appointments will be rescheduled out of the 240 total appointments during next week. Explain whether the prediction is reasonable.

Method 1: Use a proportion.

$$\frac{11}{100} = \frac{x}{240}$$

Write a proportion. 11 out of 100 is how many out of 240?

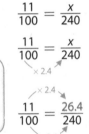

$$\frac{11}{100} = \frac{x}{240}$$

> 26.4 is the average number of patients that would call to reschedule.

$$\frac{11}{100} = \frac{26.4}{240}$$

Since 100 times 2.4 is 240, multiply 11 times 2.4 to find the value of x.

$$x = 26.4$$

Method 2: Use a percent equation.

$$0.11 \cdot 240 = x$$ Find 11% of 240.

$$26.4 = x$$ Solve for x.

The prediction of 23 is reasonable but a little low, because 23 is a little less than 26.4.

Reflect

2. Does 26.4 make sense for the number of patients? Explain.

_____

_____

YOUR TURN ⤵

3. In emails to monthly readers of a newsletter 3% of the emails come back undelivered. The editor predicts that if he sends out 12,372 emails, he will receive 437 notices for undelivered email. Do you agree with his prediction?

Explain. _____

_____

Making a Quantitative Prediction

You can use proportional reasoning to make quantitative predictions and compare options in real-world situations.

EXAMPLE 3 · Problem Solving

TEKS 7.6.H

An online poll for a movie site shows its polling results for a new movie. If a newspaper surveys 150 people leaving the movie, how many people can it predict will like the movie based on the online poll? Is the movie site's claim accurate if the newspaper finds that 104 people say they like the movie?

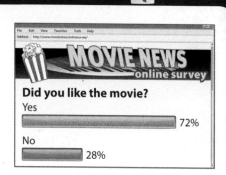

MOVIE NEWS
online survey

Did you like the movie?

Yes — 72%

No — 28%

Analyze Information

The **answer** is a prediction of how many people out of 150 will like the movie based on the online poll. Also tell whether the 104 people that say they like the movie is enough to support the movie site's claim.

List the important information:

- The online poll says 72% of movie goers like the new movie.
- A newspaper surveys 150 people.

Formulate a Plan

Use a proportion to calculate 72% of the 150 people surveyed.

Solve

$$\frac{72}{100} = \frac{x}{150}$$

Set up a proportion. 72 out of 100 is how many out of 150?

$$\frac{72}{100} = \frac{x}{150}$$
$\times 1.5$

$$\frac{72}{100} = \frac{108}{150}$$
$\times 1.5$

Since 100 times 1.5 is 150, multiply 72 times 1.5 to find the value of x.

$$x = 108$$

The newspaper can predict that 108 out of 150 people will say they like the movie, based on the online poll.

Justify and Evaluate

Since 108 is close to 104, the newspaper survey and the online poll show that about the same percent of people like the movie.

My Notes

Math On the Spot

my.hrw.com

© Houghton Mifflin Harcourt Publishing Company

YOUR TURN

4. On average, 24% of customers who buy shoes in a particular store buy two or more pairs. One weekend, 350 customers purchased shoes. How many can be predicted to buy two or more pairs? If 107 customers buy more than two pairs, did more customers than normal buy two or more pairs?

_____

_____

Guided Practice

1. A baseball player reaches first base 30% of the times he is at bat. Out of 50 times at bat, about how many times will the player reach first base? (Example 1)

_____

2. The experimental probability that it will rain on any given day in Houston, Texas, is about 15%. Out of 365 days, about how many days can residents predict rain? (Example 1)

_____

3. A catalog store has 6% of its orders returned for a refund. The owner predicts that a new candle will have 812 returns out of the 16,824 sold. Do you agree with this prediction? Explain. (Example 2)

_____

_____

4. On a toy assembly line, 3% of the toys are found to be defective. The quality control officer predicts that 872 toys will be found defective out of 24,850 toys made. Do you agree with this prediction? Explain. (Example 2)

_____

_____

5. A light-rail service claims to be on time 98% of the time. If Jeanette takes the light-rail 40 times one month, how many times can she predict she will be on time? Is the light-rail's claim accurate if she is late 6 times? (Example 3)

_____

_____

6. On average, a college claims to accept 18% of its applicants. If the college has 5,000 applicants, predict how many will be accepted. If 885 applicants are accepted, is the college's claim accurate? (Example 3)

_____

_____

? ESSENTIAL QUESTION CHECK-IN

7. How do you make predictions using experimental probability?

_____

_____

_____

5.4 Independent Practice

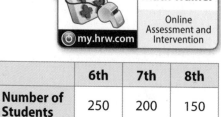

Personal Math Trainer

Online Assessment and Intervention

my.hrw.com

TEKS 7.6.C, 7.6.H, 7.6.I

The table shows the number of students in a middle school at the beginning of the year and the percentage that can be expected to move out of the area by the end of the year.

	6th	7th	8th
Number of Students	250	200	150
% Moves	2%	4%	8%

8. How many 7th grade students are expected to move by the end of the year? If 12 students actually moved, did more or fewer 7th grade students move than expected? Justify your answer.

_____

_____

9. **Critique Reasoning** The middle school will lose some of its funding if 50 or more students move away in any year. The principal claims he only loses about 30 students a year. Do the values in the table support his claim? Explain.

_____

_____

10. **Represent Real-World Problems** An airline knows that, on average, the probability that a passenger will not show up for a flight is 6%. If an airplane is fully booked and holds 300 passengers, how many seats are expected to be empty? If the airline overbooked the flight by 10 passengers, about how many passengers are expected to show up for the flight? Justify your answer.

_____

_____

_____

_____

11. **Draw Conclusions** In a doctor's office, an average of 94% of the clients pay on the day of the appointment. If the office has 600 clients per month, how many are expected not to pay on the day of the appointment? If 40 clients do not pay on the day of their appointment in a month, did more or fewer than the average not pay?

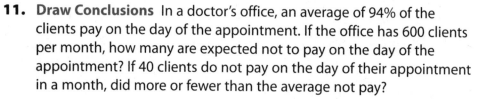

_____

12. Counterexamples The soccer coach claimed that, on average, only 80% of the team comes to practice each day. The table shows the number of students that came to practice for 8 days. If the team has 20 members, how many team members should come to practice to uphold the coach's claim? Was the coach's claim accurate? Explain your reasoning.

	1	2	3	4	5	6	7	8
Number of Students	18	15	18	17	17	19	20	20

_____

_____

13. What's the Error? Ronnie misses the school bus 1 out of every 30 school days. He sets up the proportion $\frac{1}{30} = \frac{180}{x}$ to predict how many days he will miss the bus in the 180-day school year. What is Ronnie's error?

_____

 FOCUS ON HIGHER ORDER THINKING

Work Area

14. Persevere in Problem Solving A gas pump machine rejects 12% of credit card transactions. If this is twice the normal rejection rate for a normal gas pump, how many out of 500 credit card transactions would a

normal gas pump machine reject? _____

15. Make Predictions An airline's weekly flight data showed a 98% probability of being on time. If this airline has 15,000 flights in a year, how many flights would you predict to arrive on time? Explain whether you can use the data to predict whether a specific flight with this airline will be on time.

_____

_____

_____

16. Draw Conclusions An average response rate for a marketing letter is 4%, meaning that 4% of the people who receive the letter respond to it. A company writes a new type of marketing letter, sends out 2,400 of them, and gets 65 responses. Explain whether the new type of letter would be considered to be a success.

_____

_____

_____

Ready to Go On?

Personal
Math Trainer

Online Assessment
and Intervention

my.hrw.com

5.1 Probability

1. Josue tosses a coin and spins the spinner at the right. What are all the possible outcomes? _____

5.2 Experimental Probability of Simple Events

2. While bowling with friends, Brandy rolls a strike in 6 out of 10 frames. What is the experimental probability that Brandy will roll a strike in the first frame of the next game? _____

3. Ben is greeting customers at a music store. Of the first 20 people he sees enter the store, 13 are wearing jackets and 7 are not. What is the experimental probability that the next person to enter the store will be wearing a jacket? _____

5.3 Experimental Probability of Compound Events

4. Auden rolled two number cubes and recorded the results.

Roll #1	Roll #2	Roll #3	Roll #4	Roll #5	Roll #6	Roll #7
2, 1	4, 5	3, 2	2, 2	1, 3	6, 2	5, 3

What is the experimental probability that the sum of the next two numbers rolled is more than 5? _____

5.4 Making Predictions with Experimental Probability

5. A player on a school baseball team reaches first base $\frac{3}{10}$ of the time he is at bat. Out of 80 times at bat, about how many times would you predict he will reach first base? _____

? ESSENTIAL QUESTION

6. How is experimental probability used to make predictions?

_____

_____

_____

Selected Response

1. A frozen yogurt shop offers scoops in cake cones, waffle cones, or cups. You can get vanilla, chocolate, strawberry, pistachio, or coffee flavored frozen yogurt. If you order a single scoop, how many outcomes are in the sample space?

(A) 3   (C) 8

(B) 5   (D) 15

2. A bag contains 7 purple beads, 4 blue beads, and 4 pink beads. What is the probability of **not** drawing a pink bead?

(A) $\frac{4}{15}$ (C) $\frac{8}{15}$

(B) $\frac{7}{15}$ (D) $\frac{11}{15}$

3. During the month of June, Ava kept track of the number of days she saw birds in her garden. She saw birds on 18 days of the month. What is the experimental probability that she will see birds in her garden on July 1?

(A) $\frac{1}{18}$ (C) $\frac{1}{2}$

(B) $\frac{2}{5}$ (D) $\frac{3}{5}$

4. A rectangle has a width of 4 inches and a length of 6 inches. A similar rectangle has a width of 12 inches. What is the length of the similar rectangle?

(A) 8 inches   (C) 14 inches

(B) 12 inches   (D) 18 inches

5. The experimental probability of hearing thunder on any given day in Ohio is 30%. Out of 600 days, on about how many days can Ohioans expect to hear thunder?

(A) 90 days   (C) 210 days

(B) 180 days   (D) 420 days

6. Isidro tossed two coins several times and then recorded the results in the table below.

Toss 1	Toss 2	Toss 3	Toss 4	Toss 5
H; T	T; T	T; H	H; T	H; H

What is the experimental probability that both coins will land on the same side on Isidro's next toss?

(A) $\frac{1}{5}$ (C) $\frac{3}{5}$

(B) $\frac{2}{5}$ (D) $\frac{4}{5}$

Gridded Response

7. Magdalena had a spinner that was evenly divided into sections of red, blue, and green. She spun the spinner and tossed a coin several times. The table below shows the results.

Trial 1	Trial 2	Trial 3	Trial 4	Trial 5
blue; T	green; T	green; H	red; T	blue; H

Given the results, what is the experimental probability of spinning blue? Write an answer as a decimal.

<table>
<tr><td>⊕</td><td>⓪</td><td>⓪</td><td>⓪</td><td>⓪</td><td>•</td><td>⓪</td><td>⓪</td></tr>
<tr><td>⊖</td><td>①</td><td>①</td><td>①</td><td>①</td><td></td><td>①</td><td>①</td></tr>
<tr><td></td><td>②</td><td>②</td><td>②</td><td>②</td><td></td><td>②</td><td>②</td></tr>
<tr><td></td><td>③</td><td>③</td><td>③</td><td>③</td><td></td><td>③</td><td>③</td></tr>
<tr><td></td><td>④</td><td>④</td><td>④</td><td>④</td><td></td><td>④</td><td>④</td></tr>
<tr><td></td><td>⑤</td><td>⑤</td><td>⑤</td><td>⑤</td><td></td><td>⑤</td><td>⑤</td></tr>
<tr><td></td><td>⑥</td><td>⑥</td><td>⑥</td><td>⑥</td><td></td><td>⑥</td><td>⑥</td></tr>
<tr><td></td><td>⑦</td><td>⑦</td><td>⑦</td><td>⑦</td><td></td><td>⑦</td><td>⑦</td></tr>
<tr><td></td><td>⑧</td><td>⑧</td><td>⑧</td><td>⑧</td><td></td><td>⑧</td><td>⑧</td></tr>
<tr><td></td><td>⑨</td><td>⑨</td><td>⑨</td><td>⑨</td><td></td><td>⑨</td><td>⑨</td></tr>
</table>

Theoretical Probability and Simulations

ESSENTIAL QUESTION

How can you use theoretical probability to solve real-world problems?

Real-World Video

Many carnival games rely on theoretical probability to set the chance of winning fairly low. Understanding how the game is set up might help you be more likely to win.

my.hrw.com

GO DIGITAL
my.hrw.com

my.hrw.com
Go digital with your write-in student edition, accessible on any device.

Math On the Spot
Scan with your smart phone to jump directly to the online edition, video tutor, and more.

Animated Math
Interactively explore key concepts to see how math works.

Personal Math Trainer
Get immediate feedback and help as you work through practice sets.

Are YOU Ready?

Complete these exercises to review skills you will need for this chapter.

Fractions, Decimals, and Percents

EXAMPLE Write $\frac{3}{8}$ as a decimal and a percent.

$$\begin{array}{r} 0.375 \\ 8)\overline{3.000} \\ -2\,4 \\ \hline 60 \\ -56 \\ \hline 40 \\ -40 \\ \hline 0 \end{array}$$

$0.375 = 37.5\%$.

Write the fraction as a division problem.
Write a decimal point and zeros in the dividend.
Place a decimal point in the quotient.
Divide as with whole numbers.

Write the decimal as a percent.

Write each fraction as a decimal and a percent.

1. $\frac{3}{4}$ _____   **2.** $\frac{2}{5}$ _____   **3.** $\frac{9}{10}$ _____   **4.** $\frac{7}{20}$ _____

5. $\frac{7}{8}$ _____   **6.** $\frac{1}{20}$ _____   **7.** $\frac{19}{25}$ _____   **8.** $\frac{23}{50}$ _____

Operations with Fractions

EXAMPLE

$$1 - \frac{7}{12} = \frac{12}{12} - \frac{7}{12}$$

$$= \frac{12 - 7}{12}$$

$$= \frac{5}{12}$$

Use the denominator of the fraction to write 1 as a fraction.
Subtract the numerators.

Simplify.

Find each difference.

9. $1 - \frac{1}{5}$ _____   **10.** $1 - \frac{2}{9}$ _____   **11.** $1 - \frac{8}{13}$ _____   **12.** $1 - \frac{3}{20}$ _____

Multiply Fractions

EXAMPLE

$$\frac{4}{15} \times \frac{5}{6} = \frac{\overset{2}{\cancel{4}}}{\underset{3}{\cancel{15}}} \times \frac{\overset{1}{\cancel{5}}}{\underset{3}{\cancel{6}}}$$

$$= \frac{2}{9}$$

Divide by the common factors.

Simplify.

Multiply. Write each product in simplest form.

13. $\frac{8}{15} \times \frac{5}{8}$ _____   **14.** $\frac{2}{9} \times \frac{3}{4}$ _____   **15.** $\frac{9}{16} \times \frac{12}{13}$ _____   **16.** $\frac{7}{10} \times \frac{5}{28}$ _____

Reading Start-Up

Vocabulary

Review Words

   complement
   (complemento)

✔ compound event *(suceso compuesto)*

✔ event *(suceso)*

   experiment *(experimento)*

✔ outcome *(resultado)*

✔ simple event *(suceso simple)*

   probability *(probabilidad)*

Preview Words

   theoretical probability *(probabilidad teórica)*

Visualize Vocabulary

Use the ✔ words to complete the graphic.

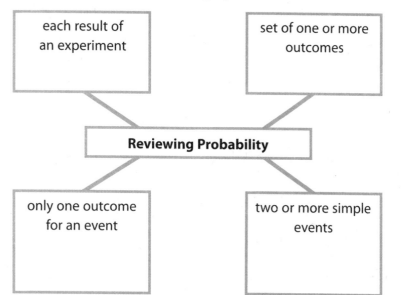

each result of an experiment		set of one or more outcomes
	Reviewing Probability	
only one outcome for an event		two or more simple events

Understand Vocabulary

Match the term on the left to the correct expression on the right.

1. compound event

2. theoretical probability

3. complement

A. The set of all outcomes that are not the desired event.

B. An event made of two or more simple events.

C. The ratio of the number of equally likely outcomes in an event to the total number of possible outcomes.

Active Reading

Two-Panel Flip Chart Create a two-panel flip chart, to help you understand the concepts in this module. Label one flap "Simple Events" and the other flap "Compound Events." As you study each lesson, write important ideas under the appropriate flap. Include information that will help you remember the concepts later when you look back at your notes.

Unpacking the TEKS

Understanding the TEKS and the vocabulary terms in the TEKS will help you know exactly what you are expected to learn in this module.

TEKS 7.6.D

Make predictions and determine solutions using theoretical probability for simple and compound events.

Key Vocabulary

simple event *(suceso simple)*
An event consisting of only one outcome.

compound event *(suceso compuesto)*
An event made of two or more simple events.

theoretical probability *(probabilidad teórica)*
The ratio of the number of equally likely outcomes in an event to the total number of possible outcomes.

What It Means to You

You will use theoretical probabilities to make predictions and solve problems.

UNPACKING EXAMPLE 7.6.D

Find the theoretical probability of rolling a number greater than 2 on a number cube.

There are four ways the event can occur: 3, 4, 5, 6.

There are six possible outcomes: 1, 2, 3, 4, 5, 6.

$$P \text{ (greater than 2)} = \frac{\text{number of ways the event can occur}}{\text{total number of equally likely outcomes}}$$

$$= \frac{4}{6} = \frac{2}{3}$$

The theoretical probability of rolling a number greater than 2 is $\frac{2}{3}$.

TEKS 7.6.E

Find the probabilities of a simple event and its complement and describe the relationship between the two.

Key Vocabulary

complement *(complemento)*
The set of all outcomes that are *not* the desired event.

What It Means to You

You will find the probabilities of a simple event and its complement.

UNPACKING EXAMPLE 7.6.E

Tara has a bag that contains 8 white marbles, 10 green marbles, and 7 red marbles. She selects a marble at random. Find the probability that the marble is red, and the probability that it is not red.

$$P(\text{red}) = \frac{\text{number of red marbles}}{\text{total number of marbles}}$$

$$= \frac{7}{25}$$

$$P \text{ (not red)} = 1 - P \text{ (red)} = 1 - \frac{7}{25} = \frac{25}{25} - \frac{7}{25} = \frac{18}{25}$$

The probability that the marble is red is $\frac{7}{25}$, and the probability that it is not red is $\frac{18}{25}$.

Visit **my.hrw.com** to see all the **TEKS** unpacked.

my.hrw.com

TEKS
Proportionality—
7.6.I Determine . . .
theoretical probabilities
related to simple and
compound events using data
and sample spaces. Also
7.6.A, 7.6.D, 7.6.E

LESSON 6.1 Theoretical Probability of Simple Events

ESSENTIAL QUESTION

How can you find the theoretical probability of a simple event?

EXPLORE ACTIVITY 1   7.6.I

Finding Theoretical Probability

In previous lessons, you found probabilities based on observing data, or experimental probabilities. In this lesson, you will find *theoretical probabilities*.

At a school fair, you have a choice of spinning Spinner A or Spinner B. You win an MP3 player if the spinner lands on a section with a star in it. Which spinner should you choose if you want a better chance of winning?

A Complete the table.

	Spinner A	Spinner B
Total number of outcomes		
Number of sections with stars		
P(winning MP3) $= \dfrac{\text{number of sections with stars}}{\text{total number of outcomes}}$		

B Compare the ratios for Spinner A and Spinner B.

The ratio for Spinner _____ is greater than the ratio for Spinner _____.

I should choose _____ for a better chance of winning.

Spinner A

Spinner B

Reflect

1. *Theoretical probability* is a way to describe how you found the chance of winning an MP3 player in the scenario above. Using the spinner example to help you, explain in your own words how to find the theoretical probability of an event.

_____

_____

_____

_____

Math Talk
Mathematical Processes

Describe a way to change Spinner B to make your chances of winning equal to your chances of not winning? Explain.

Calculating Theoretical Probability of Simple Events

Theoretical probability is the probability that an event occurs when all of the outcomes of the experiment are equally likely.

Theoretical Probability

$$P(\text{event}) = \frac{\text{number of ways the event can occur}}{\text{total number of equally likely outcomes}}$$

Probability can be written as a fraction, a decimal, or a percent. For example, the probability you win with Spinner B is $\frac{5}{16}$. You can also write that as 0.3125 or as 31.25%.

EXAMPLE 1   Real World   TEKS 7.6.I

A bag contains 6 red marbles and 12 blue ones. You select one marble at random from the bag. What is the probability that you select a red marble? Write your answer in simplest form.

STEP 1   Find the number of ways the event can occur, that is, the number of red marbles: 6

STEP 2   Add to find the total number of equally likely outcomes.

number of red marbles	+	number of blue marbles	=	total number of marbles
6	+	12	=	**18**

There are 18 possible outcomes in the sample space.

STEP 3   Find the probability of selecting a red marble.

$$P(\text{red marble}) = \frac{\text{number of red marbles}}{\text{total number of marbles}} = \frac{6}{18}$$

The probability that you select a red marble is $\frac{6}{18}$, or $\frac{1}{3}$.

Math Talk
Mathematical Processes

Describe a situation that has a theoretical probability of $\frac{1}{4}$.

YOUR TURN

2. You roll a number cube one time. What is the probability that you roll a 3 or 4? Write your answer in simplest form.

$$P(\text{rolling a 3 or 4}) = \frac{\boxed{}}{\boxed{}} = \frac{\boxed{}}{\boxed{}} = \frac{\boxed{}}{\boxed{}}$$

3. How is the sample space for an event related to the formula for theoretical probability? _____

_____

© Houghton Mifflin Harcourt Publishing Company

Comparing Theoretical and Experimental Probability

Now that you have calculated theoretical probabilities, you may wonder how theoretical and experimental probabilities compare.

Six students are performing in a talent contest. You roll a number cube to determine the order of the performances.

STEP 1 You roll the number cube once. Complete the table of theoretical probabilities for the different outcomes.

Number	1	2	3	4	5	6
Theoretical probability						

STEP 2 Predict the number of times each number will be rolled out of 30 total rolls.

1: ☐ times   3: ☐ times   5: ☐ times

2: ☐ times   4: ☐ times   6: ☐ times

STEP 3 Roll a number cube 30 times. Complete the table for the frequency of each number and then find its experimental probability.

Number	1	2	3	4	5	6
Frequency						
Experimental probability						

STEP 4 Look at the tables you completed. How do the experimental probabilities compare with the theoretical probabilities?

_____

_____

STEP 5 By performing more trials, you tend to get experimental results that are closer to the theoretical probabilities. Combine your frequency results from **Step 3** with those of your classmates to make one table for the class. How do the class experimental probabilities compare with the theoretical probabilities?

_____

_____

Reflect

4. Could the experimental probabilities ever be exactly equal to the theoretical probability? If so, how likely is it? If not, why not?

_____

_____

Guided Practice

At a school fair, you have a choice of randomly picking a ball from Basket A or Basket B. Basket A has 5 green balls, 3 red balls, and 8 yellow balls. Basket B has 7 green balls, 4 red balls, and 9 yellow balls. You can win a digital book reader if you pick a red ball. (Explore Activity 1)

	Basket A	Basket B
Total number of outcomes		
Number of red balls		
$P(\text{win}) =$ $\dfrac{\text{number of red balls}}{\text{total number of outcomes}}$		

1. Complete the chart. Write each answer in simplest form.

2. Which basket should you choose if you want the better chance of winning? _____

A spinner has 11 equal-sized sections marked 1 through 11. Find each probability. (Example 1)

3. You spin once and land on an odd number.

$P(\text{odd}) = \dfrac{\text{number of \_\_\_\_\_ sections}}{\text{total number of \_\_\_\_\_}} = \dfrac{\boxed{}}{\boxed{}}$

4. You spin once and land on an even number.

$P(\text{even}) = \dfrac{\text{number of \_\_\_\_\_ sections}}{\text{total number of \_\_\_\_\_}} = \dfrac{\boxed{}}{\boxed{}}$

You roll a number cube once.

5. What is the theoretical probability that you roll a 3 or 4? (Example 1) _____

6. Suppose you rolled the number cube 199 more times. Would you expect the experimental probability of rolling a 3 or 4 to be the same as your answer to Exercise 5? (Explore Activity 2)

_____

? ESSENTIAL QUESTION CHECK-IN

7. How can you find the probability of a simple event if the total number of equally likely outcomes is 20?

_____

6.1 Independent Practice

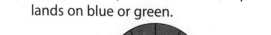 **TEKS** 7.6.I, 7.6.A, 7.6.D, 7.6.E

Find the probability of each event. Write each answer as a fraction in simplest form, as a decimal to the nearest hundredth, and as a percent to the nearest whole number.

8. You spin the spinner shown. The spinner lands on yellow.

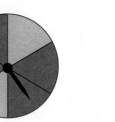

_____

9. You spin the spinner shown. The spinner lands on blue or green.

_____

10. A jar contains 4 cherry cough drops and 10 honey cough drops. You choose one cough drop without looking. The cough drop is cherry.

_____

11. You pick one card at random from a standard deck of 52 playing cards. You pick a black card.

_____

12. There are 12 pieces of fruit in a bowl. Five are lemons and the rest are limes. You choose a piece of fruit without looking. The piece of fruit is a lime.

_____

13. You choose a movie CD at random from a case containing 8 comedy CDs, 5 science fiction CDs, and 7 adventure CDs. The CD is **not** a comedy.

_____

14. You roll a number cube. You roll a number that is greater than 2 and less than 5.

_____

15. **Communicate Mathematical Ideas** The theoretical probability of a given event is $\frac{9}{13}$. Explain what each number represents.

_____

_____

_____

16. Leona has 4 nickels, 6 pennies, 4 dimes, and 2 quarters in a change purse. Leona lets her little sister Daisy pick a coin at random. If Daisy is equally likely to pick each type of coin, what is the probability that her coin is worth more than five cents? Explain.

_____

_____

Work Area

17. Critique Reasoning A bowl of flower seeds contains 5 petunia seeds and 15 begonia seeds. Riley calculated the probability that a randomly selected seed is a petunia seed as $\frac{1}{3}$. Describe and correct Riley's error.

_____

_____

_____

_____

18. There are 20 seventh graders and 15 eighth graders in a club. A club president will be chosen at random.

a. Analyze Relationships Compare the probabilities of choosing a seventh grader or an eighth grader.

_____

_____

b. Critical Thinking If a student from one grade is more likely to be chosen than a student from the other, is the method unfair? Explain.

_____

_____

A jar contains 8 red marbles, 10 blue ones, and 2 yellow ones. One marble is chosen at random. The color is recorded in the table, and then it is returned to the jar. This is repeated 40 times.

Red	Blue	Yellow
14	16	10

19. Communicate Mathematical Ideas Use proportional reasoning to explain how you know that for each color, the theoretical and experimental probabilities are not the same.

_____

_____

_____

_____

20. Persevere in Problem Solving For which color marble is the experimental probability closest to the theoretical probability? Explain.

_____

_____

TEKS
Proportionality—
7.6.I Determine . . . theoretical probabilities related to simple and compound events using data and sample spaces. *Also 7.6.A, 7.6.D, 7.6.E*

? ESSENTIAL QUESTION

How do you find the probability of a compound event?

EXPLORE ACTIVITY 🔲 **TEKS** 7.6.I

Finding Probability Using a Table

Recall that a compound event consists of two or more simple events. To find the probability of a compound event, you write a ratio of the number of ways the compound event can happen to the total number of equally likely possible outcomes.

Jacob rolls two fair number cubes. Find the probability that the sum of the numbers he rolls is 8.

STEP 1 Use the table to find the sample space for rolling a particular sum on two number cubes. Each cell is the sum of the first number in that row and column.

STEP 2 How many possible outcomes are in the sample space? _____

STEP 3 Circle the outcomes that give the sum of 8.

STEP 4 How many ways are there to roll a sum of 8? _____

STEP 5 What is the probability of rolling a sum of 8? _____

	1	2	3	4	5	6
1						
2						
3						
4						
5						
6						

Reflect

1. Give an example of an event that is more likely than rolling a sum of 8.

   _____

2. Give an example of an event that is less likely than rolling a sum of 8.

   _____

Finding Probability Using a Tree Diagram

You can also use a tree diagram to calculate theoretical probabilities of compound events.

EXAMPLE 1 **TEKS** 7.6.I

A deli prepares sandwiches with one type of bread (white or wheat), one type of meat (ham, turkey, or chicken), and one type of cheese (cheddar or Swiss). Each combination is equally likely. Find the probability of choosing a sandwich at random and getting turkey and Swiss on wheat bread.

STEP 1 Make a tree diagram to find the sample space for the compound event.

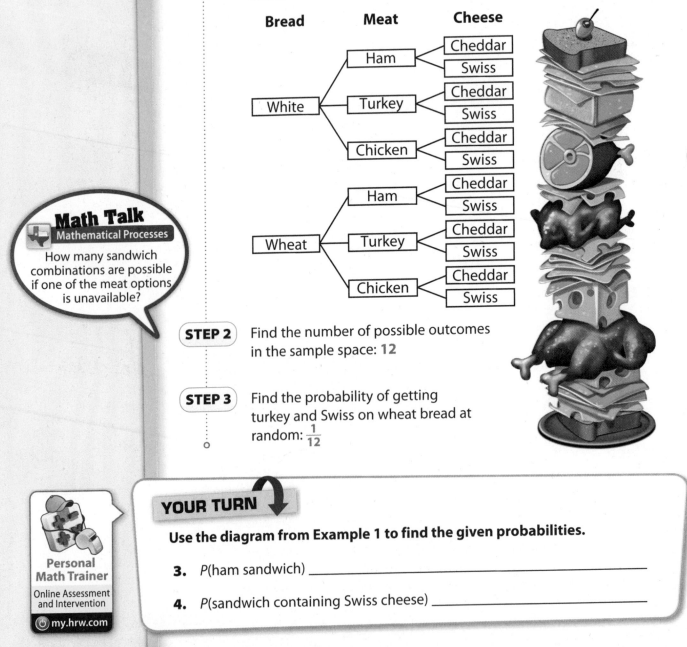

Math Talk
Mathematical Processes

How many sandwich combinations are possible if one of the meat options is unavailable?

STEP 2 Find the number of possible outcomes in the sample space: **12**

STEP 3 Find the probability of getting turkey and Swiss on wheat bread at random: $\frac{1}{12}$

Personal Math Trainer

Online Assessment and Intervention

⊙ my.hrw.com

YOUR TURN

Use the diagram from Example 1 to find the given probabilities.

3. *P*(ham sandwich) _____

4. *P*(sandwich containing Swiss cheese) _____

Finding Probability Using a List

One way to provide security for a locker or personal account is to assign it an access code number known only to the owner.

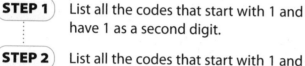

EXAMPLE 2 🌐 Real World   ⬛ **TEKS** 7.6.D

My Notes

The combination for Khiem's locker is a 3-digit code that uses the numbers 1, 2, and 3. Any of these numbers may be repeated. Find the probability that Khiem's randomly-assigned number is 222.

Make an organized list to find the sample space.

| STEP 1 | List all the codes that start with 1 and have 1 as a second digit. |

1	1	1
1	1	2
1	1	3

| STEP 2 | List all the codes that start with 1 and have 2 as a second digit. |

1	2	1
1	2	2
1	2	3

| STEP 3 | List all the codes that start with 1 and have 3 as a second digit. |

1	3	1
1	3	2
1	3	3

| STEP 4 | You have now listed all the codes that start with 1. Repeat Steps 1–3 for codes that start with 2, and then for codes that start with 3. |

2	1	1		2	2	1		2	3	1
2	1	2		2	2	2		2	3	2
2	1	3		2	2	3		2	3	3

3	1	1		3	2	1		3	3	1
3	1	2		3	2	2		3	3	2
3	1	3		3	2	3		3	3	3

> Notice that there are 3 possible first numbers, 3 possible second numbers, and 3 possible third numbers, or $3 \times 3 \times 3 = 27$ numbers in all.

| STEP 5 | Find the number of outcomes in the sample space by counting all the possible codes. There are **27** such codes. |

| STEP 6 | Find the probability that Khiem's locker code is 222. |

$$P(\text{Code 222}) = \frac{\text{number of favorable outcomes}}{\text{total number of possible outcomes}} = \frac{1}{27}$$

Math Talk
Mathematical Processes

How could you find the probability that Khiem's locker code includes exactly two 1s?

YOUR TURN ↪

5. Martha types a 4-digit code into a keypad to unlock her car doors. The code uses the numbers 1 and 0. If the digits are selected at random, what is the probability of getting a code with exactly two 0s? _____

Personal Math Trainer

Online Assessment and Intervention

⏱ my.hrw.com

Drake rolls two fair number cubes. (Explore Activity)

1. Complete the table to find the sample space for rolling a particular product on two number cubes.

2. What is the probability that the product of the two numbers Drake rolls is a multiple of 4? _____

3. What is the probability that the product of the two numbers Drake rolls is less than 13? _____

	1	2	3	4	5	6
1						
2						
3						
4						
5						
6						

You flip three coins and want to explore probabilities of certain events. (Examples 1 and 2)

4. Complete the tree diagram and make a list to find the sample space.

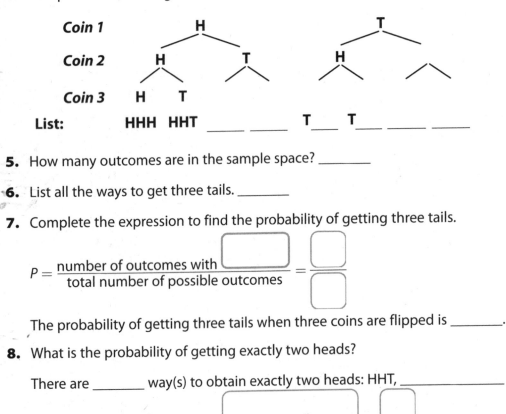

Coin 1   H   T

Coin 2   H   T   H

Coin 3   H   T

List: HHH   HHT   ____ ____   T___ T___ ____ ____

5. How many outcomes are in the sample space? _____

6. List all the ways to get three tails. _____

7. Complete the expression to find the probability of getting three tails.

$$P = \frac{\text{number of outcomes with } \boxed{}}{\text{total number of possible outcomes}} = \frac{\boxed{}}{\boxed{}}$$

The probability of getting three tails when three coins are flipped is _____.

8. What is the probability of getting exactly two heads?

There are _____ way(s) to obtain exactly two heads: HHT, _____

$$P = \frac{\text{number of outcomes with } \boxed{}}{\text{total number of possible outcomes}} = \frac{\boxed{}}{\boxed{}}$$

? ESSENTIAL QUESTION CHECK-IN

9. There are 6 ways a given compound event can occur. What else do you need to know to find the theoretical probability of the event?

_____

6.2 Independent Practice

TEKS 7.6.I, 7.6.A, 7.6.D, 7.6.E

Personal
Math Trainer

Online
Assessment and
Intervention

my.hrw.com

In Exercises 10–12, use the following information. Mattias gets dressed in the dark one morning and chooses his clothes at random. He chooses a shirt (green, red, or yellow), a pair of pants (black or blue), and a pair of shoes (checkered or red).

10. Use the space below to make a tree diagram to find the sample space.

11. What is the probability that Mattias picks an outfit at random that includes

red shoes? _____

12. What is the probability that no part of

Mattias's outfit is red? _____

13. Rhee and Pamela are two of the five members of a band. Every week, the band picks two members at random to play on their own for five minutes. What is the probability that Rhee and Pamela are

chosen this week? _____

14. Ben rolls two number cubes. What is the probability that the sum of the numbers he

rolls is less than 6? _____

15. Nhan is getting dressed. He considers two different shirts, three pairs of pants, and three pairs of shoes. He chooses one of each of the articles at random. What is the probability that he will wear his jeans but not his sneakers?

Shirt	Pants	Shoes
collared	khakis	sneakers
T-shirt	jeans	flip-flops
	shorts	sandals

_____

16. Communicate Mathematical Ideas A ski resort has 3 chair lifts, each with access to 6 ski trails. Explain how you can find the number of possible outcomes when choosing a chair lift and a ski trail without making a list, a tree diagram, or table.

_____

_____

_____

_____

17. Explain the Error For breakfast, Sarah can choose eggs, granola or oatmeal as a main course, and orange juice or milk for a drink. Sarah says that the sample space for choosing one of each contains $3^2 = 9$ outcomes. What is her error? Explain.

_____

_____

_____

18. **Represent Real-World Problems** A new shoe comes in two colors, black or red, and in sizes from 5 to 12, including half sizes. If a pair of the shoes is chosen at random for a store display, what is the probability it will be

    red and size 9 or larger? _____

19. **Analyze Relationships** At a diner, Sondra tells the server, "Give me one item from each column." Gretchen says, "Give me one main dish and a vegetable." Who has a greater probability of getting a meal that includes salmon? Explain.

Main Dish	Vegetable	Side
Pasta	Carrots	Tomato soup
Salmon	Peas	Tossed salad
Beef	Asparagus	
Pork	Sweet potato	

_____

_____

20. The digits 1 through 5 are used for a set of locker codes.

    a. **Look for a Pattern** Suppose the digits cannot repeat. Find the number of possible two-digit codes and three-digit codes. Describe any pattern and use it to predict the number of possible five-digit codes.

    _____

    _____

    _____

    b. **Look for a Pattern** Repeat part **a**, but allow digits to repeat.

    _____

    _____

    c. **Justify Reasoning** Suppose that a gym plans to issue numbered locker codes by choosing the digits at random. Should the gym use codes in which the digits can repeat or not? Justify your reasoning.

    _____

    _____

    _____

Making Predictions with Theoretical Probability

TEKS
Proportionality—
7.6.H Solve problems using qualitative and quantitative predictions and comparisons from simple experiments.
Also 7.6.D, 7.6.I

? **ESSENTIAL QUESTION**

How do you make predictions using theoretical probability?

Using Theoretical Probability to Make a Quantitative Prediction

You can make quantitative predictions based on theoretical probability just as you did with experimental probability earlier.

Math On the Spot

⏻ my.hrw.com

EXAMPLE 1 *Real World*

TEKS 7.6.H

My Notes

A **You roll a standard number cube 150 times. Predict how many times you will roll a 3 or a 4.**

The probability of rolling a 3 or a 4 is $\frac{2}{6} = \frac{1}{3}$.

Method 1: Set up a proportion.

$$\frac{1}{3} = \frac{x}{150}$$ Write a proportion. 1 out of 3 is how many out of 150?

$$\frac{1}{3} = \frac{x}{150}$$
$\times 50$

$\times 50$
$$\frac{1}{3} = \frac{50}{150}$$ Since 3 times 50 is 150, multiply 1 times 50 to find the value of x.

$$x = 50$$

Method 2: Set up an equation and solve.

P(rolling a 3 or 4) · Number of events = Prediction

$$\frac{1}{3} \cdot 150 = x$$ Multiply the probability by the total number of rolls.

$$50 = x$$ Solve for x.

You can expect to roll a 3 or a 4 about 50 times out of 150.

B Celia volunteers at her local animal shelter. She has an equally likely chance to be assigned to the dog, cat, bird, or reptile section. If she volunteers 24 times, about how many times should she expect to be assigned to the dog section?

Set up a proportion. The probability of being assigned to the dog section is $\frac{1}{4}$.

$$\frac{1}{4} = \frac{x}{24}$$ Write a proportion. 1 out of 4 is how many out of 24?

$$\frac{1}{4} = \frac{x}{24}$$
$$\times 6$$

$$\times 6$$
$$\frac{1}{4} = \frac{x}{24}$$ Since 4 times 6 is 24, multiply 1 times 6 to find the value of x.

$$x = 6$$

Celia can expect to be assigned to the dog section about 6 times out of 24.

Personal Math Trainer

Online Assessment and Intervention

(⏻) my.hrw.com

YOUR TURN

1. Predict how many times you will roll a number less than 5 if you roll a standard number cube 250 times.

   _____

2. You flip a fair coin 18 times. About how many times would you expect heads to appear?

   _____

Math On the Spot

(⏻) my.hrw.com

Using Theoretical Probability to Make a Qualitative Prediction

Earlier, you learned how to make predictions using experimental probability. You can use theoretical probabilities in the same way to help you predict or compare how likely events are.

EXAMPLE 2 Real World

TEKS 7.6.H

A Herschel pulls a sock out of his drawer without looking and puts it on. The sock is black. There are 7 black socks, 8 white socks, and 5 striped socks left in the drawer. He pulls out a second sock without looking. Is it likely that he will be wearing matching socks to school?

Find the theoretical probability that Herschel picks a matching sock and the probability that he picks one that does not match.

$P(\text{matching}) = \frac{7}{20}$ $P(\text{not matching}) = 1 - \frac{7}{20} = \frac{13}{20}$

> $P(\text{not matching}) = 1 - P(\text{matching})$

The probability that Herschel picks a matching sock is about half the probability that he picks one that does not match. It is **not** likely that he will be wearing matching socks to school.

B All 2,000 customers at a gym are randomly assigned a 3-digit security code that they use to access their online accounts. The codes are made up of the digits 0 through 4, and the digits can be repeated. Is it likely that fewer than 10 of the customers are issued the code 103?

Set up a proportion. The probability of the code 103 is $\frac{1}{125}$.

$\frac{1}{125} = \frac{x}{2,000}$ Write a proportion. 1 out of 125 is how many out of 2,000?

$\frac{1}{125} \overset{\times 16}{=} \frac{16}{2,000}$ Since 125 times 16 is 2,000, multiply 1 times 125 to find the value of x.

> There are 5 possible first numbers, 5 possible second numbers, and 5 possible third numbers. So, there are $5 \times 5 \times 5 = 125$ possible security codes.

It is **not** likely that fewer than 10 of the customers get the same code. It is more likely that 16 members get the code 103.

YOUR TURN

3. A bag of marbles contains 8 red marbles, 4 blue marbles, and 5 white marbles. Tom picks a marble at random. Is it more likely that he picks a red marble or a marble of another color?

_____

4. At a fundraiser, a school group charges $6 for tickets for a "grab bag." You choose one bill at random from a bag that contains 40 $1 bills, 20 $5 bills, 5 $10 bills, 5 $20 bills, and 1 $100 bill. Is it likely that you will win enough to pay for your ticket? Justify your answer.

_____

_____

_____

Personal Math Trainer

Online Assessment and Intervention

my.hrw.com

1. Bob works at a construction company. He has an equally likely chance of being assigned to work different crews every day. He can be assigned to work on crews building apartments, condominiums, or houses. If he works 18 days a month, about how many times should he expect to be assigned to the house crew? (Example 1)

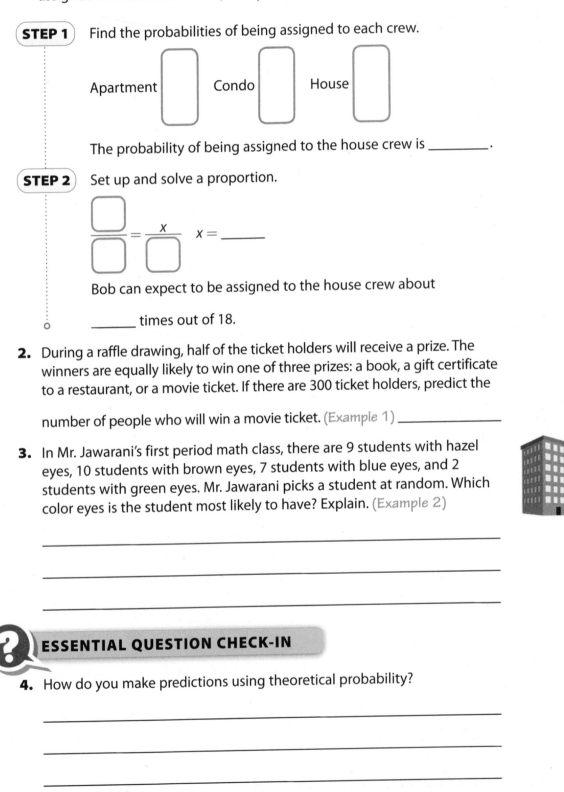

STEP 1 Find the probabilities of being assigned to each crew.

Apartment ☐ Condo ☐ House ☐

The probability of being assigned to the house crew is _____.

STEP 2 Set up and solve a proportion.

$$\frac{\boxed{}}{\boxed{}} = \frac{x}{\boxed{}} \qquad x = \underline{\qquad}$$

Bob can expect to be assigned to the house crew about

_____ times out of 18.

2. During a raffle drawing, half of the ticket holders will receive a prize. The winners are equally likely to win one of three prizes: a book, a gift certificate to a restaurant, or a movie ticket. If there are 300 ticket holders, predict the

number of people who will win a movie ticket. (Example 1) _____

3. In Mr. Jawarani's first period math class, there are 9 students with hazel eyes, 10 students with brown eyes, 7 students with blue eyes, and 2 students with green eyes. Mr. Jawarani picks a student at random. Which color eyes is the student most likely to have? Explain. (Example 2)

_____

_____

_____

? ESSENTIAL QUESTION CHECK-IN

4. How do you make predictions using theoretical probability?

_____

_____

6.3 Independent Practice

TEKS 7.6.H, 7.6.D, 7.6.I

Personal Math Trainer

Online Assessment and Intervention

my.hrw.com

5. A bag contains 6 red marbles, 2 white marbles, and 1 gray marble. You randomly pick out a marble, record its color, and put it back in the bag. You repeat this process 45 times. How many white or gray marbles do you expect to get?

_____

6. Using the blank circle below, draw a spinner with 8 equal sections and 3 colors—red, green, and yellow. The spinner should be such that you are equally likely to land on green or yellow, but more likely to land on red than either on green or yellow.

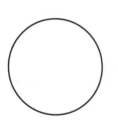

Use the following for Exercises 7–9. In a standard 52-card deck, half of the cards are red and half are black. The 52 cards are divided evenly into 4 suits: spades, hearts, diamonds, and clubs. Each suit has three face cards (jack, queen, king), and an ace. Each suit also has 9 cards numbered from 2 to 10.

7. Dawn draws 1 card, replaces it, and draws another card. Is it more likely that she draws 2 red cards or 2 face cards?

_____

_____

8. Luis draws 1 card from a deck, 39 times. Predict how many times he draws an ace.

_____

9. Suppose a solitaire player has played 1,000 games. Predict how many times the player turned over a red card as the first card.

_____

10. John and O'Neal are playing a board game in which they roll two number cubes. John needs to get a sum of 8 on the number cubes to win. O'Neal needs a sum of 11. If they take turns rolling the number cube, who is more likely to win? Explain.

_____

_____

_____

11. Every day, Navya's teacher randomly picks a number from 1 to 20 to be the number of the day. The number of the day can be repeated. There are 180 days in the school year. Predict how many days the number of

the day will be greater than 15. _____

12. Eben rolls two standard number cubes 36 times. Predict how many times he will

roll a sum of 4. _____

13. Communicate Mathematical Ideas Can you always show that a prediction based on theoretical probability is true by performing the event often enough? If so, explain why. If not, describe a situation that justifies your response.

_____

_____

_____

_____

_____

14. Represent Real-World Problems Give a real-world example of an experiment in which all of the outcomes are not equally likely. Can you make a prediction for this experiment, using theoretical probability?

_____

_____

_____

_____

_____

15. Critical Thinking Pierre asks Sherry a question involving the theoretical probability of a compound event in which you flip a coin and draw a marble from a bag of marbles. The bag of marbles contains 3 white marbles, 8 green marbles, and 9 black marbles. Sherry's answer, which is correct, is $\frac{12}{40}$. What was Pierre's question?

_____

_____

_____

16. Make a Prediction Horace is going to roll a standard number cube and flip a coin. He wonders if it is more likely that he rolls a 5 **and** the coin lands on heads, or that he rolls a 5 **or** the coin lands on heads. Which event do you think is more likely to happen? Find the probability of both events to justify or reject your initial prediction.

_____

_____

_____

_____

17. Communicate Mathematical Ideas Cecil solved a theoretical prediction problem and got this answer: "The spinner will land on the red section 4.5 times." Is it possible to have a prediction that is not a whole number? If so, give an example.

_____

_____

_____

_____

© Houghton Mifflin Harcourt Publishing Company

LESSON 6.4 Using Technology to Conduct a Simulation

TEKS Proportionality—
7.6.B Select and use different simulations to represent simple and compound events with and without technology.

? ESSENTIAL QUESTION

How can you use technology simulations to estimate probabilities?

Designing and Conducting a Simulation for a Simple Event

You can use a graphing calculator or computer to generate random numbers and conduct a simulation.

Math On the Spot
my.hrw.com

EXAMPLE 1 Real World

TEKS 7.6.B

A cereal company is having a contest. There are codes for winning prizes in 30% of its cereal boxes. Find the experimental probability of having to buy *exactly* 3 boxes of cereal before you find a winning code.

STEP 1 Choose a model.

The probability of finding a winning code is $30\% = \frac{3}{10}$.

Use whole numbers from 1 to 10.
Let three numbers represent buying a box with a winning code.

Winning code: 1, 2, 3   Nonwinning code: 4, 5, 6, 7, 8, 9, 10

STEP 2 Generate random numbers from 1 to 10 until you get one that represents a box with a winning code. Record how many boxes you bought before finding a winning code.

5 numbers generated: 9, 6, 7, 8, 1 — 1 represents a box with a winning code.

STEP 3 Perform multiple trials by repeating Step 2.

STEP 4 Find the experimental probability.

In 1 of 10 trials, you bought exactly 3 boxes of cereal before finding a winning code. The experimental probability is $\frac{1}{10}$, or 10%.

Animated Math
my.hrw.com

Trial	Numbers generated	Boxes bought
1	9, 6, 7, 8, 1	5
2	2	1
3	10, 4, 8, 1	4
4	4, 10, 7, 1	4
5	2	1
6	4, 3	2
7	3	1
8	7, 5, 2	3
9	8, 5, 4, 8, 10, 3	6
10	9, 1	2

Trial 8 represents a winning code after buying 3 boxes.

YOUR TURN

1. An elephant has a 50% chance of giving birth to either a male or to a female calf. Use a simulation to find the experimental probability that the elephant gives birth to 3 male calves before having a female calf. (*Hint:* Use 0s and 1s. Let 0 represent a male calf, and 1 represent a female calf. Generate random numbers until you get a 1.)

Trial	Numbers generated	3 Males first
1		
2		
3		
4		
5		

Trial	Numbers generated	3 Males first
6		
7		
8		
9		
10		

Math Talk
Mathematical Processes

Could you generate random numbers from a list of more than 2 numbers? Explain.

Math On the Spot

⏻ my.hrw.com

Designing and Conducting a Simulation for a Compound Event

You can use random numbers to simulate compound events as well as simple events.

EXAMPLE 2  TEKS 7.6.B

Suppose that there is a 20% chance that a particular volcano will erupt in any given decade. Find the experimental probability that the volcano will erupt in at least 1 of the next 5 decades.

STEP 1 Choose a model.

The probability of an eruption is $20\% = \frac{1}{5}$. Use whole numbers from 1 to 5.

Let 1 represent a decade with an eruption.

Let 2, 3, 4, and 5 represent a decade without an eruption.

STEP 2 Generate 5 random numbers from 1 to 5. Record the number of decades with an eruption.

5 numbers generated: 3, 1, 3, 4, 2   Eruption decades: 1

STEP 3 Perform multiple trials by repeating Step 2. Calculate the percent of trials in which there was an eruption in at least 1 of the 5 decades.

Trial	Numbers generated	Eruption decades
1	3, 1, 3, 4, 2	1
2	3, 2, 2, 4, 5	0
3	1, 3, 3, 2, 5	1
4	5, 3, 4, 5, 4	0
5	5, 5, 3, 2, 4	0

Trial	Numbers generated	Eruption decades
6	2, 3, 3, 4, 2	0
7	1, 2, 4, 1, 4	2
8	1, 3, 2, 1, 5	2
9	1, 2, 4, 2, 5	1
10	5, 5, 3, 2, 4	0

In 5 out of the 10 trials, there was an eruption in at least 1 of the 5 decades. The experimental probability of an eruption in at least 1 of the next 5 decades is $\frac{5}{10} = 50\%$.

YOUR TURN

2. Matt guesses the answers on a quiz with 5 true-false questions. The probability of guessing a correct answer on each question is 50%. Use a simulation to find an experimental probability that he gets at least 2 questions right. (*Hint:* Use 0s and 1s. Let 0s represent incorrect answers, and 1s represent correct answers. Perform 10 trials, generating 5 random numbers in each, and count the number of 1s.)

Trial	Numbers generated	Correct answers
1		
2		
3		
4		
5		

Trial	Numbers generated	Correct answers
6		
7		
8		
9		
10		

Personal Math Trainer

Online Assessment and Intervention

ⓑ my.hrw.com

There is a 30% chance that T'Shana's county will have a drought during any given year. She performs a simulation to find the experimental probability of a drought in at least 1 of the next 4 years. (Examples 1 and 2)

1. T'Shana's model involves the whole numbers from 1 to 10. Complete the description of her model.

   Let the numbers 1 to 3 represent

   and the numbers 4 to 10 represent

   Perform multiple trials, generating [ ] random numbers each time.

2. Suppose T'Shana used the model described in Exercise 1 and got the results shown in the table. Complete the table.

Trial	Numbers generated	Drought years
1	10, 3, 5, 1	
2	10, 4, 6, 5	
3	3, 2, 10, 3	
4	2, 10, 4, 4	
5	7, 3, 6, 3	

Trial	Numbers generated	Drought years
6	8, 4, 8, 5	
7	6, 2, 2, 8	
8	6, 5, 2, 4	
9	2, 2, 3, 2	
10	6, 3, 1, 5	

3. According to the simulation, what is the experimental probability that there will be a drought in the county in at least 1 of the next 4 years? _____

4. You want to generate random numbers to simulate an event with a 75% chance of occurring. Describe a model you could use.

   _____

   _____

   _____

   _____

6.4 Independent Practice

 TEKS 7.6.B

Personal Math Trainer

Online Assessment and Intervention

my.hrw.com

Every contestant on a game show has a 40% chance of winning. In the simulation below, the numbers 1–4 represent a winner, and the numbers 5–10 represent a nonwinner. Numbers were generated until one that represented a winner was produced.

Trial	Numbers generated
1	7, 4
2	6, 5, 2
3	1
4	9, 1
5	3

Trial	Numbers generated
6	8, 8, 6, 2
7	2
8	5, 9, 4
9	10, 3
10	1

5. In how many of the trials did it take exactly 4 contestants to get a winner? _____

6. Based on the simulation, what is the experimental probability that it will take exactly 4 contestants to get a winner? _____

Over a 100-year period, the probability that a hurricane struck Rob's city in any given year was 20%. Rob performed a simulation to find an experimental probability that a hurricane would strike the city in at least 4 of the next 10 years. In Rob's simulation, 1 represents a year with a hurricane.

Trial	Numbers generated
1	2, 5, 3, 2, 5, 5, 1, 4, 5, 2
2	1, 1, 5, 2, 2, 1, 3, 1, 1, 5
3	4, 5, 4, 5, 5, 4, 3, 5, 1, 1
4	1, 5, 5, 5, 1, 2, 2, 3, 5, 3
5	5, 1, 5, 3, 5, 3, 4, 5, 3, 2

Trial	Numbers generated
6	1, 1, 5, 5, 1, 4, 2, 2, 3, 4
7	2, 1, 5, 3, 1, 5, 1, 2, 1, 4
8	2, 4, 3, 2, 4, 4, 2, 1, 3, 1
9	3, 2, 1, 4, 5, 3, 5, 5, 1, 2
10	3, 4, 2, 4, 3, 5, 2, 3, 5, 1

7. According to Rob's simulation, what was the experimental probability that a hurricane would strike the city in at least 4 of the next 10 years? _____

8. Analyze Relationships Suppose that over the 10 years following Rob's simulation, there was actually 1 year in which a hurricane struck. How did this compare to the results of Rob's simulation?

_____

_____

9. **Communicate Mathematical Ideas** You generate three random whole numbers from 1 to 10. Do you think that it is unlikely or even impossible that all of the numbers could be 10? Explain?

_____

_____

_____

_____

_____

10. Erika collects baseball cards, and 60% of the packs contain a player from her favorite team. Use a simulation to find an experimental probability that she has to buy exactly 2 packs before she gets a player from her favorite team.

_____

_____

H.O.T. FOCUS ON HIGHER ORDER THINKING

Work Area

11. **Represent Real-World Problems** When Kate plays basketball, she usually makes 37.5% of her shots. Describe a simulation that you could use to find the experimental probability that she makes at least 3 of her next 10 shots.

_____

_____

_____

_____

_____

_____

12. **Justify Reasoning** George and Susannah used a simulation to simulate the flipping of 8 coins 50 times. In all of the trials, at least 5 heads came up. What can you say about their simulation? Explain.

_____

_____

_____

_____

 **Ready to Go On?**

Personal Math Trainer
Online Assessment and Intervention
🔘 my.hrw.com

6.1, 6.2 Theoretical Probability of Simple and Compound Events

Find the probability of each event. Write your answer as a fraction, as a decimal, and as a percent.

1. You choose a marble at random from a bag containing 12 red, 12 blue, 15 green, 9 yellow, and 12 black marbles. The marble is red. _____

2. You draw a card at random from a shuffled deck of 52 cards. The deck has four 13-card suits (diamonds, hearts, clubs, spades). The card is a diamond or a spade. _____

6.3 Making Predictions with Theoretical Probability

3. A bag contains 23 red marbles, 25 green marbles, and 18 blue marbles. You choose a marble at random from the bag. What color marble will you most likely choose? _____

6.4 Using Technology to Conduct a Simulation

4. Bay City has a 20% chance of having a flood in any given decade. The table shows the results of a simulation using random numbers to find the experimental probability that there will be a flood in Bay City in at least 1 of the next 5 decades. In the table, the number 1 represents a decade with a flood. The numbers 2 through 5 represent a decade without a flood.

Trial	Numbers generated	Trial	Numbers generated
1	2, 2, 5, 5, 5	6	4, 2, 2, 5, 4
2	3, 2, 3, 5, 4	7	1, 3, 2, 4, 4
3	5, 5, 5, 4, 3	8	3, 5, 5, 2, 1
4	5, 1, 3, 3, 5	9	4, 3, 3, 2, 5
5	4, 5, 5, 3, 2	10	5, 4, 1, 2, 1

According to the simulation, what is the experimental probability of a flood in Bay City in at least 1 of the next 5 decades? _____

? ESSENTIAL QUESTION

5. How can you use theoretical probability to make predictions in real-world situations?

_____

_____

MODULE 6 MIXED REVIEW

Texas Test Prep

Personal
Math Trainer

Online
Assessment and
Intervention

my.hrw.com

Selected Response

1. What is the probability of flipping two fair coins and having both show tails?

Ⓐ $\frac{1}{8}$ Ⓒ $\frac{1}{3}$

Ⓑ $\frac{1}{4}$ Ⓓ $\frac{1}{2}$

2. A bag contains 8 white marbles and 2 black marbles. You pick out a marble, record its color, and put the marble back in the bag. If you repeat this process 45 times, how many times would you expect to remove a white marble from the bag?

Ⓐ 9   Ⓒ 36

Ⓑ 32   Ⓓ 40

3. Philip rolls a standard number cube 24 times. Which is the best prediction for the number of times he will roll a number that is even and less than 4?

Ⓐ 2   Ⓒ 4

Ⓑ 3   Ⓓ 6

4. A set of cards includes 24 yellow cards, 18 green cards, and 18 blue cards. What is the probability that a card chosen at random is **not** green?

Ⓐ $\frac{3}{10}$ Ⓒ $\frac{3}{5}$

Ⓑ $\frac{4}{10}$ Ⓓ $\frac{7}{10}$

5. A rectangle made of square tiles measures 10 tiles long and 8 tiles wide. What is the width of a similar rectangle whose length is 15 tiles?

Ⓐ 3 tiles   Ⓒ 13 tiles

Ⓑ 12 tiles   Ⓓ 18.75 tiles

6. You buy a game that originally cost $35. It was on sale at 20% off. You paid 6% tax on the sale price. What was the total amount that you paid?

Ⓐ $29.68   Ⓒ $44.10

Ⓑ $37.10   Ⓓ $44.52

7. The Fernandez family drove 273 miles in 5.25 hours. How far would they have driven at that rate in 4 hours?

Ⓐ 208 miles   Ⓒ 280 miles

Ⓑ 220 miles   Ⓓ 358 miles

8. There are 20 tennis balls in a bag. Five are orange, 7 are white, 2 are yellow, and 6 are green. You choose one at random. Which color ball are you **least** likely to choose?

Ⓐ green   Ⓒ white

Ⓑ orange   Ⓓ yellow

Gridded Response

9. Gibley's frozen yogurt cones come in 3 flavors (chocolate, vanilla, and strawberry) with 4 choices of topping (sprinkles, strawberries, nuts, and granola). You choose a cone at random. What is the probability, expressed as a decimal, that you get a cone with strawberry topping?

⊕	⓪	⓪	⓪	⓪	•	⓪	⓪
⊖	①	①	①	①		①	①
	②	②	②	②		②	②
	③	③	③	③		③	③
	④	④	④	④		④	④
	⑤	⑤	⑤	⑤		⑤	⑤
	⑥	⑥	⑥	⑥		⑥	⑥
	⑦	⑦	⑦	⑦		⑦	⑦
	⑧	⑧	⑧	⑧		⑧	⑧
	⑨	⑨	⑨	⑨		⑨	⑨

MODULE 5 Experimental Probability

? ESSENTIAL QUESTION

How can you use experimental probability to solve real-world problems?

EXAMPLE 1

What is the probability of picking a red marble from a jar with 5 green marbles and 2 red marbles?

$$P(\text{picking a red marble}) = \frac{\text{number of red marbles}}{\text{total number of marbles}}$$

$$= \frac{2}{7} \quad \text{There are 2 red marbles.}$$
$$\text{The total number of marbles is } 2 + 5 = 7.$$

EXAMPLE 2

For one month, a doctor recorded information about new patients as shown in the table.

	Senior	Adult	Young adult	Child
Female	5	8	2	14
Male	3	10	1	17

What is the experimental probability that his next new patient is a female adult?

$$P\left(\begin{array}{c}\text{new patient is a}\\\text{female adult}\end{array}\right) = \frac{\text{number of female adults}}{\text{total number of patients}}$$

$$P = \frac{8}{60} = \frac{2}{15}$$

What is the experimental probability that his next new patient is a child?

$$P\left(\begin{array}{c}\text{new patient is}\\\text{a child}\end{array}\right) = \frac{\text{number of children}}{\text{total number of patients}}$$

$$P = \frac{31}{60}$$

EXERCISES

Find the probability of each event. (Lesson 5.1)

1. Rolling a 5 on a fair number cube.

_____

2. Picking a 7 from a standard deck of 52 cards. A standard deck includes 4 cards of each number from 2 to 10.

_____

3. Picking a blue marble from a bag of 4 red marbles, 6 blue marbles, and 1 white marble.

_____

4. Rolling a number greater than 7 on a 12-sided number cube.

_____

5. Christopher picked coins randomly from his piggy bank and got the numbers of coins shown in the table. Find each experimental probability. (Lessons 5.2, 5.3)

Penny	Nickel	Dime	Quarter
7	2	8	6

a. The next coin that Christopher picks is a quarter. _____

b. The next coin that Christopher picks is not a quarter. _____

c. The next coin that Christopher picks is a penny or a nickel. _____

6. A grocery store manager found that 54% of customers usually bring their own bags. In one afternoon, 82 out of 124 customers brought their own grocery bags. Did a greater or lesser number of people than usual bring their own bags? (Lesson 5.4)

_____

MODULE 6 # Theoretical Probability

Key Vocabulary
theoretical probability
(probabilidad teórica)

ESSENTIAL QUESTION

How can you use theoretical probability to solve real-world problems?

EXAMPLE 1

A. Lola rolls two fair number cubes. What is the probability that the two numbers Lola rolls include at least one 4 and have a product of at least 16?

There are 5 pairs of numbers that include a 4 and have a product of at least 16:

$(4, 4), (4, 5), (4, 6), (5, 4), (6, 4)$

Find the probability.

$P = \dfrac{\text{number of possible ways}}{\text{total number of possible outcomes}} = \dfrac{5}{36}$

	1	2	3	4	5	6
1	1	2	3	4	5	6
2	2	4	6	8	10	12
3	3	6	9	12	15	18
4	4	8	12	16	20	24
5	5	10	15	20	25	30
6	6	12	18	24	30	36

B. Suppose Lola rolls the two number cubes 180 times. Predict how many times she will roll two numbers that include a pair of numbers like the ones described above.

One way to answer is to write and solve an equation.

$\dfrac{5}{36} \times 180 = x$ Multiply the probability by the total number of rolls.

$25 = x$ Solve for x.

Lola can expect to roll two numbers that include at least one 4 and have a product of 16 or more about 25 times.

EXAMPLE 2

A store has a sale bin of soup cans. There are 6 cans of chicken noodle soup, 8 cans of split pea soup, 8 cans of minestrone, and 13 cans of vegetable soup. Find the probability of picking each type of soup at random. Then predict what kind of soup a customer is most likely to pick.

$P(\text{chicken noodle}) = \frac{6}{35}$ $P(\text{split pea}) = \frac{8}{35}$

$P(\text{minestrone}) = \frac{8}{35}$ $P(\text{vegetable}) = \frac{13}{35}$

The customer is most likely to pick vegetable soup. That is the event that has the greatest probability.

EXERCISES

Find the probability of each event. (Lessons 6.1, 6.2)

1. Graciela picks a white mouse at random from a bin of 8 white mice, 2 gray mice, and 2 brown mice.

_____

2. Theo spins a spinner that has 12 equal sections marked 1 through 12. It does **not** land on 1.

_____

3. Tania flips a coin three times. The coin lands on heads twice and on tails once, not necessarily in that order.

_____

4. Students are randomly assigned two-digit codes. Each digit is either 1, 2, 3, or 4. Guy is given the number 11.

_____

5. Patty tosses a coin and rolls a number cube. (Lesson 6.3)

   a. Find the probability that the coin lands on heads and the cube lands on an even number.

_____

   b. Patty tosses the coin and rolls the number cube 60 times. Predict how many times the coin will land on heads and the cube will land on an even number.

_____

6. Rajan's school is having a raffle. The school sold raffle tickets with 3-digit numbers. Each digit is either 1, 2, or 3. The school also sold 2 tickets with the number 000. Which number is more likely to be picked, 123 or 000? (Lesson 6.3)

_____

© Houghton Mifflin Harcourt Publishing Company

7. Suppose you know that over the last 10 years, the probability that your town would have at least one major storm was 40%. Describe a simulation that you could use to find the experimental probability that your town will have at least one major storm in at least 3 of the next 5 years. *(Lesson 6.4)*

_____

_____

_____

_____

Unit 3 Performance Tasks

1. **CAREERS IN MATH** | Meteorologist A meteorologist predicts a 20% chance of rain for the next two nights, and a 75% chance of rain on the third night.

a. On which night is it most likely to rain? On that night, is it *likely* to rain or *unlikely* to rain?

_____

b. Tara would like to go camping for the next 3 nights, but will not go if it is likely to rain on all 3 nights. Should she go? Use probability to justify your answer.

_____

_____

2. Sinead tossed 4 coins at the same time. She did this 50 times, and 6 of those times, all 4 coins showed the same result (heads or tails).

a. Find the experimental probability that all 4 coins show the same result when tossed.

_____

b. Can you determine the experimental probability that **no** coin shows heads? Explain.

_____

c. Suppose Sinead tosses the coins 125 more times. Use experimental probability to predict the number of times that all 4 coins will show heads or tails. Show your work.

_____

Selected Response

1. A pizza parlor offers thin, thick, and traditional style pizza crusts. You can get pepperoni, beef, mushrooms, olives, or peppers for toppings. You order a one-topping pizza. How many outcomes are in the sample space?

  (A) 3   (C) 8

  (B) 5   (D) 15

2. A bag contains 9 purple marbles, 2 blue marbles, and 4 pink marbles. The probability of randomly drawing a blue marble is $\frac{2}{15}$. What is the probability of **not** drawing a blue marble?

  (A) $\frac{2}{15}$

  (B) $\frac{4}{15}$

  (C) $\frac{11}{15}$

  (D) $\frac{13}{15}$

3. During the month of April, Dora kept track of the bugs she saw in her garden. She saw a ladybug on 23 days of the month. What is the experimental probability that she will see a ladybug on May 1?

  (A) $\frac{1}{23}$

  (B) $\frac{7}{30}$

  (C) $\frac{1}{2}$

  (D) $\frac{23}{30}$

4. Ryan flips a coin 8 times and gets tails all 8 times. What is the experimental probability that Ryan will get heads the next time he flips the coin?

  (A) 1   (C) $\frac{1}{8}$

  (B) $\frac{1}{2}$ (D) 0

5. Jay tossed two coins several times and then recorded the results in the table below.

Coin Toss Results				
Toss 1	Toss 2	Toss 3	Toss 4	Toss 5
H; H	H; T	T; H	T; T	T; H

What is the experimental probability that the coins will land on different sides on his next toss?

  (A) $\frac{1}{5}$

  (B) $\frac{2}{5}$

  (C) $\frac{3}{5}$

  (D) $\frac{4}{5}$

6. A used guitar is on sale for $280. Derek offers the seller $\frac{3}{4}$ of the advertised price. How much does Derek offer for the guitar?

  (A) $180

  (B) $210

  (C) $240

  (D) $270

7. What is the probability of tossing two fair coins and having exactly one land tails side up?

  (A) $\frac{1}{8}$

  (B) $\frac{1}{4}$

  (C) $\frac{1}{3}$

  (D) $\frac{1}{2}$

8. Find the percent change from 60 to 96.

  (A) 37.5% decrease

  (B) 37.5% increase

  (C) 60% decrease

  (D) 60% increase

9. Jason, Erik, and Jamie are friends in art class. The teacher randomly chooses 2 of the 21 students in the class to work together on a project. What is the probability that two of these three friends will be chosen?

Ⓐ $\frac{1}{105}$

Ⓑ $\frac{1}{70}$

Ⓒ $\frac{34}{140}$

Ⓓ $\frac{4}{50}$

10. Philip rolls a number cube 12 times. Which is the best prediction for the number of times that he will roll a number that is odd and less than 5?

Ⓐ 2   Ⓒ 4

Ⓑ 3   Ⓓ 6

Gridded Response

11. A bag contains 6 white beads and 4 black beads. You pick out a bead at random, record its color, and put the bead back in the bag. You repeat this process 35 times. How many times would you expect to remove a white bead from the bag?

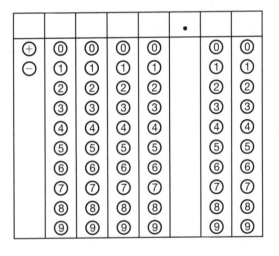

12. A set of cards includes 20 yellow cards, 16 green cards, and 24 blue cards. What is the probability, written in decimal form, that a blue card is chosen at random?

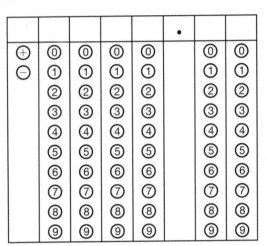

 Estimate your answer before solving the problem. Use your estimate to check the reasonableness of your answer.

13. A survey reveals that one airline's flights have a 92% probability of being on time. Out of 4,000 flights in a year, how many flights would you predict to arrive on time?

Multiple Representations of Linear Relationships

MODULE 7
Linear Relationships
TEKS 7.7

MODULE 8
Equations and Inequalities
TEKS 7.10.A, 7.10.B, 7.10.C, 7.11.A, 7.11.B

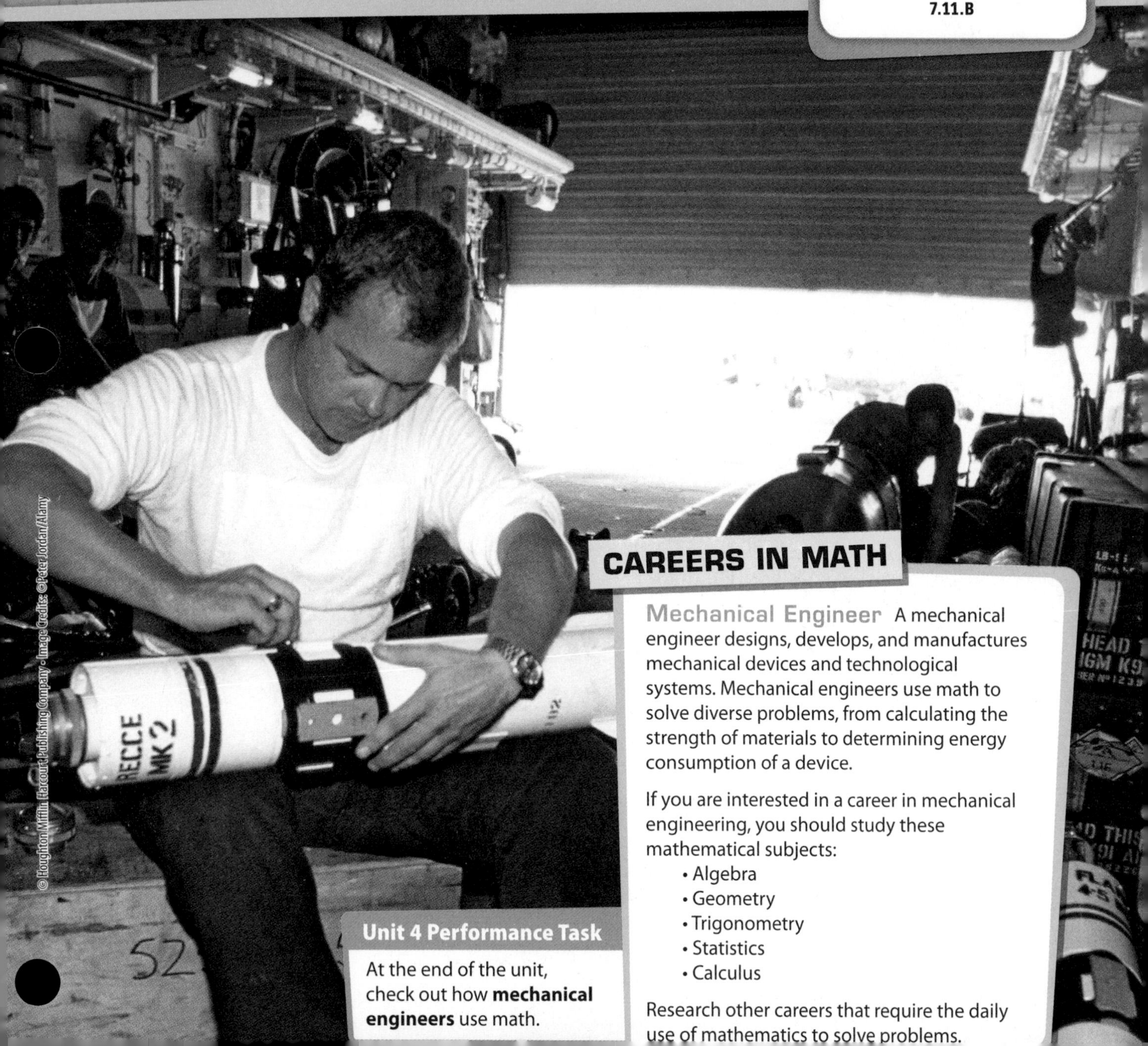

CAREERS IN MATH

Mechanical Engineer A mechanical engineer designs, develops, and manufactures mechanical devices and technological systems. Mechanical engineers use math to solve diverse problems, from calculating the strength of materials to determining energy consumption of a device.

If you are interested in a career in mechanical engineering, you should study these mathematical subjects:
- Algebra
- Geometry
- Trigonometry
- Statistics
- Calculus

Research other careers that require the daily use of mathematics to solve problems.

Unit 4 Performance Task

At the end of the unit, check out how **mechanical engineers** use math.

Use the puzzle to preview key vocabulary from this unit. Unscramble the circled letters to answer the riddle at the bottom of the page.

As one quantity changes by a constant amount, the other quantity also changes by a constant amount. (Lesson 7.1)

— — —◯— — —

— — — — —◯— — — — —

A special type of linear relationship in which the rate of change is constant, or one in which the ratio of one quantity to the other is constant. (Lesson 7.1)

— — — —◯— — — — — —

— — — — —◯— — — —

An equation with more than one operation. (Lesson 8.1)

— — — — — — — —◯— — — — —◯

A variable whose value is less than zero. (Lesson 8.1)

— —◯— — — — — — — —◯—

A variable whose value is greater than zero. (Lesson 8.1)

—◯— — —◯— — — — —◯— —

Q: Why does the sum of −4 and 3 complain more than the sum of −3 and 5?

A: It's the ___ ___ ___ ___ ___ ___ ___ ___ ___ ___!

Linear Relationships

? **ESSENTIAL QUESTION**

How can you use linear relationships to solve real-world problems?

Real-World Video

A kayaker can use the linear relationship between distance, rate, and time to find out how far she can travel. All linear relationships can be described by an equation in the form of $y = mx + b$.

my.hrw.com

© Houghton Mifflin Harcourt Publishing Company • ©Bob Daemmrich/Alamy Images

GO DIGITAL
my.hrw.com

my.hrw.com

Go digital with your write-in student edition, accessible on any device.

Math On the Spot

Scan with your smart phone to jump directly to the online edition, video tutor, and more.

Animated Math

Interactively explore key concepts to see how math works.

Personal Math Trainer

Get immediate feedback and help as you work through practice sets.

221

Are YOU Ready?

Complete these exercises to review skills you will need for this chapter.

Personal Math Trainer

Online Assessment and Intervention

my.hrw.com

Evaluate Expressions

EXAMPLE $3(4) + 7 = 12 + 7$ Multiply first.
                          $= 19$ Then add.

Evaluate each expression.

1. $2(5) + 11$ _____

2. $9(6) - 5$ _____

3. $4(12) - 15$ _____

4. $-6(2) + 13$ _____

5. $7(-4) - 8$ _____

6. $-2(-5) + 7$ _____

Function Tables

EXAMPLE   Find a rule relating the given values.

y is 5 times x.

x	1	2	3	4
y	5	10	15	20

Find a rule relating the given values.

7.

x	1	2	3	4
y	3	6	9	12

_____

8.

x	1	2	3	4
y	9	10	11	12

_____

Graph Ordered Pairs (First Quadrant)

EXAMPLE

Graph point $A(4, 3)$.
Start at the origin.
Move 4 units right.
Then move 3 units up.

Graph each point on the coordinate grid above.

9. $B(9, 0)$

10. $C(2, 7)$

11. $D(0, 5)$

12. $E(6, 2)$

© Houghton Mifflin Harcourt Publishing Company

Reading Start-Up

Visualize Vocabulary

Use the ✔ words to complete the third column of the chart.

Reviewing Proportional Relationships		
Definition	**Example**	**Review Word**
A comparison of two quantities by division.	2 to 4	
A ratio of two quantities that have different units.	8 ounces in 1 cup	
A statement that two rates or ratios are equivalent.	$\frac{2}{4} = \frac{1}{2}$	

Vocabulary

Review Words
   constant (*constante*)
✔ proportion (*proporción*)
   proportional relationship (*relación proporcional*)
✔ rate (*tasa*)
   rate of change (*tasa de cambio*)
✔ ratio (*razón*)
   unit rates (*tasas unitaria*)

Preview Words
   constant of proportionality (*constante de proporcionalidad*)
   equation (*ecuación*)
   linear relationship (*relación lineal*)

Understand Vocabulary

Answer each question with the correct preview word.

1. What is a mathematical statement that two expressions are equal?

   _____

2. What is a constant ratio of two variables that are related

   proportionally? _____

Active Reading

Tri-Fold Before beginning the module, create a tri-fold to help you learn the concepts and vocabulary in this module. Fold the paper into three sections. Label the columns "What I Know," "What I Need to Know," and "What I Learned." Complete the first two columns before you read. After studying the module, complete the third column.

Unpacking the TEKS

Understanding the TEKS and the vocabulary terms in the TEKS will help you know exactly what you are expected to learn in this module.

TEKS 7.7

Represent linear relationships using verbal descriptions, tables, graphs, and equations that simplify to the form $y = mx + b$.

What It Means to You

You will use a variety of methods to represent linear relationships.

UNPACKING EXAMPLE 7.7

Charia orders T-shirts from a Web site that charges $8 per shirt. She also chooses expedited shipping that costs an additional $15.

A. Use a table to show how much Charia would pay for different numbers of T-shirts.

T-Shirts	Total cost ($)
1	$15 + 8(1) = 23$
2	$15 + 8(2) = 31$
3	$15 + 8(3) = 39$
4	$15 + 8(4) = 47$
5	$15 + 8(5) = 55$
6	$15 + 8(6) = 63$

B. Write the linear relationship as an equation.

The total cost is $8 times the number of shirts plus $15 for shipping. The linear equation is $y = 8x + 15$.

C. Graph the linear relationship.

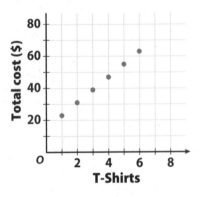

Visit **my.hrw.com** to see all the **TEKS** unpacked.

my.hrw.com

Linear Relationships in the Form $y = mx + b$

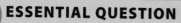 **TEKS**
Expressions, equations, and relationships—7.7 The student applies mathematical process standards to represent linear relationships using multiple representations....

? **ESSENTIAL QUESTION**

How do you use tables and verbal descriptions to describe a linear relationship?

EXPLORE ACTIVITY  **TEKS** 7.7

Discovering Linear Relationships

Many real-world situations can be described by linear relationships.

Jodie pays $5 per ticket for a play and a one-time $2 convenience fee. The table shows the total cost for different numbers of tickets.

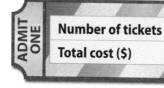

Number of tickets	1	2	3	4	5
Total cost ($)	7	12	17	22	27

A Describe a pattern for the row showing the number of tickets bought.

_____

B Describe the pattern for the row showing total cost.

_____

_____

C Out of the total cost paid, how much does the actual ticket account for?

_____

Reflect

1. How much more than $5 does Jodie pay for one ticket? What if she buys 5 tickets? Explain.

_____

_____

_____

2. **Analyze Relationships** Describe the total amount paid in dollars based on the number of tickets.

_____

Representing Linear Relationships Using a Table

In a **linear relationship** between two quantities, as one quantity changes by a constant amount, the other quantity also changes by a constant amount. Proportional relationships are a special kind of linear relationship.

EXAMPLE 1 Real World

TEKS 7.7

A man's shoe size is approximately 3 times his foot length in inches minus 22. Use a table to represent the relationship between foot length and shoe size.

STEP 1 Make a table. Label the top row Foot length (in.) and the bottom row Shoe size.

STEP 2 Enter some foot lengths in inches. Since it is impossible to have a negative shoe size, pick a foot length that when multiplied by 3 will be greater than 22.

Think:

$3 \times 7 = 21$ $21 - 22 = -1$; this cannot be a man's shoe size.

$3 \times 8 = 24$ $24 - 22 = 2$; start the table at 8 inches.

> Remember that a man's shoe size is 3 times his foot length in inches minus 22.

> **Math Talk**
> Mathematical Processes
>
> Why is foot length on the top and shoe size on the bottom?

STEP 3 Make a table relating foot length to show size.

Foot length (in.)	8	9	10	11	12
Shoe size	2	5	8	11	14

Reflect

3. **Analyze Relationships** If someone had a foot length of 13 inches, how can you use the table to determine his shoe size?

_____

_____

4. **Critical Thinking** Foot lengths do not have to be whole numbers. Give an example of a non-whole number foot length you could have chosen when filling in the table and find the approximate shoe size. What should a person do if their foot length does not correspond to a whole or half shoe size? Explain.

_____

_____

_____

5. Lea's house is 350 meters from her friend's house. Lea walks to her friend's house at a constant rate of 50 meters per minute. Use a table to represent the relationship between time and the distance Lea has left to walk to her friend's house.

Personal Math Trainer

Online Assessment and Intervention

my.hrw.com

Representing Linear Relationships Using a Verbal Description

Just as you can create a table given a verbal description of a linear relationship, you can also create a verbal description given a table. To do so, look for patterns so that you can determine how a change in one quantity affects another. Then put the patterns into words by making a general statement about the relationship.

Math On the Spot

my.hrw.com

EXAMPLE 2 Real World

TEKS 7.7

Luis will participate in a walkathon for charity. He received a pledge from his aunt, and the table shows the relationship between the miles walked by Luis and the amount his aunt pledged.

Use the table to give a verbal description of the relationship between miles walked and amount pledged.

Miles walked	1	2	3	4	5
Amount pledged ($)	31.50	33	34.50	36	37.50

My Notes

STEP 1 Look for patterns in the different values for miles walked and amount pledged.

$33 - 31.50 = 1.50$ Find the difference in the amounts pledged.

$2 - 1 = 1$ Find the difference in the number of miles walked.

$\frac{1.50}{1} = 1.50$ Find the rate that represents the amount pledged per mile walked.

In the table, each value for the number of miles walked is 1 greater than the previous one, and each amount pledged is $1.50 greater than the previous one.

STEP 2 Determine how much more money than $1.50 Luis's aunt is pledging for 1 mile walked.

> Luis's aunt only gives the additional $30 one time.

$31.50 − $1.50 = $30

Luis's aunt gives an additional $30 more than the $1.50 per mile.

STEP 3 Give a verbal description for the relationship between the miles walked by Luis and amount of money pledged by his aunt.

Luis's aunt pledged $30 plus an additional $1.50 for each mile he walks.

Reflect

6. **Make a Prediction** How could you find the amount pledged by Luis's aunt if Luis walks 7 miles? What is the amount pledged?

_____

_____

_____

7. **What If...?** Luis's mother decides to also pledge $15 plus and additional $3 per mile. If Luis wants to earn the same amount from his mother and his aunt, how far must he walk? What is the amount he will earn from

each person? _____

YOUR TURN

The relationship between the cost of an online advertisement for a movie and the number of times it is clicked on is shown in the table.

8. Use the table to give a verbal description of the relationship.

Number of clicks	10	20	30	40	50
Cost ($)	150.50	151	151.50	152	152.50

_____

9. What is the cost for the advertisement if it is clicked 1000 times?

_____

10. Is there a lower limit for the number of clicks? Is there an upper limit? Explain.

_____

_____

_____

_____

Personal Math Trainer

Online Assessment and Intervention

ⓗ my.hrw.com

© Houghton Mifflin Harcourt Publishing Company

1. The age of a cat 2 years or older can be approximately converted into human years by multiplying by 4 and adding 16. Use a table to represent the relationship between cat age and human years. (Example 1)

Label the rows of the table.

Choose numbers to represent the ages of the cat. Choose numbers that are 2 or greater, since the relationship described is only for cats 2 years or older.

Complete the table by calculating the value for Human years based on the description.

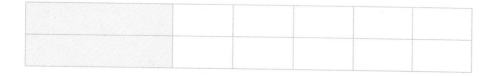

2. The yearly cost of a community college based on the number of credits taken is shown in the table. Use the table to give a verbal description of the relationship between credits and cost. (Explore Activity and Example 2)

Credits	3	6	9	12	15
Cost ($)	175	250	325	400	475

STEP 1 Look for patterns in the different values for credits and cost.

Each value for credits is _____ greater than the previous one,

and each value for cost is _____ greater than the previous one.

This means that 1 credit corresponds to _____ in cost.

STEP 2 Determine how many more dollars than _____ that it costs to take 3 credits.

It costs _____ − _____ = _____ more than _____ to take 3 credits.

STEP 3 Give a verbal description for the relationship between credits and cost.

The yearly cost of the community college is _____ plus

_____ for each credit taken.

? ESSENTIAL QUESTION CHECK-IN

3. When using tables and verbal descriptions to describe a linear relationship, why is it useful to convert from one to another?

_____

_____

7.1 Independent Practice

TEKS 7.7

Personal
Math Trainer

Online
Assessment and
Intervention

my.hrw.com

A teacher is making multiple copies of a 1-page homework assignment.
The time it takes her in seconds is 2 times the number of copies she
makes plus 3.

4. What does the 3 represent in this scenario? What does the 2 represent?

_____

_____

_____

5. What is the total number of seconds it takes for the teacher to make
1 copy? 2 copies? 3 copies? By how many seconds does the total time
increase for each copy?

_____

_____

_____

6. Represent Real-World Problems Represent the relationship between
the number of copies made and time in seconds in the table below.

Rosalee parks at a metered space that still has some time left. She adds
some dimes to the meter. The table below represents the number of
minutes left based on the number of dimes inserted into the meter.

Dimes	4	8	12	16	20
Minutes	22	38	54	70	86

7. How many minutes does 1 dime correspond to?

_____

8. Based on your answer to exercise 7, how many minutes should you
receive for inserting 4 dimes?

_____

_____

9. Analyze Relationships Give a verbal description of the relationship between dimes and the number of minutes left on the meter.

_____

_____

10. Look at your answer for exercise 9. What does each of the numbers in the answer represent?

_____

_____

_____

_____

The cost in dollars of a loaf of bread in a bakery is equal to 2 minus 0.25 times the number of days since it was baked.

11. What is different about this description compared to most of the other descriptions you have seen in this lesson?

_____

_____

_____

12. Make a Conjecture Is there a point at which the linear relationship between days and dollars no longer makes sense?

_____

_____

_____

_____

13. Represent Real-World Problems Represent the relationship between days and dollars in the table below.

14. Find the number of days it will take the price to reach $0.25.

_____

The relationship between the number of years since a tree was transplanted and its height in inches is shown in the table.

Years	2	4	5	8	9
Height (in.)	34	50	58	82	90

15. What is different about this table compared to the other tables you have seen in this lesson?

_____

_____

16. Analyze Relationships Can you give a description of the relationship between the years since the tree was transplanted and its height in inches? If so, what is it?

_____

_____

_____

17. Communicate Mathematical Ideas Suppose you are analyzing the relationship between time and distance given in a table, and there are 4 values for each quantity. You divide distance 2 minus distance 1 by time 2 minus time 1. You then divide distance 4 minus distance 3 by time 4 minus time 3 and get a different answer. What can you say about the relationship? Explain.

_____

_____

18. Persevere in Problem Solving There is a linear relationship between a salesperson's sales and her weekly income. If her sales are $200, her income is $500, and if her sales are $1,200, her income is $600. What is the relationship between sales and income?

_____

19. Critique Reasoning Molly orders necklace kits online. The cost of the necklace kits can be represented by a linear relationship. Molly's order of 3 kits cost $12.50. Another order of 5 kits cost $17.50. Molly decides that the kits cost $5 each. Is she correct? Explain.

_____

_____

Work Area

LESSON 7.2 Writing and Graphing Equations in the Form $y = mx + b$

TEKS
Expressions, equations, and relationships—7.7 The student is expected to represent linear relationships using verbal descriptions, tables, graphs, and equations that simplify to the form $y = mx + b$.

? **ESSENTIAL QUESTION**

How do you write and graph a linear relationship?

EXPLORE ACTIVITY  **TEKS 7.7**

Graphing Linear Relationships

Teresa signs up for a membership to rent video games. The company charges $5 per month and $2 per video game. Graph a linear relationship between the number of games Teresa rents and her monthly cost.

STEP 1 Make a table. Record different values for the linear relationship.

Number of video games rented	Monthly cost ($)
0	$5 + 2(0) = 5$
1	$5 + 2(1) =$
2	$5 + 2(\quad) =$
3	$5 + 2(\quad) =$
4	$5 + 2(\quad) =$

> To find the monthly cost, multiply the number of video games rented by 2 and then add 5.

STEP 2 Use the table to create ordered pairs:

$(0, 5), (1, 7), (2, 9), (3, 11), (4, 13)$

Plot each ordered pair on the coordinate grid.

Total Cost for Video Game Rental

Reflect

1. Do the values between the points make sense in this context? Explain.

_____

_____

© Houghton Mifflin Harcourt Publishing Company • Image Credits: ©Asia Images Group/Getty Images

Writing Linear Relationships

You can write an equation to describe a linear relationship. The equation of a linear relationship is $y = mx + b$, where m is the rate of change and b is the value of y when x is 0.

EXAMPLE 1 Real World

TEKS 7.7

Anthony runs a bicycle courier company that charges $3 per delivery plus $0.50 per mile. Write an equation to describe the linear relationship.

STEP 1 Make a table. Record different values for the linear relationship.

Distance (miles)	Cost ($)
0	$3 + 0.5(0) = 3$
1	$3 + 0.5(1) = 3.5$
2	$3 + 0.5(2) = 4$
3	$3 + 0.5(3) = 4.5$
4	$3 + 0.5(4) = 5$

Math Talk
Mathematical Processes

Would all values between the given distances make sense? Explain.

STEP 2 Write an equation for the delivery cost y for x miles traveled.

When distance is 0, the cost is $3. With each additional mile, the cost increases by $0.50.

Cost	=	$0.50	times	number of miles	plus	$3 charge
↓	↓	↓	↓	↓	↓	↓
y	=	0.5	·	x	+	3

The equation is $y = 0.5x + 3$.

YOUR TURN

Write an equation to describe the linear relationship.

2. The temperature of a pot of water is 45 °F. The temperature increases by 20 °F per minute when being heated.

_____

3. A bamboo reed is planted when it is 12 centimeters tall. It grows 2.2 centimeters per week.

_____

Personal Math Trainer

Online Assessment and Intervention

⏻ my.hrw.com

Representing Linear Relationships Using Multiple Representations

There are several ways to represent a linear relationship.

Math On the Spot
my.hrw.com

EXAMPLE 2 · Real World

TEKS 7.7

Charlie starts with $350 in his savings account. He withdraws $15 per week from his account. Represent the relationship using a table, an equation, and a graph.

STEP 1 Make a table. Record different values for the linear relationship.

STEP 2 Write an equation for the amount of money y in the savings after x weeks.

$350 minus $15 times the number of weeks

$y = 350 - 15x$

Week	Amount ($)
0	$350 - 15(0) = 350$
1	$350 - 15(1) = 335$
2	$350 - 15(2) = 320$
3	$350 - 15(3) = 305$
4	$350 - 15(4) = 290$

STEP 3 Use the table to create ordered pairs and then plot the data.

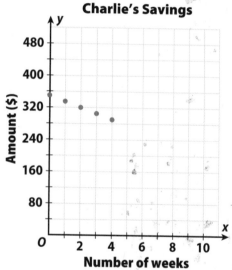

Charlie's Savings

Reflect

4. Does it make sense to connect the points on the graph with a line? Explain.

_____

_____

5. Does an ordered pair with a negative y-value make sense in the situation?

_____

_____

Animated Math
my.hrw.com

Personal
Math Trainer
Online Assessment
and Intervention
my.hrw.com

 **YOUR TURN**

6. A bicycle rental company charges $18 to rent a bicycle, plus $7 for every two hours of rental time. Represent the relationship using a table, an equation, and a graph.

Hours rented	Cost ($)
0	
2	
4	
6	
8	

Equation: _____

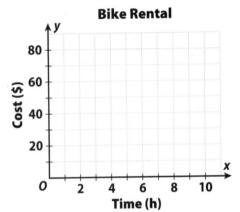

Bike Rental

Guided Practice

Graph the linear relationship. (Explore Activity)

1. A pool contains 5 liters of water, and 10 liters of water are being poured into the pool every 5 minutes.

Write an equation to describe the linear relationships. (Example 1)

2. A moving company charges a $50 flat fee and $55 per hour to move.

$y =$ _____ $x +$ _____

3. Anne has $250 in a savings account. She withdraws $5 per month.

$y =$ _____ $x +$ _____

4. Erin owns $375 worth of comic books. She spends $15 every week on new comic books. Represent the relationship using a table and an equation. (Example 2)

$y =$ _____ $x +$ _____

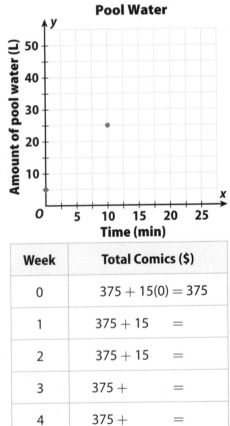

Pool Water

Week	Total Comics ($)
0	$375 + 15(0) = 375$
1	$375 + 15$ $=$
2	$375 + 15$ $=$
3	$375 +$ $=$
4	$375 +$ $=$

? ESSENTIAL QUESTION CHECK-IN

5. How can you use a table of data to write and graph a linear relationship?

_____

_____

7.2 Independent Practice

TEKS 7.7

Personal Math Trainer

Online Assessment and Intervention

my.hrw.com

A cab company charges a $3.50 boarding fee and $0.50 per mile.

6. Write an equation to describe the relationship between the cost of the cab ride and the number of miles traveled.

_____

7. Graph the linear relationship.

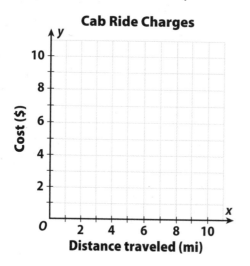

Cab Ride Charges

Cost ($) vs Distance traveled (mi)

8. Draw Conclusions Does it make sense to draw a line through the points? Explain.

_____

_____

_____

9. What If? Suppose that the boarding fee was changed to $5. How would the graph change?

_____

_____

_____

For 10–13 write an equation to represent the given linear relationship. Then state the meaning of the given ordered pair.

10. A plain medium pizza costs $8.00. Additional toppings cost $0.85 each. (4, 11.4)

_____

_____

11. Luis joined a gym that charges a membership fee of $99.95 plus $7.95 per month. (9, 171.5)

_____

_____

12. A tank currently holds 35 liters of water, and water is pouring into the tank at 15 liters per minute. (5.5, 117.5)

_____

_____

13. Jonas is riding his bicycle at 18 kilometers per hour, and he has already ridden for 40 kilometers. (6, 148)

_____

_____

_____

14. Analyze Relationships How can you use an equation of a linear relationship to verify the points on the graph of the relationship?

_____

_____

_____

_____

15. **Multiple Representations** A furniture salesperson earns $750 per week plus a 15% commission on all sales made during the week.

   a. Complete the table of data.

Weekly Sales ($)	Earnings ($)
0	
1,000	
2,000	
3,000	
4,000	

   b. Graph the values in the table.

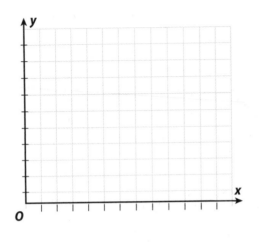

   c. Write a linear equation to describe the relationship.

   _____

16. **Make a Conjecture** Can you draw a straight line through the points? Explain.

   _____

   _____

Work Area

17. **Analyze Relationships** What are the advantages of portraying a linear relationship as a table, graph, or equation?

   _____

   _____

   _____

   _____

18. **Critical Thinking** Describe when it would be more useful to represent a linear relationship with an equation than with a graph.

   _____

   _____

19. **Communicate Mathematical Ideas** How can you determine when to draw a line through the points on the graph of a linear relationship?

   _____

   _____

Ready to Go On?

Personal Math Trainer

Online Assessment and Intervention

my.hrw.com

7.1 Linear Relationships in the Form $y = mx + b$

1. Darice also took a break after riding 10 miles. The table below shows the rate at which Darice rides her bicycle after the break.

Time after break (min)	1	2	3	4	5	6
Total distance (mi)	$10\frac{1}{4}$	$10\frac{1}{2}$	$10\frac{3}{4}$	11	$11\frac{1}{4}$	$11\frac{1}{2}$

Write a verbal description of the relationship between the time she rides and the distance she travels.

_____

_____

7.2 Writing and Graphing Equations in the Form $y = mx + b$

Emir started out a card game with 500 points. For every hand he won, he gained 100 points.

2. Complete the table.

Hands won	Points
0	
1	
2	
3	
4	

3. Plot the points on the graph.

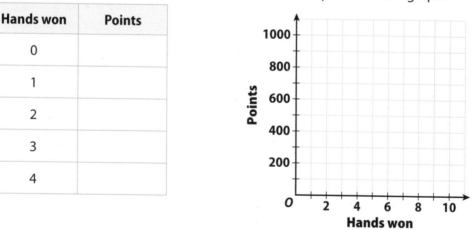

4. Write an equation for the linear relationship. _____

? ESSENTIAL QUESTION

5. What are some of the ways you can represent real-world linear relationships?

_____

_____

_____

Selected Response

1. Which description corresponds to the relationship shown in the table?

Hours	5	10	15	20
Pay	$50	$90	$130	$170

Ⓐ earning $10 an hour

Ⓑ earning $8 an hour plus a $10 bonus

Ⓒ earning $7 an hour plus a $15 bonus

Ⓓ earning $9 an hour

2. Which equation represents the same linear relationship as the graph below?

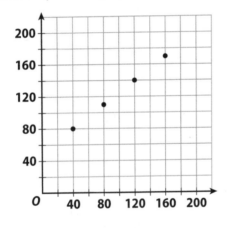

Ⓐ $y = 1.2x + 32$ Ⓒ $y = 0.75x + 50$

Ⓑ $y = 1.5x + 20$ Ⓓ $y = 0.8x + 45$

3. Omar began the week with $25. He took a city bus to and from school, paying $1.25 for each trip. Let x be the number of trips he took and y be the amount of money he had left at the end of the week. Which equation represents the relationship in the situation?

Ⓐ $y = 1.25x + 25$ Ⓒ $x = 25 - 1.25y$

Ⓑ $y = 25 - 1.25x$ Ⓓ $y = 1.25x - 25$

4. Which table represents the same linear relationship as the equation $y = 5x + 7$?

Ⓐ
x	0	1	2	3
y	0	5	10	15

Ⓑ
x	2	3	4	5
y	17	22	27	32

Ⓒ
x	1	2	3	4
y	12	19	26	33

Ⓓ
x	1	2	3	4
y	12	17	24	31

5. Selina is planning to paint a large picture on a wall. She draws a smaller version first. The drawing is 8 inches by 6 inches. If the scale of the drawing is 2 in: 1 ft, what is the area of the actual picture on the wall?

Ⓐ 4 feet   Ⓒ 48 square inches

Ⓑ 3 feet   Ⓓ 12 square feet

Gridded Response

6. The equation $y = 3.5x - 210$ represents the profit made by a manufacturer that sells products for $3.50 each, where y is the profit and x is the number of units sold. What is the profit in dollars when 80 units are sold?

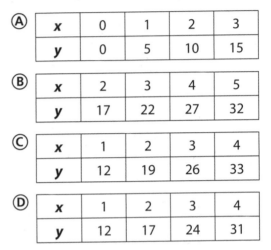

Equations and Inequalities

ESSENTIAL QUESTION

How can you use equations and Inequalities to solve real-world problems?

Real-World Video

When you take a taxi, you will be charged an initial fee plus a charge per mile. To describe situations like this, you can write a two-step equation.

ⓞ my.hrw.com

GO DIGITAL

my.hrw.com

 my.hrw.com

Go digital with your write-in student edition, accessible on any device.

 Math On the Spot

Scan with your smart phone to jump directly to the online edition, video tutor, and more.

 Animated Math

Interactively explore key concepts to see how math works.

 Personal Math Trainer

Get immediate feedback and help as you work through practice sets.

Are YOU Ready?

Complete these exercises to review skills you will need for this chapter.

Inverse Operations

> **EXAMPLE**
> $3x = 24$ x is multiplied by 3.
> $\dfrac{3x}{3} = \dfrac{24}{3}$ Use the inverse operation, division.
>   Divide both sides by 3.
> $x = 8$
>
> $z + 6 = 4$ 6 is added to z.
> $\underline{-6 = -6}$ Use the inverse operation, subtraction.
> $z = -2$ Subtract 6 from both sides.

Solve each equation, using inverse operations.

1. $9w = -54$ _____

2. $b - 12 = 3$ _____

3. $\dfrac{n}{4} = -11$ _____

Locate Points on a Number Line

> **EXAMPLE**
>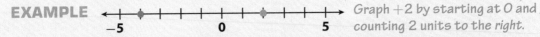
> Graph +2 by starting at 0 and counting 2 units to the right.
>
> Graph −4 by starting at 0 and counting 4 units to the left.

Graph each number on the number line.

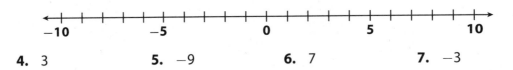

4. 3   **5.** −9   **6.** 7   **7.** −3

Solve and Graph Inequalities

> **EXAMPLE**
> $-3d \geq -18$ d is multiplied by −3.
> $\dfrac{-3d}{-3} \geq \dfrac{-18}{-3}$ Divide both sides by −3.
>   When you multiply or divide both sides by a negative
> $d \leq 6$ number, reverse the direction of the inequality.

8. $4p > 20$ _____

9. $m - 7 \leq 3$ _____

10. $\dfrac{s}{-2} < 9$ _____

11. $r + 6 \leq -7$ _____

12. $\dfrac{h}{4} > -5$ _____

13. $-y \leq 2$ _____

Reading Start-Up

Visualize Vocabulary

Use the ✔ words to complete the graphic. You may put more than one word in each box.

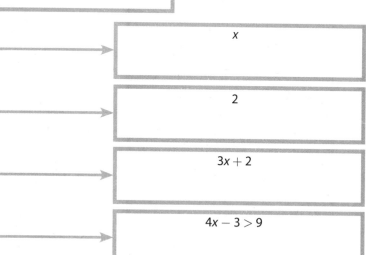

Expressions and Inequalities

x

2

$3x + 2$

$4x - 3 > 9$

Vocabulary

Review Words
- ✔ algebraic expression *(expresión algebraica)*
- coefficient *(coeficiente)*
- ✔ constant *(contante)*
- ✔ equation *(ecuación)*
- greater than *(mayor que)*
- ✔ inequality *(desigualdad)*
- integers *(entero)*
- less than *(menor que)*
- operations *(operaciones)*
- solution *(solución)*
- ✔ variable *(variable)*

Understand Vocabulary

Complete each sentence, using the review words.

1. A value of the variable that makes the equation true is a _____.

2. The set of all whole numbers and their opposites are _____.

3. An _____ is an expression that contains at least one variable.

Active Reading

Layered Book Before beginning the module, create a layered book to help you learn the concepts in this module. At the top of the first flap, write the title of the module, "Equations and Inequalities." Then label each flap with one of the lesson titles in this module. As you study each lesson, write important ideas, such as vocabulary and formulas, under the appropriate flap.

Unpacking the TEKS

Understanding the TEKS and the vocabulary terms in the TEKS will help you know exactly what you are expected to learn in this module.

TEKS 7.10.A

Write one-variable, two-step equations and inequalities to represent constraints or conditions within problems.

Key Vocabulary

equation *(ecuación)*
A mathematical sentence that shows that two expressions are equivalent.

variable *(variable)*
A symbol used to represent a quantity that can change.

What It Means to You

You will write an equation or inequality to solve a real-world problem.

UNPACKING EXAMPLE 7.10.A

To rent a certain car for a day costs $39 plus $0.29 for every mile the car is driven. Write an algebraic equation to show how much it costs to rent the car for a day.

The cost to rent the car for a day is

$$C = 39 + 0.29m$$

where C is the cost in dollars and m is the number of miles driven.

TEKS 7.11.B

Determine if the given value(s) make(s) one-variable, two-step equations and inequalities true.

Key Vocabulary

inequality *(desigualdad)*
A mathematical sentence that shows the relationship between quantities that are not equivalent.

What It Means to You

You will determine if an equation or inequality is true given the value of a variable.

UNPACKING EXAMPLE 7.11.B

Determine whether the inequality $\frac{y}{5} - 14 > -7$ is true for $y = 20$ and for $y = 55$.

$\underline{y = 20}$

$$\frac{y}{5} - 14 \overset{?}{>} -7$$

$$\frac{20}{5} - 14 \overset{?}{>} -7$$

$$4 - 14 \overset{?}{>} -7$$

$$-10 \overset{?}{>} -7 \; \textbf{✗}$$

$\underline{y = 55}$

$$\frac{y}{5} - 14 \overset{?}{>} -7$$

$$\frac{55}{5} - 14 \overset{?}{>} -7$$

$$11 - 14 \overset{?}{>} -7$$

$$-3 \overset{?}{>} -7 \; \textbf{✔}$$

The equation is true for $y = 55$ but not for $y = 20$.

Visit **my.hrw.com** to see all the **TEKS** unpacked.

⏻ my.hrw.com

Writing Two-Step Equations

TEKS
Expressions, equations, and relationships—
7.10.A Write one-variable, two-step equations ... to represent constraints or conditions within problems. *Also 7.10.C, 7.11.A.*

? ESSENTIAL QUESTION

How do you write a two-step equation?

EXPLORE ACTIVITY TEKS 7.11.A

Modeling Two-Step Equations

You can use algebra tiles to model two-step equations.

KEY

+ = positive variable

− = negative variable

+ = 1   − = −1

Use algebra tiles to model 3x − 4 = 5.

A How can you model the left side of the equation?

_____

B How can you model the right side of the equation?

_____

C Use algebra tiles or draw them to model the equation on the mat.

Math Talk
Mathematical Processes

Why is the mat divided into two equal halves with a line?

Reflect

1. **What If?** How would you change the equation in the Explore Activity to model −3x + 4 = 5?

_____

_____

_____

Writing Two-Step Equations

You can write two-step equations to represent real-world problems by translating the words of the problems into numbers, variables, and operations.

EXAMPLE 1 | Real World

TEKS 7.10.A

A one-year membership to Metro Gym costs $460. There is a fee of $40 when you join, and the rest is paid monthly. Write an equation to represent what you will pay monthly for the yearlong membership. Write an equation that would help members find how much they pay per month.

STEP 1 Identify what you are trying to find. This will be the variable in the equation.

Let m represent the amount of money members pay per month.

STEP 2 Identify important information in the problem that can be used to help write an equation.

one-time joining fee: **$40**
fee charged for 1 year: **$12 · m**
total cost for the year: **$460**

> Convert 1 year into 12 months to find how much members pay per month.

STEP 3 Use words in the problem to tie the information together and write an equation.

One-time joining fee	plus	**12**	times	monthly cost	equals	**$460**
↓	↓	↓	↓	↓	↓	↓
$40	+	12	·	m	=	$460

The equation $40 + 12m = 460$ can help members find out their monthly fee.

Reflect

2. **Multiple Representations** Why would this equation for finding the monthly fee be difficult to model with algebra tiles?

_____

3. Can you rewrite the equation in the form $52m = 460$? Explain.

_____

_____

YOUR TURN

4. Billy has a gift card with a $150 balance. He buys several video games that cost $35 each. After the purchases, his gift card balance is $45. Write an equation to help find out how many video games Billy bought.

_____

Personal Math Trainer
Online Assessment and Intervention
⊙ my.hrw.com

Math On the Spot
⊙ my.hrw.com

Writing a Verbal Description of a Two-Step Equation

You can also write a verbal description to fit a two-step equation.

EXAMPLE 2 Real World   TEKS 7.10.C

Write a corresponding real-world problem to represent $5x + 50 = 120$.

STEP 1 Analyze what each part of the equation means mathematically.

x is the solution of the problem, the quantity you are looking for.

$5x$ means that, for a reason given in the problem, the quantity you are looking for is multiplied by 5.

$+ 50$ means that, for a reason given in the problem, 50 is added to $5x$.

$= 120$ means that after multiplying the solution x by 5 and adding 50 to it, the result is 120.

STEP 2 Think of some different situations in which a quantity x might be multiplied by 5.

You have x number of books, each weighing 5 pounds, and you want to know their total weight.	You save $5 each week for x weeks and want to know the total amount you have saved.

STEP 3 Build on the situation and adjust it to create a verbal description that takes all of the information of the equation into account.

- A publisher ships a package of x number of books each weighing 5 pounds, plus a second package weighing 50 pounds. The total weight of both packages is 120 pounds. How many books are being shipped?

- Leon receives a birthday gift of $50 from his parents. Each week he saves $5. How many weeks will it take for him to save $120?

© Houghton Mifflin Harcourt Publishing Company

My Notes

YOUR TURN

5. Write a real-world problem that can be represented by $10x + 40 = 100$.

_____

_____

Guided Practice

Draw algebra tiles to model the given two-step equation. (Explore Activity)

1. $2x + 5 = 7$

2. $-3 = 5 - 4x$

3. A group of adults plus one child attend a movie at Cineplex 15. Tickets cost $9 for adults and $6 for children. The total cost for the movie is $78. Write an equation to find the number of adults in the group. (Example 1) _____

4. Break down the equation $2x + 10 = 16$ to analyze each part. (Example 2)

   x is _____ of the problem.

   $2x$ is the quantity you are looking for _____.

   $+$ **10** means 10 is _____. $=$ **16** means the _____ is 16.

5. Write a corresponding real-world problem to represent $2x - 125 = 400$.

   (Example 2) _____

   _____

? ESSENTIAL QUESTION CHECK-IN

6. Describe the steps you would follow to write a two-step equation you can use to solve a real-world problem.

   _____

   _____

   _____

8.1 Independent Practice

TEKS 7.10.A, 7.10.C, 7.11.A

Personal Math Trainer

Online Assessment and Intervention

my.hrw.com

7. Describe how to model $-3x + 7 = 28$ with algebra tiles.

_____

_____

_____

8. Val rented a bicycle while she was on vacation. She paid a flat rental fee of $55.00, plus $8.50 each day. The total cost was $123. Write an equation you can use to find the number of days she rented the bicycle.

_____

9. A restaurant sells a coffee refill mug for $6.75. Each refill costs $1.25. Last month Keith spent $31.75 on a mug and refills. Write an equation you can use to find the number of refills that Keith bought.

_____

10. A gym holds one 60-minute exercise class on Saturdays and several 45-minute classes during the week. Last week all of the classes lasted a total of 285 minutes. Write an equation you can use to find the number of weekday classes.

_____

11. Multiple Representations There are 172 South American animals in the Springdale Zoo. That is 45 more than half the number of African animals in the zoo. Write an equation you could use to find n, the number of African animals in the zoo.

_____

12. A school bought $548 in basketball equipment and uniforms costing $29.50 each. The total cost was $2,023. Write an equation you can use to find the number of uniforms the school purchased.

_____

13. Financial Literacy Heather has $500 in her savings account. She withdraws $20 per week for gas. Write an equation Heather can use to see how many weeks it will take her to have a balance of $220.

_____

14. Critique Reasoning For $9x + 25 = 88$, Deena wrote the situation "I bought some shirts at the store for $9 each and received a $25 discount. My total bill was $88. How many shirts did I buy?"

a. What mistake did Deena make?

_____

_____

_____

b. Rewrite the equation to match Deena's situation.

_____

c. How could you rewrite the situation to make it fit the equation?

_____

_____

_____

_____

_____

15. Multistep Sandy charges each family that she babysits a flat fee of $10 for the night and an extra $5 per child. Kimmi charges $25 per night, no matter how many children a family has.

a. Write a two-step equation that would compare what the two girls charge and find when their fees are the same. _____

b. How many children must a family have for Sandy and Kimmi to charge the same amount? _____

c. The Sanderson family has five children. Which babysitter should they choose if they wish to save some money on babysitting, and why?

_____

_____

 FOCUS ON HIGHER ORDER THINKING

16. Analyze Relationships Each student wrote a two-step equation. Peter wrote the equation $4x - 2 = 10$, and Andres wrote the equation $16x - 8 = 40$. The teacher looked at their equations and asked them to compare them. Describe one way in which the equations are similar.

_____

_____

_____

_____

17. What's the Error? Damon has 5 dimes and some nickels in his pocket, worth a total of $1.20. To find the number of nickels Damon has, a student wrote the equation $5n + 50 = 1.20$. Find the error in the student's equation.

_____

_____

_____

18. Represent Real-World Problems Write a real-world problem you could answer by solving the equation $-8x + 60 = 28$.

_____

_____

_____

_____

Solving Two-Step Equations

TEKS
Expressions, equations, and relationships—7.10.B Represent solutions for one-variable, two-step equations and inequalities on number lines. *Also 7.11.A, 7.11.B*

? ESSENTIAL QUESTION

How do you solve a two-step equation?

Modeling and Solving Two-Step Equations

You can solve two-step equations using algebra tiles.

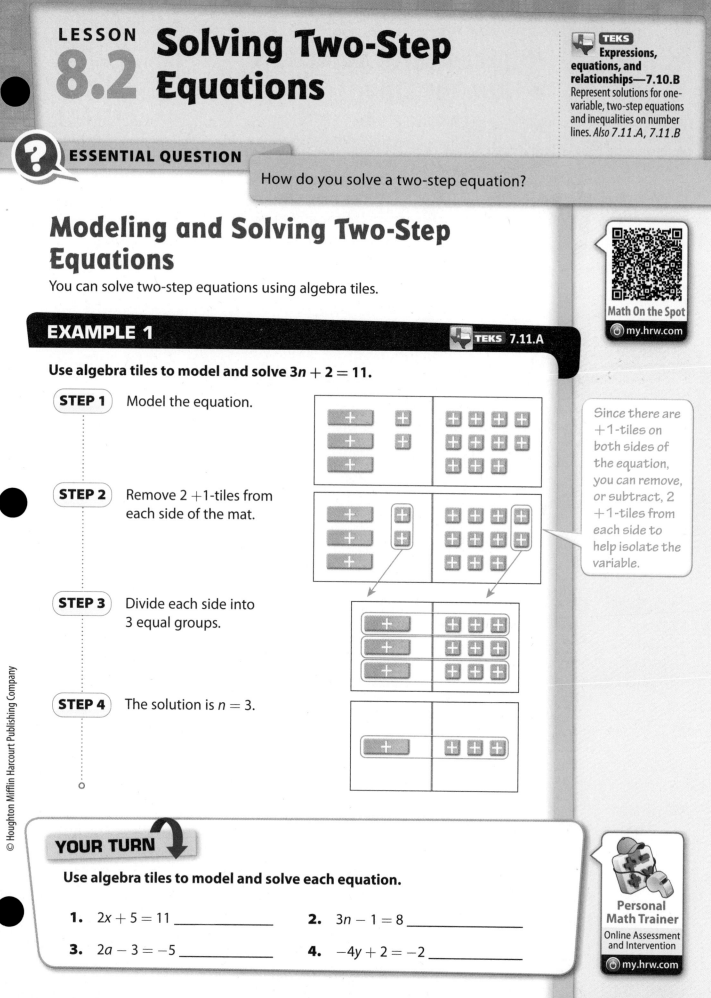

EXAMPLE 1   TEKS 7.11.A

Use algebra tiles to model and solve $3n + 2 = 11$.

STEP 1   Model the equation.

STEP 2   Remove 2 +1-tiles from each side of the mat.

Since there are +1-tiles on both sides of the equation, you can remove, or subtract, 2 +1-tiles from each side to help isolate the variable.

STEP 3   Divide each side into 3 equal groups.

STEP 4   The solution is $n = 3$.

YOUR TURN

Use algebra tiles to model and solve each equation.

1. $2x + 5 = 11$ _____

2. $3n - 1 = 8$ _____

3. $2a - 3 = -5$ _____

4. $-4y + 2 = -2$ _____

Math On the Spot
my.hrw.com

Personal Math Trainer
Online Assessment and Intervention
my.hrw.com

Representing Solutions on a Number Line

You have used inverse operations to solve equations with one operation. You can use the same method to solve equations with more than one operation. After solving, you can represent the solution on a number line.

EXAMPLE 2 *Real World*   🔲 **TEKS** 7.10.B

Tony carried 5 identical baseball bats to a ball game inside a carrying case weighing 12 ounces. The combined weight of the bats and the case was 162 ounces. How much did each bat weigh? Graph the solution on a number line.

STEP 1   Write an equation to represent the problem.
Let $w =$ the weight of a bat in ounces.

5 times the weight of each bat **plus** 12 oz **is** 162 oz.

$$5w \qquad\qquad + \ 12 \ = 162$$

> It is helpful to reverse the order of operations when solving equations that have more than one operation.

STEP 2   Use inverse operations to solve the equation.

$$5w + 12 = 162 \qquad \text{Subtract 12 from both sides.}$$
$$\underline{-12 \quad -12}$$
$$5w \qquad = 150$$
$$\frac{5w}{5} = \frac{150}{5} \qquad \text{Divide both sides by 5.}$$
$$w = 30$$

Each bat weighed 30 ounces

STEP 3   Graph the solution on a number line.

```
←——+——+——+——◆——+——+——+——+——+——+——→
    0   20   40   60   80  100
```

Reflect

5. **Analyze Relationships** Describe how you could find the weight of one baseball bat using only arithmetic. Compare your method with the one used in Example 2.

_____

_____

_____

_____

_____

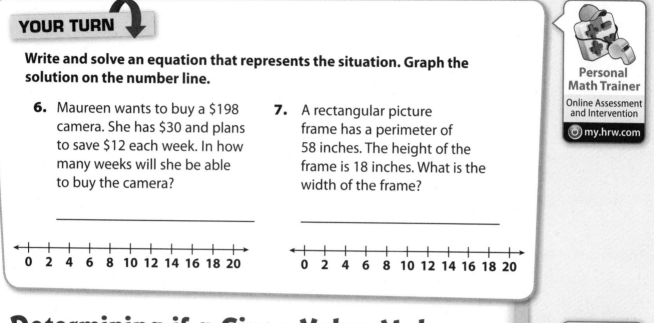

Write and solve an equation that represents the situation. Graph the solution on the number line.

6. Maureen wants to buy a $198 camera. She has $30 and plans to save $12 each week. In how many weeks will she be able to buy the camera?

_____

7. A rectangular picture frame has a perimeter of 58 inches. The height of the frame is 18 inches. What is the width of the frame?

_____

Determining if a Given Value Makes an Equation True

You can use substitution to decide whether a given value is the solution of an equation.

EXAMPLE 3 Real World   TEKS 7.11.B

After first doubling the weight being pulled by a dog sled, the sled driver removes 20 pounds. The final weight of the dog sled is 180 pounds. The equation $2w - 20 = 180$ can be used to find w, the initial weight of the sled. Determine which, if any, of these values is a solution: $w = 60$; $w = 80$; $w = 100$.

STEP 1 Substitute each value for w in the equation $2w - 20 = 180$.

$w = 60$	$w = 80$	$w = 100$
$2(60) - 20 = 180$	$2(80) - 20 = 180$	$2(100) - 20 = 180$

STEP 2 Evaluate to see if a true equation results.

$2(60) - 20 \overset{?}{=} 180$	$2(80) - 20 \overset{?}{=} 180$	$2(100) - 20 \overset{?}{=} 180$
$120 - 20 \overset{?}{=} 180$	$160 - 20 \overset{?}{=} 180$	$200 - 20 \overset{?}{=} 180$
$100 \overset{?}{=} 180$ ✗	$140 \overset{?}{=} 180$ ✗	$180 \overset{?}{=} 180$ ✓
not true	*not* true	true

The initial weight of the sled was 100 pounds.

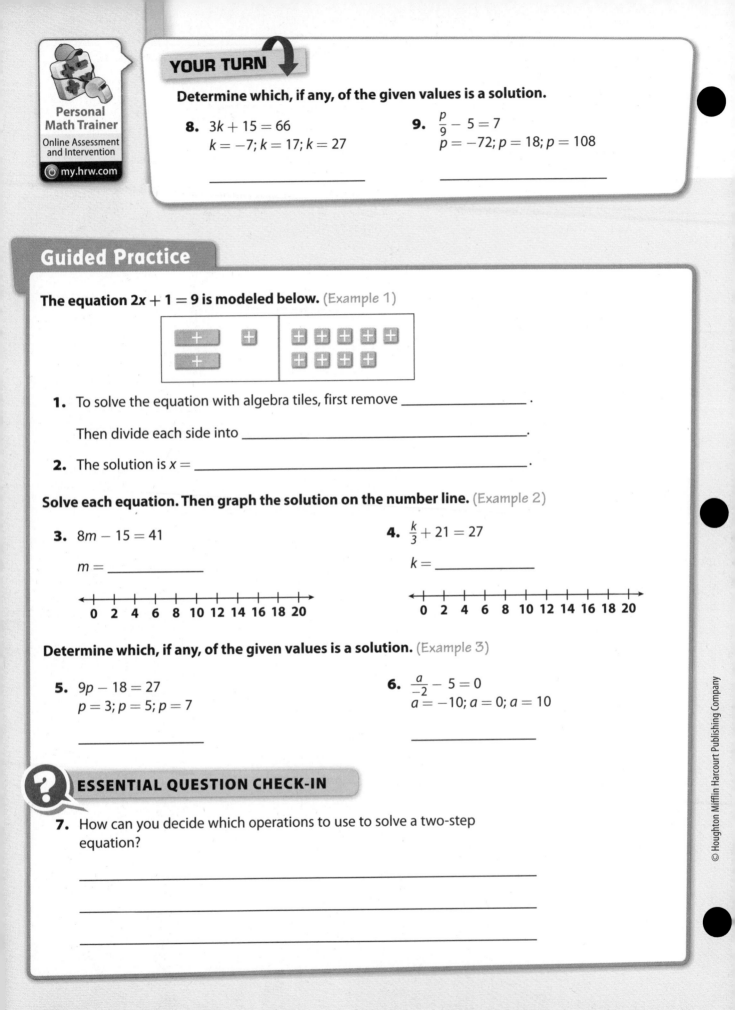

YOUR TURN

Determine which, if any, of the given values is a solution.

8. $3k + 15 = 66$
$k = -7; k = 17; k = 27$

_____

9. $\dfrac{p}{9} - 5 = 7$
$p = -72; p = 18; p = 108$

_____

Guided Practice

The equation $2x + 1 = 9$ is modeled below. (Example 1)

1. To solve the equation with algebra tiles, first remove _____ .

Then divide each side into _____ .

2. The solution is $x =$ _____ .

Solve each equation. Then graph the solution on the number line. (Example 2)

3. $8m - 15 = 41$

$m =$ _____

0 2 4 6 8 10 12 14 16 18 20

4. $\dfrac{k}{3} + 21 = 27$

$k =$ _____

0 2 4 6 8 10 12 14 16 18 20

Determine which, if any, of the given values is a solution. (Example 3)

5. $9p - 18 = 27$
$p = 3; p = 5; p = 7$

_____

6. $\dfrac{a}{-2} - 5 = 0$
$a = -10; a = 0; a = 10$

_____

? ESSENTIAL QUESTION CHECK-IN

7. How can you decide which operations to use to solve a two-step equation?

_____

_____

_____

8.2 Independent Practice

TEKS 7.10.B, 7.11.A, 7.11.B

Solve.

8. $9s + 3 = 57$

9. $4d + 6 = 42$

10. $-3y + 12 = -48$

11. $\frac{k}{2} + 9 = 30$

12. $\frac{g}{3} - 7 = 15$

13. $\frac{z}{5} + 3 = -35$

14. $-9h - 15 = 93$

15. $24 + \frac{n}{4} = 10$

16. $-17 + \frac{b}{8} = 13$

17. $-5 = 9 + \frac{c}{4}$

18. $-3 + \frac{p}{7} = -5$

19. $46 = -6t - 8$

20. After making a deposit, Puja had $264 in her savings account. She noticed that if she added $26 to the amount originally in the account and doubled the sum, she would get the new amount. How much did she originally have in the account?

21. The current temperature in Smalltown is 20 °F. This is 6 degrees less than twice the temperature that it was six hours ago. What was the temperature in Smalltown six hours ago?

22. Daphne gave away 3 more than half of her apples. She gave away 17 apples in all. How many apples did Daphne have originally?

23. Artaud noticed that if he takes the opposite of his age and adds 40 he gets the number 28. How old is Artaud?

24. Sven has 11 more than twice as many customers as when he started selling newspapers. He now has 73 customers. How many did he have when he started?

25. Paula bought a ski jacket on sale for $6 less than half its original price. She paid $88 for the jacket. What was the original price?

26. Michelle has a starting balance on a gift card for $300. She buys several dresses at $40 a piece. After her purchases she has $140 left on the gift card. How many dresses did she buy?

Use a calculator to solve each equation.

27. $-5.5x + 0.56 = -1.64$

28. $-4.2x + 31.5 = -65.1$

29. $\frac{k}{5.2} + 81.9 = 47.2$

30. Write a two-step equation involving multiplication and subtraction that has a solution of $x = 7$.

_____

31. Write a two-step equation involving division and addition that has a solution of $x = -25$

_____

32. **Reason Abstractly** The formula $F = 1.8C + 32$ allows you to find the Fahrenheit (F) temperature for a given Celsius (C) temperature. Solve the equation for C to produce a formula for finding the Celsius temperature for a given Fahrenheit temperature.

_____

33. **Reason Abstractly** The equation $P = 2(\ell + w)$ can be used to find the perimeter P of a rectangle with length ℓ and width w. Solve the equation for w to produce a formula for finding the width of a rectangle given its perimeter and length.

_____

34. **Critique Reasoning** A student's solution to the equation $3x + 2 = 15$ is shown. Describe the error that the student made.

$$3x + 2 = 15 \qquad \text{Divide both sides by 3.}$$
$$x + 2 = 5 \qquad \text{Subtract 2 from both sides.}$$
$$x = 3$$

_____

_____

35. **Multiple Representations** Explain how you could use the work backward problem-solving strategy to solve the equation $\frac{x}{4} - 6 = 2$.

_____

_____

_____

_____

36. **Reason Abstractly** Solve the equation $ax + b = c$ for x.

_____

Work Area

Writing Two-Step Inequalities

TEKS
Expressions, equations, and relationships—7.10.A
Write one-variable, two-step ... inequalities to represent constraints or conditions within problems. *Also 7.10.C.*

? **ESSENTIAL QUESTION**

How do you write a two-step inequality?

EXPLORE ACTIVITY **TEKS** 7.10.A

Modeling Two-Step Inequalities

You can use algebra tiles to model two-step inequalities.

Use algebra tiles to model $2k + 5 \geq -3$.

A Using the line on the mat, draw in the inequality symbol shown in the inequality.

B How can you model the left side of the inequality?

_____

C How can you model the right side of the inequality?

_____

D Use algebra tiles or draw them to model the inequality on the mat.

Reflect

1. **Multiple Representations** How does your model differ from the one you would draw to model the equation $2k + 5 = -3$?

_____

_____

_____

2. Why might you need to change the inequality sign when you solve an inequality using algebra tiles?

_____

_____

_____

Writing Two-Step Inequalities

You can write two-step inequalities to represent real-world problems by translating the words of the problems into numbers, variables, and operations.

EXAMPLE 1 **TEKS** 7.10.A

A mountain climbing team is camped at an altitude of 18,460 feet on Mount Everest. The team wants to reach the 29,029-foot summit within 6 days. Write an inequality to find the average number of feet per day the team must climb to accomplish its objective.

STEP 1 Identify what you are trying to find. This will be the variable in the inequality.

Let *d* represent the average altitude the team must gain each day.

STEP 2 Identify important information in the problem that you can use to write an inequality.

starting altitude: **18,460 ft**   target altitude: **29,029 ft**
number of days times altitude gained to reach target altitude: $6 \cdot d$

STEP 3 Use words in the problem to tie the information together and write an inequality.

starting altitude	+	number of days	times	altitude gain	is greater than or equal to	target altitude
↓	↓	↓	↓	↓	↓	↓
18,460	+	6	×	d	≥	29,029

$$18,460 + 6d \geq 29,029$$

Math Talk
Mathematical Processes

Why is the inequality sign ≥ used, rather than an equal sign?

YOUR TURN

3. The 45 members of the glee club are trying to raise at least $6,000 so they can compete in the state championship. They already have $1,240. What inequality can you write to find the amount each member must raise, on

   average, to meet the goal? _____

4. Ella has $40 to spend at the State Fair. Admission is $6 and each ride costs $3. Write an inequality to find the greatest number of rides she can go on.

   _____

© Houghton Mifflin Harcourt Publishing Company • Image Credits: © Photographers Choice RF/SuperStock

Writing a Verbal Description of a Two-Step Inequality

You can also write a verbal description to fit a two-step inequality.

EXAMPLE 2 Real World   **TEKS** 7.10.C

Write a corresponding real-world problem to represent $2x + 20 \leq 50$.

STEP 1 Analyze what each part of the inequality means mathematically.

> x is the solution of the problem, the quantity you are looking for.
>
> $2x$ means that, for a reason given in the problem, the quantity you are looking for is multiplied by 2.
>
> $+ 20$ means that, for a reason given in the problem, 20 is added to $2x$.
>
> ≤ 50 means that after multiplying the solution x by 2 and adding 20 to it, the result can be no greater than 50.

STEP 2 Think of some different situations in which a quantity x is multiplied by 2.

You run x miles per day for 2 days. So, $2x$ is the total distance run.	You buy 2 items each costing x dollars. So, $2x$ is the total cost.

STEP 3 Build on the situation and adjust it to create a verbal description that takes all of the information into account.

- Tomas has run 20 miles so far this week. If he intends to run 50 miles or less, how many miles on average should he run on each of the 2 days remaining in the week?

- Manny buys 2 work shirts that are each the same price. After using a $20 gift card, he can spend no more than $50. What is the maximum amount he can spend on each shirt?

YOUR TURN

Write a real-world problem for each inequality.

5. $3x + 10 > 30$

_____

_____

_____

_____

6. $5x - 50 \leq 100$

_____

_____

_____

_____

Draw algebra tiles to model each two-step inequality. (Explore Activity)

1. $4x - 5 < 7$

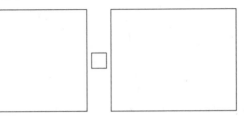

2. $-3x + 6 > 9$

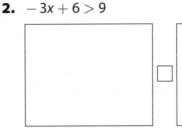

3. The booster club needs to raise at least $7,000 for new football uniforms. So far, they have raised $1,250. Write an inequality to find the average amounts each of the 92 members can raise to meet the club's objective. (Example 1)

Let a represent the amount each member must raise.

amount to be raised: _____   amount already raised: _____   number of members: _____

Use clues in the problem to write an inequality.

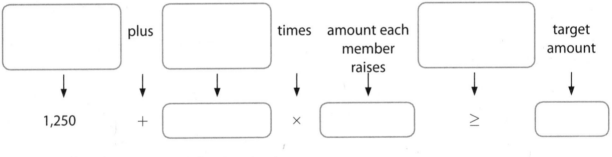

The inequality that represents the situation is _____.

4. Analyze what each part of $7x - 18 \leq 32$ means mathematically. (Example 2)

x is _____. $7x$ is _____.

-18 means that _____.

≤ 32 means that _____

5. Write a real-world problem to represent $7x - 18 \leq 32$.

_____

? ESSENTIAL QUESTION CHECK-IN

6. Describe the steps you would follow to write a two-step inequality you can use to solve a real-world problem.

_____

_____

8.3 Independent Practice

TEKS 7.10.A, 7.10.C

Personal Math Trainer

Online Assessment and Intervention

my.hrw.com

7. Three friends earned more than $200 washing cars. They paid their parents $28 for supplies and divided the rest of money equally. Write an inequality to find possible amounts each friend earned. Identify what your variable represents.

_____

_____

8. Nick has $7.00. Bagels cost $0.75 each, and a small container of cream cheese costs $1.29. Write an inequality to find the numbers of bagels Nick can buy. Identify what your variable represents.

_____

_____

9. Chet needs to buy 4 work shirts, all costing the same amount. The total cost before Chet applies a $25 gift certificate can be no more than $75. Write an inequality to find the possible amounts that Chet pays per shirt. Identify what your variable represents.

_____

_____

10. Due to fire laws, no more than 720 people may attend a performance at Metro Auditorium. The balcony holds 120 people. There are 32 rows on the ground floor, each with the same number of seats. Write an inequality to find the numbers of people that can sit in a ground-floor row if the balcony is full. Identify what your variable represents.

_____

_____

11. Liz earns a salary of $2,100 per month, plus a commission of 5% of her sales. She wants to earn at least $2,400 this month. Write an inequality to find amounts of sales that will meet her goal. Identify what your variable represents.

_____

_____

12. Lincoln Middle School plans to collect more than 2,000 cans of food in a food drive. So far, 668 cans have been collected. Write an inequality to find numbers of cans the school can collect on each of the final 7 days of the drive to meet this goal. Identify what your variable represents.

_____

_____

13. Joanna joins a CD club. She pays $7 per month plus $10 for each CD that she orders. Write an inequality to find how many CDs she can purchase in a month if she spends no more than $100. Identify what your variable represents.

_____

_____

14. Lionel wants to buy a belt that costs $22. He also wants to buy some shirts that are on sale for $17 each. He has $80. What inequality can you write to find the number of shirts he can buy? Identify what your variable represents.

_____

_____

15. Write and solve a real-world problem that can be represented by $15x - 20 \leq 130$.

_____

_____

_____

Analyze Relationships Write $>$, $<$, $\geq$, or $\leq$ in the blank to express the given relationship.

16. m is at least 25 m _____ 25

17. k is no greater than 9 k _____ 9

18. p is less than 48 p _____ 48

19. b is no more than -5 b _____ -5

20. h is at most 56 h _____ 56

21. w is no less than 0 w _____ 0

22. Critical Thinking Marie scored 95, 86, and 89 on three science tests. She wants her average score for 6 tests to be at least 90. What inequality can you write to find the average scores that she can get on her next three tests to meet this goal? Use s to represent the lowest average score.

_____

_____

H.O.T.   **FOCUS ON HIGHER ORDER THINKING**

Work Area

23. Communicate Mathematical Ideas Write an inequality that expresses the reason the lengths 5 feet, 10 feet, and 20 feet could not be used to make a triangle. Explain how the inequality demonstrates that fact.

_____

_____

_____

_____

24. Analyze Relationships The number m satisfies the relationship $m < 0$. Write an inequality expressing the relationship between $-m$ and 0. Explain your reasoning.

_____

_____

_____

25. Analyze Relationships The number n satisfies the relationship $n > 0$. Write three inequalities to express the relationship between n and $\frac{1}{n}$.

_____

Solving Two-Step Inequalities

TEKS
Expressions, equations, and relationships—
7.11.A Model and solve one-variable, two-step inequalities. Also 7.10.B, 7.11.B

? ESSENTIAL QUESTION

How do you solve a two-step inequality?

Modeling and Solving Two-Step Inequalities

You can solve two-step inequalities using algebra tiles. The method is similar to the one you used to solve two-step equations.

Math On the Spot

my.hrw.com

EXAMPLE 1

TEKS 7.11.A

Use algebra tiles to model and solve $4d - 3 \geq 9$.

STEP 1 Model the inequality. Use a "$\geq$" symbol between the mats.

STEP 2 Add three +1 tiles to both sides of the mat.

STEP 3 Remove zero pairs from the left side of the mat.

STEP 4 Divide each side into 4 equal groups.

STEP 5 The solution is $d \geq 3$.

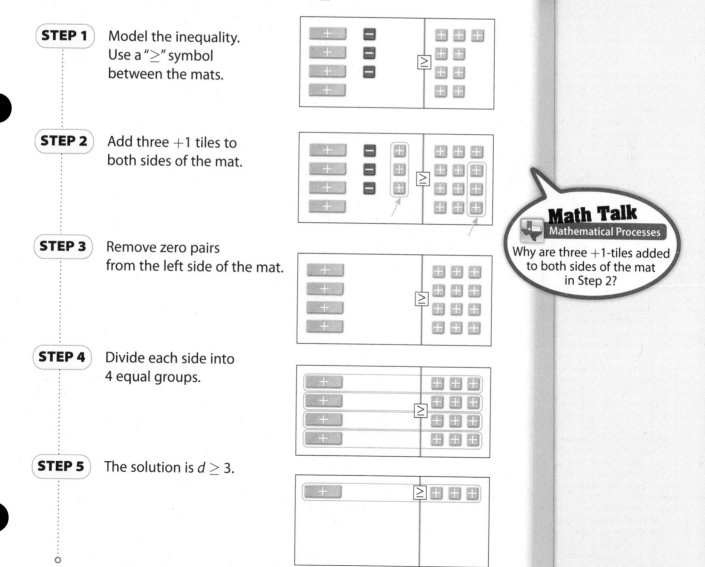

Math Talk
Mathematical Processes

Why are three +1-tiles added to both sides of the mat in Step 2?

YOUR TURN

Use algebra tiles to model and solve each inequality.

1. $2x + 7 > 11$ _____

2. $5h - 4 \geq 11$ _____

Solving and Interpreting Solutions

You can apply what you know about solving two-step equations and one-step inequalities to solving two-step inequalities.

EXAMPLE 2 Real World   **TEKS** 7.10.B, 7.11.A

Serena wants to complete the first 3 miles of a 10-mile run in 45 minutes or less running at a steady pace. The inequality $10 - 0.75p \leq 7$ can be used to find p, the pace, in miles per hour, she can run to reach her goal. Solve the inequality. Then graph and interpret the solution.

My Notes

STEP 1 Use inverse operations to solve the inequality.

$$10 - 0.75p \leq 7$$

$$\underline{-10} \qquad\qquad \underline{-10} \qquad \text{Subtract 10 from both sides.}$$

$$-0.75p \leq -3$$

$$\frac{-0.75p}{-0.75} \geq \frac{-3}{-0.75} \qquad \begin{array}{l}\text{Divide both sides by } -0.75. \\ \text{Reverse the inequality symbol.}\end{array}$$

$$p \geq 4$$

STEP 2 Graph the inequality and interpret the circle and the arrow.

Serena can meet her goal by running
at a pace of 4 miles per hour.

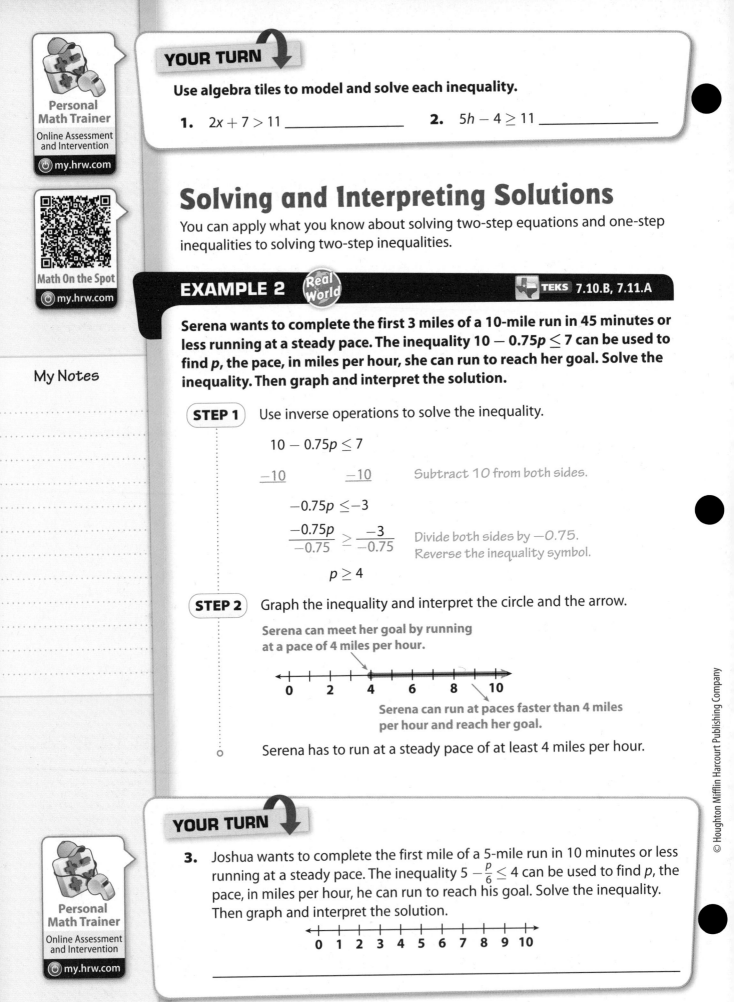

Serena can run at paces faster than 4 miles
per hour and reach her goal.

Serena has to run at a steady pace of at least 4 miles per hour.

YOUR TURN

3. Joshua wants to complete the first mile of a 5-mile run in 10 minutes or less running at a steady pace. The inequality $5 - \frac{p}{6} \leq 4$ can be used to find p, the pace, in miles per hour, he can run to reach his goal. Solve the inequality. Then graph and interpret the solution.

Determining if a Given Value Makes the Inequality True

You can use substitution to decide whether a given value is the solution of an inequality.

EXAMPLE 3 *Real World*   **TEKS** 7.11.B

At Gas 'n' Wash, gasoline sells for $4.00 a gallon and a car wash costs $12. Harika wants to have her car washed and keep her total purchase under $60. The inequality $4g + 12 < 60$ can be used to find g, the number of gallons of gas she can buy. Determine which, if any, of these values is a solution: $g = 10$; $g = 11$; $g = 12$.

STEP 1   Substitute each value for g in the inequality $4g + 12 < 60$.

$g = 10$	$g = 11$	$g = 12$
$4(10) + 12 < 60$	$4(11) + 12 < 60$	$4(12) + 12 < 60$

STEP 2   Evaluate each expression to see if a true inequality results.

$4(10) + 12 \overset{?}{<} 60$	$4(11) + 12 \overset{?}{<} 60$	$4(12) + 12 \overset{?}{<} 60$
$40 + 12 \overset{?}{<} 60$	$44 + 12 \overset{?}{<} 60$	$48 + 12 \overset{?}{<} 60$
$52 \overset{?}{<} 60$	$56 \overset{?}{<} 60$	$60 \overset{?}{<} 60$
true ✓	true ✓	*not* true ✗

So, Harika can buy 10 or 11 gallons of gas but not 12 gallons.

Check: Solve and graph the inequality.

$4g + 12 < 60$

$\qquad 4g < 48$

$\qquad\quad g < 12$

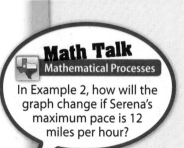

Math Talk
Mathematical Processes

In Example 2, how will the graph change if Serena's maximum pace is 12 miles per hour?

The closed circle at zero represents the minimum amount she can buy, zero gallons. She cannot buy a negative number of gallons. The open circle at 12 means that she can buy any amount up to but not including 12 gallons.

YOUR TURN

Circle any given values that make the inequality true.

4. $3v - 8 > 22$

$v = 9; v = 10; \ v = 11$

5. $5h + 12 \le -3$

$h = -3; h = -4; h = -5$

Guided Practice

1. Describe how to solve the inequality $3x + 4 < 13$ using algebra tiles. (Example 1)

_____

_____

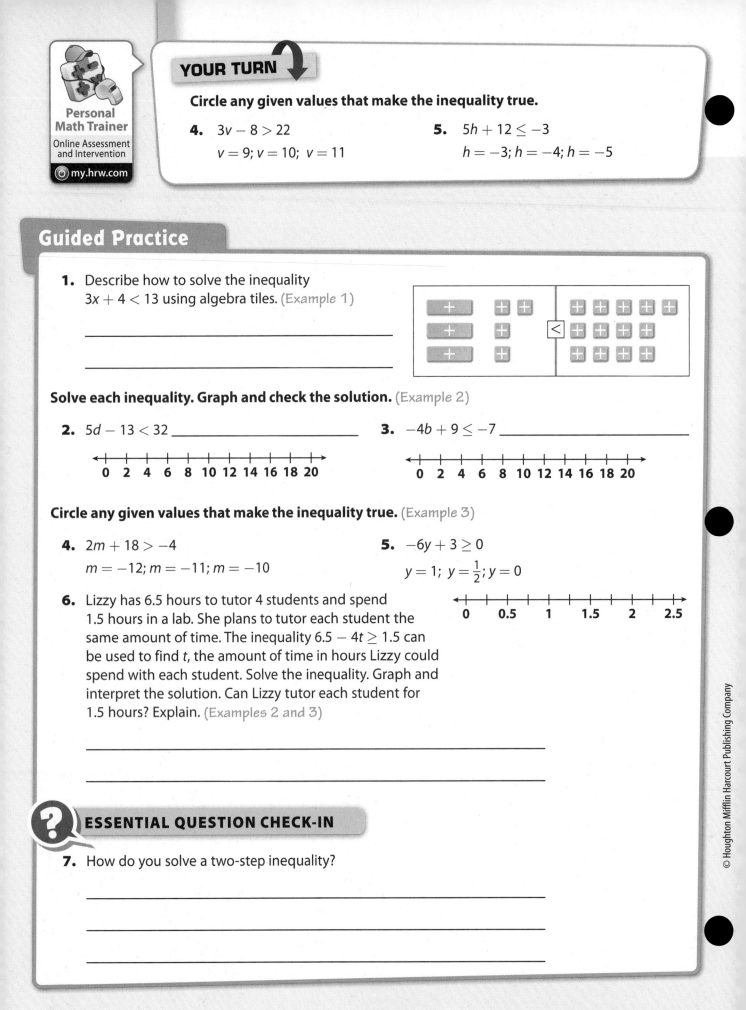

Solve each inequality. Graph and check the solution. (Example 2)

2. $5d - 13 < 32$ _____

0 2 4 6 8 10 12 14 16 18 20

3. $-4b + 9 \le -7$ _____

0 2 4 6 8 10 12 14 16 18 20

Circle any given values that make the inequality true. (Example 3)

4. $2m + 18 > -4$

$m = -12; m = -11; m = -10$

5. $-6y + 3 \ge 0$

$y = 1; \ y = \frac{1}{2}; y = 0$

6. Lizzy has 6.5 hours to tutor 4 students and spend 1.5 hours in a lab. She plans to tutor each student the same amount of time. The inequality $6.5 - 4t \ge 1.5$ can be used to find t, the amount of time in hours Lizzy could spend with each student. Solve the inequality. Graph and interpret the solution. Can Lizzy tutor each student for 1.5 hours? Explain. (Examples 2 and 3)

0   0.5   1   1.5   2   2.5

_____

_____

? ESSENTIAL QUESTION CHECK-IN

7. How do you solve a two-step inequality?

_____

_____

_____

© Houghton Mifflin Harcourt Publishing Company

8.4 Independent Practice

TEKS 7.10.B, 7.11.A, 7.11.B

Solve each inequality. Graph and check the solution.

8. $2s + 5 \geq 49$ _____

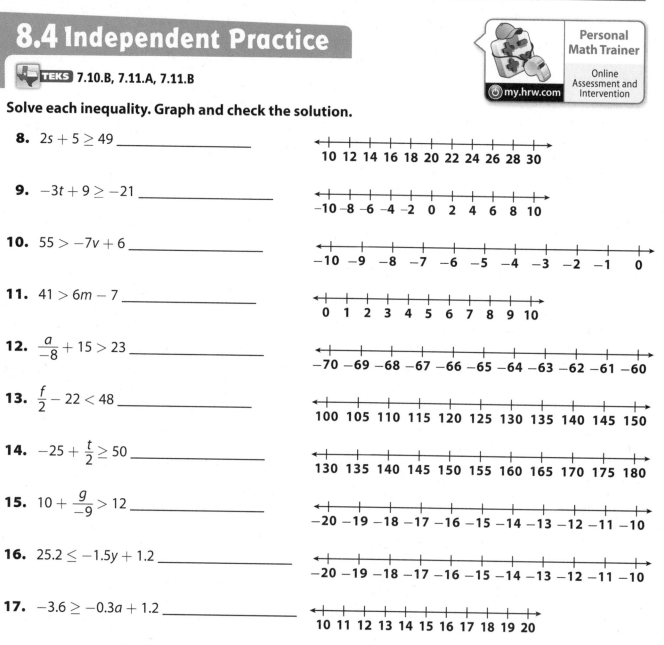

10 12 14 16 18 20 22 24 26 28 30

9. $-3t + 9 \geq -21$ _____

−10 −8 −6 −4 −2 0 2 4 6 8 10

10. $55 > -7v + 6$ _____

−10 −9 −8 −7 −6 −5 −4 −3 −2 −1 0

11. $41 > 6m - 7$ _____

0 1 2 3 4 5 6 7 8 9 10

12. $\dfrac{a}{-8} + 15 > 23$ _____

−70 −69 −68 −67 −66 −65 −64 −63 −62 −61 −60

13. $\dfrac{f}{2} - 22 < 48$ _____

100 105 110 115 120 125 130 135 140 145 150

14. $-25 + \dfrac{t}{2} \geq 50$ _____

130 135 140 145 150 155 160 165 170 175 180

15. $10 + \dfrac{g}{-9} > 12$ _____

−20 −19 −18 −17 −16 −15 −14 −13 −12 −11 −10

16. $25.2 \leq -1.5y + 1.2$ _____

−20 −19 −18 −17 −16 −15 −14 −13 −12 −11 −10

17. $-3.6 \geq -0.3a + 1.2$ _____

10 11 12 13 14 15 16 17 18 19 20

18. **What If?** The perimeter of a rectangle is at most 80 inches. The length of the rectangle is 25 inches. The inequality $80 - 2w \geq 50$ can be used to find w, the width of the rectangle in inches. Solve the inequality and interpret the solution. How will the solution change if the width must be at least 10 inches and a whole number?

_____

_____

_____

19. Interpret the Answer Grace earns $7 for each car she washes. She always saves $25 of her weekly earnings. This week, she wants to have at least $65 in spending money. How many cars must she wash? Write and solve an inequality to represent this situation. Interpret the solution in context.

_____

_____

H.O.T.   **FOCUS ON HIGHER ORDER THINKING**

20. Critical Thinking Is there any value of x with the property that $x < x - 1$? Explain your reasoning.

_____

_____

_____

21. Analyze Relationships A *compound inequality* consists of two simple inequalities joined by the word "*and*" or "*or*." Graph the solution sets of each of these compound inequalities.

  a. $x > 2$ and $x < 7$

  b. $x < 2$ or $x > 7$

            0   1   2   3   4   5   6   7   8   9   10

  c.   Describe the solution set of the compound inequality $x < 2$ and $x > 7$.

_____

  d.   Describe the solution set of the compound inequality $x > 2$ or $x < 7$.

_____

22. Communicate Mathematical Ideas Joseph used the problem-solving strategy Work Backward to solve the inequality $2n + 5 < 13$. Shawnee solved the inequality using the algebraic method you used in this lesson. Compare the two methods.

_____

_____

_____

_____

_____

_____

Ready to Go On?

Personal Math Trainer

Online Assessment and Intervention

my.hrw.com

8.1 Writing Two-Step Equations

1. Jerry started doing sit-ups every day. The first day he did 15 sit-ups. Every day after that he did 2 more sit-ups than he had done the previous day. Today Jerry did 33 sit-ups. Write an equation that could be solved to find the number of days Jerry has been doing sit-ups since the first day.

_____

8.2 Solving Two-Step Equations

Solve.

2. $5n + 8 = 43$ _____

3. $\frac{y}{6} - 7 = 4$ _____

4. $8w - 15 = 57$ _____

5. $\frac{g}{3} + 11 = 25$ _____

6. $\frac{f}{5} - 22 = -25$ _____

7. $-4p + 19 = 11$ _____

8.3 Writing Two-Step Inequalities

8. Eddie scored at least 27 points more than half of what Duncan scored. Eddie scored 58 points. Write an inequality that could be solved to find the numbers of points that Duncan could have scored.

_____

8.4 Solving Two-Step Inequalities

Solve.

9. $2s + 3 > 15$ _____

10. $\frac{d}{12} - 6 < 1$ _____

11. $6w - 18 \geq 36$ _____

12. $\frac{z}{4} + 22 \leq 38$ _____

13. $\frac{b}{9} - 34 < -36$ _____

14. $-2p + 12 > 8$ _____

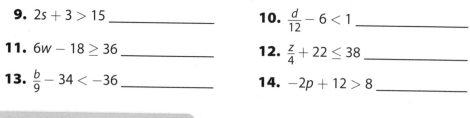

ESSENTIAL QUESTION

15. How can you use two-step equations and inequalities to represent and solve real-world problems?

_____

_____

MODULE 8 MIXED REVIEW

Texas Test Prep

Personal
Math Trainer

Online
Assessment and
Intervention

my.hrw.com

Selected Response

1. A taxi cab costs $1.50 for the first mile and $0.75 for each additional mile. Which equation could be solved to find how many miles you can travel in a taxi for $10, if x is the number of additional miles?

    Ⓐ $1.5x + 0.75 = 10$

    Ⓑ $0.75x + 1.5 = 10$

    Ⓒ $1.5x - 0.75 = 10$

    Ⓓ $0.75x - 1.5 = 10$

2. Tony operates a skate rental company. He charges an equipment fee of $3 plus $6 per hour. Which equation represents this linear relationship?

    Ⓐ $y = 6x + 3$

    Ⓑ $y = 3x + 6$

    Ⓒ $y = -6x + 3$

    Ⓓ $y = 3x - 3$

3. Which equation has $x = 8$ for a solution?

    Ⓐ $2x + 3 = 13$

    Ⓑ $4x + 6 = 38$

    Ⓒ $3x - 5 = 29$

    Ⓓ $5x - 8 = 48$

4. Which inequality has the following graphed solution?

    Ⓐ $3x + 8 \leq 2$

    Ⓑ $4x + 12 < 4$

    Ⓒ $2x + 5 \leq 1$

    Ⓓ $3x + 6 < 3$

5. Which represents the solution for the inequality $3x - 7 > 5$?

    Ⓐ $x < 4$

    Ⓑ $x \leq 4$

    Ⓒ $x > 4$

    Ⓓ $x \geq 4$

6. The 30 members of a choir are trying to raise at least $1,500 to cover travel costs to a singing camp. They have already raised $600. Which inequality could you solve to find the average amounts each member can raise in order to meet the goal?

    Ⓐ $30x + 600 > 1,500$

    Ⓑ $30x + 600 \geq 1,500$

    Ⓒ $30x + 600 < 1,500$

    Ⓓ $30x + 600 \leq 1,500$

Gridded Response

7. Mrs. Drennan keeps a bag of small prizes to distribute to her students. She likes to keep at least three times as many prizes in the bag as she has students. The bag currently has 72 prizes in it. Mrs. Drennan has 26 students. What is the least amount of prizes Mrs. Drennan needs to buy?

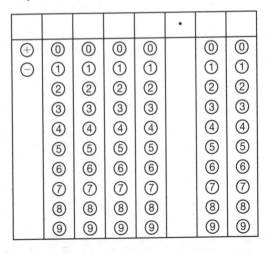

Key Vocabulary
linear relationship *(relación lineal)*

? ESSENTIAL QUESTION

How can you use linear relationships to solve real-world problems?

EXAMPLE

Ross earns a set rate of $10 for babysitting, plus $6 per hour. Represent the relationship using a table, an equation, and a graph of the linear relationship.

Hours	Amount ($)
0	$10
1	$16
2	$22
3	$28
4	$34

Babysitting Fees

(4, 34)
(3, 28)
(2, 22)
(1, 16)
(0, 10)

Write an equation for the amount *y* in dollars earned for *x* hours.

Amount = $10 + $6 per hour

$y = 10 + 6x$

EXERCISES

1. The cost of a box of cupcakes is $1.50 per cupcake plus $3. Complete the table to represent the linear relationship. (Lesson 7.1)

Number of cupcakes	1	2	3	4
Cost of cupcakes ($)				

2. The score a student receives on a standardized test is based on the number of correct answers, as shown in the table. Use the table to give a verbal description of the relationship between correct answers and score. (Lesson 7.1)

Correct answers	5	10	15	20	25
Score	210	220	230	240	250

3. Steve is saving for his daughter's college education. He opens an account with $2,400 and deposits $40 per month. Represent the relationship using a table and an equation. (Lesson 7.2)

_____

4. Tonya has a 2-page story she wants to expand. She plans to write 3 pages per day until it is done. Represent the relationship using a table, an equation, and a graph. (Lesson 7.2)

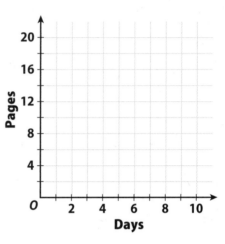

_____

Equations and Inequalities

? ESSENTIAL QUESTION

How can you use equations and inequalities to solve real-world problems?

EXAMPLE 1

A clothing store sells clothing for 2 times the wholesale cost plus $10. The store sells a pair of pants for $48. How much did the store pay for the pants? Represent the solution on a number line.

Let w represent the wholesale cost of the pants, or the price paid by the store.

$2w + 10 = 48$

$2w = 38$ Subtract 10 from both sides.

$w = 19$ Divide both sides by 2.

The store paid $19 for the pants.

EXAMPLE 2

Determine which, if any, of these values makes the inequality $-7x + 42 \leq 28$ true: $x = -1, x = 2, x = 5$.

$-7(-1) + 42 \leq 28$ $-7(2) + 42 \leq 28$ $-7(5) + 42 \leq 28$

$x = 2$ and $x = 5$

Substitute each value for x in the inequality and evaluate the expression to see if a true inequality results.

EXERCISES

1. The cost of a ticket to an amusement park is $42 per person. For groups of up to 8 people, the cost per ticket decreases by $3 for each person in the group. Marcos's ticket cost $30. Write and solve an equation to find the number of people in Marcos's group. (Lessons 8.1, 8.2)

_____

Solve each equation. Graph the solution on a number line.
(Lesson 8.2)

2. $8x - 28 = 44$

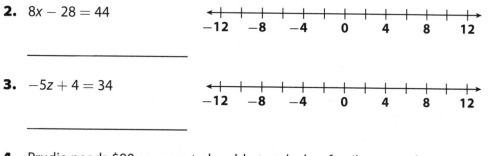

_____

3. $-5z + 4 = 34$

_____

4. Prudie needs $90 or more to be able to take her family out to dinner. She has already saved $30 and wants to take her family out to eat in 4 days. (Lesson 8.3)

   a. Suppose that Prudie saves the same each day. Write an inequality to find how much she needs to save each day.

   _____

   b. Suppose that Prudie saves $18 each day. Will she have enough money to take her family to dinner in 4 days? Explain.

   _____

Solve each inequality. Graph and check the solution. (Lesson 8.4)

5. $15 + 5y > 45$

   _____

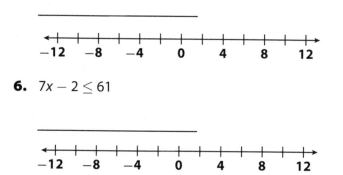

6. $7x - 2 \leq 61$

   _____

1. **CAREERS IN MATH** Mechanical Engineer A mechanical engineer is testing the amount of force needed to make a spring stretch by a given amount. The force y is measured in units called *Newtons*, abbreviated N. The stretch x is measured in centimeters. Her results are shown in the graph.

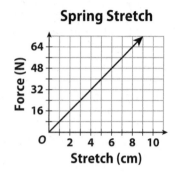

Spring Stretch

a. Write an equation for the line. Explain, using the graph and then using the equation, why the relationship is proportional.

_____

_____

_____

_____

b. Identify the rate of change and the constant of proportionality.

_____

c. What is the meaning of the constant of proportionality in the context of the problem?

_____

2. A math tutor charges $30 for a consultation, and then $25 per hour. An online tutoring service charges $30 per hour.

a. Does either service represent a proportional relationship? Explain.

_____

_____

_____

_____

b. Write an equation for the cost c of h hours of tutoring for each service. Which service charges less for 4 hours of tutoring? Show your work.

_____

_____

_____

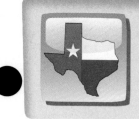
Selected Response

1. Which description corresponds to the relationship shown in the table?

Hours	5	10	15	20
Pay	$50	$85	$120	$155

- (A) earning $10 per hour
- (B) earning $8 per hour plus $10 in tips
- (C) earning $7 per hour plus $15 in tips
- (D) earning $8.50 per hour

2. Timothy began the week with $35. He bought lunch at school, paying $2.25 for each meal. Let x be the number of meals he bought at school and y be the amount of money he had left at the end of the week. Which equation represents the relationship in the situation?

- (A) $y = 2.25x + 35$
- (C) $x = 35 - 2.25y$
- (B) $y = 35 - 2.25x$
- (D) $y = 2.25x - 35$

3. Which table represents the linear relationship described by the equation $y = 3x + 9$?

(A)

x	0	1	2	3
y	0	2	6	9

(B)

x	2	3	4	5
y	15	18	21	24

(C)

x	1	2	3	4
y	12	21	30	39

(D)

x	1	2	3	4
y	9	18	27	36

4. A taxi costs $1.65 for the first mile and $0.85 for each additional mile. Which equation could be solved to find the number x of additional miles traveled in a taxi given that the total cost of the trip is $20?

- (A) $1.65x + 0.85 = 20$
- (B) $0.85x + 1.65 = 20$
- (C) $1.65x - 0.85 = 20$
- (D) $0.85x - 1.65 = 20$

5. A bag contains 7 purple beads, 4 blue beads, and 7 pink beads. What is the probability of **not** drawing a blue bead?

- (A) $\frac{4}{18}$
- (C) $\frac{11}{18}$
- (B) $\frac{7}{18}$
- (D) $\frac{14}{18}$

6. Which equation has the solution $x = 12$?

- (A) $4x + 3 = 45$
- (B) $3x + 6 = 42$
- (C) $2x - 5 = 29$
- (D) $5x - 8 = 68$

7. The 23 members of the school jazz band are trying to raise at least $1,800 to cover the cost of traveling to a competition. The members have already raised $750. Which inequality could you solve to find the amount that each member should raise to meet the goal?

- (A) $23x + 750 > 1,800$
- (B) $23x + 750 \geq 1,800$
- (C) $23x + 750 < 1,800$
- (D) $23x + 750 \leq 1,800$

8. What is the solution of the inequality $2x - 9 < 7$?

Ⓐ $x < 8$

Ⓑ $x \leq 8$

Ⓒ $x > 8$

Ⓓ $x \geq 8$

9. Carter rolls a fair number cube 18 times. Which is the best prediction for the number of times he will roll a number that is odd and less than 3?

Ⓐ 2

Ⓑ 3

Ⓒ 4

Ⓓ 5

10. Which inequality has the solution shown?

Ⓐ $3x + 5 < 2$

Ⓑ $4x + 12 < 4$

Ⓒ $2x + 5 \leq 1$

Ⓓ $3x + 6 \leq 3$

Gridded Response

11. What is the greatest whole number value that makes the inequality $4x + 4 \leq 12$ true?

12. The rectangles shown are similar. The dimensions are given in inches.

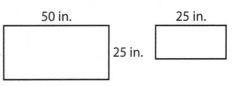

What is the width of the smaller rectangle?

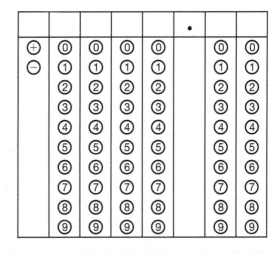

Hot Tip! Gridded responses can be positive or negative numbers. Enter any negative signs in the first column. Check your work!

13. What is the solution to the equation $8x - 11 = 77$?

Geometric Relationships

MODULE 9
Applications of Geometry Concepts
⊕ **TEKS** 7.8.C, 7.9.B, 7.9.C, 7.11.C

MODULE 10
Volume and Surface Area
⊕ **TEKS** 7.8.A, 7.9.A, 7.9.D

CAREERS IN MATH

Product Design Engineer A product design engineer works to design and develop manufactured products and equipment. A product design engineer uses math to design and modify models, and to calculate costs in producing their designs.

If you are interested in a career in product design engineering, you should study these mathematical subjects:
- Algebra
- Geometry
- Trigonometry
- Statistics
- Calculus

Research other careers that require the use of mathematics to design and modify products.

Unit 5 Performance Task

At the end of the unit, check out how **product design engineers** use math.

Vocabulary Preview

Use the puzzle to preview key vocabulary from this unit. Unscramble the circled letters to answer the riddle at the bottom of the page.

1. NEONGTURC LANSEG

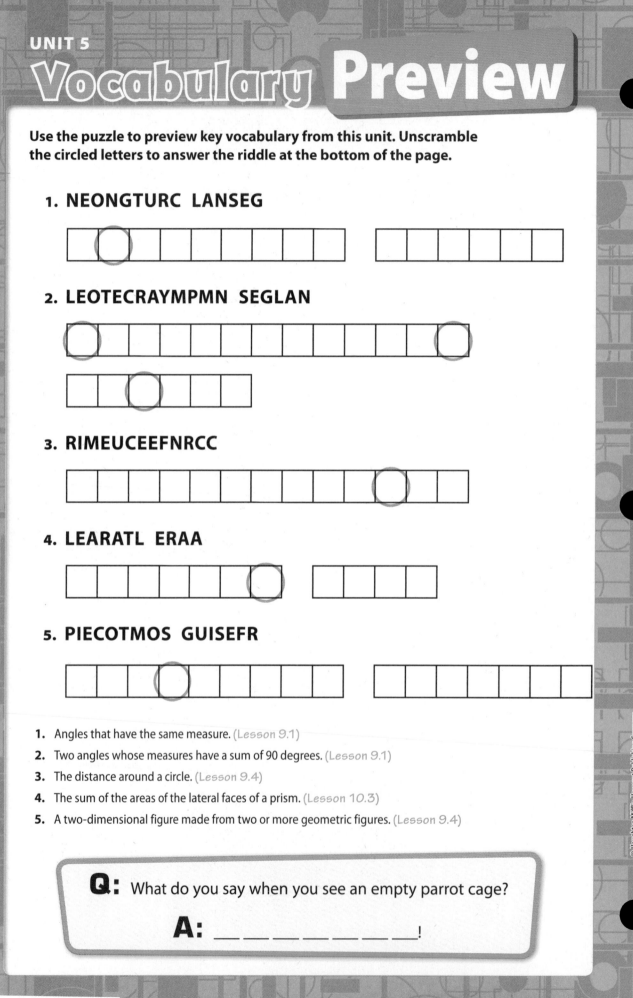

2. LEOTECRAYMPMN SEGLAN

3. RIMEUCEEFNRCC

4. LEARATL ERAA

5. PIECOTMOS GUISEFR

1. Angles that have the same measure. (Lesson 9.1)
2. Two angles whose measures have a sum of 90 degrees. (Lesson 9.1)
3. The distance around a circle. (Lesson 9.4)
4. The sum of the areas of the lateral faces of a prism. (Lesson 10.3)
5. A two-dimensional figure made from two or more geometric figures. (Lesson 9.4)

Q: What do you say when you see an empty parrot cage?

A: ___ ___ ___ ___ ___ ___ ___ ___!

Applications of Geometry Concepts

? ESSENTIAL QUESTION

How can you apply geometry concepts to solve real-world problems?

Real-World Video

my.hrw.com

A 16-inch pizza has a diameter of 16 inches. You can use the diameter to find circumference and area of the pizza. You can also determine how much pizza is in one slice of different sizes of pizzas.

GO DIGITAL
my.hrw.com

my.hrw.com

Go digital with your write-in student edition, accessible on any device.

Math On the Spot

Scan with your smart phone to jump directly to the online edition, video tutor, and more.

Animated Math

Interactively explore key concepts to see how math works.

Personal Math Trainer

Get immediate feedback and help as you work through practice sets.

279

Are YOU Ready?

Complete these exercises to review skills you will need for this chapter.

Personal Math Trainer

Online Assessment and Intervention

my.hrw.com

Multiply with Fractions and Decimals

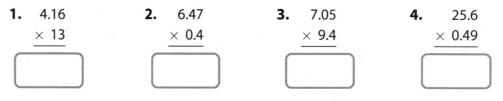

EXAMPLE		
	7.3	Multiply as you would with whole numbers.
	× 2.4	Count the total number of decimal places in the two factors.
	2 9 2	
	+ 1 4 6	Place the decimal point in the product so that there are the
	1 7.5 2	same number of digits after the decimal point.

Multiply.

1. 4.16
   × 13

2. 6.47
   × 0.4

3. 7.05
   × 9.4

4. 25.6
   × 0.49

Area of Squares, Rectangles, and Triangles

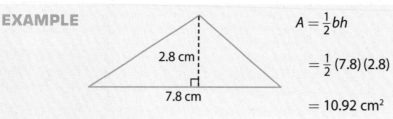

EXAMPLE

2.8 cm

7.8 cm

$A = \frac{1}{2}bh$ Use the formula for area of a triangle.

$= \frac{1}{2}(7.8)(2.8)$ Substitute for each variable.

$= 10.92 \text{ cm}^2$ Multiply.

Find the area of each figure.

5. triangle with base 14 in. and height 10 in. _____

6. square with sides of 3.5 ft _____

7. rectangle with length $8\frac{1}{2}$ in. and width 6 in. _____

8. triangle with base 12.5 m and height 2.4 m _____

Reading Start-Up

© Houghton Mifflin Harcourt Publishing Company

Vocabulary

Review Words

acute angle *(ángulo agudo)*
✔ circumference *(circunferencia)*
✔ diameter *(diámetro)*
obtuse angle *(ángulo obtuso)*
✔ pi *(pi)*
✔ radius *(radio)*
right angle *(ángulo recto)*
vertex *(vértice)*

Preview Words

adjacent angles *(ángulos adyacentes)*
complementary angles *(ángulos complementarios)*
congruent angles *(ángulos congruentes)*
supplementary angles *(ángulos suplementarios)*
vertical angles *(ángulos opuestos por el vértice)*

Visualize Vocabulary

Use the ✔ words to complete the graphic. You will put one word in each oval.

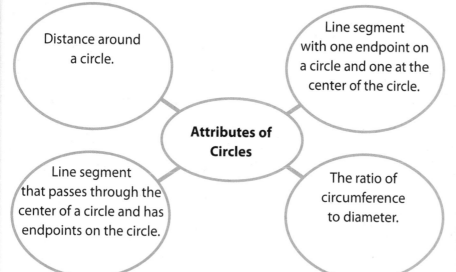

Distance around a circle.

Line segment with one endpoint on a circle and one at the center of the circle.

Attributes of Circles

Line segment that passes through the center of a circle and has endpoints on the circle.

The ratio of circumference to diameter.

Understand Vocabulary

Complete each sentence, using the preview words.

1. _____ are angles that have the same measure.

2. _____ are two angles whose measures have a sum of 90°.

Active Reading

Four-Corner Fold Before beginning the module, create a four-corner fold to help you organize what you learn. As you study this module, note important ideas, such as vocabulary, properties, and formulas, on the flaps. Use one flap for each lesson in the module. You can use your FoldNote later to study for tests and complete assignments.

Unpacking the TEKS

Understanding the TEKS and the vocabulary terms in the TEKS will help you know exactly what you are expected to learn in this module.

TEKS 7.11.C

Write and solve equations using geometry concepts, including the sum of the angles in a triangle, and angle relationships.

Key Vocabulary

supplementary angles
(ángulos suplementarios)
Two angles whose measures have a sum of 180°.

complementary angles
(ángulos complementarios)
Two angles whose measures add to 90°.

vertical angles (ángulos opuestos por el vértice)
A pair of opposite congruent angles formed by intersecting lines.

What It Means to You

You will learn about supplementary, complementary, vertical, and adjacent angles. You will solve simple equations to find the measure of an unknown angle in a figure.

UNPACKING EXAMPLE 7.11.C

Line $n \parallel$ line p. Find the measure of angle 2.

Corresponding angles are congruent.

$m\angle 1 = 55°$

Adjacent angles formed by two intersecting lines are supplementary.

$m\angle 1 + m\angle 2 = 180°$

$55° + m\angle 2 = 180°$ Substitute.

$m\angle 2 = 180° - 55°$

$= 125°$

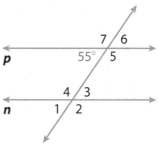

TEKS 7.9.B

Determine the circumference and area of circles.

Key Vocabulary

area (área)
The number of square units needed to cover a given surface.

circumference (circunferencia)
The distance around a circle.

What It Means to You

You will use formulas to solve problems involving the area and circumference of circles.

UNPACKING EXAMPLE 7.9.B

Lily is drawing plans for a circular fountain. The diameter of the fountain is 20 feet. What is the approximate circumference?

$C = \pi d$

$C \approx 3.14 \cdot 20$ Substitute.

$C \approx 62.8$

The circumference of the fountain is about 62.8 feet.

Visit **my.hrw.com** to see all the **TEKS** unpacked.

⊙ my.hrw.com

TEKS
Equations, expressions, and relationships—7.11.C
Write and solve equations using geometry concepts, including the sum of the angles in a triangle, and angle relationships.

ESSENTIAL QUESTION

How can you use angle relationships to solve problems?

EXPLORE ACTIVITY   **TEKS** 7.11.C

Measuring Angles

It is useful to work with pairs of angles and to understand how pairs of angles relate to each other. **Congruent angles** are angles that have the same measure.

STEP 1 Using a ruler, draw a pair of intersecting lines. Label each angle from 1 to 4.

STEP 2 Use a protractor to help you complete the chart.

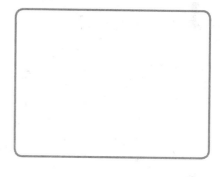

Angle	Measure of Angle
m∠1	
m∠2	
m∠3	
m∠4	
m∠1 + m∠2	
m∠2 + m∠3	
m∠3 + m∠4	
m∠4 + m∠1	

Reflect

1. **Conjecture** Share your results with other students. Make a conjecture about pairs of angles that are opposite each other.

   _____

   _____

2. **Conjecture** When two lines intersect to form two angles, what conjecture can you make about the pairs of angles that are next to each other?

   _____

   _____

Angle Pairs and One-Step Equations

Vertical angles are the opposite angles formed by two intersecting lines. Vertical angles are congruent because the angles have the same measure. **Adjacent angles** are pairs of angles that share a vertex and one side but do not overlap.

Complementary angles are two angles whose measures have a sum of 90°. **Supplementary angles** are two angles whose measures have a sum of 180°. You discovered in the Explore Activity that adjacent angles formed by two intersecting lines are supplementary.

EXAMPLE 1

TEKS 7.11.C

Use the diagram.

A Name a pair of vertical angles.

∠AFB and ∠DFE

B Name a pair of adjacent angles.

∠AFB and ∠BFD

C Name a pair of supplementary angles.

∠AFB and ∠BFD

D Find the measure of ∠AFB.

Use the fact that ∠AFB and ∠BFD in the diagram are supplementary angles to find m∠AFB.

$$m\angle AFB + m\angle BFD = 180°$$ They are supplementary angles.

$$x + 140° = 180°$$ $m\angle BFD = 50° + 90° = 140°$

$$\underline{-140°\ \ -140°}$$ Subtract 140° from both sides.

$$x = 40°$$

The measure of ∠AFB is 40°.

My Notes

Reflect

3. Analyze Relationships What is the relationship between ∠AFB and ∠BFC? Explain.

_____

_____

4. Draw Conclusions Are ∠AFC and ∠BFC adjacent angles? Why or why not?

_____

_____

YOUR TURN

Use the diagram.

5. Name a pair of supplementary angles.

_____

6. Name a pair of vertical angles.

_____

7. Find the measure of ∠CGD. _____

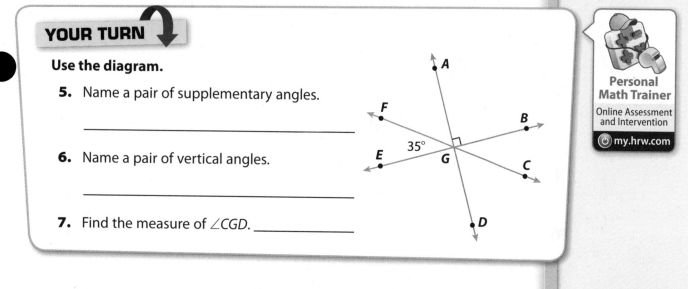

Angle Pairs and Two-Step Equations

Sometimes solving an equation is only the first step in using an angle relationship to solve a problem.

EXAMPLE 2

TEKS 7.11.C

Math On the Spot

⏻ my.hrw.com

A **Find the measure of ∠EHF.**

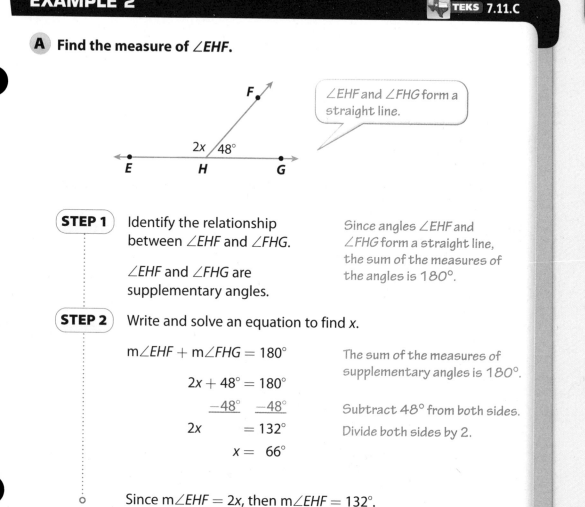

∠EHF and ∠FHG form a straight line.

STEP 1 Identify the relationship between ∠EHF and ∠FHG.

∠EHF and ∠FHG are supplementary angles.

Since angles ∠EHF and ∠FHG form a straight line, the sum of the measures of the angles is 180°.

STEP 2 Write and solve an equation to find x.

$$m\angle EHF + m\angle FHG = 180°$$

$$2x + 48° = 180°$$

$$\underline{-48° \quad -48°}$$

$$2x \quad = 132°$$

$$x = \ 66°$$

The sum of the measures of supplementary angles is 180°.

Subtract 48° from both sides.

Divide both sides by 2.

Since m∠EHF = 2x, then m∠EHF = 132°.

B Find the measure of ∠ZXY.

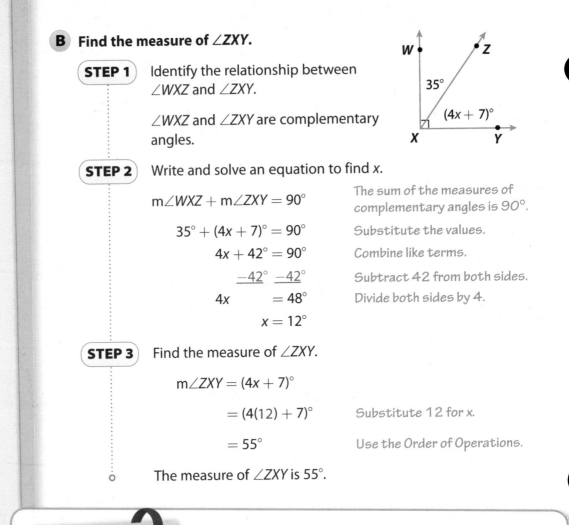

STEP 1 Identify the relationship between ∠WXZ and ∠ZXY.

∠WXZ and ∠ZXY are complementary angles.

STEP 2 Write and solve an equation to find x.

$m∠WXZ + m∠ZXY = 90°$ The sum of the measures of complementary angles is 90°.

$35° + (4x + 7)° = 90°$ Substitute the values.

$4x + 42° = 90°$ Combine like terms.

$\underline{-42° \quad -42°}$ Subtract 42 from both sides.

$4x \quad\quad = 48°$ Divide both sides by 4.

$x = 12°$

STEP 3 Find the measure of ∠ZXY.

$m∠ZXY = (4x + 7)°$

$= (4(12) + 7)°$ Substitute 12 for x.

$= 55°$ Use the Order of Operations.

The measure of ∠ZXY is 55°.

YOUR TURN

8. Find the measure of ∠JML.

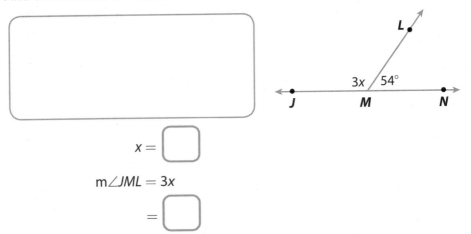

$x = \boxed{}$

$m∠JML = 3x$

$= \boxed{}$

9. **Critique Reasoning** Cory says that to find m∠JML above you can stop when you get to the solution step $3x = 126°$. Explain why this works.

_____

_____

_____

© Houghton Mifflin Harcourt Publishing Company

Using Angle Measures in Triangles

You learned earlier that the sum of the measures of the angles in any triangle is 180°. You can use this property in many real-world situations.

EXAMPLE 3 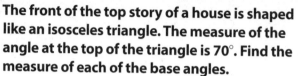 **TEKS** 7.11.C

The front of the top story of a house is shaped like an isosceles triangle. The measure of the angle at the top of the triangle is 70°. Find the measure of each of the base angles.

STEP 1 Make a sketch.

C

$70°$

x x

A B

STEP 2 Write an equation.

$m\angle A + m\angle B + m\angle C = 180°$ *The sum of the angle measures in a triangle is 180°.*

$x + x + 70° = 180°$ *Substitute values.*

STEP 3 Solve the equation to find x.

$x + x + 70° = 180°$

$2x + 70° = 180°$ *Combine like terms.*

$\underline{-70° \quad -70°}$ *Subtract 70° from both sides.*

$2x = 110°$

$\dfrac{2x}{2} = \dfrac{110°}{2}$ *Divide both sides of the equation by 2.*

$x = 55°$

Each of the base angles measures 55°.

YOUR TURN

Use the diagram.

10. Find the value of x. _____

11. Find the measures of

    $\angle A$ and $\angle B$. _____

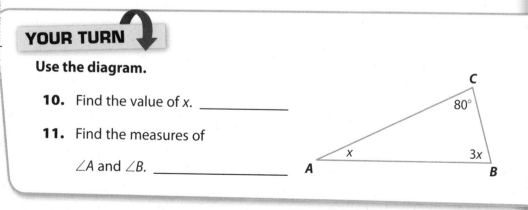

Personal Math Trainer

Online Assessment and Intervention

my.hrw.com

For Exercises 1–2, use the figure. (Example 1)

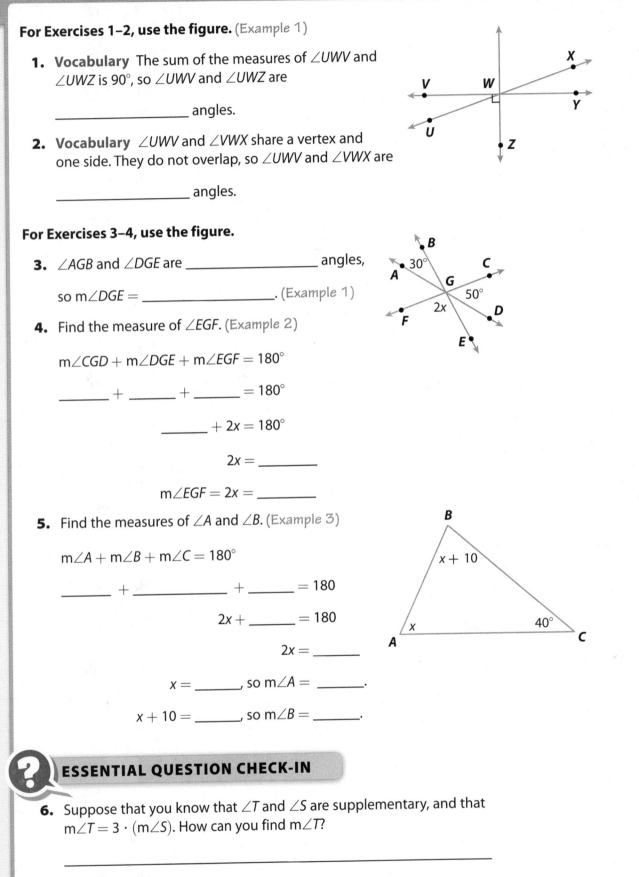

1. **Vocabulary** The sum of the measures of ∠UWV and ∠UWZ is 90°, so ∠UWV and ∠UWZ are

   _____ angles.

2. **Vocabulary** ∠UWV and ∠VWX share a vertex and one side. They do not overlap, so ∠UWV and ∠VWX are

   _____ angles.

For Exercises 3–4, use the figure.

3. ∠AGB and ∠DGE are _____ angles,

   so m∠DGE = _____. (Example 1)

4. Find the measure of ∠EGF. (Example 2)

   m∠CGD + m∠DGE + m∠EGF = 180°

   _____ + _____ + _____ = 180°

   _____ + 2x = 180°

   2x = _____

   m∠EGF = 2x = _____

5. Find the measures of ∠A and ∠B. (Example 3)

   m∠A + m∠B + m∠C = 180°

   _____ + _____ + _____ = 180

   2x + _____ = 180

   2x = _____

   x = _____, so m∠A = _____.

   x + 10 = _____, so m∠B = _____.

? ESSENTIAL QUESTION CHECK-IN

6. Suppose that you know that ∠T and ∠S are supplementary, and that m∠T = 3 · (m∠S). How can you find m∠T?

   _____

   _____

9.1 Independent Practice

TEKS 7.11.C

Personal Math Trainer

Online Assessment and Intervention

my.hrw.com

For Exercises 7–11, use the figure.

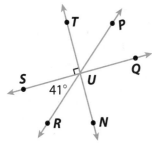

7. Name a pair of adjacent angles. Explain why they are adjacent.

_____

_____

_____

8. Name a pair of acute vertical angles.

_____

9. Name a pair of supplementary angles.

_____

10. Justify Reasoning Find m∠QUR. Justify your answer.

_____

_____

_____

_____

_____

11. Draw Conclusions Which is greater, m∠TUR or m∠RUQ? Explain.

_____

_____

_____

_____

Solve for each indicated angle measure or variable in the figure.

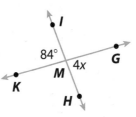

12. x _____

13. m∠KMH _____

Solve for each indicated angle measure or variable in the figure.

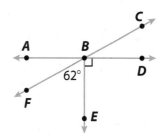

14. m∠CBE _____

15. m∠ABF _____

16. m∠CBA _____

Solve for each indicated angle measure or variable in the figure.

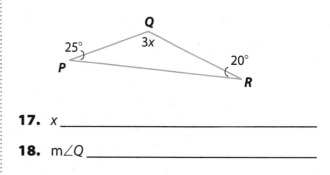

17. x _____

18. m∠Q _____

Let △ABC be a right triangle with m∠C = 90°.

19. **Critical Thinking** An equilateral triangle has three congruent sides and three congruent angles. Can △ABC be an equilateral triangle? Explain your reasoning.

_____

_____

20. **Counterexample** An isosceles triangle has two congruent sides, and the angles opposite those sides are congruent. River says that right triangle ABC cannot be an isosceles triangle. Give a counterexample to show that his statement is incorrect.

_____

_____

21. **Make a Conjecture** In a scalene triangle, no two sides have the same length, and no two angles have the same measure. Do you think a right triangle can be a scalene triangle? Explain your reasoning.

_____

_____

_____

_____

22. **Represent Real-World Problems** The railroad tracks meet the road as shown. The town will allow a parking lot at angle J if the measure of angle J is greater than 38°. Can a parking lot be built at angle J? Why or why not?

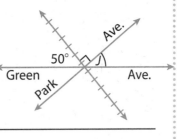

_____

_____

23. **Analyze Relationships** In triangle XYZ, m∠X = 30°, and all the angles have measures that are whole numbers. Angle Y is an obtuse angle. What is the greatest possible measure that angle Z can have? Explain your answer.

_____

_____

_____

TEKS
Equations, expressions, and relationships—
7.9.B Determine the circumference ... of circles.

? ESSENTIAL QUESTION

How do you find the circumference of a circle?

Finding Circumference Using Diameter

As you learned earlier, the ratio of the circumference to the diameter $\frac{C}{d}$ is the same for all circles. This ratio is called π or *pi*, and you can approximate it as 3.14 or as $\frac{22}{7}$. You can use π to find a formula for circumference.

For any circle, $\frac{C}{d} = \pi$. Solve the equation for C to give an equation for the circumference of a circle in terms of the diameter.

$\frac{C}{d} = \pi$ — The ratio of the circumference to the diameter is π.

$\frac{C}{d} \times d = \pi \times d$ — Multiply both sides by d.

$C = \pi d$ — Simplify.

Math On the Spot
my.hrw.com

EXAMPLE 1
TEKS 7.9.B

Find the circumference of the circle to the nearest hundredth. Use 3.14 or $\frac{22}{7}$ for π.

STEP 1 Identify the diameter of the circle.

$d = 8$ in.

8 in.

STEP 2 Use the formula.

$C = \pi d$

$C = \pi(8)$ — Substitute 8 for d.

$C \approx 3.14(8)$ — Substitute 3.14 for π.

$C \approx 25.12$ — Multiply.

The circumference is about 25.12 inches.

Math Talk
Mathematical Processes
Explain why you wouldn't want to use $\frac{22}{7}$ as an approximation for π in this problem.

Reflect

1. What value of π could you use to estimate the circumference? _____

2. **Checking for Reasonableness** How do you know your answer is reasonable?

_____

© Houghton Mifflin Harcourt Publishing Company

YOUR TURN

3. Find the circumference of the circle to the nearest hundredth.

11 cm

_____

Finding Circumference Using Radius

Since the diameter of a circle is the same as 2 times the radius, you can substitute $2r$ in the equation for d.

$C = \pi d$

$C = \pi(2r)$ Substitute $2r$ for d.

$C = 2\pi r$ Use the Commutative Property.

The two equivalent formulas for circumference are $C = \pi d$ or $C = 2\pi r$.

EXAMPLE 2   Real World   **TEKS** 7.9.B

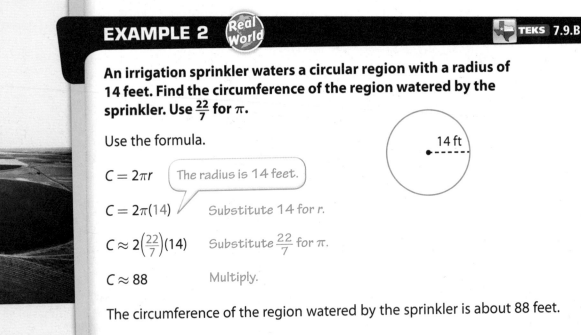

An irrigation sprinkler waters a circular region with a radius of 14 feet. Find the circumference of the region watered by the sprinkler. Use $\frac{22}{7}$ for π.

Use the formula.

$C = 2\pi r$ The radius is 14 feet.

$C = 2\pi(14)$ Substitute 14 for r.

$C \approx 2\left(\frac{22}{7}\right)(14)$ Substitute $\frac{22}{7}$ for π.

$C \approx 88$ Multiply.

The circumference of the region watered by the sprinkler is about 88 feet.

Reflect

4. **Analyze Relationships** When is it logical to use $\frac{22}{7}$ instead of 3.14 for π?

_____

YOUR TURN

5. Find the circumference of the circle.

21 cm

_____

© Houghton Mifflin Harcourt Publishing Company • Image Credits: ©Corbis

Using Circumference

Given the circumference of a circle, you can use the appropriate circumference formula to find the radius or the diameter of the circle. You can use that information to solve problems.

EXAMPLE 3 · Real World

TEKS 7.9.B

A circular pond has a circumference of 628 feet. A model boat is moving directly across the pond, along a radius, at a rate of 5 feet per second. How long does it take the boat to get from the edge of the pond to the center?

STEP 1 Find the radius of the pond.

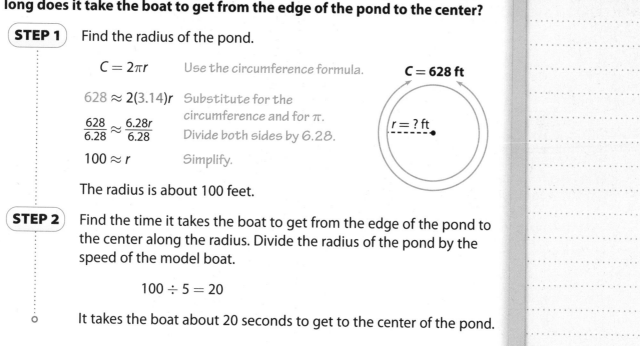

$C = 2\pi r$ Use the circumference formula.

$628 \approx 2(3.14)r$ Substitute for the circumference and for π.

$\dfrac{628}{6.28} \approx \dfrac{6.28r}{6.28}$ Divide both sides by 6.28.

$100 \approx r$ Simplify.

$C = 628$ ft

$r = ?$ ft

The radius is about 100 feet.

STEP 2 Find the time it takes the boat to get from the edge of the pond to the center along the radius. Divide the radius of the pond by the speed of the model boat.

$$100 \div 5 = 20$$

It takes the boat about 20 seconds to get to the center of the pond.

Reflect

6. **Analyze Relationships** Dante checks the answer to Step 1 by multiplying it by 6 and comparing it with the given circumference. Explain why Dante's estimation method works. Use it to check Step 1.

   _____

7. **What If?** Suppose the model boat were traveling at a rate of 4 feet per second. How long would it take the model boat to get from the edge of

   the pond to the center? _____

YOUR TURN

8. A circular garden has a circumference of 44 yards. Lars is digging a straight line along a diameter of the garden at a rate of 7 yards per hour. How many hours will it take him to dig across the garden?

   _____

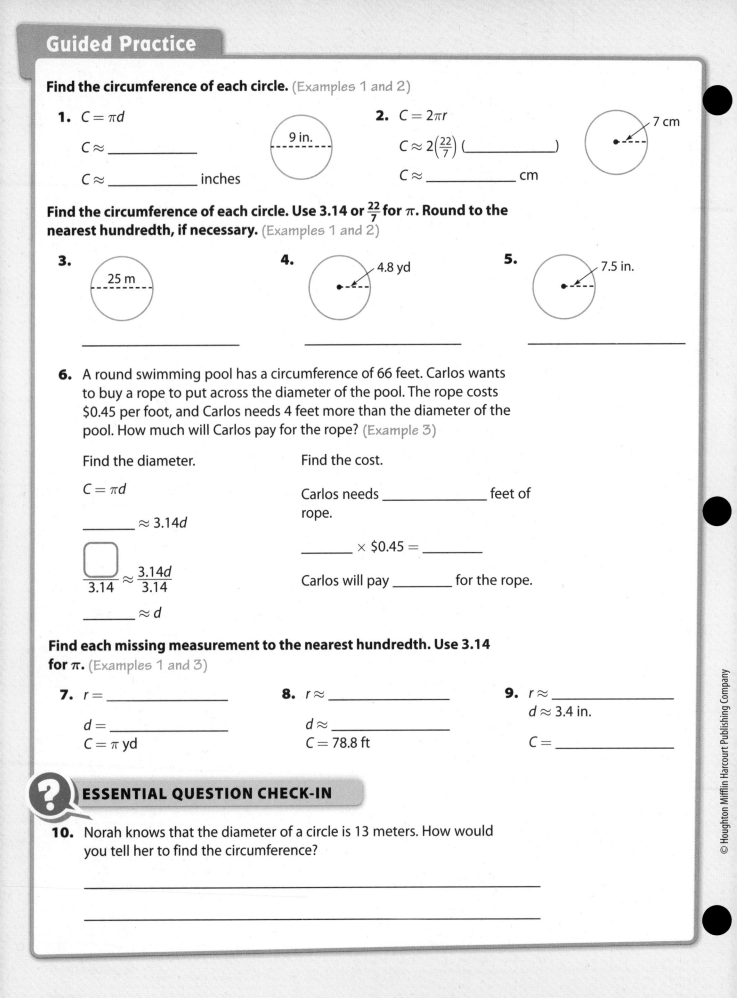

Find the circumference of each circle. (Examples 1 and 2)

1. $C = \pi d$

$C \approx$ _____

$C \approx$ _____ inches

9 in.

2. $C = 2\pi r$

$C \approx 2\left(\frac{22}{7}\right)$ (_____)

$C \approx$ _____ cm

7 cm

Find the circumference of each circle. Use 3.14 or $\frac{22}{7}$ for π. Round to the nearest hundredth, if necessary. (Examples 1 and 2)

3.

25 m

_____

4.

4.8 yd

_____

5.

7.5 in.

_____

6. A round swimming pool has a circumference of 66 feet. Carlos wants to buy a rope to put across the diameter of the pool. The rope costs $0.45 per foot, and Carlos needs 4 feet more than the diameter of the pool. How much will Carlos pay for the rope? (Example 3)

Find the diameter.

$C = \pi d$

_____ $\approx 3.14d$

$\dfrac{\boxed{}}{3.14} \approx \dfrac{3.14d}{3.14}$

_____ $\approx d$

Find the cost.

Carlos needs _____ feet of rope.

_____ $\times \$0.45 =$ _____

Carlos will pay _____ for the rope.

Find each missing measurement to the nearest hundredth. Use 3.14 for π. (Examples 1 and 3)

7. $r =$ _____

$d =$ _____

$C = \pi$ yd

8. $r \approx$ _____

$d \approx$ _____

$C = 78.8$ ft

9. $r \approx$ _____

$d \approx 3.4$ in.

$C =$ _____

? ESSENTIAL QUESTION CHECK-IN

10. Norah knows that the diameter of a circle is 13 meters. How would you tell her to find the circumference?

_____

_____

Name _____ Class _____ Date _____

9.2 Independent Practice

TEKS 7.9.B

Personal
Math Trainer

Online
Assessment and
Intervention

my.hrw.com

Find the circumference of each circle. Use 3.14 or $\frac{22}{7}$ for π. Round to the nearest hundredth, if necessary.

11.

5.9 ft

_____

12.

56 cm

_____

13.

35 in.

_____

14. In Exercises 11–13, for which problems did you use $\frac{22}{7}$ for π? Explain your choice.

_____

_____

_____

15. A circular fountain has a radius of 9.4 feet. Find its diameter and circumference to the nearest hundredth.

_____

16. Find the radius and circumference of a CD with a diameter of 4.75 inches.

_____

17. A dartboard has a diameter of 18 inches. What is its radius and circumference?

_____

18. Multistep Randy's circular garden has a radius of 1.5 feet. He wants to enclose the garden with edging that costs $0.75 per foot. About how much will the edging cost? Explain.

_____

_____

19. Represent Real-World Problems The Ferris wheel shown makes 12 revolutions per ride. How far would someone travel during one ride?

_____

diameter 63 feet

20. The diameter of a bicycle wheel is 2 feet. About how many revolutions does the wheel make to travel 2 kilometers? Explain. Hint: 1 km = 3,280 ft

_____

_____

_____

21. Multistep A map of a public park shows a circular pond. There is a bridge along a diameter of the pond that is 0.25 mi long. You walk across the bridge, while your friend walks halfway around the pond to meet you at the other side of the bridge. How much farther does your friend walk?

_____

© Houghton Mifflin Harcourt Publishing Company

22. Architecture The Capitol Rotunda connects the House and the Senate sides of the U.S. Capitol. Complete the table. Round your answers to the nearest foot.

Capitol Rotunda Dimensions	
Height	180 ft
Circumference	301.5 ft
Radius	
Diameter	

 FOCUS ON HIGHER ORDER THINKING

23. Multistep A museum groundskeeper is creating a semicircular statuary garden with a diameter of 30 feet. There will be a fence around the garden. The fencing costs $9.25 per linear foot. About how much will the fencing cost altogether?

_____

24. Critical Thinking Sam is placing rope lights around the edge of a circular patio with a diameter of 18 feet. The lights come in lengths of 54 inches. How many strands of lights does he need to surround the patio edge?

_____

25. Represent Real-World Problems A circular path 2 feet wide has an inner diameter of 150 feet. How much farther is it around the outer edge of the path than around the inner edge?

_____

26. Critique Reasoning A gear on a bicycle has the shape of a circle. One gear has a diameter of 4 inches, and a smaller one has a diameter of 2 inches Justin says that the circumference of the larger gear is 2 inches more than the circumference of the smaller gear. Do you agree? Explain your answer.

_____

_____

_____

_____

27. Persevere in Problem Solving Consider two circular swimming pools. Pool A has a radius of 12 feet, and Pool B has a diameter of 7.5 meters. Which pool has a greater circumference? How much greater? Justify your answers.

_____

_____

_____

_____

Work Area

TEKS
Equations, expressions, and relationships—7.8.C
Use models to determine the approximate formulas for the ... area of a circle and connect the models to the actual formulas. *Also 7.9.B*

? **ESSENTIAL QUESTION**

How do you find the area of a circle?

EXPLORE ACTIVITY 1 TEKS 7.8.C

Exploring Area of Circles

You can use what you know about circles and π to help find the formula for the area of a circle.

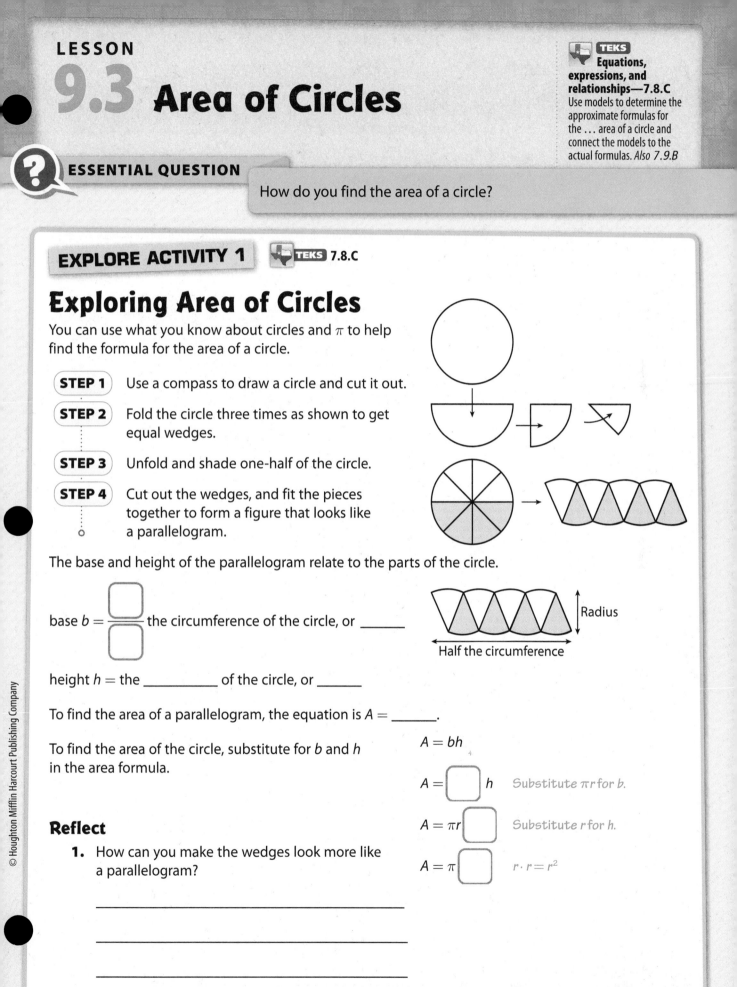

STEP 1 Use a compass to draw a circle and cut it out.

STEP 2 Fold the circle three times as shown to get equal wedges.

STEP 3 Unfold and shade one-half of the circle.

STEP 4 Cut out the wedges, and fit the pieces together to form a figure that looks like a parallelogram.

The base and height of the parallelogram relate to the parts of the circle.

Radius

Half the circumference

base $b = \dfrac{\square}{\square}$ the circumference of the circle, or _____

height $h =$ the _____ of the circle, or _____

To find the area of a parallelogram, the equation is $A =$ _____.

To find the area of the circle, substitute for b and h in the area formula.

$A = bh$

$A = \boxed{}\, h$ *Substitute πr for b.*

$A = \pi r \boxed{}$ *Substitute r for h.*

$A = \pi \boxed{}$ $r \cdot r = r^2$

Reflect

1. How can you make the wedges look more like a parallelogram?

_____

_____

_____

Math On the Spot
my.hrw.com

Finding the Area of a Circle

Area of a Circle

The area of a circle is equal to π times the radius squared.

$$A = \pi r^2$$

Remember that area is given in square units.

EXAMPLE 1 Real World

TEKS 7.9.B

A biscuit recipe calls for the dough to be rolled out and circles to be cut from the dough. The biscuit cutter has a radius of 4 cm. Find the area of the biscuit once it is cut. Use 3.14 for π.

$A = \pi r^2$	Use the formula.
$A = \pi(4)^2$	Substitute. Use 4 for r.
$A \approx 3.14 \times 4^2$	Substitute. Use 3.14 for π.
$A \approx 3.14 \times 16$	Evaluate the power.
$A \approx 50.24$	Multiply.

The area of the biscuit is about 50.24 cm².

Math Talk
Mathematical Processes

If the radius increases by 1 centimeter, how does the area of the top of the biscuit change?

Reflect

2. Compare finding the area of a circle when given the radius with finding the area when given the diameter.

_____

_____

_____

3. Why do you evaluate the power in the equation before multiplying?

_____

_____

Personal Math Trainer

Online Assessment and Intervention

my.hrw.com

YOUR TURN

4. A circular pool has a radius of 10 feet. What is the area of the pool? Use 3.14 for π. _____

© Houghton Mifflin Harcourt Publishing Company • Image Credits: Zigzag Mountain Art/Shutterstock

Finding the Relationship between Circumference and Area

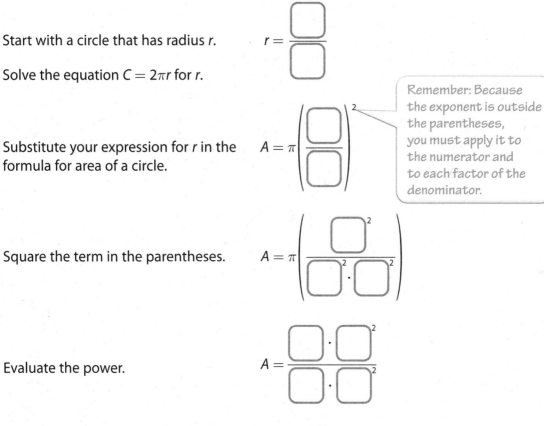

You can use what you know about circumference and area of circles to find a relationship between them.

Find the relationship between the circumference and area of a circle.

Start with a circle that has radius r. $r = \dfrac{\boxed{}}{\boxed{}}$

Solve the equation $C = 2\pi r$ for r.

Substitute your expression for r in the formula for area of a circle.

$$A = \pi\left(\dfrac{\boxed{}}{\boxed{}}\right)^2$$

> Remember: Because the exponent is outside the parentheses, you must apply it to the numerator and to each factor of the denominator.

Square the term in the parentheses.

$$A = \pi\left(\dfrac{\boxed{}^2}{\boxed{}^2 \cdot \boxed{}^2}\right)$$

Evaluate the power.

$$A = \dfrac{\boxed{} \cdot \boxed{}^2}{\boxed{} \cdot \boxed{}^2}$$

Simplify.

$$A = \dfrac{\boxed{}^2}{\boxed{} \cdot \boxed{}}$$

Solve for C^2. $C^2 = 4\,\boxed{}\,\boxed{}$

The circumference of the circle squared is equal to

_____.

Reflect

5. Does this formula work for a circle with a radius of 3 inches? Show your work.

Guided Practice

Find the area of each circle. Round to the nearest tenth if necessary. Use 3.14 for π.
(Explore Activity 1)

1.
14 m _____

2.
12 mm _____

3.
20 yd _____

Solve. Use 3.14 for π. (Example 1)

4. A clock face has a radius of 8 inches. What is the area of the clock face? Round your answer to the nearest hundredth. _____

5. A DVD has a diameter of 12 centimeters. What is the area of the DVD? Round your answer to the nearest hundredth. _____

6. A company makes steel lids that have a diameter of 13 inches. What is the area of each lid? Round your answer to the nearest hundredth. _____

Find the area of each circle. Give your answers in terms of π.
(Explore Activity 2)

7. $C = 4\pi$

$A =$ _____

8. $C = 12\pi$

$A =$ _____

9. $C = \frac{\pi}{2}$

$A =$ _____

10. A circular pen has an area of 64π square yards. What is the circumference of the pen? Give your answer in terms of π.
(Explore Activity 2) _____

? ESSENTIAL QUESTION CHECK-IN

11. What is the formula for the area A of a circle in terms of the radius r? _____

9.3 Independent Practice

Personal Math Trainer

Online Assessment and Intervention

TEKS 7.8.C, 7.8.B

12. The most popular pizza at Pavone's Pizza is the 10-inch personal pizza with one topping. What is the area of a pizza with a diameter of 10 inches? Round your answer to the nearest hundredth.

_____

13. A hubcap has a radius of 16 centimeters. What is the area of the hubcap? Round your answer to the nearest hundredth.

16 cm

_____

14. A stained glass window is shaped like a semicircle. The bottom edge of the window is 36 inches long. What is the area of the stained glass window? Round your answer to the nearest hundredth.

_____

15. Analyze Relationships The point (3, 0) lies on a circle with the center at the origin. What is the area of the circle to the nearest hundredth?

_____

16. Multistep A radio station broadcasts a signal over an area with a radius of 50 miles. The station can relay the signal and broadcast over an area with a radius of 75 miles. How much greater is the area of the broadcast region when the signal is relayed? Round your answer to the nearest square mile.

_____

17. Multistep The sides of a square field are 12 meters. A sprinkler in the center of the field sprays a circular area with a diameter that corresponds to a side of the field. How much of the field is **not** reached by the sprinkler? Round your answer to the nearest hundredth.

_____

18. Justify Reasoning A small silver dollar pancake served at a restaurant has a circumference of 2π inches. A regular pancake has a circumference of 4π inches. Is the area of the regular pancake twice the area of the silver dollar pancake? Explain.

_____

_____

_____

_____

_____

19. Analyze Relationships A bakery offers a small circular cake with a diameter of 8 inches. It also offers a large circular cake with a diameter of 24 inches. Does the top of the large cake have three times the area of that of the small cake? If not, how much greater is its area? Explain.

_____

_____

_____

_____

_____

_____

20. Communicate Mathematical Ideas You can use the formula $A = \frac{C^2}{4\pi}$ to find the area of a circle given the circumference. Describe another way to find the area of a circle when given the circumference.

_____

_____

_____

21. Draw Conclusions Mark wants to order a pizza. Which is the better deal? Explain.

_____

_____

_____

Donnie's Pizza Palace		
Diameter (in.)	12	18
Cost ($)	10	20

22. Multistep A bear was seen near a campground. Searchers were dispatched to the region to find the bear.

a. Assume the bear can walk in any direction at a rate of 2 miles per hour. Suppose the bear was last seen 4 hours ago. How large an area must the searchers cover? Use 3.14 for π. Round your answer to the

nearest square mile. _____

b. What If? How much additional area would the searchers have to

cover if the bear were last seen 5 hours ago? _____

 **FOCUS ON HIGHER ORDER THINKING**

23. Analyze Relationships Two circles have the same radius. Is the combined area of the two circles the same as the area of a circle with twice the radius? Explain.

_____

_____

24. Look for a Pattern How does the area of a circle change if the radius is multiplied by a factor of n, where n is a whole number?

_____

25. Represent Real World Problems The bull's-eye on a target has a diameter of 3 inches. The whole target has a diameter of 15 inches. What part of the whole target is the bull's-eye? Explain.

_____

Work Area

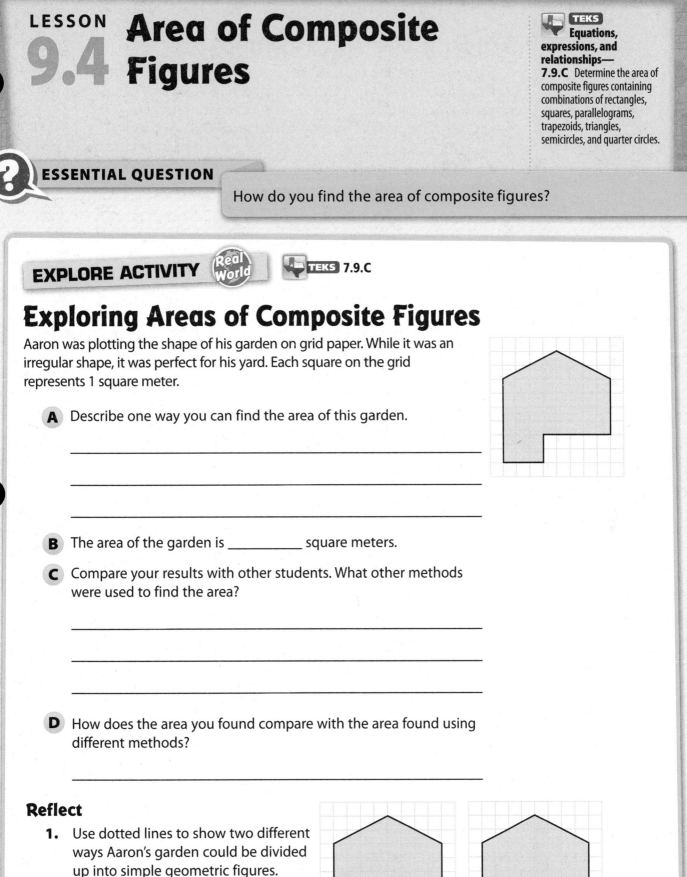

Area of Composite Figures

TEKS
Equations, expressions, and relationships—
7.9.C Determine the area of composite figures containing combinations of rectangles, squares, parallelograms, trapezoids, triangles, semicircles, and quarter circles.

ESSENTIAL QUESTION

How do you find the area of composite figures?

EXPLORE ACTIVITY *Real World* TEKS 7.9.C

Exploring Areas of Composite Figures

Aaron was plotting the shape of his garden on grid paper. While it was an irregular shape, it was perfect for his yard. Each square on the grid represents 1 square meter.

A Describe one way you can find the area of this garden.

_____

_____

_____

B The area of the garden is _____ square meters.

C Compare your results with other students. What other methods were used to find the area?

_____

_____

_____

D How does the area you found compare with the area found using different methods?

_____

Reflect

1. Use dotted lines to show two different ways Aaron's garden could be divided up into simple geometric figures.

Finding the Area of a Composite Figure

A composite figure is made up of simple geometric shapes. To find the area of a composite figure or other irregular-shaped figure, divide it into simple, nonoverlapping figures. Find the area of each simpler figure, and then add the areas together to find the total area of the composite figure.

Use the chart below to review some common area formulas.

Shape	Area Formula
triangle	$A = \frac{1}{2}bh$
square	$A = s^2$
rectangle	$A = \ell w$
parallelogram	$A = bh$
trapezoid	$A = \frac{1}{2}h(b_1 + b_2)$

EXAMPLE 1   Real World

TEKS 7.9.C

Find the area of the figure.

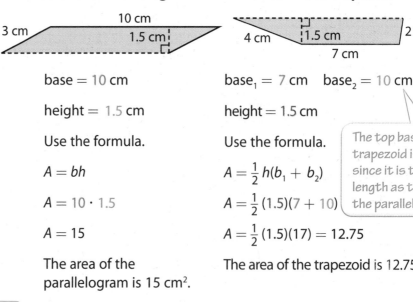

STEP 1 Separate the figure into smaller, familiar figures: a parallelogram and a trapezoid.

STEP 2 Find the area of each shape.

Area of the Parallelogram

base = 10 cm

height = 1.5 cm

Use the formula.

$A = bh$

$A = 10 \cdot 1.5$

$A = 15$

The area of the parallelogram is 15 cm².

Area of the Trapezoid

base₁ = 7 cm   base₂ = 10 cm

height = 1.5 cm

Use the formula.

$A = \frac{1}{2}h(b_1 + b_2)$

$A = \frac{1}{2}(1.5)(7 + 10)$

$A = \frac{1}{2}(1.5)(17) = 12.75$

The area of the trapezoid is 12.75 cm².

> The top base of the trapezoid is 10 cm since it is the same length as the base of the parallelogram.

STEP 3 Add the areas to find the total area.

$A = 15 + 12.75 = 27.75$ cm²

The area of the figure is 27.75 cm².

YOUR TURN

Find the area of each figure. Use 3.14 for π.

2.

2 ft
8 ft
3 ft
4 ft
3 ft
3 ft
8 ft

3.

10 m

10 m

Using Area to Solve Problems

EXAMPLE 2 Real World

TEKS 7.9.C

A banquet room is being carpeted. A floor plan of the room is shown at right. Each unit represents 1 yard. The carpet costs $23.50 per square yard. How much will it cost to carpet the room?

STEP 1 Separate the composite figure into simpler shapes as shown by the dashed lines: a parallelogram, a rectangle, and a triangle.

STEP 2 Find the area of the simpler figures. Count units to find the dimensions.

Parallelogram	Rectangle	Triangle
$A = bh$	$A = \ell w$	$A = \frac{1}{2}bh$
$A = 4 \cdot 2$	$A = 6 \cdot 4$	$A = \frac{1}{2}(1)(2)$
$A = 8 \text{ yd}^2$	$A = 24 \text{ yd}^2$	$A = 1 \text{ yd}^2$

STEP 3 Find the area of the composite figure.

$A = 8 + 24 + 1 = 33$ square yards

STEP 4 Calculate the cost to carpet the room.

Area · Cost per yard = Total cost

33 · $23.50 = $775.50

The cost to carpet the banquet room is $775.50.

Math Talk
Mathematical Processes

Describe how you can estimate the cost to carpet the room.

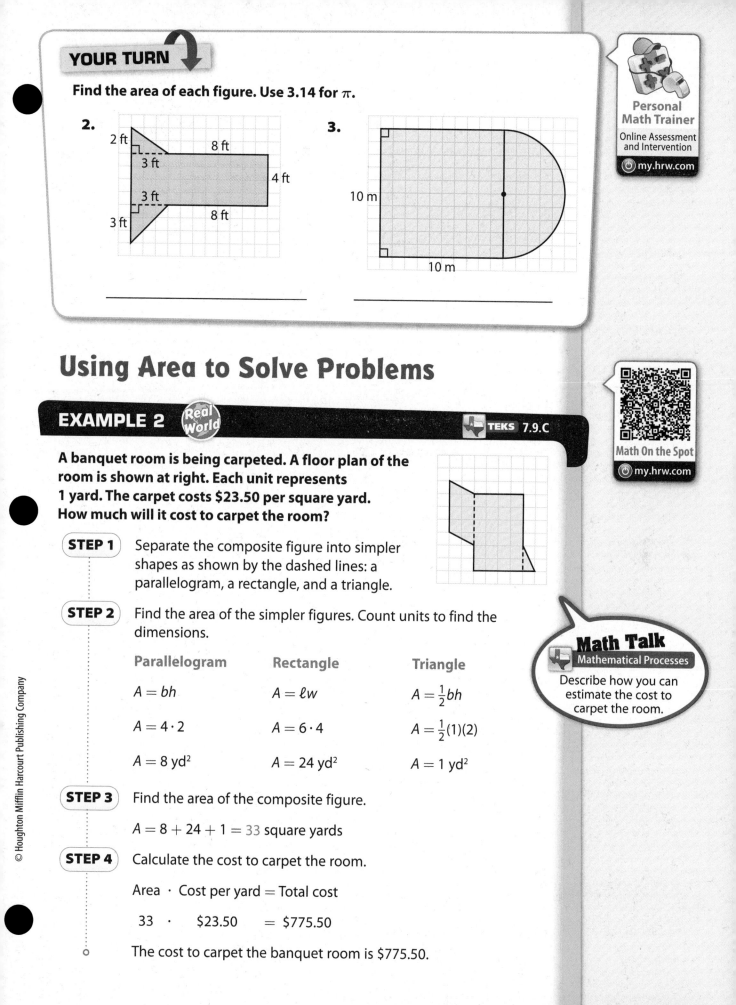

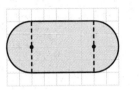

YOUR TURN

4. A window is being replaced with tinted glass. The plan at the right shows the design of the window. Each unit length represents 1 foot. The glass costs $28 per square foot. How much will it cost to replace the glass? Use 3.14 for π.

_____

Guided Practice

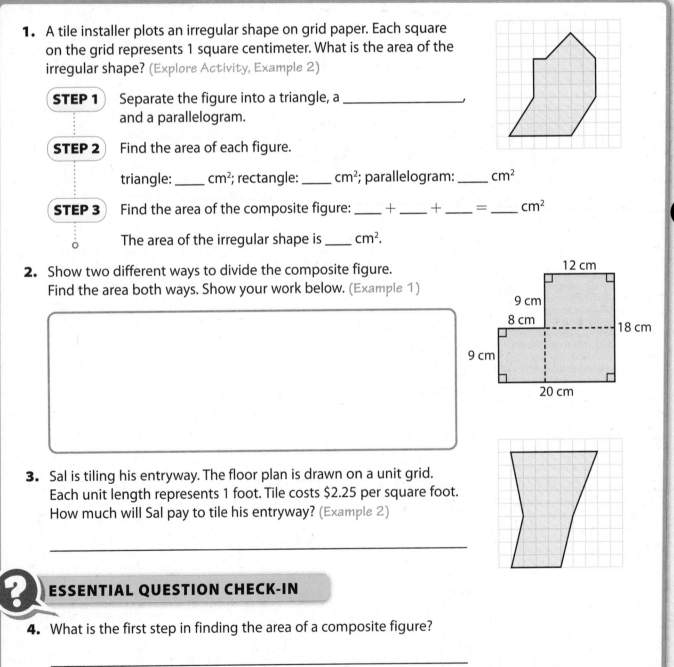

1. A tile installer plots an irregular shape on grid paper. Each square on the grid represents 1 square centimeter. What is the area of the irregular shape? (Explore Activity, Example 2)

   STEP 1 Separate the figure into a triangle, a _____, and a parallelogram.

   STEP 2 Find the area of each figure.

   triangle: _____ cm²; rectangle: _____ cm²; parallelogram: _____ cm²

   STEP 3 Find the area of the composite figure: ____ + ____ + ____ = ____ cm²

   The area of the irregular shape is ____ cm².

2. Show two different ways to divide the composite figure. Find the area both ways. Show your work below. (Example 1)

   12 cm
   9 cm
   8 cm
   18 cm
   9 cm
   20 cm

3. Sal is tiling his entryway. The floor plan is drawn on a unit grid. Each unit length represents 1 foot. Tile costs $2.25 per square foot. How much will Sal pay to tile his entryway? (Example 2)

   _____

? **ESSENTIAL QUESTION CHECK-IN**

4. What is the first step in finding the area of a composite figure?

   _____

9.4 Independent Practice

TEKS 7.9.C

5. A banner is made of a square and a semicircle. The square has side lengths of 26 inches. One side of the square is also the diameter of the semicircle. What is the total area of the banner? Use 3.14 for π.

_____

6. Multistep Erin wants to carpet the floor of her closet. A floor plan of the closet is shown.

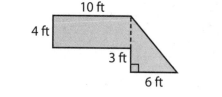

a. How much carpet does Erin need?

_____

b. The carpet Erin has chosen costs $2.50 per square foot. How much will it cost her to carpet the floor?

_____

7. Multiple Representations Hexagon *ABCDEF* has vertices *A*(−2, 4), *B*(0, 4), *C*(2, 1), *D*(5, 1), *E*(5, −2), and *F*(−2, −2). Sketch the figure on a coordinate plane. What is the area of the hexagon?

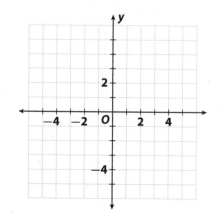

8. A field is shaped like the figure shown. What is the area of the field? Use 3.14 for π.

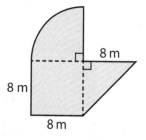

_____

9. A bookmark is shaped like a rectangle with a semicircle attached at both ends. The rectangle is 12 cm long and 4 cm wide. The diameter of each semicircle is the width of the rectangle. What is the area of the bookmark? Use 3.14 for π.

_____

10. Multistep Alex is making 12 pennants for the school fair. The pattern he is using to make the pennants is shown in the figure. The fabric for the pennants costs $1.25 per square foot. How much will it cost Alex to make 12 pennants?

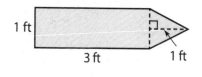

_____

11. Reasoning A composite figure is formed by combining a square and a triangle. Its total area is 32.5 ft². The area of the triangle is 7.5 ft². What is the length of each side of the square? Explain.

_____

_____

_____

_____

12. Represent Real-World Problems Christina plotted the shape of her garden on graph paper. She estimates that she will get about 15 carrots from each square unit. She plans to use the entire garden for carrots. About how many carrots can she expect to grow? Explain.

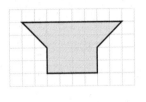

_____

_____

_____

13. Analyze Relationships The figure shown is made up of a triangle and a square. The perimeter of the figure is 56 inches. What is the area of the figure? Explain.

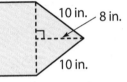

10 in. 8 in.

10 in.

_____

_____

_____

_____

14. Critical Thinking The pattern for a scarf is shown at right. What is the area of the scarf? Use 3.14 for π.

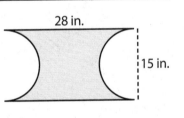

28 in.

15 in.

15. Persevere in Problem Solving The design for the palladium window shown includes a semicircular shape at the top. The bottom is formed by squares of equal size. A shade for the window will extend 4 inches beyond the perimeter of the window, shown by the dashed line around the window. Each square in the window has an area of 100 in².

a. What is the area of the window? Use 3.14 for π.

_____

b. What is the area of the shade? Round your answer to the nearest whole number.

_____

Ready to Go On?

9.1 Angle Relationships

Use the diagram to name a pair of each type of angle.

1. Supplementary angles _____

2. Complementary angles _____

3. Vertical angles _____

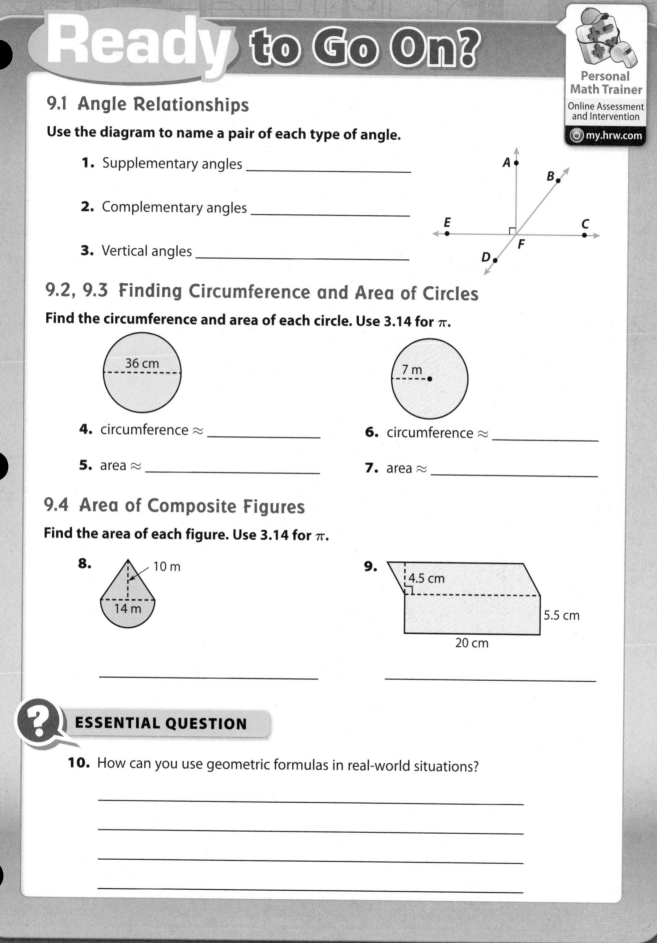

9.2, 9.3 Finding Circumference and Area of Circles

Find the circumference and area of each circle. Use 3.14 for π.

36 cm

7 m

4. circumference ≈ _____

5. area ≈ _____

6. circumference ≈ _____

7. area ≈ _____

9.4 Area of Composite Figures

Find the area of each figure. Use 3.14 for π.

8.   10 m

14 m

9.   4.5 cm

5.5 cm

20 cm

_____

_____

? ESSENTIAL QUESTION

10. How can you use geometric formulas in real-world situations?

_____

_____

_____

_____

Selected Response

Use the diagram for Exercises 1–3.

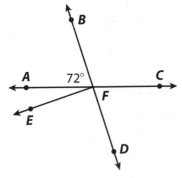

1. What is the measure of ∠BFC?

Ⓐ 18°　　　　Ⓒ 108°

Ⓑ 72°　　　　Ⓓ 144°

2. Which describes the relationship between ∠BFA and ∠CFD?

Ⓐ adjacent angles

Ⓑ complementary angles

Ⓒ supplementary angles

Ⓓ vertical angles

3. Which information would allow you to identify ∠BFA and ∠AFE as complementary angles?

Ⓐ m∠AFE = 108°

Ⓑ ∠DFE is a right angle.

Ⓒ ∠BFA and ∠BFC are supplementary angles.

Ⓓ ∠BFA and ∠BFC are adjacent angles.

4. David pays $7 per day to park his car. He uses a debit card each time. By what amount does his bank account change due to parking charges over a 40-day period?

Ⓐ −$280　　　Ⓒ $47

Ⓑ −$47　　　　Ⓓ $280

5. What is the circumference of the circle? Use 3.14 for π.

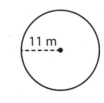

Ⓐ 34.54 m

Ⓑ 69.08 m

Ⓒ 379.94 m

Ⓓ 1,519.76 m

6. What is the area of the circle? Use 3.14 for π.

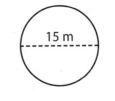

Ⓐ 23.55 m²　　　Ⓒ 176.625 m²

Ⓑ 47.1 m²　　　　Ⓓ 706.5 m²

Gridded Response

7. Find the area in square meters of the figure below? Use 3.14 for π.

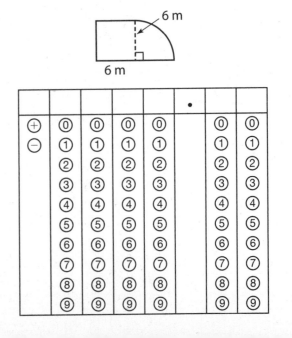

Volume and Surface Area

? ESSENTIAL QUESTION

How can you use volume and surface area to solve real-world problems?

Real-World Video

There are famous pyramids around the world. The glass and metal square pyramid in the courtyard of the Louvre Palace in Paris is the main entrance to the Louvre Museum.

⏻ my.hrw.com

G⊙ DIGITAL

my.hrw.com

my.hrw.com

Go digital with your write-in student edition, accessible on any device.

Math On the Spot

Scan with your smart phone to jump directly to the online edition, video tutor, and more.

Animated Math

Interactively explore key concepts to see how math works.

Personal Math Trainer

Get immediate feedback and help as you work through practice sets.

Complete these exercises to review skills you will need for this chapter.

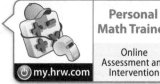

Write a Mixed Number as an Improper Fraction

EXAMPLE $3\frac{5}{8} = 1 + 1 + 1 + \frac{5}{8}$ Write the whole number as a sum of ones.

$= \frac{8}{8} + \frac{8}{8} + \frac{8}{8} + \frac{5}{8}$ Use the denominator of the fraction to write equivalent fractions for the ones.

$= \frac{29}{8}$ Add the numerators.

Write each mixed number as an improper fraction.

1. $1\frac{9}{10}$ _____ **2.** $2\frac{3}{4}$ _____ **3.** $4\frac{1}{6}$ _____ **4.** $7\frac{2}{9}$ _____

Use Repeated Multiplication

EXAMPLE $3 \times 3 \times 3$ Multiply the first two factors.

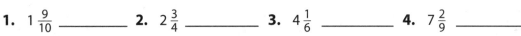

9×3 Multiply the result by the next factor.

27 Continue until there are no more factors to multiply.

Find each product.

5. $8 \times 8 \times 8$ **6.** $5 \times 5 \times 5$ **7.** $5.1 \times 5.1 \times 5.1$ **8.** $4 \times 4 \times 4 \times 4$

_____ _____ _____ _____

Multiply Fractions

EXAMPLE  $\frac{5}{6} \times \frac{3}{10} = \frac{\overset{1}{5}}{\underset{2}{6}} \times \frac{\overset{1}{3}}{\underset{2}{10}}$ Divide by the common factors.

$= \frac{1}{4}$ Simplify.

Multiply. Write each product in simplest form.

9. $\frac{1}{2} \times \frac{1}{3}$ _____ **10.** $\frac{3}{4} \times \frac{5}{6}$ _____ **11.** $\frac{9}{10} \times \frac{15}{16}$ _____ **12.** $\frac{2}{5} \times \frac{5}{12}$ _____

13. $\frac{4}{7} \times \frac{3}{16}$ _____ **14.** $\frac{5}{12} \times \frac{3}{20}$ _____ **15.** $\frac{3}{8} \times \frac{3}{5}$ _____ **16.** $\frac{5}{9} \times \frac{7}{10}$ _____

Reading Start-Up

Visualize Vocabulary

Use the ✔ words to complete the graphic. You will put one word in each oval.

```
        Volume of a Prism
           V = Bh
```

The capacity of a three-dimensional shape.

The area of the bottom of a three-dimensional shape.

Distance from the bottom to the top of a shape measured perpendicular to the base.

Understand Vocabulary

Match the term on the left to the correct expression on the right.

1. lateral faces

2. surface area

3. lateral area

A. Parallelograms that form the sides of a prism and connect the bases.

B. The sum of the areas of all lateral faces in a prism.

C. The sum of all of the areas of all of the faces of a prism.

Active Reading

Booklet Before beginning the module, create a booklet to help you learn the concepts in this module. Write the main idea of each lesson on one page of the booklet. As you study each lesson, write important details that support the main idea, such as vocabulary and formulas. Refer to your finished booklet as you work on assignments and study for tests.

Vocabulary

Review Words
✔ base *(base)*
   face *(cara)*
✔ height *(altura)*
   prism *(prisma)*
   rectangular prism *(prisma rectangular)*
   right triangle *(triángulo rectángulo)*
   triangular prism *(prisma triangular)*
✔ volume *(volumen)*

Preview Words
   lateral area *(área lateral)*
   lateral faces *(cara lateral)*
   net *(plantlla)*
   pyramid *(pirámide)*
   surface area *(área total)*

MODULE 10
Unpacking the TEKS
Understanding the TEKS and the vocabulary terms in the TEKS will help you know exactly what you are expected to learn in this module.

TEKS 7.9.A

Solve problems involving the volume of rectangular prisms, triangular prisms, rectangular pyramids, and triangular pyramids.

Key Vocabulary

volume *(volumen)*
The number of cubic units needed to fill a given space.

What It Means to You

You will use edge lengths to find the volume of prisms and pyramids.

UNPACKING EXAMPLE 7.9.A

Maurice sets up a tent that has the shape of a rectangular pyramid. The base is 7 feet by 6 feet, and the height is 5 feet. What is the volume of the tent?

$$V_{pyramid} = \frac{1}{3} Bh \qquad B = base\ area;\ h = height$$

$$V_{pyramid} = \frac{1}{3}(7 \cdot 6) \cdot 5 = \frac{1}{3} \cdot 210 = 70$$

The volume of the tent is 70 ft^3.

TEKS 7.9.D

Solve problems involving the lateral and total surface area of a rectangular prism, rectangular pyramid, triangular prism, and triangular pyramid by determining the area of the shape's net.

Key Vocabulary

net *(plantilla)*
An arrangement of two-dimensional figures that can be folded to form a polyhedron.

surface area *(área total)*
The sum of the areas of the faces, or surfaces, of a three-dimensional figure.

Visit **my.hrw.com** to see all the **TEKS** unpacked.

my.hrw.com

What It Means to You

You will use nets to find the surface area of three-dimensional figures in real-world and mathematical problems.

UNPACKING EXAMPLE 7.9.D

Julie is wrapping a present for a friend. Find the surface area of the box.

5 in. 21 in. 11 in.

Draw a net to help you see each face of the prism.

5 in. A 5 in.
11 in. 11 in.
21 in.
B C D E
F
5 in.

Use the formula $A = lw$ to find the area of each face.

A: $A = 11 \times 5 = 55$

B: $A = 21 \times 11 = 231$

C: $A = 21 \times 5 = 105$

D: $A = 21 \times 11 = 231$

E: $A = 21 \times 5 = 105$

F: $A = 11 \times 5 = 55$

$S = 55 + 231 + 105 + 231 + 105 + 55 = 782$

The surface area is 782 in^2.

© Houghton Mifflin Harcourt Publishing Company • Image Credits: ©Morgan Lane Photography/Alamy Images

LESSON

10.1 Volume of Rectangular Prisms and Pyramids

TEKS
Equations, expressions, and relationships—7.8.A
Model the relationship between the volume of a rectangular prism and a rectangular pyramid having both congruent bases and heights and connect that relationship to the formulas. *Also 7.9.A*

? **ESSENTIAL QUESTION**

How do you find the volume of a rectangular prism and a rectangular pyramid?

Finding the Volume of a Rectangular Prism

Remember that the volume of a rectangular prism is given by the formula $V = \ell \times w \times h$, or $V = \ell wh$.

The base of a rectangular prism is a rectangle with length ℓ and width w, so the area of the base B is equal to ℓw. The volume formula can also be written as $V = Bh$. In fact, the volume of any prism is the product of the base B and the height h. Remember that volume is given in cubic units.

Math On the Spot
⏱ my.hrw.com

Volume of a Prism

The volume V of a prism is the area of its base B times its height h.

$V = Bh$

EXAMPLE 1

TEKS 7.9.A

Find the volume of the rectangular prism.

STEP 1 Find the area of the base.

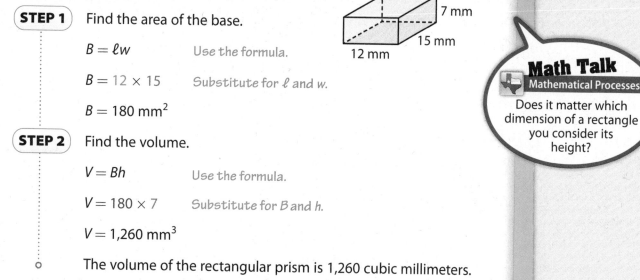

7 mm
15 mm
12 mm

$B = \ell w$ *Use the formula.*

$B = 12 \times 15$ *Substitute for ℓ and w.*

$B = 180 \text{ mm}^2$

Math Talk
Mathematical Processes

Does it matter which dimension of a rectangle you consider its height?

STEP 2 Find the volume.

$V = Bh$ *Use the formula.*

$V = 180 \times 7$ *Substitute for B and h.*

$V = 1,260 \text{ mm}^3$

The volume of the rectangular prism is 1,260 cubic millimeters.

Reflect

1. **What If?** If you know the volume V and the height h of a prism, how would you find the area of the base B?

_____

_____

Personal Math Trainer

Online Assessment and Intervention

my.hrw.com

YOUR TURN

2. Use the formula $V = Bh$ to find the volume of a gift box that is 3.5 inches high, 7 inches long, and 6 inches wide.

_____

EXPLORE ACTIVITY 1 TEKS 7.9.A

Nets

A **net** is a two-dimensional pattern of shapes that can be folded into a three-dimensional figure. The shapes in the net become the faces of the three-dimensional figure.

STEP 1 Copy Net A and Net B on graph paper, and cut them out along the blue lines.

One of these nets can be folded along the black lines to make a cube. Which net will

not make a cube? _____

Net A

Net B

STEP 2 See if you can find another net that can be folded into a cube.

Draw a net that you think will make a cube on your graph paper, and then cut it out. Can you fold it into a cube? Sketch your net below.

STEP 3 Compare your results with several of your classmates. How many different nets for a cube did you and your classmates find?

_____

© Houghton Mifflin Harcourt Publishing Company

Reflect

3. What shapes will appear in a net for a rectangular prism that is not a cube? How many of these shapes will there be?

_____

How do you know that each net cannot be folded into a cube without actually cutting and folding it?

4.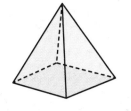

5.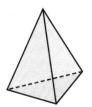

_____   _____

_____   _____

6. **Make a Conjecture** If you draw a net for a cylinder, such as a soup can, how many two-dimensional geometric shapes would this net have? Name the shapes in the net for a cylinder.

_____

_____

Exploring the Volume of a Rectangular Pyramid

A **pyramid** is a three-dimensional shape whose base is a polygon and whose other faces are all triangles. Like a prism, a pyramid is named by the shape of its base.

Rectangular Pyramid   **Triangular Pyramid**   **Pentagonal Pyramid**

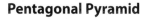

The faces of a pyramid that are not the base have a common vertex, called the vertex of the pyramid. The perpendicular distance from the vertex to the base is the height of the pyramid.

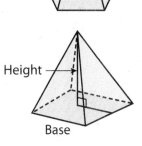

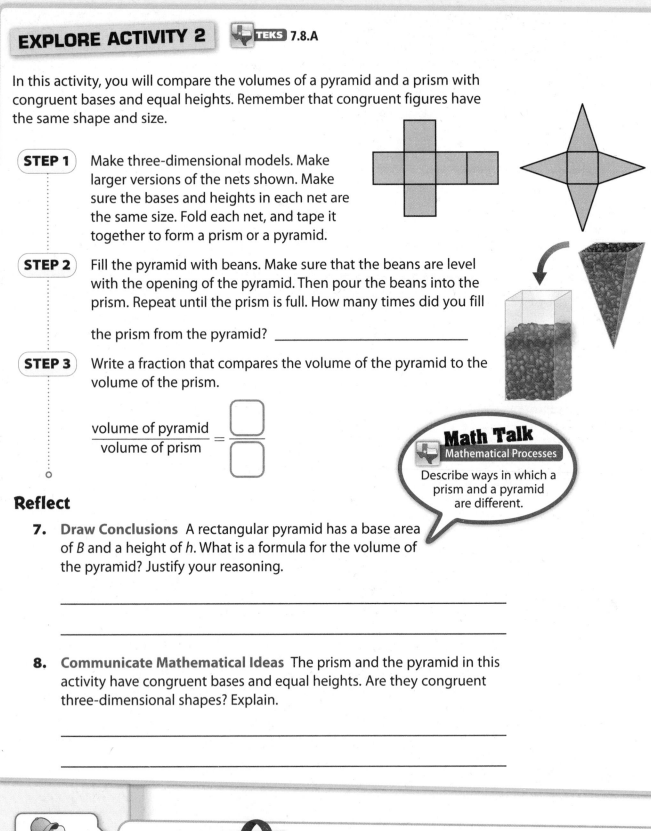

EXPLORE ACTIVITY 2   TEKS 7.8.A

In this activity, you will compare the volumes of a pyramid and a prism with congruent bases and equal heights. Remember that congruent figures have the same shape and size.

STEP 1   Make three-dimensional models. Make larger versions of the nets shown. Make sure the bases and heights in each net are the same size. Fold each net, and tape it together to form a prism or a pyramid.

STEP 2   Fill the pyramid with beans. Make sure that the beans are level with the opening of the pyramid. Then pour the beans into the prism. Repeat until the prism is full. How many times did you fill

the prism from the pyramid? _____

STEP 3   Write a fraction that compares the volume of the pyramid to the volume of the prism.

$$\frac{\text{volume of pyramid}}{\text{volume of prism}} = \frac{\square}{\square}$$

Math Talk
Mathematical Processes

Describe ways in which a prism and a pyramid are different.

Reflect

7. **Draw Conclusions** A rectangular pyramid has a base area of B and a height of h. What is a formula for the volume of the pyramid? Justify your reasoning.

_____

_____

8. **Communicate Mathematical Ideas** The prism and the pyramid in this activity have congruent bases and equal heights. Are they congruent three-dimensional shapes? Explain.

_____

_____

Personal Math Trainer

Online Assessment and Intervention

⏻ my.hrw.com

YOUR TURN

9. The volume of a rectangular prism is $4\frac{1}{2}$ in^3. What is the volume of a rectangular pyramid with a congruent base and the same height? Explain your reasoning.

_____

Solving Volume Problems

You can use the formulas for the volume of a rectangular prism and the volume of a rectangular pyramid to solve problems.

Math On the Spot

my.hrw.com

> ### Volume of a Rectangular Pyramid
>
> The volume V of a pyramid is one-third the area of its base B times its height h.
>
> $V = \frac{1}{3}Bh$

EXAMPLE 2 Real World

TEKS 7.9.A

A Kyle needs to build a crate in the shape of a rectangular prism. The crate must have a volume of $38\frac{1}{2}$ cubic feet, and a base area of $15\frac{2}{5}$ square feet. Find the height of the crate.

$V = Bh$ Use the formula.

$38\frac{1}{2} = 15\frac{2}{5} \cdot h$ Substitute for V and B.

$\frac{77}{2} = \frac{77}{5}h$ Change the mixed numbers to fractions.

$\frac{5}{77} \cdot \frac{77}{2} = \frac{77}{5}h \cdot \frac{5}{77}$ To divide both sides by $\frac{77}{5}$, multiply both sides by the reciprocal.

$\frac{5}{2} = h$

The height of the crate must be $\frac{5}{2}$, or $2\frac{1}{2}$, feet.

B A glass paperweight in the shape of a rectangular pyramid has a base that is 4 inches by 3 inches and a height of 5 inches. Find the volume of the paperweight.

$V = \frac{1}{3}Bh$ Use the formula.

$V = \frac{1}{3} \cdot 12 \cdot 5$ Think: $B = \ell w = 4 \cdot 3 = 12$

$V = 20$

The paperweight has a volume of 20 cubic inches.

YOUR TURN

10. A rectangular prism has a volume of 160 cubic centimeters and a height of 4 centimeters. What is the area of its base? _____

11. A square pyramid has a base edge of 5.5 yards and a height of 3.25 yards. Find the volume of the pyramid to the nearest tenth. _____

Personal Math Trainer

Online Assessment and Intervention

my.hrw.com

1. Find the volume of the rectangular prism. (Example 1)

$V = Bh$

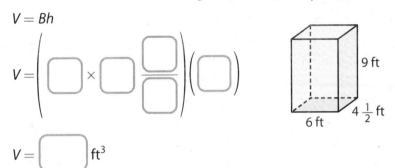

$V = \left(\boxed{} \times \boxed{} \dfrac{\boxed{}}{\boxed{}} \right) \left(\boxed{} \right)$

$V = \boxed{}$ ft³

9 ft

$4\frac{1}{2}$ ft

6 ft

Identify the three-dimensional shape that can be formed from each net.
(Explore Activity 1 and Explore Activity 2)

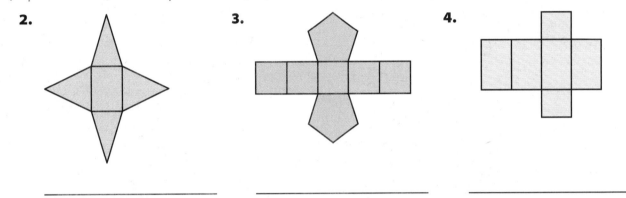

2.

3.

4.

_____   _____   _____

5. The volume of a rectangular prism is 161.2 m³. The prism has a base that is 5.2 m by 3.1 m. Find the height of the prism. (Example 2)

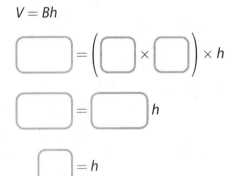

$V = Bh$

$\boxed{} = \left(\boxed{} \times \boxed{} \right) \times h$

$\boxed{} = \boxed{} \, h$

$\boxed{} = h$

The height of the prism is _____.

? ESSENTIAL QUESTION CHECK-IN

6. Explain how to use models to show the relationship between the volume of a rectangular prism and a rectangular pyramid with congruent bases and heights.

_____

_____

10.1 Independent Practice

TEKS 7.8.A, 7.9.A

Personal Math Trainer

Online Assessment and Intervention

my.hrw.com

8. Explain the Error A student found the volume of a rectangular pyramid with a base area of 92 square meters and a height of 54 meters to be 4,968 cubic meters. Explain and correct the error.

_____

_____

9. A block of marble is in the shape of a rectangular prism. The block is 3 feet long, 2 feet wide, and 18 inches high. What is the

volume of the block? _____

10. Multistep Curtis builds a doghouse with base shaped like a cube and a roof shaped like a pyramid. The cube has an edge length of $3\frac{1}{2}$ feet. The height of the pyramid is 5 feet. Find the volume of the doghouse rounded to the nearest tenth.

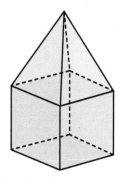

_____

11. Miguel has an aquarium in the shape of a rectangular prism. The base is 30.25 inches long and 12.5 inches wide. The aquarium is 12.75 inches high. What is the volume of the aquarium to the nearest cubic inch?

_____

12. After a snowfall, Sheree built a snow pyramid. The pyramid had a square base with side lengths of 32 inches and a height of 28 inches. What was the volume of the pyramid to the nearest cubic inch?

_____

13. A storage chest has the shape of a rectangular prism with the dimensions shown. The volume of the storage chest is 18,432 cubic inches. What is its height?

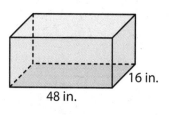

16 in.

48 in.

_____

14. Draw Conclusions A shipping company ships certain boxes at a special rate. The boxes must not have a volume greater than 2,500 cm³. Can the box shown be shipped at the special rate? Explain.

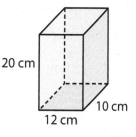

20 cm

10 cm

12 cm

_____

15. Communicate Mathematical Ideas Is the figure shown a prism or a pyramid? Justify your answer.

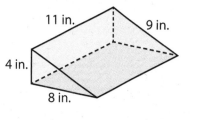

11 in.   9 in.

4 in.

8 in.

_____

_____

_____

16. A cereal box can hold 144 cubic inches of cereal. Suppose the box is 8 inches long and 1.5 inches wide. How tall is the box?

_____

17. A shed in the shape of a rectangular prism has a volume of 1,080 cubic feet. The height of the shed is 8 feet, and the width of its base is 9 feet. What is the length of the shed?

_____

 FOCUS ON HIGHER ORDER THINKING

18. Draw Conclusions Sue has a plastic paperweight shaped like a rectangular pyramid. The volume is 120 cubic inches, the height is 6 inches, and the length is 10 inches. She has a gift box that is a rectangular prism with a base that is 6 inches by 10 inches. How tall

must the box be for it to hold the pyramid? _____

19. Represent Real-World Problems A public swimming pool is in the shape of a rectangular prism. The pool is 20 meters long and 16 meters wide. The pool is filled to a depth of 1.75 meters.

a. Find the volume of water in the pool. _____

b. A cubic meter of water has a mass of 1,000 kilograms. Find the mass

of the water in the pool. _____

20. Analyze Relationships There are two glass pyramids at the Louvre Museum in Paris, France. The outdoor pyramid has a square base with side lengths of 35.4 meters and a height of 21.6 meters. The indoor pyramid has a square base with side lengths of 15.5 meters and a height of 7 meters. How many times as great is the volume of the outdoor pyramid than that of the indoor pyramid?

_____

21. Persevere in Problem Solving A small solid pyramid was installed on top of the Washington Monument in 1884. The square base of the pyramid is 13.9 centimeters on a side, and the height of the pyramid is 22.6 centimeters. The pyramid has a mass of 2.85 kilograms.

a. Find the volume of the pyramid. Round to the nearest hundredth.

_____

b. Find the mass of the pyramid in grams. _____

c. Science The _density_ of a substance is the ratio of its mass to its volume. Find the density of the pyramid in grams per cubic centimeter. Round to the nearest hundredth.

_____

Work Area

LESSON
10.2 Volume of Triangular Prisms and Pyramids

TEKS
Equations, expressions, and relationships—7.9.A Solve problems involving the volume of rectangular prisms, triangular prisms, rectangular pyramids, and triangular pyramids. *Also 7.8.B*

? ESSENTIAL QUESTION

How do you find the volume of a triangular prism or a triangular pyramid?

Finding the Volume of a Triangular Prism

The volume V of a prism is the area of its base B times its height h, or $V = Bh$.

EXAMPLE 1
TEKS 7.9.A

Find the volume of the triangular prism.

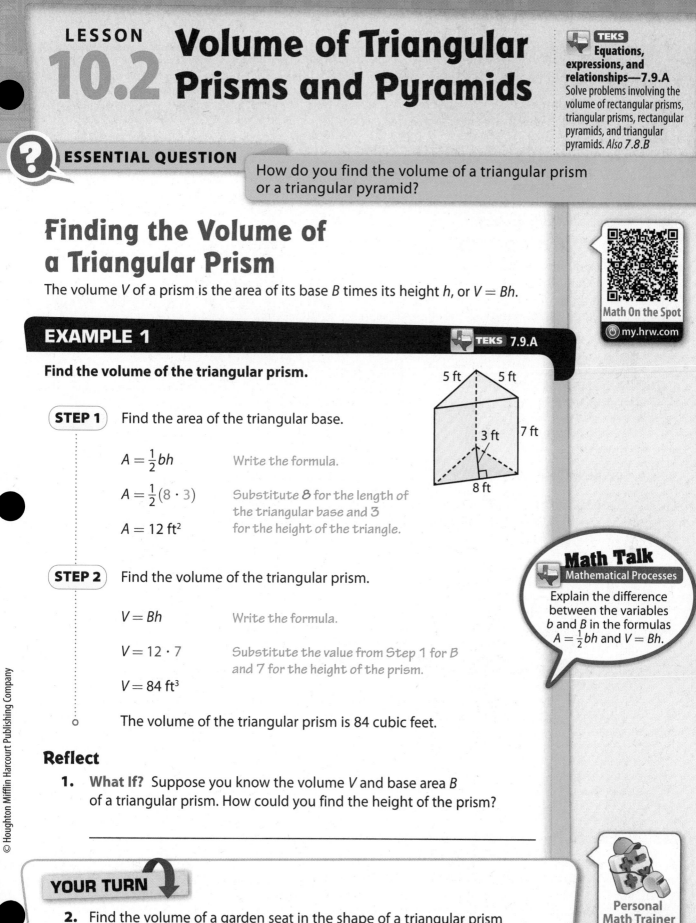

5 ft 5 ft
3 ft 7 ft
8 ft

STEP 1 Find the area of the triangular base.

$A = \frac{1}{2}bh$ *Write the formula.*

$A = \frac{1}{2}(8 \cdot 3)$ *Substitute 8 for the length of the triangular base and 3 for the height of the triangle.*

$A = 12$ ft²

STEP 2 Find the volume of the triangular prism.

$V = Bh$ *Write the formula.*

$V = 12 \cdot 7$ *Substitute the value from Step 1 for B and 7 for the height of the prism.*

$V = 84$ ft³

The volume of the triangular prism is 84 cubic feet.

Math Talk
Mathematical Processes

Explain the difference between the variables b and B in the formulas $A = \frac{1}{2}bh$ and $V = Bh$.

Reflect

1. **What If?** Suppose you know the volume V and base area B of a triangular prism. How could you find the height of the prism?

_____

YOUR TURN

2. Find the volume of a garden seat in the shape of a triangular prism with a height of 30 inches and a base area of 72 in².

_____

Personal Math Trainer

Online Assessment and Intervention

⏱ my.hrw.com

Math On the Spot

⏱ my.hrw.com

Exploring the Volume of a Triangular Pyramid

Previously you explored the volumes of rectangular prisms and pyramids. Now you will repeat the same activity with triangular pyramids and prisms that have the same height and congruent bases.

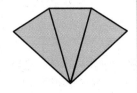

STEP 1   Make three-dimensional models. Make larger versions of the nets shown. Make sure the bases and heights in each net are the same size. Fold each net, and tape it together to form an open prism or pyramid.

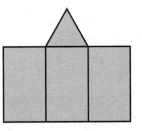

STEP 2   Fill the pyramid with beans. Make sure that the beans are level with the opening of the pyramid. How many pyramids full of beans do you think

it will take to fill the prism? _____

Pour the beans into the prism. Repeat until the prism is full.

Was your conjecture supported? _____

STEP 3   Write a fraction that compares the volume of the pyramid to the

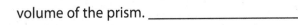

volume of the prism. _____

Reflect

3. **Analyze Relationships** Does it appear that the relationship between the volume of triangular pyramids and prisms is the same as that for rectangular pyramids and prisms?   _____

4. **Draw Conclusions** Write a formula for the volume of a triangular pyramid with a base area of B and a height of h.   _____

Personal Math Trainer

Online Assessment and Intervention

⊙ my.hrw.com

YOUR TURN

5.   The volume of a triangular pyramid is 13.5 m³. What is the volume of a triangular prism with a congruent base and the same height? Explain.

_____

Solving Volume Problems

As you solve volume problems, you will use the volume formulas you have learned. You will also need to use the formula for the area of a triangle: $A = \frac{1}{2}bh$.

EXAMPLE 2 Real World

TEKS 7.9.A

Mr. Martinez is building wooden shapes for a sculpture in the park. His plans show a triangular pyramid and a triangular prism, and each shape is 5 feet high. The base of each shape is a triangle with a base of 2.5 feet and a height of 2 feet. How much greater than the volume of the pyramid is the volume of the prism?

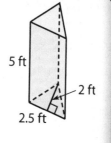

5 ft
2 ft
2.5 ft

My Notes

STEP 1   The triangular base is the same for both shapes. Find the area of the base B.

$A = \frac{1}{2}bh$ *The area A of the triangle is the same as B in $V = Bh$.*

$A = \frac{1}{2}(2.5)(2) = 2.5$ *Substitute the values for b and h of the triangle.*

5 ft
2 ft
2.5 ft

The area of the base B for both shapes is 2.5 ft².

STEP 2   Find the volume of the prism.

$V = Bh$ *Use the formula.*

$V = (2.5) \times 5 = 12.5$ *Substitute the value for B and h of the prism.*

The volume of the prism is 12.5 ft³.

STEP 3   Find the volume of the pyramid.

Volume of pyramid $= \frac{1}{3} \cdot$ volume of prism

$= \frac{1}{3} \cdot 12.5 \approx 4.2$ *Substitute and calculate.*

The volume of the pyramid is approximately 4.2 ft³.

STEP 4   Compare the volumes.

Volume of prism − volume of pyramid $= 12.5 - 4.2 = 8.3$

The volume of the prism is 8.3 ft³ greater than that of the pyramid.

© Houghton Mifflin Harcourt Publishing Company

YOUR TURN

6. How much greater is the volume of a triangular prism with base area of 14 cm² and height of 4.8 cm than the volume of a triangular pyramid with the same height and base area?

_____

1. Find the volume of the triangular prism. (Example 1)

Find the area of the base of the prism.

Use the equation $A =$ _____ bh.

$A =$ ____ (____) (____) $=$ ____ in²

Find the volume of the prism. Use the equation $V = Bh$.

$V = \left(\underline{\quad}\right)\left(\underline{\quad}\right) =$ ____ in³

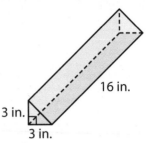

16 in.

3 in.

3 in.

2. A triangular pyramid and a triangular prism have congruent bases and the same height. The triangular pyramid has a volume of 90 m³. Find the volume of the prism. (Explore Activity)

The volume of the prism is _____ because the volume of the prism

is _____ times the volume of the pyramid.

3. In Exercise 2, how much greater is the volume of the prism than the volume of the pyramid? (Example 2)

_____

Find the volume of each figure.

4.

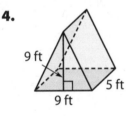

9 ft

5 ft

9 ft

5.

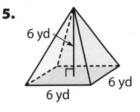

6 yd

6 yd

6 yd

6. 7 in.   10 in.

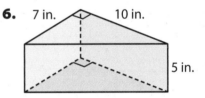

5 in.

_____   _____   _____

? **ESSENTIAL QUESTION CHECK-IN**

7. A pyramid has a base that is a triangle. The length of the base of the triangle is 5 meters, and the height of the triangle is 12 meters. The height of the pyramid is 10 meters. How would you explain to a friend how to find the volume of the pyramid?

_____

_____

_____

_____

10.2 Independent Practice

TEKS 7.9.A, 7.8.B

Personal Math Trainer

Online Assessment and Intervention

my.hrw.com

8. A trap for insects is in the shape of a triangular prism. The area of the base is 3.5 in² and the height of the prism is 5 in. What is the volume of this trap?

_____

9. Arletta built a cardboard ramp for her little brothers' toy cars. Identify the shape of the ramp. Then find its volume.

_____

6 in.

25 in.

7 in.

10. **Represent Real-World Problems** Sandy builds this shape of four congruent triangles using clay and toothpicks. The area of each triangle is 17.6 cm², and the height of the shape is 5.2 cm. What three-dimensional figure does the shape Sandy built resemble? If this were a solid shape, what would be its volume? Round your answer to the nearest tenth.

_____

11. **Draw Conclusions** Would tripling the height of a triangular prism triple its volume? Explain.

_____

12. The Jacksons went camping in a state park. One of the tents they took is shown. What is the volume of the tent?

_____

3.5 ft

6 ft

4.5 ft

13. Shawntelle is solving a problem involving a triangular pyramid. You hear her say that "bee" is equal to 24 inches. How can you tell if she is talking about the base area B of the pyramid or about the base b of the triangle?

_____

_____

14. Alex made a sketch for a homemade soccer goal he plans to build. The goal will be in the shape of a triangular prism. The legs of the right triangles at the sides of his goal measure 4 ft and 8 ft, and the opening along the front is 24 ft. How much space is contained within this goal?

_____

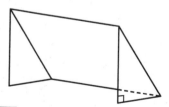

15. A plastic puzzle in the shape of a triangular prism has bases that are equilateral triangles with side lengths of 4 inches and a height of 3.5 inches. The height of the prism is 5 inches. Find the volume of the prism.

_____

16. **Persevere in Problem Solving** Lynette's grandmother has a metal doorstop with the dimensions shown. Find the volume of the metal in the doorstop. The metal in the doorstop has a mass of about 8.6 grams per cubic centimeter. Find the mass of the doorstop.

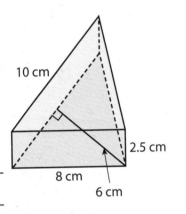

10 cm

2.5 cm

8 cm

6 cm

_____

_____

17. **Make a Conjecture** Don and Kayla each draw a triangular pyramid that has a volume of 100 cm³. They do not draw identical shapes. Give a set of possible dimensions for each pyramid.

_____

_____

18. **Multistep** Don's favorite cheese snack comes in a box of six pieces. Each piece of cheese has the shape of a triangular prism that is 2 cm high. The triangular base of the prism has a height of 5 cm and a base of 4 cm. Find the volume of cheese in the box.

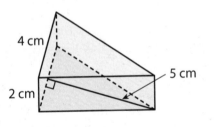

4 cm

5 cm

2 cm

_____

_____

19. **Analyze Relationships** What effect would doubling all the dimensions of a triangular pyramid have on the volume of the pyramid? Explain your reasoning.

_____

_____

_____

_____

Lateral and Total Surface Area

TEKS
Equations, expressions, and relationships—
7.9.D Solve problems involving the lateral and total surface area of a rectangular prism, rectangular pyramid, triangular prism, and triangular pyramid by determining the area of the shape's net.

? ESSENTIAL QUESTION

How do you find the lateral and total surface area of rectangular and triangular prisms or pyramids?

Lateral and Total Surface Area of a Prism

The **lateral faces** of a prism are parallelograms that connect the bases. Each face that is not a base is a lateral face. The sum of the areas of all the lateral faces is the **lateral area** of the prism. The **surface area** is the sum of areas of all of the surfaces of a figure expressed in square units. The total surface area of a prism can be found by finding the sum of the lateral area and the area of the bases.

Lateral face

Base

You can find the lateral area and total surface area of a prism by using a net.

Math On the Spot
⊙ my.hrw.com

EXAMPLE 1

TEKS 7.9.A

A net of a rectangular prism is shown. Use the net to find the lateral area and the total surface area of the prism. Each square represents one square inch. The blue regions are the bases, and the green regions are the lateral faces.

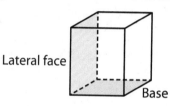

STEP 1 Find the lateral area of the rectangular prism. There are two 2 in. by 5 in. rectangles, and two 2 in. by 6 in. rectangles.

$2 \cdot (2 \cdot 5) = 20 \text{ in}^2$
$2 \cdot (2 \cdot 6) = 24 \text{ in}^2$.

The lateral area is $20 + 24 = 44 \text{ in}^2$.

STEP 2 Find the total surface area of the rectangular prism.

Each base is 5 inches by 6 inches. $2 \cdot (5 \cdot 6) = 60 \text{ in}^2$.

The total surface area is $44 + 60 = 104 \text{ in}^2$.

Math Talk
Mathematical Processes

Explain how the total surface area of a prism differs from the lateral area.

YOUR TURN

1. Use the net to find the lateral area and the total surface area of the triangular prism described by the net.

   _____

   _____

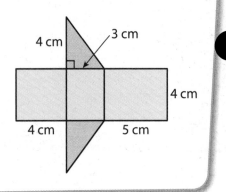

Lateral and Total Surface Area of a Pyramid

In a rectangular pyramid, the base is a rectangle, and the lateral faces are triangles. The lateral area and the total surface area are defined in the same way as they are for a prism.

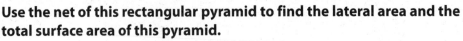

EXAMPLE 2 TEKS 7.9.D

Use the net of this rectangular pyramid to find the lateral area and the total surface area of this pyramid.

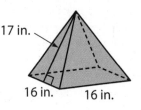 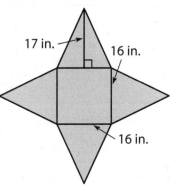

STEP 1 Find the lateral area of the rectangular pyramid.

There are four triangles with base 16 in. and height 17 in.

The lateral area is $4 \times \frac{1}{2}(16)(17) = 544$ in^2.

STEP 2 Find the total surface area of the rectangular pyramid.

The area of the base is $16 \times 16 = 256$ in^2.

The total surface area is $544 + 256 = 800$ in^2.

Reflect

2. How many surfaces does a triangular pyramid have? What shape are they?

   _____

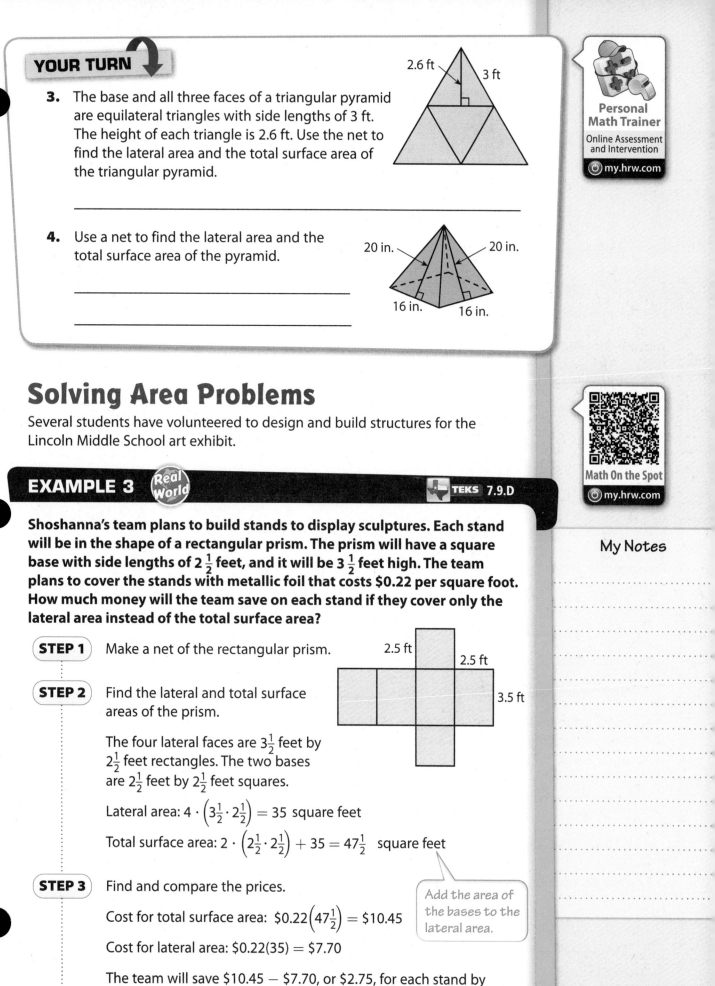

3. The base and all three faces of a triangular pyramid are equilateral triangles with side lengths of 3 ft. The height of each triangle is 2.6 ft. Use the net to find the lateral area and the total surface area of the triangular pyramid.

2.6 ft   3 ft

_____

Personal Math Trainer

Online Assessment and Intervention

my.hrw.com

4. Use a net to find the lateral area and the total surface area of the pyramid.

20 in.   20 in.

16 in.   16 in.

_____

_____

Solving Area Problems

Several students have volunteered to design and build structures for the Lincoln Middle School art exhibit.

EXAMPLE 3 *Real World*   **TEKS** 7.9.D

Math On the Spot

my.hrw.com

Shoshanna's team plans to build stands to display sculptures. Each stand will be in the shape of a rectangular prism. The prism will have a square base with side lengths of $2\frac{1}{2}$ feet, and it will be $3\frac{1}{2}$ feet high. The team plans to cover the stands with metallic foil that costs $0.22 per square foot. How much money will the team save on each stand if they cover only the lateral area instead of the total surface area?

My Notes

STEP 1   Make a net of the rectangular prism.

2.5 ft
2.5 ft
3.5 ft

STEP 2   Find the lateral and total surface areas of the prism.

The four lateral faces are $3\frac{1}{2}$ feet by $2\frac{1}{2}$ feet rectangles. The two bases are $2\frac{1}{2}$ feet by $2\frac{1}{2}$ feet squares.

Lateral area: $4 \cdot \left(3\frac{1}{2} \cdot 2\frac{1}{2}\right) = 35$ square feet

Total surface area: $2 \cdot \left(2\frac{1}{2} \cdot 2\frac{1}{2}\right) + 35 = 47\frac{1}{2}$ square feet

STEP 3   Find and compare the prices.

Cost for total surface area: $0.22\left(47\frac{1}{2}\right) = \$10.45$

> Add the area of the bases to the lateral area.

Cost for lateral area: $0.22(35) = \$7.70$

The team will save $10.45 − $7.70, or $2.75, for each stand by covering only the lateral area.

YOUR TURN

5. Kwame's team will make two triangular pyramids to decorate the entrance to the exhibit. They will be wrapped in the same metallic foil. Each base is an equilateral triangle. If the base has an area of about 3.9 square feet, how much will the team save altogether by covering only the lateral area of the two pyramids?

6.1 ft

3 ft

The foil costs $0.22 per square foot. _____

Guided Practice

A three-dimensional figure is shown sitting on a base. (Example 1)

1. The figure has a total of _____ rectangular faces.

2. Of the total number of faces, _____ are lateral faces.

3. The figure is a _____.

4. Sketch a net of the figure.

5. The lateral area of the prism is _____.

6. The total surface area is _____.

3

7

6

A triangular prism is shown. (Example 2)

7. Identify the number and type of faces of the prism.

_____

8. Find the lateral area of the prism. _____

9. Find the total surface area of the prism. _____

10. Use a net to find the total surface area of the pyramid. Then find the cost of wrapping the pyramid completely in gold foil that costs $0.05 per square centimeter. (Examples 2 and 3)

_____

4.3 cm   6 cm   4.3 cm   4 cm   3 cm

12 cm   10 cm   10 cm

? ESSENTIAL QUESTION CHECK-IN

11. How do you find the lateral and total surface area of a triangular pyramid?

_____

_____

10.3 Independent Practice

TEKS 7.9.D

Personal
Math Trainer
Online
Assessment and
Intervention
my.hrw.com

12. Use a net to find the lateral area and the total surface area of the cereal box.

Lateral area: _____

Total surface area: _____

Yums
12 in.
2 in.
8 in.

13. Describe a net for the shipping carton shown.

_____

_____

3.6 in.
SEND IT
15 in.
3 in.
4 in.

14. A shipping carton is in the shape of a triangular prism. Use a net to find the lateral area and the total surface area of the carton.

Lateral area: _____

Total surface area: _____

15. Victor wrapped this gift box with adhesive paper (with no overlaps). How much paper did he use?

_____

5 in.
6 in.
8 in.

16. **Vocabulary** Name a three-dimensional shape that has four triangular faces and one rectangular face.

_____

17. Cindi wants to cover the top and sides of this box with glass tiles that are 1 cm square. How many tiles will she need?

_____

9 cm
20 cm
15 cm

18. A glass paperweight has the shape of a triangular prism. The bases are equilateral triangles with side lengths of 4 inches and heights of 3.5 inches. The height of the prism is 5 inches. Find the lateral area and the total surface area of the paperweight.

_____

19. The doghouse shown has a floor, but no windows. Find the total surface area of the doghouse (including the door).

_____

2 ft
2.5 ft
2.5 ft
2 ft
4 ft
3 ft

20. Describe the simplest way to find the total surface area of a cube.

_____

21. Communicate Mathematical Ideas Describe how you approach a problem involving lateral area and total surface area. What do you do first? In what ways can you use the figure that is given with a problem? What are some shortcuts that you might use when you are calculating these areas?

_____

_____

_____

_____

_____

_____

 FOCUS ON HIGHER ORDER THINKING

22. Persevere in Problem Solving A pedestal in a craft store is in the shape of a triangular prism. The bases are right triangles with side lengths of 12 cm, 16 cm, and 20 cm. The store owner used 192 cm^2 of burlap cloth to cover the lateral area of the pedestal. Find the height of the pedestal.

_____

23. Communicate Mathematical Ideas The base of Prism A has an area of 80 ft^2, and the base of Prism B has an area of 80 ft^2. The height of Prism A is the same as the height of Prism B. Is the base of Prism A congruent to the base of Prism B? Explain.

_____

_____

_____

_____

24. Critique Reasoning A triangular pyramid is made of 4 equilateral triangles. The sides of the triangles measure 5 m, and the height of each triangle is 4.3 m. A rectangular prism has a height of 4.3 m and a square base that is 5 m on each side. Susan says that the total surface area of the prism is more than twice the total surface area of the pyramid. Is she correct? Explain.

_____

_____

_____

_____

Ready to Go On?

Personal Math Trainer

Online Assessment and Intervention

⊙ my.hrw.com

10.1 Volume of Rectangular Prisms and Pyramids

Find the volume of each figure.

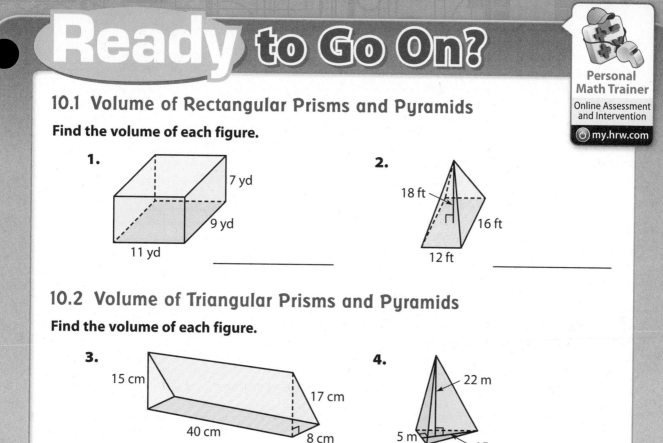

1.

7 yd
9 yd
11 yd

_____

2.

18 ft
16 ft
12 ft

_____

10.2 Volume of Triangular Prisms and Pyramids

Find the volume of each figure.

3.

15 cm
17 cm
40 cm
8 cm

_____

4.

22 m
5 m
15 m

_____

10.3 Lateral and Total Surface Area

Find the lateral and total surface area of each figure using its net.

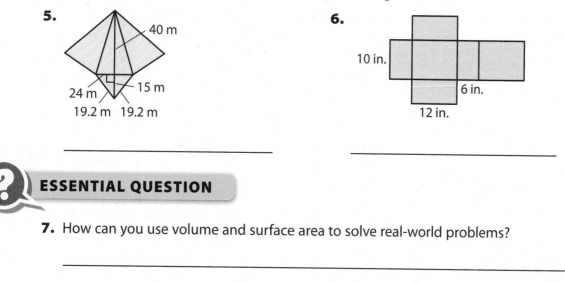

5.

40 m
24 m   15 m
19.2 m   19.2 m

_____

6.

10 in.
6 in.
12 in.

_____

? ESSENTIAL QUESTION

7. How can you use volume and surface area to solve real-world problems?

_____

_____

_____

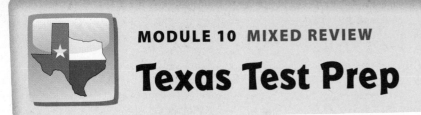

Selected Response

1. The volume of a triangular pyramid is 232 cubic units. The area of the base of the pyramid is 29 square units. What is the height of the pyramid?

Ⓐ 8 units Ⓒ 16 units

Ⓑ 12 units Ⓓ 24 units

2. What is the volume of a rectangular prism that has a length of 8.5 centimeters (cm), a width of 3.2 centimeters, and a height of 6 centimeters?

Ⓐ 19.2 cm³ Ⓒ 51 cm³

Ⓑ 27.2 cm³ Ⓓ 163.2 cm³

3. What is the volume of the rectangular pyramid shown?

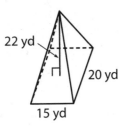

22 yd

20 yd

15 yd

Ⓐ 1,650 yd³ Ⓒ 3,300 yd³

Ⓑ 2,200 yd³ Ⓓ 6,600 yd³

4. A circle has a circumference of 56π centimeters (cm). What is the radius of the circle?

Ⓐ 28 cm Ⓒ 88 cm

Ⓑ 56 cm Ⓓ 112 cm

5. What is the volume of a triangular prism that has a height of 45 meters and has a base with an area of 20 square meters?

Ⓐ 225 m³ Ⓒ 450 m³

Ⓑ 300 m³ Ⓓ 900 m³

6. What is the total surface area of the square pyramid whose net is shown?

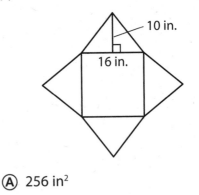

10 in.

16 in.

Ⓐ 256 in²

Ⓑ 336 in²

Ⓒ 576 in²

Ⓓ 896 in²

Gridded Response

7. What is the lateral area in square meters of the prism?

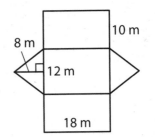

10 m

8 m

12 m

18 m

⊕	⓪	⓪	⓪	⓪	•	⓪	⓪
⊖	①	①	①	①		①	①
	②	②	②	②		②	②
	③	③	③	③		③	③
	④	④	④	④		④	④
	⑤	⑤	⑤	⑤		⑤	⑤
	⑥	⑥	⑥	⑥		⑥	⑥
	⑦	⑦	⑦	⑦		⑦	⑦
	⑧	⑧	⑧	⑧		⑧	⑧
	⑨	⑨	⑨	⑨		⑨	⑨

© Houghton Mifflin Harcourt Publishing Company

Study Guide Review

MODULE 9 **Applications of Geometry Concepts**

? **ESSENTIAL QUESTION**

How can you apply geometry concepts to solve real-world problems?

EXAMPLE 1

Find (a) the value of x and (b) the measure of $\angle APY$.

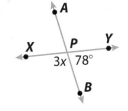

a. $\angle XPB$ and $\angle YPB$ are supplementary.

$$3x + 78° = 180°$$

$$3x = 102°$$

$$x = 34°$$

b. $\angle APY$ and $\angle XPB$ are vertical angles.

$$m\angle APY = m\angle XPB = 3x = 102°$$

EXAMPLE 2

Find the area of the composite figure. It consists of a semicircle and a rectangle.

10 cm

6 cm

Area of semicircle $= 0.5(\pi r^2)$

$$\approx 0.5(3.14)25$$

$$\approx 39.25 \text{ cm}^2$$

Area of rectangle $= \ell w$

$$= 10(6)$$

$$= 60 \text{ cm}^2$$

The area of the composite figure is approximately 99.25 square centimeters.

EXERCISES

1. Find the value of y and the measure of $\angle YPS$ (Lesson 9.1)

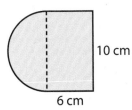

$y =$ _____

$m \angle YPS =$ _____

Find the circumference and area of each circle. Round to the nearest hundredth. (Lessons 9.2, 9.3)

2.

22 in.

_____

3.

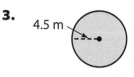
4.5 m

_____

Find the area of each composite figure. Round to the nearest hundredth if necessary. (Lesson 9.4)

4.

9 in.

9 in.

13 in.

Area _____

5.

20 cm

16 cm

Area _____

Key Vocabulary
lateral area (*área lateral*)
lateral faces (*cara lateral*)
net (*plantilla*)
pyramid (*pirámide*)
total surface area (*área de superficie total*)

? ESSENTIAL QUESTION

How can you use volume and surface area to solve real-world problems?

EXAMPLE

The height of the figure whose net is shown is 8 feet. Identify the figure. Then find its volume, lateral area, and total surface area.

The figure is a rectangular pyramid.

Volume $= \frac{1}{3}Bh$	**Lateral Area**	**Total Surface Area**
$= \frac{1}{3}(144)(8)$	$4\left(\frac{1}{2}\right)(12)(8) = 192$	$192 + 12^2 = 192 + 144$
$= 384$		$= 336$

8 ft

12 ft

The volume of the rectangular pyramid is 384 cubic feet, the lateral surface area is 192 square feet, and the total surface area is 336 square feet.

EXERCISES

1. Identify the figure represented by the net. Then find its lateral area and total surface area. (Lesson 10.3)

_____

_____

_____

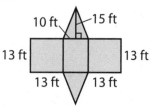
10 ft   15 ft
13 ft   13 ft
13 ft   13 ft

© Houghton Mifflin Harcourt Publishing Company

Find the volume of each figure. (Lessons 10.1, 10.2)

2.

12 in.

5 in.

7 in.

_____

3.

9 m

6 m

4 m

_____

4. The volume of a rectangular pyramid is 1.32 cubic inches. The height of the pyramid is 1.1 inches and the length of the base is 1.2 inches.

Find the width of the base of the pyramid. (Lesson 10.1) _____

5. The volume of a triangular prism is 264 cubic feet. The area of a base of the prism is 48 square feet. Find the height of the prism.

(Lesson 10.2) _____

Unit 5 Performance Tasks

1. **CAREERS IN MATH** | Product Design Engineer Miranda is a product design engineer working for a sporting goods company. She designs a tent in the shape of a triangular prism. The dimensions of the tent are shown in the diagram.

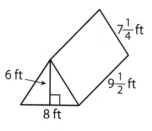

$7\frac{1}{4}$ ft

6 ft

$9\frac{1}{2}$ ft

8 ft

a. Draw a net of the triangular prism and label the dimensions.

b. How many square feet of material does Miranda need to make the tent (including the floor)? Show your work.

_____

c. What is the volume of the tent? Show your work.

_____

d. Suppose Miranda wants to increase the volume of the tent by 10%. The specifications for the height (6 feet) and the width (8 feet) must stay the same. How can Miranda meet this new requirement? Explain.

_____

_____

2. Li is making a stand to display a sculpture made in art class. The stand will be 45 centimeters wide, 25 centimeters long, and 1.2 meters high.

a. What is the volume of the stand? Write your answer in cubic centimeters.

_____

b. Li needs to fill the stand with sand so that it is heavy and stable. Each piece of wood is 1 centimeter thick. The boards are put together as shown in the figure, which is not drawn to scale. How many cubic centimeters of sand does she need to fill the stand? Explain how you found your answer.

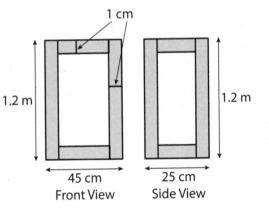

_____

_____

_____

_____

_____

_____

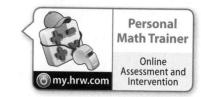
Selected Response

1. The dimensions of the pyramid are given in centimeters (cm). What is the volume of the pyramid?

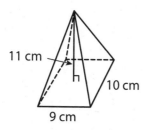

11 cm
10 cm
9 cm

- Ⓐ 222.5 cubic centimeters
- Ⓑ 330 cubic centimeters
- Ⓒ 445 cubic centimeters
- Ⓓ 990 cubic centimeters

2. The volume of a triangular pyramid is 437 cubic units. The height of the pyramid is 23 units. What is the area of the base of the pyramid?

- Ⓐ 6.3 square units
- Ⓒ 38 square units
- Ⓑ 19 square units
- Ⓓ 57 square units

> **Hot Tip!**
>
> **Make sure you look at all the answer choices before making your decision. Try substituting each answer choice into the problem if you are unsure of the answer.**

3. What is the lateral surface area of the square pyramid whose net is shown?

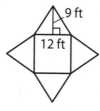

9 ft
12 ft

- Ⓐ 216 square feet
- Ⓑ 388 square feet
- Ⓒ 568 square feet
- Ⓓ 776 square feet

4. A one-topping pizza costs $15.00. Each additional topping costs $1.25. Let x be the number of additional toppings. You have $20 to spend. Which equation can you solve to find the number of additional toppings you can get on your pizza?

- Ⓐ $15x + 1.25 = 20$
- Ⓑ $1.25x + 15 = 20$
- Ⓒ $15x - 1.25 = 20$
- Ⓓ $1.25x - 15 = 20$

5. A bank offers a home improvement loan with simple interest at an annual rate of 12%. J.T. borrows $14,000 over a period of 3 years. How much will he pay back altogether?

- Ⓐ $15,680
- Ⓑ $17,360
- Ⓒ $19,040
- Ⓓ $20,720

6. What is the volume of a triangular prism that is 75 centimeters long and that has a base with an area of 30 square centimeters?

- Ⓐ 2.5 cubic centimeters
- Ⓑ 750 cubic centimeters
- Ⓒ 1,125 cubic centimeters
- Ⓓ 2,250 cubic centimeters

7. The radius of the circle is given in meters. What is the circumference of the circle? Use 3.14 for π.

(A) 25.12 meters

(B) 50.24 meters

(C) 200.96 meters

(D) 803.84 meters

8. The dimensions of the figure are given in millimeters. What is the area of the two-dimensional figure?

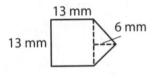

(A) 39 square millimeters

(B) 169 square millimeters

(C) 208 square millimeters

(D) 247 square millimeters

Gridded Response

9. What is the measure in degrees of an angle that is supplementary to a 74° angle?

10. What is the volume in cubic centimeters of a rectangular prism that has a length of 6.2 centimeters, a width of 3.5 centimeters, and a height of 10 centimeters?

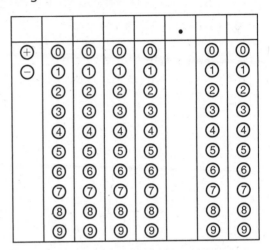

 It is helpful to draw or redraw a figure. Answers to geometry problems may become clearer as you redraw the figure.

11. What is the area of the circle in square meters? Use 3.14 for π.

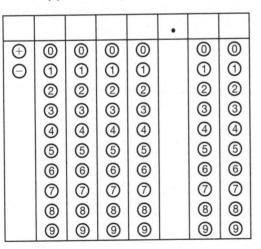

Measurement and Data

MODULE 11

Analyzing and Comparing Data

TEKS 7.6.G, 7.12.A

MODULE 12

Random Samples and Populations

TEKS 7.6.F, 7.12.B, 7.12.C

CAREERS IN MATH

Entomologist An entomologist is a biologist who studies insects. These scientists analyze data and use mathematical models to understand and predict the behavior of insect populations.

If you are interested in a career in entomology, you should study these mathematical subjects:
- Algebra
- Trigonometry
- Probability and Statistics
- Calculus

Research other careers that require the analysis of data and use of mathematical models.

Unit 6 Performance Task

At the end of the unit, check out how **entomologists** use math.

Vocabulary Preview

Use the puzzle to preview key vocabulary from this unit. Unscramble the circled letters to answer the riddle at the bottom of the page.

Across

3. A sample in which every person, object, or event has an equal chance of being selected (2 words). (Lesson 12.1)

5. A display that shows how the values in a data set are distributed (2 words). (Lesson 11.3)

6. A display in which each piece of data is represented by a dot above a number line (2 words). (Lesson 11.2)

Down

1. A round chart divided into pieces that represent a portion of a set of data (2 words). (Lesson 11.1)

2. The entire group of objects, individuals, or events in a set of data. (Lesson 12.1)

4. Part of a population chosen to represent the entire group. (Lesson 12.1)

Q: Where do cowboys who love statistics live?

A: on the ___ ___ ___ ___ ___!

Analyzing and Comparing Data

? ESSENTIAL QUESTION

How can you solve real-world problems by analyzing and comparing data?

Real-World Video

Scientists place radio frequency tags on some animals within a population of that species. Then they track data, such as migration patterns, about the animals.

⏻ my.hrw.com

GO DIGITAL

my.hrw.com

Go digital with your write-in student edition, accessible on any device.

my.hrw.com

Math On the Spot

Scan with your smart phone to jump directly to the online edition, video tutor, and more.

Animated Math

Interactively explore key concepts to see how math works.

Personal Math Trainer

Get immediate feedback and help as you work through practice sets.

© Houghton Mifflin Harcourt Publishing Company • Image Credits: ©Mike Veitch

Are YOU Ready?

Complete these exercises to review skills you will need for this chapter.

Personal Math Trainer

Online Assessment and Intervention

my.hrw.com

Fractions, Decimals, and Percents

EXAMPLE   Write $\frac{13}{20}$ as a decimal and a percent.

$$
\begin{array}{r}
0.65 \\
20\overline{)13.00} \\
-12\,0 \\
\hline
1\,00 \\
-1\,00 \\
\hline
0
\end{array}
$$

Write the fraction as a division problem. Write a decimal point and zeros in the dividend.
Place a decimal point in the quotient.

$0.65 = 65\%$ Write the decimal as a percent.

Write each fraction as a decimal and a percent.

1. $\frac{7}{8}$ _____

2. $\frac{4}{5}$ _____

3. $\frac{1}{4}$ _____

4. $\frac{3}{10}$ _____

5. $\frac{19}{20}$ _____

6. $\frac{7}{25}$ _____

7. $\frac{37}{50}$ _____

8. $\frac{29}{100}$ _____

Find the Median and Mode

EXAMPLE   17, 14, 13, 16, 13, 11

11, 13, 13, 14, 16, 17

median $= \frac{13 + 14}{2}$

$= 13.5$

mode $= 13$

Order the data from least to greatest.

The median is the middle number or the average of the two middle numbers.
The mode is the number or numbers, if any, that appear most frequently.

Find the median and the mode of the data.

9. 11, 17, 7, 6, 7, 4, 15, 9 _____

10. 43, 37, 49, 51, 56, 40, 44, 50, 36 _____

Find the Mean

EXAMPLE   17, 14, 13, 16, 13, 11

mean $= \frac{17 + 14 + 13 + 16 + 13 + 11}{6}$

$= \frac{84}{6}$

$= 14$

The mean is the sum of the data values divided by the number of values.

Find the mean of the data.

11. 9, 16, 13, 14, 10, 16, 17, 9 _____

12. 108, 95, 104, 96, 97, 106, 94 _____

Reading Start-Up

Visualize Vocabulary

Use the ✔ words to complete the right column of the chart.

Statistical Data		
Definition	**Example**	**Review Word**
A group of facts.	Grades on history exams: 85, 85, 90, 92, 94	
The middle value of a data set.	85, 85, 90, 92, 94	
The number or category that occurs most frequently in a data set.	85, 85, 90, 92, 94	
A value that summarizes a set of values, found through addition and division.	Results of the survey show that students typically spend 5 hours a week studying.	

Understand Vocabulary

Complete each sentence using the preview words.

1. A display that uses values from a data set to show how the

values are spread out is a _____.

2. A _____ uses vertical or horizontal bars to display data.

Active Reading

Layered Book Before beginning the module, create a layered book to help you learn the concepts in this module. Label each flap with lesson titles from this module. As you study each lesson, write important ideas, such as vocabulary and formulas, under the appropriate flap. Refer to your finished layered book as you work on exercises from this module.

Unpacking the TEKS

Understanding the TEKS and the vocabulary terms in the TEKS will help you know exactly what you are expected to learn in this module.

TEKS 7.6.G

Solve problems using data represented in bar graphs, dot plots, and circle graphs, including part-to-whole and part-to-part comparisons and equivalents.

What It Means to You

You will solve problems using data provided in bar graphs, dot plots, and circle graphs.

UNPACKING EXAMPLE 7.6.G

Antonia asked students at her school which of five professional sports they enjoyed watching the most. Her results are shown in the circle graph.

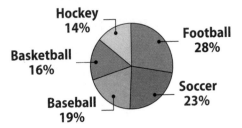

Which two sports were favored by more than half of the students in the survey?
football and soccer, 28% + 23% = 51%

TEKS 7.12.A

Compare two groups of numeric data using comparative dot plots or box plots by comparing their shapes, centers, and spreads.

What It Means to You

You will compare two groups of data using dot plots or box plots.

UNPACKING EXAMPLE 7.12.A

The box-and-whisker plots show the distribution of the number of fish caught per trip by two fishing charters.

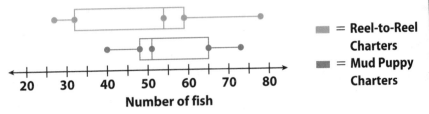

Which fishing charter appears to be more predictable in the number of fish that might be caught on a fishing trip?
Mud Puppy Charters

Visit **my.hrw.com** to see all the **TEKS** unpacked.

⏱ my.hrw.com

Analyzing Categorical Data

TEKS
Proportionality—
7.6.G Solve problems using data represented in bar graphs, dot plots, and circle graphs, including part-to-whole and part-to-part comparisons and equivalents.

? ESSENTIAL QUESTION

How do you use proportional reasoning to solve problems involving graphs of data?

EXPLORE ACTIVITY   **TEKS** 7.6.G

Solving Problems Involving Dot Plots

The students in a class were surveyed to find out how many people live in their households. Household members might include parents, step parents, guardians, and siblings, as well as extended family, such as grandparents. The results of the survey are shown in the dot plot.

Number of People in Household

A How many students were surveyed? How do you know?

_____

B What percent of the class has a household of 3 or fewer people?

Set up a proportion to find the percent: $\dfrac{\boxed{}}{25} \overset{\times 4}{\underset{\times 4}{=}} \dfrac{x}{100}$

> The numerator is the number of people with a household of 3 or fewer. Be sure to include all the appropriate data.

$x = \boxed{}$

$\dfrac{\boxed{}}{100} = \boxed{}$%.

Reflect

1. Critical Thinking What percent of households with 4 or fewer people have exactly 2 people?

_____

Solving Problems Involving Bar Graphs

Bar graphs organize data into categories, and show the frequency for each category. You identify the frequency for each category by comparing the height of each bar to its scale.

EXAMPLE 1 Real World

TEKS 7.6.G

Three boys and three girls ran for 7th grade class president. The boys are Andrew, Derrick, and Miguel. The girls are Becky, Dora, and Trisha. The results of the election are shown in the bar graph. Which is greater — the percent of total votes for boys that Derrick received, or the percent of total votes for girls that Dora received?

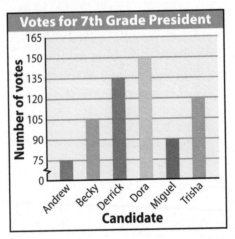

STEP 1 Calculate the percent of total votes for boys that Derrick received. Set up a ratio:

$$\frac{\text{Number of votes for Derrick}}{\text{Total number of votes for boy candidates}} = \frac{135}{75 + 135 + 90} = \frac{135}{300}$$

Set up a proportion to find the percent: $\frac{135 \div 3}{300 \div 3} = \frac{x}{100}$: $x = 45$

Derrick received 45% of the total votes for boys.

STEP 2 Calculate the percent of total votes for girls that Dora received. Set up a ratio:

$$\frac{\text{Number of votes for Dora}}{\text{Total number of votes for girl candidates}} = \frac{150}{105 + 150 + 120} = \frac{150}{375}$$

Set up a proportion to find the percent: $\frac{150 \div 3.75}{375 \div 3.75} = \frac{x}{100}$: $x = 40$

Dora received 40% of the total votes for girls.

STEP 3 Compare the percents calculated in the previous two steps.

Because 45% is greater than 40%, the percent of votes for boys that Derrick received is greater.

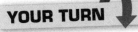

2. In Example 1, Calculate the percent of total votes that Dora received.

_____

Personal Math Trainer

Online Assessment and Intervention

⬤ my.hrw.com

Solving Problems Involving Circle Graphs

A **circle graph** shows how a set of data is divided into parts. The entire circle contains 100% of the data. Each section of the circle represents one part of the entire data set. Data values are often given as percents.

Math On the Spot

⬤ my.hrw.com

EXAMPLE 2 · Real World

TEKS 7.6.G

There are 5,000 tickets available for a concert. The percent of available tickets belonging to each ticket type is shown in the circle graph. Calculate the number of tickets available for each type of ticket.

> Circle graphs are sometimes called pie charts.

Ticket Types

Platinum 2%
Club 8%
Floor 16%
Lower level 30%
Upper level 44%

Math Talk
Mathematical Processes

How could you estimate the percents if they were not labeled on the circle graph?

STEP 1 Write a ratio to represent each type of ticket.

Floor: $16\% = \frac{16}{100}$ **Lower level:** $30\% = \frac{30}{100}$

Platinum: $2\% = \frac{2}{100}$ **Upper level:** $44\% = \frac{44}{100}$

Club: $8\% = \frac{8}{100}$

STEP 2 Set up and solve a proportion to find the number of each type of ticket.

Floor: $\frac{16}{100} \overset{\times 50}{\underset{\times 50}{=}} \frac{x}{5,000}$; $x = 800$ Lower level: $\frac{30}{100} \overset{\times 50}{\underset{\times 50}{=}} \frac{x}{5,000}$; $x = 1,500$

Platinum: $\frac{2}{100} \overset{\times 50}{\underset{\times 50}{=}} \frac{x}{5,000}$; $x = 100$ Upper level: $\frac{44}{100} \overset{\times 50}{\underset{\times 50}{=}} \frac{x}{5,000}$; $x = 2,200$

Club: $\frac{8}{100} \overset{\times 50}{\underset{\times 50}{=}} \frac{x}{5,000}$; $x = 400$

The floor has 800 tickets, the lower level has 1,500, the upper level has 2,200, the club has 400, and the platinum section has 100.

Personal Math Trainer

Online Assessment and Intervention

my.hrw.com

YOUR TURN

3. What percentage of sold tickets not on the floor were platinum tickets? Round to the nearest percent.

_____

Guided Practice

1. The students in a class were asked which hand they preferred to use for writing. The bar graph shows the results. Of the students who had a preference, what percent chose the left hand? (Example 1)

STEP 1 Find the total number of students who had a preference.

Left _____ Right _____ Total _____

STEP 2 Set up a proportion and find the percent.

_____

Of the students that had a preference, _____ chose the left hand.

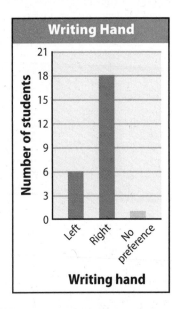

Writing Hand

Number of students

Writing hand

2. There are 20,000 members of a zoo. The percent of members having each membership type is shown in the circle graph. How many members have a contributor membership? What percentage of the noncontributory memberships are individual memberships? Round to the nearest percent. (Example 2)

_____

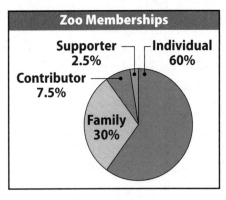

Zoo Memberships

Supporter 2.5% — Individual 60%

Contributor 7.5%

Family 30%

? **ESSENTIAL QUESTION CHECK-IN**

3. When solving proportions based on data from graphs, why do you often convert from fractions and percents to decimals?

_____

_____

© Houghton Mifflin Harcourt Publishing Company

11.1 Independent Practice

TEKS 7.6.G

Personal
Math Trainer

Online
Assessment and
Intervention

my.hrw.com

The number of computers sold at an electronics store for each day of a week is shown in the dot plot.

4. What percent of all computers sold during the entire week were sold on Friday?

_____

5. What percent of computers sold on weekdays were sold on Tuesday? Round to the nearest percent.

_____

6. **Multiple Representations** Suppose the data described above for the electronics store were represented with a bar graph instead of a dot plot. Would there be any advantages or disadvantages?

_____

_____

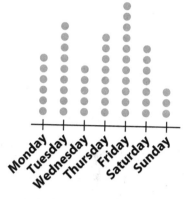

Number of Computers Sold

The number of states in the United States that are primarily in each of the time zones is shown in the bar graph.

7. The continental United States is all states except Hawaii and Alaska. What percent of the continental states are primarily in the Eastern time zone?

_____

8. Is the percent of the continental states primarily in the Eastern time zone greater than or less than the percent of **all** states that are in the Mountain or Central time zone?

_____

9. **What If?** Suppose the horizontal scale of the bar graph had intervals of 1 instead of 4. Would there be any advantages to having that scale? Would there be any disadvantages?

_____

_____

_____

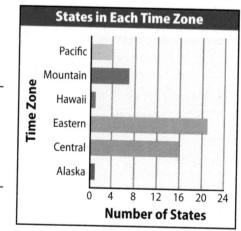

All of the boys attending a prom wore a tuxedo. The circle graph shows the number of boys wearing each of the different bow tie colors.

10. **Make a Conjecture** Estimate the percent of boys wearing black bow ties by comparing the black section of the graph to the whole graph.

_____

_____

_____

_____

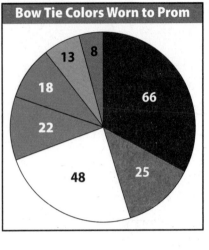

Bow Tie Colors Worn to Prom

13 8
18
66
22
48 25

11. Calculate the percent of boys wearing each bow tie color. How does the percent wearing black bow ties compare to your estimate?

_____

_____

_____

H.O.T. **FOCUS ON HIGHER ORDER THINKING**

Work Area

12. **Communicate Mathematical Ideas** A dot plot shows the number of pizzas sold at a local restaurant each day one week. One column of dots on the plot is much taller than the others. Explain what that means in the context of the data and of percents. Then describe how that same category would be noticeable on a circle graph of the same data.

_____

_____

_____

13. **Analyze Relationships** What is the relationship between the degree measure of the angle formed by the straight edges of a section of a circle graph and the percent of the data that the section represents?

_____

_____

14. **Multiple Representations** A bar graph has 8 bars, all the same height. Suppose that a circle graph were used instead of a bar graph to represent the data. What percent of the data would each piece represent?

_____

_____

Comparing Data Displayed in Dot Plots

TEKS
Measurement and data—7.12.A Compare two groups of numeric data using comparative dot plots or box plots by comparing their shapes, centers, and spreads.

? ESSENTIAL QUESTION

How do you compare two sets of data displayed in dot plots?

EXPLORE ACTIVITY  TEKS 7.12.A

Analyzing Dot Plots

You can use dot plots to analyze a data set, especially with respect to its center and spread.

People once used body parts for measurements. For example, an inch was the width of a man's thumb. In the 12th century, King Henry I of England stated that a yard was the distance from his nose to his outstretched arm's thumb. The dot plot shows the different lengths, in inches, of the "yards" for students in a 7th grade class.

A Describe the shape of the dot plot. Are the dots evenly distributed or grouped on one side?

_____

B What value best describes the center of the data? Explain how you chose this value.

_____

_____

C Describe the spread of the dot plot. Are there any outliers?

_____

_____

Reflect

1. Calculate the mean, median, and range of the data in the dot plot.

_____

Comparing Dot Plots Visually

You can compare dot plots visually using various characteristics, such as center, spread, and shape.

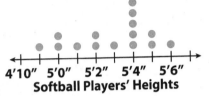

EXAMPLE 1 Real World

TEKS 7.12.A

The dot plots show the heights of 15 high school basketball players and the heights of 15 high school softball players.

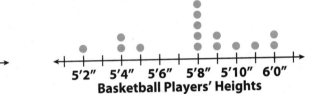

Softball Players' Heights

Basketball Players' Heights

A **Visually compare the shapes of the dot plots.**

Softball: All the data is 5'6" or less.
Basketball: Most of the data is 5'8" or greater.
As a group, the softball players are shorter than the basketball players.

B **Visually compare the centers of the dot plots.**

Softball: The data is centered around 5'4".
Basketball: The data is centered around 5'8".
This means that the most common height for the softball players is 5 feet 4 inches, and for the basketball players 5 feet 8 inches.

C **Visually compare the spreads of the dot plots.**

Softball: The spread is from 4'11" to 5'6".
Basketball: The spread is from 5'2" to 6'0".
There is a greater spread in heights for the basketball players.

YOUR TURN

2. Visually compare the dot plot of heights of field hockey players to the dot plots for softball and basketball players.

Field Hockey Players' Heights

Shape: _____

_____

Center: _____

_____

Spread: _____

_____

© Houghton Mifflin Harcourt Publishing Company

Comparing Dot Plots Numerically

You can also compare the shape, center, and spread of two dot plots numerically by calculating values related to the center and spread. Remember that outliers can affect your calculations.

EXAMPLE 2 Real World

TEKS 7.12.A

Numerically compare the dot plots of the number of hours a class of students exercises each week to the number of hours they play video games each week.

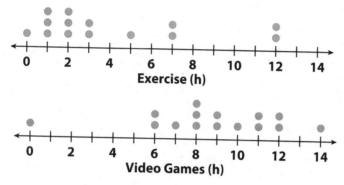

A Compare the shapes of the dot plots.

Exercise: Most of the data is less than 4 hours.
Video games: Most of the data is 6 hours or greater.

B Compare the centers of the dot plots by finding the medians.

Median for exercise: 2.5 hours. Even though there are outliers at 12 hours, most of the data is close to the median.
Median for video games: 9 hours. Even though there is an outlier at 0 hours, these values do not seem to affect the median.

C Compare the spreads of the dot plots by calculating the range.

Exercise range with outlier: $12 - 0 = 12$ hours
Exercise range without outlier: $7 - 0 = 7$ hours
Video games range with outlier: $14 - 0 = 14$ hours
Video games range without outlier: $14 - 6 = 8$ hours

Math Talk
Mathematical Processes

How do outliers affect the results of this data?

YOUR TURN

3. Calculate the median and range of the data in the dot plot. Then compare the results to the dot plot for Exercise in Example 2.

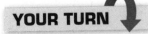

Internet Usage (h)

_____

_____

_____

The dot plots show the number of miles run per week for two different classes. For 1–5, use the dot plots shown.

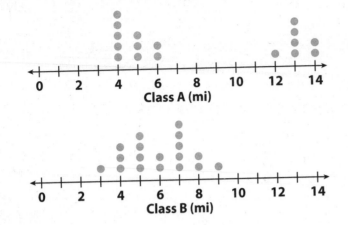

1. Compare the shapes of the dot plots.

_____

_____

2. Compare the centers of the dot plots.

_____

_____

3. Compare the spreads of the dot plots.

_____

_____

4. Calculate the medians of the dot plots.

_____

5. Calculate the ranges of the dot plots.

_____

? ESSENTIAL QUESTION CHECK-IN

6. What do the medians and ranges of two dot plots tell you about the data?

_____

_____

_____

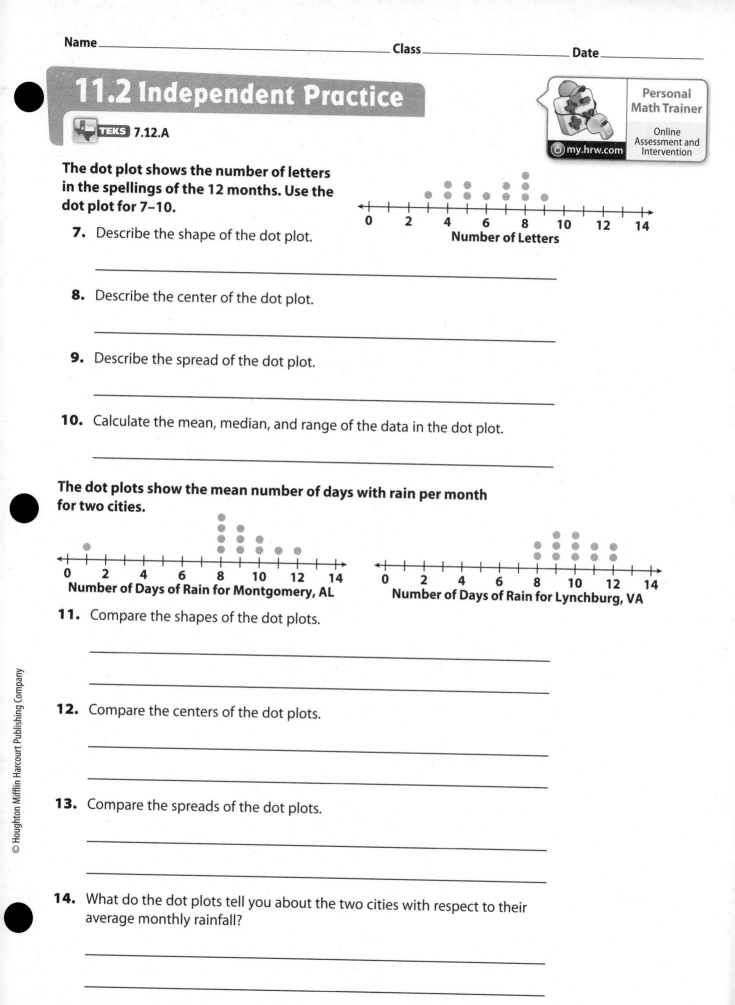

11.2 Independent Practice

TEKS 7.12.A

Personal
Math Trainer

Online
Assessment and
Intervention

my.hrw.com

The dot plot shows the number of letters in the spellings of the 12 months. Use the dot plot for 7–10.

0   2   4   6   8   10   12   14
Number of Letters

7. Describe the shape of the dot plot.

_____

8. Describe the center of the dot plot.

_____

9. Describe the spread of the dot plot.

_____

10. Calculate the mean, median, and range of the data in the dot plot.

_____

The dot plots show the mean number of days with rain per month for two cities.

0   2   4   6   8   10   12   14
Number of Days of Rain for Montgomery, AL

0   2   4   6   8   10   12   14
Number of Days of Rain for Lynchburg, VA

11. Compare the shapes of the dot plots.

_____

_____

12. Compare the centers of the dot plots.

_____

_____

13. Compare the spreads of the dot plots.

_____

_____

14. What do the dot plots tell you about the two cities with respect to their average monthly rainfall?

_____

_____

© Houghton Mifflin Harcourt Publishing Company

The dot plots show the shoe sizes of two different groups of people.

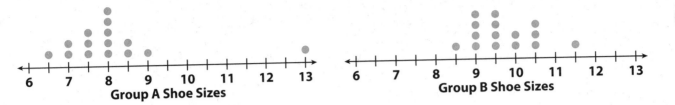

Group A Shoe Sizes

Group B Shoe Sizes

15. Compare the shapes of the dot plots.

_____

_____

16. Compare the medians of the dot plots.

_____

17. Compare the ranges of the dot plots (with and without the outliers).

_____

_____

18. Make A Conjecture Provide a possible explanation for the results of the dot plots.

_____

_____

H.O.T. FOCUS ON HIGHER ORDER THINKING

19. Analyze Relationships Can two dot plots have the same median and range but have completely different shapes? Justify your answer using examples.

_____

_____

_____

_____

20. Draw Conclusions What value is most affected by an outlier, the median or the range? Explain. Can you see these effects in a dot plot?

_____

_____

_____

Work Area

Comparing Data Displayed in Box Plots

TEKS
Measurement and data—7.12.A Compare two groups of numeric data using comparative dot plots or box plots by comparing their shapes, centers, and spreads.

? ESSENTIAL QUESTION

How do you compare two sets of data displayed in box plots?

EXPLORE ACTIVITY Real World **TEKS** 7.12.A

Analyzing Box Plots

Box plots show five key values to represent a set of data, the least and greatest values, the lower and upper quartile, and the median. To create a box plot, arrange the data in order, and divide them into four equal-size parts or quarters. Then draw the box and the whiskers as shown.

The number of points a high school basketball player scored during the games he played this season are organized in the box plot shown.

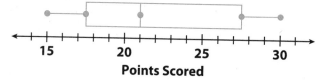

A Find the least and greatest values.

Least value: _____   Greatest value: _____

B Find the median and describe what it means for the data.

_____

_____

_____

C Find and describe the lower and upper quartiles.

_____

_____

_____

Math Talk
Mathematical Processes

How do the lengths of the whiskers compare? Explain what this means.

D The interquartile range is the difference between the upper and lower quartiles, which is represented by the length of the box. Find the interquartile range.

$Q_3 - Q_1 =$ _____ − _____ = _____

Reflect

1. Why is one-half of the box wider than the other half of the box?

_____

_____

Math On the Spot

⏻ my.hrw.com

Box Plots with Similar Variability

You can compare two box plots numerically according to their centers, or medians, and their spreads, or variability. Range and interquartile range (IQR) are both measures of spread. Data sets with similar variability should have box plots of similar sizes.

EXAMPLE 1 Real World   TEKS 7.12.A

My Notes

The box plots show the distribution of times spent shopping by two different groups.

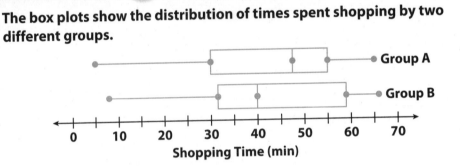

A Compare the shapes of the box plots.

The positions and lengths of the boxes and whiskers appear to be very similar. In both plots, the right whisker is shorter than the left whisker.

B Compare the centers of the box plots.

Group A's median, 47.5, is greater than Group B's, 40. This means that the median shopping time for Group A is 7.5 minutes more.

C Compare the spreads of the box plots.

The box shows the interquartile range. The boxes are similar in length.

Group A: 55 − 30 = 25 min   Group B: 59 − 32 = 27 min

The length of a box plus its whiskers shows the range of a data set. The two data sets have similar ranges.

Math Talk

Mathematical Processes

Which store has the shopper who shops longest? Explain how you know.

Reflect

2. Which group has the greater variability in the bottom 50% of shopping times? The top 50% of shopping times? Explain how you know.

_____

_____

© Houghton Mifflin Harcourt Publishing Company

YOUR TURN

3. The box plots show the distribution of weights in pounds of two different groups of football players. Compare the shapes, centers, and spreads of the box plots.

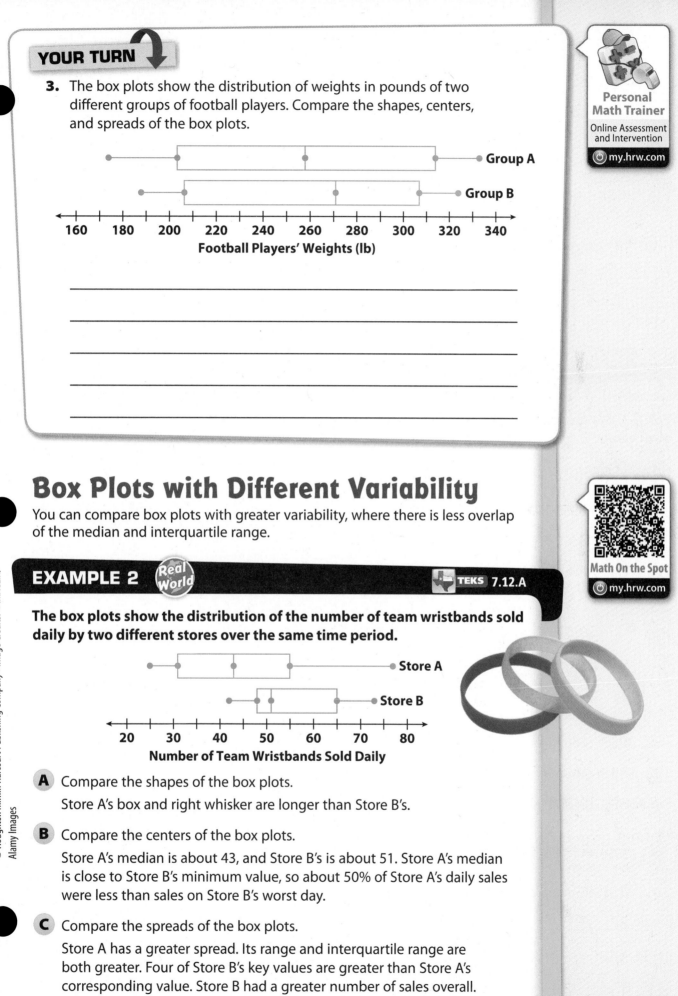

Football Players' Weights (lb)

_____

_____

_____

_____

Box Plots with Different Variability

You can compare box plots with greater variability, where there is less overlap of the median and interquartile range.

EXAMPLE 2 · Real World

TEKS 7.12.A

Math On the Spot

my.hrw.com

The box plots show the distribution of the number of team wristbands sold daily by two different stores over the same time period.

Number of Team Wristbands Sold Daily

A Compare the shapes of the box plots.

Store A's box and right whisker are longer than Store B's.

B Compare the centers of the box plots.

Store A's median is about 43, and Store B's is about 51. Store A's median is close to Store B's minimum value, so about 50% of Store A's daily sales were less than sales on Store B's worst day.

C Compare the spreads of the box plots.

Store A has a greater spread. Its range and interquartile range are both greater. Four of Store B's key values are greater than Store A's corresponding value. Store B had a greater number of sales overall.

YOUR TURN

4. Compare the shape, center, and spread of the data in the box plot with the data for Stores A and B in the two box plots in Example 2.

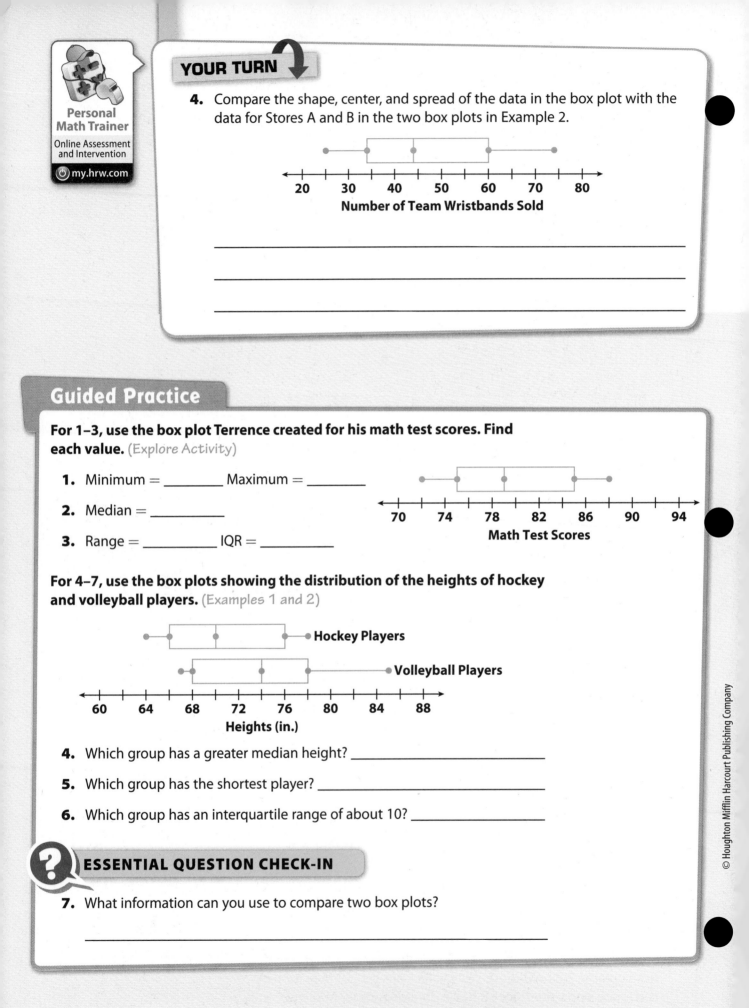

Number of Team Wristbands Sold

_____

_____

_____

Guided Practice

For 1–3, use the box plot Terrence created for his math test scores. Find each value. (Explore Activity)

1. Minimum = _____ Maximum = _____

2. Median = _____

3. Range = _____ IQR = _____

Math Test Scores

For 4–7, use the box plots showing the distribution of the heights of hockey and volleyball players. (Examples 1 and 2)

Hockey Players

Volleyball Players

Heights (in.)

4. Which group has a greater median height? _____

5. Which group has the shortest player? _____

6. Which group has an interquartile range of about 10? _____

? ESSENTIAL QUESTION CHECK-IN

7. What information can you use to compare two box plots?

_____

11.3 Independent Practice

TEKS 7.12.A

Personal Math Trainer

Online Assessment and Intervention

my.hrw.com

For 8–11, use the box plots of the distances traveled by two toy cars that were jumped from a ramp.

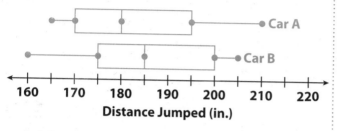

8. Compare the minimum, maximum, and median of the box plots.

_____
_____
_____
_____
_____

9. Compare the ranges and interquartile ranges of the data in box plots.

_____
_____
_____

10. What do the box plots tell you about the jump distances of two cars?

_____
_____
_____
_____

11. Critical Thinking What do the whiskers tell you about the two data sets?

_____
_____
_____
_____
_____

For 12–14, use the box plots to compare the costs of leasing cars in two different cities.

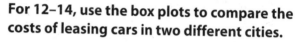
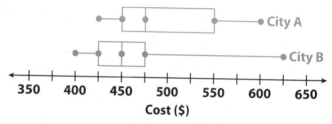

12. In which city could you spend the least amount of money to lease a car? The greatest?

_____
_____
_____

13. Which city has a higher median price? How much higher is it?

_____

14. Make a Conjecture In which city is it more likely to choose a car at random that leases for less than $450? Why?

_____
_____
_____
_____

15. Summarize Look back at the box plots for 12–14 on the previous page. What do the box plots tell you about the costs of leasing cars in those two cities?

_____

_____

_____

_____

H.O.T. FOCUS ON HIGHER ORDER THINKING

16. Draw Conclusions Two box plots have the same median and equally long whiskers. If one box plot has a longer box than the other box plot, what does this tell you about the difference between the data sets?

_____

_____

17. Communicate Mathematical Ideas What can you learn about a data set from a box plot? How is this information different from a dot plot?

_____

_____

_____

_____

_____

_____

_____

_____

_____

_____

18. Analyze Relationships In mathematics, *central tendency* is the tendency of data values to cluster around some central value. What does a measure of variability tell you about the central tendency of a set of data? Explain.

_____

_____

_____

Ready to Go On?

Personal Math Trainer

Online Assessment and Intervention

my.hrw.com

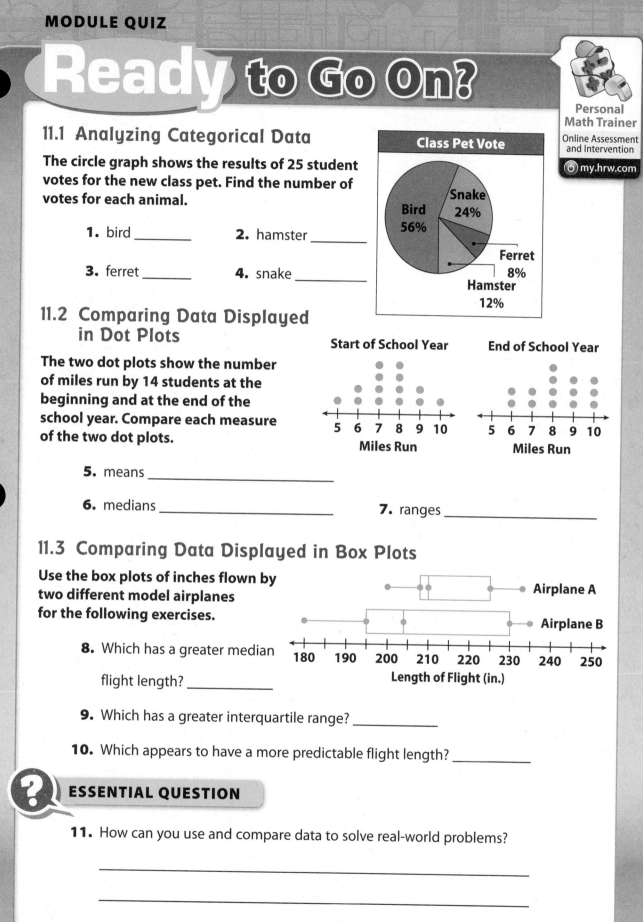

11.1 Analyzing Categorical Data

The circle graph shows the results of 25 student votes for the new class pet. Find the number of votes for each animal.

Class Pet Vote

Bird 56%

Snake 24%

Ferret 8%

Hamster 12%

1. bird _____
2. hamster _____
3. ferret _____
4. snake _____

11.2 Comparing Data Displayed in Dot Plots

The two dot plots show the number of miles run by 14 students at the beginning and at the end of the school year. Compare each measure of the two dot plots.

Start of School Year

5 6 7 8 9 10
Miles Run

End of School Year

5 6 7 8 9 10
Miles Run

5. means _____

6. medians _____

7. ranges _____

11.3 Comparing Data Displayed in Box Plots

Use the box plots of inches flown by two different model airplanes for the following exercises.

Airplane A

Airplane B

180 190 200 210 220 230 240 250
Length of Flight (in.)

8. Which has a greater median flight length? _____

9. Which has a greater interquartile range? _____

10. Which appears to have a more predictable flight length? _____

ESSENTIAL QUESTION

11. How can you use and compare data to solve real-world problems?

_____

_____

Selected Response

Chelsea is reading a 250-page book that is divided into five chapters. For 1–3, use the bar graph below.

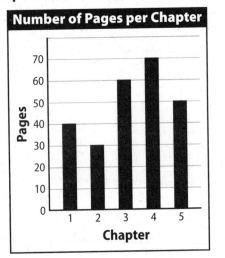

Number of Pages per Chapter

1. What percent of the book's pages are in Chapter 4?

Ⓐ 24%   Ⓒ 35%

Ⓑ 28%   Ⓓ 70%

2. What percent of the book's pages are in Chapters 3 and 4?

Ⓐ 24%   Ⓒ 52%

Ⓑ 28%   Ⓓ 65%

3. If Chelsea has read through the first half of Chapter 3, what percent of the book has she read?

Ⓐ 25%   Ⓒ 44%

Ⓑ 40%   Ⓓ 52%

4. What is $-3\frac{1}{2}$ written as a decimal?

Ⓐ −3.05   Ⓒ −0.35

Ⓑ −3.5   Ⓓ −0.035

5. Which is a true statement based on the dot plots below?

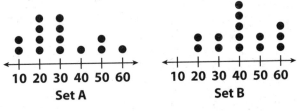

Set A   **Set B**

Ⓐ Set A has the lesser range.

Ⓑ Set B has the greater median.

Ⓒ Set A has the greater mean.

Ⓓ Set B is less symmetric than Set A

Gridded Response

6. The dot plot shows the number of pencils each boy has at his desk in class.

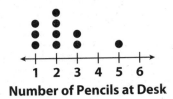

Number of Pencils at Desk

Find the median for the number of pencils.

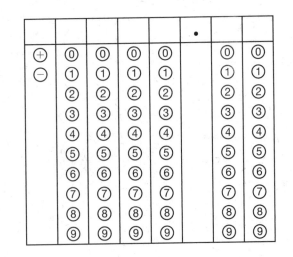

Random Samples and Populations

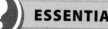

ESSENTIAL QUESTION

How can you use random samples and populations to solve real-world problems?

Real-World Video

Scientists study animals like dolphins to learn more about characteristics such as behavior, diet, and communication. Acoustical data (recordings of dolphin sounds) can reveal the species that made the sound.

my.hrw.com

GO DIGITAL
my.hrw.com

my.hrw.com

Go digital with your write-in student edition, accessible on any device.

Math On the Spot

Scan with your smart phone to jump directly to the online edition, video tutor, and more.

Animated Math

Interactively explore key concepts to see how math works.

Personal Math Trainer

Get immediate feedback and help as you work through practice sets.

Are YOU Ready?

Complete these exercises to review skills you will need for this module.

Fractions, Decimals, and Percents

EXAMPLE

Write $\frac{19}{25}$ as a decimal and a percent.

$$\begin{array}{r} 0.76 \\ 25\overline{)\ 19.00} \\ -17\,5 \\ \hline 1\,50 \\ -1\,50 \\ \hline 0 \end{array}$$

Write the fraction as a division problem.
Write a decimal point and zeros in the dividend.
Place a decimal point in the quotient.

$0.76 = 76\%$ Write the decimal as a percent.

Write each fraction as a decimal and a percent.

1. $\frac{1}{2}$ _____

2. $\frac{3}{4}$ _____

3. $\frac{2}{5}$ _____

4. $\frac{7}{10}$ _____

Find the Range

EXAMPLE

29, 26, 21, 30, 32, 19

19, 21, 26, 29, 30, 32   Order the data from least to greatest.

range $= 32 - 19$
$= 13$

The range is the difference between the greatest and the least data values.

Find the range of the data.

5. 52, 48, 57, 47, 49, 60, 59, 51 _____

6. 5, 9, 13, 6, 4, 5, 8, 12, 12, 6 _____

7. 97, 106, 99, 97, 115, 95, 108, 100 _____

8. 27, 13, 35, 19, 71, 12, 66, 47, 39 _____

Find the Mean

EXAMPLE

21, 15, 26, 19, 25, 14

mean $= \dfrac{21 + 15 + 26 + 19 + 25 + 14}{6}$

$= \dfrac{120}{6}$

$= 20$

The mean is the sum of the data values divided by the number of values.

Find the mean of each set of data.

9. 3, 5, 7, 3, 6, 4, 8, 6, 9, 5 _____

10. 8.1, 9.4, 11.3, 6.7, 6.2, 7.5 _____

Reading Start-Up

Visualize Vocabulary

Use the ✔ words to complete the right column of the chart.

Box Plots to Display Data	
Definition	**Review Word**
A display that uses values from a data set to show how the values are spread out.	
The middle value of a data set.	
The median of the lower half of the data.	
The median of the upper half of the data.	

Understand Vocabulary

Complete each sentence, using the preview words.

1. An entire group of objects, individuals, or events is a

   _____.

2. A _____ is part of the population chosen to represent the entire group.

3. A sample that does not accurately represent the population is a

   _____.

© Houghton Mifflin Harcourt Publishing Company

Vocabulary

Review Words

✔ box plot (*diagrama de caja*)

data (*datos*)

dot plot (*diagrama de puntos*)

interquartile range (*rango entre cuartiles*)

✔ lower quartile (*cuartil inferior*)

✔ median (*mediana*)

mode (*moda*)

spread (*dispersión*)

survey (*encuesta*)

✔ upper quartile (*cuartil superior*)

Preview Words

biased sample (*muestra sesgada*)

population (*población*)

random sample (*muestra aleatoria*)

sample (*muestra*)

Active Reading

Three-Panel Flip Chart Before beginning the module, create a three-panel flip chart to help you organize what you learn. Label each flap with one of the lesson titles from this module. As you study each lesson, write important ideas, such as vocabulary, properties, and formulas, under the appropriate flap.

MODULE 12

Unpacking the TEKS

Understanding the TEKS and the vocabulary terms in the TEKS will help you know exactly what you are expected to learn in this module.

© Houghton Mifflin Harcourt Publishing Company

TEKS 7.12.B

Use data from a random sample to make inferences about a population.

Key Vocabulary

population *(población)*
The entire group of objects or individuals considered for a survey.

sample *(muestra)*
A part of the population.

random sample
(muestra aleatoria)
A sample in which each individual or object in the entire population has an equal chance of being selected.

What It Means to You

You will use data collected from a random sample to make inferences about a population.

UNPACKING EXAMPLE 7.12.B

Alexi surveys a random sample of 80 students at his school and finds that 22 of them usually walk to school. There are 1,760 students at the school. Predict the number of students who usually walk to school.

$$\frac{\text{number in sample who walk}}{\text{size of sample}} = \frac{\text{number in population who walk}}{\text{size of population}}$$

$$\frac{22}{80} = \frac{x}{1,760}$$

$$x = \frac{22}{80} \cdot 1,760$$

$$x = \frac{38,720}{80} = 484$$

Approximately 484 students usually walk to school.

TEKS 7.12.C

Compare two populations based on data in random samples from these populations, including informal comparative inferences about differences between the two populations.

What It Means to You

You will compare two populations based on random samples.

UNPACKING EXAMPLE 7.12.C

Melinda surveys a random sample of 16 students from two college dorms to find the average number of hours of sleep they get. Use the results shown in the dot plots to compare the two populations.

Average Daily Hours of Sleep

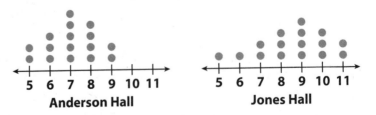

Anderson Hall   **Jones Hall**

Students in Jones Hall tend to sleep more than students in Anderson Hall, and the variation in the amount of sleep is greater for students in Jones Hall.

Visit **my.hrw.com** to see all the **TEKS** unpacked.

my.hrw.com

Populations and Samples

TEKS Proportionality—
7.6.F Use data from a random sample...

? ESSENTIAL QUESTION

How can you use a sample to gain information about a population?

EXPLORE ACTIVITY   **TEKS** 7.6.F

Random and Non-Random Sampling

When information is being gathered about a group, the entire group of objects, individuals, or events is called the **population**. A **sample** is part of the population that is chosen to represent the entire group.

A vegetable garden has 36 tomato plants arranged in a 6-by-6 array. The gardener wants to know the average number of tomatoes on the plants. Each white cell in the table represents a plant. The number in the cell tells how many tomatoes are on that particular plant.

Because counting the number of tomatoes on all of the plants is too time-consuming, the gardener decides to choose plants at random to find the average number of tomatoes on them.

To simulate the random selection, roll two number cubes 10 times. Find the cell in the table identified by the first and second number cubes. Record the number in each randomly selected cell.

						First Number Cube
8	9	13	18	24	15	1
34	42	46	20	13	41	2
29	21	14	45	27	43	3
22	45	46	41	22	33	4
12	42	44	17	42	11	5
18	26	43	32	33	26	6
Second Number Cube 1	2	3	4	5	6	

A What is the average number of tomatoes on the 10 plants that were randomly selected?

_____

B Alternately, the gardener decides to choose the plants in the first row. What is the average number of tomatoes on these plants?

_____

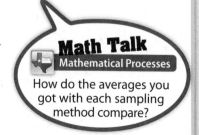

Math Talk
Mathematical Processes

How do the averages you got with each sampling method compare?

Reflect

1. How do the averages you got with each sampling method compare to the average for the entire population, which is 28.25?

_____

_____

2. Why might the first method give a closer average than the second method?

_____

_____

Math On the Spot

my.hrw.com

Random Samples and Biased Samples

A sample in which every person, object, or event has an equal chance of being selected is called a **random sample**. A random sample is more likely to be representative of the entire population than other sampling methods. When a sample does not accurately represent the population, it is called a **biased sample**.

EXAMPLE 1 Real World
TEKS 7.6.F

Identify the population. Determine whether each sample is a random sample or a biased sample. Explain your reasoning.

A Roberto wants to know the favorite sport of adults in his hometown. He surveys 50 adults at a baseball game.

The population is adults in Roberto's hometown.

The sample is biased.

Think: People who don't like baseball will be not be represented in this sample.

Math Talk

Mathematical Processes

Why do you think samples are used? Why not survey each member of the population?

B Paula wants to know the favorite type of music for students in her class. She puts the names of all students in a hat, draws 8 names, and surveys those students.

The population is students in Paula's class.

The sample is random.

Think: Each student has an equal chance of being selected.

Reflect

3. You want to know the preferred practice day of all the players in a soccer league. How might you select a random sample?

_____

_____

Determine whether each sample is a random or biased sample. Explain your reasoning.

4. A librarian randomly chooses 100 books from the library's database to calculate the average length of a library book.

_____

Bias in Survey Questions

Once you have selected a representative sample of the population, be sure that the data is gathered without bias. Make sure that the survey questions themselves do not sway people to respond a certain way.

EXAMPLE 2 Real World

TEKS 7.6.F

In Madison County, residents were surveyed about a new skateboard park. Determine whether each survey question may be biased. Explain.

A Would you like to waste the taxpayers' money to build a frivolous skateboard park?

This question is biased. It discourages residents from saying yes to a new skateboard park by implying it is a waste of money.

B Do you favor a new skateboard park?

This question is not biased. It does not include an opinion on the skateboard park.

C Studies have shown that having a safe place to go keeps kids out of trouble. Would you like to invest taxpayers' money to build a skateboard park?

This question is biased. It leads people to say yes because it mentions having a safe place for kids to go and to stay out of trouble.

Determine whether each question may be biased. Explain.

5. When it comes to pets, do you prefer cats?

_____

6. What is your favorite season?

_____

_____

1. Follow each method described below to collect data to estimate the average shoe size of seventh grade boys. (Explore Activity)

Method 1

Ⓐ Randomly select 6 seventh grade boys and ask each his shoe size. Record your results in a table like the one shown.

Random Sample of Seventh Grade Male Students	
Student	Shoe Size

_____

Ⓑ Find the mean of this data. Mean:

_____

Method 2

Ⓐ Find the 6 boys in your math class with the largest shoes and ask their shoe size. Record your results in a table like the one shown in Method 1.

_____

Ⓑ Find the mean of this data. Mean: _____

2. Method 1 produces results that are ⎡ **more / less** ⎤ representative of the

   entire student population because it is a ⎡ **random / biased** ⎤ sample.
   (Example 1)

3. Method 2 produces results that are ⎡ **more / less** ⎤ representative of the

   entire student population because it is a ⎡ **random / biased** ⎤ sample.
   (Example 1)

4. Heidi decides to use a random sample to determine her classmates' favorite color. She asks, "Is green your favorite color?" Is Heidi's question biased? If so, give an example of an unbiased question that would serve Heidi better. (Example 2)

_____

? ESSENTIAL QUESTION CHECK-IN

5. How can you select a sample so that the information gained represents the entire population?

_____

_____

12.1 Independent Practice

TEKS 7.6.F

Personal Math Trainer

Online Assessment and Intervention

my.hrw.com

6. Paul and his friends average their test grades and find that the average is 95. The teacher announces that the average grade of all of her classes is 83. Why are the averages so different?

_____

_____

_____

7. Nancy hears a report that the average price of gasoline is $2.82. She averages the prices of stations near her home. She finds the average price of gas to be $3.03. Why are the averages different?

_____

_____

_____

_____

For 8–11, determine whether each sample is a random sample or a biased sample. Explain.

8. Carol wants to find out the favorite foods of students at her middle school. She asks the boys' basketball team about their favorite foods.

_____

_____

9. Dallas wants to know what elective subjects the students at his school like best. He surveys students who are leaving band class.

_____

_____

10. Karim wants to know what day of the week students at his school prefer. He randomly asks students each day in the cafeteria.

_____

_____

11. Members of a polling organization survey 700 registered voters by randomly choosing names from a list of all registered voters.

_____

_____

_____

_____

Determine whether each question may be biased. Explain.

12. Joey wants to find out what sport seventh grade girls like most. He asks girls, "Is basketball your favorite sport?"

_____

_____

_____

13. Jae wants to find out what type of art her fellow students enjoy most. She asks her classmates, "What is your favorite type of art?"

_____

_____

_____

14. Draw Conclusions Determine which sampling method will better represent the entire population. Justify your answer.

Student Attendance at Football Games	
Sampling Method	**Results of Survey**
Collin surveys 78 students by randomly choosing names from the school directory.	63% attend football games.
Karl surveys 25 students that were sitting near him during lunch.	82% attend football games.

_____

_____

_____

_____

_____

_____

15. Multistep Barbara surveyed students in her school by looking at an alphabetical list of the 600 student names, dividing them into groups of 10, and randomly choosing one from each group.

a. How many students did she survey? What type of sample is this?

_____

b. Barbara found that 35 of the survey participants had pets. About what percent of the students she surveyed had pets? Is it safe to believe that about the same percent of students in the school have pets? Explain your thinking.

_____

_____

_____

16. Communicating Mathematical Ideas Carlo said a population can have more than one sample associated with it. Do you agree or disagree with his statement? Justify your answer.

_____

_____

_____

Making Inferences from a Random Sample

 TEKS
Measurement and data— 7.12.B The student applies mathematical process standards to use statistical representations to analyze data. The student is expected to use data from a random sample to make inferences about a population. *Also 7.6.F*

? **ESSENTIAL QUESTION**

How can you use a sample to gain information about a population?

EXPLORE ACTIVITY 1 **TEKS** 7.12.B

Using Dot Plots to Make Inferences

After obtaining a random sample of a population, you can use statistical representations of the data from the sample, such as a dot plot or box plot, to make inferences about the population.

Rosee asked students on the lunch line how many books they had in their backpacks. She recorded the data as a list: 2, 6, 1, 0, 4, 1, 4, 2, 2. Make a dot plot for the books carried by this sample of students.

STEP 1 Order the data from least to greatest. Find the least and greatest values in the data set.

STEP 2 Draw a number line from 0 to 6. Place a dot above each number on the number line for each time it appears in the data set.

Notice that the dot plot puts the data values in order.

Math Talk
Mathematical Processes
No students in Rosee's sample carry 3 books. Do you think this is true of all the students at the school? Explain.

Reflect

1. How are the number of dots you plotted related to the number of data values?

_____

2. Complete each qualitative inference about the population.

Most students have _____ 1 book in their backpacks.

Most students have fewer than _____ books in their backpacks.

Most students have between _____ books in their backpacks.

3. What could Rosee do to improve the quality of her data?

_____

Using Box Plots to Make Inferences

You can also analyze box plots to make inferences about a population.

The number of pets owned by a random sample of students at Park Middle school is shown below. Use the data to make a box plot.

9, 2, 0, 4, 6, 3, 3, 2, 5

STEP 1 Order the data from least to greatest. Then find the least and greatest values, the median, and the lower and upper quartiles.

The lower and upper quartiles can be calculated by finding the medians of each "half" of the number line that includes all the data.

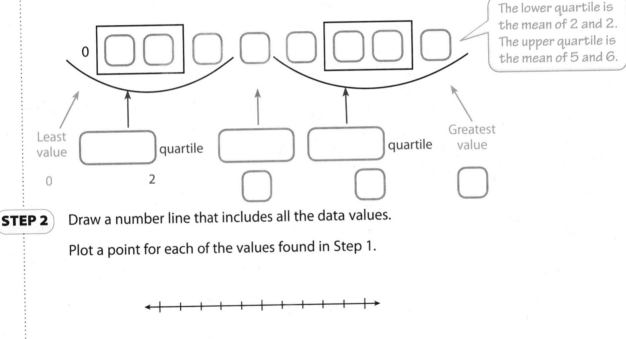

The lower quartile is the mean of 2 and 2. The upper quartile is the mean of 5 and 6.

Least value

quartile

quartile

Greatest value

0   2

STEP 2 Draw a number line that includes all the data values.

Plot a point for each of the values found in Step 1.

STEP 3 Draw a box from the lower to upper quartile. Inside the box, draw a vertical line through the median. Finally, draw the whiskers by connecting the least and greatest values to the box.

Math Talk
Mathematical Processes
What can you see from a box plot that is not readily apparent in a dot plot?

Reflect

4. Complete each qualitative inference about the population.

A good measure for the most likely number of pets is _____.

50% of the students have between _____ and 3 pets.

Almost every student in Parkview has at least _____ pet.

Using Proportions to Make Inferences

A random sample has a good chance of being representative of the population. You can use data about the sample and proportional reasoning to make inferences or predictions about the population.

EXAMPLE 1 *Real World*   TEKS 7.6.F

A shipment to a warehouse consists of 3,500 MP3 players. The manager chooses a random sample of 50 MP3 players and finds that 3 are defective. How many MP3 players in the shipment are likely to be defective?

It is reasonable to make a prediction about the population because this sample is random.

STEP 1 Set up a proportion.

$$\frac{\text{defective MP3s in sample}}{\text{size of sample}} = \frac{\text{defective MP3s in population}}{\text{size of population}}$$

STEP 2 Substitute values into the proportion.

$$\frac{3}{50} = \frac{x}{3,500}$$ Substitute the values you know. Let x represent the number of defective MP3 players in the population.

$$\frac{3 \cdot 70}{50 \cdot 70} = \frac{x}{3,500}$$ Think: What number times 50 equals 3,500?

$$\frac{210}{3,500} = \frac{x}{3,500}$$ $50 \cdot 70 = 3,500$
Multiply the numerator and denominator by 70.

$$210 = x$$

Based on the sample, you can predict that 210 MP3 players in the shipment would be defective.

Animated Math
my.hrw.com

YOUR TURN

5. **What If?** How many MP3 players in the shipment would you predict to be damaged if 6 MP3s in the sample had been damaged?

_____

Reflect

6. How could you use estimation to check if your answer is reasonable?

_____

_____

Personal Math Trainer

Online Assessment and Intervention

my.hrw.com

Patrons in the children's section of a local branch library were randomly selected and asked their ages. The librarian wants to use the data to infer the ages of all patrons of the children's section so he can select age appropriate activities. (Explore Activity 1 and 2)

7, 4, 7, 5, 4, 10, 11, 6, 7, 4

1. Make a dot plot of the sample population data.

<------|----|----|----|----|----|----|----|----|----|----|----|----|----|----|------>

2. Make a box plot of the sample population data.

<------|----|----|----|----|----|----|----|----|----|----|----|----|----|----|------>

3. The most common age of children that use the library is _____ and _____.

4. The range of ages of children that use the library is from _____ to _____.

5. The median age of children that use the library is _____.

6. A manufacturer fills an order for 4,200 smart phones. The quality inspector selects a random sample of 60 phones and finds that 4 are defective. How many smart phones in the order are likely to be defective? (Example 1)

About _____ smart phones in the order are likely to be defective.

7. Part of the population of 4,500 elk at a wildlife preserve is infected with a parasite. A random sample of 50 elk shows that 8 of them are infected. How many elk are likely to be infected? (Example 1)

_____

? **ESSENTIAL QUESTION CHECK-IN**

8. How can you use a random sample of a population to make predictions?

_____

_____

_____

_____

_____

12.2 Independent Practice

TEKS 7.12.B, 7.6.F

Personal Math Trainer

Online Assessment and Intervention

my.hrw.com

9. A manager samples the receipts of every fifth person who goes through the line. Out of 50 people, 4 had a mispriced item. If 600 people go to this store each day, how many people would you expect to have a mispriced item?

_____

10. Jerry randomly selects 20 boxes of crayons from the shelf and finds 2 boxes with at least one broken crayon. If the shelf holds 130 boxes, how many would you expect to have at least one broken crayon?

_____

11. A random sample of dogs at different animal shelters in a city shows that 12 of the 60 dogs are puppies. The city's animal shelters collectively house 1,200 dogs each year. About how many dogs in all of the city's animal shelters are puppies?

_____

12. Part of the population of 10,800 hawks at a national park are building a nest. A random sample of 72 hawks shows that 12 of them are building a nest. Estimate the number of hawks building a nest in the population.

_____

13. In a wildlife preserve a random sample of the population of 150 raccoons was caught and weighed. The results, given in pounds, were 17, 19, 20, 21, 23, 27, 28, 28, 28 and 32. Jean made the qualitative statement, "The average weight of the raccoon population is 25 pounds." Is her statement reasonable? Explain.

_____

_____

_____

14. Greta collects the number of miles run each week from a random sample of female marathon runners. Her data is shown below. She made the qualitative statement, "25% of female marathoners run 13 or more miles a week." Is her statement reasonable? Explain. Data: 13, 14, 18, 13, 12, 17, 15, 12, 13, 19, 11, 14, 14, 18, 22, 12

_____

_____

_____

15. A random sample of 20 of the 200 students at Garland Elementary is asked how many siblings each has. The data was ordered as shown. Make a dot plot of the data. Then make a qualitative statement about the population. Data: 0, 1, 1, 1, 1, 1, 1, 2, 2, 2, 2, 2, 3, 3, 3, 3, 4, 4, 4, 6

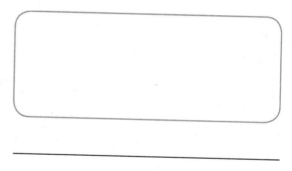

_____

_____

16. Linda collects a random sample of 12 of the 98 Wilderness Club members' ages. She makes an inference that most wilderness club members are between 20 and 40 years old. Describe what a box plot that would confirm Linda's inference should look like.

_____

_____

_____

17. What's the Error? Kudrey was making a box plot. He first plotted the least and greatest data values. He then divided the distance into half, and then did this again for each half. What did Kudrey do wrong and what did his box plot look like?

_____

_____

_____

_____

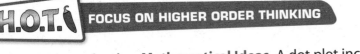

Work Area

18. Communicating Mathematical Ideas A dot plot includes all of the actual data values. Does a box plot include any of the actual data values?

_____

_____

_____

_____

19. Make a Conjecture Sammy counted the peanuts in several packages of roasted peanuts. He found that the bags had 102, 114, 97, 85, 106, 120, 107, and 111 peanuts. Should he make a box plot or dot plot to represent the data? Explain your reasoning.

_____

_____

_____

_____

_____

20. Represent Real-World Problems The salaries for the eight employees at a small company are $20,000, $20,000, $22,000, $24,000, $24,000, $29,000, $34,000 and $79,000. Make a qualitative inference about a typical salary at this company. Would an advertisement that stated that the average salary earned at the company is $31,500 be misleading? Explain.

_____

_____

_____

TEKS
Measurement and data—7.12.C Compare two populations based on data in random samples from these populations, including informal comparative inferences about differences between the two populations.

? ESSENTIAL QUESTION

How can you use random samples to compare two populations?

EXPLORE ACTIVITY 1 **TEKS** 7.12.C

Using Dot Plots to Compare Populations

You can compare two populations by taking a random sample of each population and comparing the samples using dot plots.

A test prep company gives its students a Pretest before the course and a Posttest after the course is completed. The test prep company picks a random sample of 10 students from each testing session.

Pretest Scores
520, 510, 550, 580, 600, 480, 480, 460, 460, 640

Posttest Scores
510, 480, 510, 610, 590, 670, 550, 560, 600, 610

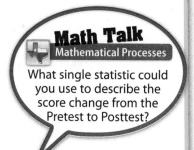

Math Talk
Mathematical Processes

What single statistic could you use to describe the score change from the Pretest to Posttest?

A Make a dot plot for the sample of Pretest scores.

```
←+—+—+—+—+—+—+—+—+—+—+—+—+→
  460  480  500  520  540  560  580  600  620  640  660  680
```

B Make a dot plot for the sample of Posttest scores.

```
←+—+—+—+—+—+—+—+—+—+—+—+—+→
  460  480  500  520  540  560  580  600  620  640  660  680
```

C Compare the dot plots. The plots have a similar [**center / spread**],

but the Posttest values are shifted to the _____ .

Reflect

1. What can you infer about the populations by comparing the dot plots for the samples?

_____

Using Box Plots to Compare Populations

You can also compare two populations using random samples and box plots.

A survey of 7th graders asks girls and boys how many baseball caps they own.

Girls	Boys
8, 6, 4, 18, 3, 7, 5, 8, 8, 7	9, 18, 9, 7, 10, 15, 18, 10, 9, 12

A Make a box plot for the number of baseball caps girls own.

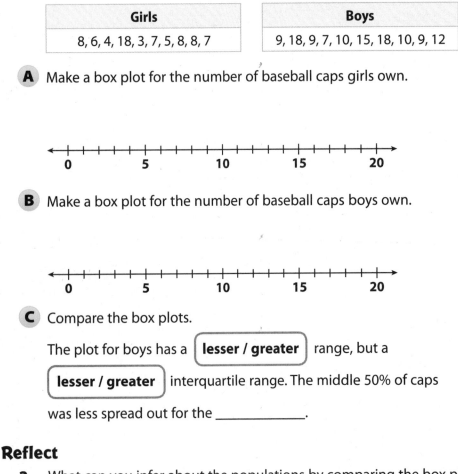

B Make a box plot for the number of baseball caps boys own.

C Compare the box plots.

The plot for boys has a ⬭ **lesser / greater** ⬭ range, but a

⬭ **lesser / greater** ⬭ interquartile range. The middle 50% of caps

was less spread out for the _____.

Reflect

2. What can you infer about the populations by comparing the box plots for the samples? Justify your answer.

_____

_____

_____

_____

_____

Real World   TEKS 7.12.B, 7.12.C

Using Statistical Measures to Compare Populations

You can use the means and ranges of two random samples to compare the populations that the random samples represent.

Paula and Daniel wanted to determine the average word length in two books. They took a random sample of 12 words each and counted the length of each word from each book.

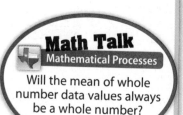

Math Talk
Mathematical Processes
Will the mean of whole number data values always be a whole number? Explain.

Book 1 Word length
3, 7, 5, 2, 4, 3, 1, 6, 4, 8, 2, 3

Book 2 Word length
5, 4, 3, 6, 4, 5, 5, 2, 3, 4, 2, 5

STEP 1 Calculate the mean for Book 1.

$$\frac{3 + 7 + 5 }{\boxed{}} = \frac{\boxed{}}{\boxed{}} = \boxed{}$$

The mean for Book 1 is _____ letters long.

STEP 2 Find the range for Book 1.

$$\boxed{} - \boxed{} = \boxed{}$$ *Subtract the least word length from the greatest word length.*

STEP 3 Calculate the mean for Book 2.

$$\frac{5 + 4 + 3 }{\boxed{}} = \frac{\boxed{}}{\boxed{}} = \boxed{}$$

The mean for Book 2 is _____ letters long.

STEP 4 Find the range for Book 2.

$$\boxed{} - \boxed{} = \boxed{}$$ *Subtract the least word length from the greatest word length.*

You can infer from the mean of each population that the overall average word length for Book 1 is | **less than / the same as / greater than** | the average word length for Book 2.

You can infer from the range of each population that the length of the words in Book 1 varies | **less than / in the same way as / more than** | Book 2.

Reflect

3. What are the populations from which the samples were taken?

_____

_____

Guided Practice

Carol wants to know how many people live in each household in her town. She conducts two random surveys of 10 people each and asks how many people live in their home. Her results are listed below. Use the data for 1–6.

(Explore Activities 1, 2 and 3)

Sample A: 1, 6, 2, 4, 4, 3, 5, 5, 2, 8

1. Make a dot plot for Sample A.

Sample B: 3, 4, 5, 4, 3, 2, 4, 5, 4, 4

2. Make a dot plot for Sample B.

```
<---+--+--+--+--+--+--+--+--+--+--+--->
    0  1  2  3  4  5  6  7  8  9  10
```

```
<---+--+--+--+--+--+--+--+--+--+--+--->
    0  1  2  3  4  5  6  7  8  9  10
```

3. Find the mean and range for Sample A.

   Mean: _____   Range: _____

4. Find the mean and range for Sample B.

   Mean: _____   Range: _____

5. What can you infer about the population based on Sample A? Explain.

_____

_____

_____

_____

6. What can you infer about the population based on Sample B? Explain.

_____

_____

_____

_____

? ESSENTIAL QUESTION CHECK-IN

7. How can you use random samples to compare two populations?

_____

_____

_____

12.3 Independent Practice

Personal
Math Trainer

Online
Assessment and
Intervention

my.hrw.com

TEKS 7.12.C

The high school is buying shoes for the boy's football team and boy's soccer team. The sizes of a random sample of the players' feet is shown.

Football Team Shoe Sizes	Soccer Team Shoe Sizes
6, 8, 9, 10, 10, 10, 10, 10, 11, 11, 13	3, 5, 5, 6, 6, 6, 6, 6, 7, 8, 10

8. Find the mean for both lists. What can you infer about the populations by comparing the means?

_____

_____

9. Find the range of both lists. What can you infer about the populations by comparing the ranges?

_____

_____

10. Make a box plot for each sample.

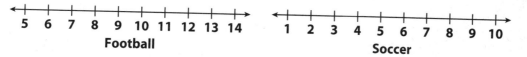

Football   Soccer

11. **Draw Conclusions** Compare the box plots. What do you notice from the visual comparison?

_____

_____

Mrs. Garcia asked a random sample of her students the number of books they read over the summer. Use these data for 12–14.

Number of Books Read by Class A	Number of Books Read by Class B
9, 7, 10, 9, 9, 2, 3, 4, 4, 8	1, 3, 9, 9, 1, 10, 2, 3, 4, 10

12. Make dot plots for each sample to illustrate the books read in each class.

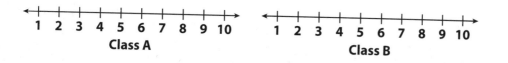

Class A   Class B

13. Describe two similarities and two differences between the dot plots.

14. **Make a Conjecture** Without doing any calculations, can you tell which class has read more books? Explain. What calculation would you perform to verify your response?

H.O.T. FOCUS ON HIGHER ORDER THINKING

Work Area

15. **Communicate Mathematical Ideas** Compare plotting points on a number line with plotting points on a dot plot.

16. **Analyze Relationships** If you are given a box plot without any numbers on the number line, what can you tell about the data used to make the plot?

17. **Draw Conclusions** Using at least ten points, create two distinct data sets with the same mean and range. Will their dot plots be the same? Could their box plots be the same?

Ready to Go On?

12.1 Populations and Samples

1. A company uses a computer to identify their 600 most loyal customers from its database and then surveys those customers to find out how they like their service. Identify the population and determine whether the sample is random or biased.

_____

_____

_____

12.2 Making Inferences from a Random Sample

2. A university has 30,330 students. In a random sample of 270 students, 18 speak three or more languages. Predict the number of students at

the university who speak three or more languages. _____

12.3 Comparing Populations

3. The box plot shows data that was collected on two basketball players over 20 randomly selected games in order to analyze the number of points each player has scored per game over his career. Make an inference from this data.

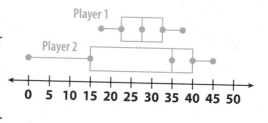

_____

_____

? ESSENTIAL QUESTION

4. How can you use random samples to compare populations and make inferences?

_____

_____

_____

_____

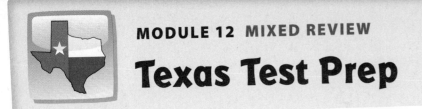

MODULE 12 MIXED REVIEW

Texas Test Prep

Personal
Math Trainer

Online
Assessment and
Intervention

my.hrw.com

Selected Response

1. The box plot shows the results from a survey in which 50 of the school's 7th graders were asked about their height. Which could you infer based on the box plot below?

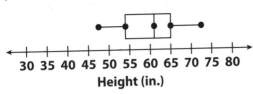

30 35 40 45 50 55 60 65 70 75 80
Height (in.)

Ⓐ Most 7th graders are at least 65 inches tall.

Ⓑ Most 7th graders are at least 54 inches tall.

Ⓒ Almost no 7th graders are less than 60 inches tall.

Ⓓ Almost no 7th graders are more than 60 inches tall.

2. A middle school has 490 students. Mae surveys a random sample of 60 students and finds that 24 of them have pet dogs. How many students are likely to have pet dogs?

Ⓐ 98 Ⓒ 245

Ⓑ 196 Ⓓ 294

3. Caitlyn finds that the experimental probability of her making a three-point shot is 30%. Out of 500 three-point shots, about how many could she predict she would make?

Ⓐ 100 Ⓒ 125

Ⓑ 115 Ⓓ 150

4. Which of the following is a random sample?

Ⓐ A radio DJ asks the first 10 listeners who call in if they liked the last song.

Ⓑ 20 customers at a chicken restaurant are surveyed on their favorite food.

Ⓒ Members of a polling organization survey 800 registered voters by randomly choosing names from a list of all registered voters.

Ⓓ Rebecca used an email poll to survey 100 students about how often they use the internet.

Gridded Response

5. Mary wanted to know the amount of time 7th grade students spend on homework each week, so she surveyed 20 students at random. The results are shown below.

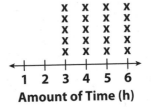

1 2 3 4 5 6
Amount of Time (h)

There are 164 students in the 7th grade. Predict how many 7th grade students spend 5 hours on homework in a week.

					•		
⊕	⓪	⓪	⓪	⓪		⓪	⓪
⊖	①	①	①	①		①	①
	②	②	②	②		②	②
	③	③	③	③		③	③
	④	④	④	④		④	④
	⑤	⑤	⑤	⑤		⑤	⑤
	⑥	⑥	⑥	⑥		⑥	⑥
	⑦	⑦	⑦	⑦		⑦	⑦
	⑧	⑧	⑧	⑧		⑧	⑧
	⑨	⑨	⑨	⑨		⑨	⑨

Key Vocabulary

circle graph (*gráfica circular*)

? ESSENTIAL QUESTION

How can you solve real-world problems by analyzing and comparing data?

EXAMPLE 1

There are 500 students at Trenton Middle School. The percent of students in each grade level is shown in the circle graph. Calculate the number of students in each grade.

$43\% = 0.43$ $31\% = 0.31$ $26\% = 0.26$

$0.43 \times 500 = 215$ $0.31 \times 500 = 155$ $0.26 \times 500 = 130$

There are 215 6th graders, 155 7th graders, and 130 8th graders.

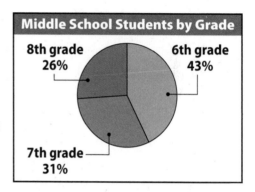

Middle School Students by Grade

8th grade 26%

6th grade 43%

7th grade 31%

EXAMPLE 2

The box plots show the amount that each employee from the same office donated to two charities. Compare the shapes, centers and spreads of the box plots.

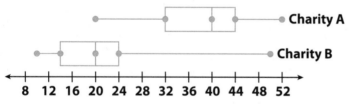

Charity A

Charity B

8 12 16 20 24 28 32 36 40 44 48 52

Shapes: The lengths of the boxes are similar, as are the overall lengths of the graphs. The whiskers for the two graphs are very different. The whiskers for Charity A are similar in length. The left whisker for Charity B is much shorter than the right one.

Centers: The median for Charity A is $40, and for Charity B is $20. That means the median donor gave $20 more for Charity A.

Spreads: The interquartile range for Charity A is $44 - 32 = 12$. The interquartile range for Charity B is slightly less, $24 - 14 = 10$.

The donations varied more for Charity B and were lower overall.

EXERCISES

1. Five candidates are running for the position of School Superintendent. Find the percent of votes that each candidate received. (Lesson 11.1)

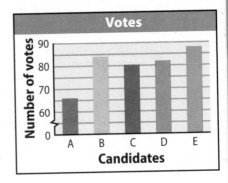

_____

_____

_____

The dot plots show the number of hours a group of students spend online each week, and how many hours they spend reading. Compare the dot plots visually. (Lesson 11.2)

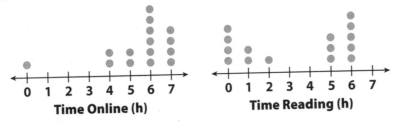

2. Compare the shapes, centers, and spreads of the dot plots.

Shape: _____

_____

Center: _____

_____

Spread: _____

_____

3. Calculate the medians of the dot plots. _____

4. Calculate the ranges of the dot plots. _____

The box plots show the math and reading scores on a standardized test for a group of students. Use the box plots shown to answer the following questions. (Lesson 11.3)

5. Compare the maximum and minimum values of the box plots.

_____

6. Compare the interquartile range of the box plots.

_____

Random Samples and Populations

? **ESSENTIAL QUESTION**

How can you use random samples and populations to solve real-world problems?

EXAMPLE

An engineer at a lightbulb factory chooses a random sample of 100 lightbulbs from a shipment of 2,500 and finds that 2 of them are defective. How many lightbulbs in the shipment are likely to be defective?

$$\frac{\text{defective lightbulbs}}{\text{size of sample}} = \frac{\text{defective lightbulbs in population}}{\text{size of population}}$$

$$\frac{2}{100} = \frac{x}{2,500}$$

$$\frac{2 \cdot 25}{100 \cdot 25} = \frac{x}{2,500}$$

$$x = 50$$

In a shipment of 2,500 lightbulbs, 50 are likely to be defective.

EXERCISES

1. Molly uses the school directory to select 25 students at random from her school for a survey on which sports people like to watch on television. She calls the students and asks them, "Do you think basketball is the best sport to watch on television?" (Lesson 12.1)

   a. Did Molly survey a random sample or a biased sample of the students at her school?

   _____

   b. Was the question she asked an unbiased question? Explain your answer.

   _____

2. There are 2,300 licensed dogs in Clarkson. A random sample of 50 of the dogs in Clarkson shows that 8 have ID microchips implanted. How many dogs in Clarkson are likely to have ID microchips implanted? (Lesson 12.2)

   _____

3. Mr. Puccia teaches Algebra 1 and Geometry. He randomly selected 10 students from each class. He asked the students how many hours they spend on math homework in a week. He recorded each set of data in a list. (Lesson 12.3)
Algebra 1: 4, 0, 5, 3, 6, 3, 2, 1, 1, 4
Geometry: 7, 3, 5, 6, 5, 3, 5, 3, 6, 5

a. Make a dot plot for Algebra 1. Then find the mean and the range for Algebra 1.

_____

Algebra 1

b. Make a dot plot for Geometry. Then find the mean and the range for Geometry.

_____

Geometry

c. What can you infer about the students in the Algebra 1 class compared to the students in the Geometry class?

_____

_____

Unit 6 Performance Tasks

1. **CAREERS IN MATH** Entomologist An entomologist is studying how two different types of flowers appeal to butterflies. The box-and-whisker plots show the number of butterflies who visited one of two different types of flowers in a field. The data were collected over a two-week period, for one hour each day.

a. Find the median, range, and interquartile range for each data set.

_____

_____

b. Which measure makes it appear that flower type A had a more consistent number of butterfly visits? Which measure makes it appear that flower type B did? If you had to choose one flower as having the more consistent visits, which would you choose? Explain your reasoning.

_____

_____

_____

_____

© Houghton Mifflin Harcourt Publishing Company

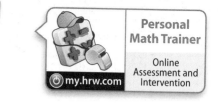
Selected Response

1. Which is a true statement based on the dot plots below?

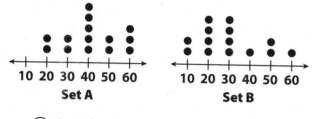

Set A

Set B

- Ⓐ Set B has the greater range.
- Ⓑ Set B has the greater median.
- Ⓒ Set B has the greater mean.
- Ⓓ Set A is less symmetric than Set B.

2. Which is a solution to the equation $7g - 2 = 47$?

- Ⓐ $g = 5$
- Ⓑ $g = 6$
- Ⓒ $g = 7$
- Ⓓ $g = 8$

3. Which is a true statement based on the box plots below?

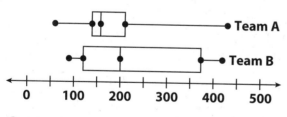

Team A

Team B

- Ⓐ The data for Team B have the greater range.
- Ⓑ The data for Team A are more symmetric.
- Ⓒ The data for Team B have the greater interquartile range.
- Ⓓ The data for Team A have the greater median.

4. Which is a random sample?

- Ⓐ 10 students in the Spanish Club are asked how many languages they speak.
- Ⓑ 20 customers at an Italian restaurant are surveyed on what their favorite food is.
- Ⓒ 15 students were asked what their favorite color is.
- Ⓓ 10 customers at a pet store were asked whether or not they had pets.

5. Find the percent change from 84 to 63.

- Ⓐ 30% decrease
- Ⓑ 30% increase
- Ⓒ 25% decrease
- Ⓓ 25% increase

6. A survey asked 100 students in a school to name the temperature at which they feel most comfortable. The box plot below shows the results for temperatures in degrees Fahrenheit. Which could you infer based on the box plot below?

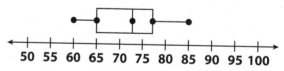

- Ⓐ Most students prefer a temperature less than 65 degrees.
- Ⓑ Most students prefer a temperature of at least 70 degrees.
- Ⓒ Almost no students prefer a temperature of less than 75 degrees.
- Ⓓ Almost no students prefer a temperature of more than 65 degrees.

7. The box plots below show data from a survey of students under 14 years old. They were asked on how many days in a month they read and draw. Based on the box plots, which is a true statement about students?

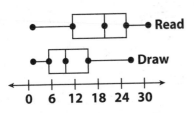

A Most students draw at least 12 days a month.

B Most students read less than 12 days a month.

C Most students read more often than they draw.

D Most students draw more often than they read.

Use logic to eliminate answer choices that are incorrect. This will help you to make an educated guess if you are having trouble with the question.

8. Which describes the relationship between ∠NOM and ∠JOK in the diagram?

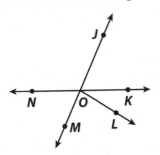

A adjacent angles

B complementary angles

C supplementary angles

D vertical angles

Gridded Response

9. Katie is reading a 200-page book that is divided into five chapters. The bar graph shows the number of pages in each chapter.

What percent of the pages are in Chapter 2?

+	⓪	⓪	⓪	⓪	•	⓪	⓪
−	①	①	①	①		①	①
	②	②	②	②		②	②
	③	③	③	③		③	③
	④	④	④	④		④	④
	⑤	⑤	⑤	⑤		⑤	⑤
	⑥	⑥	⑥	⑥		⑥	⑥
	⑦	⑦	⑦	⑦		⑦	⑦
	⑧	⑧	⑧	⑧		⑧	⑧
	⑨	⑨	⑨	⑨		⑨	⑨

10. Lee Middle School has 420 students. Irene surveys a random sample of 45 students and finds that 18 of them have pet cats. How many students are likely to have pet cats?

+	⓪	⓪	⓪	⓪	•	⓪	⓪
−	①	①	①	①		①	①
	②	②	②	②		②	②
	③	③	③	③		③	③
	④	④	④	④		④	④
	⑤	⑤	⑤	⑤		⑤	⑤
	⑥	⑥	⑥	⑥		⑥	⑥
	⑦	⑦	⑦	⑦		⑦	⑦
	⑧	⑧	⑧	⑧		⑧	⑧
	⑨	⑨	⑨	⑨		⑨	⑨

Personal Financial Literacy

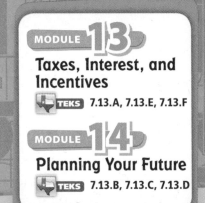

MODULE 13
Taxes, Interest, and Incentives
TEKS 7.13.A, 7.13.E, 7.13.F

MODULE 14
Planning Your Future
TEKS 7.13.B, 7.13.C, 7.13.D

CAREERS IN MATH

Freelance Computer Programmer

A computer programmer translates commands into code, a language that a computer understands. Programmers work on a variety of tasks, from creating computer games to testing software. A freelance programmer doesn't work for a specific company; this gives the freelancer more flexibility with his or her work schedule. Computer programmers use mathematical logic when writing or altering code.

If you are interested in a career as a computer programmer, you should study these mathematical subjects:

- Algebra
- Geometry
- Trigonometry
- Calculus
- Discrete Math

Research other careers that require the understanding of mathematical logic.

Unit 7 Performance Task

At the end of the unit, check out how a **freelance computer programmer** uses math.

© Houghton Mifflin Harcourt Publishing Company • Image Credits: ©alexFIC/Alamy

Vocabulary Preview

Use the puzzle to preview key vocabulary from this unit. Unscramble the circled letters within found words to answer the riddle at the bottom of the page.

```
S  T  Ⓔ  S  S  A  Y  N  F  N  M  B  S  K  U
M  Y  J  I  R  Z  K  W  I  Q  C  E  H  Y  F
F  S  R  N  D  N  M  R  J  A  Ⓢ  V  F  C  A
S  K  K  S  P  S  O  D  A  N  W  J  I  Z  R
A  F  B  P  E  M  K  C  E  B  W  H  Q  E  M
O  R  Z  R  P  A  U  P  V  N  K  H  Q  B  O
I  V  N  P  B  G  X  N  E  C  Z  W  O  U  R
N  G  P  G  M  E  N  R  J  A  K  Z  X  D  P
P  Ⓔ  Z  M  D  D  C  E  C  A  U  K  L  G  X
H  Q  T  E  L  I  Ⓐ  B  I  L  I  Ⓣ  I  E  S
C  K  Ⓧ  W  Ⓝ  T  U  L  J  G  C  B  Y  T  K
M  I  P  C  O  K  Y  G  K  T  U  C  U  C  L
F  G  O  K  P  R  J  W  W  K  R  Y  R  D  L
C  M  G  J  Q  U  Ⓣ  P  P  W  U  N  A  B  Z
E  Y  F  M  C  T  L  H  Y  E  H  S  M  U  C
```

- The things you own that have a positive cash value. (Lesson 14.3)
- The amount of money you earn. (Lesson 14.1)
- A plan for managing your money to help you reach your financial goals. (Lesson 14.1)
- Debts you owe that have a negative cash value. (Lesson 14.3)
- Expenses that occur regularly and stay the same (2 words). (Lesson 14.1)
- The difference between assets and liabilities (2 words). (Lesson 14.3)

Q: What did the fisherman give to the IRS?

A: His ___ ___ ___ ___ ___ ___ ___ ___!

Taxes, Interest, and Incentives

ESSENTIAL QUESTION

How can you solve real-world problems involving taxes, interest, and incentives?

Real-World Video

You can invest money in savings accounts, certificates of deposit (CDs), and bonds. Each type of investment earns simple or compound interest, so your money grows over time.

ⓞ my.hrw.com

© Houghton Mifflin Harcourt Publishing Company • Image Credits: ©NAN/Alamy Images

GO DIGITAL
my.hrw.com

my.hrw.com	Math On the Spot	Animated Math	Personal Math Trainer
Go digital with your write-in student edition, accessible on any device.	Scan with your smart phone to jump directly to the online edition, video tutor, and more.	Interactively explore key concepts to see how math works.	Get immediate feedback and help as you work through practice sets.

Complete these exercises to review skills you will need for this chapter.

Personal Math Trainer

Online Assessment and Intervention

my.hrw.com

Percents and Decimals

> **EXAMPLE** $125\% = 100\% + 25\%$ Write the percent as the sum of 1 whole and a percent remainder.
>
> $= \frac{100}{100} + \frac{25}{100}$ Write the percents as fractions.
>
> $= 1 + 0.25$ Write the fractions as decimals.
>
> $= 1.25$ Simplify.

Write each percent as a decimal.

1. 45% _____   **2.** 91% _____   **3.** 8% _____   **4.** 111% _____

Write each decimal as a percent.

5. 0.79 _____   **6.** 0.8 _____   **7.** 0.05 _____   **8.** 1.98 _____

Decimal Operations

> **EXAMPLE** $25.9 - 3.24 \rightarrow$ $\begin{array}{r} 25.90 \\ -\ 3.24 \\ \hline 22.66 \end{array}$ To add or subtract decimals, align the decimal points. Add zeros if necessary.

Find each sum or difference.

9. $11.9 - 7.6$ _____   **10.** $24.1 - 9.25$ _____   **11.** $45 - 10.6$ _____

12. $6.04 - 3.5$ _____   **13.** $5.17 - 5.09$ _____   **14.** $100 - 3.77$ _____

Multiply with Fractions and Decimals

> **EXAMPLE** $\begin{array}{r} 5.9 \\ \times\ 3.6 \\ \hline 3\,5\,4 \\ +\ 1\,7\,7 \\ \hline 2\,1.2\,4 \end{array}$ Multiply as you would with whole numbers. Count the total number of decimal places in the two factors. Write the same total number of decimal places in the product.

Multiply.

15. $\begin{array}{r} 2.77 \\ \times\ 24 \end{array}$ **16.** $\begin{array}{r} 9.95 \\ \times\ 0.7 \end{array}$ **17.** $\begin{array}{r} 12.04 \\ \times\ 3.2 \end{array}$ **18.** $\begin{array}{r} 38.4 \\ \times\ 0.72 \end{array}$

▢   ▢   ▢   ▢

© Houghton Mifflin Harcourt Publishing Company

Reading Start-Up

Visualize Vocabulary

Use the ✔ words to complete the graphic. You will put a different word in each box.

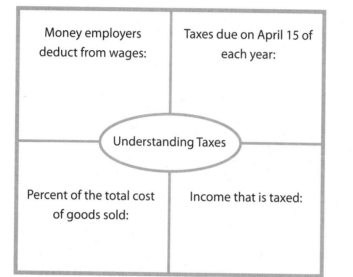

Money employers deduct from wages:	Taxes due on April 15 of each year:
Percent of the total cost of goods sold:	Income that is taxed:

Understanding Taxes

Understand Vocabulary

Complete each sentence using the preview words.

1. The amount of money earned by bank customers based on the amount of principal in their savings account is _____.

2. _____ is interest paid only on the principal, according to an agreed upon interest rate.

Vocabulary

Review Words

deductions (deducciones)

✔ federal withholding (retención fiscal federal)

gross pay (paga bruta)

✔ income tax (impuesto sobre la renta)

net pay (paga neta)

principal (capital)

✔ sales tax (impuesto sobre la venta)

✔ taxable income (ingreso sujeto a impuestos)

unit price (precio por unidad)

Preview Words

compound interest (interés compuesto)

interest (interés)

simple interest (interés simple)

Active Reading

Tri-Fold Before beginning the module, create a tri-fold to help you learn the concepts and vocabulary in this module. Fold the paper into three sections. Label the columns "What I Know," "What I Need to Know," and "What I Learned." Complete the first two columns before you read. After studying the module, complete the third column.

© Houghton Mifflin Harcourt Publishing Company

Module 13 **403**

Unpacking the TEKS

Understanding the TEKS and the vocabulary terms in the TEKS will help you know exactly what you are expected to learn in this module.

© Houghton Mifflin Harcourt Publishing Company

TEKS 7.13

Develop an economic way of thinking and problem solving useful in one's life as a knowledgeable consumer and investor.

Key Vocabulary

taxable income
(ingreso sujeto a impuestos)
The total amount of income minus deductions.

sales tax
(impuesto sobre la venta)
A percent of the total cost of goods and services.

principal *(capital)*
The money you put in a savings account.

interest *(interés)*
Money paid to you by the bank to allow them to borrow your money.

simple interest *(interés simple)*
Interest paid only on the original principal.

compound interest
(interés compuesto)
Interest paid on the principal and on the interest an account has earned.

What It Means to You

You will learn how each of the following standards related to 7.13 is designed to help you understand your taxes, interest and incentives.

7.13.A Calculate the sales tax for a given purchase and calculate income tax for earned wages.

7.13.E Calculate and compare simple interest and compound interest earnings.

7.13.F Analyze and compare monetary incentives, including sales, rebates, and coupons.

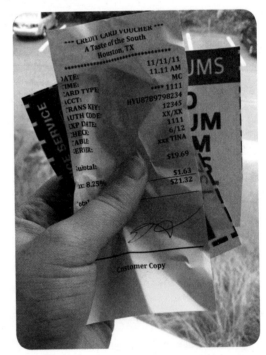

Visit **my.hrw.com** to see all the **TEKS** unpacked.

my.hrw.com

Calculating Sales and Income Tax

TEKS
Personal financial literacy—
7.13.A Calculate the sales tax for a given purchase and calculate income tax for earned wages.

? **ESSENTIAL QUESTION**

How do you calculate sales tax and income tax?

Calculating Sales Tax

Sales tax is a tax imposed by state or local governments. It is collected by the seller or service provider. The tax is a percent of the total cost of goods and services. Sales tax rates vary by region and not all items are taxable.

Math On the Spot
my.hrw.com

EXAMPLE 1 _Real World_   **TEKS** 7.13.A

Rafiq purchases products from a nursery for his yard. The table shows his purchases and the prices. The sales tax rate is 7.5%. Find the total cost of his purchase, including tax.

STEP 1   Find the tax on each item.

Black-Eyed Susan: ($6.25 · 2) · 7.5%

$12.50 · 0.075 = 0.9375 = 0.94

> **Math Talk**
> **Mathematical Processes**
> What is another way to find the total cost?

STEP 2   Add the subtotal and the tax on each item to find its total price. Add to find the total cost of his purchase.

$12.50 + 0.94 = $13.44

Item	Unit price	Number	Subtotal	Tax (7.5%)	Total
Black-Eyed Susan	$6.25	2	$12.50	$0.94	$13.44
Coneflower	$6.99	5	$34.95	$2.62	$37.57
Mexican White Oak	$29.99	1	$29.99	$2.25	$32.24
				Total cost	$83.25

The total cost of his purchase is $83.25.

> Multiply the subtotal for each product by the tax rate of 7.5%, or 0.075.

YOUR TURN

1.   **What If?** Suppose Rafiq returned to the nursery and bought a second tree priced at $49.99 and two packages of fertilizer priced at $12.99 each. Find the total cost of his purchase, including tax. _____

Personal
Math Trainer
Online Assessment and Intervention
my.hrw.com

Calculating Withholding

Most workers pay yearly federal income taxes based on the wages, or pay, they earn. Employers deduct money called federal **withholding** from workers' wages, and send it to the federal government as partial payment of the workers' yearly income tax. Each year around April 15, workers submit a federal income tax return. At that time, they may owe additional taxes or may get a refund depending on several factors, including the amount already paid through withholding.

A worker's pay before any amounts are deducted, or taken out, is called **gross pay**. **Net pay** is gross pay less all deductions, including withholding.

$$\boxed{\textit{net pay}} = \boxed{\textit{gross pay}} - \boxed{\textit{total deductions}}$$

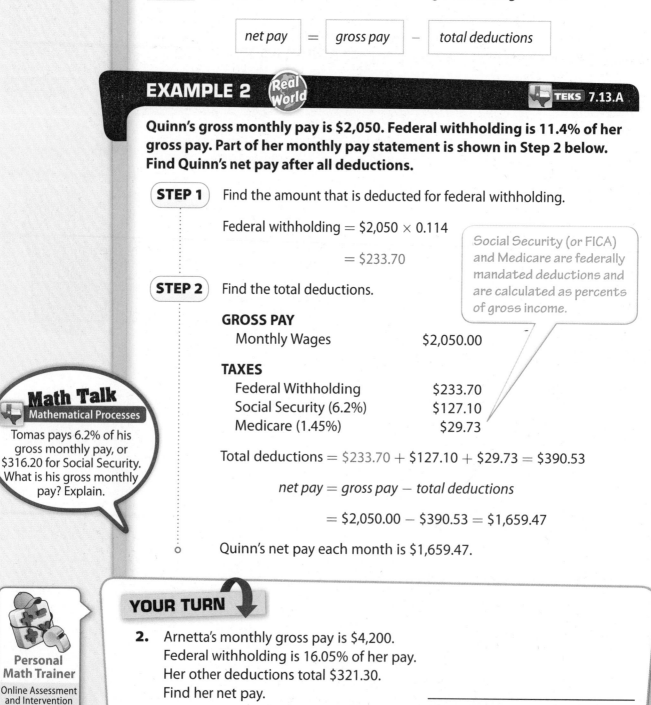

EXAMPLE 2 Real World · · · · · · · · · · · · · · · · TEKS 7.13.A

Quinn's gross monthly pay is $2,050. Federal withholding is 11.4% of her gross pay. Part of her monthly pay statement is shown in Step 2 below. Find Quinn's net pay after all deductions.

STEP 1 Find the amount that is deducted for federal withholding.

Federal withholding = $2,050 × 0.114

= $233.70

> Social Security (or FICA) and Medicare are federally mandated deductions and are calculated as percents of gross income.

STEP 2 Find the total deductions.

GROSS PAY
Monthly Wages $2,050.00

TAXES
Federal Withholding $233.70
Social Security (6.2%) $127.10
Medicare (1.45%) $29.73

Total deductions = $233.70 + $127.10 + $29.73 = $390.53

net pay = gross pay − total deductions

= $2,050.00 − $390.53 = $1,659.47

Quinn's net pay each month is $1,659.47.

Math Talk
Mathematical Processes

Tomas pays 6.2% of his gross monthly pay, or $316.20 for Social Security. What is his gross monthly pay? Explain.

YOUR TURN

2. Arnetta's monthly gross pay is $4,200.
Federal withholding is 16.05% of her pay.
Her other deductions total $321.30.
Find her net pay. _____

Calculating Income Tax

Federal income taxes are based on an individual's taxable income. **Taxable income** is the total amount of income minus deductions.

$$\boxed{\text{taxable income}} = \boxed{\text{gross income}} - \boxed{\text{total deductions}}$$

Taxpayers may take a standard deduction set by the Internal Revenue Service (IRS), or they may itemize deductions such as property taxes or medical expenses. Income tax is the product of the tax rate and the taxable income. Many taxpayers use a tax table provided by the IRS.

EXAMPLE 3   Problem Solving   TEKS 7.13.A

After deductions, Jonah has a taxable income of $26,318. He paid a total of $4,059 in federal withholding. Find the tax due on Jonah's income. Then tell whether he will have to pay an additional amount or will get a refund.

Analyze Information

Identify the important information.

- Jonah's taxable income is $26,318.
- Jonah already paid $4,059 in federal withholding.

Formulate a Plan

Use a tax table to find the amount of tax owed on $26,318. Then compare the tax due with the tax withheld.

Solve

STEP 1 Use a tax table to find the tax for a gross income of $26,318.

If line 43 (taxable income is —		And you are single
At least	**But less than**	**Your tax is —**
26,200	26,250	3,509
26,250	26,300	3,516
26,300	26,350	3,524
26,350	26,400	3,531

$26,318 is between 26,300 and 26,350.

STEP 2 Compare the tax due of $3,524 with the tax withheld of $4,059.

$4,059 − $3,524 = $535

Jonah paid $535 more than he owes.

Justify and Evaluate

Jonah paid $4,059. His tax from the tax table was $3,524, which is a lesser number. This means Jonah paid more in taxes than he owes. He will get $535 back as a refund.

YOUR TURN

3. Glenda's taxable income is $26,222. She paid $2,640 in federal withholding. Find the tax due on Glenda's income. Then tell whether she will have to pay an additional amount or will get a refund. Use the tax table in Example 3.

_____

Guided Practice

Find each amount. Use a sales tax rate of 8%. (Example 1)

	Product description	Unit price	Number	Subtotal	Tax (8%)	Total
1.	Pens (3 pack)	$3.59	3	$10.77		
2.	Notebooks (2 pack)	$1.99	2	$3.98		
3.	Backpack	$44.99	1	$44.99		
4.	Highlighters (4 pack)	$5.15	1	$5.15		
5.					Total cost	

6. Juan earns a monthly salary of $3,200. Federal withholding is 14.1% of his gross pay. Juan has a total of $244.80 deducted for Social Security and Medicare. Find his net pay. (Example 2)

_____

7. Lizaveta's taxable income is $26,380. She paid $2,940 in federal withholding. Use a problem solving model to determine whether she will have to pay an additional amount or will get a refund. Use the tax table in Example 3. (Example 3)

_____

? ESSENTIAL QUESTION CHECK-IN

8. Suppose the sales tax rate in your area is 7.5%. Explain how to determine the total cost, including tax, of an eReader that costs $125.

_____

_____

_____

_____

13.1 Independent Practice

TEKS 7.13.A

Personal Math Trainer

Online Assessment and Intervention

my.hrw.com

9. Roland is purchasing pottery supplies for his pottery class. He buys a portable pottery wheel for $382.00, modeling clay for $12.00, and a pottery tool set for $16.14. If the tax rate is 8.25%, find the total tax he paid. Then find the total cost of his purchases.

_____

10. Megna has $300 to buy a digital camera. She finds one she likes that costs $275.

   a. Suppose the tax rate is 7.3%. Does Megna have enough to buy the camera? Explain.

_____

   b. Megna discovers that the digital camera needs a memory card. She finds a memory card on sale for $9.99 plus tax. Can Megna afford the card?

_____

_____

11. Casey is looking at the used car shown. Suppose that Casey is able to get $1,200 in trade for his old vehicle. The sales tax rate is 7.75%. How much will Casey pay in taxes on the reduced sales price?

_____

12. **What's the Error?** Lauren wants to buy 3 shirts at $15.00 each. At home, she calculates the total cost as $46.20, using the sales tax rate of 8%. At the store, the cashier tells Lauren the total cost is $48.60. Who is wrong and what mistake did he or she make?

_____

13. Camden earns $25 per hour, and works 40 hours a week.

   a. Camden gets paid every 2 weeks. Federal withholding is 15.6% of his gross pay, Social Security is 6.2% of his gross pay, and Medicare is 1.45%. Find Camden's net pay after 2 weeks. Show your work.

_____

   b. **What If** Suppose Camden gets a raise of $5 per hour and pays 17.2% of his gross pay in federal withholding. What would his net pay for 2 weeks be? Make sure to factor in his social security and Medicare withholdings.

14. Critique Reasoning Samantha said adding 6% to the cost of an item for sales tax makes the total cost 106% of the original price. Joshua disagrees. Is Samantha's reasoning accurate? Explain.

_____

_____

_____

15. After deductions, Elizabeth's taxable income was $28,536. She had $344 withheld each month for taxes. Use the tax table shown to find how much she will get as a refund or owe.

If line 43 (taxable income is —		And you are single
At least	But less than	Your tax is —
28,400	28,450	3,839
28,450	28,500	3,846
28,500	28,550	3,854
28,550	28,600	3,861

_____

 FOCUS ON HIGHER ORDER THINKING

16. Persevere in Problem Solving A family buys groceries for $149.98, including $10.07 in taxes. The bill includes $26.95 worth of items that are not taxable. Find the sales tax rate. Round your answer to the nearest tenth of a percent.

_____

17. Multistep Suppose the personal income tax rate is changed to a flat rate of 15% of one's taxable income. Use the tax table in problem 15 to investigate the effect of the change in the rate on a single taxpayer with a taxable income of $28,443.

_____

_____

_____

18. Represent Real-World Problems You have $3,000 to spend on a laptop. Suppose the tax rate is 6.78%. What is the maximum you can spend on a laptop if you know you will also be purchasing a $25 case? Explain.

_____

_____

_____

Work Area

LESSON
13.2
Calculating and Comparing Simple and Compound Interest

TEKS
Personal financial literacy—
7.13.E Calculate and compare simple interest and compound interest earnings.

? ESSENTIAL QUESTION

How do you calculate simple and compound interest?

Calculating Simple Interest

Recall that the money you put in a savings account is called *principal*. The bank pays you *interest* at an agreed upon *interest rate*. *Simple interest* is interest paid only on the principal, and is paid out to the person who owns the account. It is not kept on deposit to earn more interest.

Math On the Spot

(•) my.hrw.com

EXAMPLE 1   Real World

TEKS 7.13.E

Roberto's parents open a savings account for him on his birthday. The account earns simple interest at an annual rate of 5%. They deposit $100 and will deposit $100 on each birthday after that. Roberto will make no withdrawals from the account for at least 10 years. Make a table to show how the interest accumulates over five years.

Deposit phase	Beginning balance for new phase $	Amount deposited $	New balance $	Interest rate %	Amount of interest earned $
1	0	100	100	5	5
2	100	100	200	5	10
3	200	100	300	5	15
4	300	100	400	5	20
5	400	100	500	5	25
				Total	75

Roberto earns a total of $75 in interest over the five years.

Reflect

1. **Make a Prediction** Predict how much simple interest Roberto will have earned after the tenth year. Suppose he continues to make no withdrawals. _____

YOUR TURN

2. Each year Amy deposits $100 into an account that earns simple interest at an annual rate of 8%. How much interest will she earn over the first five years? How much will be in her account after that time? _____

Personal
Math Trainer
Online Assessment and Intervention
(•) my.hrw.com

Lesson 13.2 **411**

Calculating Compound Interest

Most banks pay **compound interest**. That is, interest earned is kept on deposit to earn more interest. Compound interest is computed on the entire amount in the account, including the principal, and any previously interest earned.

EXAMPLE 2 *Real World*

TEKS 7.13.E

On Claudia's birthday, her parents open a savings account and deposit $100. They also deposit $100 each year after that on her birthday. The account earns interest at an annual rate of 5% compounded annually. Claudia will make no withdrawals from the account for at least 10 years. Make a table to find the ending balance in Claudia's account after 5 years.

Deposit phase	Beginning balance for new phase $	Amount deposited $	New balance $	Interest rate %	Amount of interest earned $	Ending balance $
1	0.00	100	100.00	5	5.00	105.00
2	105.00	100	205.00	5	10.25	215.25
3	215.25	100	315.25	5	15.76	331.01
4	331.01	100	431.01	5	21.55	452.56
5	452.56	100	552.56	5	27.63	580.19

The total amount in the account at the end of the fifth year is $580.19.

Math Talk
Mathematical Processes

How can you find the total amount of interest that accumulates over the five years?

Reflect

3. Does the balance of Claudia's account change by the same amount each year? Explain why or why not.

_____

_____

_____

4. Would the total amount in the account after 5 years be greater if the interest rate were higher? Explain.

_____

_____

YOUR TURN

5. **What If?** Suppose the interest rate on Claudia's account is 6% instead of 5%. How much will Claudia have in her account at the end of the fifth year? How does it compare to the amount in Example 2?

_____

© Houghton Mifflin Harcourt Publishing Company

Comparing Simple and Compound Interest

Math On the Spot
⊙ my.hrw.com

You can use a formula for compound interest compounded annually to solve problems.

Compound Interest Compounded Annually

$A = P(1 + r)^t$, where P is the principal (the original amount deposited), r is the interest rate expressed as a decimal, t is the time in years, and A is the amount in the account after t years if no withdrawals are made.

EXAMPLE 3 Real World

TEKS 7.13.E

Jane has two savings accounts, Account S and Account C. Both accounts are opened with an initial deposit of $100 and an annual interest rate of 5%. No additional deposits are made, and no withdrawals are made. Account S earns simple interest, and Account C earns interest compounded annually. Which account will earn more interest after 10 years? How much more?

STEP 1 Find the total interest earned by Account S after 10 years.

Find the amount of interest earned in *one* year.

Principal	×	Interest rate	=	Interest for 1 year
$100	×	0.05	=	$5

Find the amount of interest earned in *ten* years.

Interest for 1 year	×	Number of years	=	Interest for 10 years
$5	×	10	=	$50

Account S will earn $50 after 10 years.

STEP 2 Find the final amount in Account C. Then subtract the principal to find the amount of interest earned.

$(1 + 0.05)^{10}$ means you have 10 factors of 1.05.

$A = P(1 + r)^t$ Use the compound interest formula.

$= 100 \times (1 + 0.05)^{10}$ Substitute 100 for P, 0.05 for r, 10 for t.

$= 162.89$ Calculate. Round to the nearest cent.

Account C will earn $162.89 − $100.00 = $62.89 after 10 years.

STEP 3 Compare the amounts using subtraction: $62.89 − $50 = $12.89

Account C earns $12.89 more in compound interest after 10 years than Account S earns in simple interest.

Animated Math
⊙ my.hrw.com

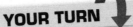

YOUR TURN

6. **What If?** Suppose the accounts in Example 3 both have interest rates of 4.5%. Which account will earn more interest after 10 years? How much more?

_____

Guided Practice

1. Each year on the same day, Hasan deposits $150 in a savings account that earns simple interest at an annual rate of 3%. He makes no other deposits or withdrawals. How much interest does his account earn after one year? After two years? After five years? (Example 1)

_____

Keri deposits $100 in an account every year on the same day. She makes no other deposits or withdrawals. The account earns an annual rate of 4% compounded annually. Complete the table. (Example 2)

	Deposit phase	Beginning balance for new phase $	Amount deposited $	New balance $	Interest rate %	Amount of interest earned $	Ending balance $
2.	1	0.00	100	100.00	4		
3.	2	104.00	100		4		
4.	3		100		4		
5.	4		100		4		
6.	5		100		4		

7. Theo deposits $2,000 deposit in a savings account earning compound interest at an annual rate of 5% compounded annually. He makes no additional deposits or withdrawals. Use the formula for compound interest to find the amount in the account after 10 years. (Example 3)

_____

(?) ESSENTIAL QUESTION CHECK-IN

8. Describe the difference between simple interest and compound interest.

_____

_____

_____

13.2 Independent Practice

TEKS 7.13.E

Personal
Math Trainer

Online
Assessment and
Intervention

my.hrw.com

Mia borrowed $5,000 from her grandparents to pay college expenses. She pays them $125 each month, and simple interest at an annual rate of 5% on the remaining balance of the loan at the end of each year.

9. How many months will it take her to pay the loan off? Explain.

_____

10. For how many years will she pay interest? Explain.

_____

_____

_____

_____

11. How much simple interest will she pay her grandparents altogether? Explain.

_____

_____

12. Roman saves $500 each year in an account earning interest at an annual rate of 4% compounded annually. How much interest will the account earn at the end of each of the first 3 years?

_____

13. Jackson started a savings account with $25. He plans to deposit $25 each month for the next 12 months, then continue those monthly deposits in following years. The account earns interest at an annual rate of 4% compounded annually, based on his final yearly balance. Fill in the chart to find out how much money he will have in the account after 3 years.

Deposit phase	Beginning balance for new phase $	Amount deposited by year end $	New balance $	Interest rate %	Amount of interest earned $	Ending balance $
1	25.00	300.00	325.00	4		
2						
3						

14. **Communicate Mathematical Ideas** Look back at Exercise 13. Suppose Jackson increased the initial deposit by $75, but made the same monthly deposits. Would the balance at the end of every year increase by $75?

_____

_____

_____

15. Account A and Account B both have a principal of $1,000 and an annual interest rate of 4%. No additional deposits or withdrawals are made. Account A earns simple interest. Account B earns interest compounded annually. Compare the amounts in the two accounts after 20 years. Which earns more interest? How much more?

_____

 FOCUS ON HIGHER ORDER THINKING

16. **Justify Reasoning** Luisa deposited $2,000 in an account earning simple interest at an annual rate of 5%. She made no additional deposits and no withdrawals. When she closed the account, she had earned a total of $2,000 in interest. How long was the account open?

_____

_____

17. **Draw Conclusions** Amanda deposits $500 into a savings account earning simple interest at an annual rate of 8%. Tori deposits $1,000 into a savings account earning simple interest at an annual rate of 2.5%. Neither girl makes any additional deposits or withdrawals. Which girl's account will reach a balance of $1,500 first? Justify your answer.

_____

_____

_____

_____

18. **Persevere in Problem Solving** Gary invested $1,000 in an account earning interest at an annual rate of 5% compounded annually. Each year, he deposited an additional $1,000, and made no withdrawals. When he closed the account, he had a balance of $4,525.64. Make a table similar to the one in Example 2 to help you estimate how long the money was in the account. How much interest would Gary earn in that same time if he invests $10,000 and deposits $10,000 into the account each year?

_____

Making Purchasing Decisions

TEKS
Personal financial literacy—7.13.F Analyze and compare monetary incentives, including sales, rebates, and coupons.

? ESSENTIAL QUESTION

How do you decide on the best purchase among various options?

Using Unit Prices

You often need to make purchasing decisions based upon price. Finding the lower unit price is often the way to determine the better buy.

EXAMPLE 1 *Real World*

TEKS 7.13.F

Math On the Spot
⊙ my.hrw.com

Silvie went to a local warehouse store to buy her family's favorite sports drink. Which of the two options described below is the better buy?

Value Pack	Sport Pack
24 0.5-liter bottles	18 0.75-liter bottles
$9.24	$11.88

STEP 1 Find the total amount of the sports drink in each purchase.

> Multiply the number of bottles by the number of ounces.

Value Pack: 24(0.5) = 12 liters

Sport Pack: 18(0.75) = 13.5 liters

STEP 2 Find each unit price.

Value Pack

$$\frac{\$9.24}{12 \text{ liters}} = \$0.77 \text{ per liter}$$

Sports Pack

$$\frac{\$11.88}{13.5 \text{ liters}} = \$0.88 \text{ per liter}$$

The Value Pack is a better buy, because $0.77 < $0.88.

Math Talk
Mathematical Processes

Suppose a very large box of cereal has a lower unit price than a small box. Why might the small box be the better choice for you?

YOUR TURN

1. **Financial Literacy** Manny must choose between a pack of four 6.5-ounce containers of yogurt for $3.77 or three 8-ounce containers at $1.29 each. Which is the better buy? Why?

_____

_____

Personal Math Trainer
Online Assessment and Intervention
⊙ my.hrw.com

Analyzing Sales

Sales and discounts may affect your choice when considering several purchase options. Some discounts are fixed amounts, while others are percents or fractions of the original price.

EXAMPLE 2 (Real World)

TEKS 7.13.F

Nathan plans on hiking this summer and wants to buy a solar charger for his cell phone and notebook computer. He finds the charger that he wants at two stores. Which store has the lower price for the charger?

	Regular price	Discount
Kitt's	$89.99	30% off
Rec Plus	$79.99	$15 off

STEP 1 Find the discount price at each store.

Kitt's

$$\frac{\text{discount}}{\text{price}} = \frac{\text{regular} - \text{discount}}{\text{price}}$$
$$= \$89.99 - 0.3(\$89.99)$$
$$= \$89.99 - \$26.997$$
$$= \$62.993$$

To the nearest cent, the discount price at Kitt's is $62.99.

Rec Plus

$$\frac{\text{discount}}{\text{price}} = \frac{\text{regular} - \text{discount}}{\text{price}}$$
$$= \$79.99 - \$15.00$$
$$= \$64.99$$

The discount price at Rec Plus is $64.99.

STEP 2 Compare the discounted prices.

Kitt's offers the lower price, because $62.99 < $64.99.

Reflect

2. **Critical Thinking** Why might Nathan choose the higher priced item?

_____

_____

_____

YOUR TURN

3. Nathan finds a backpack at Kitt's that is regularly $84.99, but is on sale for $\frac{1}{3}$ off. The same backpack is regularly $72.99 at Rec Plus but is on sale for 25% off. Which is a better buy? Explain.

_____

Comparing Sales, Rebates, and Coupons

When you buy an item on sale or use a discount coupon, you pay less than full price for the item and generally pay tax on the sale price. When you get a *rebate*, you usually pay full price for the item and the tax on that price, and then get a refund later.

EXAMPLE 3 🌎 *Real World*   TEKS 7.13.F

Cedelia can get the same running shoes at two different stores. She wants to get two pairs of the same style. Which is the better buy?

Go Run	Shoe Shoppe
Reg. price: $109	Reg. price: $89
Take $5 off 1 pair.	Mail-in rebate: $30 per pair (limit 2)
Buy 1 pair, get 1 pair free.	

Go Run

Regular price: $109

$5 off: − 5

Total: $104

Shoe Shoppe

Regular price: $89

Rebate: − 30

Total: $59

She pays $104 for 2 pairs.   She pays 2 × $59 = $118 for 2 pairs.

Go Run has the better buy because $104 < $118.

Reflect

4. What If? Suppose the total price at Shoe Shoppe had been $103? What are some conditions of a rebate that would make it a better decision to buy the shoes at Go Run?

_____

_____

_____

YOUR TURN

5. Greta wants to buy 3 jars of honey. Food Mart sells it for $8.99 with a "Buy 2, get 1 free" offer. Leona's sells it for $8.49 with a coupon for 50% off with a limit of 2 coupons. Which store has the better deal?

_____

Personal Math Trainer

Online Assessment and Intervention

my.hrw.com

Which is the better buy? Write an inequality to justify your answer.

1. The Corner Store sells 4 bottles of energy drink for $11.56. Bev's sells 6 bottles for $17.94. Which is the better buy? (Example 1)

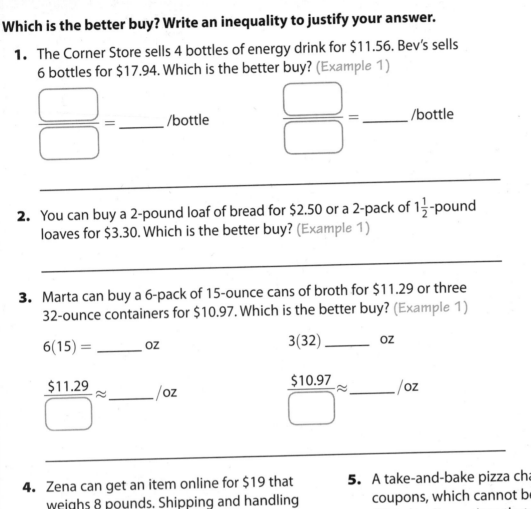

$\dfrac{\boxed{}}{\boxed{}}$ = _____ /bottle $\dfrac{\boxed{}}{\boxed{}}$ = _____ /bottle

_____

2. You can buy a 2-pound loaf of bread for $2.50 or a 2-pack of $1\frac{1}{2}$-pound loaves for $3.30. Which is the better buy? (Example 1)

_____

3. Marta can buy a 6-pack of 15-ounce cans of broth for $11.29 or three 32-ounce containers for $10.97. Which is the better buy? (Example 1)

6(15) = _____ oz   3(32) _____ oz

$\dfrac{\$11.29}{\boxed{}} \approx$ _____ /oz $\dfrac{\$10.97}{\boxed{}} \approx$ _____ /oz

_____

4. Zena can get an item online for $19 that weighs 8 pounds. Shipping and handling costs $0.49 per pound. She can also buy the same item locally for $26.95, and she has a $5 off coupon. Which is the better buy? (Example 2)

_____

5. A take-and-bake pizza chain has several coupons, which cannot be used together. J.D. is buying a pizza that costs $17.90. Should he use a $5 off coupon or a 35% off coupon? (Example 2)

_____

6. The King family buys an HDTV selling for $825 at PanView with a 20% off coupon and a rebate of $125. They later see the TV on sale at Rey's TVs for $555. Did they get the better deal? (Example 3)

_____

7. Credit card A has an annual fee of $50 but gives you a rebate at the end of the year of 2% of your total purchases. Credit card B has no annual fee or rebate. If you spend about $150 a month, which card is better for you? (Example 3)

_____

? ESSENTIAL QUESTION CHECK-IN

8. Is the lower unit price always the best buy?

_____

_____

13.3 Independent Practice

Personal Math Trainer

Online Assessment and Intervention

my.hrw.com

TEKS 7.13.F

9. Store 1 has a price of $99 on an MP3 player. Store 2 is offering the same MP3 player at a sale price of 25% off their regular price of $125. Jerusha wants to buy an MP3 player. From which store should she buy it? Explain.

_____

10. **Multistep** Randy wants trail mix for his hiking trip. The ready-made trail mix costs $8.95 for 1.5 pounds. The costs of the bulk ingredients to make one pound of trail mix are as follows: salted peanuts—$1.25, raisins—$1.70, sunflower seeds—$0.50, cashews—$0.87, and almonds—$0.65. If Randy plans to take 6 pounds of trail mix, which option is cheaper? How much does he save by choosing the cheaper option?

_____

11. Tyron and Penelope both bought 4-wheelers. Tyron paid $199 up front, and will pay the remainder in 12 payments of $50 each. Penelope paid nothing up front, and will make 18 payments of $49. Who got the better buy? Explain.

_____

12. **Financial Literacy** T'Shonda is buying a laptop computer. She will pay 8% sales tax on the price before any rebates. Where will she get a better buy? Explain.

XYZ-Tronic

Price $629
Mail-in rebate: $150

Tec-U-Comp

Reg. price $649

Discount 25% off

_____

_____

13. **Critical Thinking** What single discount is equal to a discount of $\frac{1}{4}$ off followed by an additional 10% off the sale price?

_____

14. **Make a Conjecture** John is comparing the prices of two bags of the same cereal. He notices that the larger bag holds 10 more ounces and costs $1.50 more. How can he use the unit price of the smaller bag to decide the better buy? Explain.

_____

_____

_____

15. Draw Conclusions Mr. Jaros has the following options for buying a digital video recorder and access to the recording service for 2 years.

DiV: $49.99 digital video recorder, 2-year subscription at $16.98 a month

TVU: Free digital video recorder, 2-year commitment at $19.95 a month

a. Which is the better deal? Explain.

_____

b. What If? Suppose each offer were for 1 year. Would that change your answer? Explain.

_____

c. Make a Conjecture Find the difference in monthly rates. Divide the cost of the DiV digital video recorder by the difference and round up to the nearest whole number. What does this quotient represent?

_____

_____

16. Analyze Relationships Sandy wants to buy 5 pounds of apples. She has a coupon for $1.00 off for every 3 pounds of apples. She gets to the store and discovers that apples are on sale for $0.75 a pound. Is it cheaper for her to buy 5 pounds or 6 pounds? Explain.

_____

_____

17. Draw Conclusions Two stores have a sale on T-shirts originally priced at $8.50. Yeager's has a "Buy 2, get 1 free" sale. Gample's has a 30% off sale. Dirk wants to buy only 2 T-shirts. Which is the better buy for him? Explain your reasoning.

_____

_____

18. Represent Real-World Problems Suppose you are buying books from an online store, and the total price of your books is $39. Orders of $50 or more for eligible items qualify for free shipping. Would you buy more to qualify for free shipping? Or would you check out with only the books you have in your shopping cart? Explain your answer.

_____

_____

_____

_____

13.1 Calculating Sales and Income Tax

1. Marcel bought a new hat for $21.99 and 2 pairs of socks for $3.99 each. What is the total price, including a 7.5% sales tax? _____

For 2–3, use the tax table shown. Jennifer computed her taxable income as $24,382 and paid $3,115 in federal withholding.

If line 43 (taxable income is –		And you are single
At least	**But less than**	**Your tax is –**
24,250	24,300	3,216
24,300	24,350	3,224
24,350	24,400	3,231

2. How much federal income tax is Jennifer required to pay? _____

3. Determine whether Jennifer still owes money or will get a refund,

and what amount that is. _____

13.2 Calculating and Comparing Simple and Compound Interest

4. Two savings accounts each start with a $200 principal and have an interest rate of 5%. One account earns simple interest and the other is compounded annually. Which account will earn more interest over 10 years? How much more?

_____

13.3 Making Purchasing Decisions

5. Brenda wants to buy a sweater that is regularly priced at $27. She can apply one of two coupons, $5 off or 25% off. Which should she use? _____

❓ ESSENTIAL QUESTION

6. How can you use your knowledge of taxes and simple and compound interest to help you make informed decisions in the real-world?

_____

_____

MODULE 13 MIXED REVIEW

Texas Test Prep

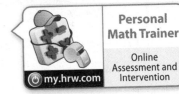

Personal
Math Trainer

Online
Assessment and
Intervention
my.hrw.com

Selected Response

1. Tela bought a backpack for $34.99 and 3 notebooks for $1.89 each. What is the total price, including a 8% sales tax?

Ⓐ $38.77
Ⓒ $41.87
Ⓑ $40.66
Ⓓ $43.91

Taylor's gross monthly pay is $2,500. Use this information for 2–4.

2. Taylor pays 15.6% of his monthly income for federal withholding. How much federal withholding does he pay?

Ⓐ $32.50
Ⓒ $390
Ⓑ $375
Ⓓ $2,110

3. How much does Taylor pay for Medicare, which is 1.45% of his monthly salary?

Ⓐ $30.56
Ⓒ $2,140.56
Ⓑ $36.25
Ⓓ $2,536.25

4. How much does Taylor pay for Social Security, which is 6.2% of his monthly salary?

Ⓐ $130.82
Ⓒ $2,240.82
Ⓑ $155
Ⓓ $2,655

5. Kit can purchase a 6-pound item from several different retailers. Which is the best buy?

Ⓐ Buy online for $24 plus pay shipping and handling costs of $0.79 per pound.

Ⓑ Buy online for $25 plus pay shipping and handling costs of $0.49 per pound.

Ⓒ Pay at a local store with a regular price of $32.95 and a $5-off coupon.

Ⓓ Pay at a local store with a regular price of $40 on sale for 25% off.

6. Each year on the same day, Lia deposits $225 in an account that earns simple interest at a rate of 4%. How much interest does her account earn after 10 years?

Ⓐ $9
Ⓒ $234
Ⓑ $90
Ⓓ $495

7. Omar deposits $300 in an account earning 3% interest compounded annually. How much interest will the account earn after 5 years if he makes no withdrawals?

Ⓐ $45
Ⓒ $345
Ⓑ $47.78
Ⓓ $347.78

Gridded Response

8. Carey computed her taxable income as $27,342 and paid $4,127 in federal withholding. Use the tax table to find the amount in dollars Carey will get as a refund.

If line 43 (taxable income is –		And you are single
At least	But less than	Your tax is –
27,200	27,250	3,659
27,250	27,300	3,666
27,300	27,350	3,674
27,350	27,400	3,681

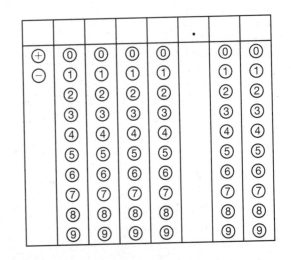

© Houghton Mifflin Harcourt Publishing Company

Planning Your Future

? ESSENTIAL QUESTION

How can you use mathematics to plan for a successful financial future?

Real-World Video

Creating and sticking to a household budget is an important part of smart spending and saving. Having a plan for how much you can spend on various expenses helps you control your debt.

my.hrw.com

GO DIGITAL
my.hrw.com

my.hrw.com

Go digital with your write-in student edition, accessible on any device.

Math On the Spot

Scan with your smart phone to jump directly to the online edition, video tutor, and more.

Animated Math

Interactively explore key concepts to see how math works.

Personal Math Trainer

Get immediate feedback and help as you work through practice sets.

Are YOU Ready?

Complete these exercises to review skills you will need for this chapter.

Personal Math Trainer
Online Assessment and Intervention
my.hrw.com

Compare and Order Decimals

EXAMPLE

tens	ones	·	tenths	hundredths	thousandths
4	6	·	0	3	8
4	6	·	0	5	1

Compare tens: $4 = 4$
Compare ones: $6 = 6$
Compare tenths: $0 = 0$
Compare hundredths: $5 > 3$
So, $46.051 > 46.038$

Compare. Write > or <.

1. 4.051 ◯ 4.501

2. 73.090 ◯ 73.089

Whole Number Operations

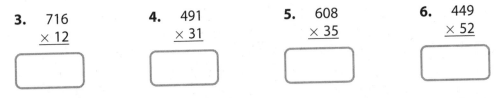

EXAMPLE

$$
\begin{array}{r}
420 \\
\times\ 58 \\
\hline
3360 \\
+\ 21000 \\
\hline
24,360
\end{array}
$$

← 8 × 420
← 50 × 420
← (8 × 420) + (50 × 420)

Find each product.

3. 716
× 12

4. 491
× 31

5. 608
× 35

6. 449
× 52

Find the Percent of a Number

EXAMPLE 15% of 70 = ?

Write the percent as a decimal. 15% = 0.15

Multiply.

$$
\begin{array}{r}
70 \\
\times\ 0.15 \\
\hline
10.5
\end{array}
$$

Find each percent.

7. 40% of 30 _____

8. 9% of 26 _____

9. 48% of 130 _____

10. 66% of 29 _____

11. 140% of 12 _____

12. 100% of 584 _____

Reading Start-Up

Visualize Vocabulary

Use the ✔ words to complete the graphic. You will put a different one in each box.

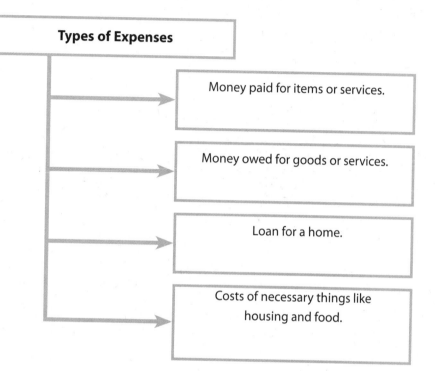

Types of Expenses

Money paid for items or services.

Money owed for goods or services.

Loan for a home.

Costs of necessary things like housing and food.

Vocabulary

Review Words

checking account (*cuenta corriente*)

✔ cost of living (*costo de vida*)

✔ credit card (*tarjeta de crédito*)

✔ debt (*deuda*)

deposit (*depósito*)

✔ expenses (*gastos*)

✔ mortgage (*hipoteca*)

salary (*salario*)

Preview Words

assets (*activos*)

budget (*presupuesto*)

fixed expenses (*gastos fijos*)

income (*ingreso*)

liabilities (*pasivo*)

net worth (*patrimonio neto*)

savings (*ahorros*)

variable expense (*gasto variable*)

Understand Vocabulary

Complete each sentence, using the preview words.

1. _____ occur regularly and stay the same.

2. A plan to help you reach your financial goals is a _____.

Active Reading

Layered Book Before beginning the module, create a layered book to help you learn the concepts in this module. At the top of the first flap, write the title of the module, "Planning Your Future." Then label each flap with one of the lesson titles in this module. As you study each lesson, write important ideas, such as vocabulary and formulas, under the appropriate flap.

Unpacking the TEKS

Understanding the TEKS and the vocabulary terms in the TEKS will help you know exactly what you are expected to learn in this module.

TEKS 7.13

Develop an economic way of thinking and problem solving useful in one's life as a knowledgeable consumer and investor.

Key Vocabulary

budget *(presupuesto)*
A plan to help you reach your financial goals.

income *(ingreso)*
The amount of money you earn.

assets *(activos)*
Things you own, which have a positive cash value.

liabilities *(pasivo)*
The debts you owe, which have a negative cash value.

net worth *(patrimonio neto)*
Difference between assets and liabilities.

What It Means to You

You will learn how each of the following standards related to 7.13 is designed to help you understand how to plan for your future.

7.13.B Identify the components of a personal budget, including income, planned savings for college, retirement, and emergencies; taxes; and fixed and variable expenses, and calculate what percent each category comprises of the total budget.

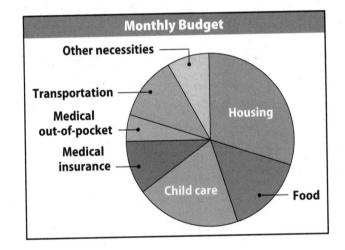

Monthly Budget

Other necessities • Transportation • Medical out-of-pocket • Medical insurance • Child care • Food • Housing

7.13.C Create and organize a financial assets and liabilities record and construct a net worth statement.

7.13.D Use a family budget estimator to determine the minimum household budget and average hourly wage needed for a family to meet its basic needs in the student's city or another large city nearby.

FOR SALE SOLD

Visit **my.hrw.com** to see all the **TEKS** unpacked.

my.hrw.com

14.1 Personal Budgets

TEKS
Personal financial literacy—7.13.B
Identify the components of a personal budget including income, planned savings for college, retirement, and emergencies, taxes, and fixed and variable expenses, and calculate what percentage each category comprises of the total budget.

? **ESSENTIAL QUESTION**

How do you identify the components of a personal budget?

EXPLORE ACTIVITY 1 Real World TEKS 7.13.B

Identifying the Components of a Personal Budget

It can be tough to reach a long-term goal without making a plan for how to get there. A **budget** is a plan to help you reach your financial goals.

Some of the components of a budget are **income**, or the amount of money you earn, and expenses, or how much you spend. Expenses can include **planned savings** for college, retirement, emergencies, and taxes. The goal of a budget is to spend no more than you earn, and save some additional money if you can.

Jenna is saving for a tablet for college. She is making a 4-week budget. The budget shows her total income and the various expenses she has, including saving for the tablet.

STEP 1 Enter the total amount that Jenna will earn babysitting for 4 weekends in the table.

Income is added to the total amount available.

Expenses are subtracted from the total amount available.

Jenna's 4-Week Budget

Description	Income (+)	Expenses (−)	Amount Available
Earnings ($25 babysitting each weekend)			$100
College fund			$80
Entertainment			
Savings for tablet			
Snacks			

STEP 2 Enter Jenna's expenses and planned savings in the Expenses column.

Expenses: entertainment—$15   snacks—$10

Planned savings: college fund—$20   tablet—$25

STEP 3 Complete the Amount Available column by adding each row of income and subtracting each row of expenses.

How much money does Jenna have available at the end of 4 weeks? What could she do with it?

_____

_____

Reflect

1. **What If?** What if Jenna misses a weekend babysitting? How would that affect the budget?

_____

_____

Math On the Spot

⏻ my.hrw.com

Identifying Types of Expenses

There are two different types of expenses: fixed expenses and variable expenses. **Fixed expenses,** such as car and house payments, occur regularly and do not change from month to month. A **variable expense,** such as purchases of food or gas, occurs regularly and is necessary for living, but you have some control over the amount.

EXAMPLE 1 Real World

TEKS 7.13.B

Math Talk
Mathematical Processes

Why do planned savings items go in the expense column instead of the income column?

A The table shows Garrett's monthly budget. To earn money, he mows lawns. Identify Garrett's fixed and variable expenses.

Garrett's Monthly Budget			
Description	**Income (+)**	**Expenses (−)**	**Amount Available**
Earnings ($30 per mowed lawn, 8 lawns)	$240		$240
Clothes		$40	$200
Monthly guitar rental fee		$15	$185
Savings for a car		$30	$155
Entertainment (movies, computer games)		$50	$105
Emergency savings		$10	$95

Fixed expenses: guitar rental fee, savings for a car, emergency savings

Variable expenses: clothes, entertainment

B The table shows Mrs. Everdeen's monthly budget. Identify Mrs. Everdeen's fixed and variable expenses.

Mrs. Everdeen's Monthly Budget			
Description	Income (+)	Expenses (−)	Amount Available
Wages	$2,500		$2,500
Taxes		$550	$1,950
Rent		$850	$1,100
Utilities (water, electricity)		$70	$1,030
Groceries & household supplies		$425	$605
Auto insurance		$50	$555
Retirement savings		$150	$405
Clothing		$100	$305

Fixed expenses: taxes, retirement savings, rent, auto insurance

Variable expenses: utilities, groceries and household supplies, clothing

Reflect

2. How are these budgets different?

_____

_____

_____

YOUR TURN

3. Malina is making a budget. The table shows the categories of expenses in her budget. In the second column of the table, use an F to mark fixed expenses and a V to mark variable expenses.

Expenses	
Snacks	
Weekly flute lesson	
Saving for a new flute	
Entertainment	
Savings for college	
Monthly bus pass	

Personal Math Trainer

Online Assessment and Intervention

my.hrw.com

Analyzing a Family Budget

One way to present a budget is in a circle graph. You can see at a glance which categories take the greatest part of the family's resources. You can also work backward from a circle graph to figure out exactly how much money is in each category.

Use the circle graph to complete the table for the Baker family's monthly budget. Their net monthly income is $4,000.

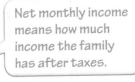
Net monthly income means how much income the family has after taxes.

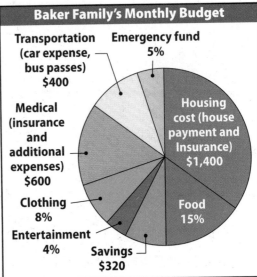

Baker Family's Monthly Budget

Transportation (car expense, bus passes) $400

Medical (insurance and additional expenses) $600

Clothing 8%

Entertainment 4%

Savings $320

Emergency fund 5%

Housing cost (house payment and Insurance) $1,400

Food 15%

STEP 1 Enter the income in the table.

STEP 2 Enter the percent or amount of money for each category from the circle graph in the table.

STEP 3 Calculate the amount of money or the percent for each category in the table.

STEP 4 Determine which expenses are fixed and which are variable. Place X's in the appropriate columns.

STEP 5 Complete the Amount Available column.

Item	Amount ($)	Percent (%)	Fixed Expense	Variable Expense	Amount Available ($)
Net monthly income					
Housing cost					
Food					
Savings					
Entertainment					
Clothing					
Medical					
Transportation					
Emergency fund					

Reflect

4. Analyze Relationships One month, the family must make an emergency car repair for $305. Are they able to pay for it out of the fixed emergency fund for that month? If not, how can they afford it?

_____

_____

_____

_____

5. The family wants to make a trip to Houston to visit the NASA Space Center. What are some ways they can save without using all of the allotted $160 for entertainment?

_____

_____

_____

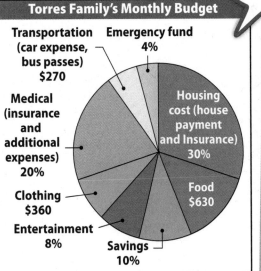

Math Talk
Mathematical Processes

What if the cost of transportation for the Torres family rises by $90? How can they adjust the budget to cover this increased cost?

YOUR TURN

For 6–8, use the circle graph of the Torres family's monthly budget. Their net monthly income is $4,500.

6. How much does the Torres family spend on housing each month?

_____

7. What percent of the budget does the Torres family spend on food? clothing?

_____

8. During a thunderstorm, lighting strikes a large tree in the Torres family's backyard. The tree needs to be removed. The cost to remove the tree is $500. Is there enough money budgeted in the allotted emergency fund? Explain. If not, how much more does the family need, and how could they find the money for it?

_____

_____

_____

Torres Family's Monthly Budget

Transportation (car expense, bus passes) $270

Emergency fund 4%

Medical (insurance and additional expenses) 20%

Housing cost (house payment and Insurance) 30%

Clothing $360

Food $630

Entertainment 8%

Savings 10%

© Houghton Mifflin Harcourt Publishing Company

Personal Math Trainer

Online Assessment and Intervention

ⓗ my.hrw.com

Sofia is creating a budget to save $250 for a week of soccer camp. She earns money by working as a mother's helper on Saturday mornings and Wednesday afternoons. She earns $20 each time she works. She wants to save $12.50 a week for the camp. Her mother wants her to save $5 a week for college. She is planning on spending $5 a week for snacks and $10 a week for entertainment.

1. Complete the table. (Explore Activity 1)

Sofia's 4-Week Budget			
Description	Income (+)	Expenses (−)	Amount Available
Earnings			
Savings for soccer camp			
Savings for college			
Entertainment			
Snacks			

2. Circle the variable expenses in Sofia's budget. (Example 1)

3. If Sofia decides to take piano lessons at the community center for $5 a week, would that be a fixed expense or a variable expense?

 (Example 1)

For 4–5, use the circle graph of the Talbot family's monthly budget. Their monthly income is $3,200.
(Explore Activity 2)

4. What percent of the Talbot family budget is spent on rent? _____

5. If the Talbots did not have to make a credit card payment, and instead put that money into savings, how much would they be able to save each month? _____

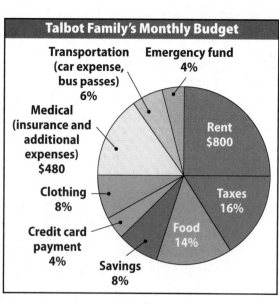

Talbot Family's Monthly Budget

Transportation (car expense, bus passes) 6%
Emergency fund 4%
Medical (insurance and additional expenses) $480
Clothing 8%
Credit card payment 4%
Savings 8%
Food 14%
Taxes 16%
Rent $800

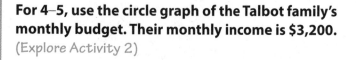

❓ ESSENTIAL QUESTION CHECK-IN

6. How does a budget help an individual or a family manage their finances?

_____

_____

_____

14.1 Independent Practice

Personal Math Trainer

Online Assessment and Intervention

my.hrw.com

TEKS 7.13.B

For 7–8, use the table.

Kareem's 4-Week Budget			
Description	Income (+)	Expenses (−)	Amount Available
Earnings	$300		
Savings for swim camp		$40	
Savings for college		$25	
Computer (software, equipment)		$50	
Entertainment (movies, sporting events)		$40	

7. Complete the Amount Available column in the table.

8. The swim camp costs $280. How long will it take Kareem to save enough for the camp? Show your work.

_____

For 9–12, use the circle graph for the Moore family's monthly budget. Their monthly income is $5,000.

9. What percent of the Moore's income goes to taxes?   _____

10. How much does the Moore family spend each year on insurance?   _____

11. Draw Conclusions Emily says that the Moore family spends $300 more on recreation than on transportation. Is she right? Explain.

_____

_____

_____

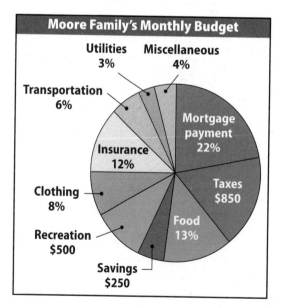

Moore Family's Monthly Budget

Utilities 3%
Miscellaneous 4%
Transportation 6%
Mortgage payment 22%
Insurance 12%
Taxes $850
Clothing 8%
Food 13%
Recreation $500
Savings $250

12. Communicate Mathematical Ideas The Moore's monthly income increases by $500, but the mortgage expense stays the same. Explain how to find what percent of the budget the mortgage payment would now be.

_____

_____

H.O.T. FOCUS ON HIGHER ORDER THINKING

The circle graph shows the Rivera family's monthly budget. Their monthly income is $4,500. The table shows the budget for the Wagner family. Their monthly income is $4,200.

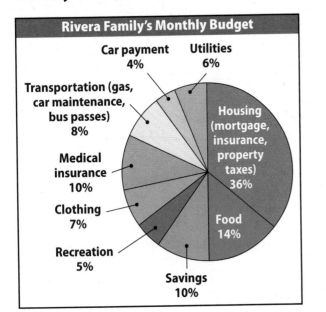

Rivera Family's Monthly Budget

- Car payment 4%
- Utilities 6%
- Transportation (gas, car maintenance, bus passes) 8%
- Medical insurance 10%
- Clothing 7%
- Recreation 5%
- Savings 10%
- Food 14%
- Housing (mortgage, insurance, property taxes) 36%

Wagner Family's Monthly Budget	
Description	**Expenses (—)**
Rent	$1,134
Medical insurance	$504
Medical expenses	$210
Transportation	$630
Food & household supplies	$588
Clothing	$252
Utilities	$336
Miscellaneous	$126
Retirement savings	$168
Emergency savings	$252

13. Analyze Relationships Which family pays a greater part of their income for transportation (including car payments)? Explain your conclusion.

_____

_____

_____

14. Multistep Over a year, which family pays more for medical insurance? How much more?

_____

_____

_____

15. Multiple Representations Compare the two budgets. What are the advantages and disadvantages of each type of presentation?

_____

_____

_____

_____

Work Area

TEKS
Personal financial literacy—7.13.D Use a family budget estimator to determine the minimum household budget and average hourly wage needed for a family to meet its basic needs in the student's city or another large city nearby.

? ESSENTIAL QUESTION

How do you plan a personal budget?

EXPLORE ACTIVITY 1 *Real World* **TEKS** 7.13.D

Exploring a Family Budget

A family budget is a financial plan based on the amount of money needed to live. In general, the total family income must meet or exceed the total family expenses. The number of children, employment benefits such as insurance, and where the family lives all affect the budget.

The Jones family includes two parents and two children. The family lives in Beaumont, Texas. They have an employer-sponsored insurance plan where the employer pays 100% of one parent's insurance premium and 50% of the rest of the family's premiums.

A The table shows the *minimum* monthly expenses, rounded to the nearest dollar, for the family. The data is based on an online family budget estimator. Use this information to fill out the first column of rows 1–7 of the form given on the next page.

Jones Family's Monthly Expenses	
Description	**Expense ($)**
Housing	$593
Food	$491
Child Care	$594
Medical Costs (insurance and out of pocket expenses)	$462
Transportation	$322
Other Necessities	$309
Total Monthly Expenses	**$2,771**
Federal Taxes (payroll and income)	$282
Federal Tax Credits	(−$345)
Necessary Monthly Income (including taxes and credits)	**$2,708**
Household Hourly Wage	**$16**

Tax credits help give back money to families. A *tax credit* is deducted from the total amount a taxpayer owes.

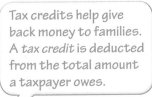

Household hourly wage is the necessary *combined* hourly wage needed for the family.

Family Name _____   City or Town _____

Number of Parents _____   Number of Children _____

Employer Paid Insurance (y/n) _____

Description	Minimum Monthly Budget Estimate	Actual Budget
1. Housing		
2. Food		
3. Childcare		
4. Medical Costs		
5. Transportation		
6. Other Necessities		
7. Total Federal Tax Impact		
8. Retirement Savings (9% of monthly income)		
9. Emergency Fund (3% of monthly income)		
10. College Savings: $30 per child		

> To find the total federal tax impact, find the sum of the federal taxes and federal tax credits. This can be a negative number, which is considered a credit.

B What is the combined household hourly wage for the Joneses? What does this mean if both parents are looking for a job and Mr. Jones finds a job paying $10 per hour?

_____

_____

C The Joneses earn $600 more each month than the necessary monthly income. This allows them to save for retirement, emergencies, and college. Complete the chart for 8–10.

Personal Math Trainer

Online Assessment and Intervention

my.hrw.com

YOUR TURN

1. Mr. Wilson and his daughter Shannon live in El Paso, Texas. Mr. Wilson's employer pays 100% of his health insurance premium and 50% of his daughter's. Use an online family budget estimator to estimate the minimum necessary monthly income and the hourly household wage for this family.

_____

Exploring a Family Budget in Different Cities

Living in different parts of the country or the state can mean different budgets for even the same family. This may be because housing is more expensive in one area compared to another, or perhaps transportation costs are generally higher because most people live in the suburbs and have a further commute to work.

The Jones family is considering a move to the Dallas–Fort Worth area. The table shows the expenses from the table in Activity 1, as well as the data from an online family budget estimator for living in the Dallas–Fort Worth area.

Math Talk
Mathematical Processes

How might you determine if one online estimator is more accurate or reliable than another?

A Fill in the missing blanks for the Dallas–Fort Worth area. Round to the nearest dollar.

Beaumont, Texas		Dallas–Fort Worth, Texas	
Description	**Expense ($)**	**Description**	**Expense ($)**
Housing	$593	Housing	$781
Food	$491	Food	$491
Childcare	$594	Childcare	$1,021
Medical Costs	$462	Medical Costs	$462
Transportation	$322	Transportation	$403
Other Necessities	$309	Other Necessities	$360
Total Monthly Expenses	**$2,771**	**Total Monthly Expenses**	
Federal Taxes (payroll and income)	$282	Federal Taxes (payroll and income)	$492
Federal Tax Credits	(−$345)	Federal Tax Credits	(−$267)
Total Required Income	**$2,708**	**Total Required Income**	
Household Hourly Wage	$16	Household Hourly Wage	$22

B Compare the cost of living in Beaumont to the cost of living in the Dallas–Fort Worth area.

_____

_____

_____

Animated Math

⏱ my.hrw.com

© Houghton Mifflin Harcourt Publishing Company

YOUR TURN

2. Mr. Wilson and his daughter are thinking of moving to Austin. Use an online family budget estimator to compare the monthly required income in Austin with your results for the monthly required income you found for the Wilsons in El Paso.

_____

_____

_____

Guided Practice

1. Mr. and Mrs. Dominguez have three children. They live in Corpus Christi, Texas. Their employers do not pay any of their health insurance. Use an online family budget estimator to estimate each of the following for the Dominguez family. Fill in the chart for Corpus Christi. (Explore Activity 1)

Description	Corpus Christi, TX Expenses ($)	Lubbock, TX Expenses ($)
Housing		
Food		
Child Care		
Medical Costs		
Transportation		
Other Necessities		
Total Monthly Expenses		
Total Federal Tax Impact		
Necessary monthly income		
Household Hourly Wage		

2. Complete the chart to show how the Dominguez family's budget might change if they move to Lubbock, TX. (Explore Activity 2).

3. How does the amount needed to live in Lubbock differ from the amount needed to live in Corpus Christi? (Explore Activity 2)

_____

_____

14.2 Independent Practice

TEKS 7.13.D

Personal Math Trainer

Online Assessment and Intervention

my.hrw.com

4. **Multistep** Andre and his parents are comparing family budgets in Midland, Texas, and San Antonio, Texas. Andre does not have any siblings. His parents have an employer-sponsored health plan.

   a. Use an online family budget estimator to complete the table.

Item	Midland, TX	San Antonio, TX
Housing		
Food		
Child Care		
Medical Costs		
Transportation		
Other Necessities		
Total Monthly Expenses		
Necessary Monthly Income		
Necessary Annual Income		

   b. How do the monthly expenses in San Antonio compare to those in Midland?

   _____

   _____

   _____

   _____

5. **Justify Reasoning** Jolene and her two children live in Texarkana, Texas. Jolene has employer-sponsored health insurance. She earns an annual salary of $68,000. How does her monthly income compare to the necessary monthly income to live in Texarkana? Use an online family budget estimator to estimate the necessary monthly income. Explain your thinking.

   _____

   _____

   _____

6. Choose a city in Texas that you would like to live in as a single adult, after graduating from college. Use an online family budget estimator to compare possible budgets with and without employer-sponsored health insurance.

Description	With health insurance	Without health insurance
Housing		
Food		
Medical Costs		
Transportation		
Other Necessities		
Total Monthly Expenses		
Necessary Monthly Income		
Household Hourly Wage		

 FOCUS ON HIGHER ORDER THINKING

7. Draw Conclusions Luke earns an hourly wage of $14 and works 160 hours per month. He is a single adult living in Odessa, Texas. He does not have employer-sponsored health insurance. Luke's expenses follow the budget outlined in an online family budget estimator, except that his rent is $435 and he spends about $230 on other necessities. Does Luke have enough additional money each month to buy a computer with monthly payments of $216? Explain.

_____

_____

_____

8. Analyze Relationships The Richardson family has two parents and two children. Their company is opening branches in Houston, McAllen, and Denison. The family needs to move to one of the cities. They use an online family budget estimator for no employer insurance to help compare living expenses in each city. In Houston, they estimate they will exceed the estimated budget by $1,600. The salary offer for Houston is $68,000. In McAllen, they estimate they will exceed the estimated budget by $1,300. The salary offer for McAllen is $62,000. In Denison, they estimate they will exceed the estimated budget by $1,400. The salary offer for Denison is $67,000. If the family wants to save as much money as possible, which city should they choose? Explain.

_____

_____

Work Area

Constructing a Net Worth Statement

TEKS
Personal financial literacy— 7.13.C Create and organize a financial assets and liabilities record and construct a net worth statement.

ESSENTIAL QUESTION

How do you create a net worth statement?

EXPLORE ACTIVITY  TEKS 7.13.C

Identifying Financial Assets and Liabilities

Assets are the things you own. They have a positive cash value. Examples of assets are goods that are paid for and owned, such as houses, cars or bicycles, positive bank accounts, and savings bonds.

Liabilities are the debts you owe. They have a negative cash value. Examples of liabilities are car loans, house mortgages, credit card debt, or student loans.

For each description in the table below, decide whether the item is an asset or a liability. Explain your reasoning.

Description	Asset or Liability	Reasoning
Money in a savings account	Asset	It is money I have saved to use at a later time.
Car loan	Liability	I owe the bank money for the car.
Mountain bike		I own the bike.
Rent		
Credit card bill	Liability	
Savings bond	Asset	

Math Talk
Mathematical Processes

Is the money you have in your wallet an asset or a liability? Explain.

Reflect

1. **Critical Thinking** How do you decide if something like a computer is an asset or a liability?

_____

_____

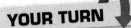

YOUR TURN

Determine whether each described item is an asset or a liability. Explain your reasoning.

2. George leases a car for $175 per month.

_____

_____

3. Morgana pays cash for a new flat screen television.

_____

_____

Constructing a Net Worth Statement

Net worth is the difference between assets and liabilities. In personal finance, the value of a person's assets minus the value of all of a person's liabilities will give their net worth.

EXAMPLE 1 *Real World*   TEKS 7.13.C

Use the information below to construct a net worth statement to find Toni's current net worth.

Toni paid off her motorcycle, which is worth $6,000. She owes 12 monthly installments of $65 each for her computer. She pays $45 per month for her cell phone and her contract lasts 1 year. She has $584 in her checking account and $1,255 in her savings account. Toni owes $173 on her credit card. Her electronic appliances are valued at $1,641. Her share of the rent and utilities for the apartment she shares with roommates is $425 per month, and her lease lasts for another 6 months.

STEP 1 List and total Toni's assets.

Description	Value
Motorcycle	$6,000
Checking account	$584
Savings account	$1,255
Electronic appliances	$1,641
Total	**$9,480**

Math Talk

Mathematical Processes

If an item has a value of a certain amount but money is still owed on it, how can you find the net worth of the item?

© Houghton Mifflin Harcourt Publishing Company • Image Credits: ©Design Pics Inc./Alamy Images

STEP 2 List and total Toni's liabilities.

Description	Value
Computer payments	$780
Cell phone bill	$540
Credit card debt	$173
Rent and utilities	$2,550
Total	**$4,043**

$65 × 12 = $780

$45 × 12 = $540

$425 × 6 = $2,550

STEP 3 Subtract total liabilities from total assets to find Toni's net worth.

Net worth = value of assets − value of liabilities

Net worth = $9,480 − $4,043   *Substitute the values.*

Net worth = $5,437   *Subtract.*

Toni's current net worth is $5,437.

Reflect

4. **Critical Thinking** Why is the monthly payment for Toni's computer loan multiplied by 12 to find the total liability?

   _____

   _____

   _____

5. **What If?** What if Toni did not own her motorcycle? Suppose she bought it with a loan and must make monthly payments of $240 per month for 2 more years. How will this change her current net worth? Explain.

   _____

   _____

   _____

   _____

Math Talk
Mathematical Processes

What does it mean to have a negative net worth? Explain.

YOUR TURN

6. Andre owns a condominium with a value of $145,000. He has a stock portfolio worth $8,300. He owes $3,700 on his car, which is valued at $9,500. He has $7,200 in student loans to repay. He has a credit card balance of $4,372. He also has $2,600 in a bank account. Construct a net worth statement to find Andre's net worth.

   _____

Personal Math Trainer

Online Assessment and Intervention

ⓦ my.hrw.com

1. Complete the table below. For each description, either decide whether the item is an asset or a liability or explain the reasoning. (Explore Activity)

Description	Asset or Liability	Reasoning
Home mortgage		It is money I must pay every month.
Car		I own the car.
Checking account		It is money I have earned.
College tuition		It is money I must pay to attend college.
Furniture	Asset	
Monthly gym membership	Liability	

2. Rachel lives in a home with a value of $195,000 and has a mortgage of $160,000. She has electronic equipment worth $2,325. She is paying off the equipment with a loan of $875. Her car, which she owns, is worth $9,300. She has $6,890 in a bank account and $1,437 on her credit card. She owes $4,800 in student loans. She has a piano worth $1,200. Construct a net worth statement to find Rachel's net worth. (Example 1)

STEP 1 List Rachel's assets and their values.

_____

_____

STEP 2 Find the total of Rachel's assets. _____

STEP 3 List Rachel's liabilities and their values.

_____

_____

STEP 4 Find the total of Rachel's liabilities. _____

STEP 5 Find Rachel's net worth.

Net worth = _____ − _____

Rachel's net worth is _____.

? ESSENTIAL QUESTION CHECK-IN

3. How can you calculate your net worth?

_____

14.3 Independent Practice

Personal Math Trainer

Online Assessment and Intervention

my.hrw.com

4. Communicate Mathematical Ideas Travis pays cash for an e-reader. The value of the e-reader is $1,200. He buys a stereo system with his credit card. The value of the stereo system is $2,300. Is the e-reader an asset or a liability? Is the stereo system an asset or a liability? Explain.

_____

_____

_____

5. Estimate your net worth.

a. Create a table like the one below. List your assets. Include items such as your clothes, shoes, furniture, electronics (for example, a computer or a stereo), sports equipment, a musical instrument, money in a savings account, and savings bonds. Estimate the values.

Description	Value
Total	

b. Create a table like the one below. List your liabilities. Include items such as any money borrowed from your parents, pre-ordering video games, or belonging to a club with monthly dues. Estimate the values.

Description	Value
Total	

c. What is your approximate net worth? _____

6. Analyze Relationships In 2011, according to the Federal Reserve, the median net worth of people under age 35 was $14,200. The median net worth of those from 35 to 44 was $69,400.

a. About how many times as great was the net worth of those from 35 to 44 as compared to those under 35?

_____

b. Why do you think the median net worth is so much greater?

_____

_____

7. Critique Reasoning Paul has a stock portfolio worth $21,000. His home is valued at $325,000. His car is valued at $18,000. He owes $322,000 on his mortgage and $16,250 on his car loan. His credit card debt is $11,750. He owes student loans of $17,300. Because the value of his home and his car exceed their loans and his stock portfolio exceeds his credit card and student loan debt, Paul says he has a positive net worth. Is this true? Explain.

_____

_____

_____

_____

8. Explain the Error Jessie wants to buy a guitar. She has enough money in her bank accounts to pay cash for a new guitar for $1,150 or a used guitar for $500. Jessie wants to choose the guitar that has a better impact on her net worth. Why is this not a good approach for making the decision?

_____

_____

_____

_____

9. Multistep Carla has a scooter worth $3,200. Her computer is worth $900. She owes $800 on her scooter and $483 on her credit card. Her personal property has a value of $2,100. She has $3,000 in her bank accounts and a mutual fund valued at $4,600. She wants to take out a $2,800 loan to buy some new appliances. The value of the appliances after purchase will go down 20%. How will the purchase of the appliances change Carla's net worth? Explain.

_____

_____

_____

_____

10. Critical Thinking Do you think it is a good idea to track net worth monthly? Why?

_____

_____

_____

_____

Ready to Go On?

Personal Math Trainer

Online Assessment and Intervention

⏻ my.hrw.com

14.1 Personal Budgets

For 1–3, use the following information on the Plimpton family's monthly budget.

Their net monthly income is $4,500. They have an emergency fund that is 6% of their monthly budget and they have a savings of 7% per month. Medical costs are $675 per month, housing is $1,485, and transportation costs $450. Food accounts for 17% of the monthly budget and they spend 5% on entertainment. They also spend 7% of the budget on clothing each month.

1. How much does the Plimpton family spend on clothing each month? _____

2. How much does the Plimpton family spend on entertainment each year? _____

3. How much more does the Plimpton family spend on food than on savings each month? _____

4. What percent of the net monthly income goes to housing? _____

14.2 Planning a Budget

5. Ms. Wofford and her two sons live in Lubbock, Texas, where she makes $3,200 a month. She is thinking of transferring to Abilene and uses an online family budget estimator to see her potential monthly expenses. Use the table below. Is a transfer to Abilene a good financial move for the Woffords? Explain.

Description	Lubbock Monthly Budget Estimate	Abilene Monthly Budget Estimate
Total monthly expenses	$2,951	$2,775
Necessary monthly income	$3,111	$2,812

_____

_____

14.3 Constructing a Net Worth Statement

6. Calvin lives in a home with a value of $185,000 and has a mortgage of $145,000. He has a stock portfolio worth $11,700. He owns his car, which is valued at $10,500. He has $15,300 in student loans to repay. He has a credit card balance of $6,228. He also has $3,400 in a bank account. What is Calvin's net worth? _____

Selected Response

1. Which of the following is an example of income?

   Ⓐ insurance

   Ⓑ emergency savings

   Ⓒ wages

   Ⓓ taxes

2. Which of the following is an example of a variable expense?

   Ⓐ weekly martial arts lesson

   Ⓑ rent

   Ⓒ entertainment

   Ⓓ monthly bus pass

3. A boating company on the lake charges a $10 equipment fee and $5.50 per hour to rent a canoe. Write the equation of the linear relationship.

   Ⓐ $y = 10x + 5.5$

   Ⓑ $y = 10x + 55$

   Ⓒ $y = 55x + 10$

   Ⓓ $y = 5.5x + 10$

4. Barry owns a home with a value of $170,000. He owes $4,400 on his car, which is valued at $11,500. He has $9,500 in student loans to repay. He owns $3,300 worth of musical equipment. He has a credit card balance of $2,117. He also has $2,900 in a bank account. What is Barry's net worth?

   Ⓐ $157,483   Ⓒ $171,683

   Ⓑ $165,883   Ⓓ $175,917

5. Which of the following is an example of an asset?

   Ⓐ car loan   Ⓒ credit card bill

   Ⓑ savings bond   Ⓓ rent

Gridded Response

6. The Garza family consists of two adults and two children. Their current monthly income is $4,800. The circle graph shows their monthly budget. How much money in dollars do the Garzas spend on housing each month?

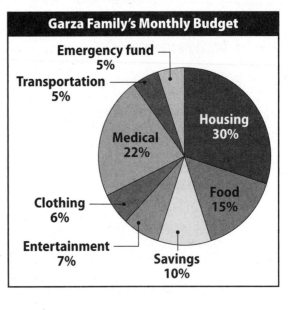

Garza Family's Monthly Budget

Emergency fund 5%
Transportation 5%
Medical 22%
Housing 30%
Clothing 6%
Food 15%
Entertainment 7%
Savings 10%

 **MODULE 13** Taxes, Interest, and Incentives

Key Vocabulary

compound interest (*interés compuesto*)

federal withholding (*retención fiscal federal*)

gross pay (*paga bruta*)

interest (*interés*)

net pay (*paga neta*)

sales tax (*impuesto sobre la venta*)

simple interest (*interés simple*)

taxable income (*ingreso sujeto a impuestos*)

? ESSENTIAL QUESTION

How can you solve real-world problems involving taxes, interest, and incentives?

EXAMPLE 1

Samuel puts $5,000 into a savings account that earns simple interest at an annual rate of 1.2% for 5 years. Tinos puts the same amount into a savings account that earns interest at an annual rate of 1.2% compounded annually for 5 years. Which account will earn more interest after 5 years?

Samuel

Use the formula for simple interest.

$I = P \times r \times t$

$I = \$5,000 \times 0.012 \times 5 = \$300$

Samuel earns $300 in interest.

Tinos

Use the formula for compound interest.

$A = P(1 + r)^t$

$A = \$5,000(1.012)^5 = \$5,307.29$

Tinos earns $5,307.29 − $5,000 = $307.29.

Tinos's account will earn more interest than Samuel's account.

EXERCISES

1. Find the sales tax for each product, using a sales tax rate of 8.5%. Then find the product's total price and the total for the entire purchase. Round to the nearest hundredth. (Lesson 13.1)

Item	Unit Price ($)	Number	Subtotal ($)	Tax ($)	Total ($)
Basketball	8.95	3	26.85		
Tennis balls (3 pack)	3.88	5	19.40		
				Total	

2. Claire earns a monthly paycheck of $2,900. Federal withholding is 12.8% of her gross pay. Complete the table. (Lesson 13.1)

Gross Pay	
Taxes	
Federal Income Tax	
Social Security	$179.80
Medicare	$42.05
Net Pay	

3. Bette has $10,000 to put into savings accounts. She puts half into an account that earns simple interest at an annual rate of 3.1%. She puts the other half into an account that earns interest at an annual rate of 2.6% compounded annually. After 10 years, which account will earn more money? How much more? *(Lesson 13.2)*

_____

4. Barack can buy a four pack of mangos for $2.76 or a six pack of mangos for $4.32. Which is the better buy? Explain. *(Lesson 13.3)*

_____

_____

MODULE **14** **Planning Your Future**

? ESSENTIAL QUESTION

How can you use mathematics to plan for a successful financial future?

EXAMPLE 1

The circle graph shows the Morales family's monthly budget. Their fixed expenses are housing, savings, and an emergency fund. Use the graph to find the amount the family spends on fixed expenses.

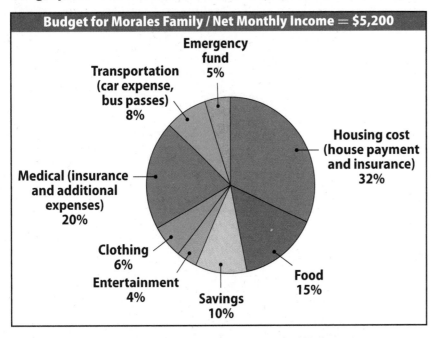

Budget for Morales Family / Net Monthly Income = $5,200

Emergency fund 5%
Transportation (car expense, bus passes) 8%
Housing cost (house payment and insurance) 32%
Medical (insurance and additional expenses) 20%
Clothing 6%
Entertainment 4%
Savings 10%
Food 15%

Item	Percent	Amount Available
Housing cost	32%	$1,664
Savings	10%	$520
Emergency fund	5%	$260

EXERCISES

For 1–3, use the graph from the Example. (Lessons 14.1)

1. How much money does the Morales family spend on clothing each month?

   _____

2. How much more money does the Morales family spend on food than on entertainment?

   _____

3. The air conditioning in the Morales's house is broken. The repair service estimated that the cost of repairing it is $1,040. How many months of emergency funds will the family use to fix the air conditioning?

   _____

4. Mr. and Mrs. Clark have two children. They live in Waco, Texas. They may move to Austin to be closer to their parents. Their employers pay for 100% of one parent's health insurance premium and 50% of the premium for other family members. Use an online family budget estimator to estimate to the nearest dollar, the following for the Clark family in Waco and in Austin. (Lesson 14.2)

   _____

Item	Monthly Estimated Budget for Waco ($)	Monthly Estimated Budget for Austin ($)
Housing		
Food		
Child Care		
Medical Insurance		
Medical Out-of-pocket		
Transportation		
Other Necessities		
Total monthly expenses		
Total Federal Tax Impact		
Necessary monthly income		
Household Hourly Wage		

5. Rashid paid off his car, which is worth $6,500. He has a credit card balance of $325. He has $4,250 in his savings account and $672 in his checking account. He owes $3,600 in student loans. He lives with his parents. What is Rashid's net worth? (Lesson 14.3)

   _____

1. **CAREERS IN MATH** | Freelance Computer Programmer Andre works as a freelance computer programmer, and his laptop has stopped working. He is purchasing a new laptop, which he needs to have in 2 days in order to meet a job deadline. He lives in Massachusetts, which has a 6.25% sales tax. He is considering these three options for the purchase:

> Buy it online for $1,499, pay sales tax, and pay $24 priority shipping.
> Buy it in Massachusetts for $1,479.
> Buy it in New Hampshire for $1,549 with no sales tax.

a. Calculate the total cost for each option. Which is the best deal?

_____

_____

b. List other factors that relate to the purchase that could also affect Andre's decision.

_____

_____

_____

_____

_____

2. Grant is going to purchase several large pizzas for a party. He has two options for local pizza shops as described below.

> Hank's Pizza: For every two pizzas, get a third at half price.
> Antonio's: 20% off of all orders of $40 or more.

a. Write a paragraph that describes the other information Grant needs in order to compare these options. Include both facts that relate to the pizzas and facts that relate to the event.

_____

_____

_____

_____

b. Suppose large pizzas cost $13 at each shop. Compare the total cost at each shop for 3 pizzas and for 6 pizzas.

_____

_____

UNIT 7 MIXED REVIEW
Texas Test Prep

Personal
Math Trainer

Online
Assessment and
Intervention

my.hrw.com

Selected Response

Evan makes $2,800 a month and has $750 withheld as federal income tax. Use this information for 1–3.

1. How much does Evan pay for Social Security, which is 6.2% of his monthly salary?

  Ⓐ $127.10   Ⓒ $2,626.40

  Ⓑ $173.60   Ⓓ $2,672.90

2. How much does Evan pay for Medicare, which is 1.45% of his monthly salary?

  Ⓐ $29.73   Ⓒ $2,759.40

  Ⓑ $40.60   Ⓓ $2,770.27

3. What is Evan's net monthly pay?

  Ⓐ $1,835.80   Ⓒ $2,050

  Ⓑ $1,876.40   Ⓓ $2,585.80

4. Which of the following is **not** an example of a fixed expense?

  Ⓐ weekly martial arts lesson

  Ⓑ monthly bus pass

  Ⓒ vacation

  Ⓓ rent

5. Bonnie deposits $180 in a savings account that earns simple interest at an annual rate of 3%. How much interest does her account earn after 10 years?

  Ⓐ $0.54

  Ⓑ $5.40

  Ⓒ $54

  Ⓓ $540

6. Shelby can purchase a 4-pound item from several different retailers. Which is the best buy?

  Ⓐ online for $19, plus shipping and handling costs $0.89 per pound

  Ⓑ online for $20, plus shipping and handling costs $0.59 per pound

  Ⓒ $29.95 with a $5-off coupon

  Ⓓ regularly priced for $30 on sale for 25% off

7. Which of the following is **not** an example of an expense?

  Ⓐ savings

  Ⓑ entertainment

  Ⓒ wages

  Ⓓ snacks

8. Mr. Burr and his daughter live in Corpus Christi, Texas. Mr. Burr's employer pays 100% of his insurance premium and 50% of the premiums for the rest of the family. His total monthly expenses according to an online family budget estimator are about $2,100. His payroll and income taxes are $257 and he gets tax credits of $245, what is his necessary monthly income?

  Ⓐ $2,088   Ⓒ $2,817

  Ⓑ $2,112   Ⓓ $3,827

9. Which represents the solution for the inequality $6x - 9 < 9$?

  Ⓐ $x < 3$

  Ⓑ $x \leq 3$

  Ⓒ $x > 3$

  Ⓓ $x \geq 3$

10. Anthony owns a home with a value of $140,000. He also owns a motorcycle worth $7,000. He has $22,500 in student loans to repay. He owes 9 monthly payments of $55 each for his keyboard. He has a credit card balance of $785. He also has $3,400 in a bank account. What is Anthony's net worth?

Ⓐ $112,620 Ⓒ $126,620

Ⓑ $119,820 Ⓓ $128,190

11. What is the volume of a triangular prism that has a height of 36 meters and a base with an area of 15 square meters?

Ⓐ 180 m³

Ⓑ 270 m³

Ⓒ 360 m³

Ⓓ 540 m³

12. Which of the following is an example of an asset?

Ⓐ student loan

Ⓑ money in a savings account

Ⓒ credit card debt

Ⓓ house mortgage

13. A bag contains 3 white marbles and 6 black marbles. You pick out a marble, record its color, and put the marble back in the bag. If you repeat this process 36 times, how many times would you expect to remove a black marble from the bag?

Ⓐ 9

Ⓑ 12

Ⓒ 24

Ⓓ 27

Gridded Response

14. Neelie bought a pair of shorts for $17.99 and 2 T-shirts for $6.89 each. What is the total price in dollars including an 8% sales tax?

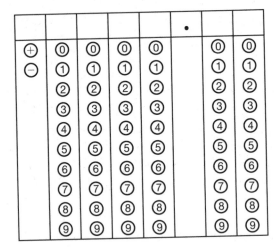

 Underline key words given in the test question so you know for certain what the question is asking.

15. Len deposited $400 into an account earning interest at an annual rate of 2.5% compounded annually. What is the amount of interest in dollars that the account will earn after 5 years?

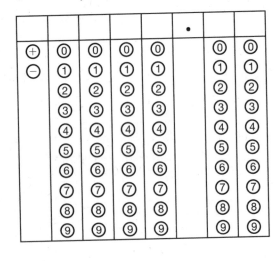

UNIT 1 Selected Answers

MODULE 1

LESSON 1.1

Your Turn

4. 0.571428… **5.** 0.333… **6.** 0.45
7. 2.75; terminating decimal
8. 7.333…; repeating decimal

Guided Practice

1. 0.6; terminating **2.** 0.89;
terminating **3.** 0.333…; repeating
4. 0.2525…; repeating
5. 0.7777…; repeating **6.** 0.36;
terminating **7.** 0.04; terminating
8. 0.14204545…; repeating
9. 0.012; terminating **10.** 11.166…
11. 2.9 **12.** 8.23 **13.** 7.2
14. 54.2727… **15.** 3.0555…
16. 3.666… **17.** 12.875

Independent Practice

19. $\frac{5}{11}$; 0.4545…; repeating
21. $\frac{4}{11}$; 0.3636…; repeating **23.** $\frac{11}{11}$;
1; terminating **25a.** $\frac{39}{8}$ **b.** 4.875
27. Ben is taller because 5.3125
> 5.291$\overline{6}$… . **29.** When the
denominator is 3, 6, 7, or 9, the
result will be a repeating decimal.
31. No; although the digits follow
a pattern, the same combination
of digits do not repeat.

LESSON 1.2

Your Turn

1. integer, rational number
2. rational number **3.** rational
number **4.** whole number,
integer, rational number **6.** True

Guided Practice

1. integer, rational number
2. rational number **3.** rational
number **4.** rational number
6. True **7.** whole numbers
8. integers

Independent Practice

11. rational number **13.** rational
number

15.

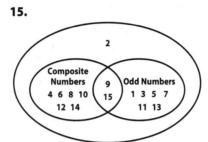

17. True **19.** False **21.** whole
numbers **25.** A mixed number
has two parts, a whole number (or
integer) and a fraction. A whole
number or integer has only one
part, the number itself.

LESSON 1.3

Your Turn

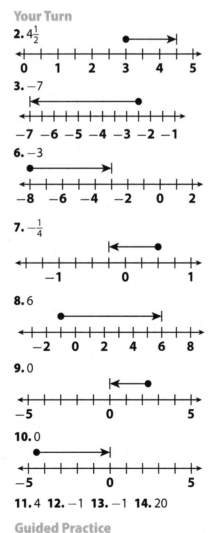

2. $4\frac{1}{2}$

3. −7

6. −3

7. −$\frac{1}{4}$

8. 6

9. 0

10. 0

11. 4 **12.** −1 **13.** −1 **14.** 20

Guided Practice

1. −4.5

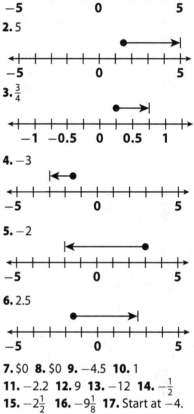

2. 5

3. $\frac{3}{4}$

4. −3

5. −2

6. 2.5

7. $0 **8.** $0 **9.** −4.5 **10.** 1
11. −2.2 **12.** 9 **13.** −12 **14.** −$\frac{1}{2}$
15. −2$\frac{1}{2}$ **16.** −9$\frac{1}{8}$ **17.** Start at −4.
Move 6 units to the right because
6 is positive. The sum is 2.

Independent Practice

19. $12.75 **21.** 1$\frac{1}{2}$ miles **23.** 30 +
15 + (−25) = 20; the final score is
20 points **25.** June: $306.77, July:
$301.50, Aug: $337.88 **27.** opposite
or additive inverse

LESSON 1.4

Your Turn

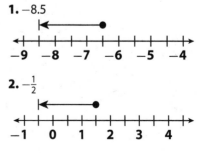

1. −8.5

2. −$\frac{1}{2}$

Selected Answers

3. −7.75

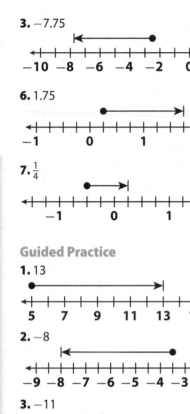

6. 1.75

7. $\frac{1}{4}$

Guided Practice

1. 13

2. −8

3. −11

4. −4

5. −36 **6.** −7.7 **7.** 1 **8.** 79
9. $2\frac{7}{9}$ **10.** $78\frac{1}{2}$ **11.** 1.5 meters
12. $17\frac{1}{2}$ yards loss **13.** 543 feet
14. took out $75.15

Independent Practice

17. −25.65 − 16.5 + 12.45; −29.7
ft; the diver is 29.7 ft below the
surface. **19a.** −$43.30
b. −$68.30 **c.** $68.30 **21.** 65,233
ft; 96,000 ft; 96,000 ft (Mars);
30,767 ft **23a.** 5 − 7.2 + 2.2
b. He is exactly where he started
because 5 − 7.2 + 2.2 = 0.

LESSON 1.5

Your Turn

1. −7

2. 3.75

4. $-\frac{2}{7}$ **5.** $\frac{2}{5}$ **6.** $-\frac{1}{2}$

Guided Practice

1. $-3\frac{1}{3}$

2. $-\frac{3}{4}$

3. $1\frac{5}{7}$

4. 3

5. −12 **6.** −9 **7.** 6.8 **8.** 4.32
9. 6 **10.** −7.2 **11.** $\frac{1}{3}, \frac{1}{4}$ **12.** $\frac{12}{35}; -\frac{4}{5}$
13. $-\frac{5}{12}$ **14.** $\frac{2}{7}$ **15.** 4(−3.50) = −14;
$14
16. 18(−100) = −1,800; $1,800

Independent Practice

21. The submarine would be 975
feet below sea level, or −975
feet. **25.** 13.5 points

LESSON 1.6

Your Turn

5. −0.7 **6.** $\frac{35}{48}$ **7.** −11

Guided Practice

1. −0.8 **2.** $-\frac{1}{7}$ **3.** −8 **4.** $-\frac{502}{3}$
5. −375 **6.** 7 **7.** $-\frac{4}{21}$ **8.** −400
9. −0.875 liter per day **10.** −45.75
÷ 5 = −9.15; $9.15 per day, on
average **11.** −0.55 miles per minute

Independent Practice

13. −20 **15.** 20 **17.** −0.1 **19.** $\frac{5}{9}$
21. 4.5 **23.** $-1\frac{3}{4}$ yards **25a.** $250
b. $1,050 **c.** −$70 **31.** Yes, since
an integer divided by an integer
is a ratio of two integers and
the denominator is not zero, the
number is rational by definition.

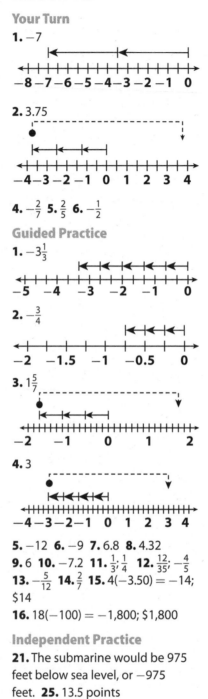

UNIT 2 Selected Answers

MODULE 2

LESSON 2.1

Your Turn
3. $\frac{1}{6} \div \frac{1}{4} = \frac{1}{6} \times \frac{4}{1} = \frac{4}{6} = \frac{2}{3}; \frac{2}{3}$ acre per hour **4.** 4 ounces **5.** the second tank

Guided Practice
2. $2\frac{4}{5}$ miles per hour **3.** $\frac{15}{16}$ page per minute **4.** $\frac{1}{2}$ foot per hour
5. $2\frac{1}{2}$ square feet per hour
6. Brand A: 720 mg/pickle, Brand B: 650 mg/pickle; Brand B
7. Ingredient C: $\frac{3}{8}$ cup/serving, Ingredient D: $\frac{4}{9}$ cup/serving; Ingredient C

Independent Practice
9a. On Call: about $2.86 per hour; Talk Time: $2.50 per hour
b. Talk Time; their rate per hour is lower. **c.** Multiply 0.05 times 60 because there are 60 minutes in 1 hour. **d.** The unit rate is $3 per hour, so it is not a better deal. **11.** $\frac{5 \text{ songs}}{1 \text{ commercial}}$ **13.** Faster; he typed 50 words per minute before and 60 words per minute after.

LESSON 2.2

Your Turn
3. No; the rates are not equal because her speed changed.
4. Each rate is equal to $\frac{1 \text{ adult}}{12 \text{ students}}$. The relationship is proportional; $a = \frac{1}{12}s$.

Guided Practice
1. 45; 90; 2; 45; 135; 3; 45; 180; 4; 45
2. $k = 5$; $y = 5x$ **3.** $k = \frac{1}{4}$; $y = \frac{1}{4}x$

Independent Practice
5. $y = 18.50x$ **7.** Rent-All has the best deal because it has the lowest rate per day ($18.50).

9. The rates have the same unit rate, $6.25 per hour. **11.** x is the number of hours Steven babysits, and y is the amount he charges; the equation is $y = 6.25x$. **13.** 150 feet per minute; 9,000 feet per hour **15.** Feet per minute

LESSON 2.3

Your Turn
1. No; A line drawn through the points does not go through the origin.

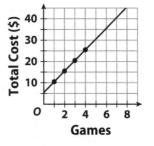

4a. The bicyclist rides 60 miles in 4 hours. **b.** 15 **c.** $y = 15x$

Guided Practice
1. 9; 195; 325; 650; proportional; pages is always 65 times the number of hours. **2.** 3; 8; 15; 37.50; proportional; earnings are always 7.5 times the number of hours. **3.** not proportional; the line will not pass through the origin. **4.** proportional; the line will pass through the origin.
5. $y = 3.5x$ **6.** $y = \frac{1}{4}x$

Independent Practice
9. Horse A takes about 4 minutes. Horse B takes about 2.5 minutes. **11.** Horse A: $y = 3$ miles; Horse B: $y = 4\frac{4}{5}$ miles **13.** Yes; A graph of miles traveled compared to number of hours will form a line that passes through the origin.

15a.

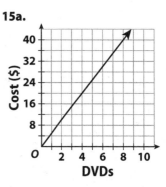

b. Sample answer: (4, 20); 4 DVDs cost $20. **17.** Yes. The graph is a line that passes through the origin. **21.** If the values in the "Time" column are the same, each value in the "Distance" column for Car 4 will be twice the corresponding value for Car 2.

MODULE 3

LESSON 3.1

Your Turn
2. 5.676 **3.** 4.27 **4.** 9 **5.** 7.40
7. 64.55

Guided Practice
1. 8.05; 5 miles; 1.61 km **2.** 18.95; 5 gallons; 3.79 L **3.** 30.48 **4.** 1.816
5. 18.28 **6.** 340.8 **7.** 4.73 **8.** 437.64
9. 2.64 **10.** 450 **11.** 64.96
12. 6,211.18

Independent Practice
15. one inch **17.** one mile
19. one liter **21.** four liters
23. 22.7 kg **25.** 2-liter juice bottle **27.** 2.75 pounds **29a.** Yes; Two half-gallon containers will hold one gallon, which is about 3.79 liters. **b.** No; A gallon jug can hold 3.79 liters, so a half-gallon jug would hold half of that, which is only 1.895 liters. **31a.** 4.47
b. 125.16 **33.** Multiply the number of pounds by 0.454; 3.8 kg

LESSON 3.2

Your Turn

2. 23% **4.** 33% **5.** 37.5%
8. $548.90 **9.** $349.30

Guided Practice

1. 60% **2.** 50% **3.** 74% **4.** 11%
5. 8% **6.** 220% **7.** 78% **8.** 20%
9. 28% **10.** 50% **11.** 9% **12.** 67%
13. 100% **14.** 83% **15.** $9.90
16. 36 cookies **17.** 272 pages
18. 42 members **19.** $27,840
20. 1,863 songs **21.** 26 miles

Independent Practice

25a. Amount of change = 1;
percent decrease = $\frac{1}{5}$ = 20%
27a. They have the same. $100 +
$10 = $110 and $100 + 10%
($100) = $110. **b.** Sylvia has more.
Leroi has $110 + $10 = $120, and
Sylvia has $110 + 10%($110) =
$121. **29.** No. Each withdrawal is
less than the previous, so there
will be a little money left.

LESSON 3.3

Your Turn

2a. $1c + 0.1c$; $1.1c$ **b.** $30.80
3a. 200% **b.** $1c + 2c$; $3c$
5a.

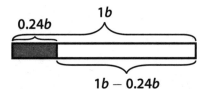

b. $0.76b$ **6a.** $1p - 0.05p$, $0.95p$
b. $14.25

Guided Practice

1a. $0.35s$ **b.** $1s + 0.35s$ or $1.35s$
c. $43.20 **d.** $11.20 **2.** $2.70;
$20.70 **3.** $9.45; $31.95 **4.** $25.31;
$59.06 **5.** $24.75; $99.74 **6.** $48.60;
$97.20 **7.** $231.25; $416.25 **8.** $35.10
9. $59.63 **10.** $13.43 **11.** $70.00

Independent Practice

13a. $0.46b$ **b.** $1b - 0.46b$ or $0.54b$
c. $15.66 **d.** $13.34 **17.** Either buy
3, get one free or $\frac{1}{4}$ off. Either case

would result in a discount of 25%,
which is better than 20%.
19. No; first change: 20.1%
decrease; second change:
25.1% increase. The second
percent change is greater.

LESSON 3.4

Your Turn

1. $1; $21 **3.** $80; $480 **4.** $34.13

Guided Practice

1. $1.50 **2.** $10.50 **3.** $0.40 **4.** $33
5. $0.80 **6.** $10 **7a.** $3.08 **b.** $47.07
8. $86.83 **9.** $700 **10.** $715 **11a.**
$18 **b.** $19.53 **12.** $37.86

Independent Practice

15. $82.58 **17.** $75.14 **19.** $1,076.25
21a. Multiply Sandra's height by
0.10 and add the product to 4 to
get Pablo's height. Then multiply
Pablo's height by 0.08 and add
the product to Pablo's height to
get Michaela's height. **b.** about
4 feet 9 inches **23a.** $101.49
b. $109.39 **c.** Digital camera; the
total cost is $7.90 less. **d.** $109.61

LESSON 4.1

Your Turn

2. No; the measures of
corresponding angles are not
equal. **3.** Yes; the corresponding
angle measures are equal, and
the ratio of corresponding sides
is 1:4. **4.** Yes; all the angles are
right angles, and the ratio of the
corresponding sides is 1:3. **5.** No;
6:6 is not equal to 3:18, so the
sides are not proportional.

Guided Practice

1. 21 tiles **2.** No; the measures
of corresponding angles are not
equal. **3.** Yes; all the angles are
right angles, and the ratio of the
corresponding sides is 2:3.

Independent Practice

5. true **7.** The Dance Class; the
ratios of the corresponding sides
are both 11:10. **9.** Yes **11.** Yes
13. No; the ratio of the short
sides is 4:5 and the ratio of the
long sides is 10:8. They are not
equal. **15.** 1. Check that the
corresponding angle measures for
the figures are equal. 2. Check that
corresponding side lengths in the
figures are proportional.

LESSON 4.2

Your Turn

2. 59°, 3 cm **3.** 120°, 180 cm **4.** 28 ft
5. 8 ft **6.** 18 ft

Guided Practice

1. $z = 20$ m; $d = 53°$ **2.** $t = 24$ in.;
$s = 85°$ **3.** $t = 32$ in.; $x = 46°$
4. $x = 100$ ft; $a = 84°$ **5.** $y = 9.5$ in.;
$x = 90°$ **6.** $q = 10$ cm; $f = 90°$
7. 35 feet

Independent Practice

9. 9 ft **11.** 21 m **13a.** 7.5 inches,
8 inches, 9 inches, 10.5 inches,
and 12 inches **b.** 4 inches **c.**
Because every edge on a cube has
the same length. **15.** $y = 56$ m;
$s = 58°$ **19.** No, it is not possible.
When the sun is directly overhead,
objects do not cast shadows that
have measurable lengths.

LESSON 4.3

Your Turn

5. length: about 17.3 feet; width:
about 13.3 feet; area: 230.1 square
feet. **6.** The length is 22 feet, and
the width is 10 feet. The area is 22
feet × 10 feet, or 220 square feet.

Guided Practice

1a. The wall is 30 feet long. **b.** 1.5
in. **2.** The length is 28 feet, and
the width is 14 feet. The area is
28 feet × 14 feet, or 392 square
feet. **3.** length: 25 meters; width:
15 meters; area: 375 square meters

4a.

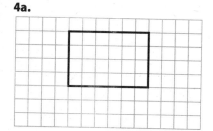

b. Length is 36 m and width is 24 m, using both scales.

Independent Practice

7. The scale drawing is 24 units by 15 units. **9.** Because the scale is 10 cm:1 mm and because 10 cm is longer than 1 mm, the drawing will be larger. **11a.** 6 toothpicks tall **b.** approximately 5 cotton swabs tall

LESSON 4.4

Your Turn

4. Yes, the two circles are proportional. **5.** 3.5 m

Guided Practice

1. circumference **2.** diameter **3.** 3.14; $\frac{22}{7}$ **4.** yes; $\frac{100}{10}$, $\frac{50}{5}$ **5.** Yes, all circles are similar. Their shapes are the same, though the sizes are different. **6.** 2 cm

Independent Practice

9. about 3 feet **11.** No **13a.** 314 in. **b.** Half a foot is 6 inches, so each brick is 6 inches long. He would need 52.3 bricks. **c.** 53 × 0.68 = $36.04 **d.** The circumference would change to 157 inches, which means he would only need 27 bricks, so his new cost would be $18.36. **15.** Yes

UNIT 3 — Selected Answers

© Houghton Mifflin Harcourt Publishing Company

MODULE 5

LESSON 5.1

Your Turn

3. as likely as not; $\frac{1}{2}$ **4.** $\frac{1}{2}$ **5.** $\frac{1}{3}$
7. $\frac{7}{8}$ **8.** $\frac{1}{2}$

Guided Practice

1. 8; 5; 7; 1; 3; 2; 4; 6 **2.** impossible;
0 **3.** as likely as not; $\frac{1}{2}$ **4.** certain; 1
5. unlikely; close to 0 **6.** $\frac{2}{5}$ **7.** $\frac{1}{4}$ **8.** $\frac{5}{6}$
9. $\frac{2}{3}$ **10.** $\frac{4}{5}$ **11.** $\frac{12}{13}$

Independent Practice

13. $\frac{2}{13}$; The event can occur in 8
ways. There are 52 outcomes in
the sample space $\frac{8}{52} = \frac{2}{13}$.
15. No, it is unlikely that
she will have oatmeal for
breakfast. **19a.** $\frac{8}{14} = \frac{4}{7}$ **b.** $8 - 1$
$= 7$ blue coins and $6 + 3 = 9$ red
coins; $\frac{9}{16}$ **c.** $8 + 3 = 11$ blue coins
and $6 - 1 = 5$ red coins; $\frac{5}{16}$
21. Yes

LESSON 5.2

Your Turn

7. red: $\frac{1}{3}$, yellow: $\frac{7}{15}$, blue: $\frac{1}{5}$ **8.** Let
1 and 2 represent red, let 3 and 4
represent white, and let 5 and 6
represent blue.

Guided Practice

1b. The probability of both Heads
and Tails would get close to $\frac{1}{2}$.
2. Write "yes" on 6 of the index
cards, and write "no" on 4 of the
index cards. Results will vary.

Independent Practice

7. $\frac{1}{20}, \frac{19}{20}$ **9.** $\frac{2}{5}$; 16 aces; $\frac{2}{5}$ of 40
is 16. **11.** She did not add 40 and
60 to find the total number of
trials. $P(\text{heads}) = \frac{40}{100}$

LESSON 5.3

Your Turn

1. $\frac{60}{100} = \frac{3}{20} = 15\%$ **3.** $\frac{12}{75} = \frac{4}{25}$

Guided Practice

1. $\frac{50}{400} = \frac{1}{8}$

Independent Practice

5. $\frac{60}{400} = \frac{3}{20}$ **7.** 12; The total is the
product of 3 page count choices
and 4 color choices, which is 12.
13. No, because coins are fair and
the probabilities do not appear to
be equally likely.

LESSON 5.4

Your Turn

1. 132 customers **3.** No; about
371 e-mails out of 12,372
will come back undelivered.
The prediction is high. **4.** 84
customers; Yes, $107 > 84$, so more
customers than normal bought
two or more pairs.

Guided Practice

1. 15 times **2.** about 55 days
3. No, about 1,009 candles out
of 16,824 will be returned. The
prediction is low. **4.** No, about
746 toys out of 24,850 will be
defective. The prediction is
high. **5.** 39 times; No, the
light-rail's claim is higher than
the actual 85%. **6.** 900 students;
Yes, the college's claim is close to
the number actually accepted.

Independent Practice

9. Yes; 6th grade: $\frac{2}{100} = \frac{x}{250} \rightarrow x = 5$;
7th grade: $\frac{4}{100} = \frac{x}{200} \rightarrow x = 8$; 8th
grade: $\frac{8}{100} = \frac{x}{250} \rightarrow x = 12$
11. 36 clients; more than average
did not pay. **13.** He set up the
fraction incorrectly; it should be
$\frac{1}{30} = \frac{x}{180}$. **15.** 14,700 on-time
flights

MODULE 6

LESSON 6.1

Your Turn

2. $\frac{1}{3}$ **3.** The total number of
outcomes in the sample space is
the denominator of the formula
for theoretical probability.

Guided Practice

1.

	Basket A	Basket B
Total number of outcomes	16	20
Number of red balls	3	4
$P(\text{win}) =$ number of red balls / total number of outcomes	$\frac{3}{16}$	$\frac{4}{20} = \frac{1}{5}$

2. Basket B **3.** odd, 6; sections,
11 **4.** even, 5; sections, 11
5. $\frac{2}{6} = \frac{1}{3}$

Independent Practice

9. $\frac{2}{3}$, 0.67, 67% **11.** $\frac{1}{2}$, 0.50, 50%
13. $\frac{3}{5}$, 0.60, 60% **15.** 9 represents
the ways the event can occur; 13
represents the number of equally
likely outcomes.

LESSON 6.2

Your Turn

3. $\frac{4}{12} = \frac{1}{3}$ **4.** $\frac{6}{12} = \frac{1}{2}$ **5.** $\frac{3}{8}$

Guided Practice

1.

	1	2	3	4	5	6
1	1	2	3	4	5	6
2	2	4	6	8	10	12
3	3	6	9	12	15	18
4	4	8	12	16	20	24
5	5	10	15	20	25	30
6	6	12	18	24	30	36

2. $\frac{15}{36}$ **3.** $\frac{23}{36}$

4.

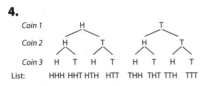

Coin 1	H	T
Coin 2	H T	H T
Coin 3	H T H T	H T H T
List:	HHH HHT HTH HTT	THH THT TTH TTT

5. 8 **6.** TTT **7.** 3 tails; $\frac{1}{8}$; $\frac{1}{8}$
8. 3; HTH, THH; exactly 2 heads; $\frac{3}{8}$

Independent Practice
11. $\frac{1}{2}$ **13.** $\frac{1}{10}$ **15.** $\frac{2}{9}$ **17.** Because
there are 3 choices for the first
item and 2 for the second,
there are $3 \cdot 2 = 6$ possible
outcomes. **19.** Neither

LESSON 6.3

Your Turn
1. about 167 times **2.** about 9
times **3.** more likely that he picks
a marble of another color **4.** No

Guided Practice
1. $\frac{1}{3}, \frac{1}{3}, \frac{1}{3}, \frac{1}{3}$; 1, 3, 18, 6, 6 **2.** 50
people **3.** brown; $P(\text{hazel}) = \frac{9}{28}$,
$P(\text{brown}) = \frac{10}{28}$, $P(\text{blue}) = \frac{7}{28}$, and

$P(\text{green}) = \frac{2}{28}$. The event with the
greatest probability is choosing a
person with brown eyes.

Independent Practice
5. 15 white or gray marbles **7.** It is
more likely that she draws 2 red
cards. **9.** 500 times **11.** 45 days
17. Yes, but only theoretically
because in reality, nothing can
occur 0.5 time.

LESSON 6.4

Guided Practice
1. years with a drought; years
without a drought; 4

2.

Trial	Numbers generated	Drought years
1	10,3,5,1	2
2	10,4,6,5	0
3	3,2,10,3	3
4	2,10,4,4	1
5	7,3,6,3	2

Trial	Numbers generated	Drought years
6	8,4,8,5	0
7	6,2,2,8	2
8	6,5,2,4	1
9	2,2,3,2	4
10	6,3,1,5	2

3. 80%

Independent Practice
5. 1 trial **7.** 20%

 Selected Answers

UNIT 4 Selected Answers

MODULE 7

LESSON 7.1

Your Turn

8. The cost of the advertisement is $150 plus $0.05 for each click.
9. $150 + 1000 \times \$0.05 = \$150 + \$50 = \$200$

Guided Practice

2. 3, $75, $25; $75, $175, $75, $100, $75; $100, $25 **3.** Converting from a table helps to generalize the relationship. Converting from a verbal description helps to see specific values in a table.

Independent Practice

5. It takes the teacher 5 seconds to make 1 copy, 7 seconds to make 2 copies, and 9 seconds to make 3 copies. The total time increases by 2 seconds for each copy. **7.** 1 dime corresponds to $\frac{38-22}{8-4} = \frac{16}{4} = 4$ minutes. **9.** The number of minutes left on the meter is 4 times the number of dimes plus 6 more minutes. **11.** In this description, as one quantity increases, the other quantity decreases. **15.** In this table, the value for years does not change by the same amount.

LESSON 7.2

Your Turn

2. $y = 20x + 45$ **3.** $y = 2.2x + 12$
6. $y = 3.5x + 18$

Hours rented	Cost ($)
0	18
2	25
4	32
6	39
8	46

Bike Rental

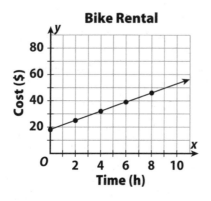

Guided Practice

1.

Pool Water

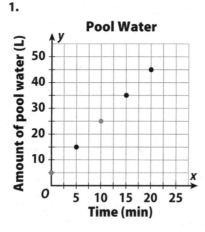

2. 55; 50
3. −5; 250
4. 15; 375

Week	Total Comics ($)
0	375 + 15(0) = 375
1	375 + 15(1) = 390
2	375 + 15(2) = 405
3	375 + 15(3) = 420
4	375 + 15(4) = 435

Independent Practice

7.

Cab Ride Charges

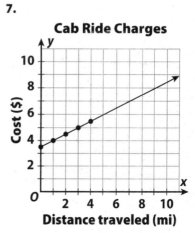

11. $y = 7.95x + 99.95$ **13.** $y = 18x + 40$

15a.

Weekly Sales ($)	Earnings ($)
0	750.00
1,000	900.00
2,000	1,050.00
3,000	1,200.00
4,000	1,350.00

c. $y = 0.15x + 750$

MODULE 8

LESSON 8.1

Your Turn

4. $150 − 35x = 45$

Guided Practice

1.

2.

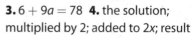

3. $6 + 9a = 78$ **4.** the solution; multiplied by 2; added to 2x; result

Independent Practice

7. three negative variable tiles and seven $+1$-tiles on one side of a line and 28 $+1$-tiles on the other side **9.** $1.25r + 6.75 = 31.75$ **11.** $\frac{1}{2}n + 45 = 172$ **13.** $500 - 20x = 220$ **15a.** $10 + 5c = 25$ **b.** 3 children **c.** They should choose Kimmi because she charges only $25. If they chose Sandy, they would pay $35. **17.** Part of the equation is written in cents and part in dollars. All of the numbers in the equation should be written either in cents or in dollars.

LESSON 8.2

Your Turn

1. $x = 3$ **2.** $n = 3$ **3.** $a = -1$
4. $y = 1$
6. 14 weeks

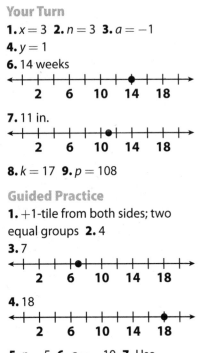

7. 11 in.

8. $k = 17$ **9.** $p = 108$

Guided Practice

1. $+1$-tile from both sides; two equal groups **2.** 4
3. 7

4. 18

5. $p = 5$ **6.** $a = -10$ **7.** Use the inverse operations of the operations indicated in the problem. Usually it is best to use addition and subtraction before multiplication and division.

Independent Practice

9. $d = 9$ **11.** $k = 42$ **13.** $z = -190$
15. $n = -56$ **17.** $c = -56$
19. $t = -9$ **21.** $13°F$ **23.** 12 years old **25.** $188 **27.** $x = 0.4$
29. $k = -180.44$ **32.** $C = \frac{F - 32}{1.8}$

LESSON 8.3

Your Turn

3. $1{,}240 + 45a \geq 6{,}000$
4. $6 + 3n \leq 40$

Guided Practice

1.

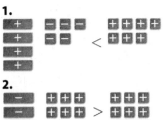

2.

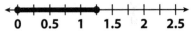

3. $7,000; $1,250; 92; $1{,}250 + 92a \geq 7{,}000$ **4.** The solution of the problem; the solution multiplied by 7; 18 is subtracted from $7x$; the result can be no greater than 32.

Independent Practice

7. $3a + 28 > 200$; $a = $ possible amounts each friend earned
9. $25 + 4a \leq 75$; $a = $ the maximum amount each shirt can cost
11. $120 + 32n \leq 720$; $n = $ the number of people in each row
13. $7 + 10c \leq 100$; $c = $ the number of CDs she buys **17.** $\leq$
19. $\leq$ **21.** $\geq$ **25.** $n > \frac{1}{n}$ if $n > 1$; $n < \frac{1}{n}$ if $n < 1$; $n = \frac{1}{n}$ if $n = 1$

LESSON 8.4

Your Turn

1. $x > 2$ **2.** $h \geq 3$ **3.** $p \geq 6$; Joshua has to run at a steady pace of at least 6 mi/h. **4.** $v = 11$ **5.** $h = -3$; $h = -4$; $h = -5$

Guided Practice

1. Remove four $+1$-tiles from both sides, then divide each side into three equal groups; $x < 3$
2. $d < 9$

3. $b \geq 4$

4. $m = -10$ **5.** $y = \frac{1}{2}$; $y = 0$
6. $t \leq 1.25$; Lizzy can spend from 0 to 1.25 h with each student. No; 1.5 h per student will exceed Lizzy's available time.

Independent Practice

9. $t \leq 10$ **11.** $m < 8$ **13.** $f < 140$ **15.** $g < -18$ **17.** $a \geq 16$ **19.** $7n - 25 \geq 65$; $n \geq 12\frac{6}{7}$; Grace must wash at least 13 cars, because n must be a whole number.
21c. There is no number that satisfies both inequalities. **d.** The solution set is all numbers.

UNIT 5 **Selected Answers**

 MODULE **9**

LESSON 9.1

Your Turn

5. Sample answer: ∠FGA and ∠AGC **6.** Sample answer: ∠FGE and ∠BGC **7.** 55° **8.** 42°; 126°
9. Sample answer: You can stop at the solution step where you find the value of 3x because the measure of ∠JML is equal to 3x. **10.** 25° **11.** 25°, 75°

Guided Practice

1. complementary **2.** adjacent **3.** vertical; 30° **4.** 50°, 30°, 2x; 80°; 100°; 100° **5.** x, x + 10, 40; 50; 130; 65, 65°; 75, 75°

Independent Practice

11. m∠RUQ **13.** 96° **15.** 28°
17. 45° **19.** No **21.** Yes **23.** 59°

LESSON 9.2

Your Turn

3. about 34.54 cm **5.** about 132 cm
8. about 2 hours

Guided Practice

1. 3.14(9); 28.26 **2.** 7; 44
3. 78.5 m **4.** 30.14 yd **5.** 47.1 in.
6. 66; 66; 21; 21 + 4 = 25; 25; $11.25; $11.25 **7.** 0.5 yd; 1 yd
8. 12.55 ft; 25.10 ft **9.** 1.7 in.; 10.68 in.

Independent Practice

11. 18.53 ft **13.** 110 in.
15. d = 18.80 ft; $C \approx$ 59.03 ft
17. r = 9 in.; $C \approx$ 56.52 in.
19. about 2,376 feet **21.** about 0.14 mi **23.** about $713.18
25. 12.56 feet **27.** Pool B; about 0.57 m or 1.84 ft

LESSON 9.3

Your Turn

4. 314 ft²

Guided Practice

1. 153.9 m² **2.** 452.2 mm²
3. 314 yd² **4.** 200.96 in² **5.** 113.04 cm² **6.** 132.67 in² **7.** 4π square units **8.** 36π square units
9. $\frac{\pi}{16}$ square units **10.** 16π yd

Independent Practice

13. 803.84 cm² **15.** 28.26 square units **17.** 30.96 m² **19.** No; the top of the large cake has an area 9 times that of the small cake. The area of the top of the large cake is 144π in² and that of the small cake is 16π in². **21.** The 18-inch pizza is a better deal because it costs about 8¢ per square inch while the 12-inch pizza costs about 9¢ per square inch. **23.** No; the combined area is 2πr² while the area of a circle with twice the radius is 4πr². **25.** $\frac{\pi (1.5)^2}{\pi (7.5)^2} = \frac{2.25}{56.25}$ = $\frac{1}{25}$ or 0.04 or 4%

LESSON 9.4

Your Turn

2. 51.5 ft² **3.** 139.25 m² **4.** $911.68

Guided Practice

1. rectangle; 4; 15; 15; 4; 15; 15; 34; 34 **3.** $97.88

Independent Practice

5. 941.33 in²
7. 30 square units

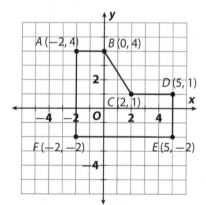

9. 60.56 cm² **11.** 5 ft; 32.5 ft² − 7.5 ft² = 25 ft²; 25 ft² is area of the square, so each side of the square is 5 ft because 5 × 5 = 25 **15a.** 2,228 in² **b.** 3,016 in²

MODULE **10**

LESSON 10.1

Your Turn

2. 147 in³ **9.** 1$\frac{1}{2}$ in³; the volume is one-third that of the prism.
10. 40 cm² **11.** 32.8 yd³

Guided Practice

2. rectangular pyramid
3. pentagonal prism **4.** rectangular prism **5.** 10 m **7.** $V = \frac{1}{3}bh$

Independent Practice

9. 9 ft³ **11.** 4,821 in³ **13.** 24 in.
15. prism **17.** 15 ft **19a.** 560 m³
b. 560,000 kg **21a.** 1,455.52 cm³
b. 2,850 g **c.** 1.96 g/ cm³

LESSON 10.2

Your Turn

2. The volume of the garden seat is 2,160 in³. **5.** 40.5 m³; the volume is 3 times that of the pyramid.
6. 67.2 − 22.4 = 44.8; volume of the prism is 44.8 cm³ greater.

Guided Practice

2. 270 m³; 3 **3.** The volume of the prism is 180 m³ greater. **4.** 202.5 ft³
5. 72 yd³ **6.** 175 in³

Independent Practice

9. triangular prism; 525 in³ **11.** yes; $V = Bh$ so $B(3h) = 3Bh = 3V$
13. Because the measurement is in units, and not square units, she must mean the base, b. **15.** 35 in³

LESSON 10.3

Your Turn

1. lateral area: 48 cm² ; total surface area: 60 cm² **3.** Lateral area: 11.7 ft²; total surface area: 15.6 ft² **4.** Lateral area: 640 in², total surface area: 896 in² **5.** $1.72

Guided Practice

1. 6 **2.** 4 **3.** rectangular prism

4.

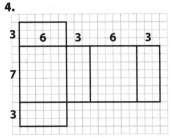

5. 78 square units **6.** 162 square units **7.** two triangular faces, three rectangular faces **8.** 69.6 cm² **9.** 81.6 cm² **10.** 340 cm²; $17

Independent Practice

13. The net includes two congruent triangles with base 4 in. and height 3 in., one 15 in. by 4 in. rectangle, and two congruent 15 in. by 3.6 in. rectangles. **15.** 236 in² **17.** 930 tiles **19.** 66 ft² **23.** Not necessarily; the bases may be different shapes. For example, a 2 × 8 rectangle and a 4 × 4 square have the same area, but are not congruent.

MODULE 11

LESSON 11.1

Your Turn

2. the percent of votes for girls that Becky received **3.** Floor: 480, lower: 900, upper: 1,320; club: 240; platinum: 60

Guided Practice

1. 6; 18; 24; $\frac{6}{24} = \frac{x}{100}$; $x = 25$; 25%; 25% **2.** 1,500 members

Independent Practice

5. greater than **7.** 43.75%
11. Black: 33%; Gray: 12.5%; White: 24%; Blue: 11%; Red: 9%; Green: 6.5%; Purple: 4%. The percent wearing black bow ties is the same as the estimate. **13.** The percent is equal to the degree measure divided by 360 and then multiplied by 100.

LESSON 11.2

Your Turn

2. Dot plots for field hockey players and softball players have a similar spread.; Center of the field hockey dot plot is less than the center for softball or basketball players.; Dot plots for field hockey players and softball players have a similar spread. **3.** median: 6h, range: 10h; If you remove the outliers, the range is 4 hours. The median is greater than the median for exercise. The range is less than for exercise.

Guided Practice

1. Class A: clustered around two areas; Class B: clustered in one area **2.** Class A: center is at about 9 mi; Class B: center is at about 6 mi **3.** Class A: spread from 4 to 14 mi, a wide gap with no data; Class B: spread from 3 to 9 mi
4. The median for both dot plots is 6 miles. **5.** Range for Class A: 10 mi; range for Class B: 6 mi

Independent Practice

7. The dots have a relatively even spread, with a peak at 8 letters.
9. The dots spread from 3 to 9 letters. **11.** AL: clustered in one small interval with an outlier to the left; VA: relatively uniform in height over the same interval
13. AL: spreads from 1 to 12 days of rain, an outlier at 1; VA: spreads from 8 to 12 days of rain
15. Group A: clustered to the left of size 9; Group B: clustered to the right of size 9 **17.** Group A: range with outlier = 6.5, without outlier = 2.5; Group B: range = 3 **19.** Yes; one group of five students could have the following number of pets: 1, 2, 3, 4, 5. Another group of five students could have the following number of pets: 1, 3, 3, 3, 5. For both groups of students, the median would be 3 and the range would be 4.

LESSON 11.3

Your Turn

4. Sample answer: The shape is similar to Store A's. The median is greater than Store A's and less than Store B's. The interquartile range is about the same as Store A's and longer than B's.

Guided Practice

1. 72; 88 **2.** 79 **3.** 16; 10
4. Volleyball players **5.** Hockey players **6.** Both groups

Independent Practice

9. Both cars have ranges of 45 in. Both cars have interquartile ranges of 25 in. **11.** Car A has less variability in the lowest quarter of its data and greater variability in the highest quarter of its data. The variability is reversed for Car B.
13. City A; $25

MODULE 12

LESSON 12.1

Your Turn

4. The sample is not biased. It is a random sample. **5.** The question is biased since cats are suggested. **6.** The question is not biased. It does not lead people to pick a particular season.

Guided Practice

2. more; random **3.** less; biased **4.** Yes; Sample answer: What is your favorite color?

Independent Practice

9. It is biased because students who aren't in that class won't be selected. **11.** It is a random sample because the organization selects names at random from all registered voters. **13.** Jae's question is not biased since it does not suggest a type of art to students. **15a.** 60; a random sample **b.** 58%; it appears reasonable because Barbara used a random sample and surveyed a significant percent of the students.

LESSON 12.2

Your Turn

5. 420 damaged MP3s **6.** Sample answer: 6 is a little more than 10% of 50. 10% of 3,500 is 350, and 420 is a little more than that.

Guided Practice

1.

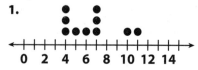

2.

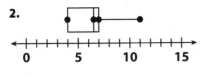

3. 4; 7 **4.** 4; 11 **5.** 6.5 **6.** 280
7. 720 elk

9. 48 people **11.** 240 puppies
13. Yes, this seems reasonable
because 25 is the median of the
data. **17.** Kudrey needs to find the
median and the lower and upper
quartiles and plot those points.
He assumed all quartiles would be
equally long when each quartile
represents an equal number of
data values. **19.** a box plot

LESSON 12.3

1.

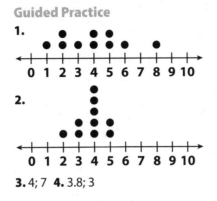

3. 4; 7 **4.** 3.8; 3

9. The range for both teams is
7. The range indicates that both
populations have a similar spread

between the largest and the
smallest size. **11.** Sample answer:
They are identical in range and
interquartile range, but have
different minimum and maximum
values.

UNIT 7 Selected Answers

MODULE 13

LESSON 13.1

Your Turn
1. $81.67 **2.** $3,204.60 **3.** $3,509; she has to pay an additional amount of $869.

Guided Practice
1. $0.86; $11.63 **2.** $0.32; $4.30 **3.** $3.60; $48.59 **4.** $0.41; $5.56 **5.** $70.08 **6.** $2,504 **7.** $3,531; she has to pay an additional $591.

Independent Practice
9. $33.84; $443.98 **11.** $914.42 **13a.** His net pay is $1,535. **b.** $1,803.60 **15.** She will get a refund of $274. **17.** Under the existing rate, the taxpayer would pay $3,839. Under the flat tax rate, the taxpayer would pay 15% of $28,443, or $4266.45. That is an increase of $427.45.

LESSON 13.2

Your Turn
2. $120; $500 **5.** $597.53; it is $17.34 more. **6.** Account C; $10.30

Guided Practice
1. $4.50; $9; $22.50 **2.** 4.00; 104.00 **3.** 204.00; 8.16; 212.16 **4.** 212.16; 312.16; 12.49; 324.65 **5.** 324.65; 424.65; 16.99; 441.64 **6.** 441.64; 541.64; 21.67; 563.31 **7.** $3,257.79

Independent Practice
9. 40 months; $5,000 ÷ $125 = 40 **11.** Year 1: 0.05($3500) = $175, Year 2: 0.05($2,000) = $100, Year 3: 0.05($500) = $25; $175 + $100 + $25 = $300 **15.** Account B earns $391.12 more interest in 20 years. **17.** Tori's

LESSON 13.3

Your Turn
1. The 4-pack; it costs $0.145/oz; the other cost is about 0.16/oz. **3.** Rec Plus; their price is $54.74, while Kitt's is $56.66. **5.** Leona's; $16.98 < $17.98

Guided Practice
1. The Corner Store; $2.89/bottle < $2.99/bottle **2.** The 2-pack; $1.10/lb < $1.25/lb **3.** 90; 96; $0.13; 90; $0.11; 96; Three 32-ounce containers; $0.11/oz < 0.13/oz **4.** Locally; $21.95 < $22.92 **5.** 35% off; $11.64 < $12.90 **6.** Yes; $535 < $555 **7.** Card B; $0/year < $14/year

Independent Practice
9. Store 2; its price is $93.75, which is less than $99. **11.** Tyron; his total is $799. Penelope's is $882. **13.** 32.5% off **15a.** DiV; the cost is $457.51. TVU's price is $478.80. **b.** Yes; DiV cost: $253.75. TVU cost: $239.40. **c.** 17; the number of months that it takes for the DiV offer to be less expensive than TVU's offer.

MODULE 14

LESSON 14.1

Your Turn
3.

Expenses	
Snacks	V
Weekly flute lesson	F
Saving for a new flute	F
Entertainment	V
Savings for college	F
Monthly bus pass	F

6. $1,350 **7.** 14%, 8% **8.** No, only $180 is budgeted so they need $500 − 180 = $320.

Guided Practice
3. fixed expense **4.** 25% **5.** $384 **6.** Sample answer: It makes the person or family aware of how much money they have coming in compared with the expenses that they have. This can help to keep a family from overspending and make it possible to plan for big purchases.

Independent Practice
9. 17% **11.** No, $300 is the amount they spend on transportation. $500 − $300 = $200, so they spend $200 more on recreation. **13.** The Wagner family; The Wagner family pays $630, which is 15% of $4,200. The Rivera Family pays 8% + 4% = 12% of $4,500.

LESSON 14.2

Your Turn
1. Sample answer: $1,844 per month; $11 per hour **2.** Sample answer: The required income increases from $1,844 to $2,543 per month and to $15 per hour from $11.

Guided Practice
3. Sample answer: Housing, childcare, and medical costs are less in Lubbock than in Corpus Christi. The other expenses are the same.

Independent Practice
4b. Sample answer: Food and other necessities are the same in both cities. Although medical costs are less in San Antonio, all the other items are more expensive than in Midland.

LESSON 14.3

Your Turn

2. It is a liability because he does not own the car and it is money he must pay every month. **3.** It is an asset because Morgana owns the television and can sell it if she wishes. **6.** $150,128

Guided Practice

2. Home: $195,000; electronics: $2,325; car: $9,300; bank account: $6,890; piano: $1,200; $214,715; Mortgage: $160,000; electronics loan: $875; credit card debt: $1,437; student loans: $4,800; $167,112; $214,715; $167,112; $47,603

Independent Practice

7. No; Paul's stock portfolio does not exceed the total of his credit card and student loan debt. His net worth is actually negative. It is −$3,300. **9.** Before the purchase, her net worth is $12,517. After the purchase it will go down $560 to $11,957, because she will gain a new asset worth $2,240 but also gain a new liability worth $2,800.

Glossary/Glosario

ENGLISH	SPANISH	EXAMPLES
absolute value The distance of a number from zero on a number line; shown by | |.	**valor absoluto** Distancia a la que está un número de 0 en una recta numérica. El símbolo del valor absoluto es | |.	$\|5\| = 5$ $\|-5\| = 5$
accuracy The closeness of a given measurement or value to the actual measurement or value.	**exactitud** Cercanía de una medida o un valor a la medida o el valor real.	
acute angle An angle that measures greater than 0° and less than 90°.	**ángulo agudo** Ángulo que mide más de 0° y menos de 90°.	
acute triangle A triangle with all angles measuring less than 90°.	**triángulo acutángulo** Triángulo en el que todos los ángulos miden menos de 90°.	
addend A number added to one or more other numbers to form a sum.	**sumando** Número que se suma a uno o más números para formar una suma.	In the expression $4 + 6 + 7$, the numbers 4, 6, and 7 are addends.
Addition Property of Equality The property that states that if you add the same number to both sides of an equation, the new equation will have the same solution.	**Propiedad de igualdad de la suma** Propiedad que establece que puedes sumar el mismo número a ambos lados de una ecuación y la nueva ecuación tendrá la misma solución.	$x \; -6 \; = \; 8$ $\underline{+6 \quad +6}$ $x \; = \; 14$
Addition Property of Opposites The property that states that the sum of a number and its opposite equals zero.	**Propiedad de la suma de los opuestos** Propiedad que establece que la suma de un número y su opuesto es cero.	$12 + (-12) = 0$
additive inverse The opposite of a number.	**inverso aditivo** El opuesto de un número.	The additive inverse of 5 is -5.
adjacent angles Angles in the same plane that have a common vertex and a common side.	**ángulos adyacentes** Angulos en el mismo plano que comparten un vértice y un lado.	$\angle 1$ and $\angle 2$ are adjacent angles.
algebraic expression An expression that contains at least one variable.	**expresión algebraica** Expresión que contiene al menos una variable.	$x + 8$ $4(m - b)$

ENGLISH	SPANISH	EXAMPLES
algebraic inequality An inequality that contains at least one variable.	**desigualdad algebraica** Desigualdad que contiene al menos una variable.	$x + 3 > 10$ $5a > b + 3$
alternate exterior angles A pair of angles on the outer side of two lines cut by a transversal that are on opposite sides of the transversal.	**ángulos alternos externos** Par de ángulos en los lados externos de dos líneas intersecadas por una transversal, que están en lados opuestos de la transversal.	 $\angle a$ and $\angle d$ are alternate exterior angles.
alternate interior angles A pair of angles on the inner sides of two lines cut by a transversal that are on opposite sides of the transversal.	**ángulos alternos externos** Par de ángulos en los lados internos de dos líneas intersecadas por una transversal, que están en lados opuestos de la transversal.	 $\angle r$ and $\angle v$ are alternate interior angles.
angle A figure formed by two rays with a common endpoint called the vertex.	**ángulo** Figura formada por dos rayos con un extremo común llamado vértice.	
arc A part of a circle named by its endpoints.	**arco** Parte de un círculo que se nombra por sus extremos.	
area The number of square units needed to cover a given surface.	**área** El número de unidades cuadradas que se necesitan para cubrir una superficie dada.	 The area is 10 square units.
arithmetic sequence A sequence in which the terms change by the same amount each time.	**sucesión aritmética** Una sucesión en la que los términos cambian la misma cantidad cada vez.	The sequence 2, 5, 8, 11, 14 … is an arithmetic sequence.
assets Items a person owns with monetary value.	**activos** Cosas que posees y que tienen valor monetario.	
Associative Property of Addition The property that states that for all real numbers a, b, and c, the sum is always the same, regardless of their grouping.	**Propiedad asociativa de la suma** Propiedad que establece que para todos los números reales a, b y c, la suma siempre es la misma sin importar cómo se agrupen.	$2 + 3 + 8 = (2 + 3) + 8 = 2 + (3 + 8)$
Associative Property of Multiplication The property that states that for all real numbers a, b, and c, their product is always the same, regardless of their grouping.	**Propiedad asociativa de la multiplicación** Propiedad que para todos los números reales a, b y c, el producto siempre es el mismo sin importar cómo se agrupen.	$2 \cdot 3 \cdot 8 = (2 \cdot 3) \cdot 8 = 2 \cdot (3 \cdot 8)$

Glossary/Glosario

ENGLISH	SPANISH	EXAMPLES

asymmetry Not identical on either side of a central line; not symmetrical.

asimetría Ocurre cuando dos lados separados por una línea central no son idénticos; falta de simetría.

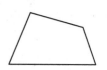

The quadrilateral has asymmetry.

---

axes The two perpendicular lines of a coordinate plane that intersect at the origin.

ejes Las dos rectas numéricas perpendiculares del plano cartesiano que se intersecan en el origen.

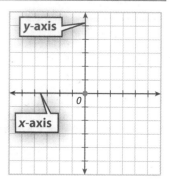

B

bar graph A graph that uses vertical or horizontal bars to display data.

gráfica de barras Gráfica en la que se usan barras verticales u horizontales para presentar datos.

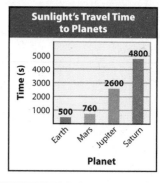

---

base-10 number system A number system in which all numbers are expressed using the digits 0–9.

sistema de base 10 Sistema de numeración en el que todos los números se expresan con los dígitos 0–9.

---

base (in numeration) When a number is raised to a power, the number that is used as a factor is the base.

base (en numeración) Cuando un número es elevado a una potencia, el número que se usa como factor es la base.

$3^5 = 3 \cdot 3 \cdot 3 \cdot 3 \cdot 3$; 3 is the base.

---

base (of a polygon) A side of a polygon.

base (de un polígono) Lado de un polígono.

---

base (of a three-dimensional figure) A face of a three-dimensional figure by which the figure is measured or classified.

base (de una figura tridimensional) Cara de una figura tridimensional a partir de la cual se mide o se clasifica la figura.

Bases of a cylinder   Bases of a prism

Base of a cone   Base of a pyramid

biased sample A sample that does not fairly represent the population.

muestra no representativa Muestra que no representa adecuadamente la población.

---

bisect To divide into two congruent parts.

trazar una bisectriz Dividir en dos partes congruentes.

$\overrightarrow{JK}$ bisects ∠LJM.

---

box-and-whisker plot A graph that shows how data are distributed by using the median, quartiles, least value, and greatest value; also called a box plot.

gráfica de mediana y rango Gráfica que muestra los valores máximo y mínimo, los cuartiles superior e inferior, así como la mediana de los datos.

---

break (graph) A zigzag on a horizontal or vertical scale of a graph that indicates that some of the numbers on the scale have been omitted.

discontinuidad (gráfica) Zig-zag en la escala horizontal o vertical de una gráfica que indica la omisión de algunos de los números de la escala.

---

budget A plan to help you reach your financial goals.

presupuesto Plan que te ayuda a obtener tus metas financieras.

C

capacity The amount a container can hold when filled.

capacidad Cantidad que cabe en un recipiente cuando se llena.

A large milk container has a capacity of 1 gallon.

Celsius A metric scale for measuring temperature in which 0 °C is the freezing point of water and 100 °C is the boiling point of water; also called *centigrade*.

Celsius Escala métrica para medir la temperatura, en la que 0 °C es el punto de congelación del agua y 100 °C es el punto de ebullición. También se llama *centígrado*.

---

center (of a circle) The point inside a circle that is the same distance from all the points on the circle.

centro (de un círculo) Punto interior de un círculo que se encuentra a la misma distancia de todos los puntos de la circunferencia.

---

center (of rotation) The point about which a figure is rotated.

centro (de una rotación) Punto alrededor del cual se hace girar una figura.

Glossary/Glosario

ENGLISH	SPANISH	EXAMPLES
central angle of a circle An angle with its vertex at the center of a circle.	**ángulo central de un círculo** Ángulo cuyo vértice se encuentra en el centro de un círculo.	
certain (probability) Sure to happen; having a probability of 1.	**seguro (probabilidad)** Que con seguridad sucederá. Representa una probabilidad de 1.	
chord A line segment with endpoints on a circle.	**cuerda** Segmento de recta cuyos extremos forman parte de un círculo.	
circle The set of all points in a plane that are the same distance from a given point called the center.	**círculo** Conjunto de todos los puntos en un plano que se encuentran a la misma distancia de un punto dado llamado centro.	
circle graph A graph that uses sectors of a circle to compare parts to the whole and parts to other parts.	**gráfica circular** Gráfica que usa secciones de un círculo para comparar partes con el todo y con otras partes.	
circumference The distance around a circle.	**circunferencia** Distancia alrededor de un círculo.	
clockwise A circular movement in the direction shown.	**en el sentido de las manecillas del reloj** Movimiento circular en la dirección que se indica.	
coefficient The number that is multiplied by the variable in an algebraic expression.	**coeficiente** Número que se multiplica por la variable en una expresión algebraica.	5 is the coefficient in 5b.
combination An arrangement of items or events in which order does not matter.	**combinación** Agrupación de objetos o sucesos en la cual el orden no es importante.	For objects A, B, C, and D, there are 6 different combinations of 2 objects: AB, AC, AD, BC, BD, CD.
commission A fee paid to a person for making a sale.	**comisión** Page que recibe una persona por realizar una venta.	
commission rate The fee paid to a person who makes a sale expressed as a percent of the selling price.	**tasa de comisión** Page que recibe una persona por hacer una venta, expresado como un porcentaje del precio de venta.	A commission rate of 5% and a sale of $10,000 results in a commission of $500.
common denominator A denominator that is the same in two or more fractions.	**común denominador** Denominador que es común a dos o más fracciones.	The common denominator of $\frac{5}{8}$ and $\frac{2}{8}$ is 8.

Glossary/Glosario

ENGLISH	SPANISH	EXAMPLES
common difference In an arithmetic sequence, the nonzero constant difference of any term and the previous term.	**diferencia común** En una sucesión aritmética, diferencia constante distinta de cero entre cualquier término y el término anterior.	In the arithmetic sequence 3, 5, 7, 9, 11, ..., the common difference is 2.
common factor A number that is a factor of two or more numbers.	**factor común** Número que es factor de dos o más números.	8 is a common factor of 16 and 40.
common multiple A number that is a multiple of each of two or more numbers.	**común múltiplo** Número que es múltiplo de dos o más números.	15 is a common multiple of 3 and 5.
Commutative Property of Addition The property that states that two or more numbers can be added in any order without changing the sum.	**Propiedad conmutativa de la suma** Propiedad que establece que sumar dos o más números en cualquier orden no altera la suma.	$8 + 20 = 20 + 8$
Commutative Property of Multiplication The property that states that two or more numbers can be multiplied in any order without changing the product.	**Propiedad conmutativa de la multiplicación** Propiedad que establece que multiplicar dos o más números en cualquier orden no altera el producto.	$6 \cdot 12 = 12 \cdot 6$
compatible numbers Numbers that are close to the given numbers that make estimation or mental calculation easier.	**números compatibles** Números que están cerca de los números dados y hacen más fácil la estimación o el cálculo mental.	To estimate $7{,}957 + 5{,}009$, use the compatible numbers 8,000 and 5,000: $8{,}000 + 5{,}000 = 13{,}000$.
complement The set of all outcomes that are not the event.	**complemento** La serie de resultados que no están en el suceso.	When rolling a number cube, the complement of rolling a 3 is rolling a 1, 2, 4, 5, or 6.
complementary angles Two angles whose measures add to 90°.	**ángulos complementarios** Dos ángulos cuyas medidas suman 90°.	
complex fraction A fraction that contains one or more fractions in the numerator, the denominator, or both.	**fracción compleja** Fracción que contiene una o más fracciones en el numerador, en el denominador, o en ambos.	
composite figure A figure made up of simple geometric shapes.	**figura compuesta** Figura formada por figuras geométricas simples.	
composite number A number greater than 1 that has more than two whole-number factors.	**número compuesto** Número mayor que 1 que tiene más de dos factores que son números cabales.	4, 6, 8, and 9 are composite numbers.

ENGLISH	SPANISH	EXAMPLES
compound event An event made up of two or more simple events.	**suceso compuesto** Suceso que consista de dos o más sucesos simples.	Rolling a 3 on a number cube and spinning a 2 on a spinner is a compound event.
compound inequality A combination of more than one inequality.	**desigualdad compuesta** Combinación de dos o más desigualdades.	$-2 \leq x < 10$
compound interest Interest earned or paid on a principal and previous earned or paid interest.	**interés compuesto** Intereses ganados o pagados sobre el capital y los intereses ya devengados. La fórmula de interés compuesto es $A = P\left(1 + \frac{r}{n}\right)^{nt}$, donde F es la cantidad final, C es el capital, i es la tasa de interés expresada como un decimal, n es la cantidad de veces que se capitaliza el interés y t es el tiempo.	
cone A three-dimensional figure with one vertex and one circular base.	**cono** Figura tridimensional con un vértice y una base circular.	
congruent Having the same size and shape, the symbol for congurent is ≅.	**congruentes** Que tiene el mismo tamaño y la misma forma, expresado por ≅.	$\triangle ABC \cong \triangle DEF$
congruent angles Angles that have the same measure.	**ángulos congruentes** Ángulos que tienen la misma medida.	$\angle ABC \cong \angle DEF$
conjecture A statement believed to be true.	**conjetura** Enunciado que se supone verdadero.	
constant A value that does not change.	**constante** Valor que no cambia.	$3, 0, \pi$
constant of proportionality A constant ratio of two variables related proportionally.	**constante de proporcionalidad** Razón constante de dos variables que están relacionadas en forma proporcional.	
constant of variation The constant k in direct and inverse variation equations.	**constante de variación** La constante k en ecuaciones de variación directa e inversa.	$y = 5x$ ↑ constant of variation
convenience sample A sample based on members of the population that are readily available.	**muestra de conveniencia** Una muestra basada en miembros de la población que están fácilmente disponibles.	

Glossary/Glosario

ENGLISH	SPANISH	EXAMPLES
coordinate One of the numbers of an ordered pair that locate a point on a coordinate graph.	**coordenada** Uno de los números de un par ordenado que ubica un punto en una gráfica de coordenadas.	
coordinate plane A plane formed by the intersection of a horizontal number line called the *x*-axis and a vertical number line called the *y*-axis.	**plano cartesiano** Plano formado por la intersección de una recta numérica horizontal llamada eje *x* y otra vertical llamada eje *y*.	
correlation The description of the relationship between two data sets.	**correlación** Descripción de la relación entre dos conjuntos de datos.	
corresponding angles (for lines) Angles in the same position formed when a third line intersects two lines.	**ángulos correspondientes (en líneas)** Ángulos en la misma posición formaron cuando una tercera línea interseca dos líneas.	$\angle 1$ and $\angle 3$ are corresponding angles.
corresponding angles (of polygons) Angles in the same relative position in polygons with an equal number of sides.	**ángulos correspondientes (en polígonos)** Ángulos que se ubican en la misma posición relativa en dos o más polígonos.	$\angle A$ and $\angle D$ are corresponding angles.
corresponding sides Matching sides of two or more polygons.	**lados correspondientes** Lados que se ubican en la misma posición relativa en dos o más polígonos.	$\overline{AB}$ and $\overline{DE}$ are corresponding sides.
counterclockwise A circular movement in the direction shown.	**en sentido contrario a las manecillas del reloj** Movimiento circular en la dirección que se indica.	
counterexample An example that shows that a statement is false.	**contraejemplo** Ejemplo que demuestra que un enunciado es falso.	
cross product The product of numbers on the diagonal when comparing two ratios.	**producto cruzado** El producto de los números multiplicados en diagonal cuando se comparan dos razones.	For the proportion $\frac{2}{3} = \frac{4}{6}$, the cross products are $2 \cdot 6 = 12$ and $3 \cdot 4 = 12$.
cube (geometric figure) A rectangular prism with six congruent square faces.	**cubo (figura geométrica)** Prisma rectangular con seis caras cuadradas congruentes.	
cube (in numeration) A number raised to the third power.	**cubo (en numeración)** Número elevado a la tercera potencia.	$5^3 = 5 \cdot 5 \cdot 5 = 125$

ENGLISH	SPANISH	EXAMPLES
cumulative frequency The frequency of all data values that are less than or equal to a given value.	**frecuencia acumulativa** La frecuencia de todos los datos que son menores que o iguales a un valor dado.	
customary system of measurement The measurement system often used in the United States.	**sistema usual de medidas** El sistema de medidas que se usa comúnmente en Estados Unidos.	inches, feet, miles, ounces, pounds, tons, cups, quarts, gallons
cylinder A three-dimensional figure with two parallel, congruent circular bases connected by a curved lateral surface.	**cilindro** Figura tridimensional con dos bases circulares paralelas y congruentes, unidas por una superficie lateral curva.	

D

decagon A polygon with ten sides.	**decágono** Polígono de 10 lados.	
decimal system A base-10 place value system.	**sistema decimal** Sistema de valor posicional de base 10.	
deductive reasoning Using logic to show that a statement is true.	**razonamiento deductivo** Uso de la lógica para demostrar que un enunciado es verdadero.	
degree The unit of measure for angles or temperature.	**grado** Unidad de medida para ángulos y temperaturas.	
denominator The bottom number of a fraction that tells how many equal parts are in the whole.	**denominador** Número de abajo de una fracción que indica en cuántas partes iguales se divide el entero.	$\frac{3}{4}$ ◄— denominator
dependent events Events for which the outcome of one event affects the probability of the second event.	**sucesos dependientes** Dos sucesos son dependientes si el resultado de uno afecta la probabilidad del otro.	A bag contains 3 red marbles and 2 blue marbles. Drawing a red marble and then drawing a blue marble without replacing the first marble is an example of dependent events.
diagonal A line segment that connects two nonadjacent vertices of a polygon.	**diagonal** Segmento de recta que une dos vértices no adyacentes de un polígono.	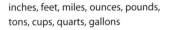
diameter A line segment that passes through the center of a circle and has endpoints on the circle, or the length of that segment.	**diámetro** Segmento de recta que pasa por el centro de un círculo y tiene sus extremos en la circunferencia, o bien la longitud de ese segmento.	
difference The result when one number is subtracted from another.	**diferencia** El resultado de restar un número de otro.	In $16 - 5 = 11$, 11 is the difference.

Glossary/Glosario

dimension The length, width, or height of a figure.

dimensión Longitud, ancho o altura de una figura.

direct variation A linear relationship between two variables, x and y, that can be written in the form $y = kx$, where k is a nonzero constant.

variacion directa Relación lineal entre dos variables, x e y, que puede expresarse en la forma $y = kx$, donde k es una constante distinta de cero.

$$y = 2x$$

Distributive Property For all real numbers, a, b, and c, $a(b + c) = ab + ac$ and $a(b - c) = ab - ac$.

Propiedad distributiva Dado números reales a, b, y c, $a(b + c) = ab + ac$ y $a(b - c) = ab - ac$.

$5(20 + 1) = 5 \cdot 20 + 5 \cdot 1$

dividend The number to be divided in a division problem.

dividendo Número que se divide en un problema de división.

In $8 \div 4 = 2$, 8 is the dividend.

divisible Can be divided by a number without leaving a remainder.

divisible Que se puede dividir entre un número sin dejar residuo.

18 is divisible by 3.

Division Property of Equality The property that states that if you divide both sides of an equation by the same nonzero number, the new equation will have the same solution.

Propiedad de igualdad de la división Propiedad que establece que puedes dividir ambos lados de una ecuación entre el mismo número distinto de cero, y la nueva ecuación tendrá la misma solución.

$4x = 12$

$\frac{4x}{4} = \frac{12}{4}$

$x = 3$

divisor The number you are dividing by in a division problem.

divisor El número entre el que se divide en un problema de división.

In $8 \div 4 = 2$, 4 is the divisor.

double-bar graph A bar graph that compares two related sets of data.

gráfica de doble barra Gráfica de barras que compara dos conjuntos de datos relacionados.

double-line graph A line graph that shows how two related sets of data change over time.

gráfica de doble línea Gráfica lineal que muestra cómo cambian con el tiempo dos conjuntos de datos relacionados.

E

edge The line segment along which two faces of a polyhedron intersect.

arista Segmento de recta donde se intersecan dos caras de un poliedro.

Edge

Glossary/Glosario

ENGLISH	SPANISH	EXAMPLES
endpoint A point at the end of a line segment or ray.	**extremo** Un punto ubicado al final de un segmento de recta o rayo.	A ●———————● B ●——————→ D
equally likely Outcomes that have the same probability.	**resultados igualmente probables** Resultados que tienen la misma probabilidad de ocurrir.	
equation A mathematical sentence that shows that two expressions are equivalent.	**ecuación** Enunciado matemático que indica que dos expresiones son equivalentes.	$x + 4 = 7$ $6 + 1 = 10 - 3$
equilateral triangle A triangle with three congruent sides.	**triángulo equilátero** Triángulo con tres lados congruentes.	
equivalent Having the same value.	**equivalentes** Que tienen el mismo valor.	
equivalent fractions Fractions that name the same amount or part.	**fracciones equivalentes** Fracciones que representan la misma cantidad o parte.	$\frac{1}{2}$ and $\frac{2}{4}$ are equivalent fractions.
equivalent ratios Ratios that name the same comparison.	**razones equivalentes** Razones que representan la misma comparación.	$\frac{1}{2}$ and $\frac{2}{4}$ are equivalent ratios.
estimate (n) An answer that is close to the exact answer and is found by rounding or other methods.	**estimación (s)** Una solución aproximada a la respuesta exacta que se halla mediante el redondeo u otros métodos.	
estimate (v) To find an answer close to the exact answer by rounding or other methods.	**estimar (v)** Hallar una solución aproximada a la respuesta exacta mediante el redondeo u otros métodos.	
evaluate To find the value of a numerical or algebraic expression.	**evaluar** Hallar el valor de una expresión numérica o algebraica.	Evaluate $2x + 7$ for $x = 3$. $2x + 7$ $2(3) + 7$ $6 + 7$ 13
even number An integer that is divisible by two.	**número par** Número entero divisible entre 2.	2, 4, 6
event An outcome or set of outcomes of an experiment or situation.	**suceso** Un resultado o una serie de resultados de un experimento o una situación.	When rolling a number cube, the event "an odd number" consists of the outcomes 1, 3, and 5.
expanded form A number written as the sum of the values of its digits.	**forma desarrollada** Número escrito como suma de los valores de sus dígitos.	236,536 written in expanded form is $200,000 + 30,000 +$ $6,000 + 500 + 30 + 6$.
experiment In probability, any activity based on chance, such as tossing a coin.	**experimento** En probabilidad, cualquier actividad basada en la posibilidad, como lanzar una moneda.	Tossing a coin 10 times and noting the number of "heads"

Glossary/Glosario

ENGLISH	SPANISH	EXAMPLES
experimental probability The ratio of the number of times an event occurs to the total number of trials, or times that the activity is performed.	**probabilidad experimental** Razón del número de veces que ocurre un suceso al número total de pruebas o al número de veces que se realiza el experimento.	Kendra attempted 27 free throws and made 16 of them. Her experimental probability of making a free throw is $\dfrac{\text{number made}}{\text{number attempted}} = \dfrac{16}{27} \approx 0.59$.
exponent The number that indicates how many times the base is used as a factor.	**exponente** Número que indica cuántas veces se usa la base como factor.	$2^3 = 2 \cdot 2 \cdot 2 = 8$; 3 is the exponent.
exponential form A number is in exponential form when it is written with a base and an exponent.	**forma exponencial** Se dice que un número está en forma exponencial cuando se escribe con una base y un exponente.	4^2 is the exponential form for $4 \cdot 4$.
expression A mathematical phrase that contains operations, numbers, and/or variables.	**expresión** Enunciado matemático que contiene operaciones, números y/o variables.	$6x + 1$

F

face A flat surface of a polyhedron.	**cara** Superficie plana de un poliedro.	Face
factor A number that is multiplied by another number to get a product.	**factor** Número que se multiplica por otro para hallar un producto.	7 is a factor of 21 since $7 \cdot 3 = 21$.
factor tree A diagram showing how a whole number breaks down into its prime factors.	**árbol de factores** Diagrama que muestra cómo se descompone un número cabal en sus factores primos.	12 $3 \cdot 4$ $2 \cdot 2$ $12 = 3 \cdot 2 \cdot 2$
factorial The product of all whole numbers except zero that are less than or equal to a number.	**factorial** El producto de todos los números cabales, excepto cero que son menores que o iguales a un número.	4 factorial $= 4! = 4 \cdot 3 \cdot 2 \cdot 1$
Fahrenheit A temperature scale in which 32 °F is the freezing point of water and 212 °F is the boiling point of water.	**Fahrenheit** Escala de temperatura en la que 32 °F es el punto de congelación del agua y 212 °F es el punto de ebullición.	
fair When all outcomes of an experiment are equally likely, the experiment is said to be fair.	**justo** Se dice de un experimento donde todos los resultados posibles son igualmente probables.	
federal withholding The amount of an employee's pay that the employer sends to the federal government as partial payment of the employee's yearly income tax.	**retención fiscal federal** Ingresos que descuenta un empleador y que envía al gobierno federal como pago parcial del impuesto sobre el salario anual del empleado.	

ENGLISH	SPANISH	EXAMPLES
first quartile The median of the lower half of a set of data; also called *lower quartile*.	**primer cuartil** La mediana de la mitad inferior de un conjunto de datos. También se llama *cuartil inferior*.	
fixed expenses Expenses that occur regularly and stay the same.	**gastos fijos** Gastos que ocurren con regularidad y se mantienen igual.	
formula A rule showing relationships among quantities.	**fórmula** Regla que muestra relaciones entre cantidades.	$A = lw$ is the formula for the area of a rectangle.
fraction A number in the form $\frac{a}{b}$, where $b \neq 0$.	**fracción** Número escrito en la forma $\frac{a}{b}$, donde $b \neq 0$.	
frequency The number of times the value appears in the data set.	**frecuencia** Cantidad de veces que aparece el valor en un conjunto de datos.	In the data set 5, 6, 6, 7, 8, 9, the data value 6 has a frequency of 2.

frequency table A table that lists items together according to the number of times, or frequency, that the items occur.

tabla de frecuencia Una tabla en la que se organizan los datos de acuerdo con el número de veces que aparece cada valor (o la frecuencia).

Data set: 1, 1, 2, 2, 3, 4, 5, 5, 5, 6, 6, 6, 6
Frequency table:

Data	1	2	3	4	5	6
Frequency	2	2	1	1	3	4

function An input-output relationship that has exactly one output for each input.

función Relación de entrada-salida en la que a cada valor de entrada corresponde exactamente un valor de salida.

function table A table of ordered pairs that represent solutions of a function.

tabla de función Tabla de pares ordenados que representan soluciones de una función.

x	3	4	5	6
y	7	9	11	13

Fundamental Counting Principle If one event has m possible outcomes and a second event has n possible outcomes after the first event has occurred, then there are $m \cdot n$ total possible outcomes for the two events.

Principio fundamental de conteo Si un suceso tiene m resultados posibles y otro suceso tiene n resultados posibles después de ocurrido el primer suceso, entonces hay $m \cdot n$ resultados posibles en total para los dos sucesos.

There are 4 colors of shirts and 3 colors of pants. There are $4 \cdot 3 = 12$ possible outfits.

G

ENGLISH	SPANISH	EXAMPLES
geometric sequence A sequence in which each term is multiplied by the same value to get the next term.	**sucesión geométrica** Una sucesión en la que cada término se multiplica por el mismo valor para obtener el siguiente término.	The sequence 2, 4, 8, 16 … is a geometric sequence.
graph of an equation A graph of the set of ordered pairs that are solutions of the equation.	**gráfica de una ecuación** Gráfica del conjunto de pares ordenados que son soluciones de la ecuación.	
greatest common factor (GCF) The largest common factor of two or more given numbers.	**máximo común divisor (MCD)** El mayor de los factores comunes compartidos por dos o más números dados.	The GCF of 27 and 45 is 9.

gross pay An employee's pay before any deductions are taken.

paga bruta Paga de un empleado antes de sustraer cualquier deducción.

H

height In a pyramid or cone, the perpendicular distance from the base to the opposite vertex.

altura En una pirámide o cono, la distancia perpendicular desde la base al vértice opuesto.

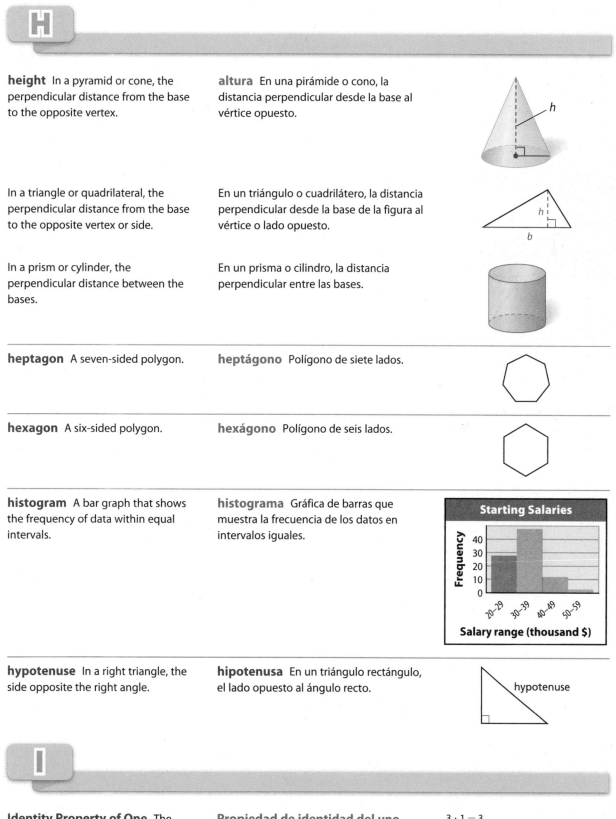

In a triangle or quadrilateral, the perpendicular distance from the base to the opposite vertex or side.

En un triángulo o cuadrilátero, la distancia perpendicular desde la base de la figura al vértice o lado opuesto.

In a prism or cylinder, the perpendicular distance between the bases.

En un prisma o cilindro, la distancia perpendicular entre las bases.

heptagon A seven-sided polygon.

heptágono Polígono de siete lados.

hexagon A six-sided polygon.

hexágono Polígono de seis lados.

histogram A bar graph that shows the frequency of data within equal intervals.

histograma Gráfica de barras que muestra la frecuencia de los datos en intervalos iguales.

hypotenuse In a right triangle, the side opposite the right angle.

hipotenusa En un triángulo rectángulo, el lado opuesto al ángulo recto.

I

Identity Property of One The property that states that the product of 1 and any number is that number.

Propiedad de identidad del uno Propiedad que establece que el producto de 1 y cualquier número es ese número.

$3 \cdot 1 = 3$
$-9 \cdot 1 = -9$

ENGLISH	SPANISH	EXAMPLES
Identity Property of Zero The property that states that the sum of zero and any number is that number.	**Propiedad de identidad del cero** Propiedad que establece que la suma de cero y cualquier número es ese número.	$5 + 0 = 5$ $-4 + 0 = -4$
image A figure resulting from a transformation.	**imagen** Figura que resulta de una transformación.	
impossible (probability) Can never happen; having a probability of 0.	**imposible (en probabilidad)** Que no puede ocurrir. Suceso cuya probabilidad de ocurrir es 0.	
improper fraction A fraction in which the numerator is greater than or equal to the denominator.	**fracción impropia** Fracción en la que el numerador es mayor que o igual al denominador.	$\frac{5}{5}$ $\frac{7}{4}$
income Money that is paid to a person for goods, services, or investments.	**ingreso** Dinero que se le paga a una persona por bienes, servicios o inversiones.	
independent events Events for which the outcome of one event does not affect the probability of the other.	**sucesos independientes** Dos sucesos son independientes si el resultado de uno no afecta la probabilidad del otro.	A bag contains 3 red marbles and 2 blue marbles. Drawing a red marble, replacing it, and then drawing a blue marble is an example of independent events.
indirect measurement The technique of using similar figures and proportions to find a measure.	**medición indirecta** La técnica de usar figuras semejantes y proporciones para hallar una medida.	
inductive reasoning Using a pattern to make a conclusion.	**razonamiento inductivo** Uso de un patrón para sacar una conclusión.	
inequality A mathematical sentence that shows the relationship between quantities that are not equivalent.	**desigualdad** Enunciado matemático que muestra una relación entre cantidades que no son equivalentes.	$5 < 8$ $5x + 2 \geq 12$
input The value substituted into an expression or function.	**valor de entrada** Valor que se usa para sustituir una variable en una expresión o función.	For the function $y = 6x$, the input 4 produces an output of 24.
integers The set of whole numbers and their opposites.	**enteros** Conjunto de todos los números cabales y sus opuestos.	$\ldots -3, -2, -1, 0, 1, 2, 3, \ldots$
interest The amount of money charged for borrowing or using money, or the amount of money earned by saving money.	**interés** Cantidad de dinero que se cobra por el préstamo o uso del dinero, o la cantidad que se gana al ahorrar dinero.	

Glossary/Glosario

ENGLISH	SPANISH	EXAMPLES

interquartile range The difference between the upper and lower quartiles in a box-and-whisker plot.

rango entre cuartiles La diferencia entre los cuartiles superior e inferior en una gráfica de mediana y rango.

Lower half   Upper half
18, ⟨23⟩, 28, 29, ⟨36⟩, 42
↑   ↑
Lower   Upper
quartile   quartile
Interquartile range: $36 - 23 = 13$

---

intersecting lines Lines that cross at exactly one point.

líneas secantes Líneas que se cruzan en un solo punto.

---

interval The space between marked values on a number line or the scale of a graph.

intervalo El espacio entre los valores marcados en una recta numérica o en la escala de una gráfica.

---

inverse operations Operations that undo each other: addition and subtraction, or multiplication and division.

operaciones inversas Operaciones que se cancelan mutuamente: suma y resta, o multiplicación y división.

Addition and subtraction are inverse operations:
$5 + 3 = 8; 8 - 3 = 5$
Multiplication and division are inverse operations:
$2 \cdot 3 = 6; 6 \div 3 = 2$

Inverse Property of Addition The sum of a number and its opposite, or additive inverse, is 0.

propiedad inversa de la suma La suma de un número y su opuesto, o inverso aditivo, es cero.

$3 + (-3) = 0; a + (-a) = 0$

---

irrational number A number that cannot be expressed as a ratio of two integers or as a repeating or terminating decimal.

número irracional Número que no puede expresarse como una razón de dos enteros ni como un decimal periódico o finito.

$\sqrt{2}, \pi$

---

isolate the variable To get a variable alone on one side of an equation or inequality in order to solve the equation or inequality.

despejar la variable Dejar sola la variable en un lado de una ecuación o desigualdad para resolverla.

$$\begin{array}{rcc} x + 7 = & & 22 \\ -7 & & -7 \\ \hline x & = & 15 \end{array}$$

---

isosceles triangle A triangle with at least two congruent sides.

triángulo isósceles Triángulo que tiene al menos dos lados congruentes.

L

lateral area The sum of the areas of the lateral faces of a prism or pyramid, or the area of the lateral surface of a cylinder or cone.

área lateral Suma de las áreas de las caras laterales de un prisma o pirámide, o área de la superficie lateral de un cilindro o cono.

12 cm
6 cm
8 cm
Lateral area $= 12(8)(2) + 12(6)(2)$
$= 336$ cm²

---

lateral face A face of a prism or a pyramid that is not a base.

Cara lateral Cara de un prisma o pirámide que no es una base.

Bases
Lateral face
Right prism

Glossary/Glosario

ENGLISH	SPANISH	EXAMPLES
least common denominator (LCD) The least common multiple of two or more denominators.	**mínimo común denominador (mcd)** El mínimo común múltiplo de dos o más denominadores.	The LCD of $\frac{3}{4}$ and $\frac{5}{6}$ is 12.
least common multiple (LCM) The least number, other than zero, that is a multiple of two or more given numbers.	**mínimo común múltiplo (mcm)** El menor de los números, distinto de cero, que es múltiplo de dos o más números.	The LCM of 10 and 18 is 90.
legs In a right triangle, the sides that include the right angle; in an isosceles triangle, the pair of congruent sides.	**catetos** En un triángulo rectángulo, los lados adyacentes al ángulo recto. En un triángulo isósceles, el par de lados congruentes.	
liability Money a person owes.	**pasivo** Dinero que debe una persona.	
like terms Terms with the same variables raised to the same exponents.	**términos semejantes** Términos que contienen las mismas variables elevada a las mismas exponentes.	In the expression $3a^2 + 5b + 12a^2$, $3a^2$ and $12a^2$ are like terms.
line A straight path that has no thickness and extends forever.	**línea** Trayectoria recta que no tiene ningún grueso y que se extiende por siempre.	
line graph A graph that uses line segments to show how data changes.	**gráfica lineal** Gráfica que muestra cómo cambian los datos mediante segmentos de recta.	
line of best fit A straight line that comes closest to the points on a scatter plot.	**línea de mejor ajuste** la línea recta que más se aproxima a los puntos de un diagrama de dispersión.	
line of reflection A line that a figure is flipped across to create a mirror image of the original figure.	**línea de reflexión** Línea sobre la cual se invierte una figura para crear una imagen reflejada de la figura original.	\n**Line of reflection**
line of symmetry The imaginary "mirror" in line symmetry.	**eje de simetría** El "espejo" imaginario en la simetría axial.	
line plot A number line with marks or dots that show frequency.	**diagrama de acumulación** Recta numérica con marcas o puntos que indican la frecuencia.	

ENGLISH	SPANISH	EXAMPLES

line segment A part of a line made of two endpoints and all points between them. | **segmento de recta** Parte de una línea con dos extremos. | A · ———— · B

line symmetry A figure has line symmetry if one-half is a mirror-image of the other half. | **simetría axial** Una figura tiene simetría axial si una de sus mitades es la imagen reflejada de la otra. |

linear equation An equation whose solutions form a straight line on a coordinate plane. | **ecuación lineal** Ecuación cuyas soluciones forman una línea recta en un plano cartesiano. | $y = 2x + 1$

linear function A function whose graph is a straight line. | **función lineal** Función cuya gráfica es una línea recta. | $y = x - 1$

linear relationship A relationship between two quantities in which one variable changes by a constant amount as the other variable changes by a constant amount. | **relación lineal** Relación entre dos cantidades en la cual una variable cambia según una cantidad constante y la otra variable también cambia según una cantidad constante. |

lower quartile The median of the lower half of a set of data. | **cuartil inferior** La mediana de la mitad inferior de un conjunto de datos. | Lower half   Upper half
18, (23), 28, 29, 36, 42
↑
Lower quartile

M

mean The sum of the items in a set of data divided by the number of items in the set; also called *average*. | **media** La suma de todos los elementos de un conjunto de datos dividida entre el número de elementos del conjunto. También se llama *promedio*. | Data set: 4, 6, 7, 8, 10
Mean:
$\frac{4 + 6 + 7 + 8 + 10}{5} = \frac{35}{5} = 7$

measure of central tendency A measure used to describe the middle of a data set; the mean, median, and mode are measures of central tendency. | **medida de tendencia dominante** Medida que describe la parte media de un conjunto de datos; la media, la mediana y la moda son medidas de tendencia dominante. |

median The middle number, or the mean (average) of the two middle numbers, in an ordered set of data. | **mediana** El número intermedio, o la media (el promedio), de los dos números intermedios en un conjunto ordenado de datos. | Data set: 4, 6, 7, 8, 10
Median: 7

metric system of measurement A decimal system of weights and measures that is used universally in science and commonly throughout the world. | **sistema métrico de medición** Sistema decimal de pesos y medidas empleado universalmente en las ciencias y comúnmente en todo el mundo. | centimeters, meters, kilometers, grams, kilograms, milliliters, liters

ENGLISH	SPANISH	EXAMPLES
midpoint The point that divides a line segment into two congruent line segments.	**punto medio** El punto que divide un segmento de recta en dos segmentos de recta congruentes.	 B is the midpoint of $\overline{AC}$.
mixed number A number made up of a whole number that is not zero and a fraction.	**número mixto** Número compuesto por un número cabal distinto de cero y una fracción.	$5\frac{1}{8}$
mode The number or numbers that occur most frequently in a set of data; when all numbers occur with the same frequency, we say there is no mode.	**moda** Número o números más frecuentes en un conjunto de datos; si todos los números aparecen con la misma frecuencia, no hay moda.	Data set: 3, 5, 8, 8, 10 Mode: 8
multiple The product of any number and any nonzero whole number is a multiple of that number.	**múltiplo** El producto de un número y cualquier número cabal distinto de cero es un múltiplo de ese número.	30, 40, and 90 are all multiples of 10.
Multiplication Property of Equality The property that states that if you multiply both sides of an equation by the same number, the new equation will have the same solution.	**Propiedad de igualdad de la multiplicación** Propiedad que establece que puedes multiplicar ambos lados de una ecuación por el mismo número y la nueva ecuación tendrá la misma solución.	$\frac{1}{3}x = 7$ $(3)(\frac{1}{3}x) = (3)(7)$ $x = 21$
Multiplication Property of Zero The property that states that for all real numbers a, $a \times 0 = 0$ and $0 \times a = 0$.	**Propiedad de multiplicación del cero** Propiedad que establece que para todos los números reales a, $a \times 0 = 0$ y $0 \times a = 0$.	$6 \cdot 0 = 0$ $-5 \cdot 0 = 0$
Multiplicative Inverse Property The product of a nonzero number and its reciprocal, or multiplicative inverse, is one.	**Propiedad inversa de la multiplicación** El producto de un número distinto a cero y su recíproco, o inverso multiplicativo, es uno.	$\frac{2}{3} \cdot \frac{3}{2} = 1; \frac{a}{b} \cdot \frac{b}{a} = 1$
mutually exclusive Two events are mutually exclusive if they cannot occur in the same trial of an experiment.	**mutuamente excluyentes** Dos sucesos son mutuamente excluyentes cuando no pueden ocurrir en la misma prueba de un experimento.	

N

ENGLISH	SPANISH	EXAMPLES
negative correlation Two data sets have a negative correlation, or relationship, if one set of data values increases while the other decreases.	**correlación negativa** Dos conjuntos de datos tienen correlación, o relación, negativa, si los valores de un conjunto aumentan a medida que los valores del otro conjunto disminuyen.	
negative integer An integer less than zero.	**entero negativo** Entero menor que cero.	← −4 −3 −2 −1 0 1 2 3 4 → −2 is a negative integer.

Glossary/Glosario

ENGLISH	SPANISH	EXAMPLES
net An arrangement of two-dimensional figures that can be folded to form a polyhedron.	**plantilla** Arreglo de figuras bidimensionales que se doblan para formar un poliedro.	
net pay The amount that remains after all deductions are taken from the gross pay.	**paga neta** Cantidad restante después de restar todas las deducciones de la paga bruta.	
net worth The difference between the monetary values of a consumer's assets and liabilities.	**patrimonio neto** Diferencia entre el valor monetario de los activos y pasivos de un consumidor.	
no correlation Two data sets have no correlation when there is no relationship between their data values.	**sin correlación** Caso en que los valores de dos conjuntos de datos no muestran ninguna relación.	
nonlinear function A function whose graph is not a straight line.	**función no lineal** Función cuya gráfica no es una línea recta.	
nonterminating decimal A decimal that never ends.	**decimal infinito** Decimal que nunca termina.	
numerator The top number of a fraction that tells how many parts of a whole are being considered.	**numerador** El número de arriba de una fracción; indica cuántas partes de un entero se consideran.	$\frac{4}{5}$ ← numerator
numerical expression An expression that contains only numbers and operations.	**expresión numérica** Expresión que incluye sólo números y operaciones.	$(2 \cdot 3) + 1$

obtuse angle An angle whose measure is greater than 90° but less than 180°.	**ángulo obtuso** Ángulo que mide más de 90° y menos de 180°.	
obtuse triangle A triangle containing one obtuse angle.	**triángulo obtusángulo** Triángulo que tiene un ángulo obtuso.	
octagon An eight-sided polygon.	**octágono** Polígono de ocho lados.	

ENGLISH	SPANISH	EXAMPLES
odd number An integer that is not divisible by two.	**número impar** Entero que no es divisible entre 2.	
odds A comparison of the number of ways an event can occur and the number of ways an event can NOT occur.	**posibilidades** Comparación del numero de las maneras que puede ocurrir un suceso y el numero de maneras que no puede ocurrir el suceso.	
opposites Two numbers that are an equal distance from zero on a number line; also called *additive inverse*.	**opuestos** Dos números que están a la misma distancia de cero en una recta numérica. También se llaman *inversos aditivos*.	5 and −5 are opposites. 5 units · 5 units −6 −5 −4 −3 −2 −1 0 1 2 3 4 5 6
order of operations A rule for evaluating expressions: first perform the operations in parentheses, then compute powers and roots, then perform all multiplication and division from left to right, and then perform all addition and subtraction from left to right.	**orden de las operaciones** Regla para evaluar expresiones: primero se hacen las operaciones entre paréntesis, luego se hallan las potencias y raíces, después todas las multiplicaciones y divisiones de izquierda a derecha y, por último, todas las sumas y restas de izquierda a derecha.	$3^2 - 12 \div 4$ $9 - 12 \div 4$ Evaluate the power. Divide. $9 - 3$ Subtract. 6
ordered pair A pair of numbers that can be used to locate a point on a coordinate plane.	**par ordenado** Par de números que sirven para ubicar un punto en un plano cartesiano.	The coordinates of *B* are (−2, 3).
origin The point where the *x*-axis and *y*-axis intersect on the coordinate plane; (0, 0).	**origen** Punto de intersección entre el eje *x* y el eje *y* en un plano cartesiano: (0, 0).	origin
outcome A possible result of a probability experiment.	**resultado** Posible resultado de un experimento de probabilidad.	When rolling a number cube, the possible outcomes are 1, 2, 3, 4, 5, and 6.
outlier A value much greater or much less than the others in a data set.	**valor extremo** Un valor mucho mayor o menor que los demás de un conjunto de datos.	Most of data Mean Outlier
output The value that results from the substitution of a given input into an expression or function.	**valor de salida** Valor que resulta después de sustituir un valor de entrada determinado en una expresión o función.	For the function $y = 6x$, the input 4 produces an output of 24.
overestimate An estimate that is greater than the exact answer.	**estimación alta** Estimación mayor que la respuesta exacta.	100 is an overestimate for the sum $23 + 24 + 21 + 22$.

P

parallel lines Lines in a plane that do not intersect.

líneas paralelas Líneas que se encuentran en el mismo plano pero que nunca se intersecan.

parallelogram A quadrilateral with two pairs of parallel sides.

paralelogramo Cuadrilátero con dos pares de lados paralelos.

pentagon A five-sided polygon.

pentágono Polígono de cinco lados.

percent A ratio comparing a number to 100.

porcentaje Razón que compara un número con el número 100.

$45\% = \frac{45}{100}$

percent of change The amount stated as a percent that a number increases or decreases.

porcentaje de cambio Cantidad en que un número aumenta o disminuye, expresada como un porcentaje.

percent of decrease A percent change describing a decrease in a quantity.

porcentaje de disminución Porcentaje de cambio en que una cantidad disminuye.

An item that costs $8 is marked down to $6. The amount of the decrease is $2 and the percent of decrease is $\frac{2}{8} = 0.25 = 25\%$.

percent of increase A percent change describing an increase in a quantity.

porcentaje de incremento Porcentaje de cambio en que una cantidad aumenta.

The price of an item increases from $8 to $12. The amount of the increase is $4 and the percent of increase is $\frac{4}{8} = 0.5 = 50\%$.

perfect square A square of a whole number.

cuadrado perfecto El cuadrado de un número cabal.

$5^2 = 25$, so 25 is a perfect square.

perimeter The distance around a polygon.

perímetro Distancia alrededor de un polígono.

perimeter = $18 + 6 + 18 + 6 = 48$ ft

permutation An arrangement of items or events in which order is important.

permutación Arreglo de objetos o sucesos en el que el orden es importante.

For objects A, B, and C, there are 6 different permutations, ABC, ACB, BAC, BCA, CAB, and CBA.

perpendicular bisector A line that intersects a segment at its midpoint and is perpendicular to the segment.

mediatriz Línea que cruza un segmento en su punto medio y es perpendicular al segmento.

Glossary/Glosario

perpendicular lines Lines that intersect to form right angles.

líneas perpendiculares Líneas que al intersecarse forman ángulos rectos.

---

pi (π) The ratio of the circumference of a circle to the length of its diameter; $\pi \approx 3.14$ or $\frac{22}{7}$.

pi (π) Razón de la circunferencia de un círculo a la longitud de su diámetro; $\pi \approx 3.14$ ó $\frac{22}{7}$.

---

plane A flat surface that has no thickness and extends forever.

plano Superficie plana que no tiene ningún grueso y que se extiende por siempre.

plane *ABC*

---

point An exact location that has no size.

punto Ubicación exacta que no tiene ninqún tamaño.

P •
point *P*

---

polygon A closed plane figure formed by three or more line segments that intersect only at their endpoints (vertices).

polígono Figura plana cerrada, formada por tres o más segmentos de recta que se intersecan sólo en sus extremos (vértices).

---

polyhedron A three-dimensional figure in which all the surfaces or faces are polygons.

poliedro Figura tridimensional cuyas superficies o caras tienen forma de polígonos.

---

population The entire group of objects or individuals considered for a survey.

población Grupo completo de objetos o individuos que se desea estudiar.

In a survey about the study habits of middle school students, the population is all middle school students.

---

positive correlation Two data sets have a positive correlation, or relationship, when their data values increase or decrease together.

correlación positiva Dos conjuntos de datos tienen una correlación, o relación, positiva cuando los valores de ambos conjuntos aumentan o disminuyen al mismo tiempo.

---

positive integer An integer greater than zero.

entero positivo Entero mayor que cero.

---

power A number produced by raising a base to an exponent.

potencia Número que resulta al elevar una base a un exponente.

$2^3 = 8$, so 2 to the 3rd power is 8.

---

precision The level of detail of a measurement, determined by the unit of measure.

precisión Detalle de una medición, determinado por la unidad de medida.

A ruler marked in millimeters has a greater level of precision than a ruler marked in centimeters.

---

prediction Something you can reasonably expect to happen in the future.

predicción Algo que se puede razonablemente esperar suceder en el futuro.

Glossary/Glosario

preimage The original figure in a transformation.

imagen original Figura original en una transformación.

Preimage

prime factorization A number written as the product of its prime factors.

factorización prima Un número escrito como el producto de sus factores primos.

$10 = 2 \cdot 5$
$24 = 2^3 \cdot 3$

prime number A whole number greater than 1 that has exactly two factors, itself and 1.

número primo Número cabal mayor que 1 que sólo es divisible entre 1 y él mismo.

5 is prime because its only factors are 5 and 1.

principal The initial amount of money borrowed or saved.

capital Cantidad inicial de dinero depositada o recibida en préstamo.

prism A polyhedron that has two congruent polygon-shaped bases and other faces that are all parallelograms.

prisma Poliedro con dos bases congruentes con forma de polígono y caras con forma de paralelogramo.

probability A number from 0 to 1 (or 0% to 100%) that describes how likely an event is to occur.

probabilidad Un número entre 0 y 1 (ó 0% y 100%) que describe qué tan probable es un suceso.

A bag contains 3 red marbles and 4 blue marbles. The probability of randomly choosing a red marble is $\frac{3}{7}$

product The result when two or more numbers are multiplied.

producto Resultado de multiplicar dos o más números.

The product of 4 and 8 is 32.

proper fraction A fraction in which the numerator is less than the denominator.

fracción propia Fracción en la que el numerador es menor que el denominador.

$\frac{3}{4}, \frac{1}{12}, \frac{7}{8}$

proportion An equation that states that two ratios are equivalent.

proporción Ecuación que establece que dos razones son equivalentes.

$\frac{2}{3} = \frac{4}{6}$

proportional relationship A relationship between two quantities in which the ratio of one quantity to the other quantity is constant.

relación proporcional Relación entre dos cantidades en que la razón de una cantidad a la otra es constante.

protractor A tool for measuring angles.

transportador Instrumento para medir ángulos.

pyramid A polyhedron with a polygon base and triangular sides that all meet at a common vertex.

pirámide Poliedro cuya base es un polígono; tiene caras triangulares que se juntan en un vértice común.

Glossary/Glosario

ENGLISH	SPANISH	EXAMPLES

Pythagorean Theorem In a right triangle, the square of the length of the hypotenuse is equal to the sum of the squares of the lengths of the legs.

Teorema de Pitágoras En un triángulo rectángulo, la suma de los cuadrados de los catetos es igual al cuadrado de la hipotenusa.

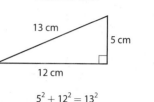

$$5^2 + 12^2 = 13^2$$
$$25 + 144 = 169$$

Q

quadrant The x- and y-axes divide the coordinate plane into four regions. Each region is called a quadrant.

cuadrante El eje x y el eje y dividen el plano cartesiano en cuatro regiones. Cada región recibe el nombre de cuadrante.

Quadrant II	Quadrant I
Quadrant III	Quadrant IV

quadratic function A function of the form $y = ax^2 + bx + c$, where $a \neq 0$.

función cuadrática Función del tipo $y = ax^2 + bx + c$, donde $a \neq 0$.

$y = 2x^2 - 12x + 10,$
$y = 3x^2$

quadrilateral A four-sided polygon.

cuadrilátero Polígono de cuatro lados.

quartile Three values, one of which is the median, that divide a data set into fourths. See also *first quartile, third quartile*.

cuartiles Cada uno de tres valores, uno de los cuales es la mediana, que dividen en cuartos un conjunto de datos. Ver también *primer cuartil, tercer cuartil*.

quotient The result when one number is divided by another.

cociente Resultado de dividir un número entre otro.

In $8 \div 4 = 2$, 2 is the quotient.

R

radical sign The symbol $\sqrt{}$ used to represent the nonnegative square root of a number.

símbolo de radical El símbolo $\sqrt{}$ con que se representa la raíz cuadrada no negativa de un número.

$\sqrt{36} = 6$

radius A line segment with one endpoint at the center of a circle and the other endpoint on the circle, or the length of that segment.

radio Segmento de recta con un extremo en el centro de un círculo y el otro en la circunferencia; o bien la longitud de ese segmento.

Radius

random sample A sample in which each individual or object in the entire population has an equal chance of being selected.

muestra aleatoria Muestra en la que cada individuo u objeto de la población tiene la misma oportunidad de ser elegido.

Mr. Henson chose a random sample of the class by writing each student's name on a slip of paper, mixing up the slips, and drawing five slips without looking.

Glossary/Glosario

ENGLISH	SPANISH	EXAMPLES
range (in statistics) The difference between the greatest and least values in a data set.	**rango (en estadística)** Diferencia entre los valores máximo y mínimo de un conjunto de datos.	Data set: 3, 5, 7, 7, 12 Range: $12 - 3 = 9$
rate A ratio that compares two quantities measured in different units.	**tasa** Una razón que compara dos cantidades medidas en diferentes unidades.	The speed limit is 55 miles per hour, or 55 mi/h.
rate of change A ratio that compares the amount of change in a dependent variable to the amount of change in an independent variable.	**tasa de cambio** Razón que compara la cantidad de cambio de la variable dependiente con la cantidad de combio de la variable independiente.	The cost of mailing a letter increased from 22 cents in 1985 to 25 cents in 1988. During this period, the rate of change was $\frac{\text{change in cost}}{\text{change in year}} = \frac{25-22}{1988-1985} = \frac{3}{3}$
rate of interest The percent charged or earned on an amount of money; see *simple interest*.	**tasa de interés** Porcentaje que se cobra por una cantidad de dinero prestada o que se gana por una cantidad de dinero ahorrada; ver *interés simple*.	
ratio A comparison of two quantities by division.	**razón** Comparación de dos cantidades mediante una división.	12 to 25, 12:25, $\frac{12}{25}$
rational number Any number that can be expressed as a ratio of two integers.	**número racional** Número que se puede escribir como una razón de dos enteros.	6 can be expressed as $\frac{6}{1}$. 0.5 can be expressed as $\frac{1}{2}$.
ray A part of a line that starts at one endpoint and extends forever in one direction.	**rayo** Parte de una recta que comienza en un extremo y se extiende infinitamente en una dirección.	
real number A rational or irrational number.	**número real** Número racional o irracional.	
reciprocal One of two numbers whose product is 1; also called *multiplicative inverse*.	**recíproco** Uno de dos números cuyo producto es igual a 1. También se llama *inverso multiplicativo*.	The reciprocal of $\frac{2}{3}$ is $\frac{3}{2}$.
rectangle A parallelogram with four right angles.	**rectángulo** Paralelogramo con cuatro ángulos rectos.	
rectangular prism A polyhedron whose bases are rectangles and whose other faces are parallelograms.	**prisma rectangular** Poliedro cuyas bases son rectángulos y cuyas caras tienen forma de paralelogramo.	
reflection A transformation of a figure that flips the figure across a line.	**reflexión** Transformación que ocurre cuando se invierte una figura sobre una línea.	
regular polygon A polygon with congruent sides and angles.	**polígono regular** Polígono con lados y ángulos congruentes.	

Glossary/Glosario

ENGLISH	SPANISH	EXAMPLES
regular pyramid A pyramid whose base is a regular polygon and whose lateral faces are all congruent.	**pirámide regular** Pirámide que tiene un polígono regular como base y caras laterales congruentes.	
relative frequency The frequency of a data value or range of data values divided by the total number of data values in the set.	**frecuencia relativa** La frecuencia de un valor o un rango de valores dividido por el número total de los valores en el conjunto.	
relatively prime Two numbers are relatively prime if their greatest common factor (GCF) is 1.	**primo relatívo** Dos números son primos relativos si su máximo común divisor (MCD) es 1.	8 and 15 are relatively prime.
repeating decimal A decimal in which one or more digits repeat infinitely.	**decimal periódico** Decimal en el que uno o más dígitos se repiten infinitamente.	$0.757575\ldots = 0.\overline{75}$
rhombus A parallelogram with all sides congruent.	**rombo** Paralelogramo en el que todos los lados son congruentes.	
right angle An angle that measures 90°.	**ángulo recto** Ángulo que mide exactamente 90°.	
right triangle A triangle containing a right angle.	**triángulo rectángulo** Triángulo que tiene un ángulo recto.	
rise The vertical change when the slope of a line is expressed as the ratio $\frac{rise}{run}$, or "rise over run."	**distancia vertical** El cambio vertical cuando la pendiente de una línea se expresa como la razón $\frac{distancia\ vertical}{distancia\ horizontal}$, o "distancia vertical sobre distancia horizontal".	For the points $(3, -1)$ and $(6, 5)$, the rise is $5 - (-1) = 6$.
rotation A transformation in which a figure is turned around a point.	**rotación** Transformación que ocurre cuando una figura gira alrededor de un punto.	
rotational symmetry A figure has rotational symmetry if it can be rotated less than 360° around a central point and coincide with the original figure.	**simetría de rotación** Ocurre cuando una figura gira menos de 360° alrededor de un punto central sin dejar de ser congruente con la figura original.	
rounding Replacing a number with an estimate of that number to a given place value.	**redondear** Sustituir un número por una estimación de ese número hasta cierto valor posicional.	2,354 rounded to the nearest thousand is 2,000, and 2,354 rounded to the nearest 100 is 2,400.

ENGLISH	SPANISH	EXAMPLES
run The horizontal change when the slope of a line is expressed as the ratio $\frac{rise}{run}$, or "rise over run."	**distancia horizontal** El cambio horizontal cuando la pendiente de una línea se expresa como la razón $\frac{distancia\ vertical}{distancia\ horizontal}$, o "distancia vertical sobre distancia horizontal".	For the points $(3, -1)$ and $(6, 5)$, the run is $6 - 3 = 3$.

S

ENGLISH	SPANISH	EXAMPLES
sales tax A percent of the cost of an item, which is charged by governments to raise money.	**impuesto sobre la venta** Porcentaje del costo de un artículo que los gobiernos cobran para recaudar fondos.	
sample A part of the population.	**muestra** Una parte de la población.	In a survey about the study habits of middle school students, a sample is a survey of 100 randomly chosen students.
sample space All possible outcomes of an experiment.	**espacio muestral** Conjunto de todos los resultados posibles de un experimento.	When rolling a number cube, the sample space is 1, 2, 3, 4, 5, 6.
savings Money that is not spent by a consumer currently, but is reserved for later use.	**ahorros** Dinero que un consumidor no gasta en el presente, pero que reserva para uso futuro.	
scale The ratio between two sets of measurements.	**escala** La razón entre dos conjuntos de medidas.	1 cm:5 mi
scale drawing A drawing that uses a scale to make an object smaller than or larger than the real object.	**dibujo a escala** Dibujo en el que se usa una escala para que un objeto se vea mayor o menor que el objeto real al que representa.	A blueprint is an example of a scale drawing.
scale factor The ratio used to enlarge or reduce similar figures.	**factor de escala** Razón que se usa para agrandar o reducir figuras semejantes.	Scale factor: 2
scale model A proportional model of a three-dimensional object.	**modelo a escala** Modelo proporcional de un objeto tridimensional.	
scalene triangle A triangle with no congruent sides.	**triángulo escaleno** Triángulo que no tiene lados congruentes.	

© Houghton Mifflin Harcourt Publishing Company

	ENGLISH	SPANISH	EXAMPLES

scatter plot A graph with points plotted to show a possible relationship between two sets of data.

diagrama de dispersión Gráfica de puntos que se usa para mostrar una posible relación entre dos conjuntos de datos.

scientific notation A method of writing very large or very small numbers by using powers of 10.

notación científica Método que se usa para escribir números muy grandes o muy pequeños mediante potencias de 10.

$12{,}560{,}000{,}000{,}000 = 1.256 \times 10^{13}$

sector A region enclosed by two radii and the arc joining their endpoints.

sector Región encerrada por dos radios y el arco que une sus extremos.

sector (data) A section of a circle graph representing part of the data set.

sector (datos) Sección de una gráfica circular que representa una parte del conjunto de datos.

The circle graph has 5 sectors.

segment A part of a line between two endpoints.

segmento Parte de una línea entre dos extremos.

sequence An ordered list of numbers.

sucesión Lista ordenada de números.

2, 4, 6, 8, 10, …

set A group of terms.

conjunto Un grupo de elementos.

side A line bounding a geometric figure; one of the faces forming the outside of an object.

lado Línea que delimita las figuras geométricas; una de las caras que forman la parte exterior de un objeto.

Side-Side-Side (SSS) A rule stating that if three sides of one triangle are congruent to three sides of another triangle, then the triangles are congruent.

Lado-Lado-Lado (LLL) Regla que establece que dos triángulos son congruentes cuando sus tres lados correspondientes son congruentes.

$\triangle ABC \cong \triangle DEF$

Glossary/Glosario

ENGLISH	SPANISH	EXAMPLES
significant digits The digits used to express the precision of a measurement.	**dígitos significativos** Dígitos usados para expresar la precisión de una medida.	0.048 has 2 significant digits. 5.003 has 4 significant digits.
similar Figures with the same shape but not necessarily the same size are similar.	**semejantes** Figuras que tienen la misma forma, pero no necesariamente el mismo tamaño.	
simple event An event consisting of only one outcome.	**suceso simple** Suceso que tiene sólo un resultado.	In the experiment of rolling a number cube, the event consisting of the outcome 3 is a simple event.
simple interest A fixed percent of the principal. It is found using the formula $I = Prt$, where P represents the principal, r the rate of interest, and t the time.	**interés simple** Un porcentaje fijo del capital. Se calcula con la fórmula $I = Cit$, donde C representa el capital, i, la tasa de interés y t, el tiempo.	$100 is put into an account with a simple interest rate of 5%. After 2 years, the account will have earned $I = 100 \cdot 0.05 \cdot 2 = \$10$.
simplest form A fraction is in simplest form when the numerator and denominator have no common factors other than 1.	**mínima expresión** Una fracción está en su mínima expresión cuando el numerador y el denominador no tienen más factor común que 1.	Fraction: $\frac{8}{12}$ Simplest form: $\frac{2}{3}$
simplify To write a fraction or expression in simplest form.	**simplificar** Escribir una fracción o expresión numérica en su mínima expresión.	
simulation A model of an experiment, often one that would be too difficult or too time-consuming to actually perform.	**simulación** Representación de un experimento, por lo regular de uno cuya realización sería demasiado difícil o llevaría mucho tiempo.	
skew lines Lines that lie in different planes that are neither parallel nor intersecting.	**líneas oblicuas** Líneas que se encuentran en planos distintos, por eso no se intersecan ni son paralelas.	 $\overrightarrow{AB}$ and $\overrightarrow{CG}$ are skew lines.
slant height of a cone The distance from the vertex of a cone to a point on the edge of the base.	**altura inclinada de un cono** Distancia desde el vértice de un cono hasta un punto en el borde de la base.	 Slant height
slant height of a pyramid The distance from the vertex of a pyramid to the midpoint of an edge of the base.	**altura inclinada de una pirámide** Distancia desde el vértice de una pirámide hasta el punto medio de una arista de la base.	 Slant height $P = 4s$

Glossary/Glosario

ENGLISH	SPANISH	EXAMPLES
slope A measure of the steepness of a line on a graph; the rise divided by the run.	**pendiente** Medida de la inclinación de una línea en una gráfica. Razón de la distancia vertical a la distancia horizontal.	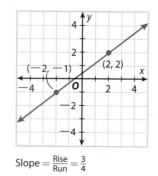 $(-2, -1)$ $(2, 2)$ Slope $= \frac{\text{Rise}}{\text{Run}} = \frac{3}{4}$
slope-intercept form A linear equation written in the form $y = mx + b$, where m represents slope and b represents the y-intercept.	**forma de pendiente-intersecciíon** Ecuación lineal escrita en la forma $y = mx + b$, donde m es la pendiente y b es la intersección con el eje y.	$y = 6x - 3$
solid figure A three-dimensional figure.	**cuerpo geométrico** Figura tridimensional.	
solution of an equation A value or values that make an equation true.	**solución de una ecuación** Valor o valores que hacen verdadera una ecuación.	Equation: $x + 2 = 6$ Solution: $x = 4$
solution of an inequality A value or values that make an inequality true.	**solución de una desigualdad** Valor o valores que hacen verdadera una desigualdad.	Inequality: $x + 3 \geq 10$ Solution: $x \geq 7$
solution set The set of values that make a statement true.	**conjunto solución** Conjunto de valores que hacen verdadero un enunciado.	Inequality: $x + 3 \geq 5$ Solution set: $x \geq 2$ $-4\ -3\ -2\ -1\ \ 0\ \ 1\ \ 2\ \ 3\ \ 4\ \ 5\ \ 6$
solve To find an answer or a solution.	**resolver** Hallar una respuesta o solución.	
sphere A three-dimensional figure with all points the same distance from the center.	**esfera** Figura tridimensional en la que todos los puntos están a la misma distancia del centro.	
square (geometry) A rectangle with four congruent sides.	**cuadrado** (en geometría) Rectángulo con cuatro lados congruentes.	
square (numeration) A number raised to the second power.	**cuadrado (en numeración)** Número elevado a la segunda potencia.	In 5^2, the number 5 is squared.
square number The product of a number and itself.	**cuadrado de un número** El producto de un número y sí mismo.	25 is a square number. $5 \cdot 5 = 25$

Glossary/Glosario

square root A number that is multiplied by itself to form a product is called a square root of that product.

raíz cuadrada El número que se multiplica por sí mismo para formar un producto se denomina la raíz cuadrada de ese producto.

$\sqrt{16} = 4$ because
$4^2 = 4 \cdot 4 = 16$

---

standard form (in numeration) A way to write numbers by using digits.

forma estándar (en numeración) Una manera de escribir números por medio de dígitos.

Five thousand, two hundred ten in standard form is 5,210.

---

stem-and-leaf plot A graph used to organize and display data so that the frequencies can be compared.

diagrama de tallo y hojas Gráfica que muestra y ordena los datos, y que sirve para comparar las frecuencias.

Stem	Leaves
3	2 3 4 4 7 9
4	0 1 5 7 7 7 8
5	1 2 2 3

Key: 3|2 means 3.2

---

straight angle An angle that measures 180°.

ángulo llano Ángulo que mide exactamente 180°.

---

subset A set contained within another set.

subconjunto Conjunto que pertenece a otro conjunto.

---

substitute To replace a variable with a number or another expression in an algebraic expression.

sustituir Reemplazar una variable por un número u otra expresión en una expresión algebraica.

Subtraction Property of Equality The property that states that if you subtract the same number from both sides of an equation, the new equation will have the same solution.

Propiedad de igualdad de la resta Propiedad que establece que puedes restar el mismo número de ambos lados de una ecuación y la nueva ecuación tendrá la misma solución.

$$\begin{array}{rcr} x + 6 = & & 8 \\ -6 & & -6 \\ \hline x = & & 2 \end{array}$$

---

sum The result when two or more numbers are added.

suma Resultado de sumar dos o más números.

The sum of $6 + 7 + 1$ is 14.

---

supplementary angles Two angles whose measures have a sum of 180°.

ángulos suplementarios Dos ángulos cuyas medidas suman 180°.

---

surface area The sum of the areas of the faces, or surfaces, of a three-dimensional figure.

área total Suma de las áreas de las caras, o superficies, de una figura tridimensional.

12 cm
6 cm
8 cm

Surface area $= 2(8)(12) + 2(8)(6) + 2(12)(6) = 432$ cm^2

T

taxable income The total amount of income minus qualifying deductions.

ingreso sujeto a impuestos Cantidad total de ingresos, menos las deducciones aplicables.

Glossary/Glosario

ENGLISH	SPANISH	EXAMPLES
term (in an expression) The parts of an expression that are added or subtracted.	**término (en una expresión)** Las partes de una expresión que se suman o se restan.	$3x^2 \;+\; 6x \;-\; 8$ Term Term Term
term (in a sequence) An element or number in a sequence.	**término (en una sucesión)** Elemento o número de una sucesión.	5 is the third term in the sequence 1, 3, 5, 7, 9, ...
terminating decimal A decimal number that ends, or terminates.	**decimal finito** Decimal con un número determinado de posiciones decimales.	6.75
tessellation A repeating pattern of plane figures that completely covers a plane with no gaps or overlaps.	**teselado** Patrón repetido de figuras planas que cubren totalmente un plano sin superponerse ni dejar huecos.	
theoretical probability The ratio of the number of ways an event can occur to the total number of equally likely outcomes.	**probabilidad teórica** Razón del numero de las maneras que puede ocurrir un suceso al numero total de resultados igualmente probables.	When rolling a number cube, the theoretical probability of rolling a 4 is $\frac{1}{6}$.
third quartile The median of the upper half of a set of data; also called *upper quartile*.	**tercer cuartil** La mediana de la mitad superior de un conjunto de datos. También se llama *cuartil superior*.	
transformation A change in the position or orientation of a figure.	**transformación** Cambio en la posición u orientación de una figura.	
translation A movement (slide) of a figure along a straight line.	**traslación** Desplazamiento de una figura a lo largo de una línea recta.	
transversal A line that intersects two or more lines.	**transversal** Línea que cruza dos o más líneas.	
trapezoid A quadrilateral with exactly one pair of parallel sides.	**trapecio** Cuadrilátero con un par de lados paralelos.	
tree diagram A branching diagram that shows all possible combinations or outcomes of an event.	**diagrama de árbol** Diagrama ramificado que muestra todas las posibles combinaciones o resultados de un suceso.	
trial Each repetition or observation of an experiment.	**prueba** Una sola repetición u observación de un experimento.	When rolling a number cube, each roll is one trial.

ENGLISH	SPANISH	EXAMPLES
triangle A three-sided polygon.	**triángulo** Polígono de tres lados.	
Triangle Sum Theorem The theorem that states that the measures of the angles in a triangle add to 180°.	**Teorema de la suma del triángulo** Teorema que establece que las medidas de los ángulos de un triángulo suman 180°.	
triangular prism A polyhedron whose bases are triangles and whose other faces are parallelograms.	**prisma triangular** Poliedro cuyas bases son triángulos y cuyas demás caras tienen forma de paralelogramo.	

U

underestimate An estimate that is less than the exact answer.	**estimación baja** Estimación menor que la respuesta exacta.	
unit conversion The process of changing one unit of measure to another.	**conversión de unidades** Proceso que consiste en cambiar una unidad de medida por otra.	
unit conversion factor A fraction used in unit conversion in which the numerator and denominator represent the same amount but are in different units.	**factor de conversión de unidades** Fracción que se usa para la conversión de unidades, donde el numerador y el denominador representan la misma cantidad pero están en unidades distintas.	$\frac{60 \text{ min}}{1\text{h}}$ or $\frac{1\text{h}}{60 \text{ min}}$
unit price A unit rate used to compare prices.	**precio unitario** Tasa unitaria que sirve para comparar precios.	
unit rate A rate in which the second quantity in the comparison is one unit.	**tasa unitaria** Una tasa en la que la segunda cantidad de la comparación es la unidad.	10 cm per minute
upper quartile The median of the upper half of a set of data.	**cuartil superior** La mediana de la mitad superior de un conjunto de datos.	Lower half Upper half 18, 23, 28, 29, (36,) 42 ↑ Upper quartile

V

variable A symbol used to represent a quantity that can change.	**variable** Símbolo que representa una cantidad que puede cambiar.	In the expression $2x + 3$, x is the variable.
variable expense Expenses that occur regularly but may change because the consumer has some control over the amount.	**gasto variable** Gasto que ocurre con regularidad y que es necesario para vivir, pero que puede cambiar debido a que el consumidor tiene algún control sobre la cantidad.	

Glossary/Glosario

ENGLISH	SPANISH	EXAMPLES

...nn diagram A diagram that is ...sed to show relationships between sets.

diagrama de Venn Diagrama que muestra las relaciones entre conjuntos.

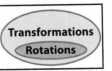

---

verbal expression A word or phrase.

expresión verbal Palabra o frase.

---

vertex On an angle or polygon, the point where two sides intersect.

vértice En un ángulo o polígono, el punto de intersección de dos lados.

A is the vertex of ∠CAB.

---

vertical angles A pair of opposite congruent angles formed by intersecting lines.

ángulos opuestos por el vértice Par de ángulos opuestos congruentes formados por líneas secantes.

∠1 and ∠3 are vertical angles.
∠2 and ∠4 are vertical angles.

---

volume The number of cubic units needed to fill a given space.

volumen Número de unidades cúbicas que se necesitan para llenar un espacio.

4 ft
3 ft
12 ft

Volume = $3 \cdot 4 \cdot 12 = 144 \text{ ft}^3$

X

---

x-axis The horizontal axis on a coordinate plane.

eje x El eje horizontal del plano cartesiano.

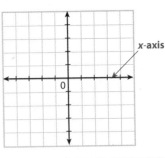

x-axis

---

x-coordinate The first number in an ordered pair; it tells the distance to move right or left from the origin, (0, 0).

coordenada x El primer número en un par ordenado; indica la distancia que debes avanzar hacia la izquierda o hacia la derecha desde el origen, (0, 0).

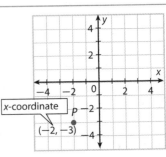

x-coordinate

P
(−2, −3)

Glossary/Glosario

ENGLISH	SPANISH	EXAMPLES

x-intercept The x-coordinate of the point where the graph of a line crosses the x-axis.

intersección con el eje x Coordenada x del punto donde la gráfica de una línea cruza el eje x.

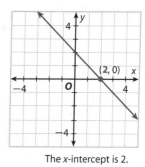

The x-intercept is 2.

Y

y-axis The vertical axis on a coordinate plane.

eje y El eje vertical del plano cartesiano.

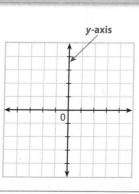

y-coordinate The second number in an ordered pair; it tells the distance to move up or down from the origin, (0, 0).

coordenada y El segundo número de un par ordenado; indica la distancia que debes avanzar hacia arriba o hacia abajo desde el origen, (0, 0).

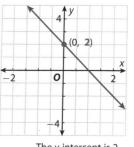

y-intercept The y-coordinate of the point where the graph of a line crosses the y-axis.

intersección con el eje y Coordenada y del punto donde la gráfica de una línea cruza el eje y.

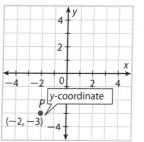

The y-intercept is 2.

Index

© Houghton Mifflin Harcourt Publishing Company

Index

Index

Index

Index

© Houghton Mifflin Harcourt Publishing Company

Index

Index

TABLE OF MEASURES

METRIC

Length

1,000 millimeters (mm) = 1 meter (m)

100 centimeters (cm) = 1 meter

10 millimeters = 1 centimeter

10 decimeters (dm) = 1 meter

1 kilometer (km) = 1000 meters

Capacity

1,000 milliliters (mL) = 1 liter (L)

100 centiliters (cL) = 1 liter

10 deciliters (dL) = 1 liter

1 kiloliter (kL) = 1,000 liters

Mass

1,000 milligrams (mg) = 1 gram (g)

100 centigrams (cg) = 1 gram

10 decigrams (dg) = 1 gram

1 kilogram (kg) = 1,000 grams

CUSTOMARY

Length

1 foot (ft) = 12 inches (in.)

1 yard (yd) = 3 feet

1 yard = 36 inches

1 mile (mi) = 5,280 feet

1 mile = 1,760 yards

Capacity

1 cup (c) = 8 fluid ounces (fl oz)

1 pint (pt) = 2 cups

1 quart (qt) = 2 pints

1 quart = 4 cups

1 gallon (gal) = 4 quarts

Weight

1 pound (lb) = 16 ounces (oz)

1 ton (T) = 2,000 pounds

TIME

1 minute (min) = 60 seconds (s)

1 hour (hr) = 60 minutes

1 day = 24 hours

1 week (wk) = 7 days

1 year (yr) = 12 months (mo)

1 year = 52 weeks

1 year = 365 days

1 leap year = 366 days

FORMULAS

Perimeter

Rectangle	$P = 2\ell + 2w$ or $P = 2(\ell + w)$
Square	$P = 4s$

Circumference

Circle	$C = 2\pi r$ or $C = \pi d$

Area

Circle	$A = \pi r^2$
Parallelogram	$A = bh$
Rectangular	$A = \ell w$ or $A = bh$
Square	$A = s^2$
Rhombus	$A = \frac{1}{2} d_1 d_2$ or $A = \frac{d_1 d_2}{2}$
Trapezoid	$A = \frac{1}{2}(b_1 + b_2)h$ or $A = \frac{(b_1 + b_2)h}{2}$
Triangle	$A = \frac{1}{2} bh$ or $A = \frac{bh}{2}$

Volume

Cylinder	$V = Bh$ or $V = \pi r^2 h$
Cube	$V = s^3$
Rectangle prism	$V = Bh$ or $V = \ell wh$
Triangular prism	$V = Bh$
Cone	$V = \frac{1}{3} Bh$ or $V = \frac{1}{3} \pi r^2 h$
Pyramid	$V = \frac{1}{3} Bh$
Sphere	$V = \frac{4}{3} \pi r^3$

Surface Area

Cylinder:

Lateral	$L = Ch$ or $L = 2\pi rh$
Total	$S = 2B + L$ or $S = 2\pi r^2 + 2\pi rh$

Prism:

Lateral	$L = Ph$
Total	$S = 2B + L$ or $S = 2B + Ph$

Other

Distance traveled	$d = 2r$
Interest (simple)	$I = Prt$
Pythagorean Theorem	$a^2 + b^2 = c^2$

SYMBOLS

$\neq$	is not equal to
$\approx$	is approximately equal to
10^2	ten squared; ten to the second power
$2.\overline{6}$	repeating decimal 2.66666...
$|-4|$	the absolute value of negative 4
$\sqrt{}$	square root

π	pi: (about 3.14)
$\perp$	is perpendicular to
$\parallel$	is parallel to
$\overleftrightarrow{AB}$	line AB
$\overrightarrow{AB}$	ray AB
$\overline{AB}$	line segment AB
$m\angle A$	measure of $\angle A$